THE
INDEPENDENT
SCHOOLS
GUIDE

Eighth Edition

THE INDEPENDENT SCHOOLS GUIDE

Eighth Edition

Publisher's note
The information supplied in this Guide has been published in good faith on the basis of information submitted by the schools listed. Neither Kogan Page nor Gabbitas Educational Consultants can guarantee the accuracy of the information in this guide and accept no responsibility for any error or misrepresentation. All liability for loss, disappointment, negligence or other damage caused by the reliance on the information contained in this Guide, or in the event of bankruptcy or liquidation or cessation of trade of any company, individual or firm mentioned, is hereby excluded.

The views expressed in this Guide are not necessarily those of the publishers.

Photographs on front cover reproduced with kind permission of Kent College, Canterbury, Kent (centre) and Rossall School, Fleetwood, Lancashire (right and left).

First published in 1995
This edition published in 2002

Kogan Page Ltd
120 Pentonville Road
London N1 9JN
Web site: www.kogan-page.co.uk

© Gabbitas and Kogan Page 2002

British Library Cataloguing in Publication Data
A CIP record for this book is available from the British Library
ISBN 0 749 437 421

Typeset by Bibliocraft Ltd, Dundee
Printed and bound by Bell and Bain Ltd., Glasgow

Contents

PART FOUR: REFERENCE SECTION

FOREWORD

Gabbitas Educational Consultants

Good schools achieve the very best for their pupils, not only in the classroom but also in the development of wider talents and abilities. Highly respected for their academic excellence, for their attention to the individual needs of each child and for the breadth of education and opportunities they offer, independent schools offer an unrivalled choice and attract an increasing number of parents every year.

Information is available from many sources, but finding the right school for your own child is not always easy.

The Independent Schools Guide combines up-to-date information with expert guidance based on over a century's experience of advising parents and students about education. As the most comprehensive directory of UK independent schools, it includes over 2,100 entries, indexed separately to enable you to use a range of starting points. The choice includes location, age range, sex, accommodation type, special needs provision, religious affiliation and scholarship and bursary opportunities. Detailed profiles of schools appear in the advertisers' section. Practical advice from our consultancy team covers all aspects of independent education, the questions to ask when making your choice, financial planning, and the special issues for parents who live overseas.

You can also search for schools online at www.gabbitas.net, the special website which accompanies this Guide and offers parents worldwide the opportunity to contact schools direct.

Established for over 125 years, Gabbitas is uniquely placed to offer parents expert independent advice based on personal knowledge of independent schools throughout the UK. Each year Gabbitas helps thousands of parents and students in the UK and abroad who seek guidance at all stages of education:

- choice of independent schools and colleges
- educational assessment services
- Sixth Form options – A levels, International Baccalaureate and vocational courses
- university and degree choices and UCAS applications
- careers assessment and guidance, job searching and interview techniques

Gabbitas also advises on transfer into the British educational system and provides guardianship services for children from overseas attending boarding schools in the UK as well as testing services to assess knowledge of English, Maths and Science. To find out more about Gabbitas, you can visit our website at www.gabbitas.co.uk or contact us at:

Gabbitas Educational Consultants
Carrington House, 126–130 Regent Street, London W1B 5EE
Tel: +44 (0)20 7734 0161 Fax: +44 (0)20 7437 1764
E-mail: admin@gabbitas.co.uk

Acknowledgements

This Guide is the product of many hours of data collection and meticulous proof-reading by staff at Gabbitas and Kogan Page, together with co-operation and contributions from a wide-ranging team of experts. Gabbitas would like to thank all those who have helped in the preparation of this Guide, in particular Towry Law Financial Services Ltd; Kent College, Canterbury and Rossall School, Fleetwood for kind permission to reproduce photographs; and the educational associations, Heads and schools who have so promptly provided the information required for publication.

Gabbitas Educational Consultants Ltd
January 2002

How To Use The Guide

About independent schools

The first part of this guide offers extensive information about independent schools, on examinations, fee-planning, scholarships and bursaries as well as guidance on choosing a school. The main index at the back contains details of all page references for each school.

Selecting schools in a particular location

If you are looking for a school in a specific area, turn to the directory section (Part Two), which is arranged geographically by town and county. Schools in London are listed under their postal areas. Each entry gives the name, address and telephone number of the school, together with the name of the Head, details of the type and age range of pupils accepted, the number of pupils, number of boarders (where applicable) and the annual fees.

Schools which have an asterisk also appear in the School Profiles section (Part Three), where advertisers provide more detailed information. These schools also have a map reference to show their exact location.

To find any other references to the school, for example to find out whether it offers scholarships or provides help for dyslexic children, turn to the appropriate index at the back.

Scholarships, bursaries and reserved entrance awards

Many schools offer scholarships for children with a particular talent, bursaries where there is financial hardship or reserved entrance awards for children with a parent in a specific profession such as the Clergy or HM Forces. The Reference Section at the back contains a complete list of schools, by county, which offer such awards.

Once you have selected a few schools for further investigation, turn to the main index to find the schools' other listings.

This section is necessarily only a brief guide to awards available. Some schools give more detailed information about scholarships and similar awards in Part Three (3.8). More specific information can be obtained from individual schools.

Religious affiliation

The index in the Reference Section (Part Four) provides a full list of schools under appropriate headings. The main index will tell you where to find further information about individual schools.

Single-sex schools

For a complete list of single-sex schools, turn to the Reference Section. Page references may be found in the main index.

Dyslexia

Most schools offer help, in varying degrees, for pupils with dyslexia. An index of these schools will be found in the Reference Section. Schools are listed by county for ease of reference. Parents should note, however, that this is intended only as a general guide. Further page references for these schools will be found in the main index.

English as a Foreign Language

Most independent schools offer assistance to overseas pupils who require special English language tuition. A list of schools, arranged by county, appears in the Reference Section.

School search online

Remember that you can also search for schools on our website at www.gabbitas.net

PART ONE: THE INDEPENDENT SECTOR

1.1
What Is An Independent School?

Independent schools educate about 7 per cent of the whole school population. While subject to certain regulations set centrally by the Department for Education and Skills (in Wales the Welsh Office Education Department – WOED), they are largely self governing and are distinct from state schools in various aspects of funding, organisation, management and regulation.

Status and funding

Independent schools are usually funded by the fees charged to parents, although some also have generous endowments which allow them to keep fees at a lower level. Most are run as charitable trusts under a Board of Governors, which constitutes the policy-making body for the school. Schools with charitable status are effectively non-profit-making concerns; any surplus funds are allocated at the discretion of the Governors. Frequently they may go towards investment in new facilities or in scholarships and bursaries for new or existing pupils. A few schools are still privately-owned.

Schools exercise individual control over the appointment of staff, financial management, administration, curriculum, admission of pupils and most other aspects of school life.

There is sometimes confusion over the terms used to describe independent schools. 'Public schools' is a term generally applied to the old-established schools in membership of the Headmasters' and Headmistresses' Conference (HMC). Many of these date back to the days when education was a luxury, received chiefly through private tutors. A public school was therefore simply a school to which the public could be admitted. Most schools now prefer to be described as 'independent'. A private school simply means any school at which fees are paid.

Organisation, management and staff

The Board of Governors is responsible for appointment of the Head, allocation of finances and for other major decisions affecting the school. In the event of a dispute between a parent and the school, for example over a pupil's breach of school rules and any disciplinary action taken as a result, the Governors are the final arbiters. Once the child is formally registered as a pupil at the school, there is in effect a formal contract between the parents and the school, the terms of which must be heeded by both parties.

Day-to-day responsibility for the running of the school is delegated to the Head, who is accountable to the Board of Governors. Other key figures in senior management include the Bursar, who has significant influence over the allocation of financial resources, and the Director of Studies, frequently appointed to manage academic life on a daily basis.

Academic staff in independent schools are not legally required to hold teaching qualifications, but schools almost always insist on a first degree in a subject which normally forms a part of the secondary school curriculum and a PGCE (Postgraduate Certificate in Education). All schools look for enthusiastic and committed staff with flair and ability. Salary scales at independent Schools tend to reflect the wide range of commitment expected of staff and are often more generous than those in the state sector, enabling schools to attract high-calibre teachers.

Curriculum, testing and assessment

Independent schools are not bound to follow the National Curriculum, although most choose to do so. Almost all are preparing pupils for the public examinations at GCSE and AS/A2 Level, or in Scotland, for Scottish National qualifications.

Assessment and monitoring of pupils' progress is a matter for individual schools to decide. There is no compulsion for pupils to sit the National Tests which are taken by pupils in state schools. In practice most schools have regular assessments throughout the term and set formal, internal examinations two or three times a year, the results of which are included in the end of term report.

Registration and inspection of independent schools

OFSTED (the Office for Standards in Education)

OFSTED is the chief body responsible for monitoring on a disinterested basis the performance of schools in England. OHMCI (the Office of Her Majesty's Chief Inspector) is the equivalent body in Wales. Both are non-ministerial government departments. Slightly different arrangements are in place in Scotland and Northern Ireland.

School inspections in the maintained sector are carried out on a six-year cycle (five-year cycle in Wales) by independent teams of inspectors. Each team is led by a Registered Inspector (RgI) trained by OFSTED/OHMCI. Other team members must also have completed the OFSTED/OHMCI training scheme. Each team must also include a lay inspector. Inspection teams are invited by OFSTED/OHMCI to tender for individual school inspections. Once the final report is published, copies are available free of charge.

Inspection of independent schools

Until January 1999, HMI inspected independent schools every five years. In January 1999 new inspection arrangements came into effect for independent schools within membership of the Independent Schools Council (ISC), but the previous system of HMI inspections remains in place for schools not in membership of ISC (see below).

Since 1980, the independent sector has also operated its own self-regulation system. When the DfES (then the Department for Education and Science) withdrew its inspection scheme for independent schools in 1978, independent schools and their associations sought to replace it with another means of monitoring and maintaining educational standards. In 1980 a new accreditation scheme was established under the auspices of the Independent Schools Joint Council (now the ISC), a national body comprising eight independent school associations: the Headmasters' and Headmistresses' Conference (HMC); the Girls' Schools Association (GSA) (including the Girls' Day School Trust GDST); the Society of Headmasters and Headmistresses of Independent School (SHMIS); the Incorporated Association of Preparatory Schools (IAPS); the Independent Schools Association (ISA); the Governing Bodies Association (GBA); the Governing Bodies of Girls' Schools Association (GBGSA) and the Independent Schools Bursars' Association (ISBA). ISC accreditation is an essential requirement for any school seeking membership of one of the ISC's constituent associations (GSA, HMC, SHMIS, IAPS and ISA). It involves a visit to the school lasting four or five days and covers all aspects, including premises, facilities, staffing and management, financial management, administration, teaching standards, accommodation, boarding facilities and pastoral care. All inspection reports are sent to OFSTED. Prior to January 1999 schools were required to publish a summary of the report, but were under no obligation to make the full report more widely available. A number of schools, however, chose to publish the full report for the benefit of parents and others who were interested. In recent years the Headmasters' and Headmistressess' Conference (HMC) developed an inspection scheme for its own member schools, similar to, but separate from, ISC inspections.

In 1996, at the request of ISC (the Accreditation Review and Consultancy Service, or ARCS) and HMC, HMI carried out an assessment of the ARCS and HMC inspection systems. This identified key strengths while also making recommendations for improvements which have since been addressed. It was subsequently agreed that from January 1999 the inspection of ISC schools should be entrusted to the Independent Schools Inspectorate (ISI), which acts as a contractor for this work and works closely with OFSTED and the DfES. ISI inspects schools on a six-year cycle and publishes report summaries and full reports, which are sent to OFSTED and the DfES and must also be made available to parents and other interested parties. ISI inspection teams are drawn from present and retired members of the ISC constituent associations and are required to reach a satisfactory standard on training courses based on OFSTED principles. In this way ISI teams combine independence and detachment with an understanding of the schools involved and it is likely that the individual associations will play an important part in offering training, peer support and advice and in following up action plans resulting from inspection. The HMC system of inspection merged with ISI in April 2000 to form a unified system.

HMI retains the right to inspect any independent school but uses its resources to monitor ISI inspection and to follow up in cases where a school shows serious deficiencies until such time as the concerns are resolved.

Inspection of publicly funded independent schools

The revised arrangements described above answer the government's wish to monitor more closely those independent schools which receive public funding (from the Assisted Places Scheme, from the Ministry of Defence and Foreign and Commonwealth boarding allowances and from the Music and Ballet and Choir School schemes). Those schools which are in membership of ISC are inspected by ISI. Schools which have five or more publicly funded pupils but are not in membership of ISC are inspected by HMI and the reports published.

Independent schools not in membership of ISC

Independent schools not in membership of ISC continue to be monitored by HMI on the same basis as before. Schools are inspected every six years. Findings are reported in confidence to the DfES and a letter is sent to the school indicating any action required, but in most cases reports are not made publicly available.

HMI also visit provisionally registered (recently established) schools every two terms, to see whether they are ready for final registration with the DfES, a legal requirement for all independent schools with five or more pupils between the ages of 5 and 16.

Annual visits are made to schools which give serious cause for concern. Schools failing to make sufficient improvement in reasonable time may be subject to eventual closure. Only in cases of ongoing concern, however, does HMI make a full inspection and publish a report.

Boarding schools

All independent schools with boarding pupils are subject to inspection by Social Services Departments. The reports are used by HMI and ISC to ensure that schools comply with statutory requirements and act upon any recommendations made.

Accreditation and inspection of independent colleges

A number of independent colleges are accredited by the BAC (British Accreditation Council) – see below. Some independent sixth-form and tutorial colleges are also in membership of CIFE (Council for Independent Further Education) – see below. All colleges taking students below the age of 16 are inspected by the DfES. Those with residential accommodation are also visited by the Department for Social Security.

Other inspecting and accrediting organisations

The British Accreditation Council (BAC)

The BAC is the main inspection and accreditation body for independent colleges accepting pupils over the age of 16. Inspections cover: premises and health and safety; administration and staffing; quality management; student welfare; and teaching and learning:

delivery and resources. Accredited colleges are re-inspected every five years, with an interim visit during the intervening period. Accreditation may be refused or withdrawn if any aspect of the college does not meet the required standards for accreditation.

Council for Independent Further Education (CIFE)

There are 31 independent sixth-form and tutorial colleges in membership of CIFE. Member colleges offer one and two-year A Level and GCSE courses, retake courses, revision courses and also one-year foundation courses for students who wish to enter a UK university but have been educated outside the British system. CIFE members are required to hold accreditation either from the BAC or from ISC. Those classified as candidate members must acquire BAC or ISC accreditation within three years.

European Council of International Schools (ECIS)

Some international schools in the UK are accredited by ECIS, a membership organisation comprising international schools in all parts of the world. As part of a range of services offered to its member schools, ECIS offers regular and associate schools a programme of evaluation and accreditation specially developed for international schools. Those schools which meet the standards for accreditation are given accredited status and in addition to regular monitoring must undergo a full re-evaluation every ten years.

Useful addresses:

Independent Schools Inspectorate (ISI)
Northway House
1379 High Road
Whetstone
London N20 9LP
Tel: (020) 8445 6262
Fax: (020) 8445 7272
Contact: Mrs M Gallagher

The Headmasters' and Headmistresses' Conference (HMC)
130 Regent Road
Leicester LE1 7PG
Tel: 0116 285 4810
Fax: 0116 247 1167
Secretary: G H Lucas

The British Accreditation Council
Westminster Central Hall
Storey's Gate
London SW1H 9NH
Tel: (020) 7233 3468
Fax: (020) 7233 3470

The Council for Independent Further Education
75 Foxbourne Road
London SW17 8EN
Tel: (020) 8767 8666
Fax: (020) 8767 9444
Executive Secretary: Dr Norma Ball

The European Council of International Schools
21 Lavant Street
Petersfield
Hampshire GU32 3EL
Tel: (01730) 268244
Fax: (01730) 267914
Website: www.ecis.org

Office for Standards in Education (OFSTED)
Alexandra House
33 Kingsway
London WC2B 6SE
Tel: (020) 7421 6800

1.2
The Independent Sector

There are over 2,200 independent schools in the UK. Schools cover all age ranges; some offer education from nursery level through to 18, others are junior or senior only. Many are day schools but a large number offer boarding or weekly boarding facilities. There is a variety of co-educational and single-sex schools; many of the latter, particularly boys' schools, offer co-education at Sixth Form level.

Age range	Type of establishment
2–7/8	Nursery or Pre-Preparatory School
7/8–13	Preparatory School
11/13–16/18	Senior School
16-18	Sixth Form

Nursery and pre-preparatory schools

Nursery education refers to schools for pupils under the age of 5, pre-preparatory education for pupils aged 5–7/8. Many preparatory schools have their own nursery and pre-prep departments.

Preparatory schools

When single-sex education was more common, it was usual for girls to remain at their prep school until the age of 11 and for boys to remain until 13. However, with the growth of co-education the options are now more flexible.

Senior schools

With the exception of a few boys' schools most girls' and co-educational senior schools now accept pupils from the age of 11. Preparation for the two-year GCSE course begins at age 14. (In Scotland pupils are prepared for Standard Grade examinations, broadly equivalent to GCSE).

Sixth Form

Changing schools at 16 after the completion of GCSEs is not unusual. Most schools admit a number of new entrants at this stage from both independent and state schools. Pupils usually follow a two-year course in preparation for AS/A2 Level (or Highers in Scotland). Some schools also offer vocational programmes including Vocational A Levels. A few UK independent schools offer the International Baccalaureate.

There is also a smaller number of independent sixth form or tutorial colleges which accept pupils from the age of about 14 upwards and provide tuition for GCSE and/or A Levels.

Why choose independent education?

Variety and choice

The independent sector includes schools of many different styles and philosophies, including both the traditional and the more liberal. Each school has its own ethos and atmosphere. Schools also vary widely in size. Some are based in towns and cities. Most boarding schools have more rural locations. Some are co-educational, others are single-sex, although many boys' schools now have co-educational Sixth Forms.

A school to suit your child

Your child's academic needs are the top priority. Not all independent schools educate highly academic children, but there is always some form of selection. While some schools will only accept pupils able to keep pace with a fast moving curriculum, there are many others which cater for children of more average ability and some which specialise in helping those in need of more individual attention in a less academic environment.

Academic success

Good independent schools enable pupils, whatever their academic ability, to achieve their best. Their success in helping children to achieve their full potential is reflected in the exam results both of highly selective schools and of schools with less competitive entry requirements where children may need more individual support and encouragement.

An all-around education

Independent schools encourage pupils to develop their strengths outside as well as inside the classroom, ensuring that special talents, in music, drama, art or sport, are nurtured and providing a range of extra-curricular activities which inspire enthusiasm for a great many wider interests.

Small classes and individual attention

Class size at the lower end of the age range normally averages 15 to 20, GCSE groups about 12 to 18 and A Level between 4 and 12, although this varies from one school to another and according to subjects. Most independent schools have a staff:pupil ratio which ensures that pupils receive plenty of individual attention in accordance with their needs.

Pastoral care

The social issues of our time present special challenges for schools. Independent schools play a vital role in building awareness, tolerance and understanding among young people in a secure but disciplined environment to help them to begin their adult lives as confident and responsible individuals.

Excellent facilities

Many schools offer first-class facilities for teaching, accommodation, sports and all aspects of school life.

Maintaining high standards

Independent schools must meet rigorous inspection criteria. Schools in membership of one of the associations which form the Independent Schools Council must conform to strict accreditation requirements and are inspected every six years by the Independent Schools Inspectorate, which works closely with OFSTED and the Department for Education and Skills. Other independent schools in England and Wales are inspected by Her Majesty's Inspectorate for OFSTED (see Section 1.1).

The boarding option

About 15 per cent of all independent school pupils are boarders. Research has shown that boarders enjoy school life and welcome the special opportunities which boarding offers, including long-lasting friendships, self-reliance and immediate access to help with studies and to a full range of facilities and activities.

The structure of boarding has changed in recent years to answer the needs of today's families. While traditional full boarding has declined in popularity, interest is growing in more flexible boarding arrangements. Flexi- and weekly boarding are now much more widely available, enabling pupils to spend more time with their families while still enjoying all the benefits of boarding life. Some schools permit pupils to board for half the week and attend as a day pupils for the remainder. Most can also offer a bed on an occasional basis, for example before a school trip or in the event of an emergency at home.

Pupils who board on a full-time basis normally enjoy busy weekends which offer access to a range of activities. A few schools timetable lessons on Saturday mornings, although this is becoming much less common as weekly boarding becomes more popular. Schools often arrange weekend trips away for boarders, for example to centres of cultural or historical interest or for activities such as walking or sailing. Otherwise pupils may be occupied with sports fixtures, musical or theatre performances or favourite hobbies. Most attend chapel on Sundays and have free time in which to study or relax.

Accommodation has improved dramatically in recent years as schools have invested in new boarding facilities. Gone are the traditional dormitories. Pupils now share well-decorated bedrooms in small groups and are encouraged to make their rooms feel homely. Sixth-form students often have single-study bedrooms in their own accommodation block and are allowed a greater degree of freedom. Houseparents provide constant care and supervision and are there to help with any problems arising. The Housemaster or Housemistress is normally assisted by a qualified Matron and one or two assistants, depending on the number of children in the House.

About 700 schools, including single-sex and co-educational schools, offer boarding places. Most also admit a significant number of day pupils. Whether you are looking for a boarding or a day place, it is wise to check the proportions of boarding and day pupils since these will influence the overall ethos and character of a school.

State-maintained and grant-maintained boarding schools

There are some 35 state-maintained or grant-maintained schools which accept boarding pupils, although day pupils are usually in the majority. UK and EU nationals with a right of residence in the UK pay only for the cost of boarding at these schools and are not charged for tuition. This means that fees, at about £5,000 annually, are much lower than those charged by independent boarding schools. For further information see the school profiles beginning on page 213 or contact the Boarding Schools Association (see page 470).

National Boarding Standards

In June 2000, the National Boarding Standards Committee submitted to the government an agreed set of minimum standards for good practice in independent and state boarding schools. The Committee, convened by the Boarding Schools' Association and the Independent Schools Council, included representatives of all independent school associations, state boarding schools, Social Services inspectors, OFSTED, the Department for Education and Skills, the Department of Health, Service Children's Education and the Independent Schools Inspectorate. The Government Version of the Standards was published for consultation in July 2001. The new standards will form the basis of all statutory and accreditation inspections and reports carried out from 1 April 2002 by the National Care Standards Commission, the new regulatory body for all residential organisations. Details can be found on the BSA website at www.boarding.org.uk or obtained from the Department of Health, tel: 08701 555455, e-mail: doh@porlog.uk.com

Curriculum, assessment and examinations

Independent schools in England and Wales are not required to teach the National Curriculum or to use the National Tests, which are compulsory for state-maintained schools. However, since most are preparing students for public examinations, they generally follow the National Curriculum, complementing it with additional options or areas of study as desired. Independent schools in Scotland are free to form their own curriculum policy but, like maintained sector schools in Scotland, they are normally preparing pupils for Standard and Higher examinations.

Nursery education

The youngest children attend either mornings or afternoons only before progressing to a full day. Emphasis is given to the development of academic, social, language and aesthetic skills through play, music, drama and handicrafts. Children may cover basic letter and number work, handwriting and spelling. Approaches vary, from traditional teaching styles to more modern methods. Montessori schools teach according to a series of principles, which centre on observation of the individual needs of each child and provision of appropriate stimuli and tasks accordingly.

Preparatory schools

Most preparatory schools are preparing pupils for the Common Entrance examination, taken at 11+, 12+ or 13+ for entry to senior boarding or day schools, although some schools, particularly city day schools, set their own entrance examinations. Some parts of the country retain the old examinations for entry to local grammar schools, which require no formal preparation. The destination of school leavers and the main academic thrust of the school may well be influenced by available provision at senior level. The Head of your child's school will want to know which senior school you have chosen when he or she

reaches the last two years of prep school. Further information about Common Entrance is given on page 41.

Pupils are normally taught by class teachers until the age of about 8. After this they may be grouped according to ability. By the age of 9 or 10 there is increasing emphasis on subject teaching by specialists and close attention to the requirements of the National Curriculum, which may be complemented by other elements such as current affairs and topical studies, group projects and field trips. Many schools encourage the development of wider talents and interests, offering a range of opportunities for children in music, art, drama and sport.

Formal assessments of academic progress and achievements as well as performance in sports and other activities are made regularly. Examinations are normally held twice a year or at the end of each term. Grades are entered in the termly report for parents.

Senior schools and Sixth Form education

Almost all senior schools in England and Wales (with a very few exceptions) are preparing pupils for the General Certificate of Secondary Education (GCSEs), taken at 16, the Advanced Subsidiary (AS) and Advanced GCE (A2) (see *Sixth Form Curriculum*). In Scotland pupils are prepared for the Scottish National Qualifications.

Pupils at the lower end of the age range are often taught in sets, a method which groups children for each subject according to their ability in that subject. Streaming, which groups children according to ability on a cross-curricular basis, is used in a smaller number of schools.

The two year GCSE course begins at 14. Most pupils take eight or nine subjects. In some cases very able children may take certain GCSE examinations after one year rather than two. In Scotland pupils normally take seven to eight Standard Grade subjects.

Assessments are examinations in each subject may take place each term. Many schools operate a tutorial system under which a House tutor is assigned to each pupil to monitor social and personal development as well as academic progress. Parents receive a full report at the end of each term. Mock examinations (in preparation for GCSE, AS/A2 or Scottish equivalents) are normally held in the spring preceding the real examinations. These are marked internally by the school and give an indication of likely performance in the summer.

Aside from academic studies, independent schools place great emphasis on an all-round education. Many excel in areas such as sport, where pupils can develop their talents through fixtures against other schools as well as county or national school championships. Most schools recognise, however, that not all pupils enjoy team games. Many offer more individual sports, including, for example, squash, horse-riding, sailing and golf. Music, art and drama are also important aspects of the curriculum and extra-curricular activities. Many schools offer individual music lessons in a range of instruments and encourage students to play in the school orchestra or other music groups or to sing in the choir. Drama is often taught to a very high standard, with performances staged for public festivals as well as in school. Many schools offer preparation for examinations set by the Associated Board of the Royal Schools of Music and the London Academy of Music and Dramatic Art (LAMDA) and there may be regular trips to galleries, concerts, the theatre or the ballet.

Sixth-form curriculum

Most sixth-form students study a combination of up to five AS Levels in the first year, which are normally reduced to two or three subjects in the final year (A2). Some Schools also offer General National Vocational Qualifications (GNVQs) For further details see page 44.

A few schools offer the International Baccalaureate, a demanding two-year course which includes six subject groups that comprise both arts and sciences. The IB is accepted as an alternative to A Levels by all British universities and as a means of entry to many universities overseas.

Some schools also run one-year courses for students who do not wish to take a full sixth-form examination course but may wish to take a general course which includes the opportunity to take additional GCSEs, supplemented by vocational options.

Boarding schools in Scotland usually follow the English examination system although many also offer Scottish qualifications. Higher examinations form the basis for entry to Higher Education and are offered in a wide range of subjects. Some schools also offer vocational programmes. See page 43 for details.

Pupils at Sixth-Form level are encouraged to develop a more independent approach to their studies, to learn how to determine priorities and manage their time wisely. As well as timetabled lessons they normally have periods set aside for private study.

Independent sixth-form colleges

Many students remain in the same school for A level studies, which offers the benefits of continuity and familiarity at a crucial stage of education. Others choose to move to a different school or college, for example if their preferred combination of subjects is not available or if a different type of environment is sought. Independent sixth-form (tutorial) colleges offer an alternative option for students who are seeking a different style of education, for whom entry to a school Sixth Form is not appropriate or in situations where a mid-course transfer to an alternative mainstream school is not possible. Most colleges offer resit and short revision courses as well as full-time one year and two year GCSE and AS/A2 courses. Tuition is in small groups with special emphasis given to exam technique and study skills. Attendance at lessons and coverage of academic work are strictly monitored, although the overall atmosphere within a college is usually less formal than that in schools.

Most independent colleges are located in major cities, including London, Oxford, Cambridge, Bristol, Birmingham and Manchester and have been established in the last 30 years. Most are day colleges but can offer assistance in finding accommodation. In recent years some colleges have taken steps to improve the availability of sports and extra-curricular activities, although few can offer the campus-style environment and full range of on-site facilities and activities offered by some schools.

For students who wish to pursue a more vocational route there is a variety of independent further education colleges. These tend to be much smaller than state-maintained further education colleges and specialise in specific areas such as Business, Secretarial Training, Computing or Beauty Therapy.

Entry requirements and when to join

Pupils under the age of 5 are rarely required to meet more than the very basic practical requirements, although the Head will wish to meet the child in advance. Some schools also set relatively simple tests. Most schools offer entry at the beginning of each term.

In the past most preparatory schools catered for pupils from 8–11/13, but today many accept pupils from the age of 3 upwards. Entry is usually dependent upon an interview with the Head and a satisfactory report from the previous school. Some schools also set verbal or written entrance tests in English and Mathematics, although pupils entering the preparatory department of a pre-preparatory school which they already attend may be exempted from such tests. It may be difficult to join a school for the final one or two years of preparatory education when pupils are approaching Common Entrance and other entrance examinations. Schools which prepare pupils primarily for Common Entrance may test older entrants more rigorously to ensure that they have the capacity to pass at 11, 12 or 13.

Senior schools generally admit pupils from 11-18, although some boys' schools still maintain the traditional age of entry at 13. Schools with their own preparatory department may offer a straightforward transfer into the senior school but most demand successful completion of entrance tests. Some schools set their own entrance tests in English, Mathematics and a general paper. Many use the Common Entrance examination.

Many senior schools also offer a range of scholarships for pupils demonstrating exceptional talent and potential in academic studies, music or art. Examinations are normally held in February and March for entry in September.

Changing schools at 15 or 17 is not generally recommended because of the likely disruption to GCSE or A Level studies, particularly if the move means a change to a different examination syllabus. If a move has to be made after age 13, it may be best to wait until after GCSEs or their equivalent have been completed.

Changing schools at 16 is quite common. Entry to the Sixth Form of most schools is dependent upon interview, together with specified results at GCSE, which will vary from one school to another. Some schools also offer scholarships at this level. Entry require-ments for independent sixth-form colleges tend to be more flexible than in schools.

Pastoral care and discipline

Many independent schools, whether boarding or day, operate a House system, which divides pupils into smaller communities to ensure a good staff:pupil ratio for pastoral care. Boarders are often accommodated in small groups with resident House staff. The House-master or Housemistress is in charge of pastoral care and will also go through the school report with each child at the end of term. House staff monitor overall progress, keep the Head informed about each child and, in boarding schools, may be the first point of contact for parents. Many schools also allocate each pupil a personal tutor, who assists with educational guidance, keeps progress and welfare under constant review and can deal with issues arising on a day-to-day basis. The Children's Act also places a legal obligation on schools to provide a statement of the policy and system of care in place for pupils. All schools are required to have a published policy on bullying.

Most schools keep rules simple, encouraging self-discipline and common sense in their pupils and giving praise for good behaviour. A pupil who has produced good work or shown particular merit in some aspect of school life may be rewarded with extra points or certain privileges. Sometimes children may contribute to a House points system, being awarded points for good work, thoughtful behaviour and for showing initiative or making a particular effort. Points might be deducted for silliness or bad behaviour. Other sanctions imposed might include limitations on leaving school premises or detention. A breach of school rules with regard to smoking or alcohol may mean suspension. Breaches involving illegal drugs may mean immediate permanent exclusion. Corporal punishment is illegal in all schools.

Religion

Spiritual growth is an important aspect of life in most independent schools, whatever their affiliation. The range includes Church of England, Roman Catholic, Quaker, Methodist, Jewish and others. Most adopt an inter-denominational approach and are happy to accept children of other faiths, but parents should check with individual schools the extent to which their child, if of a faith other than the majority of pupils, would be expected to participate in school worship. Children in a minority group can sometimes feel a little isolated in such situations. An index of schools by religious affiliations starts on page 438.

Contact with parents

Every child receives a termly report which is sent home to parents. Schools also hold parents' evenings at regular intervals to allow parents to discuss with teaching and pastoral staff any issues of concern and to be fully briefed on their child's progress. The school report will also contain results of any internal exams held during the term. Parents are often invited to attend school sporting, musical or theatrical events, whether or not their child is taking part, and sometimes to help with school projects such as trips out of school or fundraising activities.

Educational guidance and careers assessment

The value of good educational guidance cannot be overestimated, particularly in view of the complexity and variety of options now available to school leavers and the importance of making the right choice. In many schools, careers guidance has developed significantly to ensure that pupils are aware of suitable opportunities and of their own strengths and aptitudes. Provision varies, however, from one school to another. Some have well-stocked, permanently staffed careers departments and a full programme of careers guidance which includes formal assessment, talks from visiting speakers and work experience opportunities. Others may have more limited resources.

Special educational needs

The term 'special educational needs' may be applied to a whole range of individual requirements across the spectrum. The level of help available in mainstream schools varies widely depending on each school's policy on entrance requirements, the number of pupils with special needs accepted and the most appropriate type of special needs provision in the light of pupils' needs, as well as on the availability of expertise and resources. Parents of children in need of more individual attention, usually those with specific learning difficulties such as dyslexia, will find that there is a large number of mainstream independent schools which offer facilities and tuition in varying degrees. Some schools may bring in a specialist teacher to assist pupils at set times during the week.

Some may have specialist teachers permanently on the staff. Schools which accept a larger number of pupils with special needs may run a specially staffed department or unit. Parents interested in schools which offer provision in some form will find a number of these profiled in Part Three. A full list of mainstream schools offering provision for dyslexia is given in the Reference Section which begins on page 405. More detailed information is available from the Dyslexia Institute, the British Dyslexia Association and CReSTeD, details of which may be found under the Educational Associations and Useful Addresses section (Part 4). Many schools also offer English as a Foreign Language (EFL) support to students coming from overseas, although in most cases pupils will be expected to have a certain level of English on arrival. A list of schools offering EFL support appears in the Reference Section. Few mainstream independent schools have the facilities to cater for children with Statements of Special Educational Needs. Information on assessment, statementing and special schools may be found in a separate Gabbitas publication, *Schools for Special Needs – A Complete Guide*, available in bookshops or direct from Gabbitas.

Extra-curricular activities

Many schools offer an impressive range of options, from art appreciation to abseiling, from fencing to fishing, often at very high standards. Most schools have a range of musical activities – orchestras, choir, madrigal groups, wind ensembles, to name but a few; and there are usually ample opportunities for individual music tuition. Most sports form part of extra-curricular activities as well as timetabled lessons. Other alternatives might include chess, badminton, canoeing, Duke of Edinburgh Award, horse-riding, Brownies and Scout groups, ballet, cookery, gardening, trampolining, rowing, golf, billiards, furniture restoration, stamps, sailing, carpentry, model-making, DT, pottery, drama, French clubs, community service and outward bound activities. Individual schools should be happy to supply parents with a list of their activities.

School staff – who's who?

The Board of Governors

The planning and policy-making body which controls the administration and finance of the school. Some may also be parents of children at the school. They are responsible for the appointment of the Head and for all major decisions affecting the school. Governors give their time voluntarily. Many are individuals with expertise in their professional lives, for example in law or accountancy, who can contribute their knowledge for the benefit of the school.

Head

Accountable to the Governors for the safety and welfare of pupils and the competence of staff, the Head is responsible for all aspects of the day-to-day management of the school, including appointment of staff, pupil admission policy and pupil recruitment, staffing and administrative structure, curriculum content and management. As figureheads for their schools, many Heads also regard the marketing of their school as a key part of their role, although some schools now recruit staff specifically for the purpose. Most Heads also include several hours' teaching in the week, which helps them to keep in touch and get to know pupils individually.

Bursar

The Bursar, in conjunction with the Governors, is responsible for financial matters within the school and is an important member of the management team. The Bursar also takes charge of maintenance of the grounds, premises, buildings, catering and so on.

Director of Studies

Many schools now have a Director of Studies who is responsible for day-to-day curriculum matters and timetabling and for ensuring that staff are kept informed of new developments.

Registrar/Admissions Secretary

The Registrar is responsible for the admission of pupils, making arrangements for parents to visit the school and meet the Head. He or she also takes care of the practical aspects of registration and joining.

Housemaster/Housemistress

The Housemaster or Housemistress takes care of the welfare and overall progress of children in the House and is normally the first point of contact for parents. He or she will keep the Head informed of each child's progress and may often be the first to hear of any problems. Serious issues are always referred to the Head.

Subject teachers

Subject teachers are responsible for the academic progress of pupils and will produce a termly report for those taking their subject. Open evenings offer parents the opportunity to discuss any matters of concern with subject teachers.

Chaplain

The Chaplain has a special role within school. Independent of academic or disciplinary considerations, he is responsible for the spiritual development of pupils and can often provide a sympathetic ear to children who seek guidance on issues of concern.

Matron

The Matron looks after the practical aspects of boarding life, supervising and arranging laundry. Separate Houses normally have their own Matron. She often knows children individually and can provide sympathy and support for those who feel homesick or upset.

Sister

The Sister is a qualified nurse responsible for medical arrangements. She looks after pupils who may be admitted into the sanatorium with minor ailments and may require a few days in bed. Within a boarding school, serious medical matters are always referred to the school doctor and where necessary children will be taken to hospital.

Students

Independent schools encourage their pupils to take on positions of responsibility as part of school life. Senior pupils who show good sense and have contributed to the school by their achievements in academic work, musical or sporting activities for example, may be granted suitable senior positions in recognition of their efforts. Hence an excellent sportsman may be made Games Captain or an outstanding chorister Head of choir. Pupils with an excellent academic record or who deserve merit for other contributions may be given the post of Head Boy or Girl. Prefects have responsibility for some of the daily routines in school and are encouraged to set a good example to younger pupils.

What will it cost?

As a general guide, in 2001/2002 parents can expect to pay annual fees between £2,500 and £7,500 at a day preparatory school or £8,500 to £12,000 for boarding. At senior level fees range from about £5,000 to £11,000 at day schools, or £13,000 to £16,750 for a boarding place. Fees at girls' schools tend to be marginally lower than those at boys' and co-educational schools.

Fees in independent sixth-form colleges are usually charged per subject, with accommodation charged separately. The overall costs of tuition and accommodation for a student studying three subjects at A Level are broadly in line with those charged at a senior boarding school.

Parents are normally asked to pay fees in three termly instalments, one at the start of each term, although some schools may offer a choice of payment methods. If you wish to move your child to another school, the present school will normally require a full term's notice in writing. Otherwise you may find that you are charged an additional term's fees in lieu.

Parents may be asked to meet additional costs during the school year for school lunches, school trips, sports kit, music lessons and similar items, so it is important to check what is and what is not included in the basic termly fee and to take account of other essentials when estimating the overall costs. Boarders will also require additional items such as bed-linen and weekend wear.

If you live overseas, bear in mind that there will be other costs associated with a boarding education in the UK. These include the costs of guardianship, discussed in the next section, travel and any specialist dental treatment, eye tests or spectacles which your child may need while he/she is in the UK. Your child will also need a regular supply of pocket money. Schools discourage pupils from carrying large amounts of cash, but your child will probably want to buy music or clothes as well as sweets and treats.

Scholarships and bursaries

If your child is exceptionally talented in a specific area there may well be scholarship opportunities which could reduce the fees by as much as 50 per cent or possibly more. If financial hardship is an issue, bursaries may be available to help top up the shortfall. The decision to grant a bursary will be taken according to individual circumstances.

Further information about planning for school fees begins on page 33. Information on scholarship and bursary opportunities begins on page 37 and a full list of schools offering scholarships and bursaries appears in Part 4 (pp. 418–427).

1.3
Choosing Your School

"Which is the best school?"

There is no one school which can provide the best possible education for every child. Begin by working out your child's needs, then look for schools which meet these requirements. You will undoubtedly hear differing views about individual schools but remember that you are the best judge of your own child's needs. The question to ask is "Which school will suit my child best?"

When to start

For entry to preparatory school at 7 or 8, you should be thinking about your choice once your child reaches the age of about 4. This allows you to be clearer about his or her academic potential while allowing plenty of time for your research. For entry to senior schools, most parents start to look at the options two to three years ahead.

What type of school will be appropriate?

- **Single sex or co-educational:** This is really a matter of personal preference; some argue that single-sex education enables pupils to achieve at a higher level without the distraction of the opposite sex. Others believe that co-education offers a more natural environment. An index of single-sex schools appears in the Reference Section.
- **Day or boarding:** Boarding does not suit all children, but for those who enjoy it there are many benefits. For some children it may be a necessity. Ensure that your knowledge is up-to-date: most boarding schools today offer flexi-boarding or weekly boarding options which enable pupils to spend more time with their families. Some schools offer 'taster' days and weekends which enable prospective pupils to sample boarding life in advance.
- **Location:** Remember to consider the likely travelling time, particularly by car, during the morning and evening rush hours. Travel to and from school will also be

required for parents' evenings, sports days and other school events. If public transport is to be used, how easy is the journey? Schools in more rural areas often offer a minibus service. Many parents of boarders, who today generally have many opportunities to go home during the term, choose schools within about two hours' drive.

- **Religious affiliation:** Would you prefer a school of a particular denomination or are you willing to include others in your choice?

Your child's needs

Academic needs are the first priority. Be realistic about your child's potential and avoid trying to gain a place at a very academic school unless you are confident of your child's ability to cope. Consider also any other interests your child may have, for example in music or sport as well as your child's overall personality. Some children thrive in a highly active environment offering a multitude of stimuli and the company of other lively and confident youngsters. Others may benefit from being a part of a smaller school community.

Finding out

The Head of your child's present school can probably recommend suitable options, but you may also find it helpful to obtain an independent viewpoint from an educational consultant. Ask those schools which interest you to send you a prospectus. This will tell you something about the main thrust of the school, the curriculum and other areas of activity in which the school has a particular interest. If you would like independent recommendations in line with your needs you can contact Gabbitas.

Visiting schools

A personal visit is the only way to find out whether or not you like a particular school and will allow you to meet staff and pupils and experience the overall atmosphere. If possible, try to visit more than one school, so that you have a means of comparison. You may be invited to an Open Day but the best time to visit is on a normal day during term time. That way you can see the day to day routine in place and the children at their usual activities. In most cases you will meet the Head, who will want to interview your child, following which a member of staff or senior pupil may give you a tour of the school.

You might wish to ask the Head about the following:

Academic policy and destination of leavers

- Is the school's policy appropriate for your longer-term plans? Some may be preparing pupils primarily for entry to senior independent schools; others may have significant numbers whose parents are interested in good local state schools. Scholarship examinations also vary in syllabus from one school to another. Since some prep schools prepare pupils for a limited range of schools, you may wish to find out which ones are covered.

- At secondary level, what is the school's academic pace and focus?
- How many children take GCSEs and AS/A2 Levels, or their equivalents?
- How many GCSE and AS/A2 Level subjects are offered?
- How big is the Sixth Form?
- How many pupils stay on into the Sixth Form? If a large number of pupils leave after GCSE, why is this and where do they go?
- Is there any evident bias in the numbers taking certain subjects?
- What other courses are offered in the Sixth Form?
- Ask about the destinations of sixth-form leavers. What proportion go on to university or other forms of higher education? In which subject areas?

Exam results and league tables

- League tables are not always a reliable guide because they do not take into account a school's selection policy. Exam results, however, particularly if you can compare them with results in previous years, are a useful measure of the school's academic performance and any trends. Take care when interpreting the figures. A 100 per cent pass rate seems impressive, but how many pupils took the exam? Some schools pre-select candidates, which inevitably improves the pass rate statistics.

Testing and assessment

- What systems are in place to monitor performance?
- How much communication is there between staff and parents?

Educational and careers guidance

- What guidance is offered to pupils choosing subjects for examination study, higher education and career options?
- What experience do advisers have?
- What facilities are available?

Special needs

- If your child has special educational needs, exactly how will the school provide for these? The same applies if your child has any special medical or dietary requirements.

Pastoral care and boarders

- How is the welfare of students monitored?
- If your child is to be a day pupil in a boarding school, you may wish to know whether day pupils can join in with evening and weekend activities at school.
- Many working parents may find before- and after-school care facilities attractive. Some schools, particularly city day schools, offer this service.

Parents of boarders must have complete confidence in those who will be responsible for their child's welfare. Ask about the school's policy for the care and supervision of boarders.

- What is the routine at weekends? May pupils leave the premises?
- Who is on duty in the evenings, at night and at weekends? Are they suitably qualified and experienced?
- What happens in the event of an emergency? What is the school's responsibility?
- Do boarders receive regular medical and dental checks?
- Make sure that you are shown the boarding accommodation. Is it clean, warm and welcoming? Is there plenty of space for your child's clothes and personal effects? Is there a secure area for valuables?
- What are boarders permitted to bring to school? Some schools allow small pets.

Teaching staff

- Are they appropriately qualified? Are they specialists in the subjects they teach?
- How many are full-time?
- Is there a high staff turnover? If so, why?
- How is teaching organised?

Extra curricular activities

- If your child has a particular interest or strength, will the school encourage and develop it?

Discipline

- Be sure that you agree with the school's policy.

Seeing the school

- What do your first impressions tell you? Are staff and pupils polite and welcoming? Is the reception area easy to find? Are the buildings and grounds neat and well-kept?
- Is there a sense of order and purpose? What are the noise levels like?

- Do the noticeboards suggest an active, enthusiastic school?
- How do pupils respond to you? Are they articulate and confident? How do they respond to teachers in class?
- How do staff respond to the Head? Are they comfortable in his/her presence?

Registration and confirmation

Registering your child commits neither you nor the school. Schools normally charge a non-refundable registration fee, which may be anything up to £100 for a senior school. It is wise to have your child registered at more than one school in case no place is offered or available at your first choice. You will need to make up your mind about a year before your child is due to start. Once you have formally accepted a place there is a contract between you and the school. Should you change your mind, your deposit may or may not be refundable depending upon the terms set by the school. As with any contractual arrangement, ensure that you understand and accept the school's published terms and conditions before going ahead.

The final choice

After your visits, check the schools' performance against your original criteria. Each school will have its own strengths. Which are most important to you? Your child must also be happy with the final choice, but the decision must be yours. If you have difficulty deciding between two schools, the answer is to trust your instincts. The right school is the one which will allow your child to develop to his or her full potential in the company of liked and trusted staff and pupils in an environment where he or she feels happy and at home.

1.4
Coming From Overseas

If you live overseas, the best advice is to plan ahead as far as possible and at least a year in advance. This will give you a wider choice of school, allow you time to research all the options properly and make an informed choice. Parents may find it helpful to bear in mind the following aspects.

Level of English

Most independent schools will expect your child to speak some English on arrival, although additional tuition is often available in school to improve fluency and accuracy and to ensure that he or she can cope with a normal curriculum.

If your child is to board in the UK but speaks only a little or no English he or she may benefit from a short period in one of the specialist boarding schools which prepare overseas pupils for entry into mainstream boarding schools at secondary level.

Alternatively, you may wish to arrange for your child to spend the summer at one of the UK's many language schools before joining a boarding school in September. Details of suitable courses can be obtained from reputable consultants such as Gabbitas.

Academic background

If your child has been educated within the British system, it should not be difficult to join a school in the UK, although care should be taken to avoid changing schools while a student is in the middle of GCSE or A Level studies. However, if your child has not been following a British curriculum, entry to a mainstream independent school may be less straightforward. The younger your child, the easier it is likely to be for him or her to adapt to a new school environment. Prep schools may accept overseas pupils at any stage up to the final two years, when pupils are prepared for Common Entrance exams and entry may be more difficult. Senior schools, in particular, will normally look for evidence of ability and achievement comparable with pupils educated in the British system and will probably wish to test your child in English, Maths and Science before deciding whether to offer a place. Students wishing to enter the sixth-form will probably be tested in the subjects they wish to study. Recent reports and transcripts, in translation, should also be made available to schools.

If your child has been following the International Baccalaureate (IB) programme overseas, you will find a number of schools and colleges in the UK, both state and independent, which offer the IB. Details of the IB and the schools and colleges offering it are given on pages 46–53.

Length of stay

If you are planning to live in the UK for a relatively short period, perhaps no more than a year, you may find it more appropriate for your child to attend an international school. These schools specialise in educating children whose stay is limited and who regularly move around the world with their parents. Most are day schools although some also offer boarding provision. These schools tend to have a broad mix of nationalities and offer a curriculum, normally based either on the British or the American system, sufficiently flexible to allow a smooth transition afterwards into international schools elsewhere in the world. Many also offer the IB, as described above.

If your stay is relatively short and you plan to return home afterwards, you may be able to enter your child in one of the schools in the UK specifically for nationals of other countries who are based in the UK. France, Germany, Sweden, Norway, Greece and Japan are all represented. Your own embassy in London should be able to provide further details.

Location

If you are looking for a boarding school, try not to restrict your search too narrowly. Most schools, including those in the most beautiful and rural parts of the UK, are within easy reach of major transport links and the UK is well served by air, rail and road routes. In addition, most schools will make arrangements to have your child escorted between school and the airport and vice versa.

Visiting schools

Once you have decided on the most suitable type of school, you can obtain information on specific schools. Gabbitas can identify schools likely to meet your requirements, arrange for you to receive prospectuses and, if required, arrange visits for you. It is essential that you visit schools before making a choice. Try to plan your visits to school during term time. The school year in the UK begins in September and comprises three terms: early September to mid December, early January to mid March and early April to early July. There are also three half-term breaks, normally from two days to a week, at the end of October, in mid- to late February and at the end of May. Gabbitas can arrange a schedule of visits for you to ensure that you make the best use of your time in the UK.

Questions to ask

English language support

What level of English does the school expect? Is additional support available at school? How is this organised? Is there a qualified teacher?

Pupil mix

International schools naturally have pupils of many different nationalities at any one time. However, if you are looking to enter your child into a mainstream independent school, you may wish to find out how many other pupils of your nationality attend the school and what arrangements are made to encourage them to mix with English pupils.

Pastoral care

If your child has special dietary needs or is required to observe specific religious principles, is the school willing and able to cope? Would your child also be expected to take part in the school's normal worship?

If your child speaks little English, it can be very comforting during the early days when homesickness and minor worries arise, or in the event of an emergency, to have a member of staff on hand to whom the child can speak in his or her own language. Bear in mind, however, that fewer schools are likely to have staff who speak non-European languages.

Ask about arrangements for escorting your child to and from school at the beginning and end of term. Some schools have a minibus service to take children to railway stations and airports or will arrange a taxi where appropriate.

Guardianship

Most schools insist that boarding pupils whose parents live overseas have an appointed guardian living near the school who can offer a home for 'exeats' (weekends out of school), half-term breaks and at the beginning and end of term in case flights do not coincide exactly with school dates. A guardian may be a relative or friend appointed by parents, but is should be remembered that the arrangement may need to continue for some years and that guardianship is a substantial commitment.

For parents with no suitable contacts in the UK, schools may be able to assist in making arrangements. Alternatively there are independent organisations, including Gabbitas, which specialise in the provision of guardianship services. Good guardian families should offer a 'home from home', looking after the interests and welfare of your child as they would their own, providing a separate room and space for study, attending school events and parents' evenings, involving your child in all aspects of family life and encouraging him or her to feel comfortable and relaxed while away from school. Some guardianship organisations are very experienced in selecting suitable families who will offer a safe and happy home to students a long way from their own parents. The range of services offered and fees charged by different providers will vary, but you should certainly look for a service which:

- personally ensures that families are visited in their homes by an experienced member of staff and that all appropriate checks are made.
- takes a genuine interest in your child's educational and social welfare and progress.
- keeps in touch with you, your child, the school and the guardian family to ensure that all is running smoothly.
- provides, as required, administrative support and assistance with visa and travel requirements, medical and dental checks and insurance and any other matters such as the purchase of school uniform, sports kit and casual clothes.

Parents may like to know that there is now an association of guardianship service providers entitled AEGIS (the Association of Educational Guardians for International Students), of which Gabbitas is a member. The purpose of AEGIS is to promote best and legal practice in all areas of guardianship and to safeguard the welfare and happiness of overseas children attending educational institutions in the UK. Founded in November 1997, AEGIS aims to provide accreditation for all reputable guardianship organisations. Applicants for membership are required to undergo assessment and inspection to ensure that they are adhering to the AEGIS Code of Practice and fulfilling the Membership Criteria before full membership can be granted. For further details of the Gabbitas Guardianship Service, contact Jill Shilcock on +44 (0)20 7734 0161. For further information about AEGIS, contact Mrs Margaret Banks MBE, Development Director, tel: +44 (0)116 210 9893, fax: +44 (0)116 210 9894, E-mail: mrb@webleicester.co.uk

Preparing your child to come to the UK

Coming to school in a different country is an enriching and exciting experience. Learning to live in a different culture is all a part of that experience. It demands patience, tolerance and understanding on all sides. You can help your child to settle in more quickly by encouraging him or her to take a positive approach and to try to absorb the traditions and social customs of school and family life in the UK. After the first year, most children begin to feel more confident and comfortable in their surroundings, both at school and with their guardian family. A good guardianship organisation will ensure that you and your child know what to expect from life in the UK, and that you are aware of the kind of behaviour and approach which the school and guardian family will expect from your child. They will also be able to advise on aspects such as appropriate clothes to bring for a UK climate, which may be very different from that at home. Similarly, they should be able to advise on visas, UK entry requirements and related matters.

Where to go for help

You may be able to obtain information about schools from official sources in your own country. For detailed guidance and assistance in the UK you may wish to contact an independent educational consultancy such as Gabbitas which can advise you on all aspects of education in the UK and transferring into the British system.

1.5
Finding The Fees
Towry Law Financial Services Limited

How much will it cost?

You first decision is what fees you are planning to meet. Do you have a specific school or schools in mind and if so, what are the fees? Hopefully you have started planning early which means that you are unlikely to have made a final choice of school. In this case you need to work on the average or typical fees for the type of school. This can range from day preparatory to senior boarding school. If your child was born in the latter part of the year, check that you are planning for the right period, ie don't plan to provide funds a year early leaving a gap year at the end.

Next, you need to allow for inflation. A school's major cost is teacher and other salaries which tend to increase in line with earnings rather than prices. Historically, earnings rise faster than prices, so even though inflation is now relatively low it is certainly not something you can ignore.

The distinctive feature of planning for educational costs

The distinctive nature lies in the fact that you are planning for a 'known commitment'. You know that at the beginning of each term or school year, you will have a bill to pay and will need to draw on your investments.

This is where the 'reward – risk' spectrum comes in. At one end, asset backed investments offer a higher potential reward but also a degree of investment risk or potential volatility. In the longer term, such investments have been the way to achieve real growth and outpace inflation (though the past is not necessarily a guide to future performance). On the other hand, you do not want to rely on such investments if it means encashing them at the worst possible time, just after a stock market setback. Remember, because of the nature of educational planning you probably do not have any choice about when you need funds to pay a bill.

At the other end of the reward – risk spectrum are deposit accounts: just about as safe as safe can be (so long as the institution is safe) but will they even keep up with inflation?

You do not need to plump for either extreme. The answer partly depends on the period over which you are investing. If you are starting soon after birth, asset backed investment can play a larger role, giving greater potential for real growth. Nearer the time, your holdings can be switched on a phased basis into more secure investment vehicles to lock in the gains and from which you can draw during the schooling period.

An alternative approach is 'mix and match'. A mixture of asset backed investments with more secure ones will allow you to draw from the former in years when their values are high. In other years, you can draw from the more secure investments.

Existing investments

Your strategy should take into account any existing investments or savings that may be suitable. These may not have been taken out with school fees in mind. For example, you may have started a mortgage endowment some years ago which will mature during the schooling period. Will it provide a surplus?

Equity investments

Rather than investing in individual shares, most common nowadays are 'collective' investments like unit trusts (or Open Ended Investment Companies – OEICs), investment trusts or the equity funds of life insurance companies. Collective funds give access to the benefits of equity investments without the investment risk inherent in one or a small number of individual shares. They are a low cost way of spreading risk by investing in a portfolio of shares, plus the advantage of professional fund management.

Generally, these investments should only be considered if there is an investment period of at least ten years.

With profit investments

These are offered by some of the best known insurance companies and are available in both lump sum and regular premium versions. The insurance company manages a fund that is particularly widely diversified, including gilts, deposits, property, UK equities, overseas bonds, foreign currency and overseas equities.

'With profit' investments smooth the investment peaks and troughs. The surplus from the funds is distributed as a 'with profit' bonus each year. The insurance company maintains reserves and in good years part of the surplus is added to the reserves. In not so good years, the reserve is used to maintain the bonus. Because of these reserves, the financial strength of the life company is important.

In their regular premium version, these are known as with profit endowments. They are generally familiar as a predictable way of building a fund to repay a mortgage. Generally they should only be considered for a minimum period of ten years.

In their lump sum form, they are known as with profit bonds. These reserve the right to apply a 'market value adjustment' in adverse market conditions. This could reduce the amount available on encashment. Generally, they should be considered for an investment period of at least five years.

Tax efficient investments

You can invest regular contributions or a lump sum into Individual Savings Accounts (ISAs). They are generally a good idea because the tax benefits should enhance returns. You can use ISAs to accept cash deposits, equities and also 'corporate bonds'. You will need to check whether 'mini' or 'maxi' ISAs are best for you.

Any existing PEPs or TESSAs that you took out before ISAs started in 1999 and that you have kept going could, of course, be used as part of your planning.

If you are looking at least ten years ahead, you could start with equity ISAs. Nearer the time they could be transferred to corporate bond ISAs to lock in gains and for a more predictable return up to the time when you need to make withdrawals. Cash deposits are suitable for the short term. Unlike cash deposits, the capital invested in equities and corporate bonds is not guaranteed but they offer the prospect of a higher return in the medium to long term.

Expatriate parents

If you are an expatriate or offshore investor, there are offshore versions of the equity and with profit investments described above. Important considerations are your tax position whilst you are offshore and, if you will be returning to the UK during the schooling period, your UK tax position.

Late planning

If you have left it late to start planning, say within five years, you could consider the following:

- Check the school's terms for payment in advance (sometimes called composition fees schemes) as these can be attractive. Ask what happens if, for whatever reason, you switch to another school.
- Consider deposit based schemes, particularly cash deposit ISAs for tax efficiency.
- For other deposit accounts, consider postal accounts as they often offer better rates.
- National Savings, gilts and fixed interest securities could also be considered.
- Loan schemes are available whereby you arrange a 'drawdown' facility secured on your house. This assumes you have some 'free equity' (the difference between the value of the house and your mortgage) and is usually set up as a second mortgage. You can then 'drawdown' from the facility as and when you need to pay fees. Hence, you do not start paying interest sooner than necessary, keeping down the total cost. (Your home is at risk if you do not keep up repayments on a mortgage or other loan secured on it.)
- Because of the interest payments, loan schemes are costly so they should be regarded as a last resort and only after you have reviewed your finances to check that there is no alternative.

The need for protection

For most families, the major resource for educational expenses is the parent's earnings. Death or prolonged illness could destroy a well-laid plan and have a terrible effect on a family's standard of living and a child's education. You should therefore review your existing arrangements (whether from a company scheme or private) and make sure you are sufficiently protected.

University expenses

Although many of the same investment considerations apply, planning needs to cover living expenses plus a small proportion of the fees. There is a system of student loans.

Although university expenses are generally not as high as school fees, they have become more onerous in recent years, a trend that is likely to continue.

'Golden' rules of educational planning

- plan as early in the child's life as possible.
- set out what funds you need and when you need them, and plan accordingly.
- avoid or reduce tax on the investments wherever possible.
- use capital if available, particularly from grandparents.
- consult an expert, preferably an independent financial adviser.

This article briefly outlines some of the considerations and investment opportunities and does not make specific or individual recommendations. There is no one answer to suit everyone. The solution depends on a number of considerations and for a strategy tailored to your individual circumstances, seek independent financial advice.

TOWRY LAW FINANCIAL SERVICES LIMITED
REGULATED BY THE PERSONAL INVESTMENT AUTHORITY FOR INVESTMENT BUSINESS

The Personal Investment Authority does not regulate National Savings, deposits, loan schemes or tax advice.

Towry Law Financial
Services Limited,
Towry House,
Western Road,
Bracknell, RG12 1TL.
Also in Belfast, Birmingham, Glasgow, Leeds and London.
Tel: 0845 788 9933 (calls may be recorded).
E-mail: info@towrylaw.com

1.6
Scholarships, Bursaries
And Other Awards

In addition to the many financial planning schemes available, assistance with the payment of fees may be obtainable from a variety of other sources.

Scholarships

Many senior schools offer scholarship opportunities. These are awarded, at the discretion of the school, to pupils displaying particular ability or promise, either in academic subjects, as an all-rounder or in specific areas such as music or art. Candidates are normally assessed on the basis of their performance in an examination or audition. Scholarship examinations are normally held in the February or March preceding September entry. Pupils awarded scholarships in, for example, music or art, may be required to sit the Common Entrance examination to ensure that they meet the normal academic requirements of the awarding school.

Scholarships are normally offered upon the usual age of entry to the school. Some schools also offer awards for sixth-form entry, for example for students who have performed particularly well in the GCSE examinations. These awards may be restricted to pupils already attending the school or may also be open to prospective entrants coming from other schools.

Scholarships vary in value, although full-fee scholarships are now rarely available. Scholarships are awarded as a percentage of the full tuition fee to allow for inflation.

Fewer scholarships are available at preparatory school level. Choristers, however are a special category. Choir schools generally offer much reduced fees for Choristers, well below the normal day fee. Help may also be available at senior schools, although in practice it is common for choristers to gain music scholarships at their senior schools. A list of schools belonging to the Choir Schools Association appears on page 471. Details of schools specialising in the arts, dance and music appear on page 428.

For a general guide to scholarships offered by individual schools, turn to the scholarships index in the Reference Section (Part Four). More detailed information about individual school awards may be found in the section entitled Scholarship Profiles.

Bursaries

Bursaries are intended primarily to ensure that children obtain provision suited to their needs and ability in cases where parents cannot afford the normal fees. They are awarded on the basis of financial hardship, rather than particular ability. All pupils applying for a bursary, however, will be required to show, normally by passing Common Entrance or the school's own entry tests, that they meet academic requirements. The size of the award is entirely at the discretion of the school.

A list of schools able to offer bursaries is given in the Reference Section.

Reserved entrance awards

Some schools reserve awards for children with parents in a specific profession, for example in HM Forces, the clergy or in teaching. These are similar to bursaries in that the child must meet the normal entry requirements of the school, but eligibility for the award will be dependent upon fulfilment of one of the criteria stated above. Normally schools will reserve only a few places on this basis. Once a place for a specific award has been filled, it will not become available again until the pupil currently in receipt leaves the school. Hence the award may be available only once every five years or so.

A list of schools and brief summary of the reserved entrance awards offered by each is given in the Reference Section. The awards covered include those offered to children with one or both parents working in any of HM Forces, the Foreign Office, the medical profession, teaching, the clergy or as Christian missionaries.

Other awards

Schools may also offer concessions for brothers and sisters or for the children of former pupils.

The Government Assisted Places Scheme

The Government funded Assisted Places Scheme is being phased out over a period of time. The Education (Schools) Act 1997 is the legislation that provided for the scheme to be phased out and for no further intakes to assisted places after the beginning of the 1997–98 school year. However, the Government made a commitment to provide continued support for children holding assisted places at the start of the 1997–98 academic year for the remainder of the current phase of their education. The policy in relation to children in receipt of secondary education is that they are entitled to continue on their place until they reach the upper age limit of the school. For example, children in receipt of secondary education who are attending a school which provides education until age 18 are eligible to keep their place to that age. In the same way, children in receipt of secondary education who are attending a school which provides education until age 13 are eligible to hold their place until that age.

The policy with reference to children in receipt of primary education is to allow those currently holding places to remain eligible until the end of the primary phase of their education which will normally be at the end of the school year in which they reach age 11.

It is also still possible for an assisted place pupil to transfer his or her place to another school which has assisted pupils. Places can be transferred in the event of a school closure or merger, if the school notifies the Secretary of State that it no longer wishes to provide assisted places; or in cases where the Secretary of State is satisfied that it is reasonable to do so in view of the particular circumstances relating to the child.

The GDST Scholarship and Bursary Scheme

The GDST (Girls' Day School Trust), which comprises 25 independent girls' schools educating over 19,000 girls, has traditionally aimed to make its schools accessible to bright, motivated girls from families who could not afford a place at a GDST school without financial assistance. Until the Government's announcement to phase out the Assisted Places Scheme, GDST schools offered a substantial number of Assisted Places each year. With the aim of preserving most of the 3,000 places, the Trust launched in 1997 a new Scholarship and Bursary Scheme specifically designed for low-income families. Grants are only awarded at GDST schools.

Most bursaries under the Scheme will be awarded to girls from families with a total income of under £12,000, and it is unlikely that a bursary would be awarded in cases where total gross income exceeds £25,000. Bursaries are means-tested and may cover up to full fees. Scholarships, which are not means-tested, are awarded on merit and may cover up to half the fees. Most awards are available either on entry at 11 or for girls entering the Sixth Form. The Scheme is also designed to assist pupils already attending a GDST school whose parents face unexpected financial difficulties which could mean having to remove their daughter from the school and disrupt her education.

Awards are made at the discretion of individual school Heads rather than the Trust and requests for further information should therefore be directed to the Head of the school at which parents wish to apply for a place. A full list of GDST schools appears on pages 474–475.

Other government grants

Assistance with the payment of fees is also offered to personnel employed by the Foreign and Commonwealth Office and by the Ministry of Defence, where a boarding education may be the only feasible option for parents whose professional lives demand frequent moves or postings overseas.

The FCO termly boarding allowance is available to FCO parents on request and is reviewed annually. Parents in need of further information should contact the FCO Personnel Services Department on (020) 7238 4357.

Services personnel may seek guidance from Service Children's Education (UK) who can advise on choosing a boarding school and on the boarding allowance made. In 2001–2002 the boarding allowance is £2,678 per term for junior pupils and £3,382 per term for senior pupils. An allowance is also available for children with special educational needs. Further information may be obtained from HQ SCE (UK), Trenchard Lines, Upavon, Pewsey, Wiltshire SN9 6BE. Telephone: 01980 618244.

Parents may also find it helpful to consult the list of schools offering reserved entrance awards. Some schools may be able to supplement allowances offered by employers through a reserved entrance award offered to pupils who meet the relevant criteria, eg with a parent in HM Forces.

Grant-giving Trusts

There are various educational and charitable Trusts which exist to provide help with the payment of independent school fees. Usually the criteria restrict eligibility to particular groups, for example orphans, or in cases of sudden and unforeseen financial hardship. In many cases a grant may be given only to enable a child to complete the present stage of education, eg to finish a GCSE or A Level course. Applications are normally considered on an individual basis by an appointed committee. The criteria for eligibility and for the award of a grant will vary according to individual policy. In some cases several Trusts may each contribute an agreed sum towards one individual case in order to make up the fees required. It should be noted that such Trusts receive many more applications for grants than can possibly be issued and competition is fierce. Applications for financial help purely on the grounds that parents would like an independent education for their child but cannot afford it from their own resources will be rejected. Parents are advised to consider carefully before applying for an independent school place and entering a child for the entrance examination if they cannot meet the fees unaided nor demonstrate a genuine need, as defined by the criteria published by the awarding Trusts, for an independent school education. Parents may find it helpful to consult the Educational Grants Directory, published by the Directory of Social Change. For further information about charitable funding contact the Educational Grants Advisory Service, administered by Mrs Judith Crawford, 62 Park Lane, Norwich, Norfolk NR2 3EF.

Local Authority grants

Grants from Local Authorities are sometimes available where a need for a child to board can be demonstrated, for example where the child has special educational needs which cannot be met in a day school environment or where travel on a daily basis is not feasible. Such grants are few in number. Awards for boarding fees at an independent school may not be granted unless it can be shown that there is no boarding place available at one of the state boarding schools, of which there are 35 nationwide.

Awards from Local Authorities are a complex issue. Parents wishing to find out more should contact the Director of Education for the Authority in which they live.

1.7
Examinations And Qualifications
In The UK

Common Entrance

The Common Entrance examination forms the basis of entry to most independent senior schools, although some schools set their own entrance exams. Traditionally it is taken by boys at the age of 13 and by girls at the age of 11. However, with the growth of co-education at senior level the divisions have become less sharply defined and the examinations at 11+, 12+ and 13+ are open to both boys and girls.

The Common Entrance papers are set centrally by the Independent Schools' Examinations Board, which comprises members of the Headmasters' and Headmistresses' Conference (HMC), the Girls' Schools Association (GSA) and the Incorporated Association of Preparatory Schools (IAPS). The papers are marked, however, by the individual schools, which have their own marking schemes and set their own entry standards. Common Entrance is not an exam which candidates pass by reaching a national standard.

The content of the Common Entrance papers has undergone regular review and the Independent Schools Examinations Board has adapted syllabuses to bring them into line with National Curriculum requirements.

Candidates are entered for Independent Schools Examinations by their junior or preparatory schools. Parents whose children attend state primary schools should apply to the Independent School Examinations Board direct, ideally four months before the scheduled examination date. Some pupils may need additional coaching for the exam if they are not attending an independent preparatory school. To be eligible, pupils must normally have been offered a place by a senior school subject to their performance in the exam. Pupils applying for scholarships may be required to pass Common Entrance before sitting the scholarship exam. Candidates normally take the exam in their own junior or preparatory schools.

At 11+ the Common Entrance exam consists of papers in English, Mathematics and Science, and is designed to be suitable for all pupils, whether they attend independent or state schools. At 12+ papers are set in English, Mathematics, Science and Elementary French. Most pupils who take the exam at 13+ come from independent preparatory schools. Subjects are English, Mathematics, Science (Compulsory); French, History, Geography, Religious Studies, German, Spanish, Latin and Greek (Optional). English as an Additional Language is an option at 11+, 12+ and 13+.

The examination for 13+ entry takes place in February and June. For entry at 11+ the exam is held in January. For further information on Common Entrance, or copies of past papers, contact: The Administrator, Independent Schools Examinations Board, Jordan House, Christchurch Road, New Milton, Hampshire BH25 6QJ. Tel: 01425 621111, fax: 01425 620044.

General Certificate of Secondary Education (GCSE)

The GCSE examination is open to anyone, but it is normally taken by pupils at the age of 16. The GCSE forms the principal means of assessment of the two years preceding GCSE examinations (Key Stage 4) from 14-16.

Coursework also forms a part of most GCSE syllabuses, enabling pupils to gain credit from work done during the year rather than exclusively on the basis of exam performance.

GCSE results are reported on a scale of grades from A*–G.

Increasing use is being made of 'differentiated' examination papers, ie a series of tiered papers targeted at different ranges of ability within the A*–G range of the grading scale. Most large-entry GCSE subjects are examined through a foundation tier covering grades G–C and a higher tier covering grades D–A*.

Most pupils of average ability take eight or nine GCSE subjects, although some may take 10 or 11. Very able pupils may take some GCSE exams after one year. Pupils are asked to choose their subjects at 13. Schools can offer advice on those they think most suitable. A relatively new option is the GCSE (Short Course), which is designed to take only half the study time of full GCSE and is the equivalent of half a GCSE. It is graded on the same scale as a full GCSE but covers fewer topics. It can be used in various ways: to offer able students additional choices such as a second modern language or to offer a subject which could not otherwise be studied as a full GCSE because of other subject choices. It may also be attractive to students who need extra time in their studies and would be better suited to a two-year course devoted to a GCSE (Short Course) rather than a full GCSE. Short Courses are currently available in Design and Technology, Modern Foreign Languages, Information and Communication Technology, Physical Education, Religious Studies, History, Geography, Art and Design, Music, Business Studies, Electronics and Health Studies. New GCSEs in Vocational subjects will be available from September 2002. Details can be found on the Qualifications and Curriculum Authority website at www.qca.org.uk.

Qualification reforms

New arrangements for the post-16 curriculum took effect in September 2000 with the aims of broadening the sixth-form curriculum beyond the traditional three subject format, aiding progression from GCSE to A Level and helping students to make a more open-ended choice of subjects.

The reforms are designed to make it easier for students to combine A Level studies with GNVQ programmes if they wish. A common A–E grading system is used for GCE and vocational A Level qualifications.

GCE A Levels and GCE Advanced Subsidiary

Each A Level comprises six units. For each subject, three units form an Advanced Subsidiary Level (AS) course and represent the first half of the Advanced GCE (A Level) course. The remaining three units (known as A2) represent the final year's study. Successful completion of all six units is required for the award of an A Level. An A Level grade is reached by combining AS and A2 grades. AS and A Level have UCAS point scores. An AS Level receives only half the points of an A Level.

Students who do not pursue a subject beyond the first year but who successfully complete the first three units will be awarded an AS. However, completion of the three A2 units on their own does not represent a qualification.

There are a few freestanding AS subjects where no corresponding A Level is available. AS is designed to provide extra breadth to sixth form studies. Students may take four or five AS subjects in the first year of Sixth Form, but they may narrow down to three A2 in the second year.

AS units focus on material appropriate for the first year of an A Level course, and are assessed accordingly. A2 is more demanding and is assessed at full A Level standard. Overall assessment is based on examinations and/or coursework and may be made at the end of the course (linear) or at stages during the course (modular). There is a compulsory 20 per cent synoptic assessment for all modular A Levels to demonstrate understanding of the course as a whole and the connections between its different elements.

The AS and A Level is graded on a scale of A–E for passes. U (unclassified) indicates a fail. Only one re-sit of each unit is allowed, with the better result standing.

The development of key skills is integral to the new qualifications. Although not yet mandatory, it is expected that soon most college and university applicants will have evidence in their academic portfolio of at least three of the following skills: application of number, communication, information technology, improving own learning and performance, problem solving and the ability to work with others. A Key Skills Qualification is available, and students will be encouraged to build up evidence from their units and other sources towards achieving it. Based on the first three skills listed, the certificate will give a profile of the level achieved in each.

A new examination, the Advanced Extension Award, will be officially available in 2002 for the most able A Level students. Initially it will only be available for some A Level subjects.

Vocational education and training at 16+

Vocational options are available at all levels from age 16 upwards and cover a vast range of occupational areas. Qualifications are offered by three Awarding Bodies: Edexcel, AQA (Assessment and Qualifications Alliance), and OCR (Oxford, Cambridge and RSA Examinations).

Many qualifications come within a national framework, which encompasses two main forms of Award. National Vocational Qualifications, or NVQs (in Scotland, Scottish

Vocational Qualifications or SVQs), are work-based and generally taken while the candidate is in employment. The second type, the Vocational A Level (formerly the Advanced General National Vocational Qualification or GNVQ) is the one more usually available in schools and colleges and is intended to form a preparation for employment or Higher Education. It can also lead to other forms of vocational training such as Modern Apprenticeships and Foundation Modern Apprenticeships.

The body responsible for the overall framework is the Qualifications and Curriculum Authority. In Scotland the equivalent body for the SVQ/GSVQ framework is the Scottish Qualifications Authority.

GNVQs and Vocational A Levels

These qualifications have been developed in consultation with employers to offer an alternative to students who wish to remain in full time education at 16+ but seek a course that is directly related to a vocational area. Vocational A Levels take two years and students are normally expected to have achieved at least four or five GCSEs at grades A*–C or an Intermediate GNVQ. The courses are based on a modular system that allows students to complete specific units gradually and build up their qualifications to suit their individual needs.

The GNVQ is still available at two levels:

Foundation – broadly equivalent to 4 GCSEs at Grade D-G or an NVQ level 1
Intermediate – broadly equivalent to 4 GCSEs at Grade A*–C or an NVQ level 2

A new, more rigorous assessment regime has been adopted for Vocational A Levels and for Foundation and Intermediate GNVQs.

The last registrations for Foundations and Intermediate GNVQs, which are to be replaced by GCSEs in vocational subjects will be in 2003–2004.

Schools and colleges began the new Vocational A Level courses, which replaced Advanced GNVQs in September 2000.

The new advanced qualifications comprise between 3 and 12 units, depending on the level sought. The basic Vocational A Level has 6 units: the Vocational A Level (Double Award) has 12 units, and the Vocational Advanced Subsidiary (available in 4 Subjects at present) has 3 units. The units will offer the opportunity to study the six Key Skills, including application of number, communication and information technology. However, Key Skills are not separately assessed.

There are no formal examinations. Instead, students must complete projects, activities and assignments and provide evidence that the required standards have been met. Assessment of the Vocational A Level is conducted both internally and externally, and is based on criteria used to assess the students' ability to apply their skills and under-standing in a vocational context. It is not necessary for students to pass all the constituent units for the award of a Vocational A Level Certificate. Both unit grades and overall grades are now on the same A–E scale as the Advanced GCE; the broad equivalent to the old GNVQ grades being: A=Distinction, C=Merit and E=Pass. The range of Vocational A/AS subjects on offer is being reviewed along with the size of and the demand for vocational units as compared with GCE.

In Scotland, General Scottish Vocational Qualifications (GSVQs) have been brought under their new National Qualifications framework. Vocational A Levels and GSVQs are recognised by universities as a basis for entry to Higher Education.

As well as qualifications within the vocational framework, the Awarding Bodies offer a range of other qualifications. Further guidance may be obtained from your school, college or careers adviser. Alternatively, contact a reputable independent consultancy such as Gabbitas.

Scottish National Qualifications

In recent years post-16 qualifications in Scotland have seen a number of reforms. Most schools still prepare students for the Standard Grade examinations taken at 16. However, under the new National Qualifications framework, SCE Higher Grades and the Certificate of Sixth Year Studies have been phased out. All students who stay on in education after Standard Grade follow a new qualifications system, beginning at one of five levels, depending on their examination results.

Access, Intermediate 1 and Intermediate 2 are progressive levels which a student might take to gain a better grounding in a subject before going on to take one of two higher levels; Higher and Advanced Higher. These top tier levels are equivalent to the SCE Higher and Certificate of Sixth Year studies. The lower three levels are not compulsory for students with aptitude, who may move straight on to study one of the Higher level courses. With the exception of the Standard Grade, each National Qualification is built on units, courses and group awards.

National Units – these are the smallest elements of a qualification and are internally assessed, mostly requiring 40 hours of study.

Courses – national courses are usually taken in S5 or S6 and at college. They are made up of three units each, and are assessed internally and by examination for which grades A–C are awarded.

Scottish Group Awards (SGAs) – these are programmes of courses and units that cover 16 broad subject areas. An SGA can be obtained within 1 year, or worked towards over a longer period.

There are seventy subjects available, including job-orientated subjects such as Travel and Tourism and traditional ones such as Maths and English. All National Qualifications have core skills embedded in them, although it is possible to take stand-alone units, for example Problem Solving, Communication, Numeracy and Information Technology.

General Scottish Vocational Qualifications (GSVQs), Lifestart, Workstart, some National Certificate Clusters, National Certificate Modules and Short Courses will be available for the last time in 2004. After this time they will be completely replaced by National Qualifications.

For further information contact the Scottish Qualifications Authority.

The International Baccalaureate

(Diploma programme)

The International Baccalaureate Organisation (IBO), a non-profit educational foundation based in Switzerland, offers the Diploma Programme for students in the final two years of secondary school in the 16–19 age range, the Middle Years Programme for students in the 11–16 age range and the Primary Years Programme for students for 3–11 years of age.

The IB Diploma is recognised and accepted by selective universities worldwide. It is offered by a small number of independent and state schools and colleges in the UK, a full list of which appears below. Worldwide there are some 1280 state and independent schools offering the IB Diploma Programme in 106 countries. The emphasis is on breadth, specialisation in specific areas, international understanding and critical thinking skills.

The IB Diploma can be an attractive alternative to A Levels for academically able students. It is a two-year course, broader in scope and more demanding than a GCE A Level syllabus and consists of six subject groups:

Group 1   language A1 (first language) including the study of selections from world literature.

Group 2   language A2, B or *ab initio* (second language).

Group 3   individuals and societies – history, geography, economics, philosophy, psychology, social anthropology, business and organisation, information technology in a global society, history of the islamic world.

Group 4   experimental sciences – biology, chemistry, physics, environmental systems, design technology.

Group 5   mathematics – mathematics, mathematical studies, mathematical methods, further mathematics, computer science.

Group 6   arts – visual arts, music, theatre arts, a third modern language, a second subject from group 3 or group 4, a school-based syllabus (SBS) approved by the IBO.

Candidates for the diploma must take one subject from each of the first five groups, and either a second subject from one of them or a group 6 subject. They must take at least three and not more than four of the six subjects at Higher Level (HL) and the others at Standards Level (SL).

Language A1 is designed for students for whom the language is normally their strongest one. Language A2 is for study by speakers with a high level of competence in the language. Language B is designed for study by students with some previous experience of learning the language. *AB initio* is a foreign language learning programme for students with no previous experience of the language and who do not normally live in a country where the language is spoken.

Candidates must also submit an extended essay in one of the IB specified subjects, follow a course in the theory of knowledge and take part in activities representing creativity, action and service (CAS).

In line with the IB's international emphasis, all subjects are offered in English, French and Spanish.

Each examined subject is graded on a scale of 1 (minimum) to 7 (maximum). Award of the Diploma requires a minimum total of 24 points out of 45 and satisfactory completion of the theory of knowledge course, the extended essay and CAS.

The Middle Years Programme (MYP), with 195 schools worldwide, is designed for students in the 11–16 age range and can, with IBO approval, be offered in any language. While all disciplines are studied thoroughly, the MYP stresses their interrelatedness. Students are encouraged to develop intercultural awareness along with genuine understanding of their own history and traditions. Fundamental importance is also attached to the firm command of one's own language and on the acquisition of a foreign language. The educational philosophy and styles of teaching and learning are consistent from one programme to another, the five-year curriculum serves as excellent preparation but is not a prerequisite for the IB Diploma Programme. Schools may subscribe to one or the other or both.

The Primary Years Programme, with 69 schools worldwide, focuses on the heart as well as the mind. It addresses social, physical, emotional and cultural needs as well as academic ones.

For further information on the IB contact the International Baccalaureate Office, Route des Morillons 15, CH-1218 Grand-Saconnex, Geneva, Switzerland. Tel: +41 22 791 7740, fax: +41 22 791 0277. E-mail: ibhq@ibo.org Web site: www.ibo.org

The following schools and colleges are authorised to participate in the International Baccalaureate in the United Kingdom:

ENGLAND

Cambridgeshire

Impington Village College
New Road
Impington
Cambridge CB4 9LX
Tel: 01223 200400
Fax: 01223 718961
E-mail: ivc45@impingtonvc.cambs-schools.net
Warden: Mrs Jacqueline Kearns
IB Co-ordinator: Mrs Sandra Morton
IB No: 0579

Turkish International Lycée
Sawston Hall
Sawston
Cambridge CB2 4JR
Tel: 01223 837597
Fax: 01223 837596
E-mail: ar70@dial.pipex.com
School Head: Dr Sinan Bayraktaroglu
IB Co-ordinator: Mrs Lorna Pepper
IB No: 1113

Cheshire

Ridge Danyers College
Cheadle Road
Cheadle Hulme
Cheshire SK8 5HA
Tel: 0161 485 4372
Fax: 0161 482 8129
E-mail: hbh@theridge.ac.uk
Head: Mr Sandy MacDonald
IB Co-ordinator: Mrs Helen Badley Hurst
IB No: 0545

Cornwall

The Bolitho School
Polwithen
Penzance TR18 4JR
Tel: 01736 363271
Fax: 01736 330960
E-mail: enquiries@bolitho.cornwall.sch.uk
Head: Mr N Johnson
IB Co-ordinator: Mrs Mowat

Truro College
College Road
Cornwall TR1 3XX
Tel: 01872 264251
Fax: 01872 222360
E-mail: andyw@trurocollege.ac.uk
Principal: Mr Jonathan Burnett
IB Co-ordinator: Mr Andy Wildin
IB No: 1077

Cumbria

Ullswater Community College
Wetheriggs Lane
Penrith
Cumbria CA11 8NG
Tel: 01768 242160
Fax: 01768 242165
Head: Mr David A Robinson
IB Co-ordinator: Mr Brian Nicholls
IB No: 0687

Devon

Exeter College
Hele Road
Exeter
Devon EX4 4JS
Tel: 01392 205341
Fax: 01392 205324
E-mail: cwillman@exe-coll.ac.uk
Principal: Dr Tim Smith
IB Co-ordinator: Mrs Claire Willman
IB No: 0695

Essex

Anglo-European School
Willow Green
Ingatestone
Essex CM4 0DJ
Tel: 01277 354018
Fax: 01277 355623
E-mail:
*   jrstrachan@angloeuropean.essex.sch.uk*
Head: Mr R Reed
IB Co-ordinator: Mrs Jane Strachan
IB No: 0078

Hampshire

Brockenhurst College
Lyndhurst Road
Hampshire SO42 72E
Tel: 01590 625555
Fax: 01590 625526
E-mail: sra@brock.ac.uk
Head: Mr Mile Snell
IB Co-ordinator: Mr David Basse
IB No: 1210

St Vincent College
Mill Lane
Gosport
Hampshire PO12 4QA
Tel: 01705 588311
Fax: 01705 511186
E-mail: exams@stvincent.ac.uk
Principal: Mrs P Lynn Lee
IB Co-ordinator: Mr Daniel Taylor
IB No: 0899

Southampton City College
St Mary Street
Southampton
Hampshire SO14 1AR
Tel: 023 8057 577339
Fax: 023 8057 57473
Email: sylvia.waghorn@southampton-city.ac.uk
Principal: Mr Philip Gibson
IB Co-ordinator: Ms Sylvia Waghorn
IB No: 0886

Hertfordshire

Goffs School
Goffs Lane
Cheshunt
Hertfordshire
EN7 5QW
Tel: 01992 424200
Fax: 01992 424201
Head: Dr John Versey
IB Co-ordinator: Ms Catriona Connolly
IB No: 1209

Haileybury
Hertford
Hertfordshire SG13 7NU
Tel: 01992 462507
Fax: 01992 470663
E-mail: timw@haileybury.herts.sch.uk
Head: Mr S A Westley
IB Co-ordinator: Mr Tim Woffenden
IB No: 1122

Hockerill Anglo-European School
Dunmow Road
Bishop's Stortford
Hertfordshire CM23 5HX
Tel: 01279 658451
Fax: 01279 755918
E-mail: admin.hockerill@thegrid.org.uk
Principal: Dr Robert Guthrie
IB Co-ordinator: Mrs Vicki Worsnop
IB No: 0815

Oaklands College
St Peters Road
St Albans
Hertfordshire AL1 3RX
Tel: 01727 737 000
Fax: 01727 737 272
Head: Mr P Fielding
IB Co-ordinator: Mr John Hill
IB No: 0593

Kent

Dartford Grammar School
West Hill
Dartford
Kent DA1 2HW
Tel: 01322 223039
Fax: 01322 291426
E-mail: aking@dgs.org.uk
Headteacher: Mr A J Smith
IB Co-ordinator: Mrs Ann King
IB No: 0866

Maidstone Grammar School
Barton Road
Maidstone
Kent ME15 7BT
Tel: 01622 752101
Fax: 01622 753680
Head: N A Turrell
IB Co-ordinator: Mr Keith Derrett
IB No: 0859

Sevenoaks School
Sevenoaks
Kent TN13 1HU
Tel: 01732 455133
Fax: 01732 456143
E-mail: sma@cs.soaks.kent.sch.uk
Head: Mr T Cookson
IB Co-ordinator: Sue Austin
IB No: 0102

Lancashire

Rossall School
Fleetwood
Lancashire FY7 8JW
Tel: 01253 877728
Fax: 01253 772052
E-mail: ib.rossall@virgin.net
Principal: Mr Richard D W Rhodes
Head: Mr S Pengelley
IB Co-ordinator: Miss Janice Kent
IB No: 1045

London

International School of London
139 Gunnersbury Avenue
London W3 8LG
Tel: (020) 8992 5823
Fax: (020) 8993 7012
E-mail: davieshuw1@yahoo.co.uk
Head: Mrs E Whelen
IB Co-ordinator: Mr Huw Davies
IB No: 0057

King's College School
Wimbledon Common
London SW19 4TT
Tel: 020 8255 5300
Fax: 020 8255 5309
E-mail: mjw@kcs.org.uk
Head: Mr A Evans
IB Co-ordinator: Mr Michael Windsor
IB No: 1262

Southbank International School
36-40 Kensington Park Road
London W11 3BU
Tel: (020) 7229 8230
Fax: (020) 7229 3784
E-mail: gma@southbank.org
Head: Mr Milton E Toubkin
IB Co-ordinator: Mrs Gwen Martinez
IB No: 0309

Woodside Park School
49 Woodside Avenue
Friern Barnet
London N12 8SY
Tel: (020) 8445 2333
Fax: (020) 8445 0835
E-mail: amalins@wpis.org
Principal: Mr Metters
IB Co-ordinator: Ms Anne Malins
IB No: 0865

Merseyside

Broadgreen High School
Queen's Drive
Liverpool
Merseyside L13 5UQ
Tel: 0151 228 6800
Fax: 0151 220 9256
E-mail: ib@rapid.co.uk
Head: Mr Ian P Andain
IB Co-ordinator: Mr Austin Patterson
IB No: 0639

Middlesex

The American Community School
108 Vine Lane, Hillingdon
Uxbridge
Middlesex UB10 0BE
Tel: 01895 818411
Fax: 01895 256974
E-mail: dhiest@acs-england.co.uk
Head: Mr Chris Taylor
IB Co-ordinator: Mr Daniel Hiest
IB No: 0152

Oxfordshire

Henley College
Deanfield Avenue
Henley-on-Thames
Oxfordshire RG9 1UH
Tel: 01491 579988
Fax: 01491 410099
Principal: Mr Graham O J Phillips
IB Co-ordinator: Mr Robin Milne
IB No: 0557

St Clare's
139 Banbury Road
Oxford OX2 7AL
Tel: 01865 552031
Fax: 01865 310002
E-mail: ib-coord@stclares.ac.uk
Principal: Mr Boyd Roberts
IB Co-ordinator: Mr Nick Lee
IB No: 0041

Rutland

Oakham School
Chapel Close
Oakham
Rutland LE15 6DT
Tel: 01572 758698
Fax: 01572 758712
E-mail: jr@oakham.rutland.sch.uk
Head: Mr A R M Little
IB Co-ordinator: Dr Jill Rutherford

Surrey

The American Community School
'Heywood'
Portsmouth Road
Cobham
Surrey KT11 1BL
Tel: 01932 867251
Fax: 01932 869791
E-mail: cworthington@acs-england.co.uk
Head: Mr T Lehman
IB Co-ordinator: Mr Craig Worthington
IB No: 0431

The American Community School
Egham
Surrey TW20 0HS
Tel: 01784 430800
Fax: 01784 430153
E-mail: jguy@acs-england.co.uk
Head: Mrs Moira Hadley
IB Co-ordinator: Ms Judith Guy
IB No: 1211

Kings College for the Arts & Technology
Southway
Guildford
Surrey GU2 8DU
Tel: 01483 458956
Fax: 01483 458957
E-mail: n.clay@kingscollegeguildford.com
IB Co-ordinator: Mr Nick Clay
IB No: 1290

Marymount International School
George Road
Kingston upon Thames
Surrey KT2 7PE
Tel: (020) 8949 0571
Fax: (020) 8336 2485
E-mail: acdean@marymount.kingston.sch.uk
Principal: Sr Rosaleen Sheridan
IB Co-ordinator: Dr Brian Johnson
IB No: 0128

Sussex

East Sussex

Hastings College of Arts & Technology
Archery Road
St Leonards on Sea
East Sussex TN38 0HX
Tel: 01424 442222
Fax: 01424 202984
E-mail: cmorrell@hastings.ac.uk
Principal: Ms Julie Walker
IB Co-ordinator: Mr Michael Coffey
IB No: 0930

West Sussex

Ardingly College
College Road
Ardingly
Haywards Heath
West Sussex RH17 6SQ
Tel: 01444 892577
Fax: 01444 892266
E-mail: widgetcat@hotmail.com
Head: Mr J R Franklin
IB Co-ordinator: Mr John Langford
IB No: 1289

West Midlands

The City Technology College
Kingshurst
P O Box 1017
Cooks Lane
Kingshurst
Birmingham B37 6NZ
Tel: 0121 770 8923
Fax: 0121 770 0879
E-mail: warda@kingshurst.ac.uk
Principal: Mrs Valerie P Bragg
IB Co-ordinator: Mrs Alison Ward
IB No: 0568

Worcestershire

Malvern College
College Road
Malvern
Worcestershire WR14 3DF
Tel: 01684 581500
Fax: 01684 581617
E-mail: jplc@malcol.org
Head: Mr H C K Carson
IB Co-ordinator: Mr John Penfold Knee
IB No: 0641

SCOTLAND

Aberdeenshire

The International School of Aberdeen
'Fairgirth'
296 North Deeside Road
Milltimber
Aberdeen AB13 0AB
Tel: 01224 732267
Fax: 01224 734879
E-mail: trevor.wilson@isa.abdn.sch.uk
Director: Dr Doug Osbo
IB Co-ordinator: Mr Trevor Wilson
IB No: 0893

WALES

Cardiff

Whitchurch High School
Penlline Road
Whitchurch
Cardiff CF4 2XJ
Tel: 029 2062 9700
Fax: 029 2062 9701
E-mail: admin@whitchurch.cardiff.sch.uk
Head: Mr G Mathewson
IB Co-ordinator: Ms E Davis
IB No: 1213

Conwy

Llandrillo College
Llandudno Road
Rhos-on-Sea
Cowlyn Bay
Conwy LL28 4HZ
Tel: 01492 542320
Fax: 01492 542053
E-mail: c.williams@llandrillo.ac.uk
Principal: Mr Huw Evans
IB Co-ordinator: Ms Melanie Monteith
IB No: 0640

South Glamorgan

United World College of the Atlantic
St Donat's Castle
Llantwit Major
South Glamorgan CF6 1WF
Tel: 01446 799006
Fax: 01446 799013
E-mail: dos@uwcac.uwc.org
Principal: Mr Colin D O Jenkins
IB Co-ordinator: Mr Gareth Rees
IB No: 0017

Swansea

Swansea College
Ty Coch Road
Sketty
Swansea SA2 9EB
Tel: 01792 284091
Fax: 01792 284074
E-mail: s.phillips@swancoll.ac.uk
Principal: Mr Keith Elliott
IB Co-ordinator: Sue Phillips
IB No: 0614

Examining and awarding bodies: useful addresses

Assessment and Qualifications Alliance (AQA)
Devas Street
Manchester M15 6EX
Tel: 0161 953 1180
Fax: 0161 273 7572
Website: www.aqa.org.uk

Stag Hill House
Guildford
Surrey GU2 5XJ
Tel: 01483 506506
Fax: 01483 300152

City & Guilds
1 Giltspur Street
London EC1A 9DD
Tel: (020) 7294 2800
Fax: (020) 7294 2405

Edexcel Foundation
Stewart House
32 Russell Square
London WC1B 5DN
Tel: 0870 240 9800
Fax: 020 7758 6960
E-mail: enquiries@edexcel.org.uk

OCR (Oxford, Cambridge and RSA Examinations)
Head Office
1 Regent Street
Cambridge CB2 1GG
Tel: 01223 553998
E-mail: cib@ocr.org.uk; helpdesk@ocr.org.uk

Qualifications and Curriculum Authority
29 Bolton Street
London W1Y 7PD
Tel: (020) 7509 5555

Scottish Qualifications Authority
Hanover House
24 Douglas Street
Glasgow G2 7NQ
Tel: 0141 242 2214
E-mail: helpdesk@sqa.org.uk

Welsh Joint Education Committee
245 Western Avenue
Cardiff CF5 2YX
Tel: 029 2026 5000
E-mail: exams@wjec.co.uk

1.8
The Sixth Form And Beyond
– a Parent's Guide

If you have a son or daughter studying for GCSEs, he or she, like most 15 and 16 year olds, is probably still some way from decisions about higher education and careers. At this stage there is, of course, plenty of room for the development of ideas and interests, and it is important to have an open mind about all the options. Some preliminary planning, however, is essential.

Choosing the right sixth-form options is becoming increasingly significant as the range widens to give students access to higher education and careers, not just through AS/A2 Levels, but also via other routes including vocational programmes. Students who have given some thought to their future plans, to their own strengths and personal qualities, will find it easier to identify broad potential career areas. This in turn will enable them to choose suitable sixth-form and higher education options which still offer the flexibility to allow for the development of their skills and personality over the next few years. At the same time, extra-curricular activities, relevant work experience and other research will help to test long-term interest in specific career areas and to build up vital complementary personal and practical skills.

Good advice is essential. Some schools have excellent careers guidance programmes and materials and may also arrange talks from visiting speakers and work experience opportunities. Others may have more limited resources. Computerised careers assessments are often used in schools. These are not designed to provide all the answers, and it is vital that they should form part of a much more extensive discussion that includes consideration of academic achievements and aspirations, attitudes, interests and any special needs.

Your son or daughter may also find it helpful to speak to an independent consultant, who can offer a fresh, objective view and perhaps a wider perspective of the possibilities, such as the merits of moving to a different school, into a sixth-form college or joining an apprentice scheme.

Choosing sixth-form options

The main options available after GCSE are: Advanced Subsidiary GCE (AS) and Advanced GCE (A2); in Scotland, National Qualifications (Highers); the International Baccalaureate

(IB); and Vocational A Levels (formerly Advanced GNVQs). The basic structure of these courses is covered in Part 1.7.

All can be used as a means of entry to British universities. The IB, as its name implies, is an international qualification and is also recognised for admission purposes by universities worldwide. Unlike the other options above, however, the IB Diploma course is not widely available in the UK. A list of UK schools and colleges authorised to run the IB Diploma course is given on pages 47–53.

The Government's reforms to post-16 education, discussed in Part 1.7, are designed to broaden the sixth-form curriculum and to enable students to combine academic and vocational options.

Before making a choice, students may find it helpful to consider the following:

Subjects or areas of study

Is depth or breadth the most important factor? A Levels offer a high degree of specialisation. The IB is a demanding academic qualification but covers a wider range of subjects in less depth. A vocational course will probably have a focus on a particular career area such as Business, Leisure & Tourism or Information Technology.

Course load

Under the new framework, most students are taking four AS choices in the lower sixth and are continuing three of these subjects as A2s in the upper sixth, thus emerging from school with three full A levels and one AS in a fourth subject. Because of the diversity of the new sixth form programme, universities are still fairly undecided on the entry requirements they will set for a specific course; indeed these are likely to vary from one applicant to another. The equivalent of three A level passes is likely to remain the core requirement, with an interest in any additional qualification obtained. In this relatively uncertain climate, sixth formers should appreciate that quality is more important than quantity – in other words additional courses should not be taken if this would jeopardise the grades obtained in core subjects. Secondly, if they are in any doubt about the combination of A/AS Levels and grades which will be acceptable to a university, they should not hesitate to contact admission staff or seek other forms of professional advice.

Availability

Is the required course available at your child's present school or, if not, at another school or college locally? Is living away from home an option? Vocational A Level courses are widely available in maintained colleges. Some vocational courses are also offered by a much smaller number of independent schools.

Assessment method and course structure

Some students will prefer regular assessment through submission of coursework or projects rather than exam-based assessment. Many A Level courses, traditionally assessed through a final exam, now include coursework as part of the assessment. The IB is assessed chiefly by examinations. Vocational A Levels are assessed largely on coursework.

Academic ability

A Level courses often demand a good deal of reading and the ability to write well-argued essays, but some students may prefer a more practical approach.

Future plans

Students aiming for a specific career should check whether their preferred options are suitable. Those still undecided should choose a programme which allows some flexibility.

Which A Levels?

It is natural for students to want to continue with subjects they enjoy. Clearly, a high GCSE result suggests that a similar result may be expected at A Level. This is important, of course, but students must also consider whether or not their preferred combination of subjects is suitable for higher education or career plans. It is also possible to take A Level courses in subjects not previously studied.

Career choice

Some careers, typically medicine or architecture, demand a specific degree. This may limit, or sometimes dictate, the choice of A Level subjects and students must be confident that they can do well in these. If career plans are undecided, it is wise to choose subjects which will leave a number of options open.

Ability

It is advisable to have achieved at least a grade B at GCSE in any subjects being considered for A Level (ideally grade A in Maths, Science and Modern Languages). Some A Level subjects such as Economics can be taken without any previous knowledge, but students should consider what skills are required, eg numerical, analytical or essay-writing, and whether or not it will suit them.

Different examining bodies may assess the same subject in different ways. If your son or daughter has concerns about a final exam-based assessment, he or she might consider a syllabus which offers a modular structure and a higher degree of assessment though coursework. Remember, however, that if all the subjects chosen are assessed on this basis, the workload and the pressure to meet deadlines during the course could be very heavy.

Interest

Genuine interest is essential if a student is to feel motivated throughout the two-year course and achieve high grades. Students in a dilemma over the choice between a subject they enjoy and a subject which they feel they ought to do might be well advised to opt for the former, but should check that this is suitable for their future plans.

Subject combinations

If no specific combination is demanded, how can students ensure a suitable choice? At least two subjects should be complementary, ie two arts/social sciences or two sciences. It is quite common for students to combine arts and sciences. It should be remembered that even those career areas which do not demand specific degree courses may still require certain skills, which some A Levels subjects will develop better than others.

If a particular degree course does not require an A Level in the subject, eg Psychology, it may be better to choose a different A Level subject or perhaps a complementary vocational option and so demonstrate a wider knowledge/skills base to university admissions tutors.

Other matters to consider include the timetabling restraints at school, which may make a certain combination impossible, in which case students may have to compromise or change to a school or college with greater flexibility, and the school's record of success in A Level grades in the subjects chosen.

Where shall I study?

Staying on into the Sixth Form of the present school does have advantages, including continuity and familiarity with surroundings, staff and fellow students. It is not unusual, however, for students to change schools at 16. Some may be looking for a course, subjects or combination of subjects not available at their present school; others may simply want a change of atmosphere or a different style of education.

If a change to a different school is sought, consider the school's academic pace and examination results, its university entry record, the criteria for entry to the Sixth Form and the availability of places, the size of the Sixth Form and of the teaching groups and, where appropriate, the opportunities to develop skills or pursue interests aside from A Level studies.

Independent sixth-form or tutorial colleges offer an alternative environment and are described on page 16. There are also specialist independent colleges which focus on specific vocational areas such as business, accountancy or computing.

Maintained sixth-form colleges offer a wide range of A Levels and, increasingly, vocational options such as Vocational A Levels. They may have between 500 and 1,000 students and because of their size can normally offer quite extensive facilities. However, teaching groups may be much larger than those in the independent sector.

Maintained further education colleges are available in all parts of the country and offer a vast range of A Levels and vocational courses to students of all ages, many on a part-time basis. Colleges can be huge in size and may occupy several sites. Some also offer degree and diploma courses and may therefore be able to offer extensive facilities and resources, particularly for vocational studies. The age range of such colleges is much wider than in the independent sector, so it is also important to check that there is a suitable system of pastoral care for 16–18 year olds.

There are also Modern Apprenticeship schemes which incorporate employment with part-time study. The best source of information on these is usually the local careers office. Such programmes have a national NVQ rating equivalent to GCSE or sixth form studies depending on the level and the content.

The university challenge

Access to degree courses in the UK is now wider than ever before. Despite continuing pressures on graduate employment opportunities and the introduction of tuition fees, students entering higher education have reached record numbers.

Higher education offers a unique range of academic, career and social opportunities. However, poor preparation for university can prove disastrous. There are growing concerns about the rising number of students – currently nearly one in five– who do not complete their degree courses, together with demands for a full analysis of the reasons why. These may be many and varied, but it is clear that the sense of having made the wrong choice is an often-cited factor.

Why does your son or daughter want to go to university? Is he or she genuinely motivated, keen to study a particular subject in depth, to qualify for a specific career or simply to take advantage of all the benefits which university life offers? All these are valid, but some students may apply to university largely because they feel under pressure at home and/or at school to do so. Timing is also important. Students still unsure what to study should not rush into decisions. It may be better to take a year out and to use the additional time constructively before making a choice.

Most schools encourage students to begin thinking seriously about higher education soon after entering the Sixth Form. During the spring and summer terms of the Lower Sixth, students should be doing their research. Information is available from reference guides, from the Internet and from university prospectuses. Most universities organise open days, when students can visit and talk to staff and students. This means that students should be well-prepared for the autumn when application forms should be sent to UCAS (the Universities and Colleges Admissions Service): by 15th October for applications that include Oxford, Cambridge or Medicine and by 15th January for all other applications (with the exception of some for Art and Design).

Support and guidance from school, from external advisers and from parents is essential throughout this period, but the final choice of course and university lies with the student, and he or she should be taking an active part in the process. So what are the key points to consider?

Which course?

Is a specific degree necessary for a specific career? In some cases, typically Medicine, yes. In many cases, however, including law, students have more flexibility. If there are no specific requirements, prospective employers will often take account of the quality of degree obtained and the reputation of the university as much as the subject studied, and will look for other skills and qualities which match their requirements. This means that students should take a subject in which they expect to do well rather than something which they may, perhaps wrongly, believe to be 'the right thing'. It is also important to demonstrate a breadth of knowledge and skills, for example interpersonal skills, language skills, commercial awareness or an understanding of science or information technology, in addition to the subject studied. There are differing views over the importance of taking some career-related degree subjects, for example, Business Studies or Media/Communication Studies. Some employers may prefer to employ graduates with a wider education background and train them in-house. Others may prefer applicants to be able to demonstrate practical knowledge and interest. Taking the above examples, this might include work experience with a company or involvement with the university newspaper or radio station.

Sandwich courses, offered mainly in science, engineering and social sciences, include work experience as part of the course. This can help employment prospects, enhance practical skills and allow students to test their interest in a particular career before committing themselves. In some cases placements may turn into permanent positions with the same employer after graduation. Some students, however, may not want to delay graduation (a sandwich course may take an extra year), and may dislike the disruption between work and study. Many universities also offer students the opportunity to study abroad as part of their course, regardless of whether they are concentrating on modern languages.

Specialisation

Students have a choice of studying one subject (single honours) or a combination (joint honours or a modular degree). A combined course offers more breadth and the opportunity to follow complementary studies, but almost always means a heavier workload.

For students unsure about taking a subject not studied at school or going directly into a specialised field, for example Civil Engineering, a more general foundation year may be helpful in providing essential core skills before deciding on a specialisation.

Checking course content

Courses with the same name may be very different in content, so it is essential to read the prospectus for details. Modern language degrees, for example, vary widely in focus. Some place particular emphasis on practical language skills and an understanding of current affairs; others may have a more traditional emphasis on literature. Course titles like Communication Studies can also mean a wide variety of things.

Entry requirements

What subjects and grades does the course specify? Is the student likely to achieve these grades or should he or she look for a course with less stringent entry requirements? Remember that published grades are given only as a guide and may be adjusted upwards or downwards when offers are made to individual students. With the variety of Sixth Form programmes being taken under this new system, we strongly recommend students contact universities direct to find out what they may be expected to achieve. For arts A Level students who wish to take a degree in a science-based subject such as Medicine or Engineering, one year conversion courses are available, but students will be expected to have good GCSE grades in Maths and Science. Many modern language courses do not require previous knowledge, although evidence of competency in another foreign language is usually essential.

Which university?

Quality and reputation are as important for the individual course and department as for the institution as a whole. Beware of published league tables, which will not necessarily answer your questions. Find out about the career or employment destinations of recent graduates. This information may be available direct from the university or in one of the many published handbooks. If you have in mind a particular career or employer, it may be useful to contact the recruitment department to find out their views on specific universities or degree courses. You may also want to ask the university about the teaching styles, methods of assessment and the level of supervision available.

There is, of course, much more to finding the right university than simply the course. Aspects such as accommodation (both on and off campus), location or social atmosphere, can generate just as much anxiety and dissatisfaction if things go wrong and may just as likely lead to abandonment of the course.

Some students may be attracted to a collegiate style university such as Oxford, Cambridge or London. Others may prefer a self-contained campus where all academic, social and other facilities are available on-site. Some may prefer a big city environment; others a smaller, more rural location. Living costs are a further important but often neglected issue. What is the quality and frequency of local transport? Is a car necessary? How safe is the area after dark? How important is the distance from home? What other facilities are offered to cater for individual hobbies and interests?

Finding out more

There are, of course, many other options and issues which your son or daughter may want to discuss. These might include the pros and cons of taking a year out after school and how to make the best use of it, sponsorship to help finance a degree course, presenting a well-structured and effective UCAS application, interview techniques, CV writing and job applications.

This article can offer no more than a general guide to the many factors involved in education and career planning; every student's needs are different.

Advice should be available from your child's school. Expert, independent guidance is also available from Gabbitas, who can advise students who are unhappy at university as well as recent graduates and those looking for a career move in later life. If you would like to know more about the Gabbitas Advisory and Careers Assessment Services, please telephone Wendy Fidler on (020) 7734 0161.

Note on information given in the directory section

Type of school

The directory comprises schools listed within the Department for Education and Skills Register of Independent Schools. State schools, Foundation schools, special schools, independent further education colleges and overseas schools are not included, unless they have a profile in Part Three.

Each school is given a brief description, which explains whether the school is single-sex or co-educational. In some cases single-sex schools take small numbers of the opposite sex within a specified age range. These are indicated where appropriate, eg: Boys boarding and day 3–18 (Day girls 16–18)

Schools are described as 'boarding' (which indicates boarding pupils only), 'boarding and day', 'day and boarding' (indicating a predominance of day pupils) or 'day' only.

Number of boarders

Where appropriate these are divided into full boarders (F) and weekly boarders (W). Weekly boarding arrangements vary according to individual school policy.

Fees

All fees are given annually from September 2001 unless otherwise stated. It should be remembered, however, that some schools increase fees during the year and the figures shown may therefore be subject to change after September 2001. Where the date given is other than September 2001, the information provided is the latest available from the school. Figures are shown for full boarding (FB), weekly boarding (WB) and day fees. In some instances the fees for full and weekly boarding are the same (F/WB). A minimum and a maximum fee are given for each range. These figures are intended as a guide only. For more precise information schools should be contacted direct.

School profiles

* denotes that the school has a profile in Part Three.

PART TWO: FULL GEOGRAPHIC DIRECTORY

2.1
ENGLAND

(* Denotes school has a profile in Part Three)

BEDFORDSHIRE

BEDFORD

ACORN SCHOOL
15 St Andrews Road, Bedford,
Bedfordshire MK40 2LL
Tel: (01234) 343449
Head: Mrs M Mason
Type: Co-educational Day 2–8
No of pupils: 130
Fees: (September 01)
Day £2940 – £3555

BEDFORD HIGH SCHOOL*
Bromham Road, Bedford,
Bedfordshire MK40 2BS
Tel: (01234) 360221
Head: Mrs G Piotrowska
Type: Girls Day and Boarding 7–18
No of pupils: 883
No of boarders: F119 W9
Fees: (September 01) FB £11145 –
£13269 WB £10995 – £13119 Day
£5175 – £7299

BEDFORD MODERN SCHOOL
Manton Lane, Bedford, Bedfordshire
MK41 7NT
Tel: (01234) 332500
Head: Mr S Smith
Type: Boys Day and Boarding 7–18
No of pupils: 1090 *No of boarders:* F50
Fees: (September 01)
FB £10605 – £12570 Day £4995 –
£6960

BEDFORD PREPARATORY
SCHOOL
De Parys Avenue, Bedford,
Bedfordshire MK40 2TU
Tel: (01234) 362274
Head: Mr C Godwin
Type: Boys Boarding and Day 7–13
No of pupils: 446
No of boarders: F21 W11
Fees: (September 01) FB £10620 –
£15570 WB £10110 – £15060 Day
£6390 – £9870

BEDFORD SCHOOL
De Parys Avenue, Bedford,
Bedfordshire MK40 2TU
Tel: (01234) 362200
Head: Dr I P Evans
Type: Boys Day and Boarding 13–18
No of pupils: 1099
No of boarders: F160 W49
Fees: (September 01) FB £15570 WB
£15060 Day £9870

BEDFORD SCHOOL STUDY
CENTRE*
67 De Parys Avenue, Bedford,
Bedfordshire MK40 2TR
Tel: (01234) 362300
Head: Mrs O Heffill
Type: Co-educational Boarding 11–17
No of pupils: B18 G12
No of boarders: F30
Fees: (September 01) FB £20100

DAME ALICE HARPUR
SCHOOL
Cardington Road, Bedford,
Bedfordshire MK42 OBX
Tel: (01234) 340871
Head: Mrs J Berry
Type: Girls Day 7–18
No of pupils: 954
Fees: (September 01)
Day £4845 – £6690

PILGRIMS PRE-PREPARATORY
SCHOOL
Brickhill Drive, Bedford,
Bedfordshire MK41 7QZ
Tel: (01234) 369555
Head: Mrs H Bell
Type: Co-educational Day 0–7
No of pupils: B164 G123
Fees: (September 01)
Day £2688 – £4290

POLAM SCHOOL
45 Lansdowne Road, Bedford,
Bedfordshire MK40 2BY
Tel: (01234) 261864
Head: Mr A R Brown
Type: Co-educational Day 3–9
No of pupils: B120 G120
Fees: (September 01)
Day £2109 – £3618

RUSHMOOR SCHOOL
58–60 Shakespeare Road, Bedford,
Bedfordshire MK40 2DL
Tel: (01234) 352031
Head: Mr P J Owen
Type: Co-educational Day Boys 11–16
Girls 3–10
No of pupils: B297 G12
Fees: (September 01)
Day £2760 – £5760

DUNSTABLE

ST GEORGE'S
28 Priory Road, Dunstable,
Bedfordshire LU5 4HR
Tel: (01582) 661471
Head: Mrs Plater
Type: Co-educational Day 2–11
No of pupils: B65 G65
Fees: (September 01)
Day £1560 – £3765

LUTON

BROADMEAD SCHOOL
Tennyson Road, Luton, Bedfordshire
LU1 3RR
Tel: (01582) 722570
Head: Mr A F Compton
Type: Co-educational Day 2–11
No of pupils: B65 G65
Fees: (September 01) Day £3213

MOORLANDS SCHOOL
Leagrave Hall, Luton, Bedfordshire
LU4 9LE
Tel: (01582) 573376
Head: Mr A Cook
Type: Co-educational Day 2–11
No of pupils: B178 G180
Fees: (September 01)
Day £3654 – £3894

SHEFFORD

EAST LODGE SCHOOL
Ampthill Road, Campton, Shefford,
Bedfordshire SG17 5BH
Tel: (01462) 812644
Head: Mrs V A Green
Type: Co-educational Day 3–8
No of pupils: 55
Fees: (September 01)
Day £1280 – £2995

WESTONING

PHOENIX SCHOOL
Flitwick Road, Westoning,
Bedfordshire MK45 5AA
Tel: (01525) 718241
Head: Mrs S Harral
Type: Co-educational Day 2–6
No of pupils: 49
Fees: (September 01)
Day £3735 – £3795

BERKSHIRE

ASCOT

HEATHFIELD SCHOOL*
London Road, Ascot, Berkshire
SL5 8BQ
Tel: (01344) 898343
Head: Mrs H M Wright
Type: Girls Boarding 11–18
No of pupils: 221
No of boarders: F221
Fees: (September 01) FB £17325

HURST LODGE*
Bagshot Road, Ascot, Berkshire
SL5 9JU
Tel: (01344) 622154
Principals: Mrs A M Smit and
Miss V Smit
Type: Girls Day and Boarding 2½–18
(Boys 2½–7)
No of pupils: B20 G230
No of boarders: F10 W13
Fees: (September 01) FB £13545
Day £2535 – £7950

LICENSED VICTUALLERS'
SCHOOL*
London Road, Ascot, Berkshire
SL5 8DR
Tel: (01344) 882770
Head: Mr I A Mullins
Type: Co-educational Boarding and
Day 4–18
No of pupils: B460 G312
No of boarders: F70 W110
Fees: (September 01) F/WB £11805 –
£13065 Day £4480 – £7410

MARIST CONVENT SENIOR
SCHOOL
Kings Road, Sunninghill, Ascot,
Berkshire SL5 7PS
Tel: (01344) 624291
Head: Mr K McCloskey
Type: Girls Day 11–18
No of pupils: 335
Fees: (September 01) On application

PAPPLEWICK*
Ascot, Berkshire SL5 7LH
Tel: (01344) 621488
Head: Mr D R Llewellyn
Type: Boys Boarding and Day 7–13
No of pupils: 209
No of boarders: F134
Fees: (September 01) FB £13200
Day £10140

ST GEORGE'S SCHOOL*
Ascot, Berkshire SL5 7DZ
Tel: (01344) 629900
Head: Mrs J Grant Peterkin
Type: Girls Boarding and Day 11–18
No of pupils: 300
No of boarders: F140
Fees: (September 01) FB £16050
Day £10275

ST MARY'S SCHOOL, ASCOT*
St Mary's Road, Ascot, Berkshire
SL5 9JF
Tel: (01344) 293614
Head: Mrs M Breen
Type: Girls Boarding 11–18
No of pupils: 351
No of boarders: F324
Fees: (September 01) FB £16440
Day £11040

BRACKNELL

LAMBROOK HAILEYBURY
Winkfield Row, Bracknell, Berkshire
RG42 6LU
Tel: (01344) 882717
Head: Mr R J G Deighton
Type: Co-educational Boarding and
Day 4–13
No of pupils: B268 G80
No of boarders: F13 W22
Fees: (September 01)
FB £10200 – £11925
Day £5100 – £8550

MEADOWBROOK
MONTESSORI SCHOOL
Malt Hill Road, Warfield, Bracknell,
Berkshire RG42 6JQ
Tel: (01344) 890869
Head: Mrs S Gunn
Type: Co-educational Day 3–11
No of pupils: B50 G50
Fees: (September 01)
Day £650 – £1700

MORTARBOARD NURSERY
SCHOOL
Berkshire Guide Centre,
Windlesham Road, Priestwood,
Bracknell, Berkshire RG42 1GG
Tel: (01344) 450922
Head: Mrs M Baster
Type: Co-educational Day 2–5
No of pupils: B20 G20
Fees: (September 01)
Day £647 – £2049

NEWBOLD SCHOOL
Popeswood Road, Binfield,
Bracknell, Berkshire RG42 4AH
Tel: (01344) 421088
Head: Mr M Brooks
Type: Co-educational Day 3–11
No of pupils: 95
Fees: (September 01)
Day £1800 – £2310

CROWTHORNE

OUR LADY'S PREPARATORY
SCHOOL
The Avenue, Crowthorne, Berkshire
RG45 6PB
Tel: (01344) 773394
Head: Mrs E A Rhodes
Type: Co-educational Day 3–11
No of pupils: B55 G55
Fees: (September 01)
Day £2007 – £3177

WELLINGTON COLLEGE
Crowthorne, Berkshire RG45 7PU
Tel: (01344) 444 012
Head: Mr A H Monro
Type: Boys Boarding and Day 13–18
(Co-ed VIth Form)
No of pupils: B735 G51
No of boarders: F643
Fees: (September 01) FB £17610
Day £13560 *MRS. R. Walker*
[pwr@wellingtoncollege.org.uk]

MAIDENHEAD

CLAIRES COURT SCHOOL
Ray Mill Road East, Maidenhead,
Berkshire SL6 8TE
Tel: (01628) 411470
Head: Mr J T Wilding
Type: Boys Day 11–18 (Co-ed VIth
Form)
No of pupils: B356 G31
Fees: (September 01)
Day £6165 – £7290

CLAIRES COURT SCHOOLS,
THE COLLEGE
1 College Avenue, Maidenhead,
Berkshire SL6 6AW
Tel: (01628) 411480
Head: Mrs A C Pitts
Type: Girls Day 3–16 (Boys 3–5)
No of pupils: B117 G265
Fees: (September 01)
Day £4860 – £7110

HERRIES SCHOOL
Dean Lane, Cookham Dean,
Maidenhead, Berkshire SL6 9BD
Tel: (01628) 483350
Head: Mrs A Warnes
Type: Co-educational Day 2–11
No of pupils: B48 G62
Fees: (September 01)
Day £1070 – £1500

HIGHFIELD SCHOOL
2 West Road, Maidenhead, Berkshire
SL6 1PD
Tel: (01628) 624918
Head: Mrs C M A Lane
Type: Co-educational Day Boys 3–5
Girls 3–11
No of pupils: B12 G193
Fees: (September 01)
Day £1852 – £5130

RIDGEWAY SCHOOL
(CLAIRES COURT JUNIOR)
Maidenhead Thicket, Maidenhead,
Berkshire SL6 3QE
Tel: (01628) 411490
Head: Miss K M Boyd
Type: Boys Day 5–11
No of pupils: 230
Fees: (September 01) On application

ST PIRAN'S PREPARATORY
SCHOOL*
Gringer Hill, Maidenhead, Berkshire
SL6 7LZ
Tel: (01628) 627316
Head: Mr J Carroll
Type: Co-educational Day 3–13
No of pupils: B258 G105
Fees: (September 01)
Day £3780 – £6870

SILCHESTER HOUSE
SCHOOL
Silchester House, Bath Road, Taplow,
Maidenhead, Berkshire SL6 0AP
Tel: (01628) 620549
Head: Mrs D J Austen
Type: Co-educational Day 2–12
No of pupils: B92 G78
Fees: (September 01)
Day £1825 – £5770

WINBURY SCHOOL
Hibbert Road, Bray, Maidenhead,
Berkshire SL6 1UU
Tel: (01628) 627412
Head: Mrs P L Prewett
Type: Co-educational Day 2–8
No of pupils: B50 G40
Fees: (September 01)
Day £1125 – £3600

NEWBURY

BROCKHURST & MARLSTON
HOUSE PRE-PREPARATORY
SCHOOL
Ridge House, Cold Ash, Newbury,
Berkshire RG18 9HX
Tel: (01635) 200293
Head: Mrs R A Fleming
Type: Co-educational Day 3–6
No of pupils: B35 G35
Fees: (September 01)
Day £1026 – £5010

BROCKHURST SCHOOL
Hermitage, Newbury, Berkshire
RG18 9UL
Tel: (01635) 200293
Head: Mr D J W Fleming
Type: Boys Boarding and Day 3–13
No of pupils: 148
No of boarders: F30 W40
Fees: (September 01) FB £11970
Day £5010 – £8811

CHEAM SCHOOL*
Headley, Newbury, Berkshire
RG19 8LD
Tel: (01635) 268381
Head: Mr M R Johnson
Type: Co-educational Boarding and
Day 3–13
No of pupils: B210 G143
No of boarders: F58 W35
Fees: (September 01) FB £13050
Day £5520 – £9660

DOWNE HOUSE SCHOOL*
Cold Ash, Thatcham, Newbury,
Berkshire RG18 9JJ
Tel: (01635) 200286
Head: Mrs E McKendrick
Type: Girls Boarding and Day 11–18
No of pupils: 526
No of boarders: F515
Fees: (September 01) FB £17490
Day £12678

GREENHILL PRE-PREP AND
NURSERY SCHOOL
Horris Hill, Newtown, Newbury,
Berkshire RG20 9DJ
Tel: (01635) 43420
Head: Mrs M Piotrowsky
Type: Co-educational Day 3–8
No of pupils: 55
Fees: (September 01)
Day £2175 – £5550

HORRIS HILL
Newtown, Newbury, Berkshire
RG20 9DJ
Tel: (01635) 40594
Head: Mr N J Chapman
Type: Boys Boarding and Day 7–13
No of pupils: 125
No of boarders: F105
Fees: (September 01) FB £13200
Day £10200

MARLSTON HOUSE SCHOOL

Hermitage, Newbury, Berkshire
RG18 9UL
Tel: (01635) 200293
Head: Mrs C Riley
Type: Girls Boarding and Day 6–13
No of pupils: 85
No of boarders: F8 W12
Fees: (September 01) FB £10260
Day £5160 – £7770

ST GABRIEL'S SCHOOL

Sandleford Priory, Newbury,
Berkshire RG20 9BD
Tel: (01635) 40663
Head: Mr A Jones
Type: Girls Day 3–18 (Boys 3–8)
No of pupils: B18 G456
Fees: (September 01)
Day £4890 – £6987

ST MICHAELS SCHOOL

Harts Lane, Burghclere, Newbury,
Berkshire RG15 9JW
Tel: (01635) 278137
Head: Father B Lorber
Type: Co-educational Boarding and
Day 7–18
No of pupils: B37 G35
No of boarders: F23 W33
Fees: (September 01) FB £4000 –
£7950 WB £4000 – £7500 Day £3000

THORNGROVE SCHOOL

The Mount, Highclere, Newbury,
Berkshire RG20 9PS
Tel: (01635) 253172
Head: Mr & Mrs N J Broughton
Type: Co-educational Day 2–13
No of pupils: B114 G86
Fees: (September 01)
Day £4575 – £6210

READING

THE ABBEY SCHOOL

Kendrick Road, Reading, Berkshire
RG1 5DZ
Tel: (0118) 987 2256
Head: Miss B C L Sheldon
Type: Girls Day 4–18
No of pupils: 994
Fees: (September 01)
Day £5400 – £6300

ALDER BRIDGE SCHOOL

Bridge House, Mill Lane, Padworth,
Reading, Berkshire RG7 4JU
Tel: (0118) 971 4471
Head: Mrs D K Pike
Type: Co-educational Day 3–13
No of pupils: B36 G31
Fees: (September 01)
Day £1170 – £3510

BRADFIELD COLLEGE

Bradfield, Reading, Berkshire
RG7 6AU
Tel: (0118) 964 4510
Head: Mr P B Smith
Type: Boys Boarding and Day 13–18
(Co-ed VIth Form)
No of pupils: B480 G120
No of boarders: F570
Fees: (September 01) FB £17430
Day £13944

CHILTERN COLLEGE SCHOOL

16 Peppard Road, Caversham,
Reading, Berkshire RG4 8JZ
Tel: (0118) 947 1847
Head: Mrs P Ardrey
Type: Co-educational Day 4–11
No of pupils: 80
Fees: (September 01) Day £3750

CROSFIELDS SCHOOL

Shinfield, Reading, Berkshire
RG2 9BL
Tel: (0118) 987 1810
Head: Mr J P Wansey
Type: Boys Day 4–13
No of pupils: 410
Fees: (September 01)
Day £4080 – £7290

DOLPHIN SCHOOL

Hurst, Reading, Berkshire RG10 0BP
Tel: (0118) 934 1277
Head: Dr N Follett and Mrs H Brough
Type: Co-educational Day 3–13
No of pupils: B142 G140
Fees: (September 01)
Day £3135 – £6225

ELSTREE SCHOOL

Woolhampton, Reading, Berkshire
RG7 5TD
Tel: (0118) 971 3302
Head: Mr S M Hill
Type: Boys Boarding and Day 3–13
(Girls 3–7)
No of pupils: B240 G20
No of boarders: F100 W10
Fees: (September 01) FB £12600
Day £5325 – £9045

FOXLEY PNEU SCHOOL

Manor Drive, Shurlock Row,
Reading, Berkshire RG10 0PX
Tel: (0118) 934 3578
Head: Miss M J Fallon
Type: Co-educational Day 3–5
No of pupils: B15 G15
Fees: (September 01)
Day £1750 – £3000

HEMDEAN HOUSE SCHOOL

Hemdean Road, Caversham,
Reading, Berkshire RG4 7SD
Tel: (0118) 947 2590
Head: Mrs J Harris
Type: Co-educational Day Boys 2–11
Girls 2–16
No of pupils: B50 G120
Fees: (September 01)
Day £2820 – £4050

THE HIGHLANDS SCHOOL

Wardle Avenue, Tilehurst, Reading,
Berkshire RG31 6JR
Tel: (0118) 942 7186
Head: Mrs C A Bennett
Type: Co-educational Day Boys 3–7
Girls 3–11
No of pupils: B39 G108
Fees: (September 01)
Day £2475 – £3385

LEIGHTON PARK SCHOOL

Shinfield Road, Reading, Berkshire
RG2 7ED
Tel: (0118) 987 9600
Head: Mr J Dunston
Type: Co-educational Boarding and
Day 11–18
No of pupils: B235 G135
No of boarders: F115 W70
Fees: (September 01)
FB £13338 – £15693
WB £12006 – £14121
Day £9333 – £10989

THE ORATORY PREPARATORY SCHOOL

Goring Heath, Reading, Berkshire
RG8 7SF
Tel: (0118) 984 4511
Head: Mr D L Sexon
Type: Co-educational Day and
Boarding 3–13
No of pupils: B272 G83
No of boarders: F53
Fees: (September 01) FB £10695
Day £2175 – £7725

THE ORATORY SCHOOL

Woodcote, Reading, Berkshire
RG8 0PJ
Tel: (01491) 680207
Head: Mr C I Dytor
Type: Boys Boarding and Day 11–18
No of pupils: 398
No of boarders: F234
Fees: (September 01)
FB £13185 – £16755
Day £9615 – £13185

PADWORTH COLLEGE
Padworth, Reading, Berkshire
RG7 4NR
Tel: (0118) 983 2644
Head: Mr E Reynolds
Type: Girls Boarding and Day 14–20
No of pupils: 100
No of boarders: F95
Fees: (September 01) FB £14400
Day £7000 – £7200

PANGBOURNE COLLEGE*
Pangbourne, Reading, Berkshire
RG8 8LA
Tel: (0118) 984 2101
Head: Dr K Greig
Type: Co-educational Boarding and
Day 11–18
No of pupils: B301 G87
No of boarders: F221
Fees: (September 01)
FB £11595 – £15960
Day £8130 – £11190

PRESENTATION COLLEGE
63 Bath Road, Reading, Berkshire
RG30 2BB
Tel: (0118) 957 2861
Head: Mr F Loveder
Type: Boys Day 4–18 (Co-ed VIth
Form)
No of pupils: 347
Fees: (September 01)
Day £3600 – £4950

QUEEN ANNE'S SCHOOL*
6 Henley Road, Caversham, Reading,
Berkshire RG4 6DX
Tel: (0118) 918 7300
Head: Mrs D Forbes
Type: Girls Boarding and Day 11–18
No of pupils: 324
No of boarders: F125 W40
Fees: (September 01) F/WB £16026
Day £10836

READING BLUE COAT SCHOOL*
Holme Park, Sonning, Reading,
Berkshire RG4 6SU
Tel: (0118) 944 1005
Head: Mr S J W McArthur
Type: Boys Day 11–18 (Co-ed VIth
Form)
No of pupils: 600
Fees: (September 01) Day £7530

ST ANDREW'S SCHOOL
Buckhold, Pangbourne, Reading,
Berkshire RG8 8QA
Tel: (0118) 974 4276
Head: Mr J M Snow
Type: Co-educational Day and
Boarding 3–13
No of pupils: B171 G119
No of boarders: W35
Fees: (September 01)
WB £10095 – £10455
Day £1950 – £8250

ST EDWARD'S SCHOOL
64 Tilehurst Road, Reading,
Berkshire RG30 2JH
Tel: (0118) 957 4342
Head: Mr P Keddie
Type: Boys Day 5–13
No of pupils: 113
Fees: (September 01)
Day £4080 – £5085

ST JOSEPH'S CONVENT SCHOOL
Upper Redlands Road, Reading,
Berkshire RG1 5JT
Tel: (0118) 966 1000
Head: Mrs V M Brookes
Type: Girls Day 3–18
No of pupils: B9 G442
Fees: (September 01)
Day £2370 – £6135

THE ARK SCHOOL
School Road, Padworth, Reading,
Berkshire RG7 4JA
Tel: (0118) 983 4802
Head: Mrs P A Oakley
Type: Co-educational Day 0–11
No of pupils: B53 G58
Fees: (September 01) On application

SANDHURST

EAGLE HOUSE
Sandhurst, Berkshire GU47 8PH
Tel: (01344) 772134
Head: Mr S J Carder
Type: Co-educational Day and
Boarding 3–13
No of pupils: B240 G70
No of boarders: F18 W17
Fees: (September 01) F/WB £12300
Day £5250 – £8745

SLOUGH

ETON END PNEU
35 Eton Road, Datchet, Slough,
Berkshire SL3 9AX
Tel: (01753) 541075
Head: Mrs B E Ottley
Type: Girls Day 3–11 (Boys 3–7)
No of pupils: B70 G165
Fees: (September 01)
Day £3255 – £5190

LANGLEY MANOR SCHOOL
St Marys Road, Langley, Slough,
Berkshire SL3 6BZ
Tel: (01753) 825368
Head: Mrs J Sculpher
Type: Co-educational Day 3–11
No of pupils: B140 G123
Fees: (September 01) On application

LONG CLOSE SCHOOL
Upton Court Road, Slough,
Berkshire SL3 7LU
Tel: (01753) 520095
Head: Mr M H Kneath
Type: Co-educational Day 2–13
No of pupils: B172 G64
Fees: (September 01)
Day £3486 – £6939

ST BERNARD'S PREPARATORY SCHOOL
Hawtrey Close, Slough, Berkshire
SL1 1TB
Tel: (01753) 521821
Head: Mrs M F Casey
Type: Co-educational Day 3–11
No of pupils: B120 G90
Fees: (September 01)
Day £4050 – £4485

SUNNINGDALE

SUNNINGDALE SCHOOL
Sunningdale, Berkshire SL5 9PY
Tel: (01344) 620159
Head: Mr T M E Dawson and
Mr A J N Dawson
Type: Boys Boarding 8–13
No of pupils: 100
No of boarders: F100
Fees: (September 01) FB £10650

TWYFORD

CEDAR PARK DAY NURSERY
Bridge Farm Road, Twyford,
Berkshire RG10 9PP
Tel: (0118) 934 0118
Head: Mrs Kim Hambridge
Type: Co-educational Day 0–5
No of pupils: 86
Fees: (September 01)
Day £8160 – £8640

WINDSOR

THE BRIGIDINE SCHOOL
Queensmead, Kings Road, Windsor,
Berkshire SL4 2AX
Tel: (01753) 863779
Head: Mrs M B Cairns
Type: Girls Day 3–18 (Boys 3–7)
No of pupils: B4 G276
Fees: (September 01)
Day £4875 – £7050

ETON COLLEGE
Windsor, Berkshire SL4 6DW
Tel: (01753) 671000
Head: Mr J E Lewis
Type: Boys Boarding 12–18
No of pupils: 1285
No of boarders: F1285
Fees: (September 01) FB £17604

ST GEORGE'S SCHOOL
Windsor Castle, Windsor, Berkshire
SL4 1QF
Tel: (01753) 865553
Head: Mr J R Jones
Type: Co-educational Boarding and
Day 3–13
No of pupils: B186 G76
No of boarders: F23 W12
Fees: (September 01)
FB £11460 WB £11190
Day £2400 – £8505

ST JOHN'S BEAUMONT
Windsor, Berkshire SL4 2JN
Tel: (01784) 432428
Head: Mr D St Gogarty
Type: Boys Boarding and Day 4–13
No of pupils: 333
No of boarders: F28 W26
Fees: (September 01) On application

UPTON HOUSE SCHOOL
115 St Leonard's Road, Windsor,
Berkshire SL4 3DF
Tel: (01753) 862610
Head: Mrs M Collins
Type: Girls Day 3–11 (Boys 3–7)
No of pupils: B50 G148
Fees: (September 01)
Day £2265 – £5475

WOKINGHAM

BEARWOOD COLLEGE
Bearwood, Wokingham, Berkshire
RG41 5BG
Tel: (0118) 978 6915
Head: Mr S Aiano
Type: Co-educational Boarding and
Day 11–18
No of pupils: B263 G68
No of boarders: F98 W32
Fees: (September 01) F/WB £12450 –
£13875
Day £7650 – £8250

HOLME GRANGE SCHOOL
Heathlands Road, Wokingham,
Berkshire RG40 3AL
Tel: (0118) 978 1566
Head: Mr N J Brodrick
Type: Co-educational Day 3–13
No of pupils: B180 G142
Fees: (September 01)
Day £2484 – £6324

LUCKLEY-OAKFIELD
SCHOOL*
Luckley Road, Wokingham,
Berkshire RG40 3EU
Tel: (0118) 978 4175
Head: Mr R C Blake
Type: Girls Day and Boarding 11–18
No of pupils: 280
No of boarders: F25 W38
Fees: (September 01)
FB £13131 WB £12117
Day £7695

LUDGROVE
Wokingham, Berkshire RG40 3AB
Tel: (0118) 978 9881
Head: Mr G W P Barber and
Mr C N J Marston
Type: Boys Boarding 8–13
No of pupils: 199
No of boarders: F199
Fees: (September 01) FB £13050

WAVERLEY SCHOOL
Waverley Way, Finchampstead,
Wokingham, Berkshire RG40 4YD
Tel: (0118) 973 1121
Head: Mr S G Melton
Type: Co-educational Day 3–11
No of pupils: B78 G78
Fees: (September 01)
Day £1920 – £5361

WHITE HOUSE
PREPARATORY SCHOOL
Finchampstead Road, Wokingham,
Berkshire RG40 3HD
Tel: (0118) 978 5151
Head: Mrs M L Blake
Type: Girls Day 3–11 (Boys 3–4)
No of pupils: B2 G135
Fees: (September 01)
Day £4785 – £5385

BRISTOL

BRISTOL

AMBERLEY HOUSE SCHOOL
42 Apsley Road, Clifton, Bristol
BS8 2SU
Tel: (0117) 973 5515
Head: Mrs H Tallis
Type: Co-educational Day 2–11
No of pupils: B60 G36
Fees: (September 01)
Day £2190 – £3000

BADMINTON SCHOOL
Westbury-on-Trym, Bristol BS9 3BA
Tel: (0117) 905 5200
Head: Mrs J Scarrow
Type: Girls Boarding and Day 4–18
No of pupils: 390
No of boarders: F170 W36
Fees: (September 01)
FB £11340 – £16680
Day £4410 – £9390

BRISTOL CATHEDRAL
SCHOOL
College Square, Bristol BS1 5TS
Tel: (0117) 929 1872
Head: Mr K J Riley
Type: Boys Day 10–18 (Co-ed VIth
Form)
No of pupils: B425 G15
Fees: (September 01) Day £5598

BRISTOL GRAMMAR SCHOOL

University Road, Bristol BS8 1SR
Tel: (0117) 973 6006
Head: Dr D J Mascord
Type: Co-educational Day 7–18
No of pupils: B856 G407
Fees: (September 01) Day £5649

BRISTOL STEINER WALDORF SCHOOL

Park Place, Clifton, Bristol BS8 1JR
Tel: (0117) 926 0440
Head: Mr C Nelson
Type: Co-educational Day 3–14
No of pupils: 180
Fees: (September 01)
Day £1560 – £3300

CLEVE HOUSE SCHOOL

254 Wells Road, Bristol BS4 2PN
Tel: (0117) 977 7218
Head: Mr D Lawson and
Mrs E Lawson
Type: Co-educational Day 3–11
No of pupils: B66 G76
Fees: (September 01) Day £2685

CLIFTON COLLEGE*

32 College Road, Clifton, Bristol
BS8 3JH
Tel: (0117) 3157 000
Head: Dr M S Spurr
Type: Co-educational Boarding and
Day 13–18
No of pupils: B430 G240
No of boarders: F430
Fees: (September 01)
FB £16770 – £18030 Day £11170

CLIFTON COLLEGE PREPARATORY SCHOOL

The Avenue, Clifton, Bristol BS8 3HE
Tel: (0117) 315 7502
Head: Dr R J Acheson
Type: Co-educational Boarding and
Day 3–13
No of pupils: B332 G139
No of boarders: F61 W19
Fees: (September 01)
FB £11925 – £12406
WB £11400 – £11893
Day £3645 – £8270

CLIFTON HIGH SCHOOL

College Road, Clifton, Bristol
BS8 3JD
Tel: (0117) 973 0201
Head: Mrs M C Culligan
Type: Girls Day 3–18 (Boys 3–11)
No of pupils: B121 G622
No of boarders: F3
Fees: (September 01) FB £10725
WB £9330 Day £2610 – £6210

COLSTON'S COLLEGIATE SCHOOL

Stapleton, Bristol BS16 1BJ
Tel: (0117) 965 5207
Head: Mr D G Crawford
Type: Co-educational Boarding and
Day 3–18
No of pupils: B570 G250
No of boarders: F39
Fees: (September 01) FB £11670
Day £3900 – £5640

COLSTON'S GIRLS' SCHOOL

Cheltenham Road, Bristol BS6 5RD
Tel: (0117) 942 4328
Head: Mrs J P Franklin
Type: Girls Day 10–18
No of pupils: 450
Fees: (September 01)
Day £3675 – £5400

THE DOWNS SCHOOL

Wraxall, Bristol BS48 1PF
Tel: (01275) 852008
Head: Mr M A Gunn
Type: Co-educational Boarding and
Day 3–13
No of pupils: B220 G65
No of boarders: F25
Fees: (September 01) F/WB £9300
Day £2100 – £6225

FAIRFIELD PNEU SCHOOL

Fairfield Way, Backwell, Bristol
BS48 3PD
Tel: (01275) 462743
Head: Mrs A Nosowska
Type: Co-educational Day 3–11
No of pupils: B70 G73
Fees: (September 01)
Day £1278 – £4320

GRACEFIELD PREPARATORY SCHOOL

266 Overndale Road, Fishponds,
Bristol BS16 2RG
Tel: (0117) 956 7977
Head: Mrs J Baillie
Type: Co-educational Day 4–11
No of pupils: B45 G45
Fees: (September 01)
Day £2277 – £2487

MOUNT ZION (CHRISTIAN PRIMARY) SCHOOL

Christchurch, Redland Road,
Cotham, Bristol BS6 6AG
Tel: (0117) 942 5686
Head: Mrs C L S Vooght
Type: Co-educational Day
No of pupils: B8 G9
Fees: (September 01) Non fee-paying

OVERNDALE SCHOOL

Chapel Lane, Old Sodbury, Bristol
BS17 6NQ
Tel: (01454) 310332
Head: Mrs K Winstanley
Type: Co-educational Day 1–11
No of pupils: B55 G45
Fees: (September 01) Day £2845

QUEEN ELIZABETH'S HOSPITAL

Berkeley Place, Bristol BS8 1JX
Tel: (0117) 929 1856
Head: Mr S W Holliday
Type: Boys Day and Boarding 11–18
No of pupils: 540
No of boarders: F50 W15
Fees: (September 01) FB £10299
WB £9369 Day £5589

REDLAND HIGH SCHOOL

Redland Court, Redland, Bristol
BS6 7EF
Tel: (0117) 924 5796
Head: Mrs C Lear
Type: Girls Day 3–18
No of pupils: 677
Fees: (September 01)
Day £3450 – £5775

THE RED MAIDS' SCHOOL

Westbury-on-Trym, Bristol BS9 3AW
Tel: (0117) 962 2641
Head: Mrs I Tobias
Type: Girls Boarding and Day 11–18
No of pupils: 460
No of boarders: F80
Fees: (September 01) FB £10380
Day £5190

ST URSULA'S HIGH SCHOOL

Brecon Road, Westbury-on-Trym,
Bristol BS9 4DT
Tel: (01179) 622616
Head: Mrs M A Macnaughton
Type: Co-educational Day 3–16
No of pupils: B185 G138
Fees: (September 01)
Day £3225 – £4920

TOCKINGTON MANOR SCHOOL

Tockington, Bristol BS32 4NY
Tel: (01454) 613229
Head: Mr R G Tovey
Type: Co-educational Day and
Boarding 2–14
No of pupils: B168 G87
No of boarders: F32
Fees: (September 01)
FB £9960 – £11085
Day £4320 – £7470

TORWOOD HOUSE SCHOOL
29 Durdham Park, Redland, Bristol
BS6 6XE
Tel: (0117) 973 5620
Head: Mrs J Fairbrother
Type: Co-educational Day 0–11
No of pupils: B100 G100
Fees: (September 01)
Day £317 – £1360

CHEW MAGNA

**SACRED HEART
PREPARATORY SCHOOL**
Winford Road, Chew Magna, Bristol
BS40 8QY
Tel: (01275) 332470
Head: Mrs B Huntley
Type: Co-educational Day 3–11
No of pupils: B55 G60
Fees: (September 01)
Day £750 – £3900

BUCKINGHAMSHIRE

AMERSHAM

THE BEACON SCHOOL
Chesham Bois, Amersham,
Buckinghamshire HP6 5PF
Tel: (01494) 433654
Head: Mr M W Spinney
Type: Boys Day 3–13
No of pupils: 405
Fees: (September 01)
Day £2520 – £7590

**HEATHERTON HOUSE
SCHOOL**
Copperkins Lane, Chesham Bois,
Amersham, Buckinghamshire
HP6 5QB
Tel: (01494) 726433
Head: Mrs P K Thomson
Type: Girls Day 2–11 (Boys 2–5)
No of pupils: B30 G155
Fees: (September 01)
Day £1680 – £5451

AYLESBURY

ASHFOLD SCHOOL
Dorton, Aylesbury, Buckinghamshire
HP18 9NG
Tel: (01844) 238237
Head: Mr M Chitty
Type: Co-educational Boarding and
Day 3–13
No of pupils: B168 G86
No of boarders: W10
Fees: (September 01) WB £9465
Day £3450 – £8385

LADYMEDE
Little Kimble, Aylesbury,
Buckinghamshire HP17 0XP
Tel: (01844) 346154
Head: Mr A Witte
Type: Co-educational Day 3–11
No of pupils: B51 G99
Fees: (September 01)
Day £2400 – £5025

BEACONSFIELD

DAVENIES SCHOOL
Beaconsfield, Buckinghamshire
HP9 1AA
Tel: (01494) 685400
Head: Mr A J P Nott
Type: Boys Day 4–13
No of pupils: 313
Fees: (September 01)
Day £5835 – £6945

HIGH MARCH SCHOOL
23 Ledborough Lane, Beaconsfield,
Buckinghamshire HP9 2PZ
Tel: (01494) 675186
Head: Mrs P A Forsyth
Type: Girls Day 3–12 (Boys 3–5)
No of pupils: B16 G290
Fees: (September 01)
Day £1980 – £6180

BUCKINGHAM

AKELEY WOOD SCHOOL*
Buckingham, Buckinghamshire
MK18 5AE
Tel: (01280) 814110
Head: Mr W H Wilcox
Type: Co-educational Day 2–18
No of pupils: B445 G384
Fees: (September 01)
Day £4398 – £6450

**THE CHARMANDEAN
DYSLEXIA CENTRE***
Tile House Mansion, Lillingstone
Dayrell, Buckingham,
Buckinghamshire MK18 5AN
Tel: (01280) 860182
Head: Mr W H Wilcox
Type: Co-educational Day 7–16
No of pupils: B71 G28
Fees: (September 01) Day £8268

STOWE SCHOOL
Buckingham, Buckinghamshire
MK18 5EH
Tel: (01280) 818000
Head: Mr J G L Nichols
Type: Boys Boarding and Day 13–18
(Co-ed VIth Form)
No of pupils: B478 G102
No of boarders: F515
Fees: (September 01) FB £17580
Day £13185

CHESHAM

CHESHAM PREPARATORY SCHOOL
Orchard Leigh, Chesham,
Buckinghamshire HP5 3QF
Tel: (01494) 782619
Head: Mr J Marjoribanks
Type: Co-educational Day 5–13
No of pupils: B226 G160
Fees: (September 01)
Day £4185 – £4995

FARNHAM ROYAL

CALDICOTT SCHOOL*
Crown Lane, Farnham Royal,
Buckinghamshire SL2 3SL
Tel: (01753) 649300
Head: Mr S J G Doggart
Type: Boys Boarding and Day 7–13
No of pupils: 250
No of boarders: F140
Fees: (September 01) FB £12081
Day £9063

DAIR HOUSE SCHOOL TRUST LTD
Bishops Blake, Beaconsfield Road,
Farnham Royal, Buckinghamshire
SL2 3BY
Tel: (01753) 643964
Head: Mrs L J Hudson
Type: Co-educational Day 2–8
No of pupils: B67 G41
Fees: (September 01)
Day £2265 – £4980

GERRARDS CROSS

GAYHURST SCHOOL
Bull Lane, Gerrards Cross,
Buckinghamshire SL9 8RJ
Tel: (01753) 882690
Head: Mr A J Sims
Type: Boys Day 4–13
No of pupils: 274
Fees: (September 01)
Day £5130 – £6510

HOLY CROSS CONVENT
The Grange, Chalfont St Peter,
Gerrards Cross, Buckinghamshire
SL9 9DW
Tel: (01753) 895600
Head: Dr D Walker
Type: Girls Day 3–18
No of pupils: 260
Fees: (September 01)
Day £2424 – £5550

KINGSCOTE SCHOOL
Oval Way, Gerrards Cross,
Buckinghamshire SL9 8PZ
Tel: (01753) 885535
Head: Mrs S A Tunstall
Type: Boys Day 3–7
No of pupils: 130
Fees: (September 01)
Day £4524 – £5031

MALTMAN'S GREEN SCHOOL
Maltmans Lane, Gerrards Cross,
Buckinghamshire SL9 8RR
Tel: (01753) 883022
Head: Miss J Reynolds
Type: Girls Day 3–11
No of pupils: 385
Fees: (September 01)
Day £2100 – £6655

ST MARY'S SCHOOL
Packhorse Road, Gerrards Cross,
Buckinghamshire SL9 8JQ
Tel: (01753) 883370
Head: Mrs F Balcombe
Type: Girls Day 3–18
No of pupils: 302
Fees: (September 01)
Day £3495 – £6695

THORPE HOUSE SCHOOL
Oval Way, Gerrards Cross,
Buckinghamshire SL9 8PZ
Tel: (01753) 882474
Head: Mr A F Lock
Type: Boys Day 3–13
No of pupils: 280
Fees: (September 01)
Day £3522 – £6690

GREAT MISSENDEN

GATEWAY SCHOOL
1 High Street, Great Missenden,
Buckinghamshire HP16 9AA
Tel: (01494) 862407
Head: J L Wade
Type: Co-educational Day 2–12
No of pupils: B174 G126
Fees: (September 01) Day £5298

HIGH WYCOMBE

CROWN HOUSE SCHOOL
19 London Road, High Wycombe,
Buckinghamshire HP11 1BJ
Tel: (01494) 529927
Head: Mr L Clark
Type: Co-educational Day 4–11
No of pupils: B74 G65
Fees: (September 01) Day £4470

GODSTOWE PREPARATORY SCHOOL
Shrubbery Road, High Wycombe,
Buckinghamshire HP13 6PR
Tel: (01494) 529273
Head: Mrs F J Henson
Type: Girls Day and Boarding 3–13
(Boys 3–8)
No of pupils: B15 G446
No of boarders: F101 W35
Fees: (September 01) F/WB £12750
Day £5835 – £8880

PIPERS CORNER SCHOOL*
Pipers Lane, Great Kingshill, High
Wycombe, Buckinghamshire
HP15 6LP
Tel: (01494) 718255
Head: Mrs V M Stattersfield
Type: Girls Boarding and Day 4–18
No of pupils: 450
No of boarders: F25 W25
Fees: (September 01)
FB £10785 – £12960
WB £10650 – £12795
Day £3390 – £7770

WYCOMBE ABBEY SCHOOL
High Wycombe, Buckinghamshire
HP11 1PE
Tel: (01494) 520381
Head: Mrs P Davies
Type: Girls Boarding 11–18
No of pupils: 543
No of boarders: F525
Fees: (September 01) FB £17400
Day £16200

MILTON KEYNES

AKELEY WOOD JUNIOR SCHOOL
Wicken Park, Wicken, Milton
Keynes, Buckinghamshire
MK19 6DA
Tel: (01908) 571231
Head: Mrs S R Chaplin
Type: Co-educational Day 2–8
No of pupils: B150 G138
Fees: (September 01)
Day £2199 – £5490

BURY LAWN SCHOOL
Soskin Drive, Stantonbury Fields,
Milton Keynes, Buckinghamshire
MK14 6DP
Tel: (01404) 881702
Head: Mrs H Kiff
Type: Co-educational Day 1–18
No of pupils: B260 G170
Fees: (September 01)
Day £4440 – £6180

GROVE INDEPENDENT SCHOOL
Redland Drive, Loughton, Milton Keynes, Buckinghamshire MK5 8HD
Tel: (01908) 664336
Head: Mrs D M Berkin
Type: Co-educational Day 4–13
No of pupils: B116 G111
Fees: (September 01) Day £6300

GYOSEI INTERNATIONAL SCHOOL UK
Japonica Lane, Willen Park, Milton Keynes, Buckinghamshire MK15 9JX
Tel: (01908) 690100
Head: Mr Y Mikuriya
Type: Co-educational Boarding and Day 13–18
No of pupils: B62 G38
No of boarders: F100
Fees: (September 01) On application

MILTON KEYNES PREPARATORY SCHOOL
Tattenhoe Lane, Milton Keynes, Buckinghamshire MK3 7EG
Tel: (01908) 642111
Head: Mrs H A Pauley
Type: Co-educational Day 0–11
No of pupils: B220 G220
Fees: (September 01)
Day £3550 – £7260

SWANBOURNE HOUSE SCHOOL*
Swanbourne, Milton Keynes, Buckinghamshire MK17 0HZ
Tel: (01296) 720264
Head: Mr & Mrs S D Goodhart and Mrs J S Goodhart
Type: Co-educational Boarding and Day 3–13
No of pupils: B235 G170
No of boarders: F18 W31
Fees: (September 01) F/WB £11250
Day £4170 – £8850

THORNTON COLLEGE CONVENT OF JESUS AND MARY
Thornton, Milton Keynes, Buckinghamshire MK17 0HJ
Tel: (01280) 812610
Head: Miss A Williams
Type: Girls Day and Boarding 2–16 (Boys 2–7+)
No of pupils: B3 G287
No of boarders: F53 W13
Fees: (September 01) FB £9645 – £11100 WB £8760 – £10080
Day £4590 – £6570

NEWPORT PAGNELL

FILGRAVE SCHOOL
Filgrave, Newport Pagnell, Buckinghamshire MK16 9ET
Tel: (01234) 711534
Head: Mrs S Marriott
Type: Co-educational Day 2–11
No of pupils: B20 G21
Fees: (September 01) Day £3936

PRINCES RISBOROUGH

ST TERESA'S SCHOOL
Aylesbury Road, Princes Risborough, Buckinghamshire HP27 0JW
Tel: (01844) 345005
Head: Mrs C M Sparkes
Type: Co-educational Day 3–11
No of pupils: B92 G66
Fees: (September 01)
Day £1110 – £3855

CAMBRIDGESHIRE

CAMBRIDGE

BELLERBYS COLLEGE
Manor Campus, Arbury Road, Cambridge CB4 2JF
Tel: (01223) 517037
Head: Ms E Munro
Type: Co-educational Day 16–25
No of pupils: 300
Fees: (September 01) Day £14250

CAMBRIDGE ARTS & SCIENCES (CATS)*
Round Church Street, Cambridge CB5 8AD
Tel: (01223) 314431
Head: Miss E R Armstrong and Mr P McLaughlin
Type: Co-educational Day and Boarding 15–19
No of pupils: B101 G99
No of boarders: F170 W10
Fees: (September 01)
FB £13925 – £15650
Day £10625 – £12150

CAMBRIDGE CENTRE FOR VITH FORM STUDIES (CCSS)*
1 Salisbury Villas, Station Road, Cambridge CB1 2JF
Tel: (01223) 716890
Head: Mr P C Redhead
Type: Co-educational Boarding and Day 15–19
No of pupils: B95 G75
No of boarders: F120 W10
Fees: (September 01)
FB £12015 – £17880
Day £7230 – £11355

HORLERS PRE-PREPARATORY SCHOOL
20 Green End, Comberton, Cambridge CB3 7DY
Tel: (01223) 264564
Head: Mrs A Horler
Type: Co-educational Day 4–8
No of pupils: B15 G15
Fees: (September 01) Day £1670

THE LEYS SCHOOL*
Cambridge, Cambridgeshire CB2 2AD
Tel: (01223) 508900
Head: Rev Dr J C A Barrett
Type: Co-educational Boarding and Day 11–18
No of pupils: B325 G195
No of boarders: F280
Fees: (September 01)
FB £11400 – £15900
Day £7200 – £11850

MADINGLEY PRE-PREPARATORY SCHOOL
Cambridge Road, Madingley, Cambridge CB3 8AH
Tel: (01954) 210309
Head: Mrs P Evans
Type: Co-educational Day 2–8
No of pupils: B35 G35
Fees: (September 01) Day £3660

MANDER PORTMAN WOODWARD
3/4 Brookside, Cambridge CB2 1JE
Tel: (01223) 350158
Head: Dr N Marriott and P Hill
Type: Co-educational Day 15–19
No of pupils: B50 G50
No of boarders: F20 W20
Fees: (September 01)
F/WB £6129 – £14406
Day £2529 – £10806

THE PERSE SCHOOL
Hills Road, Cambridge CB2 2QF
Tel: (01223) 568300
Head: Mr N P V Richardson
Type: Boys Day 11–18 (Co-ed VIth Form)
No of pupils: B570 G30
Fees: (September 01)
Day £7356

THE PERSE SCHOOL FOR GIRLS
Union Road, Cambridge CB2 1HF
Tel: (01223) 359589
Head: Miss P M Kellcher
Type: Girls Day 7–18
No of pupils: 710
Fees: (September 01)
Day £5820 – £6900

ST ANDREW'S
2A Free School Lane, Cambridge CB2 3QA
Tel: (01223) 360040
Head: Mrs C Williams
Type: Co-educational Boarding and Day 14–18
No of pupils: B67 G53
No of boarders: F120
Fees: (September 01) FB £12300
Day £8100 – £9000

ST CATHERINES PREPARATORY SCHOOL
1 Brookside, Cambridge CB2 1JE
Tel: (01223) 311666
Head: Mrs D O' Sullivan
Type: Girls Day 3–11
No of pupils: 124
Fees: (September 01)
Day £4200 – £4770

ST COLETTE'S SCHOOL
Tenison Road, Cambridge CB1 2DP
Tel: (01223) 353696
Head: Mrs A C Wilson
Type: Co-educational Day 2–7
No of pupils: B80 G80
Fees: (September 01)
Day £3870 – £4440

ST FAITHS SCHOOL
Trumpington Road, Cambridge CB2 2AG
Tel: (01223) 352073
Head: Mr R A Dyson
Type: Co-educational Day 4–13
No of pupils: B325 G175
Fees: (September 01)
Day £5700 – £7200

ST JOHN'S COLLEGE SCHOOL
The Garden House, 75 Grange Road, Cambridge CB3 9AA
Tel: (01223) 353532
Head: Mr K L Jones
Type: Co-educational Day and Boarding 4–13
No of pupils: 451
No of boarders: F39
Fees: (September 01) F/WB £11679
Day £5454 – £7395

ST MARY'S SCHOOL
Bateman Street, Cambridge CB2 1LY
Tel: (01223) 353253
Head: Mrs J Triffitt
Type: Girls Day and Boarding 11–18
No of pupils: 464
No of boarders: F14 W23
Fees: (September 01)
FB £13650 – £14550 WB £11070 – £12150 Day £6180 – £6780

SANCTON WOOD SCHOOL*
2 St Paul's Road, Cambridge CB1 2EZ
Tel: (01223) 359488
Head: Mrs J Avis
Type: Co-educational Day 1–16
No of pupils: B105 G69
Fees: (September 01)
Day £4350 – £5355

ELY

THE KING'S SCHOOL
Ely, Cambridgeshire CB7 4DB
Tel: (01353) 660702
Head: Mr R H Youdale
Type: Co-educational Boarding and Day 2–18
No of pupils: B504 G402
No of boarders: F98 W108
Fees: (September 01)
F/WB £11550 – £15813
Day £5067 – £10923

HUNTINGDON

KIMBOLTON SCHOOL*
Kimbolton, Huntingdon, Cambridgeshire PE28 0EA
Tel: (01480) 860505
Head: Mr R V Peel
Type: Co-educational Boarding and Day 4–18
No of pupils: B418 G368
No of boarders: F53
Fees: (September 01) FB £12810
Day £3990 – £7710

WHITEHALL SCHOOL
117 High Street, Somersham, Huntingdon, Cambridgeshire PE28 3EH
Tel: (01487) 840966
Head: Mrs D Hutley
Type: Co-educational Day 3–11
No of pupils: B52 G57
Fees: (September 01)
Day £3165 – £3906

PETERBOROUGH

KIRKSTONE HOUSE SCHOOL
Main Street, Baston, Peterborough, Cambridgeshire PE6 9PA
Tel: (01778) 560350
Head: Mr M J Clifford
Type: Co-educational Day 3–16
No of pupils: B122 G104
Fees: (September 01)
Day £3300 – £5880

OUNDLE SCHOOL
The Great Hall, New Street, Oundle, Peterborough, Cambridgeshire PE8 4GH
Tel: (01832) 277125
Head: Dr R D Townsend
Type: Co-educational Boarding and Day 11–19
No of pupils: B642 G409
No of boarders: F828
Fees: (September 01)
FB £13182 – £17259 Day £8844

OUNDLE SCHOOL LAXTON JUNIOR
North Street, Oundle, Peterborough, Cambridgeshire PE8 4AL
Tel: (01832) 273673
Head: Miss S C Thomas
Type: Co-educational Day 4–11
No of pupils: B71 G72
Fees: (September 01)
Day £5544

PETERBOROUGH HIGH SCHOOL

Thorpe Road, Peterborough,
Cambridgeshire PE3 6JF
Tel: (01733) 343357
Head: Mrs S A Dixon
Type: Girls Day and Boarding 3–18
(Boys 3–11)
No of pupils: B55 G260
No of boarders: F32 W15
Fees: (September 01)
FB £11583 – £12342
WB £9795 – £10554
Day £3558 – £6150

WISBECH

WISBECH GRAMMAR SCHOOL

North Brink, Wisbech,
Cambridgeshire PE13 1JX
Tel: (01945) 583631 (seniors) /
475101 (j)
Head: Mr R S Repper
Type: Co-educational Day 4–18
No of pupils: B380 G366
Fees: (September 01)
Day £4335 – £6405

CHANNEL ISLANDS

ALDERNEY

ORMER HOUSE PREPARATORY SCHOOL

La Vallee, Alderney, Channel Islands
GY9 3XA
Tel: (01481) 823287
Head: Mr J M Edwards
Type: Co-educational Day 2–13
No of pupils: B28 G24
Fees: (September 01)
Day £760 – £3350

GUERNSEY

CONVENT OF MERCY

Cordier Hill, St Peter Port, Guernsey,
Channel Islands GY1 1JH
Tel: (01481) 720729
Head: Sister C Blackburn
Type: Co-educational Day 3–7
No of pupils: B57 G46
Fees: (September 01) Day £1500

ELIZABETH COLLEGE

Guernsey, Channel Islands GY1 2PY
Tel: (01481) 726544
Head: Dr N Argent
Type: Boys Day 2–18 (Co-ed VIth
Form)
No of pupils: B740 G35
Fees: (September 01)
Day £3670 – £4020

THE LADIES' COLLEGE

Les Gravees, St Peter Port, Guernsey,
Channel Islands GY1 1RW
Tel: (01481) 721602
Head: Miss M E Macdonald
Type: Girls Day 4–18
No of pupils: 479
Fees: (September 01)
Day £2760 – £3060

JERSEY

ASHDOWN SCHOOL AND NURSERY

47 St Mark's Road, Saint Helier,
Jersey, Channel Islands JE2 4LD
Tel: (01534) 734229
Head: Mrs S Wilton
Type: Co-educational Day 3–5
No of pupils: 80
Fees: (September 01) On application

BEAULIEU CONVENT SCHOOL

Wellington Road, Saint Helier, Jersey,
Channel Islands JE2 4RJ
Tel: (01534) 731280
Head: Mrs R A Hill
Type: Girls Day 4–18
No of pupils: 623
Fees: (September 01) On application

FCJ PRIMARY SCHOOL

Deloraine Road, St Saviour, Jersey,
Channel Islands JE2 7XB
Tel: (01534) 723063
Head: Sister Cecilia Connolly
Type: Co-educational Day 4–11
No of pupils: B110 G180
Fees: (September 01) Day £1965

HELVETIA HOUSE SCHOOL

14 Elizabeth Place, St Helier, Jersey,
Channel Islands JE2 3PN
Tel: (01534) 724928
Head: Mrs A E Atkinson
Type: Girls Day 4–11
No of pupils: 92
Fees: (September 01)
Day £1791 – £1812

ST GEORGE'S PREPARATORY SCHOOL

La Hague Manor, Rue de la Hague,
St Peter, Jersey, Channel Islands
JE3 7DB
Tel: (01534) 481593
Head: Mr C Blackwell
Type: Co-educational Day 3–13
No of pupils: B95 G124
Fees: (September 01)
Day £2610 – £8550

ST MICHAEL'S PREPARATORY SCHOOL

La Rue de la Houguette, St Saviour,
Jersey, Channel Islands JE2 7UG
Tel: (01534) 856904
Head: Mr R De Figueiredo
Type: Co-educational Day 3–13
No of pupils: B170 G116
Fees: (September 01)
Day £5940 – £8697

VICTORIA COLLEGE

Jersey, Channel Islands JE1 4HT
Tel: (01534) 638200
Head: Mr R Cook
Type: Boys Day 11–19
No of pupils: 625
Fees: (September 01) Day £2640

VICTORIA COLLEGE PREPARATORY SCHOOL

Pleasant Street, St Helier, Jersey,
Channel Islands ENG
Tel: (01534) 723468
Head: Mr P Stevenson
Type: Boys Day 7–11
No of pupils: 270
Fees: (September 01) Day £2478

CHESHIRE

ALDERLEY EDGE

ALDERLEY EDGE SCHOOL FOR GIRLS
Wilmslow Road, Alderley Edge,
Cheshire SK9 7QE
Tel: (01625) 583028
Head: Mrs K Mills
Type: Girls Day 3–18
No of pupils: 630
Fees: (September 01)
Day £3300 – £5130

THE RYLEYS
Ryleys Lane, Alderley Edge,
Cheshire SK9 7UY
Tel: (01625) 583241
Head: Mr P G Barrett
Type: Boys Day 3–13
No of pupils: 291
Fees: (September 01)
Day £5004 – £5565

ALTRINCHAM

ALTRINCHAM PREPARATORY SCHOOL
Marlborough Road, Bowdon,
Altrincham, Cheshire WA14 2RR
Tel: (0161) 928 3366
Head: Mr A C Potts
Type: Boys Day 4–12
No of pupils: 345
Fees: (September 01)
Day £3546 – £4047

BOWDON PREPARATORY SCHOOL FOR GIRLS
48 Stamford Road, Bowdon,
Altrincham, Cheshire WA14 2JP
Tel: (0161) 928 0678
Head: Mrs J H Tan
Type: Girls Day 2–11
No of pupils: 220
Fees: (September 01)
Day £3255 – £3375

CULCHETH HALL
Ashley Road, Altrincham, Cheshire
WA14 2LT
Tel: (0161) 928 1862
Head: Miss M A Stockwell
Type: Girls Day 2–16
No of pupils: B22 G203
Fees: (September 01)
Day £2505 – £4755

FOREST SCHOOL
Moss Lane, Timperley, Altrincham,
Cheshire WA15 6LJ
Tel: (0161) 980 4075
Head: Mrs J Quest
Type: Co-educational Day 3–11
No of pupils: B102 G73
Fees: (September 01)
Day £3120 – £3546

HALE PREPARATORY SCHOOL
Broomfield Lane, Hale, Altrincham,
Cheshire WA15 9AS
Tel: (0161) 928 2386
Head: Mr J Connor
Type: Co-educational Day 4–11
No of pupils: B101 G81
Fees: (September 01) Day £3525

LORETO PREPARATORY SCHOOL
Dunham Road, Altrincham,
Cheshire WA14 4AH
Tel: (0161) 928 8310
Head: Mrs R A Hedger
Type: Girls Day 4–11 (Boys 4–7)
No of pupils: B9 G176
Fees: (September 01) Day £2475

NORTH CESTRIAN GRAMMAR SCHOOL
Dunham Road, Altrincham,
Cheshire WA14 4AJ
Tel: (0161) 928 1856
Head: Mr D G Vanstone
Type: Boys Day 11–18
No of pupils: 310
Fees: (September 01) Day £4791

ST AMBROSE PREPARATORY SCHOOL
Hale Barns, Altrincham, Cheshire
WA15 0HE
Tel: (0161) 903 9193
Head: Mr M J Lochery
Type: Boys Day 4–11
No of pupils: 230
Fees: (September 01)
Day £3156 – £3330

CHEADLE

CHEADLE HULME SCHOOL
Claremont Road, Cheadle Hulme,
Cheadle, Cheshire SK8 6EF
Tel: (0161) 488 3330
Head: Mr P V Dixon
Type: Co-educational Day 4–18
No of pupils: B721 G675
Fees: (September 01)
Day £4623 – £5850

GREENBANK
Heathbank Road, Cheadle Hulme,
Cheadle, Cheshire SK8 6HU
Tel: (0161) 485 3724
Head: Mr K Phillips
Type: Co-educational Day 3–11
No of pupils: B102 G73
Fees: (September 01)
Day £2235 – £3900

HULME HALL SCHOOLS
75 Hulme Hall Road, Cheadle
Hulme, Cheadle, Cheshire SK8 6LA
Tel: (0161) 485 4638/3524
Head: Mr P Marland
Type: Co-educational Day 3–16
No of pupils: B199 G95
Fees: (September 01)
Day £2994 – £4785

HULME HALL SCHOOLS (JUNIOR SECTION)
75 Hulme Hall Road, Cheadle
Hulme, Cheadle, Cheshire SK8 6LA
Tel: (0161) 486 9970
Head: Mrs J Carr
Type: Co-educational Day 3–11
No of pupils: B58 G32
Fees: (September 01)
Day £2994 – £3690

LADY BARN HOUSE SCHOOL
Langlands, Schools Hill, Cheadle
Hulme, Cheadle, Cheshire SK8 1JE
Tel: (0161) 428 2912
Head: Mr E J Bonner
Type: Co-educational Day 3–11
No of pupils: B309 G210
Fees: (September 01)
Day £3423 – £3912

RAMILLIES HALL SCHOOL

Cheadle Hulme, Cheadle, Cheshire
SK8 7AJ
Tel: (0161) 485 3804
Head: Mrs A L Poole & Miss D M
Patterson
Type: Co-educational Boarding and
Day 0–13
No of pupils: B114 G71
No of boarders: F11 W4
Fees: (September 01) FB £9180
WB £8130 Day £3780 – £4935

CHESTER

ABBEY GATE COLLEGE

Saighton Grange, Saighton, Chester,
Cheshire CH3 6EG
Tel: (01244) 332077
Head: Mr E W Mitchell
Type: Co-educational Day 4–18
No of pupils: B191 G156
Fees: (September 01)
Day £3321 – £5874

ABBEY GATE SCHOOL

Victoria Road, Chester, Cheshire
CH2 2AY
Tel: (01244) 380552
Head: Mrs S Fisher
Type: Co-educational Day 3–11
No of pupils: B60 G60
Fees: (September 01)
Day £2445 – £2625

THE FIRS SCHOOL

45 Newton Lane, Chester, Cheshire
CH2 2HJ
Tel: (01244) 322443
Head: Mrs M Denton
Type: Co-educational Day 4–11
No of pupils: B118 G97
Fees: (September 01) Day £3465

HAMMOND SCHOOL

Hoole Bank House, Mannings Lane,
Chester, Cheshire CH2 2PB
Tel: (01244) 328542
Head: Mrs M P Dangerfield
Type: Co-educational Day and
Boarding 11–18
No of pupils: B26 G136
No of boarders: F33
Fees: (September 01) FB £14640
WB £12840 Day £8340

THE KING'S SCHOOL

Wrexham Road, Chester, Cheshire
CH4 7QL
Tel: (01244) 689500
Head: Mr T J Turvey
Type: Boys Day 7–18 (Girls 16–18)
No of pupils: B675 G35
Fees: (September 01)
Day £4818 – £6300

MERTON HOUSE
(DOWNSWOOD)

Downswood Drive, West Bank,
Off Abbots Park, Chester, Cheshire
CH1 4BD
Tel: (01244) 377165
Head: Mrs M Webb
Type: Co-educational Day 3–11
No of pupils: B58 G82
Fees: (September 01)
Day £2700 – £4700

THE QUEEN'S SCHOOL

City Walls Road, Chester, Cheshire
CH1 2NN
Tel: (01244) 312078
Head: Mrs C M Buckley
Type: Girls Day 5–18
No of pupils: 634
Fees: (September 01)
Day £3735 – £6450

CONGLETON

ST PETER'S NURSERY
SCHOOL

Chapel Street, Congleton, Cheshire
CW12 4AB
Tel: (01260) 276085
Head: Ms D L Birdsall
Type: Co-educational Day 0–5
No of pupils: 50
Fees: (September 01) Day £5376

HOLMES CHAPEL

TERRA NOVA SCHOOL

Jodrell Bank, Holmes Chapel,
Cheshire CW4 8BT
Tel: (01477) 571251
Head: Mr N Johnson
Type: Co-educational Boarding and
Day 3–13
No of pupils: B132 G76
No of boarders: F11 W20
Fees: (September 01)
F/WB £7185 – £10020
Day £3900 – £8100

KNUTSFORD

YORSTON LODGE SCHOOL

18 St John's Road, Knutsford,
Cheshire WA16 0DP
Tel: (01565) 633177
Head: Mr R Edgar
Type: Co-educational Day 2–11
No of pupils: B63 G61
Fees: (September 01)
Day £2250 – £2700

MACCLESFIELD

BEECH HALL SCHOOL

Beech Hall Drive, Tytherington,
Macclesfield, Cheshire SK10 2EG
Tel: (01625) 422192
Head: Mr J S Fitz-Gerald
Type: Co-educational Day 4–13
(Kindergarten 1–5)
No of pupils: B130 G62
Fees: (September 01)
Day £3495 – £5490

THE KING'S SCHOOL

Macclesfield, Cheshire SK10 1DA
Tel: (01625) 260000
Head: Dr S Coyne
Type: Co-educational Day 3–18
No of pupils: B800 G600
Fees: (September 01)
Day £3840 – £5745

MACCLESFIELD
PREPARATORY SCHOOL

142 Chester Road, Macclesfield,
Cheshire SK11 8PX
Tel: (01625) 422315
Head: Mrs J Horton
Type: Co-educational Day 0–11
No of pupils: B35 G40
Fees: (September 01)
Day £3100 – £3300

ST BRIDE'S SCHOOL

154 Cumberland Street,
Macclesfield, Cheshire SK10 1BP
Tel: (01625) 423255
Head: Mrs M Huntington
Type: Co-educational Day 2–11
No of pupils: B40 G15
Fees: (September 01)
Day £2850 – £3350

NORTHWICH

CRANSLEY SCHOOL

Belmont Hall, Great Budworth,
Northwich, Cheshire CW9 6HN
Tel: (01606) 891747
Head: Mrs H P Laidler
Type: Girls Day 3–16 (Boys 3–11)
No of pupils: B29 G175
Fees: (September 01)
Day £3420 – £5385

THE GRANGE SCHOOL
Bradburns Lane, Hartford,
Northwich, Cheshire CW8 1LU
Tel: (01606) 74007
Head: Mrs J Stephen and
Mr D K Geddes
Type: Co-educational Day 4–18
No of pupils: B572 G535
Fees: (September 01)
Day £3750 – £4905

SALE

CHRIST THE KING SCHOOL
The King's Centre, Raglan Road,
Sale, Cheshire M33 4AQ
Tel: (0161) 865 5323
Head: Mr T Giles
Type: Co-educational Day 5–16
No of pupils: B23 G21
Fees: (September 01) Day £2376

FOREST PARK SCHOOL
Lauriston House, 27 Oakfield, Sale,
Cheshire M33 6NB
Tel: (0161) 973 4835
Head: Mr L B R Groves
Type: Co-educational Day 3–11
No of pupils: B80 G60
Fees: (September 01)
Day £3120 – £3546

SANDBACH

**NORFOLK HOUSE
PREPARATORY & KIDS
CORNER NURSERY**
120 Congleton Road, Sandbach,
Cheshire CW11 1HF
Tel: (01270) 759257
Head: Mrs P M Jones
Type: Co-educational Day 0–11
No of pupils: B42 G43
Fees: (September 01) On application

SOUTH WIRRAL

MOSTYN HOUSE SCHOOL
Parkgate, South Wirral, Cheshire
CH64 6SG
Tel: (0151) 336 1010
Head: Mr A D J Grenfell
Type: Co-educational Day 4–18
No of pupils: B191 G114
Fees: (September 01)
Day £2696 – £6554

STALYBRIDGE

TRINITY SCHOOL
Birbeck Street, Stalybridge, Cheshire
SK15 1SH
Tel: (0161) 303 0674
Head: Mr W R Evans
Type: Co-educational Day 4–18
No of pupils: B80 G79
Fees: (September 01) Day £3600

STOCKPORT

BRABYNS SCHOOL
34–36 Arkwright Road, Marple,
Stockport, Cheshire SK6 7DB
Tel: (0161) 427 2395
Head: Mrs P Turner
Type: Co-educational Day 2–11
No of pupils: B75 G90
Fees: (September 01)
Day £1995 – £3246

**HILLCREST GRAMMAR
SCHOOL**
Beech Avenue, Stockport, Cheshire
SK3 8HB
Tel: (0161) 480 0329
Head: Mr D K Blackburn
Type: Co-educational Day 3–16
No of pupils: B180 G100
Fees: (September 01) Day £4380

ORIEL BANK HIGH SCHOOL
Devonshire Park Road, Davenport,
Stockport, Cheshire SK2 6JP
Tel: (0161) 483 2935
Head: Mr R A Bye
Type: Girls Day 3–16
No of pupils: 180
Fees: (September 01)
Day £2100 – £4890

**ST CATHERINE'S
PREPARATORY SCHOOL**
Hollins Lane, Marple Bridge,
Stockport, Cheshire SK6 5BB
Tel: (0161) 449 8800
Head: Mrs M A Sidwell
Type: Co-educational Day 3–11
No of pupils: B67 G85
Fees: (September 01)
Day £3195 – £3300

**STELLA MARIS JUNIOR
SCHOOL**
St Johns Road, Heaton Mersey,
Stockport, Cheshire SK4 3BR
Tel: (0161) 432 0532
Head: Mrs I L Gannon
Type: Co-educational Day 4–11
No of pupils: B51 G33
Fees: (September 01)
Day £2790 – £3105

**STOCKPORT GRAMMAR
SCHOOL**
Buxton Road, Stockport, Cheshire
SK2 7AF
Tel: (0161) 456 9000
Head: Mr I Mellor
Type: Co-educational Day 4–18
No of pupils: B729 G719
Fees: (September 01)
Day £5175 – £5508

SYDDAL PARK SCHOOL
33 Syddal Road, Bramhall,
Stockport, Cheshire SK7 1AB
Tel: (0161) 439 1751
Head: Mrs S Lay
Type: Co-educational Day 2–7
No of pupils: B32 G32
Fees: (September 01)
Day £2280 – £3180

**WOODFORD PREP &
NURSERY SCHOOL**
Chester Road, Woodford, Stockport,
Cheshire SK7 1PS
Tel: (0161) 439 9302
Head: Mrs V E Blundell
Type: Co-educational Day 2–11
No of pupils: B38 G16
Fees: (September 01)
Day £1500 – £3375

WILMSLOW

POWNALL HALL SCHOOL
Wilmslow, Cheshire SK9 5DW
Tel: (01625) 523141
Head: Mr J J Meadmore
Type: Co-educational Day 2–11
No of pupils: B156 G54
Fees: (September 01)
Day £4065 – £5655

CORNWALL

BUDE

ST PETROC'S SCHOOL
Ocean View Road, Bude, Cornwall
EX23 8NJ
Tel: (01288) 352876
Head: Mr B P Dare
Type: Co-educational Day 3–11
No of pupils: B48 G42
Fees: (September 01)
Day £2940 – £4845

LAUNCESTON

ST JOSEPH'S SCHOOL
15 St Stephen's Hill, Launceston,
Cornwall PL15 8HN
Tel: (01566) 772580
Head: Mr A R Doe
Type: Girls Day 3–16 (Boys 3–11)
No of pupils: B24 G146
Fees: (September 01)
Day £3945 – £5730

NEWQUAY

WHEELGATE HOUSE SCHOOL
Trevowah Road, Crantock, Newquay,
Cornwall TR8 5RU
Tel: (01637) 830680
Head: Mrs G Wilson
Type: Co-educational Day 2–12
No of pupils: B24 G20
Fees: (September 01)
Day £2000 – £2700

PAR

ROSELYON PREPARATORY SCHOOL
St Blazey Road, Par, Cornwall
PL24 2HZ
Tel: (01726) 812110
Head: Mr S C Bradley
Type: Co-educational Day 2–11
No of pupils: B33 G37
Fees: (September 01) Day £3741

PENZANCE

THE BOLITHO SCHOOL
Polwithen, Penzance, Cornwall
TR18 4JR
Tel: (01736) 363271
Head: Mr N Johnson
Type: Co-educational Day and
Boarding 4–18
No of pupils: B123 G124
No of boarders: F29 W20
Fees: (September 01)
FB £10350 – £11850
WB £9000 – £10500
Day £3750 – £6450

ST IVES

ST IA SCHOOL
St Ives Road, Carbis Bay, St Ives,
Cornwall TR26 2SF
Tel: (01736) 796963
Head: Mr D M P Bennett
Type: Co-educational Day 4–12
No of pupils: B25 G15
Fees: (September 01)
Day £975 – £1155

TRURO

POLWHELE HOUSE SCHOOL
Newquay Road, Truro, Cornwall
TR4 9AE
Tel: (01872) 273011
Head: Mr and Mrs R I White
Type: Co-educational Day and
Boarding 3–13
No of pupils: B96 G84
No of boarders: W10
Fees: (September 01) WB £10266 –
£11436
Day £675 – £6312

ST PIRAN'S SCHOOL
Trelissick Road, Hayle, Truro,
Cornwall TR27 4HY
Tel: (01736) 752612
Head: Mr D G Jones
Type: Co-educational Day 3–12
No of pupils: B45 G45
Fees: (September 01)
Day £2900 – £2700

TRELISKE SCHOOL
Truro, Cornwall TR1 3QN
Tel: (01872) 272616
Head: Mr R L Hollins
Type: Co-educational Day and
Boarding 3–11
No of pupils: B134 G86
No of boarders: W6
Fees: (September 01)
F/WB £8763 – £10695
Day £2304 – £5778

TRESCOL VEAN SCHOOL
Baldhu, Truro, Cornwall TR3 6EG
Tel: (01872) 560788
Head: Mrs S M Baron
Type: Co-educational Day 3–7
No of pupils: B23 G23
Fees: (September 01)
Day £1080 – £3600

TRURO HIGH SCHOOL
Falmouth Road, Truro, Cornwall
TR1 2HU
Tel: (01872) 272830
Head: Mr M McDowell
Type: Girls Boarding and Day 3–18
(Boys 3–5)
No of pupils: B5 G445
No of boarders: F31 W35
Fees: (September 01)
FB £5190 – £11130
WB £5055 – £10995
Day £3945 – £5940

TRURO SCHOOL
Trennick Lane, Truro, Cornwall
TR1 1TH
Tel: (01872) 272763
Head: Mr P K Smith
Type: Co-educational Day and
Boarding 11–18
No of pupils: B481 G283
No of boarders: F96
Fees: (September 01)
F/WB £11520 – £12327
Day £5961 – £6318

CUMBRIA

BARROW-IN-FURNESS

OUR LADY'S, CHETWYNDE
Croslands, Rating Lane, Barrow-in-Furness, Cumbria LA13 0NY
Tel: (01229) 824210
Head: Mrs M M Stones
Type: Co-educational Day 3–18
No of pupils: B292 G293
Fees: (September 01)
Day £2925 – £3025

CARLISLE

AUSTIN FRIARS SCHOOL
Etterby Scaur, Carlisle, Cumbria CA3 9PB
Tel: (01228) 528042
Head: Mr N J B O'Sullivan
Type: Co-educational Day 11–18
No of pupils: B163 G127
Fees: (September 01)
Day £3100 – £6045

LIME HOUSE SCHOOL
Holm Hill, Dalston, Carlisle, Cumbria CA5 7BX
Tel: (01228) 710225
Head: Mr N A Rice
Type: Co-educational Boarding and Day 4–18
No of pupils: B100 G80
No of boarders: F100 W10
Fees: (September 01)
FB £6000 – £9450 WB £5250 – £8700
Day £2550 – £4650

ST MONICA'S SCHOOL
Saint Ann's Hill, Carlisle, Cumbria CA3 9PL
Tel: (01228) 537458
Head: Mrs F M Willacy
Type: Co-educational Day 4–11
No of pupils: 140
Fees: (September 01) Day £3114

WELLSPRING CHRISTIAN SCHOOL
Cotehill, Carlisle, Cumbria CA4 0EA
Tel: (01228) 562023
Head: Mr A G Field
Type: Co-educational Day 3–18
No of pupils: B12 G8
Fees: (September 01)
Day £1300 – £2340

CARNFORTH

CASTERTON SCHOOL*
Kirkby Lonsdale, Carnforth, Cumbria LA6 2SG
Tel: (01524) 279200
Head: Mr A F Thomas
Type: Girls Boarding and Day 4–18
(Day boys 4–11)
No of pupils: B18 G344
No of boarders: F215 W5
Fees: (September 01)
FB £10287 – £12870 WB £10746
Day £6876 – £7920

KENDAL

HOLME PARK PREPARATORY SCHOOL
Hill Top, New Hutton, Kendal, Cumbria LA8 0AE
Tel: (01539) 721245
Head: Mr N J V Curry
Type: Co-educational Boarding and Day 3–13
No of pupils: B55 G15
No of boarders: W15
Fees: (September 01)
WB £6378 – £7015
Day £3780 – £5526

PENRITH

HUNTER HALL SCHOOL
Frenchfield, Penrith, Cumbria CA11 8UA
Tel: (01768) 891291
Head: Mrs L Dexter
Type: Co-educational Day 3–11
No of pupils: B50 G66
Fees: (September 01) Day £3690

SEASCALE

HARECROFT HALL SCHOOL
Gosforth, Seascale, Cumbria CA20 1HS
Tel: (01946) 725220
Head: Mr D G Hoddy
Type: Co-educational Boarding and Day 2–16
No of pupils: B49 G47
No of boarders: F13 W6
Fees: (September 01)
FB £8895 – £9747 WB £8490 – £9375
Day £4395 – £6195

SEDBERGH

SEDBERGH SCHOOL
Sedbergh, Cumbria LA10 5HG
Tel: (01539) 620535
Head: Mr C H Hirst
Type: Co-educational Boarding and Day 8–18
No of pupils: B342 G40
No of boarders: F362
Fees: (September 01)
FB £10320 – £16500
Day £7020 – £12195

ST BEES

ST BEES SCHOOL*
St Bees, Cumbria CA27 0DS
Tel: (01946) 822263
Head: Mr P J Capes
Type: Co-educational Boarding and Day 11–18
No of pupils: B184 G112
No of boarders: F92 W46
Fees: (September 01)
FB £11355 – £15513
WB £9840 – £13974
Day £7800 – £9909

WIGTON

ST URSULAS CONVENT SCHOOL
Burnfoot, Wigton, Cumbria CA7 9HL
Tel: (01697) 344359
Head: Mr M L Penrice
Type: Co-educational Day 2–11
No of pupils: B50 G33
Fees: (September 01) Day £2940

WINDERMERE

WINDERMERE ST ANNE'S SCHOOL*
Windermere, Cumbria LA23 1NW
Tel: (01539) 446164
Head: Miss W A Ellis
Type: Co-educational Boarding and Day 2–18
No of pupils: B117 G222
No of boarders: F80 W14
Fees: (September 01)
FB £11664 – £12312
WB £11616 – £11664
Day £3402 – £6804

DERBYSHIRE

ASHBOURNE

ASHBOURNE PNEU SCHOOL
St Monica's House, Windmill Lane,
Ashbourne, Derbyshire DE6 1EY
Tel: (01335) 343294
Head: Mr M A Broadbent
Type: Co-educational Day 0–13
No of pupils: 60
Fees: (September 01) On application

BAKEWELL

ST ANSELM'S
Bakewell, Derbyshire DE45 1DP
Tel: (01629) 812734
Head: Mr R J Foster
Type: Co-educational Boarding and
Day 7–13
No of pupils: B110 G83
No of boarders: F85
Fees: (September 01) FB £10950
Day £7380 – £9300

CHESTERFIELD

BARLBOROUGH HALL
SCHOOL*
Barlborough, Chesterfield,
Derbyshire S43 4TJ
Tel: (01246) 810511
Head: Mrs W Parkinson
Type: Co-educational Day and
boarding 3–11
No of pupils: B118 G86
No of boarders: F1
Fees: (September 01)
Day £3585 – £5310

ST JOSEPH'S CONVENT
42 Newbold Road, Chesterfield,
Derbyshire S41 7PL
Tel: (01246) 232392
Head: Mrs B Deane
Type: Co-educational Day 2–11
No of pupils: B69 G66
Fees: (September 01)
Day £2600 – £3500

ST PETER & ST PAUL
SCHOOL
Brambling House, Hady Hill,
Chesterfield, Derbyshire S41 0EF
Tel: (01246) 278522
Head: Mrs B Beet
Type: Co-educational Day 2–11
No of pupils: B82 G91
Fees: (September 01) Day £3276

DERBY

DERBY GRAMMAR SCHOOL
FOR BOYS
Rykneld Road, Littleover, Derby,
Derbyshire DE23 7BH
Tel: (01332) 523027
Head: Mr R D Waller
Type: Boys Day 7–18
No of pupils: 300
Fees: (September 01)
Day £4620 – £5775

DERBY HIGH SCHOOL
Hillsway, Littleover, Derby,
Derbyshire DE3 7DT
Tel: (01332) 514267
Head: Dr G H Goddard
Type: Girls Day 3–18 (Boys 3–11)
No of pupils: B98 G490
Fees: (September 01)
Day £4545 – £5685

EMMANUEL SCHOOL
Juniper Lodge, 43 Kedleston Road,
Derby, Derbyshire DE22 1FP
Tel: (01332) 340505
Head: Mr D Snowdon
Type: Co-educational Day 4–11
No of pupils: B27 G19
Fees: (September 01) On application

FOREMARKE HALL
Milton, Derby, Derbyshire DE65 6EJ
Tel: (01283) 703269
Head: Mr P Brewster
Type: Co-educational Boarding and
Day 3–13
No of pupils: B231 G130
No of boarders: F42 W33
Fees: (September 01) F/WB £10560
Day £4572 – £7800

MORLEY HALL
PREPARATORY SCHOOL
Hill House, Morley Road,
Chaddesden, Derby, Derbyshire
DE21 4QZ
Tel: (01332) 674501
Head: Mrs R N Hassell
Type: Co-educational Day 3–11
No of pupils: 90
Fees: (September 01)
Day £2202 – £3162

OCKBROOK SCHOOL
The Settlement, Ockbrook, Derby,
Derbyshire DE7 3RJ
Tel: (01332) 673532
Head: Miss D P Bolland
Type: Girls Day and Boarding 3–18
No of pupils: B40 G460
No of boarders: F18
Fees: (September 01) F/WB £10380
Day £4740 – £3960

THE OLD VICARAGE
SCHOOL
11 Church Lane, Darley Abbey,
Derby, Derbyshire DE22 1EW
Tel: (01332) 557130
Head: Mr G C Holbrow and
Mrs M Holbrow
Type: Co-educational Day 3–11
No of pupils: B44 G44
Fees: (September 01)
Day £3990 – £4275

HEANOR

MICHAEL HOUSE STEINER
SCHOOL
The Field, Shipley, Heanor,
Derbyshire DE75 7JH
Tel: (01773) 718050
Head: Ms E Conway
Type: Co-educational Day 4–16
No of pupils: B88 G73
Fees: (September 01)
Day £1350 – £3300

ILKESTON

GATEWAY CHRISTIAN
SCHOOL
Moor Lane, Dale Abbey, Ilkeston,
Derbyshire DE7 4PP
Tel: (0115) 944 0609
Head: Miss C Hahner
Type: Co-educational Day 3–11
No of pupils: B13 G8
Fees: (September 01) Day £1650

MATLOCK

ST ELPHIN'S SCHOOL
Darley Dale, Matlock, Derbyshire
DE4 2HA
Tel: (01629) 733263
Head: Mrs E Taylor
Type: Girls Boarding and Day 2–18
(Boys 2–7)
No of pupils: B31 G172
No of boarders: F20 W17
Fees: (September 01)
F/WB £10650 – £15180
Day £3750 – £8340

REPTON

REPTON SCHOOL
The Hall, Repton, Derbyshire
DE65 6FH
Tel: (01283) 559222
Head: Mr G E Jones
Type: Co-educational Boarding and
Day 13–18
No of pupils: B335 G196
No of boarders: F370
Fees: (September 01) FB £16065
Day £11910

ST WYSTAN'S SCHOOL
High Street, Repton, Derbyshire
DE65 6GF
Tel: (01283) 703258
Head: Mr C Sanderson
Type: Co-educational Day 2–11
No of pupils: B65 G53
Fees: (September 01)
Day £1965 – £3930

SPINKHILL

MOUNT ST MARY'S COLLEGE*
Spinkhill, Derbyshire S21 3YL
Tel: (01246) 433388
Head: Mr P G MacDonald
Type: Co-educational Boarding and
Day 11–18
No of pupils: B190 G100
No of boarders: F116 W36
Fees: (September 01)
FB £9195 – £12510
WB £8130 – £11085
Day £6045 – £6990

DEVON

ASHBURTON

SANDS SCHOOL
Greylands, 48 East Street,
Ashburton, Devon TQ13 7AX
Tel: (01364) 653666
Head: Mr S Bellamy
Type: Co-educational Day 10–16
No of pupils: B36 G34
Fees: (September 01)
Day £4500

BARNSTAPLE

ST MICHAEL'S
Tawstock Court, Barnstaple, Devon
EX31 3HY
Tel: (01271) 343242
Head: Mr J W Pratt
Type: Co-educational Day and
Boarding 0–13
No of pupils: B133 G83
No of boarders: W4
Fees: (September 01)
WB £10380 – £10695
Day £3225 – £7011

WEST BUCKLAND PREPARATORY SCHOOL
West Buckland, Barnstaple, Devon
EX32 0SX
Tel: (01598) 760545
Head: Mr A Moore
Type: Co-educational Day and
Boarding 3–11
No of pupils: B109 G82
No of boarders: F8 W2
Fees: (September 01)
FB £8085 – £9450
Day £3075 – £5625

WEST BUCKLAND SCHOOL
Barnstaple, Devon EX32 0SX
Tel: (01598) 760281
Head: Mr J Vick
Type: Co-educational Boarding and
Day 3–18
No of pupils: B448 G349
No of boarders: F121
Fees: (September 01)
FB £8085 – £12510
Day £3075 – £7050

BEAWORTHY

SHEBBEAR COLLEGE
Shebbear, Beaworthy, Devon
EX21 5HJ
Tel: (01409) 281228
Head: Mr L D Clark
Type: Co-educational Boarding and
Day 3–18
No of pupils: B102 G92
No of boarders: F60 W14
Fees: (September 01)
FB £8310 – £12900
WB £6825 – £10020
Day £2250 – £6660

BIDEFORD

EDGEHILL COLLEGE
Northdown Road, Bideford, Devon
EX39 3LY
Tel: (01237) 471701
Head: Mrs E M Burton
Type: Co-educational Boarding and
Day 2–18
No of pupils: B202 G244
No of boarders: F89 W8
Fees: (September 01) FB £10014 –
£13851 WB £9051 – £12504
Day £3645 – £7527

GRENVILLE COLLEGE
Bideford, Devon EX39 3JR
Tel: (01237) 472212
Head: Dr M C V Cane
Type: Co-educational Boarding and
Day 3–18
No of pupils: B231 G160
No of boarders: F90 W17
Fees: (September 01)
FB £10860 – £13986
WB £8142 – £10485
Day £2904 – £6924

CHULMLEIGH

OSHO KO HSUAN SCHOOL
Chawleigh, Chulmleigh, Devon
EX18 7EX
Tel: (01769) 580896
Head: Mr K Bartlam
Type: Co-educational Boarding 7–16
No of pupils: B14 G15
No of boarders: F26 W3
Fees: (September 01) FB £7200
WB £5850 Day £4050

DAWLISH

LANHERNE NURSERY AND JUNIOR SCHOOL
18 Longlands, Dawlish, Devon
EX7 9NG
Tel: (01626) 863091
Head: Mr R Hazeldene
Type: Co-educational Day 1–11
No of pupils: 58
Fees: (September 01) On application

EXETER

BENDARROCH SCHOOL
Aylesbeare, Exeter, Devon EX5 2BY
Tel: (01395) 233553
Head: Mr N R Home
Type: Co-educational Day 5–13
No of pupils: B20 G20
Fees: (September 01)
Day £2800 – £3150

BRAMDEAN PREPARATORY & GRAMMAR SCHOOL
Richmond Lodge, Homefield Road,
Heavitree, Exeter, Devon EX1 2QR
Tel: (01392) 273387
Head: Mr D A Connett
Type: Co-educational Boarding and
Day 3–18
No of pupils: B120 G80
No of boarders: W25
Fees: (September 01) WB £8085
Day £3234 – £5214

ELM GROVE SCHOOL
Elm Grove Road, Topsham, Exeter,
Devon EX3 0EQ
Tel: (01392) 873031
Head: Mrs K M Parsons and
Mr B E Parsons
Type: Co-educational Day 2–8
No of pupils: B30 G30
Fees: (September 01)
Day £2400

EMMANUEL SCHOOL
36–38 Blackboy Road, Exeter, Devon
EX4 6SZ
Tel: (01392) 258150
Head: Mr P J Gedye
Type: Co-educational Day 4–16
No of pupils: B40 G23
Fees: (September 01)
Day £1680 – £2448

EXETER CATHEDRAL SCHOOL
The Chantry, Palace Gate, Exeter,
Devon EX1 1HX
Tel: (01392) 255298
Head: Mr C I S Dickinson
Type: Co-educational Day and
Boarding 3–13
No of pupils: B127 G75
No of boarders: F26 W4
Fees: (September 01)
FB £8835 – £9000 WB £8460 – £8625
Day £3195 – £5505

EXETER JUNIOR SCHOOL
Victoria Park Road, Exeter, Devon
EX2 4NS
Tel: (01392) 258712
Head: Miss M Taylor
Type: Co-educational Day 7–11
No of pupils: B97 G22
Fees: (September 01) Day £5040

EXETER SCHOOL
Exeter, Devon EX2 4NS
Tel: (01392) 273679
Head: Mr N W Gamble
Type: Co-educational Day 7–18
No of pupils: B680 G124
Fees: (September 01)
Day £5040 – £5955

EXETER TUTORIAL COLLEGE
44/46 Magdalen Road, Exeter, Devon
EX2 4TE
Tel: (01392) 278101
Head: Mr K D Jack
Type: Co-educational Day 15+
No of pupils: B30 G35
Fees: (September 01) On application

HYLTON KINDERGARTEN & PRE-PREPARATORY SCHOOL
13A Lyndhurst Road, Exeter, Devon
EX2 4PA
Tel: (01392) 254755
Head: Mrs R C Leveridge
Type: Co-educational Day 2–8
No of pupils: 75
Fees: (September 01)
Day £244 – £2625

MAGDALEN COURT SCHOOL
Mulberry House, Victoria Park Road,
Exeter, Devon EX2 4NU
Tel: (01392) 494919
Head: Mr J G Bushrod
Type: Co-educational Day 2–18
No of pupils: B85 G80
Fees: (September 01)
Day £2950 – £6000

THE MAYNARD SCHOOL
Denmark Road, Exeter, Devon
EX1 1SJ
Tel: (01392) 273417
Head: Dr D West
Type: Girls Day 7–18
No of pupils: 475
Fees: (September 01)
Day £4890 – £6120

NEW SCHOOL
Exe Vale, Exminster, Exeter, Devon
EX6 8AT
Tel: (01392) 496122
Head: Mrs G Redman
Type: Co-educational Day 4–8
No of pupils: B32 G31
Fees: (September 01)
Day £2235 – £2835

ST MARGARET'S SCHOOL
147 Magdalen Road, Exeter, Devon
EX2 4TS
Tel: (01392) 273197
Head: Mrs M D'Albertanson
Type: Girls Day 7–18
No of pupils: 420
Fees: (September 01)
Day £3150 – £5880

ST WILFRID'S SCHOOL
25 St David's Hill, Exeter, Devon
EX4 4DA
Tel: (01392) 276171
Head: Mrs A E M Macdonald-Dent
Type: Co-educational Day 5–16
No of pupils: B75 G60
Fees: (September 01)
Day £2835 – £4536

EXMOUTH

CASTLE DOWN SCHOOL
Littleham Road, Exmouth, Devon
EX8 2RD
Tel: (01395) 269998
Head: Miss H Lee
Type: Co-educational Day 3–7
No of pupils: B27 G18
Fees: (September 01)
Day £1650 – £2805

THE DOLPHIN SCHOOL
Raddenstile Lane, Exmouth, Devon
EX8 2JH
Tel: (01395) 272418
Head: Mrs J Bishop
Type: Co-educational Day 3–11
No of pupils: B43 G42
Fees: (September 01)
Day £1200 – £3225

ST PETER'S SCHOOL
Harefield, Lympstone, Exmouth,
Devon EX8 5AU
Tel: (01395) 272148
Head: Mr C N Abram
Type: Co-educational Day and
Boarding 3–13
No of pupils: B134 G113
No of boarders: W20
Fees: (September 01) WB £9150
Day £3900 – £6375

HONITON

MANOR HOUSE SCHOOL
Springfield House, Honiton, Devon
EX14 9TL
Tel: (01404) 42026
Head: Mr S J Bage
Type: Co-educational Day 3–11
No of pupils: B65 G65
Fees: (September 01)
Day £2940 – £4050

NEWTON ABBOT

ABBOTSBURY SCHOOL
90 Torquay Road, Newton Abbot,
Devon TQ12 2JD
Tel: (01626) 352164
Head: Mr R J Manley
Type: Co-educational Day 2–7
No of pupils: B50 G50
Fees: (September 01)
Day £573 – £1785

LUSTLEIGH SCHOOL
Church House, Lustleigh, Newton
Abbot, Devon TQ13 9TJ
Tel: (01647) 277399
Head: Mrs J Dennis
Type: Co-educational Day 3–5
No of pupils: 9
Fees: (September 01) On application

ST BERNARD'S PREPARATORY SCHOOL
9 Courtenay Road, Newton Abbot,
Devon TQ12 1HP
Tel: (01626) 365424
Head: Mr R Dudley-Cooke
Type: Co-educational Day 2–11
No of pupils: B50 G70
Fees: (September 01)
Day £780 – £3741

STOVER SCHOOL
Newton Abbot, Devon TQ12 6QG
Tel: (01626) 354505
Head: Mr P E Bujak
Type: Girls Boarding and Day 2–18
No of pupils: B14 G357
No of boarders: F41 W52
Fees: (September 01) FB £7845 –
£11985 WB £9585 – £10785
Day £2085 – £5985

WOLBOROUGH HILL SCHOOL
South Road, Newton Abbot, Devon
TQ12 1HH
Tel: (01626) 354078
Head: Mr D L Tyler
Type: Co-educational Day 3–11
No of pupils: B91 G35
Fees: (September 01)
Day £3990 – £5790

PAIGNTON

TOWER HOUSE SCHOOL
Fisher Street, Paignton, Devon
TQ4 5EW
Tel: (01803) 557077
Head: Mr M Robinson
Type: Co-educational Day 2–16
No of pupils: B130 G130
Fees: (September 01)
Day £2994 – £4581

PLYMOUTH

FLETEWOOD SCHOOL
88 North Road East, Plymouth,
Devon PL4 6AN
Tel: (01752) 663782
Head: Mr J Martin
Type: Co-educational Day 3–11
No of pupils: B35 G35
Fees: (September 01) Day £2070

KING'S SCHOOL
Hartley Road, Mannamead,
Plymouth, Devon PL3 5LW
Tel: (01752) 771789
Head: Mrs J Lee
Type: Co-educational Day 3–11
No of pupils: B98 G74
Fees: (September 01)
Day £2655 – £2985

PLYMOUTH COLLEGE
Ford Park, Plymouth, Devon
PL4 6RN
Tel: (01752) 203300
Head: Mr A J Morsley
Type: Co-educational Day and
Boarding 11–18
No of pupils: B405 G174
No of boarders: F50 W14
Fees: (September 01)
FB £12867 – £13230
WB £12795 – £13158
Day £6546 – £6909

PLYMOUTH COLLEGE PREPARATORY SCHOOL
Hartley Road, Plymouth, Devon
PL3 5LW
Tel: (01752) 772283
Head: Mrs P Roberts
Type: Co-educational Day 3–11
No of pupils: 328
Fees: (September 01)
Day £3162 – £4845

ST DUNSTAN'S ABBEY SCHOOL
The Millfields, Plymouth, Devon
PL1 3JL
Tel: (01752) 201350
Head: Mrs T Smith
Type: Girls Day and Boarding 2–18
No of pupils: 309
No of boarders: F39 W6
Fees: (September 01)
FB £9690 – £12228
WB £8208 – £10746
Day £3759 – £6297

SIDMOUTH

ST JOHN'S SCHOOL
Broadway, Sidmouth, Devon
EX10 8RG
Tel: (01395) 513984
Head: Mr N R Pockett
Type: Co-educational Day and
Boarding 2–13
No of pupils: B127 G123
No of boarders: F50 W10
Fees: (September 01) FB £10212
WB £9561 Day £1611 – £5670

TAVISTOCK

KELLY COLLEGE
Tavistock, Devon PL19 0HZ
Tel: (01822) 813127
Head: M M Steed
Type: Co-educational Boarding and
Day 11–18
No of pupils: B220 G150
No of boarders: F105 W80
Fees: (September 01)
FB £13050 – £15600
WB £1200 – £15000
Day £6600 – £9900

KELLY COLLEGE JUNIOR SCHOOL
Hazeldon House, Parkwood Road,
Tavistock, Devon PL19 0JS
Tel: (01822) 612919
Head: Mr R P Jeynes
Type: Co-educational Boarding and
Day 2–11
No of pupils: B64 G62
No of boarders: W1
Fees: (September 01)
FB £10650 – £10875
WB £9600 – £9825
Day £3300 – £4425

MOUNT HOUSE SCHOOL
Tavistock, Devon PL19 9JL
Tel: (01822) 612244
Head: Mr C D Price
Type: Co-educational Boarding and
Day 3–13
No of pupils: B175 G75
No of boarders: F103
Fees: (September 01)
FB £10992 Day £3912 – £8241

TEIGNMOUTH

BUCKERIDGE INTERNATIONAL COLLEGE
Trinity School, Buckeridge Road,
Teignmouth, Devon TQ14 8LY
Tel: (01626) 774138
Head: Mr C Ashby
Type: Co-educational Boarding and
Day 11–19
No of pupils: B72 G45
No of boarders: F120 W2
Fees: (September 01)
FB £10980 – £12315
Day £4335 – £4995

TRINITY SCHOOL
Buckeridge Road, Teignmouth,
Devon TQ6 9RA
Tel: (01626) 774138
Head: Mr C J Ashby
Type: Co-educational Day and
Boarding 3–19
No of pupils: B235 G156
No of boarders: F120 W11
Fees: (September 01)
FB £9570 – £10680
Day £3300 – £5130

TIVERTON

BLUNDELL'S SCHOOL*
Tiverton, Devon EX16 4DN
Tel: (01884) 252543
Head: Mr J Leigh
Type: Co-educational Boarding and
Day 11–18
No of pupils: B320 G190
No of boarders: F115 W255
Fees: (September 01)
FB £10515 – £15810
WB £6664 – £14290
Day £5685 – £9825

ST AUBYN'S SCHOOL
Milestones House, Blundell's Road,
Tiverton, Devon EX16 4NA
Tel: (01884) 252393
Head: Mr N A Folland
Type: Co-educational Day 0–11
No of pupils: B171 G133
No of boarders: W3
Fees: (September 01)
Day £1044 – £5640

TORBAY

GRAMERCY HALL SCHOOL
Churston Ferrers, Torbay, Devon
TQ5 0HR
Tel: (01803) 844338
Head: Mr N Thomas
Type: Co-educational Day 3–16
No of pupils: B112 G75
No of boarders: F15 W3
Fees: (September 01) FB £8950
WB £7590 Day £3600 – £4350

TORQUAY

THE ABBEY SCHOOL
Hampton Court, St Marychurch,
Torquay, Devon TQ1 4PR
Tel: (01803) 327868
Head: Mrs J Joyce
Type: Co-educational Day 0–11
No of pupils: B68 G63
Fees: (September 01)
Day £390 – £4305

TOTNES

PARK SCHOOL
Park Road, Dartington, Totnes,
Devon TQ9 6EQ
Tel: (01803) 864588
Head: Mr R Hickman
Type: Co-educational Day 3–11
No of pupils: B29 G25
Fees: (September 01)
Day £2118 – £3021

RUDOLF STEINER SCHOOL
Hood Manor, Buckfastleigh Road,
Dartington, Totnes, Devon TQ9 6AB
Tel: (01803) 762528
Head: Mr C Cooper
Type: Co-educational Day 3–16
No of pupils: B145 G149
No of boarders: F4 W4
Fees: (September 01)
Day £2517 – £4179

ST CHRISTOPHERS SCHOOL
Mount Barton, Staverton, Totnes,
Devon TQ9 6PF
Tel: (01803) 762202
Head: Mrs J E Kenyon
Type: Co-educational Day 2–11
No of pupils: B45 G35
Fees: (September 01)
Day £2340 – £3591

DORSET

BLANDFORD FORUM

BRYANSTON SCHOOL
Blandford Forum, Dorset DT11 0PX
Tel: (01258) 452411
Head: Mr T D Wheare
Type: Co-educational Boarding and
Day 13–18
No of pupils: B377 G269
No of boarders: F573
Fees: (September 01) FB £17928
Day £13806

CLAYESMORE PREPARATORY
SCHOOL
Iwerne Minster, Blandford Forum,
Dorset DT11 8PH
Tel: (01747) 811707
Head: Mr A Roberts – Wray
Type: Co-educational Boarding and
Day 2–13
No of pupils: B185 G120
No of boarders: F57 W20
Fees: (September 01)
F/WB £10650 – £11670
Day £4050 – £8460

CLAYESMORE SCHOOL
Iwerne Minster, Blandford Forum,
Dorset DT11 8LL
Tel: (01747) 812122
Head: Mr M G Cooke
Type: Co-educational Boarding and
Day 13–18
No of pupils: B192 G107
No of boarders: F212
Fees: (September 01) FB £15600
Day £11100

HANFORD SCHOOL
Childe Okeford, Blandford Forum,
Dorset DT11 8HL
Tel: (01258) 860219
Head: Miss S Canning and
Mr & Mrs McKenzie Johnston
Type: Girls Boarding 7–13
No of pupils: 117
No of boarders: F113
Fees: (September 01) FB £10200

KNIGHTON HOUSE
Durweston, Blandford Forum,
Dorset DT11 0PY
Tel: (01258) 452065
Head: Mrs E A Heath
Type: Girls Day and Boarding 3–13
(Day boys 3–7)
No of pupils: B14 G138
No of boarders: F26 W27
Fees: (September 01) F/WB £11670
Day £1800 – £8520

MILTON ABBEY SCHOOL
Blandford Forum, Dorset DT11 0BZ
Tel: (01258) 880484
Head: Mr J Hughes-D'Aeth
Type: Boys Boarding and Day 13–18
No of pupils: 224
No of boarders: F190
Fees: (September 01) FB £16455
Day £12345

BOURNEMOUTH

THE PARK SCHOOL
Queen's Park South Drive,
Bournemouth, Dorset BH8 9BJ
Tel: (01202) 396640
Head: Mr C Cole
Type: Co-educational Day 4–12
No of pupils: B135 G129
Fees: (September 01)
Day £3075 – £4125

ST MARTIN'S SCHOOL
15 Stokewood Road, Bournemouth,
Dorset BH3 7NA
Tel: (01202) 554483
Head: Mr T B T Shenton
Type: Co-educational Day 4–12
No of pupils: B50 G50
Fees: (September 01)
Day £1350 – £3045

ST THOMAS GARNET'S
SCHOOL
Parkwood Road, Boscombe,
Bournemouth, Dorset BH5 2BH
Tel: (01202) 420172
Head: Mr P R Gillings
Type: Co-educational Day 0–11
No of pupils: B85 G87
Fees: (September 01)
Day £2400 – £3375

TALBOT HEATH
Rothesay Road, Bournemouth,
Dorset BH4 9NJ
Tel: (01202) 761881
Head: Mrs C Dipple
Type: Girls Day and Boarding 3–18
(Boys 3–7)
No of pupils: B6 G652
No of boarders: F29 W5
Fees: (September 01) FB £11805
WB £11505 Day £2175 – £6885

TALBOT HOUSE
PREPARATORY SCHOOL
8 Firs Glen Road, Bournemouth,
Dorset BH9 2LR
Tel: (01202) 510348
Head: Mrs C Oosthuizen and
Mr M Broadway
Type: Co-educational Day 3–12
No of pupils: B80 G60
Fees: (September 01)
Day £522 – £3570

WENTWORTH COLLEGE*
College Road, Bournemouth, Dorset
BH5 2DY
Tel: (01202) 423266
Head: Miss S Coe
Type: Girls Boarding and Day 11–18
No of pupils: 225
No of boarders: F40 W20
Fees: (September 01) F/WB £11550
Day £7275

CHRISTCHURCH

HOMEFIELD SCHOOL
SENIOR & PREPARATORY
Salisbury Road, Winkton,
Christchurch, Dorset BH23 7AR
Tel: (01202)479781/476644
Head: Mr A C Partridge
Type: Co-educational Boarding and
Day 3–18
No of pupils: B250 G100
No of boarders: F50 W3
Fees: (September 01) F/WB £11475
Day £2775 – £4755

DORCHESTER

DORCHESTER PREPARATORY
SCHOOL
25/26 Icen Way, Dorchester, Dorset
DT1 1EP
Tel: (01305) 264925
Head: Mr J de B Miller
Type: Co-educational Day 3–13
No of pupils: B43 G45
Fees: (September 01)
Day £1464 – £3996

SUNNINGHILL PREPARATORY SCHOOL
South Court, South Walks, Dorchester, Dorset DT1 1EB
Tel: (01305) 262306
Head: Mr C Pring
Type: Co-educational Day 3–13
No of pupils: B92 G93
Fees: (September 01)
Day £2175 – £4800

POOLE

BUCKHOLME TOWERS
18 Commercial Road, Parkstone, Poole, Dorset BH14 0JW
Tel: (01202) 742871
Head: Mrs C B M Westhead
Type: Co-educational Day 3–12
No of pupils: B70 G70
Fees: (September 01)
Day £2775 – £3255

ST JOSEPH'S CONVENT NURSERY SCHOOL
37 Parkstone Road, Poole, Dorset BH15 2NU
Tel: (01202) 670736
Head: Sister Germaine
Type: Co-educational Day 3–5
No of pupils: 40
Fees: (September 01) On application

UPLANDS SCHOOL
40 St Osmund's Road, Parkstone, Poole, Dorset BH14 9JY
Tel: (01202) 742626
Head: Mrs L Dummett
Type: Co-educational Day 2–16
No of pupils: B199 G165
Fees: (September 01)
Day £2700 – £5925

YARRELLS SCHOOL
Yarrells House, Upton, Poole, Dorset BH16 5EU
Tel: (01202) 622229
Head: Mrs Covell
Type: Co-educational Day 2–13
No of pupils: B114 G149
Fees: (September 01)
Day £1175 – £6075

SHAFTESBURY

PORT REGIS
Motcombe Park, Shaftesbury, Dorset SP7 9QA
Tel: (01747) 852566
Head: Mr P A E Dix
Type: Co-educational Boarding and Day 3–13
No of pupils: B230 G170
No of boarders: F152 W105
Fees: (September 01) F/WB £13980
Day £4650 – £10485

ST MARY'S SCHOOL*
Shaftesbury, Dorset SP7 9LP
Tel: (01747) 854005
Head: Mrs S Pennington
Type: Girls Boarding and Day 9–18
No of pupils: 340
No of boarders: F228
Fees: (September 01)
FB £13695 – £14430
Day £8910 – £9375

SHERBORNE

INTERNATIONAL COLLEGE, SHERBORNE SCHOOL*
Newell Grange, Sherborne, Dorset DT9 4EZ
Tel: (01935) 814743
Head: Dr C Greenfield
Type: Co-educational Boarding 11–17
No of pupils: B82 G38
No of boarders: F132
Fees: (September 01)
FB £19500 – £21000

ST ANTONY'S-LEWESTON PREPARATORY SCHOOL
Sherborne, Dorset DT9 6EN
Tel: (01963) 210790
Head: Mrs L M Walker
Type: Co-educational Boarding and Day Boys 2–8 Girls 2–11
No of pupils: B38 G84
No of boarders: F7
Fees: (September 01) FB £9300
Day £3870 – £5925

ST ANTONY'S-LEWESTON SCHOOL
Sherborne, Dorset DT9 6EN
Tel: (01963) 210691
Head: Mr H MacDonald
Type: Girls Boarding and Day 11–18
No of pupils: 250
No of boarders: F100
Fees: (September 01) FB £14202
Day £9444

SHERBORNE PREPARATORY SCHOOL
Acreman Street, Sherborne, Dorset DT9 3NY
Tel: (01935) 812097
Head: Mr P S Tait
Type: Co-educational Day and Boarding 2–13
No of pupils: B164 G70
No of boarders: F37 W9
Fees: (September 01)
F/WB £10440 – £11550
Day £1920 – £7710

SHERBORNE SCHOOL
Abbey Road, Sherborne, Dorset DT9 3AP
Tel: (01935) 812249
Head: Mr S F Eliot
Type: Boys Boarding 13–18
No of pupils: 520
No of boarders: F490
Fees: (September 01) FB £17700
Day £12600

SHERBORNE SCHOOL FOR GIRLS*
Bradford Road, Sherborne, Dorset DT9 3QN
Tel: (01935) 818287
Head: Mrs G Kerton-Johnson
Type: Girls Boarding and Day 11–18
No of pupils: 350
No of boarders: F328
Fees: (September 01) FB £17430
Day £12900

SWANAGE

THE OLD MALTHOUSE
Langton Matravers, Swanage, Dorset BH19 3HB
Tel: (01929) 422302
Head: Mr J H L Phillips
Type: Boys Boarding and Day 3–13 (Girls 3–9)
No of pupils: B100 G15
No of boarders: F15 W35
Fees: (September 01) F/WB £11655
Day £8835

WEYMOUTH

THORNLOW PREPARATORY SCHOOL
Connaught Road, Weymouth, Dorset DT4 0SA
Tel: (01305) 785703
Head: Mr R A Fowke
Type: Co-educational Day 3–13
No of pupils: B43 G35
Fees: (September 01) Day £1195

WIMBORNE

CANFORD SCHOOL
Wimborne, Dorset BH21 3AD
Tel: (01202) 841254
Head: Mr J D Lever
Type: Co-educational Boarding and
Day 13–18
No of pupils: B373 G204
No of boarders: F389
Fees: (September 01) FB £17355
Day £13020

CASTLE COURT PREPARATORY SCHOOL
The Knoll House, Knoll Lane, Corfe
Mullen, Wimborne, Dorset
BH21 3RF
Tel: (01202) 694438
Head: Mr R E T Nicholl
Type: Co-educational Day 3–13
No of pupils: B214 G135
Fees: (September 01)
Day £1857 – £8835

DUMPTON SCHOOL
Deans Grove House, Wimborne,
Dorset BH21 7AF
Tel: (01202) 883818
Head: Mr A G M Watson
Type: Co-educational Day 2–13
No of pupils: B185 G65
Fees: (September 01)
Day £4350 – £8335

COUNTY DURHAM

BARNARD CASTLE

BARNARD CASTLE SCHOOL
Barnard Castle, County Durham
DL12 8UN
Tel: (01833) 690222
Head: Mr M D Featherstone
Type: Co-educational Boarding and
Day 4–18
No of pupils: B430 G226
No of boarders: F176
Fees: (September 01)
FB £9084 – £11853
Day £3066 – £7017

DARLINGTON

HURWORTH HOUSE SCHOOL
The Green, Hurworth-on-Tees,
Darlington, County Durham
DL2 2AD
Tel: (01325) 720645
Head: Mr C R T Fenwick
Type: Boys Day 3–18
No of pupils: 172
Fees: (September 01)
Day £4125 – £6405

POLAM HALL
Darlington, County Durham
DL1 5PA
Tel: (01325) 463383
Head: Mrs H C Hamilton
Type: Girls Boarding and Day 4–18
No of pupils: 470
No of boarders: F40 W5
Fees: (September 01)
FB £10095 – £13155
WB £9795 – £12855
Day £2895 – £6120

RAVENTHORPE PREPARATORY SCHOOL
96 Carmel Road North, Darlington,
County Durham DL3 8JB
Tel: (01325) 463373
Head: Mrs D A Procter
Type: Co-educational Day 3–11
No of pupils: B55 G56
Fees: (September 01)
Day £2175 – £2550

DURHAM

BOW SCHOOL
South Road, Durham, County
Durham DH1 3LS
Tel: (0191) 384 8233
Head: Mr R N Baird
Type: Boys Day 3–13
No of pupils: 157
Fees: (September 01)
Day £3372 – £6309

THE CHORISTER SCHOOL
Durham, County Durham DH1 3EL
Tel: (0191) 384 2935
Head: Mr C S S Drew
Type: Co-educational Day and
Boarding 4–13
No of pupils: B143 G46
No of boarders: F20 W10
Fees: (September 01)
F/WB £4761 – £8952
Day £4272 – £6120

DURHAM HIGH SCHOOL FOR GIRLS
Farewell Hall, Durham, County
Durham DH1 3TB
Tel: (0191) 384 3226
Head: Mrs A J Templeman
Type: Girls Day 3–18
No of pupils: 530
Fees: (September 01)
Day £4080 – £6135

DURHAM SCHOOL
Durham, County Durham DH1 4SZ
Tel: (0191) 384 7977
Head: Mr M N G Kern
Type: Co-educational Boarding and
Day 11–18
No of pupils: B256 G83
No of boarders: F78
Fees: (September 01) FB £14295
Day £6465 – £9357

ESSEX

BILLERICAY

ST JOHN'S SCHOOL
Stock Road, Billericay, Essex
CM12 0AR
Tel: (01277) 623070
Head: Mrs S Hillier and
Mrs F S Armour
Type: Co-educational Day 3–16
No of pupils: B238 G164
Fees: (September 01)
Day £2775 – £5250

BRENTWOOD

BRENTWOOD SCHOOL*
Ingrave Road, Brentwood, Essex
CM15 8AS
Tel: (01277) 243243
Head: Mr J A B Kelsall
Type: Co-educational Boarding and
Day 3–18
No of pupils: B854 G546
No of boarders: F75 W20
Fees: (September 01) FB £14622
Day £8433

HERINGTON HOUSE SCHOOL
Mount Avenue, Hutton, Brentwood,
Essex CM13 2NS
Tel: (01277) 211595
Head: Mr R Dudley-Cooke
Type: Co-educational Day 3–11
No of pupils: B36 G82
Fees: (September 01)
Day £4635 – £5025

BUCKHURST HILL

BRAESIDE SCHOOL FOR GIRLS
130 High Road, Buckhurst Hill,
Essex IG9 5SD
Tel: (020) 8504 1133
Head: Mrs C Naismith
Type: Girls Day 3–16
No of pupils: 223
Fees: (September 01)
Day £3750 – £5550

DAIGLEN SCHOOL
68 Palmerston Road, Buckhurst Hill,
Essex IG9 5LG
Tel: (020) 8504 7108
Head: Mr D Wood
Type: Boys Day 4–11
No of pupils: 152
Fees: (September 01) Day £4470

LOYOLA PREPARATORY SCHOOL
103 Palmerston Road, Buckhurst
Hill, Essex IG9 5NH
Tel: (020) 8504 7372
Head: Mr P G Nicholson
Type: Boys Day 3–11 (Nursery 3–4)
No of pupils: 184
Fees: (September 01)
Day £2085 – £4170

CHELMSFORD

ELM GREEN PREPARATORY SCHOOL
Parsonage Lane, Little Baddow,
Chelmsford, Essex CM3 4SU
Tel: (01245) 225230
Head: Mrs E L Mimpriss
Type: Co-educational Day 4–11
No of pupils: B104 G115
Fees: (September 01) Day £4770

HEATHCOTE SCHOOL
Eves Corner, Danbury, Chelmsford,
Essex CM3 4QB
Tel: (01245) 223131
Head: Mrs L Mitchell-Hall
Type: Co-educational Day 2–11
No of pupils: B96 G88
Fees: (September 01) Day £4200

NEW HALL SCHOOL
Chelmsford, Essex CM3 3HT
Tel: (01245) 467588
Head: Mrs K Jeffrey
Type: Girls Boarding and Day 4–18
(Boys day 4–11)
No of pupils: B95 G546
No of boarders: F83 W29
Fees: (September 01)
FB £14220 – £14490
WB £13770 – £14040
Day £9210 – £9450

ST ANNE'S PREPARATORY SCHOOL
154 New London Road, Chelmsford,
Essex CM2 0AW
Tel: (01245) 353488
Head: Mrs Y Heaton
Type: Co-educational Day 3–11
No of pupils: B60 G90
Fees: (September 01)
Day £3600 – £3900

ST CEDD'S SCHOOL
Maltese Road, Chelmsford, Essex
CM1 2PB
Tel: (01245) 354380
Head: Mr R J Mathrick
Type: Co-educational Day 4–11
No of pupils: B166 G167
Fees: (September 01)
Day £4425 – £4785

WIDFORD LODGE
Widford Road, Chelmsford, Essex
CM2 9AN
Tel: (01245) 352581
Head: Mr S C Trowell
Type: Co-educational Day 2–11
No of pupils: B130 G65
Fees: (September 01)
Day £4020 – £5250

CHIGWELL

CHIGWELL SCHOOL
High Road, Chigwell, Essex IG7 6QF
Tel: (020) 8501 5702
Head: Mr D F Gibbs
Type: Co-educational Day and
Boarding 7–18
No of pupils: B535 G199
No of boarders: F20 W30
Fees: (September 01) FB £13122
WB £12423 – £11703
Day £5613 – £8631

GURU GOBIND SINGH KHALSA COLLEGE
Roding Lane, Chigwell, Essex
IG7 6BQ
Tel: (020) 8559 9160
Head: Mr A S Toor
Type: Co-educational Day 4–18
No of pupils: 200
Fees: (September 01) On application

CLACTON-ON-SEA

ST CLARE'S DAY NURSERY
St James' Church Hall, Tower Road,
Clacton-on-Sea, Essex CO15 1LF
Tel: (01255) 427629
Head: Mrs C Pratt
Type: Co-educational Day 2–5
No of pupils: 37
Fees: (September 01) On application

COLCHESTER

COLCHESTER HIGH SCHOOL
Wellesley Road, Colchester, Essex
CO3 3HD
Tel: (01206) 573389
Head: Mr A T Moore
Type: Boys Day 3–16 (Girls 3–11)
No of pupils: B340 G35
Fees: (September 01)
Day £1380 – £5085

HOLMWOOD HOUSE
Chitts Hill, Lexden, Colchester,
Essex CO3 5ST
Tel: (01206) 574305
Head: Mr H S Thackrah
Type: Co-educational Day and
Boarding 4–14
No of pupils: B229 G138
Fees: (September 01)
WB £10386 – £11625
Day £5049 – £8991

LITTLEGARTH SCHOOL
Horkesley Park, Nayland,
Colchester, Essex CO6 4JR
Tel: (01206) 262332
Head: Mrs E P Coley
Type: Co-educational Day 2–11
No of pupils: B153 G140
Fees: (September 01)
Day £990 – £4485

OXFORD HOUSE SCHOOL
2 Lexden Road, Colchester, Essex
CO3 3NE
Tel: (01206) 576686
Head: Mr R P Spendlove
Type: Co-educational Day 2–11
No of pupils: B65 G65
Fees: (September 01)
Day £2205 – £4335

ST MARY'S SCHOOL
91 Lexden Road, Colchester, Essex
CO3 3RB
Tel: (01206) 572544
Head: Mrs G M Mouser
Type: Girls Day 4–16
No of pupils: 520
Fees: (September 01)
Day £3870 – £5385

DUNMOW

FELSTED PREPARATORY SCHOOL
Felsted, Dunmow, Essex CM6 3JL
Tel: (01371) 820252
Head: Mr E Newton and Mr T Z Searle
Type: Co-educational Boarding and
Day 4–13
No of pupils: B210 G127
No of boarders: F33
Fees: (September 01) FB £11985
Day £3750 – £9240

FELSTED SCHOOL
Felsted, Dunmow, Essex CM6 3LL
Tel: (01371) 821594
Head: Mr S C Roberts
Type: Co-educational Boarding and
Day 13–18
No of pupils: B254 G151
No of boarders: F278
Fees: (September 01) FB £15720
Day £11490 – £12390

EPPING

COOPERSALE HALL SCHOOL
Flux's Lane, off Steward's Green
Road, Epping, Essex CM16 7PE
Tel: (01992) 577133
Head: Mrs S Bowdler
Type: Co-educational Day 3–11
No of pupils: B160 G152
Fees: (September 01)
Day £2685 – £4890

FRINTON-ON-SEA

ST PHILOMENA'S PREPARATORY SCHOOL
Hadleigh Road, Frinton-on-Sea,
Essex CO13 9HQ
Tel: (01255) 674492
Head: Mrs B Buck
Type: Co-educational Day 3–11
No of pupils: 169
Fees: (September 01) Day £2400

HALSTEAD

GOSFIELD SCHOOL
Halstead Road, Gosfield, Halstead,
Essex CO9 1PF
Tel: (01787) 474040
Head: Mrs C Goodchild
Type: Co-educational Day and
Boarding 2–18
No of pupils: B137 G90
No of boarders: F11 W5
Fees: (September 01)
FB £9300 – £10500
Day £3870 – £7080

ST MARGARET'S SCHOOL
Gosfield Hall Park, Gosfield,
Halstead, Essex CO9 1SE
Tel: (01787) 472134
Head: Mrs B Y Boyton
Type: Co-educational Day 2–11
No of pupils: B98 G102
Fees: (September 01)
Day £3375 – £5100

HARLOW

ST NICHOLAS SCHOOL
Hillingdon House, Hobbs Cross
Road, Harlow, Essex CM17 0NJ
Tel: (01279) 429910
Head: Mr G W Brant
Type: Co-educational Day 4–16
No of pupils: B160 G170
Fees: (September 01)
Day £2790 – £5610

HORNCHURCH

GOODRINGTON SCHOOL
17 Walden Road, Emerson Park,
Hornchurch, Essex RM11 2JT
Tel: (01708) 448349
Head: Mr D Morris
Type: Co-educational Day 3–11
No of pupils: B45 G34
Fees: (September 01) Day £2550

ILFORD

BEEHIVE PREPARATORY SCHOOL
233 Beehive Lane, Redbridge, Ilford,
Essex IG4 5ED
Tel: (020) 8550 3224
Head: Mr C J Beasant
Type: Co-educational Day 4–11
No of pupils: B50 G45
Fees: (September 01)
Day £2700

CLARKS PREPARATORY SCHOOL
81/85 York Road, Ilford, Essex
IG1 3AF
Tel: (020) 8478 6510
Head: Ms M L Jones
Type: Co-educational Day 1–7
No of pupils: 100
Fees: (September 01) Day £4620

CRANBROOK COLLEGE*
Mansfield Road, Ilford, Essex
IG1 3BD
Tel: (020) 8554 1757
Head: Mr C P Lacey
Type: Boys Day 4–16
No of pupils: 210
Fees: (September 01)
Day £3840 – £5019

EASTCOURT INDEPENDENT SCHOOL
1 Eastwood Road, Goodmayes,
Ilford, Essex IG3 8UW
Tel: (020) 8590 5472
Head: Mrs C Redgrave
Type: Co-educational Day 4–11
No of pupils: B171 G166
Fees: (September 01) Day £3175

GLENARM COLLEGE
20 Coventry Road, Ilford, Essex
IG1 4QR
Tel: (020) 8554 1760
Head: Mrs V Mullooly
Type: Co-educational Day 3–11
No of pupils: B54 G86
Fees: (September 01)
Day £4005 – £4305

ILFORD PREPARATORY SCHOOL
Carnegie Buildings, 785 High Road,
Ilford, Essex IG3 8RW
Tel: (020) 8599 8822
Head: Mrs B P M Wiggs
Type: Co-educational Day 3–11
No of pupils: B100 G92
Fees: (September 01)
Day £3075 – £3675

MANSFIELD INFANT COLLEGE
29 Mansfield Road, Ilford, Essex
IG1 3BA
Tel: (020) 8553 0212
Head: Ms K Ahad
Type: Co-educational Day 0–5
No of pupils: 75
Fees: (September 01) On application

PARK SCHOOL FOR GIRLS
20 Park Avenue, Ilford, Essex
IG1 4RS
Tel: (020) 8554 2466
Head: Mrs N O'Brien
Type: Girls Day 7–18
No of pupils: 235
Fees: (September 01)
Day £3720 – £4920

LEIGH-ON-SEA

COLLEGE SAINT-PIERRE
16 Leigh Road, Leigh-on-Sea, Essex
SS9 1LE
Tel: (01702) 474164
Head: Mr G Bragard
Type: Co-educational Day 2–11
No of pupils: B70 G30
Fees: (September 01)
Day £1740 – £3681

ST MICHAEL'S SCHOOL
198 Hadleigh Road, Leigh-on-Sea,
Essex SS9 2LP
Tel: (01702) 478719
Head: Mr C Maultby
Type: Co-educational Day 3–11
No of pupils: B146 G150
Fees: (September 01)
Day £3960 – £4455

LOUGHTON

OAKLANDS SCHOOL
8 Albion Hill, Loughton, Essex
IG10 4RA
Tel: (020) 8508 3517
Head: Mrs P Simmonds
Type: Co-educational Day Boys 3–7
Girls 3–11
No of pupils: B50 G192
Fees: (September 01)
Day £2745 – £4485

MALDON

MALDON COURT PREPARATORY SCHOOL
Silver Street, Maldon, Essex
CM9 4QE
Tel: (01621) 853529
Head: Mr A G Webb
Type: Co-educational Day 4–11
No of pupils: B66 G57
Fees: (September 01)
Day £3840 – £3990

ROCHFORD

CROWSTONE PREPARATORY SCHOOL (SUTTON ANNEXE)
Fleethall Lane, Shopland Road,
Rochford, Essex SS4 1LL
Tel: (01702) 540629
Head: Mr J P Thayer
Type: Co-educational Day 2–11
No of pupils: 110
Fees: (September 01)
Day £2058 – £4635

ROMFORD

GIDEA PARK COLLEGE
Balgores House, 2 Balgores Lane,
Romford, Essex RM2 5JR
Tel: (01708) 740381
Head: Mrs V S Lee
Type: Co-educational Day 2–11
No of pupils: B104 G111
Fees: (September 01) Day £4206

IMMANUEL SCHOOL
Havering Grange Centre, Havering
Road, Romford, Essex RM1 4HR
Tel: (01708) 764449
Head: Mrs H Reeves
Type: Co-educational Day 3–16
No of pupils: B63 G52
Fees: (September 01) Day £2820

RAPHAEL INDEPENDENT SCHOOL
Park Lane, Romford, Essex
RM11 1XY
Tel: (01708) 744735
Head: Mr N W Malicka
Type: Co-educational Day 3–16
No of pupils: B98 G50
Fees: (September 01)
Day £987 – £5355

ST MARY'S HARE PARK SCHOOL
South Drive, Gidea Park, Romford,
Essex RM2 6HH
Tel: (01708) 761220
Head: Mrs K Karwacinski
Type: Co-educational Day 2–11
No of pupils: 180
Fees: (September 01) Day £3195

SAFFRON WALDEN

DAME JOHANE BRADBURY'S SCHOOL
Ashdon Road, Saffron Walden, Essex
CB10 2AL
Tel: (01799) 522348
Head: Mrs R M Rainey
Type: Co-educational Day 3–11
No of pupils: B150 G165
Fees: (September 01)
Day £3828 – £5073

FRIENDS' SCHOOL
Mount Pleasant Road, Saffron
Walden, Essex CB11 3EB
Tel: 01799 525 351
Head: Mr A Waters
Type: Co-educational Boarding and
Day 3–18
No of pupils: B183 G143
No of boarders: F81 W5
Fees: (September 01)
F/WB £8919 – £13674
Day £4542 – £8205

SOUTHEND-ON-SEA

ALLEYN COURT PREPARATORY SCHOOL
Wakering Road, Great Wakering,
Southend-on-Sea, Essex SS3 0PW
Tel: (01702) 582553
Head: Mr S Bishop and Mr W Wilcox
Type: Co-educational Day 2–13
No of pupils: B146 G97
Fees: (September 01)
Day £3339 – £5904

THORPE HALL SCHOOL
Wakering Road, Southend-on-Sea,
Essex SS1 3RD
Tel: (01702) 582340
Head: Mr D W Gibbins
Type: Co-educational Day 2–16
No of pupils: B249 G144
Fees: (September 01)
Day £1980 – £4485

UPMINSTER

OAKFIELDS MONTESSORI SCHOOLS LTD
Harwood Hall, Harwood Hall Lane,
Corbets Tey, Upminster, Essex
RM14 2YG
Tel: (01708) 220117
Head: Mrs K Malandreniotis
Type: Co-educational Day 2–11
No of pupils: B84 G87
Fees: (September 01)
Day £3900 – £4260

WESTCLIFF-ON-SEA

CROWSTONE PREPARATORY SCHOOL
121–123 Crowstone Road, Westcliff-
on-Sea, Essex SS0 8LH
Tel: (01702) 346758
Head: Mr J P Thayer
Type: Co-educational Day 2–11
No of pupils: B120 G110
Fees: (September 01)
Day £870 – £4635

ST HILDA'S SCHOOL
15 Imperial Avenue, Westcliff-on-
Sea, Essex SS0 8NE
Tel: (01702) 344542
Head: Mrs S O'Riordan
Type: Girls Day 2–16 (Boys 2–7)
No of pupils: B1 G180
Fees: (September 01) On application

WESTCLIFF PREPARATORY SCHOOL
100 Crowstone Road, Westcliff-on-
Sea, Essex SS0 8LQ
Tel: (01702) 340664
Head: Rev J Goldie
Type: Co-educational Day 3–11
No of pupils: 50
Fees: (September 01)
Day £2610 – £2820

WOODFORD GREEN

AVON HOUSE
490 High Road, Woodford Green,
Essex IG8 0PN
Tel: (020) 8504 1749
Head: Mrs S Ferrari
Type: Co-educational Day 3–11
No of pupils: B146 G111
Fees: (September 01)
Day £3630 – £4875

BANCROFT'S SCHOOL
Woodford Green, Essex IG8 0RF
Tel: (020) 8505 4821
Head: Dr P R Scott
Type: Co-educational Day 7–18
No of pupils: B461 G520
Fees: (September 01)
Day £6057 – £7989

ST AUBYN'S SCHOOL
Bunces Lane, Woodford Green,
Essex IG8 9DU
Tel: (020) 8504 1577
Head: Mr G James
Type: Co-educational Day 3–13
No of pupils: B280 G180
Fees: (September 01)
Day £2040 – £5709

WOODFORD GREEN PREPARATORY SCHOOL
Glengall Road, Snakes Lane,
Woodford Green, Essex IG8 0BZ
Tel: (020) 8504 5045
Head: Mr I P Stroud
Type: Co-educational Day 3–11
No of pupils: B184 G200
Fees: (September 01)
Day £2010 – £4095

GLOUCESTERSHIRE

CHELTENHAM

AIRTHRIE SCHOOL
29 Christ Church Road,
Cheltenham, Gloucestershire
GL50 2NY
Tel: (01242) 512837
Head: Mrs A E Sullivan
Type: Co-educational Day 3–11
No of pupils: B90 G90
Fees: (September 01)
Day £3210 – £4140

BERKHAMPSTEAD SCHOOL
Pittville Circus Road, Cheltenham,
Gloucestershire GL52 2PZ
Tel: (01242) 523263
Head: Mr T R Owen
Type: Co-educational Day 3–11
No of pupils: B115 G135
Fees: (September 01)
Day £2475 – £4275

CHELTENHAM COLLEGE
Bath Road, Cheltenham,
Gloucestershire GL53 7LD
Tel: (01242) 513540
Head: Mr P A Chamberlain
Type: Co-educational Boarding and
Day 13–18
No of pupils: B368 G147
No of boarders: F349
Fees: (September 01) FB £17325
Day £13029

CHELTENHAM COLLEGE
JUNIOR SCHOOL
Thirlestaine Road, Cheltenham,
Gloucestershire GL53 7AB
Tel: (01242) 522697
Head: Mr N I Archdale
Type: Co-educational Boarding and
Day 3–13
No of pupils: B284 G203
No of boarders: F51
Fees: (September 01)
FB £9810 – £11250
Day £3030 – £9450

THE CHELTENHAM LADIES'
COLLEGE
Bayshill Road, Cheltenham,
Gloucestershire GL50 3EP
Tel: (01242) 520691
Head: Mrs V Tuck
Type: Girls Boarding and Day 11–18
No of pupils: 850
No of boarders: F610
Fees: (September 01) FB £17310
Day £11520

DEAN CLOSE PREPARATORY
SCHOOL*
Lansdown Road, Cheltenham,
Gloucestershire GL51 6QS
Tel: (01242) 512217
Head: Mr S W Baird
Type: Co-educational Boarding and
Day 2–13
No of pupils: B190 G170
No of boarders: F61
Fees: (September 01) FB £12300
Day £3960 – £8415

DEAN CLOSE SCHOOL*
Cheltenham, Gloucestershire
GL51 6HE
Tel: (01242) 522640
Head: The Revd T M Hastie-Smith
Type: Co-educational Boarding and
Day 13–18
No of pupils: B253 G207
No of boarders: F267
Fees: (September 01) FB £16800
Day £11790

THE RICHARD PATE SCHOOL
Southern Road, Cheltenham,
Gloucestershire GL53 9RP
Tel: (01242) 522086
Head: Mr E L Rowland
Type: Co-educational Day 3–11
No of pupils: B159 G137
Fees: (September 01)
Day £1650 – £4950

ST EDWARD'S SCHOOL
Cirencester Road, Cheltenham,
Gloucestershire GL53 8EY
Tel: (01242) 583955
Head: Dr A J Nash
Type: Co-educational Day 11–18
No of pupils: B418 G409
Fees: (September 01)
Day £2095 – £2450

CINDERFORD

ST ANTHONYS SCHOOL
93 Bellevue Road, Cinderford,
Gloucestershire GL14 2AA
Tel: (01594) 823558
Head: Sister M C McKenna
Type: Co-educational Day 2–11
No of pupils: B77 G74
Fees: (September 01)
Day £2160 – £2460

CIRENCESTER

HATHEROP CASTLE SCHOOL
Hatherop, Cirencester,
Gloucestershire GL7 3NB
Tel: (01285) 750206
Head: Mr P Easterbrook
Type: Co-educational Boarding and
Day 4–13
No of pupils: B115 G98
No of boarders: F24
Fees: (September 01)
F/WB £9510 – £10020
Day £3900 – £6480

INGLESIDE PNEU SCHOOL
Beeches Road, Cirencester,
Gloucestershire GL7 1BN
Tel: (01285) 654046
Head: Mrs F M M Blades
Type: Co-educational Day 4–11
No of pupils: B40 G45
Fees: (September 01)
Day £2709 – £2979

THE QUERNS SCHOOL
Querns Lane, Cirencester,
Gloucestershire GL7 1RL
Tel: (01285) 652953
Head: Mr M Whytehead
Type: Co-educational Day 4–11
No of pupils: B49 G56
Fees: (September 01)
Day £3120 – £4260

RENDCOMB COLLEGE
Rendcomb, Cirencester,
Gloucestershire GL7 7HA
Tel: (01285) 831213
Head: Mr G Holden
Type: Co-educational Boarding and
Day 4–18
No of pupils: B178 G157
No of boarders: F118 W36
Fees: (September 01)
F/WB £10875 – £13965
Day £3030 – £11070

GLOUCESTER

GLOUCESTERSHIRE ISLAMIC SECONDARY SCHOOL FOR GIRLS
Sinope Street, off Widden Street, Gloucester GL1 4AW
Tel: (01452) 300465
Head: Mrs S Maqsood
Type: Girls Day 11–16
No of pupils: 100
Fees: (September 01)
Day £650 – £750

THE KING'S SCHOOL
Pitt Street, Gloucester GL1 2BG
Tel: (01452) 337337
Head: Mr P R Lacey
Type: Co-educational Boarding and Day 3–18
No of pupils: B286 G185
No of boarders: F3 W10
Fees: (September 01)
WB £13290 – £14535
Day £3945 – £9390

SCHOOL OF THE LION
The Judges Lodgings, Spa Road, Gloucester GL1 1UY
Tel: (01452) 381601
Head: Mr N Steele
Type: Co-educational Day 3–18
No of pupils: B25 G25
Fees: (September 01) On application

WYNSTONES SCHOOL
Whaddon Green, Gloucester GL4 0UF
Tel: (01452) 429220
Head: Mrs G Kaye
Type: Co-educational Day and Boarding 3–18
No of pupils: B136 G138
No of boarders: F4 W2
Fees: (September 01)
FB £6603 – £8136 WB £5750 – £7130
Day £2220 – £4725

MORETON-IN-MARSH

THE DORMER HOUSE PNEU SCHOOL
High Street, Moreton-in-Marsh, Gloucestershire GL56 0AD
Tel: (01608) 650758
Head: Ms D A Trembath
Type: Co-educational Day 2–11
No of pupils: B60 G62
Fees: (September 01) Day £3600

KITEBROOK HOUSE
Moreton-in-Marsh, Gloucestershire GL56 0RP
Tel: (01608) 674350
Head: Mrs A McDermott
Type: Girls Boarding and Day 4–13 (Boys 4–8)
No of pupils: 150
Fees: (September 01) WB £9150
Day £2700 – £6450

NAILSWORTH

ACORN SCHOOL
Church Street, Nailsworth, Gloucestershire GL6 0BP
Tel: (01453) 836508
Head: Mr G E B Whiting
Type: Co-educational Day and Boarding 3–19
No of pupils: B41 G44
No of boarders: F2 W2
Fees: (September 01)
FB £1980 – £2700
Day £1650 – £4080

STONEHOUSE

HOPELANDS SCHOOL
38 Regent Street, Stonehouse, Gloucestershire GL10 2AD
Tel: (01453) 822164
Head: Mrs B J Janes
Type: Co-educational Day 3–11
No of pupils: B14 G55
Fees: (September 01)
Day £2775 – £3510

WYCLIFFE COLLEGE*
Stonehouse, Gloucestershire GL10 2JQ
Tel: (01453) 822432
Head: Dr R A Collins
Type: Co-educational Boarding and Day 13–18
No of pupils: B271 G152
No of boarders: F262
Fees: (September 01)
FB £16515 – £18600
Day £10755 – £11160

WYCLIFFE JUNIOR SCHOOL*
Ryeford Hall, Stonehouse, Gloucestershire GL10 2LD
Tel: (01453) 823233
Head: Mr K Melber
Type: Co-educational Boarding and Day 2–13
No of pupils: B215 G160
No of boarders: F40
Fees: (September 01)
F/WB £8460 – £10635
Day £3870 – £7545

STROUD

BEAUDESERT PARK
Minchinhampton, Stroud, Gloucestershire GL6 9AF
Tel: (01453) 832072
Head: Mr J P R Womersley
Type: Co-educational Boarding and Day 4–13
No of pupils: B212 G144
No of boarders: F10 W45
Fees: (September 01) F/WB £12210
Day £4515 – £8985

TETBURY

WESTONBIRT SCHOOL*
Tetbury, Gloucestershire GL8 8QG
Tel: (01666) 880333
Head: Mrs M Henderson
Type: Girls Boarding and Day 11–18
No of pupils: 200
No of boarders: F105 W10
Fees: (September 01) FB £15720
Day £10956

TEWKESBURY

THE ABBEY SCHOOL
Church Street, Tewkesbury, Gloucestershire GL20 5PD
Tel: (01684) 294460
Head: Mr I R Griffin and Mrs J Wilson
Type: Co-educational Day and Boarding 2–13
No of pupils: B67 G38
No of boarders: W10
Fees: (September 01)
WB £7284 – £9714
Day £1170 – £7014

BREDON SCHOOL
Pull Court, Bushley, Tewkesbury, Gloucestershire GL20 6AH
Tel: (01684) 293156
Head: Mr M Newby
Type: Co-educational Boarding and Day 8–18
No of pupils: B145 G50
No of boarders: F100 W20
Fees: (September 01)
FB £10275 – £14850
WB £9975 – £14550
Day £5250 – £10125

WOTTON-UNDER-EDGE

ROSE HILL SCHOOL
Alderley, Wotton-under-Edge,
Gloucestershire GL12 7QT
Tel: (01453) 843196
Head: Mr R C Lyne-Pirkis
Type: Co-educational Boarding and
Day 3–13
No of pupils: B136 G135
No of boarders: F48 W34
Fees: (September 01)
F/WB £8700 – £10560
Day £4500 – £7830

SOUTH GLOUCESTERSHIRE

WINTERBOURNE

SILVERHILL SCHOOL
Swan Lane, Winterbourne, South
Gloucestershire BS36 1RL
Tel: (01454) 772156
Head: Mrs C M Phillipson-Masters
Type: Co-educational Day 2–11
No of pupils: B114 G117
Fees: (September 01)
Day £3075 – £3975

HAMPSHIRE

ALDERMASTON

CEDARS SCHOOL
Church Road, Aldermaston,
Hampshire RG7 4LR
Tel: 0118 9714251
Head: Mrs A E Ludlow
Type: Co-educational Day 4–11
No of pupils: B23 G23
Fees: (September 01) Day £3600

ALDERSHOT

STOCKTON HOUSE SCHOOL
Stockton Avenue, Fleet, Aldershot,
Hampshire GU13 8NS
Tel: (01252) 616323
Head: Mrs C Tweedie-Smith
Type: Co-educational Day 2–8
No of pupils: B30 G30
Fees: (September 01)
Day £240 – £3150

ALRESFORD

**BROCKWOOD PARK
SCHOOL***
Bramdean, Alresford, Hampshire
SO24 0LQ
Tel: (01962) 771744
Head: Mr W Taylor and Mr L Peters
and Mr C Foster
Type: Co-educational Boarding 15–19
No of pupils: B28 G32
No of boarders: F52
Fees: (September 01)
FB £9400 – £10800

ALTON

ALTON CONVENT SCHOOL
Anstey Lane, Alton, Hampshire
GU34 2NG
Tel: (01420) 83878
Head: Mrs S Kirkham
Type: Girls Day 2–18 (Co-ed 2–11)
No of pupils: B98 G274
Fees: (September 01) On application

ANDOVER

FARLEIGH SCHOOL*
Red Rice, Andover, Hampshire
SP11 7PW
Tel: (01264) 710766
Head: Mr J A Allcott
Type: Co-educational Day and
Boarding 3–13
No of pupils: B253 G162
No of boarders: F38 W69
Fees: (September 01) F/WB £12210
Day £2331 – £9150

ROOKWOOD SCHOOL*
Weyhill Road, Andover, Hampshire
SP10 3AL
Tel: (01264) 325900
Head: Mrs M P Langley
Type: Co-educational Day and
Boarding Boys 3–11 Girls 3–16
No of pupils: B102 G213
No of boarders: F3 W8
Fees: (September 01)
FB £10200 – £12000
Day £870 – £6750

BASINGSTOKE

DANESHILL HOUSE
Stratfield Turgis, Basingstoke,
Hampshire RG27 0AR
Tel: (01256) 882707
Head: Mr S V Spencer
Type: Co-educational Day 3–11
No of pupils: B122 G197
Fees: (September 01)
Day £2400 – £6000

GREY HOUSE PREPARATORY
SCHOOL
Mount Pleasant Road, Hartley
Wintney, Basingstoke, Hampshire
RG27 8PW
Tel: (01252) 842353
Head: Mrs E M Purse
Type: Co-educational Day 4–11
No of pupils: B83 G69
Fees: (September 01)
Day £4128 – £5082

NORTH FORELAND LODGE
Sherfield-on-Loddon, Hook,
Basingstoke, Hampshire RG27 0HT
Tel: (01256) 884800
Head: Miss S R Cameron
Type: Girls Boarding and Day 11–18
No of pupils: 180
No of boarders: F155 W20
Fees: (September 01) FB £15600
Day £9600

CHANDLER'S FORD

KINGSMEAD DAY NURSERY
120 Kingsway, Chandler's Ford,
Hampshire SO53 5DW
Tel: (023) 8025 3815
Head: Mrs H Hancock
Type: Co-educational Day 0–5
No of pupils: 75
Fees: (September 01) On application

WOODHILL SCHOOL
61 Brownhill Road, Chandler's Ford,
Hampshire SO53 2EH
Tel: (023) 8026 8012
Head: Mrs M Dacombe
Type: Co-educational Day 3–11
No of pupils: B60 G60
Fees: (September 01) On application

EASTLEIGH

THE KING'S SCHOOL SENIOR
Lakesmere House, Allington Lane,
Fair Oak, Eastleigh, Hampshire
SO50 7DB
Tel: (023) 8060 0956
Head: Mr D Greenwood
Type: Co-educational Day 11–16
No of pupils: B59 G52
Fees: (September 01) Day £3382

SHERBORNE HOUSE SCHOOL
Lakewood Road, Chandler's Ford,
Eastleigh, Hampshire SO53 1EU
Tel: (023) 8025 2440
Head: Mrs L M Clewer
Type: Co-educational Day 3–11
No of pupils: B110 G170
Fees: (September 01)
Day £3720 – £4905

FAREHAM

BOUNDARY OAK SCHOOL
Roche Court, Fareham, Hampshire
PO17 5BL
Tel: (01329) 280955
Head: Mr R B Bliss
Type: Co-educational Boarding and
Day 3–13
No of pupils: B166 G49
No of boarders: W25
Fees: (September 01)
F/WB £7725 – £10335
Day £2190 – £7125

MEONCROSS SCHOOL
Burnt House Lane, Stubbington,
Fareham, Hampshire PO14 2EF
Tel: (01329) 662182
Head: Mr C J Ford
Type: Co-educational Day 3–16
No of pupils: B258 G227
Fees: (September 01)
Day £3900 – £5361

SEAFIELD PRE-SCHOOL
Westlands Grove, Portchester,
Fareham, Hampshire PO16 9AA
Tel: (07747) 625811
Head: Miss H C Massie
Type: Co-educational Day 2–5
No of pupils: B24 G24
Fees: (September 01) On application

WYKEHAM HOUSE SCHOOL
17 East Street, Fareham, Hampshire
PO16 0BW
Tel: (01329) 280178
Head: Mrs R M Kamaryc
Type: Girls Day 2–16
No of pupils: 320
Fees: (September 01)
Day £2313 – £5598

FARNBOROUGH

FARNBOROUGH HILL*
Farnborough, Hampshire GU14 8AT
Tel: (01252) 545197
Head: Miss J Thomas
Type: Girls Day 11–18
No of pupils: 500
Fees: (September 01) Day £6525

SALESIAN COLLEGE
Reading Road, Farnborough,
Hampshire GU14 6PA
Tel: (01252) 893000
Head: Mr P A Wilson
Type: Boys Day 11–18
No of pupils: 500
Fees: (September 01) Day £4701

FLEET

ST NICHOLAS SCHOOL
Redfields House, Redfields Lane,
Church Crookham, Fleet,
Hampshire GU52 0RF
Tel: (01252) 850121
Head: Mrs A V Whatmough
Type: Girls Day 3–16 (Boys 3–7)
No of pupils: B16 G386
Fees: (September 01)
Day £2370 – £6465

FORDINGBRIDGE

FORRES SANDLE MANOR
Fordingbridge, Hampshire SP6 1NS
Tel: (01425) 653181
Head: Mr R P Moore
Type: Co-educational Boarding and
Day 3–13
No of pupils: B136 G115
No of boarders: F50 W35
Fees: (September 01) F/WB £11835
Day £2550 – £8790

GOSPORT

MARYCOURT SCHOOL
27 Crescent Road, Alverstoke,
Gosport, Hampshire PO12 2DJ
Tel: (023) 9258 1766
Head: Mrs M Crane
Type: Co-educational Day 3–11
No of pupils: B57 G45
Fees: (September 01)
Day £1485 – £2745

HAVANT

GLENHURST SCHOOL
16 Beechworth Road, Havant,
Hampshire PO9 1AX
Tel: (023) 9248 4054
Head: Mrs E Haines
Type: Co-educational Day 3–9
No of pupils: B43 G38
Fees: (September 01)
Day £2170 – £2910

HOOK

LORD WANDSWORTH COLLEGE
Long Sutton, Hook, Hampshire
RG29 1TB
Tel: (01256) 862201
Head: Mr I G Power
Type: Co-educational Boarding and
Day 11–18
No of pupils: B365 G135
No of boarders: F52 W300
Fees: (September 01)
F/WB £13845 – £14610
Day £10425 – £10980

ST NEOT'S SCHOOL
Eversley, Hook, Hampshire
RG27 0PN
Tel: (0118) 973 2118
Head: Mr R J Thorp
Type: Co-educational Day and
Boarding 3–13
No of pupils: B150 G120
No of boarders: W28
Fees: (September 01) WB £9405
Day £2700 – £7650

LEE-ON-THE-SOLENT

ST ANNE'S NURSERY & PRE-PREPARATORY SCHOOL
13 Milvil Road, Lee-on-the-Solent,
Hampshire PO13 9LU
Tel: (023) 9255 0820
Head: Mrs A M Whitting
Type: Co-educational Day 3–8
No of pupils: B15 G15
Fees: (September 01) Day £2370

LIPHOOK

BROOKHAM SCHOOL
Highfield Lane, Liphook, Hampshire
GU30 7LQ
Tel: (01428) 722005
Head: Mrs D Jenner
Type: Co-educational Day 3–8
No of pupils: B68 G67
Fees: (September 01)
Day £1500 – £5790

HIGHFIELD SCHOOL
Liphook, Hampshire GU30 7LQ
Tel: (01428) 728000
Head: Mr P G S Evitt
Type: Co-educational Boarding and
Day 7–13
No of pupils: B111 G84
No of boarders: F94
Fees: (September 01)
FB £10800 – £12375
Day £8325 – £10875

LITTLEFIELD SCHOOL
Midhurst Road, Liphook, Hampshire
GU30 7HT
Tel: (01428) 723187
Head: Mrs E B Simpson
Type: Co-educational Day 4–11
No of pupils: B50 G48
Fees: (September 01)
Day £4380 – £4785

LYMINGTON

HORDLE WALHAMPTON SCHOOL
Walhampton, Lymington,
Hampshire SO41 5ZG
Tel: (01590) 672013
Head: Mr R H C Phillips
Type: Co-educational Boarding and
Day 2–13
No of pupils: B183 G163
No of boarders: F35 W34
Fees: (September 01) F/WB £11250
Day £4170 – £8580

NEW MILTON

BALLARD SCHOOL
Fernhill Lane, New Milton,
Hampshire BH25 5SU
Tel: (01425) 611153
Head: Mr S P Duckitt
Type: Co-educational Day 2–16
No of pupils: B200 G180
Fees: (September 01)
Day £4200 – £7590

DURLSTON COURT
Becton Lane, Barton-on-Sea, New
Milton, Hampshire BH25 7AQ
Tel: (01425) 610010
Head: Mr D C Wansey
Type: Co-educational Day 2–13
No of pupils: B125 G93
Fees: (September 01)
Day £2175 – £7650

PETERSFIELD

BEDALES SCHOOL
Petersfield, Hampshire GU32 2DG
Tel: (01730) 300100
Head: Mr K Budge
Type: Co-educational Boarding and
Day 13–18
No of pupils: B187 G208
No of boarders: F300
Fees: (September 01) FB £17814
Day £13620

CHURCHERS COLLEGE
Portsmouth Road, Petersfield,
Hampshire GU31 4AS
Tel: (01730) 263033
Head: Mr G W Buttle
Type: Co-educational Day 4–18
No of pupils: B435 G277
Fees: (September 01)
Day £3705 – £6915

CHURCHERS COLLEGE JUNIOR SCHOOL
The Spain, Petersfield, Hampshire
GU32 3LA
Tel: (01730) 263724
Head: Mrs S Rivett
Type: Co-educational Day 4–11
No of pupils: B79 G67
Fees: (September 01)
Day £3705 – £4110

DITCHAM PARK SCHOOL
Ditcham Park, Petersfield,
Hampshire GU31 5RN
Tel: (01730) 825659
Head: Mrs K S Morton
Type: Co-educational Day 4–16
No of pupils: B198 G119
Fees: (September 01)
Day £4185 – £6990

DUNHURST (BEDALES JUNIOR SCHOOL)
Alton Road, Steep, Petersfield,
Hampshire GU32 2DP
Tel: (01730) 300200
Head: Mr M Piercy
Type: Co-educational Boarding and
Day 8–13
No of pupils: B104 G90
No of boarders: F68
Fees: (September 01) FB £12243
Day £8976

PORTSMOUTH

THE PORTSMOUTH GRAMMAR SCHOOL
High Street, Portsmouth, Hampshire
PO1 2LN
Tel: (023) 9281 9125
Head: Dr T R Hands
Type: Co-educational Day 4–18
No of pupils: B850 G500
Fees: (September 01)
Day £4184 – £6726

ROOKESBURY PARK SCHOOL*
Wickham, Portsmouth, Hampshire
PO17 6HT
Tel: (01329) 833108
Head: Mrs S M Cook
Type: Co-educational Boarding and
Day 3–13
No of pupils: B20 G100
No of boarders: F30 W10
Fees: (September 01)
FB £9075 – £10500
Day £2100 – £7050

RINGWOOD

AVONLEA SCHOOL
8 Broadshard Lane, Ringwood,
Hampshire BH24 1RR
Tel: (01425) 473994
Head: Mrs E L Burdock
Type: Co-educational Day 2–11
No of pupils: B29 G54
Fees: (September 01) On application

MOYLES COURT SCHOOL
Moyles Court, Ringwood,
Hampshire BH24 3NF
Tel: (01425) 472856
Head: Mr R A Dean
Type: Co-educational Day and
Boarding 3–16
No of pupils: B105 G74
No of boarders: F48
Fees: (September 01)
FB £10320 – £12165
Day £3360 – £7185

RINGWOOD WALDORF SCHOOL
Ashley, Ringwood, Hampshire
BH24 2NN
Tel: (01425) 472664
Head: Chairman of College of
Teachers
Type: Co-educational Day 4–14
No of pupils: B100 G100
Fees: (September 01) On application

ROMSEY

EMBLEY PARK SCHOOL*
Romsey, Hampshire SO51 6ZE
Tel: (01794) 512206
Head: Mr D F Chapman
Type: Co-educational Boarding and
Day 3–18
No of pupils: B290 G140
No of boarders: F45 W45
Fees: (September 01)
F/WB £6445 – £13905
Day £2385 – £8505

STANBRIDGE EARLS SCHOOL*
Stanbridge Lane, Romsey, Hampshire
SO51 0ZS
Tel: (01794) 516777
Head: Mr N R Hall
Type: Co-educational Boarding and
Day 11–18
No of pupils: B155 G41
No of boarders: F175
Fees: (September 01)
FB £14700 – £16170
Day £10980 – £12000

THE STROUD SCHOOL
Highwood House, Romsey,
Hampshire SO51 9ZH
Tel: (01794) 513231
Head: Mr A J Dodds
Type: Co-educational Day 3–13
No of pupils: B201 G110
Fees: (September 01)
Day £2175 – £7725

SOUTHAMPTON

THE ATHERLEY SCHOOL
Grove Place, Upton Lane, Nursling,
Southampton, Hampshire SO16 0AB
Tel: (023) 8074 1629
Head: Mrs M Bradley
Type: Girls Day 3–18 (Boys 3–11)
No of pupils: B60 G340
Fees: (September 01)
Day £1498 – £2098

THE GREGG SCHOOL
Townhill Park House, Cutbush Lane,
Southampton, Hampshire SO18 2GF
Tel: (023) 8047 2133
Head: Mr R D Hart
Type: Co-educational Day 11–16
No of pupils: B193 G113
Fees: (September 01) Day £5910

KING EDWARD VI SCHOOL
Kellett Road, Southampton,
Hampshire SO15 7UQ
Tel: (023) 8070 4561
Head: Mr P B Hamilton
Type: Co-educational Day 11–18
No of pupils: B590 G370
Fees: (September 01) Day £6846

KINGS PRIMARY SCHOOL
26 Quob Lane, West End,
Southampton, Hampshire SO30 3HN
Tel: (023) 8047 2266
Head: Mr K Ford
Type: Co-educational Day 5–11
No of pupils: 130
Fees: (September 01) Day £1785

ST CHRISTOPHER'S SCHOOL
Tamarisk Gardens, Bitterne Park,
Southampton, Hampshire SO18 4RA
Tel: (023) 8067 2010
Head: Mrs J A Naulin
Type: Co-educational Day 2–7
No of pupils: B57 G78
Fees: (September 01) Day £2370

ST MARY'S COLLEGE
57 Midanbury Lane, Bitterne Park,
Southampton, Hampshire SO18 4DJ
Tel: (023) 8067 1267
Head: Rev Brot Peter
Type: Co-educational Day 3–18
No of pupils: 450
Fees: (September 01) On application

ST WINIFRED'S SCHOOL
17–19 Winn Road, Southampton,
Hampshire SO17 IEJ
Tel: (023) 8055 7352
Head: Mrs J Collins
Type: Co-educational Day 2–11
No of pupils: 125
Fees: (September 01)
Day £2700 – £3834

VINE SCHOOL
Church Lane, Curdridge,
Southampton, Hampshire SO32 2DR
Tel: (01489) 789123
Head: Mr R W Medway
Type: Co-educational Day 3–11
No of pupils: B35 G35
Fees: (September 01) On application

WOODHILL PREPARATORY SCHOOL
Brook Lane, Botley, Southampton,
Hampshire SO30 2ER
Tel: (01489) 781112
Head: Mrs M Dacombe
Type: Co-educational Day 3–11
No of pupils: B62 G48
Fees: (September 01)
Day £1539 – £3015

SOUTHSEA

MAYVILLE HIGH SCHOOL
35 St Simon's Road, Southsea,
Hampshire PO5 2PE
Tel: (023) 9273 4847
Head: Mrs L Owens
Type: Co-educational Day Boys 2–11
Girls 2–16
No of pupils: B101 G222
Fees: (September 01)
Day £3225 – £4800

PORTSMOUTH HIGH SCHOOL GDST
25 Kent Road, Southsea, Hampshire
PO5 3EQ
Tel: (023) 9282 6714
Head: Miss P Hulse
Type: Girls Day 4–18
No of pupils: 610
Fees: (September 01)
Day £3951 – £5442

ST JOHN'S COLLEGE
Grove Road South, Southsea,
Hampshire PO5 3QW
Tel: (023) 9281 5118
Head: Mr N W Thorne
Type: Co-educational Boarding and
Day 2–18
No of pupils: B386 G273
No of boarders: F66
Fees: (September 01)
FB £11172 – £12705
Day £3690 – £5397

WINCHESTER

CHILTERN TUTORIAL UNIT
c/o Otterbourne Village Hall,
Cranbourne Drive, Otterbourne,
Winchester, Hampshire SO21 2ET
Tel: (01962) 860482
Head: Mrs J Gaudie
Type: Co-educational Day 8–11
No of pupils: B12 G4
Fees: (September 01) Day £4920

NETHERCLIFFE SCHOOL
Hatherley Road, Winchester,
Hampshire SO22 6RS
Tel: (01962) 854570
Head: Mr R F Whitfield
Type: Co-educational Day 3–11
No of pupils: B88 G60
Fees: (September 01)
Day £2130 – £4380

THE PILGRIMS' SCHOOL*
3 The Close, Winchester, Hampshire
SO23 9LT
Tel: (01962) 854189
Head: Rev Dr B A Rees
Type: Boys Boarding and Day 7–13
No of pupils: 201
No of boarders: F40 W39
Fees: (September 01) FB £11730
Day £9030

PRINCE'S MEAD SCHOOL
Worthy Park House, Kingsworthy,
Winchester, Hampshire SO21 1AN
Tel: (01962) 886000
Head: Mrs D Moore
Type: Co-educational Day 3–11
No of pupils: B141 G153
Fees: (September 01)
Day £5445 – £6675

ST SWITHUN'S SCHOOL
Winchester, Hampshire SO21 1HA
Tel: (01962) 835700
Head: Dr H L Harvey
Type: Girls Boarding and Day 11–18
No of pupils: 470
No of boarders: F42 W176
Fees: (September 01) F/WB £15375
Day £9315

TWYFORD SCHOOL
Winchester, Hampshire SO21 1NW
Tel: (01962) 712269
Head: Mr P Fawkes
Type: Co-educational Day and
Boarding 3–13
No of pupils: B212 G100
No of boarders: F20 W45
Fees: (September 01) FB £12450
Day £2535 – £9150

WINCHESTER COLLEGE*
College Street, Winchester,
Hampshire SO23 9NA
Tel: (01962) 621100
Head: Dr E N Tate
Type: Boys Boarding and Day 13–18
No of pupils: 680
No of boarders: F635
Fees: (September 01) FB £18360
Day £17442

YATELEY

YATELEY MANOR PREPARATORY SCHOOL
51 Reading Road, Yateley, Hampshire
GU46 7UQ
Tel: (01252) 405500
Head: Mr F G Howard
Type: Co-educational Day 3–13
No of pupils: B344 G189
Fees: (September 01)
Day £4250 – £7062

HEREFORDSHIRE

BROMYARD

ST RICHARD'S
Bredenbury Court, Bromyard,
Herefordshire HR7 4TD
Tel: (01885) 482491
Head: Mr R E Coghlan
Type: Co-educational Boarding and
Day 3–13
No of pupils: B77 G68
No of boarders: F31 W30
Fees: (September 01) FB £10185
WB £9531 Day £2520 – £6948

HEREFORD

THE HEREFORD CATHEDRAL JUNIOR SCHOOL
28 Castle Street, Hereford,
Herefordshire HR1 2NW
Tel: (01432) 363511
Head: Mr T R Lowe
Type: Co-educational Day 3–11
No of pupils: B193 G122
Fees: (September 01)
Day £3270 – £4794

THE HEREFORD CATHEDRAL SCHOOL*
Old Deanery, Cathedral Close,
Hereford, Herefordshire HR1 2NG
Tel: (01432) 363522
Head: Dr H C Tomlinson
Type: Co-educational Day 11–18
No of pupils: B322 G272
Fees: (September 01) Day £6390

THE MARGARET ALLEN SCHOOL
32 Broomy Hill, Hereford,
Herefordshire HR4 0LH
Tel: (01432) 273594
Head: Mrs A Evans
Type: Girls Day 2–11
No of pupils: 102
Fees: (September 01)
Day £3450 – £4140

LEOMINSTER

LUCTON PIERREPONT SCHOOL
Leominster, Herefordshire HR6 9PN
Tel: (01568) 780686
Head: Mr R Cusworth
Type: Co-educational Boarding and
Day 3–16
No of pupils: B65 G55
No of boarders: F36 W14
Fees: (September 01)
FB £9039 – £10320
WB £7737 – £9039
Day £3141 – £5646

HERTFORDSHIRE

ALDENHAM

EDGE GROVE
Aldenham Village, Aldenham,
Hertfordshire WD2 8BL
Tel: (01923) 855724
Head: Mr J R Baugh
Type: Co-educational Boarding and
Day 3–13
No of pupils: B262 G61
No of boarders: F81 W39
Fees: (September 01)
F/WB £10575 – £11460
Day £4875 – £8250

BARNET

FIRST IMPRESSIONS MONTESSORI SCHOOLS
Norfolk Lodge School, Dancers Hill
Road, Barnet, Hertfordshire EN5 4RP
Tel: (020) 8447 1565
Head: Mrs L Beirne
Type: Co-educational Day 2–11
No of pupils: B60 G65
Fees: (September 01) On application

LYONSDOWN SCHOOL TRUST LTD
3 Richmond Road, New Barnet,
Barnet, Hertfordshire EN5 1SA
Tel: (020) 8449 0225
Head: Mrs R Miller
Type: Co-educational Day Boys 4–7
Girls 4–11
No of pupils: B41 G147
Fees: (September 01)
Day £4050 – £4455

NORFOLK LODGE NURSERY & PREPARATORY SCHOOL
Dancers Hill Road, Barnet,
Hertfordshire EN5 4RP
Tel: (020) 8447 1565
Head: Mrs L Beirne
Type: Co-educational Day 1–11
No of pupils: B90 G80
Fees: (September 01)
Day £930 – £4650

ST MARTHA'S SENIOR SCHOOL*
Camlet Way, Hadley, Barnet,
Hertfordshire EN5 5PX
Tel: (020) 8449 6889
Head: Ms C Burke
Type: Girls Day 11–18
No of pupils: 320
Fees: (September 01) Day £5100

BERKHAMSTED

BERKHAMSTED COLLEGIATE PREPARATORY SCHOOL
Kings Road, Berkhamsted,
Hertfordshire HP4 3YP
Tel: (01442) 358201/2
Head: Mr A J Taylor
Type: Co-educational Day 3–11
No of pupils: B235 G220
Fees: (September 01)
Day £2219 – £6657

BERKHAMSTED COLLEGIATE SCHOOL
Castle Street, Berkhamsted,
Hertfordshire HP4 2BB
Tel: (01442) 358000
Head: Dr P Chadwick
Type: Co-educational Day and
Boarding 11–18
No of pupils: B600 G400
No of boarders: F80 W10
Fees: (September 01)
F/WB £13497 – £14898
Day £7965 – £9936

EGERTON-ROTHESAY SCHOOL
Durrants Lane, Berkhamsted,
Hertfordshire HP4 3UJ
Tel: (01442) 865275
Head: Mrs N Boddam-Whetham
Type: Co-educational Day 2–18
No of pupils: B344 G176
Fees: (September 01)
Day £3435 – £7620

HARESFOOT PREPARATORY SCHOOL
Chesham Road, Berkhamsted,
Hertfordshire HP4 2SZ
Tel: (01442) 872742
Head: Mrs G R Waterhouse
Type: Co-educational Day 3–11
No of pupils: B98 G90
Fees: (September 01)
Day £4080 – £4620

MARLIN MONTESSORI SCHOOL
1 Park View Road, Berkhamsted,
Hertfordshire HP4 3EY
Tel: (01442) 866290
Head: Mrs J Harrison-Sills
Type: Co-educational Day 0–5
No of pupils: B24 G24
Fees: (September 01)
Day £924 – £4734

BISHOP'S STORTFORD

BISHOP'S STORTFORD COLLEGE
Maze Green Road, Bishop's Stortford,
Hertfordshire CM23 2PJ
Tel: (01279) 838575
Head: Mr J G Trotman
Type: Co-educational Boarding and
Day 13–18
No of pupils: B286 G106
No of boarders: F105
Fees:.(September 01) FB £13248
Day £9552

HOWE GREEN HOUSE SCHOOL
Great Hallingbury, Bishop's
Stortford, Hertfordshire CM22 7UF
Tel: (01279) 657706
Head: Mrs N R J Garrod
Type: Co-educational Day 3–11
No of pupils: B70 G65
Fees: (September 01)
Day £3810 – £6051

THE JUNIOR SCHOOL, BISHOP'S STORTFORD COLLEGE
Maze Green Road, Bishop's Stortford,
Hertfordshire CM23 2PH
Tel: (01279) 838607
Head: Mr J A Greathead
Type: Co-educational Boarding and
Day 4–13
No of pupils: B302 G146
No of boarders: F45 W10
Fees: (September 01)
F/WB £9240 – £10065
Day £4449 – £7635

BUSHEY

CKHR IMMANUEL COLLEGE
87/91 Elstree Road, Bushey,
Hertfordshire WD23 4EB
Tel: (020) 8950 0604
Head: Mr P Skelker
Type: Co-educational Day 11–18
No of pupils: B220 G170
Fees: (September 01) Day £7800

LITTLE ACORNS MONTESSORI SCHOOL
Lincolnsfields Centre, Bushey Hall
Drive, Bushey, Hertfordshire
WD2 2ER
Tel: (01923) 230705
Head: Ms J Nugent and Ms R Lau
Type: Co-educational Day 2–7
No of pupils: 24
Fees: (September 01) On application

LONGWOOD SCHOOL
Bushey Hall Drive, Bushey,
Hertfordshire WD23 2QG
Tel: (01923) 253715
Head: Mr M Livesey
Type: Co-educational Day 3–9
No of pupils: B49 G47
Fees: (September 01)
Day £2250 – £3450

THE PURCELL SCHOOL
Aldenham Road, Bushey,
Hertfordshire WD23 2TS
Tel: (01923) 331100
Head: Mr J Tolputt
Type: Co-educational Day and
Boarding 8–18
No of pupils: B59 G109
No of boarders: F100
Fees: (September 01)
FB £14013 – £16677
Day £7692 – £9993

ST HILDA'S SCHOOL
High Street, Bushey, Hertfordshire
WD23 3DA
Tel: (020) 8950 1751
Head: Mrs L Cavanagh
Type: Girls Day 3–11
No of pupils: B6 G164
Fees: (September 01)
Day £3000 – £5625

ST MARGARET'S SCHOOL
Merry Hill Road, Bushey,
Hertfordshire WD23 1DT
Tel: (020) 8901 0870
Head: Miss M de Villiers
Type: Girls Boarding and Day 4–18
No of pupils: 450
No of boarders: F45 W15
Fees: (September 01) F/WB £14085
Day £5355 – £8265

BUSHEY HEATH

WESTWOOD
6 Hartsbourne Road, Bushey Heath,
Hertfordshire WD23 1JH
Tel: (020) 8950 1138
Head: Mrs J Hill
Type: Co-educational Day 4–8
No of pupils: B36 G36
Fees: (September 01) Day £4050

ELSTREE

ALDENHAM SCHOOL*
Elstree, Hertfordshire WD6 3AJ
Tel: (01923) 858122
Head: Mr R S Harman
Type: Boys Boarding and Day 11–18
(Co-ed VIth Form)
No of pupils: B421 G20
No of boarders: F125 W15
Fees: (September 01)
FB £11100 – £15600
WB £9300 – £12900
Day £7350 – £10950

HABERDASHERS' ASKE'S BOYS' SCHOOL

Butterfly Lane, Elstree, Hertfordshire WD6 3AF
Tel: (020) 8266 1700
Head: Mr J W R Goulding
Type: Boys Day 7–18
No of pupils: 1300
Fees: (September 01)
Day £7650 – £8250

HABERDASHERS' ASKE'S SCHOOL FOR GIRLS

Aldenham Road, Elstree, Hertfordshire WD6 3BT
Tel: (020) 8266 2300
Head: Mrs P A Penney
Type: Girls Day 4–18
No of pupils: 1108
Fees: (September 01)
Day £5520 – £6525

HARPENDEN

ALDWICKBURY SCHOOL

Wheathampstead Road, Harpenden, Hertfordshire AL5 1AE
Tel: (01582) 713022
Head: Mr P H Jeffery
Type: Boys Day and Boarding 4–13 (Girls 4–7)
No of pupils: B300 G20
No of boarders: W30
Fees: (September 01)
WB £7290 – £8040
Day £5100 – £6300

HARPENDEN PREPARATORY SCHOOL

53 Luton Road, Harpenden, Hertfordshire AL5 2UE
Tel: (01582) 712361
Head: Mrs E R Broughton
Type: Co-educational Day 2–11
No of pupils: B75 G75
Fees: (September 01)
Day £1935 – £4605

KINGS SCHOOL

Elmfield, Ambrose Lane, Harpenden, Hertfordshire AL5 4DU
Tel: (01582) 767566
Head: Mr C J Case
Type: Co-educational Day 4–16
No of pupils: B73 G68
Fees: (September 01) Day £2700

ST HILDA'S SCHOOL

28 Douglas Road, Harpenden, Hertfordshire AL5 2ES
Tel: (01582) 712307
Head: Mrs M Piachaud
Type: Girls Day 2–11
No of pupils: 180
Fees: (September 01)
Day £4485 – £4575

HATFIELD

QUEENSWOOD*

Shepherds Way, Brookmans Park, Hatfield, Hertfordshire AL9 6NS
Tel: (01707) 602500
Head: Ms C Farr
Type: Girls Boarding and Day 11–18
No of pupils: 390
No of boarders: F228
Fees: (September 01)
FB £15330 – £16680
Day £10350 – £11295

HEMEL HEMPSTEAD

ABBOT'S HILL*

Bunkers Lane, Hemel Hempstead, Hertfordshire HP3 8RP
Tel: (01442) 240333
Head: Mrs K Lewis
Type: Girls Boarding and Day 11–16
No of pupils: 190
No of boarders: W30
Fees: (September 01) WB £13500
Day £8160

LOCKERS PARK

Lockers Park Lane, Hemel Hempstead, Hertfordshire HP1 1TL
Tel: (01442) 251712
Head: Mr D R Lees-Jones
Type: Boys Boarding and Day 7–13
No of pupils: 133
No of boarders: F41 W18
Fees: (September 01)
FB £10125 – £11550
Day £7125 – £8985

ST NICHOLAS HOUSE

Bunkers Lane, Hemel Hempstead, Hertfordshire HP3 8RP
Tel: (01442) 839107
Head: Mrs B B Vaughan
Type: Girls Day 3–11 (Boys 3–7)
No of pupils: B38 G165
Fees: (September 01)
Day £1630 – £2020

WESTBROOK HAY

London Road, Hemel Hempstead, Hertfordshire HP1 2RF
Tel: (01442) 256143
Head: Mr K Young
Type: Co-educational Boarding and Day 2–13
No of pupils: B181 G81
No of boarders: W15
Fees: (September 01) WB £9555
Day £1422 – £7860

HERTFORD

DUNCOMBE SCHOOL

4 Warren Park Road, Bengeo, Hertford, Hertfordshire SG14 3JA
Tel: (01992) 414100
Head: Mr D Baldwin
Type: Co-educational Day 2–11
No of pupils: B174 G170
Fees: (September 01)
Day £392 – £6228

HAILEYBURY*

Hertford, Hertfordshire SG13 7NU
Tel: (01992) 463353
Head: Mr S A Westley
Type: Co-educational Boarding and Day 11–13, 13–18
No of pupils: B400 G280
No of boarders: F400
Fees: (September 01)
FB £11160 – £17505
Day £8505 – £12750

HEATH MOUNT SCHOOL*

Woodhall Park, Watton-at-Stone, Hertford, Hertfordshire SG14 3NG
Tel: (01920) 830230
Head: Rev H J Matthews
Type: Co-educational Boarding and Day 3–13
No of pupils: B218 G143
Fees: (September 01)
WB £9762 – £11325
Day £2385 – £8130

ST JOSEPH'S IN THE PARK

St Mary's, Hertingfordbury, Hertford, Hertfordshire SG14 2LX
Tel: (01992) 581378
Head: Mrs J King
Type: Co-educational Day 3–11
No of pupils: B90 G90
Fees: (September 01) Day £1620

HITCHIN

KINGSHOTT
St Ippolyts, Hitchin, Hertfordshire
SG4 7JX
Tel: (01462) 432009
Head: Mr P R Ilott
Type: Co-educational Day 4–13
No of pupils: B215 G116
Fees: (September 01)
Day £4560 – £5880

THE PRINCESS HELENA COLLEGE
Preston, Hitchin, Hertfordshire
SG4 7RT
Tel: (01462) 432100
Head: Mrs A M Hodgkiss
Type: Girls Boarding and Day 11–18
No of pupils: 156
No of boarders: F60 W25
Fees: (September 01)
F/WB £11280 – £14175
Day £7620 – £9585

KINGS LANGLEY

RUDOLF STEINER SCHOOL
Langley Hill, Kings Langley,
Hertfordshire WD4 9HG
Tel: (01923) 262505
Type: Co-educational Day 3–19
No of pupils: 450
Fees: (September 01)
Day £2040 – £4735

LETCHWORTH

ST CHRISTOPHER SCHOOL*
Barrington Road, Letchworth,
Hertfordshire SG4 9AQ
Tel: (01462) 679301
Head: Mr C Reid
Type: Co-educational Boarding and
Day 3–18
No of pupils: B343 G249
No of boarders: F112
Fees: (September 01)
FB £12240 – £15300
Day £2040 – £8700

ST FRANCIS' COLLEGE
The Broadway, Letchworth,
Hertfordshire SG6 3PJ
Tel: (01462) 670511
Head: Miss M Hegarty
Type: Girls Boarding and Day 3–18
No of pupils: 361
No of boarders: F28 W5
Fees: (September 01)
FB £14100 – £15210
WB £11745 – £12945
Day £7200 – £8400

POTTERS BAR

LOCHINVER HOUSE SCHOOL*
Heath Road, Little Heath, Potters
Bar, Hertfordshire EN6 1LW
Tel: (01707) 653064
Head: Mr P C E Atkinson
Type: Boys Day 4–13
No of pupils: 349
Fees: (September 01)
Day £6330 – £7062

ST JOHN'S PREPARATORY SCHOOL
Brownlowes, The Ridgeway, Potters
Bar, Hertfordshire EN6 5QT
Tel: (01707) 657294
Head: Mrs C Tardios
Type: Co-educational Day 4–11
No of pupils: B248 G142
Fees: (September 01)
Day £4380 – £5700

STORMONT
The Causeway, Potters Bar,
Hertfordshire EN6 5HA
Tel: (01707) 654037
Head: Mrs M E Johnston
Type: Girls Day 4–11
No of pupils: 170
Fees: (September 01)
Day £5730 – £6090

RADLETT

MANOR LODGE SCHOOL
Rectory Lane, Ridge Hill, Radlett,
Hertfordshire WD7 9BG
Tel: (01707) 642424
Head: Mrs J M Smart
Type: Co-educational Day 4–11
No of pupils: B201 G177
Fees: (September 01)
Day £4575 – £5550

RADLETT NURSERY & INFANTS SCHOOL
Cobden Hill, Radlett, Hertfordshire
WD7 7JL
Tel: (01923) 856374
Head: Mrs J R Briggs
Type: Co-educational Day 3–7
No of pupils: B60 G50
Fees: (September 01)
Day £1485 – £1825

RADLETT PREPARATORY SCHOOL
Kendal Hall, Watling Street, Radlett,
Hertfordshire WD7 7LY
Tel: (01923) 856812
Head: Mr W N Warren
Type: Co-educational Day 4–11
No of pupils: B265 G225
Fees: (September 01) Day £4410

RICKMANSWORTH

NORTHWOOD PREPARATORY SCHOOL
Moor Farm, Sandy Lodge Road,
Rickmansworth, Hertfordshire
WD3 1LW
Tel: (01923) 825648
Head: Mr T Lee
Type: Boys Day 4–13 (Girls 3–4)
No of pupils: 300
Fees: (September 01)
Day £6240 – £6570

RICKMANSWORTH PNEU SCHOOL
88 The Drive, Rickmansworth,
Hertfordshire WD3 4DU
Tel: (01923) 772101
Head: Mrs S K Marshall-Taylor
Type: Girls Day 3–11
No of pupils: 140
Fees: (September 01)
Day £1686 – £4812

THE ROYAL MASONIC SCHOOL FOR GIRLS*
Rickmansworth Park,
Rickmansworth, Hertfordshire
WD3 4HF
Tel: (01923) 773168
Head: Mrs D Rose
Type: Girls Boarding and Day 4–18
No of pupils: 760
No of boarders: F130 W110
Fees: (September 01)
FB £6513 – £11982
WB £6513 – £11019
Day £3753 – £7374

YORK HOUSE SCHOOL
Redheath, Croxley Green,
Rickmansworth, Hertfordshire
WD3 4LW
Tel: (01923) 772395
Head: Mr P B Moore
Type: Boys Day 4–13 (Co-ed 2–5)
No of pupils: B261 G12
Fees: (September 01) Day £6078

ST ALBANS

BEECHWOOD PARK SCHOOL
Markyate, St Albans, Hertfordshire
AL3 8AW
Tel: (01582) 840333
Head: Mr D S Macpherson
Type: Co-educational Day and
Boarding 4–13
No of pupils: B306 G144
No of boarders: W50
Fees: (September 01) WB £10800
Day £5490 – £7500

HOMEWOOD INDEPENDENT SCHOOL
Hazel Road, Park Street, St Albans,
Hertfordshire AL2 2AH
Tel: (01727) 873542
Head: Mrs S King
Type: Co-educational Day 3–8
No of pupils: B33 G47
Fees: (September 01)
Day £600 – £4455

ST ALBANS HIGH SCHOOL FOR GIRLS*
Townsend Avenue, St Albans,
Hertfordshire AL1 3SJ
Tel: (01727) 853800
Head: Mrs C Y Daly
Type: Girls Day 4–18
No of pupils: 857
Fees: (September 01)
Day £5355 – £6810

ST ALBANS SCHOOL*
Abbey Gateway, St Albans,
Hertfordshire AL3 4HB
Tel: (01727) 855521
Head: Mr A R Grant
Type: Boys Day 11–18 (Co-ed VIth
Form)
No of pupils: B702 G33
Fees: (September 01) Day £7878

ST COLUMBA'S COLLEGE
King Harry Lane, St Albans,
Hertfordshire AL3 4AW
Tel: (01727) 855185
Head: Dom S Darlington
Type: Boys Day 4–18
No of pupils: 800
Fees: (September 01)
Day £4710 – £6120

TRING

THE ARTS EDUCATIONAL SCHOOL*
Tring Park, Tring, Hertfordshire
HP23 5LX
Tel: (01442) 824255
Head: Mrs J D Billing
Type: Co-educational Boarding and
Day 8–18
No of pupils: B39 G233
No of boarders: F188
Fees: (September 01)
FB £11772 – £16545
Day £6798 – £10290

ST FRANCIS DE SALES PREP SCHOOL
Aylesbury Road, Tring, Hertfordshire
HP23 4DL
Tel: (01442) 822315
Head: Mrs L Waite and Mrs L Jones
Type: Co-educational Day 2–11
No of pupils: B68 G63
Fees: (September 01)
Day £1170 – £4620

WARE

ST EDMUND'S COLLEGE*
Old Hall Green, Ware, Hertfordshire
SG11 1DS
Tel: (01920) 824247
Head: Mr D J J McEwen
Type: Co-educational Day and
Boarding 3–18
No of pupils: B340 G260
No of boarders: F120 W50
Fees: (September 01)
FB £12030 – £13605
WB £11160 – £12675
Day £4755 – £8520

WATFORD

ST ANDREW'S MONTESSORI SCHOOL
Garston Manor, High Elms Lane,
Watford, Hertfordshire WD2 0JX
Tel: (01923) 663875
Head: Mrs S O'Neill
Type: Co-educational Day 0–12
No of pupils: B29 G31
Fees: (September 01)
Day £381 – £4962

STANBOROUGH SCHOOL*
Stanborough Park, Garston,
Watford, Hertfordshire WD25 9JT
Tel: (01923) 673268
Head: Mr S Rivers
Type: Co-educational Day and
Boarding 3–18
No of pupils: B150 G150
No of boarders: F70
Fees: (September 01)
FB £11000 – £13000
WB £9000 – £10500
Day £3000 – £6000

WELWYN

SHERRARDSWOOD SCHOOL
Lockleys, Welwyn, Hertfordshire
AL6 0BJ
Tel: (01438) 714282
Head: Mrs L E Corry
Type: Co-educational Day 2–18
No of pupils: B214 G183
Fees: (September 01)
Day £4530 – £7290

ISLE OF MAN

CASTLETOWN

THE BUCHAN SCHOOL
West Hill, Castletown, Isle of Man
IM9 1RD
Tel: (01624) 822526
Head: Mr G R Shaw-Twilley
Type: Co-educational Day 4–11
No of pupils: B115 G105
Fees: (September 01)
Day £4965 – £7095

KING WILLIAM'S COLLEGE
Castletown, Isle of Man IM9 1TP
Tel: (01624) 822551
Head: Mr P D John
Type: Co-educational Boarding and
Day 11–18
No of pupils: B152 G117
No of boarders: F63
Fees: (September 01)
FB £12210 – £14895
Day £7905 – £10590

ISLE OF WIGHT

NEWPORT

WESTMONT SCHOOL
82/88 Carisbrooke Road, Newport,
Isle of Wight PO30 1BY
Tel: (01983) 523051
Head: Mr D Reading
Type: Co-educational Day 0–19
No of pupils: B53 G49
Fees: (September 01)
Day £324 – £4200

RYDE

RYDE SCHOOL
Queen's Road, Ryde, Isle of Wight
PO33 3BE
Tel: (01983) 562229
Head: Dr N J England
Type: Co-educational Day and
Boarding 3–18
No of pupils: B394 G305
No of boarders: F26 W19
Fees: (September 01)
FB £10680 – £12015
WB £10065 – £11295
Day £2385 – £5700

SANDOWN

PRIORY SCHOOL
The Broadway, Sandown,
Isle of Wight PO36 9BY
Tel: (01983) 406866
Head: Mrs E J Goldthorpe
Type: Co-educational Day 2–18
No of pupils: B56 G53
Fees: (September 01)
Day £277 – £2805

KENT

ASHFORD

ASHFORD SCHOOL
East Hill, Ashford, Kent TN24 8PB
Tel: (01233) 625171
Head: Mrs P Holloway
Type: Girls Day and Boarding 3–18
No of pupils: 510
No of boarders: F60
Fees: (September 01) FB £13200 –
£15150 WB £11895 – £13650
Day £4320 – £8700

FRIARS SCHOOL
Great Chart, Ashford, Kent TN23 3DJ
Tel: (01233) 620493
Head: Mr P M Ashley
Type: Co-educational Day 3–13
No of pupils: B150 G90
Fees: (September 01)
Day £2420 – £7410

SPRING GROVE SCHOOL
Harville Road, Wye, Ashford, Kent
TN25 5EZ
Tel: (01233) 812337
Head: Mr N Washington-Jones
Type: Co-educational Day 3–11
No of pupils: B70 G70
Fees: (September 01)
Day £1800 – £5900

BECKENHAM

EDEN PARK SCHOOL
204 Upper Elmers End Road,
Beckenham, Kent BR3 3HE
Tel: (020) 8650 0365
Head: Mrs B Hunter
Type: Co-educational Day 3–11
No of pupils: B97 G83
Fees: (September 01)
Day £2325 – £3330

ST CHRISTOPHER'S SCHOOL
49 Bromley Road, Beckenham, Kent
BR3 5PA
Tel: (020) 8650 2200
Head: Mr A Velasco
Type: Co-educational Day 3–11
No of pupils: B146 G121
Fees: (September 01)
Day £1350 – £4725

BROADSTAIRS

HADDON DENE SCHOOL
57 Gladstone Road, Broadstairs,
Kent CT10 2HY
Tel: (01843) 861176
Head: Mrs A Whitehead
Type: Co-educational Day 3–11
No of pupils: 200
Fees: (September 01)
Day £1980 – £2460

WELLESLEY HOUSE SCHOOL
Broadstairs, Kent CT10 2DG
Tel: (01843) 862991
Head: Mr R R Steel
Type: Co-educational Boarding and
Day 7–13
No of pupils: B93 G57
Fees: (September 01) FB £11250
WB £10950 Day £8850

BROMLEY

ASHGROVE SCHOOL
116 Widmore Road, Bromley, Kent
BR1 3BE
Tel: (020) 8460 4143
Head: Dr P Ash
Type: Co-educational Day 3–11
No of pupils: 118
Fees: (September 01) Day £4791

BASTON SCHOOL
Baston Road, Hayes, Bromley, Kent
BR2 7AB
Tel: (020) 8462 1010
Head: Mr C R C Wimble
Type: Girls Day 2–18
No of pupils: 153
Fees: (September 01)
Day £1377 – £6420

BICKLEY PARK SCHOOL*
24 Page Heath Lane, Bickley,
Bromley, Kent BR1 2DS
Tel: (020) 8467 2195
Head: Mr M Bruce
Type: Boys Day 2–13
No of pupils: B420 G30
Fees: (September 01)
Day £2415 – £7860

BISHOP CHALLONER SCHOOL
Bromley Road, Shortlands, Bromley,
Kent BR2 0BS
Tel: (020) 8460 3546
Head: Mr J A de Waal
Type: Co-educational Day 3–18
No of pupils: B307 G93
Fees: (September 01)
Day £3600 – £5430

BREASIDE PREPARATORY SCHOOL*
41 Orchard Road, Bromley, Kent
BR1 2PR
Tel: (020) 8460 0916
Head: Mr R O'Doherty
Type: Co-educational Day 3–11
No of pupils: B202 G98
Fees: (September 01)
Day £2730 – £5010

BROMLEY HIGH SCHOOL GDST
Blackbrook Lane, Bickley, Bromley,
Kent BR1 2TW
Tel: (020) 8468 7981
Head: Mrs L Duggleby
Type: Girls Day 4–18
No of pupils: 890
Fees: (September 01)
Day £5145 – £6624

HOLY TRINITY COLLEGE
81 Plaistow Lane, Bromley, Kent
BR1 3LL
Tel: (020) 8313 0399
Head: Mrs M Aldhouse
Type: Girls Day 2–18 (Boys 3–5)
No of pupils: B10 G550
Fees: (September 01)
Day £4212 – £5595

CANTERBURY

JUNIOR KING'S SCHOOL
Milner Court, Sturry, Canterbury,
Kent CT2 0AY
Tel: (01227) 714000
Head: Mr P M Wells
Type: Co-educational Day and
Boarding 4–13
No of pupils: B191 G158
No of boarders: F34 W25
Fees: (September 01) F/WB £11940
Day £5025 – £8430

KENT COLLEGE*
Canterbury, Kent CT2 9DT
Tel: (01227) 763231
Head: Mr E B Halse
Type: Co-educational Boarding and
Day 3–18
No of pupils: B399 G295
No of boarders: F150
Fees: (September 01) FB £15300
Day £8790

THE KING'S SCHOOL
Canterbury, Kent CT1 2ES
Tel: (01227) 595501
Head: Rev Canon K H Wilkinson
Type: Co-educational Boarding and
Day 13–18
No of pupils: B423 G339
No of boarders: F612
Fees: (September 01) FB £17985
Day £12585

PERRY COURT RUDOLF STEINER SCHOOL
Garlinge Green, Chartham,
Canterbury, Kent CT4 5RU
Tel: (01227) 738285
Head: Mrs M McIntee
Type: Co-educational Day 4–17
No of pupils: 250
Fees: (September 01)
Day £3783 – £4404

ST CHRISTOPHER'S SCHOOL
New Dover Road, Canterbury, Kent
CT1 3DT
Tel: (01227) 462960
Head: Mr David Evans
Type: Co-educational Day 2–11
No of pupils: B60 G70
Fees: (September 01)
Day £3075 – £3750

ST EDMUND'S JUNIOR SCHOOL
Canterbury, Kent CT2 8HU
Tel: (01227) 475600
Head: Mr R G Bacon
Type: Co-educational Day and
Boarding 3–13
No of pupils: B171 G96
No of boarders: F49
Fees: (September 01)
FB £11562 – £11754
Day £1800 – £8274

ST EDMUND'S SCHOOL
St Thomas Hill, Canterbury, Kent
CT2 8HU
Tel: (01227) 475600
Head: Mr A N Ridley
Type: Co-educational Day and
Boarding 13–18
No of pupils: B142 G118
No of boarders: F72
Fees: (September 01)
FB £11754 – £16815
Day £8274 – £10854

ST FAITH'S AT ASH SCHOOL
5 The Street, Ash, Canterbury, Kent
CT3 2HH
Tel: (01304) 813409
Head: Mr S G I Kerruish
Type: Co-educational Day 3–11
No of pupils: B120 G112
Fees: (September 01)
Day £1560 – £3765

VERNON HOLME (KENT COLLEGE INFANT & JUNIOR SCHOOL)
Harbledown, Canterbury, Kent
CT2 9AQ
Tel: (01227) 762436
Head: Mr A Carter
Type: Co-educational Day and
Boarding 3–11
No of pupils: B127 G106
No of boarders: F2 W1
Fees: (September 01) F/WB £11871
Day £4128 – £8133

CHISLEHURST

BABINGTON HOUSE SCHOOL
Grange Drive, Chislehurst, Kent
BR7 5ES
Tel: (020) 8467 5537
Head: Miss D Odysseas
Type: Girls Day 3–16 (Boys 3–7)
No of pupils: B60 G160
Fees: (September 01)
Day £1875 – £6300

DARUL ULOOM LONDON
Foxbury Avenue, Perry Street,
Chislehurst, Kent BR7 6SD
Tel: (020) 8295 0637
Head: Mr M Musa
Type: Boys Boarding 11+
No of pupils: 170
No of boarders: F170
Fees: (September 01)
FB £1500 – £1800

FARRINGTONS & STRATFORD HOUSE*
Perry Street, Chislehurst, Kent
BR7 6LR
Tel: (020) 8467 0256
Head: Mrs C James
Type: Girls Boarding and Day 2½–18
No of pupils: 480
No of boarders: F64 W2
Fees: (September 01)
FB £12990 – £14340
WB £12450 – £13860
Day £5100 – £7290

CRANBROOK

BEDGEBURY SCHOOL*
Bedgebury Park, Goudhurst,
Cranbrook, Kent TN17 2SH
Tel: (01580) 211221
Head: Mrs H Moriarty
Type: Girls Boarding and Day 2–18
(Boys Day 2–7)
No of pupils: B18 G375
No of boarders: F57 W74
Fees: (September 01)
F/WB £9960 – £15120
Day £2280 – £9390

BENENDEN SCHOOL
Cranbrook, Kent TN17 4AA
Tel: (01580) 240592
Head: Mrs C M Oulton
Type: Girls Boarding 11–18
No of pupils: 450
No of boarders: F450
Fees: (September 01) FB £18300

BETHANY SCHOOL
Goudhurst, Cranbrook, Kent
TN17 1LB
Tel: (01580) 211273
Head: Mr N Dorey
Type: Co-educational Boarding and
Day 11–18
No of pupils: B250 G65
No of boarders: F145
Fees: (September 01)
F/WB £13452 – £14367
Day £8646 – £9102

CRANBROOK SCHOOL*
Cranbrook, Kent TN17 3JD
Tel: (01580) 711800
Head: Mrs A Daly
Type: Co-educational Day and
Boarding 13–18
No of pupils: B403 G312
No of boarders: F245
Fees: (September 01) FB £6450

DULWICH PREPARATORY SCHOOL, CRANBROOK*
Coursehorn, Cranbrook, Kent
TN17 3NP
Tel: (01580) 712179
Head: Mr M C Wagstaffe
Type: Co-educational Day and
Boarding 3–13
No of pupils: B306 G237
No of boarders: F7 W37
Fees: (September 01) FB £12300
WB £11985 Day £2805 – £8160

DEAL

NORTHBOURNE PARK SCHOOL*
Betteshanger, Deal, Kent CT14 0NW
Tel: (01304) 611215/8
Head: Mr S Sides
Type: Co-educational Day and
Boarding 3–13
No of pupils: B128 G100
No of boarders: F49 W10
Fees: (September 01)
FB £10260 – £12555
Day £4740 – £8040

DOVER

DOVER COLLEGE*
Effingham Crescent, Dover, Kent
CT17 9RH
Tel: (01304) 205969
Head: Mr H W Blackett
Type: Co-educational Boarding and
Day 7–18
No of pupils: B166 G116
No of boarders: F100 W3
Fees: (September 01)
FB £11178 – £14250
WB £10440 – £11220
Day £4050 – £8328

DUKE OF YORK'S ROYAL MILITARY SCHOOL
Dover, Kent CT15 5EQ
Tel: (01304) 245029
Head: Mr J A Cummings
Type: Co-educational Boarding 11–18
No of pupils: B348 G152
No of boarders: F500
Fees: (September 01) FB £1200

FAVERSHAM

LORENDEN PREPARATORY SCHOOL
Painter's Forstal, Faversham, Kent
ME13 0EN
Tel: (01795) 590030
Head: Mrs M R Simmonds
Type: Co-educational Day 3–11
No of pupils: B54 G66
Fees: (September 01)
Day £3888 – £5100

FOLKESTONE

ST MARY'S WESTBROOK*
Ravenlea Road, Folkestone, Kent
CT20 2JU
Tel: (01303) 854006
Head: Mrs L A Watson
Type: Co-educational Boarding and
Day 2–16
No of pupils: B165 G119
No of boarders: F43
Fees: (September 01)
FB £10473 – £11544
Day £4347 – £7686

ST NICHOLAS NURSERY SCHOOL
18 Wiltie Gardens, Folkestone, Kent
CT19 5AX
Tel: (01303) 254578
Head: Mrs C F Carlile
Type: Co-educational Day 2–5
No of pupils: 35
Fees: (September 01) On application

GILLINGHAM

BRYONY SCHOOL
Marshall Road, Rainham,
Gillingham, Kent ME8 0AJ
Tel: (01634) 231511
Head: D E Edmunds &
Mrs M P Edmunds
Type: Co-educational Day 2–11
No of pupils: B128 G121
Fees: (September 01)
Day £2513 – £2914

GRAVESEND

BRONTE SCHOOL
7 Pelham Road, Gravesend, Kent
DA11 0HN
Tel: (01474) 533805
Head: Mr J Rose
Type: Co-educational Day 3–11
No of pupils: B64 G39
Fees: (September 01)
Day £3420 – £3975

COBHAM HALL*
Cobham, Gravesend, Kent DA12 3BL
Tel: (01474) 823371
Head: Mrs R McCarthy
Type: Girls Boarding and Day 11–18
No of pupils: 200
No of boarders: F104 W16
Fees: (September 01)
F/WB £14100 – £16200
Day £8850 – £10950

CONVENT PREPARATORY SCHOOL
46 Old Road East, Gravesend, Kent
DA12 1NR
Tel: (01474) 533012
Head: Sister Anne
Type: Co-educational Day 3–11
No of pupils: B124 G106
Fees: (September 01) Day £2760

HAWKHURST

MARLBOROUGH HOUSE SCHOOL
High Street, Hawkhurst, Kent
TN18 4PY
Tel: (01580) 753555
Head: Mr D N Hopkins
Type: Co-educational Boarding and
Day 3–13
No of pupils: B189 G137
No of boarders: W2
Fees: (September 01) WB £12030
Day £4155 – £8505

ST RONAN'S
St Ronan's Road, Hawkhurst, Kent
TN18 5DJ
Tel: (01580) 752271
Head: Mr E Yeats-Brown
Type: Co-educational Boarding and
Day 3–13
No of pupils: B125 G50
No of boarders: F18 W25
Fees: (September 01) F/WB £11115
Day £8190

LONGFIELD

STEEPHILL SCHOOL
Castle Hill, Fawkham, Longfield,
Kent DA3 7BG
Tel: (01474) 702107
Head: Mrs C Birtwell
Type: Co-educational Day 3–11
No of pupils: B50 G49
Fees: (September 01) Day £3400

MAIDSTONE

SHERNOLD SCHOOL
Hill Place, Queens Avenue,
Maidstone, Kent ME16 0ER
Tel: (01622) 752868
Head: Mrs L Dack
Type: Co-educational Day 3–11
No of pupils: B42 G95
Fees: (September 01)
Day £2850 – £3900

SUTTON VALENCE PREPARATORY SCHOOL
Underhill, Chart Sutton, Maidstone,
Kent ME17 3RF
Tel: (01622) 842117
Head: Mr A M Brooke
Type: Co-educational Day 3–11
No of pupils: B204 G147
Fees: (September 01)
Day £4350 – £6540

SUTTON VALENCE SCHOOL*
Sutton Valence, Maidstone, Kent
ME17 3HN
Tel: (01622) 842281
Head: Mr J Davies
Type: Co-educational Boarding and
Day 3–18
No of pupils: B498 G292
No of boarders: F129
Fees: (September 01)
FB £12300 – £16260
Day £2000 – £10260

RAMSGATE

THE JUNIOR SCHOOL, ST LAWRENCE COLLEGE
Ramsgate, Kent CT11 7AF
Tel: (01843) 591788
Head: Mr R Tunnicliffe
Type: Co-educational Boarding and
Day 3–13
No of pupils: B113 G93
No of boarders: F61 W2
Fees: (September 01)
FB £12480 – £16560
Day £3654 – £10632

ST LAWRENCE COLLEGE*
Ramsgate, Kent CT11 7AE
Tel: (01843) 592680
Head: Mr M Slater
Type: Co-educational Boarding and
Day 3–18
No of pupils: B239 G241
No of boarders: F179 W5
Fees: (September 01)
F/WB £12480 – £16560
Day £4494 – £10632

ROCHESTER

CEDARS SCHOOL
70 Maidstone Road, Rochester, Kent
ME1 3DE
Tel: (01634) 847163
Head: Mrs B M V Gross and
G E F Gross
Type: Co-educational Day 3–16
No of pupils: B32 G30
Fees: (September 01) On application

GAD'S HILL SCHOOL
Higham, Rochester, Kent ME3 7AA
Tel: (01474) 822366
Head: Mr D Craggs
Type: Co-educational Day 3–18
No of pupils: B80 G140
Fees: (September 01)
Day £3405 – £3897

KING'S PREPARATORY
SCHOOL, ROCHESTER
King Edward Road, Rochester, Kent
ME1 1UB
Tel: (01634) 843657
Head: Mr R Overend
Type: Co-educational Day and
Boarding 8–13
No of pupils: B177 G68
No of boarders: F12 W6
Fees: (September 01)
F/WB £11505 – £12405
Day £6870 – £7770

KING'S SCHOOL ROCHESTER
Satis House, Boley Hill, Rochester,
Kent ME1 1TE
Tel: (01634) 843913
Head: Dr I R Walker
Type: Co-educational Day and
Boarding 4–18
No of pupils: B499 G186
No of boarders: F53 W20
Fees: (September 01)
F/WB £11505 – £17385
Day £5250 – £10125

ROCHESTER INDEPENDENT
COLLEGE*
New Road House, 3 New Road,
Rochester, Kent ME1 1BD
Tel: (01634) 828115
Head: Mr S de Belder and Mr B Pain
Type: Co-educational Day and
Boarding 14–20
No of pupils: B100 G100
No of boarders: F66
Fees: (September 01)
FB £14340 – £15270
Day £9300 – £10800

ST ANDREW'S SCHOOL
24–28 Watts Avenue, Rochester,
Kent ME1 1SA
Tel: (01634) 843479
Head: Mr N D Kynaston
Type: Co-educational Day 4–11
No of pupils: B150 G160
Fees: (September 01)
Day £2646 – £2820

SEVENOAKS

COMBE BANK SCHOOL*
Sundridge, Sevenoaks, Kent
TN14 6AE
Tel: (01959) 563720
Head: Mrs R Martin
Type: Girls Day 3–18 (Boys 3–5)
No of pupils: 480
Fees: (September 01)
Day £3000 – £7845

THE GRANVILLE SCHOOL
Sevenoaks, Kent TN13 3LJ
Tel: (01732) 453039
Head: Mrs J D Evans
Type: Girls Day 3–11 (Boys 3–5)
No of pupils: B10 G190
Fees: (September 01)
Day £2400 – £6270

THE NEW BEACON
Brittains Lane, Sevenoaks, Kent
TN13 2PB
Tel: (01732) 452131
Head: Mr R Constantine
Type: Boys Day and Boarding 5–13
No of pupils: 400
No of boarders: W30
Fees: (September 01) WB £10080
Day £5250 – £6825

RUSSELL HOUSE SCHOOL
Station Road, Otford, Sevenoaks,
Kent TN14 5QU
Tel: (01959) 522352
Head: Mrs E Lindsay
Type: Co-educational Day 2–11
No of pupils: B99 G100
Fees: (September 01)
Day £5070 – £6270

ST MICHAEL'S SCHOOL
Otford Court, Otford, Sevenoaks,
Kent TN14 5SA
Tel: (01959) 522137
Head: Dr P Roots
Type: Co-educational Day 2–13
No of pupils: B223 G196
Fees: (September 01)
Day £850 – £2256

SEVENOAKS PREPARATORY
SCHOOL
Fawke Cottage, Godden Green,
Sevenoaks, Kent TN15 0JU
Tel: (01732) 762336
Head: Mr E H Oatley
Type: Co-educational Day 3–13
No of pupils: B250 G100
Fees: (September 01)
Day £4320 – £6060

SEVENOAKS SCHOOL*
Sevenoaks, Kent TN13 1HU
Tel: (01732) 455133
Head: Mr T R Cookson
Type: Co-educational Day and
Boarding 11–18
No of pupils: B504 G456
No of boarders: F333
Fees: (September 01)
FB £16194 Day £9873

SOLEFIELD SCHOOL
Solefields Road, Sevenoaks, Kent
TN13 1PH
Tel: (01732) 452142
Head: Mr P Evans
Type: Boys Day 4–13
No of pupils: 185
Fees: (September 01)
Day £1340 – £2050

WALTHAMSTOW HALL
Hollybush Lane, Sevenoaks, Kent
TN13 3UL
Tel: (01732) 451334
Head: Mrs J S Lang
Type: Girls Day 3–18
No of pupils: 435
Fees: (September 01)
Day £650 – £9105

SHEERNESS

ELLIOTT PARK SCHOOL
Marina Drive, Minster, Isle of
Sheppey, Sheerness, Kent ME12 2DP
Tel: (01795) 873372
Head: Mr R E Fielder
Type: Co-educational Day 4–11
No of pupils: 83
Fees: (September 01)
Day £2700 – £3000

SIDCUP

BENEDICT HOUSE PREPARATORY SCHOOL
1–5 Victoria Road, Sidcup, Kent
DA15 7HD
Tel: (020) 8300 7206
Head: Mrs A Brown
Type: Co-educational Day 3–11
No of pupils: B70 G70
Fees: (September 01)
Day £1845 – £3975

HARENC SCHOOL TRUST
167 Rectory Lane, Footscray, Sidcup,
Kent DA14 5BU
Tel: (020) 8309 0619
Head: Miss S Woodward
Type: Boys Day 3–11
No of pupils: 160
Fees: (September 01)
Day £3615 – £4785

MERTON COURT PREPARATORY SCHOOL
38 Knoll Road, Sidcup, Kent
DA14 4QU
Tel: (020) 8300 2112
Head: Mr D Price
Type: Co-educational Day 2–11
No of pupils: B168 G150
Fees: (September 01)
Day £4000 – £5025

WEST LODGE PREPARATORY SCHOOL
36 Station Road, Sidcup, Kent
DA15 7DU
Tel: (020) 8300 2489
Head: Mrs B A Windley
Type: Co-educational Day 3–11
No of pupils: B29 G131
Fees: (September 01)
Day £2280 – £3645

TONBRIDGE

DERWENT LODGE SCHOOL FOR GIRLS
Somerhill, Tonbridge, Kent
TN11 0NJ
Tel: (01732) 352124
Head: Mrs C M York
Type: Girls Day 7–11
No of pupils: 125
Fees: (September 01) Day £6375

FOSSE BANK NEW SCHOOL
Coldharbour Lane, Hildenborough,
Tonbridge, Kent TN11 9LE
Tel: (01732) 834212
Head: Mrs A Stables
Type: Co-educational Day 2–11
No of pupils: B60 G60
Fees: (September 01)
Day £2610 – £4350

HILDEN GRANGE SCHOOL
62 Dry Hill Park Road, Tonbridge,
Kent TN10 3BX
Tel: (01732) 352706
Head: Mr J Withers
Type: Co-educational Day 3–13
No of pupils: B204 G100
Fees: (September 01)
Day £1080 – £6825

HILDEN OAKS SCHOOL
38 Dry Hill Park Road, Tonbridge,
Kent TN10 3BU
Tel: (01732) 353941
Head: Mrs H J Bacon
Type: Co-educational Day Boys 2–7
Girls 2–11
No of pupils: B40 G135
Fees: (September 01)
Day £2025 – £5505

THE OLD VICARAGE
Marden, Tonbridge, Kent TN12 9AG
Tel: (01622) 832200
Head: Mrs P G Stevens
Type: Co-educational Boarding and
Day 8+
No of pupils: 12
No of boarders: F12
Fees: (September 01)
FB £7830 – £8100 WB £7560 – £7830

SACKVILLE SCHOOL
Tonbridge Road, Hildenborough,
Tonbridge, Kent TN11 9HN
Tel: (01732) 838888
Head: Mrs G M L Sinclair
Type: Co-educational Day 11–18
No of pupils: B124 G26
Fees: (September 01)
Day £6150 – £7500

SOMERHILL PRE-PREPARATORY
Somerhill, Tonbridge, Kent
TN11 0NJ
Tel: (01732) 352124
Head: Mrs J R Sorensen
Type: Co-educational Day 3–7
No of pupils: B149 G114
Fees: (September 01)
Day £4725 – £5460

TONBRIDGE SCHOOL
Tonbridge, Kent TN9 1JP
Tel: (01732) 365555
Head: Mr J M Hammond
Type: Boys Boarding and Day 13–18
No of pupils: 720
No of boarders: F420
Fees: (September 01) FB £17874
Day £12630

YARDLEY COURT
Somerhill, Tonbridge, Kent
TN11 0NJ
Tel: (01732) 352124
Head: Mr J T Coakley
Type: Boys Day 7–13
No of pupils: 210
Fees: (September 01)
Day £6950 – £7580

TUNBRIDGE WELLS

BEECHWOOD SACRED HEART*
12 Pembury Road, Tunbridge Wells,
Kent TN2 3QD
Tel: (01892) 532747
Head: Mr N R Beesley
Type: Girls Boarding and Day 3–18
(Boys 3–11)
No of pupils: B60 G275
No of boarders: F56 W12
Fees: (September 01)
FB £10815 – £13950
WB £9270 – £12405
Day £4440 – £8550

HOLMEWOOD HOUSE
Langton Green, Tunbridge Wells,
Kent TN3 0EB
Tel: (01892) 860000
Head: Mr A S R Corbett
Type: Co-educational Boarding and
Day 3–13
No of pupils: B296 G219
No of boarders: W26
Fees: (September 01) WB £14265
Day £3120 – £9900

KENT COLLEGE PEMBURY
Tunbridge Wells, Kent TN2 4AX
Tel: (01892) 822006
Head: Miss B J Crompton
Type: Girls Boarding and Day 3–18
No of pupils: 550
No of boarders: F50 W30
Fees: (September 01)
FB £11580 – £15075
WB £10680 – £14700
Day £4260 – £9330

THE MEAD SCHOOL
16 Frant Road, Tunbridge Wells,
Kent TN2 5SN
Tel: (01892) 525837
Head: Mrs A Culley
Type: Co-educational Day 3–11
No of pupils: B85 G85
Fees: (September 01)
Day £2460 – £5670

ROSE HILL SCHOOL
Culverden Down, Tunbridge Wells,
Kent TN4 9SY
Tel: (01892) 525591
Head: Mr P D Westcombe
Type: Co-educational Day 2–13
No of pupils: 305
Fees: (September 01)
Day £2400 – £7560

WEST WICKHAM

ST DAVID'S COLLEGE
Justin Hall, Beckenham Road, West
Wickham, Kent BR4 0QS
Tel: (020) 8777 5852
Head: Mrs S Adams and Mrs M Brabin
Type: Co-educational Day 4–11
No of pupils: B98 G71
Fees: (September 01)
Day £3384 – £3534

WESTGATE-ON-SEA

CHARTFIELD SCHOOL
45 Minster Road, Westgate-on-Sea,
Kent CT8 8DA
Tel: (01843) 831716
Head: Mrs J L Prebble
Type: Co-educational Day 4–11
No of pupils: B37 G40
Fees: (September 01)
Day £1830 – £1980

LANCASHIRE

ACCRINGTON

HEATHLAND COLLEGE
Broadoak, Sandy Lane, Accrington,
Lancashire BB5 2AN
Tel: (01254) 234284
Head: Mrs J Harrison
Type: Co-educational Day 0–11
No of pupils: B45 G45
Fees: (September 01)
Day £3075 – £3532

ASHTON-UNDER-LYNE

GRAFTON HOUSE PREPARATORY SCHOOL
1 Warrington Street, Ashton-under-
Lyne, Lancashire OL6 6XB
Tel: (0161) 343 3015
Head: Mrs J Grudgeon
Type: Co-educational Day 1–11
No of pupils: 120
Fees: (September 01)
Day £2340 – £3120

BLACKBURN

AL-ISLAH SCHOOL
108 Audley Range, Blackburn,
Lancashire BB1 1TF
Tel: (01254) 261573
Head: Mr N I Makda
Type: Co-educational Day 5–16
No of pupils: B32 G213
Fees: (September 01)
Day £400 – £725

QUEEN ELIZABETH'S GRAMMAR SCHOOL
Blackburn, Lancashire BB2 6DF
Tel: (01254) 686300
Head: Dr D S Hempsall
Type: Co-educational Day 7–18
No of pupils: B761 G32
Fees: (September 01)
Day £4485 – £5931

TAUHEEDUL ISLAM GIRLS HIGH SCHOOL
31 Bicknell Street, Blackburn,
Lancashire BB1 7EY
Tel: (01254) 54021
Head: Dr A Ghodiwala
Type: Girls Day 11–16
No of pupils: 240
Fees: (September 01) Day £600

WESTHOLME SCHOOL
Wilmar Lodge, Meins Road,
Blackburn, Lancashire BB2 6QU
Tel: (01254) 53447
Head: Mrs L Croston
Type: Girls Day 3–18 (Boys 3–7)
No of pupils: B70 G1020
Fees: (September 01)
Day £3420 – £4770

BLACKPOOL

ARNOLD SCHOOL
Lytham Road, Blackpool, Lancashire
FY4 1JG
Tel: (01253) 346391
Head: Mr W T Gillen
Type: Co-educational Day 11–18
No of pupils: B360 G437
Fees: (September 01) Day £5190

LANGDALE PREPARATORY SCHOOL
95 Warbreck Drive, Blackpool,
Lancashire FY2 9RZ
Tel: (01253) 354812
Head: Mr R A Rendell
Type: Co-educational Day 3–11
No of pupils: B50 G40
Fees: (September 01)
Day £2000 – £2300

BOLTON

BOLTON MUSLIM GIRLS SCHOOL
Swan Lane, Bolton, Lancashire
BL3 6TQ
Tel: (01204) 361103
Head: Mr I A Patel
Type: Girls Day 11–16
No of pupils: 374
Fees: (September 01) Day £800

BOLTON SCHOOL (BOYS' DIVISION)
Chorley New Road, Bolton,
Lancashire BL1 4PA
Tel: (01204) 840201
Head: Mr A W Wright
Type: Boys Day 8–18
No of pupils: 1020
Fees: (September 01)
Day £4567 – £6090

BOLTON SCHOOL (GIRLS' DIVISION)
Chorley New Road, Bolton,
Lancashire BL1 4PB
Tel: (01204) 840201
Head: Miss E J Panton
Type: Girls Day 4–18 (Boys 4–8)
No of pupils: B100 G1054
Fees: (September 01)
Day £4566 – £6090

CLEVELANDS PREPARATORY SCHOOL
Chorley New Road, Bolton,
Lancashire BL1 5DA
Tel: (01204) 843898
Head: Mrs G T Mitchell
Type: Co-educational Day 4–11
No of pupils: B94 G89
Fees: (September 01) Day £3600

LORD'S COLLEGE
53 Manchester Road, Bolton,
Lancashire BL2 1ES
Tel: (01204) 523731
Head: Mrs D Whittle
Type: Co-educational Day 10–17
No of pupils: B40 G25
Fees: (September 01) Day £1755

BURNLEY

ST JOSEPH'S CONVENT SCHOOL
Park Hill, Padiham Road, Burnley,
Lancashire BB12 6TG
Tel: (01282) 455622
Head: Sister Joan
Type: Co-educational Day 4–11
No of pupils: B73 G71
Fees: (September 01) Day £1940

SUNNY BANK PREPARATORY SCHOOL
171–173 Manchester Road, Burnley,
Lancashire BB11 4HR
Tel: (01282) 421336
Head: Mrs J M Taylor
Type: Co-educational Day 2–11
No of pupils: B35 G30
Fees: (September 01)
Day £2400 – £2460

BURY

BURY CATHOLIC PREPARATORY SCHOOL
Arden House, 172 Manchester Road,
Bury, Lancashire BL9 9BH
Tel: (0161) 764 2346
Head: Mrs S F Entwistle
Type: Co-educational Day 3–11
No of pupils: B80 G80
Fees: (September 01) Day £2880

BURY GRAMMAR SCHOOL
Tenterden Street, Bury, Lancashire
BL9 0HN
Tel: (0161) 797 2700
Head: Mr K Richards
Type: Boys Day 7–18
No of pupils: 835
Fees: (September 01)
Day £3660 – £5130

BURY GRAMMAR SCHOOL (GIRLS')
Bridge Road, Bury, Lancashire
BL9 0HH
Tel: (0161) 797 2808
Head: Miss C H Thompson
Type: Girls Day 4–18 (Boys 4–7)
No of pupils: B82 G991
Fees: (September 01)
Day £3660 – £5130

CHORLEY

CHORCLIFFE SCHOOL
The Old Manse, Park Street, Chorley,
Lancashire PR7 1ER
Tel: (01257) 268807
Head: Ms H Mayer
Type: Co-educational Day 4–16
No of pupils: 18
Fees: (September 01) Day £4500

CLITHEROE

MOORLAND SCHOOL
Ribblesdale Avenue, Clitheroe,
Lancashire BB7 2JA
Tel: (01200) 423833
Head: Mrs J E Harrison
Type: Co-educational Boarding and
Day 2–16
No of pupils: B73 G77
No of boarders: F30 W1
Fees: (September 01)
FB £9609 – £10095
WB £9500 – £9850
Day £3786 – £4533

OAKHILL COLLEGE
Wiswell Lane, Whalley, Clitheroe,
Lancashire BB7 9AF
Tel: (01254) 823546
Head: Mr P S Mahon
Type: Co-educational Day 2–16
No of pupils: B126 G96
Fees: (September 01)
Day £3762 – £5850

STONYHURST COLLEGE
Stonyhurst, Clitheroe, Lancashire
BB7 9PZ
Tel: (01254) 826345
Head: Mr A J F Aylward
Type: Co-educational Boarding and
Day 13–18
No of pupils: B326 G67
No of boarders: F300 W10
Fees: (September 01) FB £15912
WB £14334 Day £9666

FLEETWOOD

ROSSALL PREPARATORY SCHOOL
Fleetwood, Lancashire FY7 8JW
Tel: (01253) 774222
Head: Mr D Mitchell
Type: Co-educational Day and
Boarding 2–11
No of pupils: B146 G128
No of boarders: F6 W1
Fees: (September 01) FB £10485
Day £3555 – £4125

ROSSALL SCHOOL
Fleetwood, Lancashire FY7 8JW
Tel: (01253) 774201
Head: Mr G S H Pengelley
Type: Co-educational Boarding and
Day 11–18
No of pupils: B238 G177
No of boarders: F173
Fees: (September 01)
FB £10485 – £16485
Day £5460 – £7485

LANCASTER

BENTHAM GRAMMAR SCHOOL
Low Bentham, Lancaster, Lancashire
LA2 7DB
Tel: (01524) 261275
Head: Miss R E Colman
Type: Co-educational Boarding and
Day 4–18
No of pupils: B82 G58
No of boarders: F74 W7
Fees: (September 01)
FB £10125 – £12000
WB £9000 Day £4575 – £6075

LYTHAM ST ANNES

KING EDWARD VII AND QUEEN MARY SCHOOL
Clifton Drive South, Lytham
St Annes, Lancashire FY8 1DT
Tel: (01253) 736459
Head: Mr P J Wilde
Type: Co-educational Day 3–18
No of pupils: B489 G425
Fees: (September 01) Day £5040

ST ANNE'S COLLEGE GRAMMAR SCHOOL
293 Clifton Drive South, St Annes-on-Sea, Lytham St Annes, Lancashire
FY8 1HN
Tel: (01253) 725815
Head: Mr & Mrs S R Welsby
Type: Co-educational Day 2–18
No of pupils: B108 G108
Fees: (September 01)
Day £3015 – £4800

OLDHAM

FARROWDALE HOUSE PREPARATORY SCHOOL
Farrow Street, Shaw, Oldham,
Lancashire OL2 7AD
Tel: (01706) 844533
Head: Mr F G Wilkinson
Type: Co-educational Day 3–11
No of pupils: B56 G57
Fees: (September 01)
Day £2520 – £2595

GRASSCROFT INDEPENDENT SCHOOL
Lydgate Parish Hall, Stockport Road,
Lydgate, Oldham, Lancashire OL4 4JJ
Tel: (01457) 820485
Head: Mrs B Donough
Type: Co-educational Day 2–7
No of pupils: B26 G26
Fees: (September 01) Day £2838

THE HULME GRAMMAR SCHOOL
Chamber Road, Oldham, Lancashire
OL8 4BX
Tel: (0161) 624 4497
Head: Mr K E Jones
Type: Boys Day 3–18
No of pupils: 750
Fees: (September 01)
Day £3216 – £5070

THE HULME GRAMMAR SCHOOL FOR GIRLS
Chamber Road, Oldham, Lancashire
OL8 4BX
Tel: (0161) 624 2523
Head: Miss M S Smolenski
Type: Girls Day 3–18
No of pupils: 622
Fees: (September 01)
Day £3216 – £5070

SADDLEWORTH PREPARATORY SCHOOL
Huddersfield Road, Scouthead,
Oldham, Lancashire OL4 4AG
Tel: (01457) 877442
Head: Mr W K Hirst
Type: Co-educational Day 4–7
No of pupils: B27 G29
Fees: (September 01) On application

WERNETH PREPARATORY SCHOOL
Plum Street, Oldham, Lancashire
OL8 1TJ
Tel: (0161) 624 2947
Head: Mrs A S Richards
Type: Co-educational Day 3–7
No of pupils: B73 G59
Fees: (September 01)
Day £3216 – £3270

ORMSKIRK

KINGSWOOD COLLEGE AT SCARISBRICK HALL
Southport Road, Ormskirk,
Lancashire L40 9RQ
Tel: (01704) 880200
Head: Mr E J Borowski
Type: Co-educational Day 2–18
No of pupils: B274 G233
Fees: (September 01)
Day £2100 – £4425

POULTON-LE-FYLDE

EMMANUEL CHRISTIAN SCHOOL
Singleton Hall, Lodge Lane,
Singleton, Poulton-Le-Fylde,
Lancashire FY6 8LU
Tel: (01253) 882873
Head: Mr M Derry and Mrs P Derry
Type: Co-educational Day 4–16
No of pupils: B53 G60
Fees: (September 01) Day £2460

PRESTON

HIGHFIELD PRIORY SCHOOL
Fulwood Row, Fulwood, Preston,
Lancashire PR2 6SL
Tel: (01772) 709624
Head: Mr B C Duckett
Type: Co-educational Day 2–11
No of pupils: B151 G157
Fees: (September 01)
Day £3200 – £3600

KINGSFOLD CHRISTIAN SCHOOL
Moss Lane, Hesketh Bank, Preston,
Lancashire PR4 6AA
Tel: (01772) 813824
Head: Mr S D Lamin
Type: Co-educational Day 4–16
No of pupils: B30 G26
Fees: (September 01) On application

KIRKHAM GRAMMAR SCHOOL
Ribby Road, Kirkham, Preston,
Lancashire PR4 2BH
Tel: (01772) 671079
Head: Mr B Stacey
Type: Co-educational Boarding and
Day 4–18
No of pupils: B480 G470
No of boarders: F64 W10
Fees: (September 01) FB £9990
WB £9755 Day £3960 – £5280

ST PIUS X PREPARATORY SCHOOL
200 Garstang Road, Fulwood,
Preston, Lancashire PR2 8RD
Tel: (01772) 719937
Head: Miss B Banks
Type: Co-educational Day 2–11
No of pupils: B146 G148
Fees: (September 01)
Day £3000 – £3885

ROCHDALE

BEECH HOUSE SCHOOL
184 Manchester Road, Rochdale,
Lancashire OL11 4JQ
Tel: (01706) 646309
Head: Mr K Sartain
Type: Co-educational Day 3–16
No of pupils: B110 G110
Fees: (September 01)
Day £1410 – £3084

GLEBE HOUSE SCHOOL
Broadfield Stile, Rochdale,
Lancashire OL16 1UT
Tel: (01706) 645985
Head: Mr K Bayliss
Type: Co-educational Day 3–7
No of pupils: B36 G43
Fees: (September 01)
Day £2400 – £3450

STONYHURST

ST MARY'S HALL
Stonyhurst, Lancashire BB7 9PU
Tel: (01254) 826242
Head: Mr M E Higgins
Type: Co-educational Boarding and
Day 5–13
No of pupils: B148 G73
No of boarders: F64 W14
Fees: (September 01) FB £11214
WB £10383 Day £4245 – £7884

WIGAN

KINGSWAY SCHOOL
Greenough Street, Wigan,
Lancashire WN1 3SU
Tel: (01942) 244743
Head: Mrs B Jacobs
Type: Co-educational Day 3–11
No of pupils: B30 G25
Fees: (September 01) Day £1950

LEICESTERSHIRE

ASHBY-DE-LA-ZOUCH

MANOR HOUSE SCHOOL
South Street, Ashby-de-la-Zouch,
Leicestershire LE65 1BR
Tel: (01530) 412932
Head: Mr R J Sill
Type: Co-educational Day 3–14
No of pupils: B112 G113
Fees: (September 01)
Day £3387 – £4380

LEICESTER

GRACE DIEU MANOR SCHOOL
Grace Dieu, Thringstone, Leicester,
Leicestershire LE67 5UG
Tel: (01530) 222276
Head: Mr A J Borrington
Type: Co-educational Day 3–13
No of pupils: B193 G122
Fees: (September 01)
Day £3840 – £6216

IRWIN COLLEGE*
164 London Road, Leicester,
Leicestershire LE2 1ND
Tel: (0116) 255 2648
Head: Mrs L G Tonks and
Mr S Wytcherley
Type: Co-educational Boarding and
Day 14–25
No of pupils: B70 G50
No of boarders: F100
Fees: (September 01)
FB £10950 – £12000
Day £4950 – £7950

LEICESTER GRAMMAR JUNIOR SCHOOL
Evington Hall, Spencefield Lane,
Leicester, Leicestershire LE5 6HN
Tel: (0116) 210 1299
Head: Mr H McFaul
Type: Co-educational Day 3–11
No of pupils: B146 G114
Fees: (September 01) Day £4695

LEICESTER GRAMMAR SCHOOL
8 Peacock Lane, Leicester,
Leicestershire LE1 5PX
Tel: (0116) 222 0400
Head: Mr C P M King
Type: Co-educational Day 10–18
No of pupils: B400 G294
Fees: (September 01) Day £5985

LEICESTER HIGH SCHOOL FOR GIRLS
454 London Road, Leicester,
Leicestershire LE2 2PP
Tel: (0116) 270 5338
Head: Mrs P A Watson
Type: Girls Day 3–18
No of pupils: 435
Fees: (September 01)
Day £3840 – £5955

LEICESTER MONTESSORI GRAMMAR SCHOOL
140 Regent Road, Leicester,
Leicestershire LE1 7PA
Tel: (0116) 255 4443
Head: Mrs D Bailey
Type: Co-educational Day 11–18
No of pupils: 30
Fees: (September 01) On application

LEICESTER MONTESSORI SCHOOL
194 London Road, Leicester,
Leicestershire LE1 1ND
Tel: (0116) 270 6667
Head: Mrs D Bailey
Type: Co-educational Day 0–18
No of pupils: B90 G100
Fees: (September 01) On application

RATCLIFFE COLLEGE*
Fosse Way, Ratcliffe on the Wreake,
Leicester, Leicestershire LE7 4SG
Tel: (01509) 817000
Head: Mr P Farrar
Type: Co-educational Boarding and
Day 3–18
No of pupils: B360 G200
No of boarders: F86 W14
Fees: (September 01)
FB £9711 – £12207
WB £9159 – £11514
Day £935 – £8106

ST CRISPIN'S SCHOOL (LEICESTER) LTD.
6 St Mary's Road, Leicester,
Leicestershire LE2 1XA
Tel: (0116) 270 7648
Head: Mrs D Lofthouse
Type: Co-educational Day 2–16
No of pupils: B100 G20
Fees: (September 01)
Day £1743 – £5145

STONEYGATE COLLEGE
2 Albert Road, Stoneygate, Leicester,
Leicestershire LE2 2AA
Tel: (0116) 270 7414
Head: Mr J C Bourlet
Type: Co-educational Day 3–11
No of pupils: B59 G90
Fees: (September 01)
Day £3330 – £4290

STONEYGATE SCHOOL
254 London Road, Leicester,
Leicestershire LE2 1RP
Tel: (0116) 270 7536
Head: Mr J H Morris
Type: Co-educational Day 3–13
No of pupils: B263 G141
Fees: (September 01)
Day £4275 – £5760

LOUGHBOROUGH

FAIRFIELD SCHOOL
Leicester Road, Loughborough,
Leicestershire LE11 2AE
Tel: (01509) 215172
Head: Mr T A Eadon
Type: Co-educational Day 4–11
No of pupils: B245 G213
Fees: (September 01) On application

LOUGHBOROUGH GRAMMAR SCHOOL
Burton Walks, Loughborough,
Leicestershire LE11 2DU
Tel: (01509) 233233
Head: Mr P B Fisher
Type: Boys Day and Boarding 10–18
No of pupils: 970
No of boarders: F45 W20
Fees: (September 01) FB £10989
WB £9747 Day £6354

LOUGHBOROUGH HIGH SCHOOL
Burton Walks, Loughborough,
Leicestershire LE11 2DU
Tel: (01509) 212348
Head: Miss B O'Connor
Type: Girls Day 11–18
No of pupils: 555
Fees: (September 01) Day £5787

OUR LADY'S CONVENT SCHOOL
Burton Street, Loughborough,
Leicestershire LE11 2DT
Tel: (01509) 263901
Head: Sister S Fynn
Type: Girls Day 3–18 (Boys 3–5)
No of pupils: 540
Fees: (September 01)
Day £3066 – £5178

PNEU SCHOOL
8 Station Road, East Leake,
Loughborough, Leicestershire
LE12 6LQ
Tel: (01509) 852229
Head: Mrs E A Gibbs
Type: Co-educational Day 3–11
No of pupils: B46 G32
Fees: (September 01)
Day £4140 – £4200

MARKET BOSWORTH

THE DIXIE GRAMMAR SCHOOL
Market Bosworth, Leicestershire
CV13 0LE
Tel: (01455) 292244
Head: Mr R S Willmott
Type: Co-educational Day 10–18
No of pupils: B136 G148
Fees: (September 01) Day £5055

MARKET HARBOROUGH

BROOKE HOUSE COLLEGE*
Leicester Road, Market Harborough,
Leicestershire LE16 7AU
Tel: (01858) 462452
Head: Mr J Stanford
Type: Co-educational Boarding and
Day 14–19
No of pupils: B85 G65
No of boarders: F150
Fees: (September 01) FB £13860
Day £9000

UPPINGHAM

WINDMILL HOUSE SCHOOL
22 Stockerston Road, Uppingham,
Leicestershire LE15 9UD
Tel: (01572) 823593
Head: Mrs J Taylor
Type: Co-educational Day 4–11
No of pupils: B51 G41
Fees: (September 01)
Day £2355 – £3525

LINCOLNSHIRE

ALFORD

MAYPOLE HOUSE SCHOOL
Well Vale Hall, Alford, Lincolnshire
LN13 0ET
Tel: (01507) 462764
Head: Mrs A White
Type: Co-educational Day 3–16
No of pupils: B30 G20
Fees: (September 01)
Day £2160 – £2520

BOSTON

CONWAY PREPARATORY SCHOOL
Tunnard Street, Boston, Lincolnshire
PE21 6PL
Tel: (01205) 363150/355539
Head: Mr S P McElwain
Type: Co-educational Day 2–11
No of pupils: B70 G70
Fees: (September 01)
Day £273 – £2895

BOURNE

WITHAM HALL
Witham-on-the-Hill, Bourne,
Lincolnshire PE10 0JJ
Tel: (01778) 590222
Head: Mr D L Telfer & Mrs S Telfer
Type: Co-educational Boarding and
Day 3–13
No of pupils: B123 G91
No of boarders: F10 W42
Fees: (September 01) F/WB £10470
Day £4650 – £7650

GAINSBOROUGH

HANDEL HOUSE PREPARATORY SCHOOL
Northolme, Gainsborough,
Lincolnshire DN21 2JB
Tel: (01427) 612426
Head: Mrs V C Haigh
Type: Co-educational Day 3–12
No of pupils: B27 G18
Fees: (September 01)
Day £2175 – £2655

GRANTHAM

DUDLEY HOUSE SCHOOL
1 Dudley Road, Grantham,
Lincolnshire NG31 9AA
Tel: (01476) 400184
Head: Mrs P Eastwood
Type: Co-educational Day 3–11
No of pupils: B20 G22
Fees: (September 01)
Day £2580 – £2640

THE GRANTHAM PREPARATORY SCHOOL
Gorse Lane, Grantham, Lincolnshire
NG31 7UF
Tel: (01476) 593293
Head: Mrs D J Wand
Type: Co-educational Day 3–11
No of pupils: B70 G64
Fees: (September 01)
Day £3288 – £4110

LINCOLN

LINCOLN MINSTER SCHOOL
Hillside, Lindum Terrace, Lincoln,
Lincolnshire LN2 5RW
Tel: (01522) 543764/523769
Head: Mr C Rickart
Type: Co-educational Day and
Boarding 2–18
No of pupils: B307 G292
No of boarders: F42 W40
Fees: (September 01) FB £10575 –
£12270 WB £9810 – £11340
Day £4440 – £6480

ST MARY'S PREPARATORY SCHOOL
5 Pottergate, Lincoln, Lincolnshire
LN2 1PH
Tel: (01522) 524622
Head: Mr M Upton
Type: Co-educational Day 2–11
No of pupils: B150 G141
Fees: (September 01)
Day £4560 – £5610

LOUTH

GREENWICH HOUSE INDEPENDENT SCHOOL
106 High Holme Road, Louth,
Lincolnshire LN11 0HE
Tel: (01507) 609252
Head: Mrs J M Brindle
Type: Co-educational Day 0–11
No of pupils: 150
Fees: (September 01) Day £3675

SLEAFORD

THE FEN PREPARATORY SCHOOL
Side Bar Lane, Heckington Fen,
Sleaford, Lincolnshire NG34 9LY
Tel: (01529) 460966
Head: Mrs J M Dunkley
Type: Co-educational Day 2–16
No of pupils: B14 G16
Fees: (September 01) On application

SPALDING

AYSCOUGHFEE HALL SCHOOL
Welland Hall, London Road,
Spalding, Lincolnshire PE11 2TE
Tel: (01775) 724733
Head: Mr B Chittick
Type: Co-educational Day 3–11
No of pupils: B80 G80
Fees: (September 01)
Day £2686 – £3156

STAMFORD

COPTHILL SCHOOL
Barnack Road, Uffington, Stamford,
Lincolnshire PE9 4TD
Tel: (01780) 757506
Head: Mr J A Teesdale
Type: Co-educational Day 2–11
No of pupils: B152 G187
Fees: (September 01)
Day £810 – £4380

STAMFORD HIGH SCHOOL
St Martin's, Stamford, Lincolnshire
PE9 2LJ
Tel: (01780) 484200
Head: Dr P R Mason
Type: Girls Day and Boarding 11–18
No of pupils: 640
No of boarders: F60 W5
Fees: (September 01) FB £12444
WB £12396 Day £6396

STAMFORD SCHOOL
St Paul's Street, Stamford,
Lincolnshire PE9 2BS
Tel: (01780) 750300/1
Head: Dr P R Mason
Type: Boys Day and Boarding 11–18
No of pupils: 640
No of boarders: F75 W10
Fees: (September 01) FB £12444
WB £12396 Day £6396

WOODHALL SPA

ST HUGH'S SCHOOL
Cromwell Avenue, Woodhall Spa,
Lincolnshire LN10 6TQ
Tel: (01526) 352169
Head: Mr S G Greenish
Type: Co-educational Boarding and
Day 2–13
No of pupils: B90 G75
No of boarders: F20 W40
Fees: (September 01)
F/WB £9618 – £9843
Day £3936 – £7278

NORTH EAST LINCOLNSHIRE

GRIMSBY

ST JAMES' SCHOOL
18–24 Bargate, Grimsby, North East
Lincolnshire DN34 4SY
Tel: (01472) 503260
Head: Mrs S M Isaac
Type: Co-educational Day and
Boarding 3–18
No of pupils: B148 G102
No of boarders: F39 W5
Fees: (September 01)
FB £7665 – £10467
WB £7170 – £9972
Day £2805 – £6417

ST MARTIN'S PREPARATORY
SCHOOL
63 Bargate, Grimsby, North East
Lincolnshire DN34 5AA
Tel: (01472) 878907
Head: Mrs M Preston
Type: Co-educational Day 3–11
No of pupils: B109 G125
Fees: (September 01)
Day £2760 – £3150

NORTH LINCOLNSHIRE

BRIGG

BRIGG PREPARATORY
SCHOOL
Bigby Street, Brigg, North
Lincolnshire DN20 8EF
Tel: (01652) 653237
Head: Mrs P Newman
Type: Co-educational Day 3–11
No of pupils: B80 G64
Fees: (September 01) On application

KEADBY

TRENTVALE PREPARATORY
SCHOOL
Trentside, Keadby, North
Lincolnshire DN17 3EF
Tel: (01724) 782904
Head: Mr P Wright
Type: Co-educational Day 3–11
No of pupils: B45 G45
Fees: (September 01) Day £1785

SCUNTHORPE

LYNTON PREPARATORY
SCHOOL
250 Frodingham Road, Scunthorpe,
North Lincolnshire DN15 7NW
Tel: (01724) 850 881
Head: Mrs E J Broadbent
Type: Co-educational Day 3–11
No of pupils: 85
Fees: (September 01) On application

LONDON

E1

GREEN GABLES
MONTESSORI PRIMARY
SCHOOL
The Institute, 302 The Highway,
Wapping, London E1W 3DH
Tel: (020) 7488 2374
Head: Mrs J Brierley
Type: Co-educational Day 0–8
No of pupils: B24 G25
Fees: (September 01)
Day £5130 – £6960

MADNI GIRLS SCHOOL
15–17 Rampart Street, London
E1 2LA
Tel: (020) 7791 3531
Head: Mrs F R Liyawdeen
Type: Girls Day 12–18
No of pupils: 100
Fees: (September 01) On application

RIVER HOUSE MONTESSORI
SCHOOL
St Peter's Centre, Reardon Street,
Wapping, London E1W 2QH
Tel: (020) 7680 1288
Head: Ms S Greenwood
Type: Co-educational Day 2–12
No of pupils: 41
Fees: (September 01)
Day £2175 – £6520

E2

GATEHOUSE SCHOOL
Sewardstone Road, Victoria Park,
London E2 9JG
Tel: (020) 8980 2978
Head: Miss A Eversole
Type: Co-educational Day 2–11
No of pupils: B72 G88
Fees: (September 01)
Day £3750 – £5600

E4

NORMANHURST SCHOOL
68/74 Station Road, Chingford,
London E4 7BA
Tel: (020) 8529 4307
Head: Mr V Hamilton
Type: Co-educational Day 3–16
No of pupils: B131 G76
Fees: (September 01)
Day £4485 – £6510

E5

NORTH LONDON RUDOLF STEINER SCHOOL
A Steiner Waldorf Early Years
Centre, 89 Blurton Road, London
E5 0NH
Tel: (020) 8986 8968
Head: Ms G Reemer
Type: Co-educational Day 2–7
No of pupils: B26 G22
Fees: (September 01)
Day £1320 – £2496

PARAGON CHRISTIAN ACADEMY
233–241 Glyn Road, London E5 0JP
Tel: (020) 8985 1119
Head: Mr G Olson
Type: Co-educational Day 3–11
No of pupils: B17 G14
Fees: (September 01) Day £4320

E7

GRANGEWOOD INDEPENDENT SCHOOL
Chester Road, Forest Gate, London
E7 8QT
Tel: (020) 8472 3552
Head: Mrs C A Adams
Type: Co-educational Day 4–11
No of pupils: B45 G41
Fees: (September 01) Day £3582

E11

ST JOSEPH'S CONVENT SCHOOL
59 Cambridge Park, London E11 2PR
Tel: (020) 8989 4700
Head: Mrs C Youle
Type: Girls Day 3–11
No of pupils: 203
Fees: (September 01) Day £2700

E17

FOREST GIRLS' SCHOOL
Snaresbrook, London E17 3PY
Tel: (020) 8521 7477
Head: Mr A G Boggis
Type: Girls Day 11–18 (Co-ed VIth
Form)
No of pupils: 435
Fees: (September 01) Day £8148

FOREST PREPARATORY SCHOOL
Snaresbrook, London E17 3PY
Tel: (020) 8520 1744
Head: Mr M J Lovett
Type: Co-educational Day 4–11
No of pupils: B108 G100
Fees: (September 01)
Day £5151 – £6300

FOREST SCHOOL
College Place, Snaresbrook, London
E17 3PY
Tel: (020) 8520 1744
Head: Mr A G Boggis
Type: Co-educational Day and
Boarding 7–18
No of pupils: B632 G538
No of boarders: F7 W5
Fees: (September 01) F/WB £12771
Day £5151 – £8148

HYLAND HOUSE
896 Forest Road, Walthamstow,
London E17 4AE
Tel: (020) 8520 4186
Head: Mrs Abbequaye
Type: Co-educational Day 3–11
No of pupils: B55 G40
Fees: (September 01) On application

E18

SNARESBROOK COLLEGE PREPARATORY SCHOOL
75 Woodford Road, South
Woodford, London E18 2EA
Tel: (020) 8989 2394
Head: Mrs L J Chiverrell
Type: Co-educational Day 3–11
No of pupils: B76 G84
Fees: (September 01)
Day £3849 – £5154

EC1

THE CHARTERHOUSE SQUARE SCHOOL
40 Charterhouse Square, London
EC1M 6EA
Tel: (020) 7600 3805
Head: Mrs J Malden
Type: Co-educational Day 4–11
No of pupils: B80 G70
Fees: (September 01) Day £6900

THE ITALIA CONTI ACADEMY OF THEATRE ARTS
23 Goswell Road, London EC1M 7AJ
Tel: (020) 8608 0047
Head: Mr C Vote
Type: Co-educational Day 9–21
No of pupils: B45 G200
Fees: (September 01) On application

DALLINGTON SCHOOL
8 Dallington Street, London EC1V
0BW
Tel: (020) 7251 2284
Head: Mrs M C Hercules
Type: Co-educational Day 3–11
No of pupils: B102 G110
Fees: (September 01)
Day £4249 – £5763

EC2

CITY OF LONDON SCHOOL FOR GIRLS
Barbican, London EC2Y 8BB
Tel: (020) 7628 0841
Head: Dr Y Burne
Type: Girls Day 7–18
No of pupils: 689
Fees: (September 01) Day £7776

THE LYCEUM
6 Paul Street, London EC2A 4JH
Tel: (020) 7247 1588
Head: Mr J Rowe
Type: Co-educational Day 3–11
No of pupils: 128
Fees: (September 01) Day £5550

EC4

CITY OF LONDON SCHOOL
Queen Victoria Street, London EC4V 3AL
Tel: (020) 7489 0291
Head: Mr D Levin
Type: Boys Day 10–18
No of pupils: 890
Fees: (September 01) Day £8307

ST PAUL'S CATHEDRAL SCHOOL*
2 New Change, London EC4M 9AD
Tel: (020) 7248 5156
Head: Mr A H Dobbin
Type: Co-educational Boarding and Day 4–13
No of pupils: B121 G17
No of boarders: F40
Fees: (September 01) FB £4314 Day £6318 – £6810

N2

ANNEMOUNT SCHOOL
18 Holne Chase, London N2 0QN
Tel: (020) 8455 2132
Head: Mrs G Maidment
Type: Co-educational Day 2–7
No of pupils: B50 G50
Fees: (September 01) Day £3600 – £5850

KEREM HOUSE
18 Kingsley Way, London N2 0ER
Tel: (020) 8455 7524
Head: Mrs D Rose
Type: Co-educational Day 3–5
No of pupils: 96
Fees: (September 01) Day £485 – £1280

THE KEREM SCHOOL
Norrice Lea, London N2 0RE
Tel: (020) 8455 0909
Head: Mrs R Goulden
Type: Co-educational Day 4–11
No of pupils: B79 G81
Fees: (September 01) Day £4830

N3

AKIVA SCHOOL
Levy House, The Sternberg Centre, 80 East End Road, London N3 2SY
Tel: (020) 8349 4980
Head: Mrs S de Botton
Type: Co-educational Day 4–11
No of pupils: B81 G73
Fees: (September 01) Day £4560

BEIS SOROH SCHNEIRER
Finchley United Synagogue, Kinloss Gardens, London N3 3DU
Tel: (020) 8343 1190
Head: Mrs R Weiss
Type: Girls Day 3–9
No of pupils: 95
Fees: (September 01) On application

PARDES GRAMMAR BOYS' SCHOOL
Hendon Lane, London N3 1SA
Tel: (020) 8343 3568
Head: Rabbi D Dunner
Type: Boys Day 11–17
No of pupils: 450
Fees: (September 01) Day £4350

N4

HOLLY PARK MONTESSORI
The Holly Park, Methodist Church, Crouch Hill, London N4 4BY
Tel: (020) 7263 6563
Head: Mrs A Lake
Type: Co-educational Day 2–11
No of pupils: B43 G42
Fees: (September 01) Day £1032 – £4950

N5

PRIMROSE MONTESSORI SCHOOL
Congregational Church, Highbury, London N5 2TE
Tel: (020) 7359 8985
Head: Mrs L Grandson
Type: Co-educational Day 2–11
No of pupils: 110
Fees: (September 01) Day £4680

N6

CHANNING JUNIOR SCHOOL
Fairseat, 1 Highgate High Street, London N6 5JR
Tel: (020) 8342 9862
Head: Mrs J Newhan
Type: Girls Day 4–11
No of pupils: 160
Fees: (September 01) Day £7125

CHANNING SCHOOL
Highgate, London N6 5HF
Tel: (020) 8340 2328
Head: Mrs E Radice
Type: Girls Day 11–18
No of pupils: 359
Fees: (September 01) Day £7125 – £7740

HIGHGATE JUNIOR SCHOOL
Cholmeley House, 3 Bishopswood Road, Highgate, London N6 4PL
Tel: (020) 8340 9193
Head: Mr H S Evers
Type: Boys Day 7–13
No of pupils: 365
Fees: (September 01) Day £8880

HIGHGATE PRE-PREPARATORY SCHOOL
7 Bishopswood Road, Highgate, London N6 4PH
Tel: (020) 8340 9196
Head: Mrs J Challender
Type: Co-educational Day 3–7
No of pupils: B84 G46
Fees: (September 01) Day £4005 – £8055

HIGHGATE SCHOOL
North Road, London N6 4AY
Tel: (020) 8340 1524
Head: Mr R P Kennedy
Type: Boys Day 13–18
No of pupils: 550
Fees: (September 01) Day £9750

RAINBOW MONTESSORI NURSERY SCHOOL
Highgate URC, Pond Square, London N6 6BA
Tel: (020) 7328 8986
Head: Mrs L Madden
Type: Co-educational Day 2–5
No of pupils: B18 G18
Fees: (September 01) Day £2805 – £4395

N10

THE MONTESSORI HOUSE
5 Princes Avenue, Muswell Hill, London N10 3LS
Tel: (020) 8444 4399
Head: Mrs L Christoforou
Type: Co-educational Day 2–5
No of pupils: B30 G30
Fees: (September 01) Day £2190 – £5700

NORFOLK HOUSE SCHOOL
10 Muswell Avenue, London N10 2EG
Tel: (020) 8883 4584
Head: Mr R Howat
Type: Co-educational Day 4–11
No of pupils: B65 G35
Fees: (September 01) Day £5655

PRINCES AVENUE SCHOOL

5 Princes Avenue, Muswell Hill,
London N10 3LS
Tel: (020) 8444 4399
Head: Mrs L Christoforou
Type: Co-educational Day 5–7
No of pupils: B12 G12
Fees: (September 01) Day £6900

N11

WOODSIDE PARK INTERNATIONAL SCHOOL

Friern Barnet Road, London
N11 3DR
Tel: (020) 8368 3777
Head: Mr S D Anson
Type: Co-educational Day 2–18
No of pupils: B376 G184
Fees: (September 01)
Day £2730 – £9000

N14

SALCOMBE SCHOOL

224–226 Chase Side, Southgate,
London N14 4PL
Tel: (020) 8441 5282
Head: Mr A Guha
Type: Co-educational Day 2–11
No of pupils: B255 G175
Fees: (September 01) Day £4730

VITA ET PAX SCHOOL

Priory Close, Green Road,
Southgate, London N14 4AT
Tel: (020) 8449 8336
Head: Mrs M O'Connor
Type: Co-educational Day 3–11
No of pupils: B90 G90
Fees: (September 01) Day £3300

N16

LUBAVITCH HOUSE SENIOR SCHOOL FOR GIRLS

107–115 Stamford Hill, Hackney,
London N16 5RP
Tel: (020) 8800 0022
Head: Rabbi S Lew
Type: Girls Day 11–18
No of pupils: 80
Fees: (September 01) On application

MECHINAH LIYESHIVAH ZICHRON MOSHE

86 Amhurst Park, London N16 5AR
Tel: (020) 8800 5892
Head: Rabbi M Halpern
Type: Boys Day 11–16
No of pupils: 60
Fees: (September 01) On application

TAYYIBAH GIRLS SCHOOL

88 Filey Avenue, Stamford Hill,
London N16 6JJ
Tel: (020) 8880 0085
Head: Mrs N B Qureshi
Type: Girls Day 5–18
No of pupils: 247
Fees: (September 01) Day £1200

YESODEY HATORAH JEWISH SCHOOL

2–4 Amhurst Park, London N16 5AE
Tel: (020) 8800 8612
Head: Rabbi Abraham Pinter
Type: Co-educational Day 3–16
No of pupils: B250 G710
Fees: (September 01) On application

YETEV LEV DAY SCHOOL FOR BOYS

111–115 Cazenove Road, London
N16 6AX
Tel: (020) 8806 3834
Head: Mr Delange
Type: Boys Day 3–11
No of pupils: 320
Fees: (September 01) Non fee-paying

N17

PARKSIDE PREPARATORY SCHOOL

Church Lane, Bruce Grove,
Tottenham, London N17 7AA
Tel: (020) 8808 1451
Head: Mrs R E Horan-Botfield
Type: Co-educational Day 3–11
No of pupils: B27 G28
Fees: (September 01) Day £3307

N21

GRANGE PARK PREPARATORY SCHOOL

13 The Chine, Grange Park,
Winchmore Hill, London N21 2EA
Tel: (020) 8360 1469
Head: Mrs C Callegari
Type: Girls Day 4–11
No of pupils: 105
Fees: (September 01)
Day £4185 – £4485

KEBLE PREPARATORY SCHOOL

Wades Hill, Winchmore Hill,
London N21 1BG
Tel: (020) 8360 3359
Head: Mr V W P Thomas
Type: Boys Day 4–13
No of pupils: 200
Fees: (September 01)
Day £5550 – £6975

PALMERS GREEN HIGH SCHOOL

Hoppers Road, Winchmore Hill,
London N21 3LJ
Tel: (020) 8886 1135
Head: Mrs S Grant
Type: Girls Day 3–16
No of pupils: 350
Fees: (September 01)
Day £2175 – £6300

NW1

THE CAVENDISH SCHOOL*

179 Arlington Road, London
NW1 7EY
Tel: (020) 7485 1958
Head: Mrs L Hayes
Type: Girls Day 3–11
No of pupils: 180
Fees: (September 01)
Day £5424 – £5769

FRANCIS HOLLAND SCHOOL

Clarence Gate, Ivor Place, London
NW1 6XR
Tel: (020) 7723 0176
Head: Mrs G Low
Type: Girls Day 11–18
No of pupils: 380
Fees: (September 01) Day £7980

INTERNATIONAL COMMUNITY SCHOOL

4 York Terrace East, Regent's Park,
London NW1 4PT
Tel: (020) 7935 1206
Head: Mr P Hurd
Type: Co-educational Day 3–18
No of pupils: B100 G100
Fees: (September 01)
Day £6951 – £9861

NORTH BRIDGE HOUSE LOWER SCHOOL*

1 Gloucester Avenue, London
NW1 7AB
Tel: (020) 7485 0661
Head: Ms J Battye
Type: Co-educational Day Boys 8–10
Girls 8–11
No of pupils: B71 G129
Fees: (September 01) Day £6900

NORTH BRIDGE HOUSE PREP & SENIOR SCHOOL*

1 Gloucester Avenue, London
NW1 7AB
Tel: (020) 7267 6266
Head: Mr H Richardson and
Mr B Ramell
Type: Co-educational Day 10–18
No of pupils: B189 G63
Fees: (September 01) Day £7425

SYLVIA YOUNG THEATRE SCHOOL
Rossmore Road, Marylebone, London NW1 6NJ
Tel: (020) 7402 0673
Head: Mr C T Townsend
Type: Co-educational Day and Boarding 9–16
No of pupils: B55 G90
No of boarders: W15
Fees: (September 01)
Day £4050 – £6000

NW2

THE MULBERRY HOUSE SCHOOL
7 Minster Road, West Hampstead, London NW2 3SD
Tel: (020) 8452 7340
Head: Ms J Pedder and Ms B Lewis-Powell
Type: Co-educational Day 2–8
No of pupils: B114 G98
Fees: (September 01)
Day £4700 – £8648

NW3

CHALCOT MONTESSORI SCHOOL AMI
9 Chalcot Gardens, London NW3 4YB
Tel: (020) 7722 1386
Head: Ms J Morfey
Type: Co-educational Day 2–6
No of pupils: 24
Fees: (September 01)
Day £1500 – £3300

DEVONSHIRE HOUSE PREPARATORY SCHOOL*
2 Arkwright Road, Hampstead, London NW3 6AE
Tel: (020) 7435 1916
Head: Mrs S P T Donovan
Type: Co-educational Day Boys 2–13 Girls 2–11
No of pupils: B240 G190
Fees: (September 01)
Day £6600 – £7455

FINE ARTS COLLEGE
85 & 81b Belsize Park Gardens, Hampstead, London NW3 4NJ
Tel: (020) 7586 0312
Head: Ms C Cave and Mr N Cochrane
Type: Co-educational Day 15+
No of pupils: B40 G60
Fees: (September 01)
Day £3300 – £10275

THE HALL SCHOOL
23 Crossfield Road, Hampstead, London NW3 4NU
Tel: (020) 7722 1700
Head: Mr P F Ramage
Type: Boys Day 4–13
No of pupils: 420
Fees: (September 01)
Day £6600 – £8025

HAMPSTEAD HILL PRE-PREPARATORY & NURSERY SCHOOL
St Stephen's Hall, Pond Street, Hampstead, London NW3 2PP
Tel: (020) 7435 6262
Head: Mrs A Taylor
Type: Co-educational Day Boys 2–8 Girls 2–7
No of pupils: B150 G100
Fees: (September 01)
Day £5400 – £8750

HEATHSIDE PREPARATORY SCHOOL
16 New End, Hampstead, London NW3 1JA
Tel: (020) 7794 5857
Head: Mrs J White and Ms M Remus
Type: Co-educational Day 2–11
No of pupils: B54 G50
Fees: (September 01)
Day £3000 – £5250

HEREWARD HOUSE SCHOOL
14 Strathray Gardens, Hampstead, London NW3 4NY
Tel: (020) 7794 4820
Head: Mrs L Sampson
Type: Boys Day 4–13
No of pupils: 175
Fees: (September 01)
Day £6075 – £7125

LYNDHURST HOUSE PREPARATORY SCHOOL
24 Lyndhurst Gardens, Hampstead, London NW3 5NW
Tel: (020) 7435 4936
Head: Mr M O Spilberg
Type: Boys Day 7–13
No of pupils: 140
Fees: (September 01) Day £7350

MARIA MONTESSORI SCHOOL HAMPSTEAD
26 Lyndhurst Gardens, Hampstead, London NW3 5NW
Tel: (020) 7435 3646
Head: Mrs L Lawrence
Type: Co-educational Day 2–10
No of pupils: 50
Fees: (September 01) Day £4650

NORTH BRIDGE HOUSE JUNIOR SCHOOL
8 Netherhall Gardens, London NW3 5RR
Tel: (020) 7435 2884
Head: Mrs R Allsopp
Type: Co-educational Day 5–8
No of pupils: B100 G100
Fees: (September 01) On application

NORTH BRIDGE HOUSE NURSERY & KINDERGARTEN
33 Fitzjohn's Avenue, London NW3 5JY
Tel: (020) 7435 9641
Head: Mrs R Allsopp
Type: Co-educational Day 2–5
No of pupils: B116 G100
Fees: (September 01)
Day £2016 – £7425

THE PHOENIX SCHOOL
36 College Crescent, London NW3 5LF
Tel: (020) 7722 4433
Head: Mr J Clegg
Type: Co-educational Day 3–7
No of pupils: B75 G52
Fees: (September 01)
Day £1390 – £2650

THE ROYAL SCHOOL, HAMPSTEAD*
65 Rosslyn Hill, Vane Close, Hampstead, London NW3 5UD
Tel: (020) 7794 7708
Head: Mrs C A Sibson
Type: Girls Boarding and Day 4–18
No of pupils: 200
No of boarders: F30 W10
Fees: (September 01)
FB £9279 – £11529
WB £7659 – £9585
Day £4926 – £5799

ST ANTHONY'S PREPARATORY SCHOOL
90 Fitzjohns Avenue, Hampstead, London NW3 6NP
Tel: (020) 7435 0316
Head: Mr P Anderson
Type: Boys Day 5–13
No of pupils: 288
Fees: (September 01)
Day £7110 – £7305

ST MARGARET'S SCHOOL*
18 Kidderpore Gardens, London NW3 7SR
Tel: (020) 7435 2439
Head: Mrs S Meaden
Type: Girls Day 5–16
No of pupils: 150
Fees: (September 01)
Day £5250 – £5850

ST MARY'S SCHOOL HAMPSTEAD
47 Fitzjohn's Avenue, London NW3 6PG
Tel: (020) 7435 1868
Head: Mrs W Nash
Type: Girls Day 2–11 (Boys 2–7)
No of pupils: B39 G258
Fees: (September 01)
Day £3450 – £6450

SARUM HALL
15 Eton Avenue, London NW3 3EL
Tel: (020) 7794 2261
Head: Mrs C J Scott
Type: Girls Day 3–11
No of pupils: 165
Fees: (September 01)
Day £4293 – £7170

SOUTH HAMPSTEAD HIGH SCHOOL
3 Maresfield Gardens, London NW3 5SS
Tel: (020) 7435 2899
Head: Mrs V L Ainley
Type: Girls Day 4–18
No of pupils: 935
Fees: (September 01)
Day £5145 – £6624

SOUTHBANK INTERNATIONAL SCHOOL, HAMPSTEAD*
16 Netherhall Gardens, Hampstead, London NW3 5TH
Tel: (020) 7431 1200
Head: Mrs J Treftz
Type: Co-educational Day 3–14
No of pupils: B90 G86
Fees: (September 01)
Day £6150 – £12900

TREVOR ROBERTS'
57 Eton Avenue, London NW3 3ET
Tel: (020) 7586 1444
Head: Mr S Trevor-Roberts
Type: Co-educational Day 5–13
No of pupils: B98 G80
Fees: (September 01)
Day £6600 – £9000

UNIVERSITY COLLEGE SCHOOL
Frognal, Hampstead, London NW3 6XH
Tel: (020) 7435 2215
Head: Mr K J Durham
Type: Boys Day 11–18
No of pupils: 720
Fees: (September 01)
Day £9000 – £9750

UNIVERSITY COLLEGE SCHOOL, JUNIOR BRANCH
11 Holly Hill, London NW3 6QN
Tel: (020) 7435 3068
Head: Mr K J Douglas
Type: Boys Day 7–11
No of pupils: 220
Fees: (September 01) Day £9000

THE VILLAGE SCHOOL
2 Parkhill Road, Belsize Park, London NW3 2YN
Tel: (020) 7485 4673
Head: Mrs F M Prior
Type: Girls Day 4–11
No of pupils: 140
Fees: (September 01) Day £7050

WILLOUGHBY HALL DYSLEXIA CENTRE*
1 Willoughby Road, London NW3 1RP
Tel: (020) 7794 3538
Head: Mr W H Wilcox
Type: Co-educational Day 6–12
No of pupils: B24 G9
Fees: (September 01) Day £13497

NW4

THE ALBANY COLLEGE
Hendry House, 413 Hendon Way, London NW4 3LJ
Tel: (020) 8202 0822
Head: Mr D R Murduck
Type: Co-educational Day 14–19
No of pupils: B120 G80
Fees: (September 01)
Day £4000 – £9000

ALBANY COLLEGE*
21/24 Queen's Road, Hendon, London NW4 2TL
Tel: (020) 8202 5965
Head: Mr R J Arthy
Type: Co-educational Day 14–18
No of pupils: B110 G90
Fees: (September 01)
Day £4000 – £9600

HENDON PREPARATORY SCHOOL
20 Tenterden Grove, Hendon, London NW4 1TD
Tel: (020) 8203 7727
Head: Mr J Gear
Type: Co-educational Day 2–13
No of pupils: B184 G88
Fees: (September 01)
Day £6090 – £7635

THE TUITION CENTRE
Lodge House, Lodge Road, London NW4 4DQ
Tel: (020) 8203 5025
Head: Mr B Canetti
Type: Co-educational Day 15+
No of pupils: B118 G107
Fees: (September 01)
Day £2300 – £10560

NW5

L'ILE AUX ENFANTS
22 Vicar's Road, London NW5 4NL
Tel: (020) 7267 7119
Head: Mr A Hadjadj
Type: Co-educational Day 3–11
No of pupils: 200
Fees: (September 01) On application

NW6

AL-SADIQ AND AL-ZAHRA SCHOOLS
134 Salusbury Road, London NW6 6PF
Tel: (020) 7372 6760
Head: Dr M Movahedi
Type: Co-educational Day 4–16
No of pupils: B181 G201
Fees: (September 01) On application

BROADHURST SCHOOL
19 Greencroft Gardens, London NW6 3LP
Tel: (020) 7328 4280
Head: Miss D Berkery
Type: Co-educational Day 2–11
No of pupils: B70 G70
Fees: (September 01)
Day £4290 – £7260

BRONDESBURY COLLEGE FOR BOYS
8 Brondesbury Park, London NW6 7BT
Tel: (020) 8830 4522
Head: Mr Dib
Type: Boys Day 11–16
No of pupils: 119
Fees: (September 01) Day £4800

ISLAMIA GIRLS SCHOOL
129 Salisbury Road, London NW6 6PE
Tel: (020) 7372 3472
Head: Mrs B K Jones
Type: Girls Day 11–16
No of pupils: 170
Fees: (September 01) On application

NAIMA JEWISH PREPARATORY SCHOOL
21 Andover Place, London NW6 5ED
Tel: (020) 7328 2802
Head: Mrs K Peters
Type: Co-educational Day 3–11
No of pupils: B86 G86
Fees: (September 01)
Day £4560 – £5685

RAINBOW MONTESSORI JUNIOR SCHOOL
13 Woodchurch Road, West Hampstead, London NW6 3PL
Tel: (020) 7328 8986
Head: Mrs L Madden
Type: Co-educational Day 5–16
No of pupils: 50
Fees: (September 01)
Day £4530 – £6375

RAINBOW MONTESSORI NURSERY SCHOOL
St James's Hall, Sherriff Road, West Hampstead, London NW6 2AP
Tel: (020) 7328 8986
Head: Mrs L Madden
Type: Co-educational Day 2–5
No of pupils: 24
Fees: (September 01)
Day £2625 – £3600

NW7

BELMONT (MILL HILL JUNIOR SCHOOL)
Mill Hill, London NW7 4ED
Tel: (020) 8959 1431
Head: Mr J R Hawkins
Type: Co-educational Day 7–13
No of pupils: B262 G133
Fees: (September 01) Day £8439

GOODWYN SCHOOL
Hammers Lane, Mill Hill, London NW7 4DB
Tel: (020) 8959 3756
Head: Mr S W E Robertson and Mr L Wadmore
Type: Co-educational Day 3–11
No of pupils: B118 G97
Fees: (September 01)
Day £2415 – £4974

MILL HILL SCHOOL*
The Ridgeway, Mill Hill, London NW7 1QS
Tel: (020) 8959 1221
Head: Mr W R Winfield
Type: Co-educational Boarding and Day 13–18
No of pupils: B462 G148
No of boarders: F167
Fees: (September 01)
FB £16125 – £16365 Day £10464

THE MOUNT SCHOOL*
Milespit Hill, Mill Hill, London NW7 2RX
Tel: (020) 8959 3403
Head: Mrs J K Jackson
Type: Girls Day 4–18
No of pupils: 370
Fees: (September 01)
Day £5010 – £5820

ST MARTIN'S
22 Goodwyn Avenue, Mill Hill, London NW7 3RG
Tel: (020) 8959 1965
Head: Mrs A Wilson
Type: Co-educational Day 3–11
No of pupils: B50 G85
Fees: (September 01)
Day £3150 – £3345

NW8

ABERCORN PLACE SCHOOL*
28 Abercorn Place, London NW8 9XP
Tel: (020) 7286 4785
Head: Mrs A S Greystoke
Type: Co-educational Day 2–13
No of pupils: B150 G150
Fees: (September 01)
Day £4305 – £8010

THE AMERICAN SCHOOL IN LONDON*
One Waverley Place, London NW8 0NP
Tel: (020) 7449 1200
Head: Dr W C Mules
Type: Co-educational Day 4–18
No of pupils: B630 G640
Fees: (September 01)
Day £12650 – £14750

ARNOLD HOUSE SCHOOL
1, Loudoun Road, St John's Wood, London NW8 0LH
Tel: (020) 7266 4840
Head: Mr N M Allen
Type: Boys Day 5–13
No of pupils: 250
Fees: (September 01) Day £8100

ST CHRISTINA'S RC PREPARATORY SCHOOL
25 St Edmunds Terrace, Regents Park, London NW8 7PY
Tel: (020) 7722 8784
Head: Sister Mary Corr
Type: Girls Day 3–11 (Boys 3–7)
No of pupils: B40 G180
Fees: (September 01) Day £4900

ST JOHNS WOOD PRE-PREPARATORY SCHOOL
St Johns Hall, Lords Roundabout, London NW8 7NE
Tel: (020) 7722 7149
Head: Miss P Brackenbury
Type: Co-educational Day 3–8
No of pupils: B57 G25
Fees: (September 01)
Day £3180 – £5985

NW9

GOWER HOUSE SCHOOL
Blackbird Hill, London NW9 8RR
Tel: (020) 8205 2509
Head: Mr M Keane
Type: Co-educational Day 2–11
No of pupils: B120 G110
Fees: (September 01)
Day £3585 – £4485

ST NICHOLAS SCHOOL
22 Salmon Street, London NW9 8PN
Tel: (020) 8205 7153
Head: Mrs A Gregory
Type: Co-educational Day 2–11
No of pupils: B40 G40
Fees: (September 01)
Day £1785 – £3555

NW10

WELSH SCHOOL OF LONDON
Welsh School of London, c/o Stonebridge Primary School, Shakespeare Avenue, London NW10 8NG
Tel: (020) 8965 3585
Head: Miss S Edwards
Type: Co-educational Day 4–11
No of pupils: 28
Fees: (September 01) Day £1500

NW11

GOLDERS HILL SCHOOL
666 Finchley Road, London
NW11 7NT
Tel: (020) 8455 2589
Head: Mrs A Eglash
Type: Co-educational Day 2–7
No of pupils: B110 G80
Fees: (September 01)
Day £3135 – £5685

THE KING ALFRED SCHOOL*
North End Road, London NW11 7HY
Tel: (020) 8457 5200
Head: Ms L Marsden
Type: Co-educational Day 4–18
No of pupils: B248 G251
Fees: (September 01)
Day £6150 – £8790

WENTWORTH TUTORIAL COLLEGE
6–10 Brentmead Place, London
NW11 9LH
Tel: (020) 8458 8524
Head: Mr A Davies
Type: Co-educational Day 14–18
No of pupils: 150
Fees: (September 01) On application

SE1

THE SCHILLER INTERNATIONAL SCHOOL
Royal Waterloo House, 51–55
Waterloo Road, London SE1 8TX
Tel: (020) 7928 1372
Head: Mr G Selby
Type: Co-educational Day 14–18
No of pupils: 40
Fees: (September 01)
Day £9635 – £9670

SE3

BLACKHEATH HIGH SCHOOL GDST
Vanbrugh Park, Blackheath, London
SE3 7AG
Tel: (020) 8853 2929
Head: Mrs E Laws
Type: Girls Day 3–18
No of pupils: 620
Fees: (September 01)
Day £3888 – £6624

BLACKHEATH PREPARATORY SCHOOL*
4 St Germans Place, Blackheath,
London SE3 0NJ
Tel: (020) 8858 0692
Head: Mrs E Cartwright and
Mrs J Wedgeworth
Type: Co-educational Day 3–11
No of pupils: B139 G131
Fees: (September 01)
Day £2340 – £5250

HEATH HOUSE PREPARATORY SCHOOL
37 Wemyss Road, Blackheath,
London SE3 0TG
Tel: (020) 8297 1900
Head: Mr I R Laslett
Type: Co-educational Day 4–11
No of pupils: B32 G33
Fees: (September 01)
Day £5085 – £5685

THE POINTER SCHOOL
19 Stratheden Road, Blackheath,
London SE3 7TH
Tel: (020) 8293 1331
Head: Mr R J S Higgins
Type: Co-educational Day 3–11
No of pupils: B80 G80
Fees: (September 01)
Day £1194 – £5349

SE6

ST DUNSTAN'S COLLEGE
Stanstead Road, Catford, London
SE6 4TY
Tel: (020) 8516 7200
Head: Mr D I Davies
Type: Co-educational Day 4–18
No of pupils: B959 G360
Fees: (September 01)
Day £5817 – £8022

SE9

ELTHAM COLLEGE
Grove Park Road, Mottingham,
London SE9 4QF
Tel: (020) 8857 1455
Head: Mr P J Henderson
Type: Boys Day and Boarding 7–18
(Co-ed VIth Form)
No of pupils: B740 G40
No of boarders: F5 W5
Fees: (September 01) FB £16659
WB £16609 Day £8064

ST OLAVE'S PREPARATORY SCHOOL
106–110 Southwood Road, New
Eltham, London SE9 3QS
Tel: (020) 8294 8930
Head: Miss M P Taylor
Type: Co-educational Day 3–11
No of pupils: B133 G74
Fees: (September 01)
Day £2208 – £5208

SE11

TOAD HALL MONTESSORI NURSERY SCHOOL
37 St Mary's Gardens, Kennington,
London SE11 4UF
Tel: (020) 7735 5087
Head: Mrs V K Rees
Type: Co-educational Day 2–5
No of pupils: 40
Fees: (September 01)
Day £2250 – £4530

SE12

COLFE'S SCHOOL
Horn Park Lane, London SE12 8AW
Tel: (020) 8852 2283
Head: Mr A H Chicken
Type: Boys Day 3–18 (Co-ed 3–14
and 16–18)
No of pupils: B920 G114
Fees: (September 01)
Day £5112 – £7632

RIVERSTON SCHOOL
63–69 Eltham Road, London
SE12 8UF
Tel: (020) 8318 4327
Head: Mr D M Lewis
Type: Co-educational Day 1–16
No of pupils: B215 G130
Fees: (September 01) On application

SE19

VIRGO FIDELIS CONVENT
Central Hill, Upper Norwood,
London SE19 1RS
Tel: (020) 8653 2169
Head: Mr J M Noronha
Type: Co-educational Day 3–11
No of pupils: B104 G145
Fees: (September 01)
Day £340 – £1460

SE21

DUCKS (DULWICH KINDERGARTEN & INFANTS SCHOOL)*
Eller Bank, 87 College Road, London
SE21 7HH
Tel: (020) 8693 1538
Head: Mrs F Johnstone
Type: Co-educational Day 3mths–7
No of pupils: 220
Fees: (September 01) £6285

DULWICH COLLEGE*
Dulwich Common, London
SE21 7LD
Tel: (020) 8299 9263
Head: Mr G G Able
Type: Boys Day and Boarding 7–18
No of pupils: 1450
No of boarders: F110 W20
Fees: (September 01) FB £17070
WB £16395 Day £8730

DULWICH COLLEGE PREPARATORY SCHOOL
42 Alleyn Park, Dulwich, London
SE21 7AA
Tel: (020) 8670 3217
Head: Mr G Marsh
Type: Boys Day and Boarding 3–13
(Girls 3–5)
No of pupils: B795 G14
No of boarders: W25
Fees: (September 01) WB £12675
Day £2664 – £8640

OAKFIELD PREPARATORY SCHOOL
125–128 Thurlow Park Road,
Dulwich, London SE21 8HP
Tel: (020) 8670 4206
Head: Mr B Wigglesworth
Type: Co-educational Day 2–11
No of pupils: B301 G260
Fees: (September 01)
Day £3120 – £4950

ROSEMEAD PREPARATORY SCHOOL*
70 Thurlow Park Road, London
SE21 8HZ
Tel: (020) 8670 5865
Head: Mrs R L Lait
Type: Co-educational Day 3–11
No of pupils: B135 G135
Fees: (September 01)
Day £3930 – £4560

SE22

ALLEYN'S SCHOOL
Townley Road, Dulwich, London
SE22 8SU
Tel: (020) 8557 1500
Head: Dr C H R Niven
Type: Co-educational Day 4–18
No of pupils: B544 G604
Fees: (September 01)
Day £6885 – £8055

JAMES ALLEN'S GIRLS' SCHOOL
East Dulwich Grove, London
SE22 8TE
Tel: (020) 8693 1181
Head: Mrs M Gibbs
Type: Girls Day 11–18
No of pupils: 770
Fees: (September 01)
Day £7704 – £7992

JAMES ALLEN'S PREPARATORY SCHOOL
East Dulwich Grove, London
SE22 8TE
Tel: (020) 8693 0374
Head: Mr P Heyworth
Type: Co-educational Day 4–11
No of pupils: B43 G256
Fees: (September 01) Day £6483

SE24

HERNE HILL SCHOOL
127 Herne Hill, London SE24 9LY
Tel: (020) 7274 6336
Head: Mrs V Tabone & Mrs P Bennett
Type: Co-educational Day 3–7
No of pupils: B135 G135
Fees: (September 01) Day £900 –
£2220

SE26

SYDENHAM HIGH SCHOOL GDST
19 Westwood Hill, London SE26 6BL
Tel: (020) 8 768 8000
Head: Dr D Lodge
Type: Girls Day 4–18
No of pupils: 650
Fees: (September 01)
Day £5145 – £6624

SW1

EATON HOUSE SCHOOL
3 and 5 Eaton Gate, Eaton Square,
London SW1W 9BA
Tel: (020) 7730 9343
Head: Miss L Watts
Type: Boys Day 4–9
No of pupils: 250
Fees: (September 01) Day £6900

EATON SQUARE SCHOOLS
79 Eccleston Square, London
SW1V 1PP
Tel: (020) 7931 9469
Head: Miss Y Cuthbert
Type: Co-educational Day Boys 2–13
Girls 2–11
No of pupils: B245 G225
Fees: (September 01)
Day £3360 – £8400

FRANCIS HOLLAND SCHOOL
39 Graham Terrace, London
SW1W 8JF
Tel: (020) 7730 2971
Head: Miss S Pattenden
Type: Girls Day 4–18
No of pupils: 440
Fees: (September 01) Day £8700

GARDEN HOUSE BOYS' SCHOOL*
28 Pont Street, London SW1X 0AB
Tel: (020) 7589 7708
Head: Mr S Poland and Mr M Giles
Type: Boys Day 4–8
No of pupils: 100
Fees: (September 01)
Day £4050 – £8850

GARDEN HOUSE GIRLS' SCHOOL*
49–53 Sloane Gardens, London
SW1W 8ED
Tel: (020) 7730 1652
Head: Mrs J Webb and Mrs W Challen
Type: Girls Day 4–11
No of pupils: 285
Fees: (September 01)
Day £4050 – £8850

HELLENIC COLLEGE OF LONDON
67 Pont Street, London SW1X 0BD
Tel: (020) 7581 5044
Head: Mr J Wardrobe
Type: Co-educational Day 2–18
No of pupils: B95 G95
Fees: (September 01)
Day £6099 – £7632

HILL HOUSE SCHOOL
17 Hans Place, London SW1X 0EP
Tel: (020) 7584 1331
Head: Lt Col H S Townend
Type: Co-educational Day Boys 4–13
Girls 4–11
No of pupils: B610 G395
Fees: (September 01)
Day £5200 – £6160

THE KNIGHTSBRIDGE KINDERGARTEN
St Peter's Church, 119 Eaton Square,
London SW1W 9AL
Tel: (020) 7371 2306
Head: Mrs B Delfgou
Type: Co-educational Day 2–5
No of pupils: 50
Fees: (September 01) On application

MISS MORLEY'S NURSERY SCHOOL
Mrs C Spence, 18a Maunsel Street,
London SW1P 2QN
Tel: (020) 7730 5797
Head: Mrs C Spence and Ms L Spence
Type: Co-educational Day 2–5
No of pupils: 42
Fees: (September 01)
Day £1800 – £2475

MORE HOUSE
22–24 Pont Street, Chelsea, London
SW1X 0AA
Tel: (020) 7235 2855
Head: Mrs L Falconer
Type: Girls Day 11–18
No of pupils: 220
Fees: (September 01) Day £7590

SUSSEX HOUSE SCHOOL
68 Cadogan Square, Chelsea,
London SW1X 0EA
Tel: (020) 7584 1741
Head: Mr N P Kaye
Type: Boys Day 8–13
No of pupils: 180
Fees: (September 01) Day £8685

THOMAS'S KINDERGARTEN
14 Ranelagh Grove, London
SW1W 8PD
Tel: (020) 7730 3596
Head: Miss A Warwick
Type: Co-educational Day 2–5
No of pupils: B27 G27
Fees: (September 01)
Day £2190 – £2700

WESTMINSTER ABBEY CHOIR SCHOOL
Dean's Yard, London SW1P 3NY
Tel: (020) 7222 6151
Head: Mr J Curtis
Type: Boys Boarding 8–13
No of pupils: 38
No of boarders: F38
Fees: (September 01) FB £3654

WESTMINSTER CATHEDRAL CHOIR SCHOOL
Ambrosden Avenue, London
SW1P 1QH
Tel: (020) 7798 9081
Head: Mr C Foulds
Type: Boys Boarding and Day 8–13
No of pupils: 100
No of boarders: F30
Fees: (September 01) FB £4170
Day £7950

WESTMINSTER SCHOOL
17 Dean's Yard, Westminster,
London SW1P 3PB
Tel: (020) 7963 1003
Head: Mr T Jones-Parry
Type: Boys Boarding and Day 13–18
(Co-ed VIth Form)
No of pupils: B581 G104
No of boarders: F190
Fees: (September 01) FB £17712
Day £12267

WESTMINSTER UNDER SCHOOL
Adrian House, 27 Vincent Square,
London SW1P 2NN
Tel: (020) 7821 5788
Head: Mr J P Edwards
Type: Boys Day 7–13
No of pupils: 270
Fees: (September 01) Day £8484

YOUNG ENGLAND KINDERGARTEN
St Saviour's Hall, St George's Square,
London SW1V 3QW
Tel: (020) 7834 3171
Head: Mrs K C King
Type: Co-educational Day 2–5
No of pupils: B38 G37
Fees: (September 01)
Day £1950 – £2880

SW3

CAMERON HOUSE
4 The Vale, Chelsea, London
SW3 6AH
Tel: (020) 7352 4040
Head: Miss F N Stack
Type: Co-educational Day 4–11
No of pupils: B53 G63
Fees: (September 01)
Day £7605 – £8025

JAMAHIRIYA SCHOOL
Glebe Place, London SW3 5JP
Tel: (020) 7352 6642
Head: Mr Alkawash
Type: Co-educational Day 5–17
No of pupils: B100 G100
Fees: (September 01) On application

SW4

EATON HOUSE THE MANOR
58 Clapham Common Northside,
London SW4 9RU
Tel: (020) 7924 6000
Head: Mr S Hepher and Mrs S C Grave
Type: Boys Day 2–13 (Girls 2–4)
No of pupils: B360 G30
Fees: (September 01)
Day £1320 – £7350

PARKGATE HOUSE SCHOOL
80 Clapham Common North Side,
London SW4 9SD
Tel: (020) 7350 2452
Head: Ms C Shanley
Type: Co-educational Day 2–11
No of pupils: B100 G100
Fees: (September 01)
Day £2550 – £6555

SW5

COLLINGHAM
23 Collingham Gardens, London
SW5 0HL
Tel: (020) 7244 7414
Head: Mr G Hattee
Type: Co-educational Day 14–20
No of pupils: B125 G115
Fees: (September 01)
Day £9780 – £12240

SW6

AL-MUNTADA ISLAMIC SCHOOL
7 Bridges Place, Parsons Green,
London SW6 4HW
Tel: (020) 7471 8283
Head: Mr Z Chehimi
Type: Co-educational Day 4–11
No of pupils: B83 G93
Fees: (September 01) Day £1650

ERIDGE HOUSE
1 Fulham Park Road, Fulham,
London SW6 4LH
Tel: 020 7385 7173
Head: Mrs L Waring
Type: Co-educational Day 5–8
Fees: (September 01)
Day £3000 – £6600

FULHAM PREP SCHOOL
47A Fulham High Street, London
SW6 3JJ
Tel: (020) 7371 9911
Head: Mrs J Emmett
Type: Co-educational Day 5–13
No of pupils: B120 G120
Fees: (September 01)
Day £6300 – £6750

KENSINGTON PREP SCHOOL
596 Fulham Road, London SW6 5PA
Tel: (020) 7731 9300
Head: Mrs G M Lumsdon
Type: Girls Day 4–11
No of pupils: 280
Fees: (September 01) Day £6300

L'ECOLE DES PETITS
2 Hazlebury Road, London SW6 2NB
Tel: (020) 7371 8350
Head: Mrs M Otten
Type: Co-educational Day 2–6
No of pupils: B60 G65
Fees: (September 01)
Day £2970 – £4185

RISING STAR MONTESSORI SCHOOL
St Clement Church Hall, 286
Fulham Palace Road, London
SW6 6HP
Tel: (020) 7381 3511
Head: Mrs H Casson
Type: Co-educational Day 2–5
No of pupils: 24
Fees: (September 01) Day £720

SINCLAIR HOUSE SCHOOL
159 Munster Road, Fulham, London
SW6 6AD
Tel: (020) 7736 9182
Head: Mrs E A Sinclair-House
Type: Co-educational Day 2–8
No of pupils: B28 G23
Fees: (September 01)
Day £2600 – £5550

TWICE TIMES MONTESSORI SCHOOL
The Cricket Pavilion, South Park,
London SW6 3AF
Tel: (020) 7731 4929
Head: Mrs S Henderson
Type: Co-educational Day 2–5
No of pupils: B25 G25
Fees: (September 01) On application

SW7

DUFF MILLER
59 Queen's Gate, London SW7 5JP
Tel: (020) 7225 0577
Head: Mr C Denning
Type: Co-educational Day 14–18
No of pupils: B85 G85
Fees: (September 01)
Day £4095 – £10500

FALKNER HOUSE
19 Brechin Place, London SW7 4QB
Tel: (020) 7373 4501
Head: Mrs A Griggs
Type: Girls Day 3–11 (Co-ed 3–4)
No of pupils: B10 G170
Fees: (September 01) Day £8250

GLENDOWER PREPARATORY SCHOOL
87 Queen's Gate, South Kensington,
London SW7 5JX
Tel: (020) 7370 1927
Head: Mrs B Humber
Type: Girls Day 4–11
No of pupils: 185
Fees: (September 01) Day £6825

THE HAMPSHIRE SCHOOLS (KNIGHTSBRIDGE UNDER SCHOOL)
5 Wetherby Place, London SW7 4NX
Tel: (020) 7584 3297
Head: Mr A G Bray
Type: Co-educational Day 3–6
No of pupils: B45 G45
Fees: (September 01)
Day £3075 – £6285

THE HAMPSHIRE SCHOOLS (KNIGHTSBRIDGE UPPER SCHOOL)
63 Ennismore Gardens, London
SW7 1NH
Tel: (020) 7584 3297
Head: Mr A G Bray
Type: Co-educational Day 6–11
No of pupils: B56 G56
Fees: (September 01)
Day £6615 – £8520

LYCEE FRANCAIS CHARLES DE GAULLE
35 Cromwell Road, London
SW7 2DG
Tel: (020) 7584 6322
Head: Mr A Becherand
Type: Co-educational Day 4–19
No of pupils: 3115
Fees: (September 01)
Day £2541 – £4038

MANDER PORTMAN WOODWARD
24 Elvaston Place, London SW7 5NL
Tel: (020) 7584 8555
Head: Mr J Gilseman & S Boyes
Type: Co-educational Day 14–19
No of pupils: 400
Fees: (September 01)
Day £2436 – £12756

QUEEN'S GATE SCHOOL*
133 Queen's Gate, Kensington,
London SW7 5LE
Tel: (020) 7589 3587
Head: Mrs A M Holyoak
Type: Girls Day 4–18
No of pupils: 390
Fees: (September 01)
Day £6150 – £7950

ST NICHOLAS PREPARATORY SCHOOL
23 Prince's Gate, London SW7 1PT
Tel: (020) 7225 1277
Head: Mr D Wilson
Type: Co-educational Day 3–13
No of pupils: B125 G125
Fees: (September 01)
Day £3972 – £6375

ST PHILIP'S SCHOOL
6 Wetherby Place, London SW7 4ND
Tel: (020) 7373 3944
Head: Mr H Biggs-Davison
Type: Boys Day 7–13
No of pupils: 111
Fees: (September 01) Day £6900

THE VALE SCHOOL
2 Elvaston Place, London SW7 5QH
Tel: (020) 7924 6000
Head: Miss S Calder
Type: Co-educational Day 4–11
No of pupils: B50 G50
Fees: (September 01) Day £6900

WESTMINSTER TUTORS*
86 Old Brompton Road, London
SW7 3LQ
Tel: (020) 7584 1288
Head: Mr P C Brooke and
Mr J J Layland
Type: Co-educational Day 16–19
No of pupils: B60 G60
Fees: (September 01)
Day £3675 – £10650

SW8

NEWTON PREP
149 Battersea Park Road, London
SW8 4BX
Tel: (020) 7720 4091
Head: Mr R G Dell
Type: Co-educational Day 3–13
No of pupils: B259 G230
Fees: (September 01)
Day £3765 – £7530

THE WILLOW SCHOOL
c/o Clapham Baptist Church,
823–825 Wandsworth Road, London
SW8 3JL
Tel: (020) 7498 0319
Head: Miss H Irvine
Type: Co-educational Day 2–5
No of pupils: 38
Fees: (September 01)
Day £2490 – £2850

SW10

THE BOLTONS NURSERY SCHOOL
262b Fulham Road, London
SW10 9EL
Tel: (020) 7351 6993
Head: Miss N Goelz
Type: Co-educational Day 2–5
No of pupils: 32
Fees: (September 01)
Day £2700 – £5505

CHELSEA KINDERGARTEN
St Andrews Church, Park Walk,
Chelsea, London SW10 0AU
Tel: (020) 7352 4856
Head: Mrs S Stevens
Type: Co-educational Day 2–5
No of pupils: B22 G22
Fees: (September 01)
Day £3240 – £5400

PAINT POTS MONTESSORI SCHOOL CHELSEA
Chelsea Christian Centre, Edith
Grove, London SW10 0LB
Tel: (020) 7376 4571
Head: Ms G Hood
Type: Co-educational Day 2–5
No of pupils: 51
Fees: (September 01)
Day £1500 – £5070

REDCLIFFE SCHOOL*
47 Redcliffe Gardens, London
SW10 9JH
Tel: (020) 7352 9247
Head: Miss R E Cunnah
Type: Co-educational Day Boys 4–8
Girls 4–11
No of pupils: B33 G67
Fees: (September 01)
Day £3750 – £6750

SW11

DOLPHIN SCHOOL
Northcote Road Baptist Church, 106
Northcote Road, London SW11 6QP
Tel: (020) 7924 3472
Head: Mrs S Rogers
Type: Co-educational Day 4–11
No of pupils: B46 G38
Fees: (September 01)
Day £4950 – £5250

THE DOMINIE
142 Battersea Park Road, London
SW11 4NB
Tel: (020) 7720 8783
Head: Mrs L Robertson
Type: Co-educational Day 6–13
No of pupils: B22 G10
Fees: (September 01) Day £11400

EMANUEL SCHOOL
Battersea Rise, London SW11 1HS
Tel: (020) 8870 4171
Head: Mrs A Sutcliffe
Type: Co-educational Day 10–18
No of pupils: B579 G161
Fees: (September 01)
Day £7743 – £8073

NORTHCOTE LODGE*
26 Bolingbroke Grove, London
SW11 6EL
Tel: (020) 7924 7170
Head: Mr P Cheeseman
Type: Boys Day 8–13
No of pupils: 150
Fees: (September 01)
Day £7500 – £8700

THE PARK KINDERGARTEN
St Saviours' Church, 351 Battersea
Park Road, London SW11 4LH
Tel: (020) 8772 0181
Head: Miss L N Nielsen
Type: Co-educational Day 2–5
No of pupils: 30
Fees: (September 01) On application

SOUTH LONDON MONTESSORI SCHOOL
Trott Street, Battersea, London
SW11 3DS
Tel: (020) 7738 9546
Head: Mrs J Martin
Type: Co-educational Day 2–12
No of pupils: B22 G15
Fees: (September 01)
Day £2400 – £5100

THOMAS'S KINDERGARTEN, BATTERSEA
The Crypt, Saint Mary's Church,
Battersea Church Road, London
SW11 3NA
Tel: (020) 7738 0400
Head: Mrs P Smith
Type: Co-educational Day 2–5
No of pupils: B25 G25
Fees: (September 01)
Day £2190 – £2700

THOMAS'S PREPARATORY SCHOOL
28–40 Battersea High Street, London
SW11 3JB
Tel: (020) 7978 0900
Head: Mr B V R Thomas
Type: Co-educational Day 4–13
No of pupils: B267 G219
Fees: (September 01)
Day £7098 – £8310

THOMAS'S PREPARATORY SCHOOL CLAPHAM
Broomwood Road, London SW11 6JZ
Tel: (020) 7326 9300
Head: Mrs P Evelegh
Type: Co-educational Day 4–13
No of pupils: B233 G247
Fees: (September 01)
Day £6030 – £8310

SW12

BALHAM PREPARATORY SCHOOL
47a Balham High Road, London
SW12 9AW
Tel: (020) 8675 7747
Head: Mr K Bahauddin
Type: Co-educational Day 3–16
No of pupils: 360
Fees: (September 01) On application

BROOMWOOD HALL SCHOOL*

74 Nightingale Lane, London SW12 8NR
Tel: (020) 8673 1616
Head: Mrs K A H Colquhoun
Type: Co-educational Day Boys 4–8
Girls 4–13
No of pupils: B165 G225
Fees: (September 01) On application

HORNSBY HOUSE SCHOOL

Hearnville Road, London SW12 8RS
Tel: (020) 8673 7573
Head: Mrs J Strong
Type: Co-educational Day 3–11
No of pupils: B142 G115
Fees: (September 01)
Day £2625 – £6933

THE WHITE HOUSE PREP & WOODENTOPS KINDERGARTEN

24 Thornton Road, Clapham Park,
London SW12 0LF
Tel: (020) 8674 9514
Head: Mrs E Davies
Type: Co-educational Day 2–11
No of pupils: B60 G60
Fees: (September 01)
Day £2000 – £6000

SW13

THE HARRODIAN SCHOOL

Lonsdale Road, London SW13 9QN
Tel: (020) 8748 6117
Head: Mr J R Hooke
Type: Co-educational Day 5–16
No of pupils: 570
Fees: (September 01)
Day £6900 – £8850

MONTESSORI PAVILION SCHOOL

Vine Road, Recreation Ground,
London SW13 0NE
Tel: (020) 8878 9695
Head: Ms G Dashwood
Type: Co-educational Day 3–5
No of pupils: 30
Fees: (September 01) Day £2355

ST PAUL'S PREPARATORY SCHOOL

Colet Court, Lonsdale Road, London
SW13 9JT
Tel: (020) 8748 3461
Head: Mr G J Thompson
Type: Boys Day and Boarding 7–13
No of pupils: 442
Fees: (September 01) WB £8670
Day £8670

ST PAUL'S SCHOOL

Lonsdale Road, Barnes, London
SW13 9JT
Tel: (020) 8748 9162
Head: Mr R S Baldock
Type: Boys Day and Boarding 13–18
No of pupils: 818
No of boarders: W35
Fees: (September 01) F/WB £16485
Day £11085

SW14

TOWER HOUSE SCHOOL

188 Sheen Lane, London SW14 8LF
Tel: (020) 8876 3323
Head: Mr J D T Wall
Type: Boys Day 4–13
No of pupils: 186
Fees: (September 01)
Day £6690 – £6870

SW15

HURLINGHAM PRIVATE SCHOOL

95 & 97 Deodar Road, Putney,
London SW15 2NU
Tel: (020) 8874 7186
Head: Mrs D Baker
Type: Co-educational Day Boys 4–8
Girls 4–11
No of pupils: B50 G70
Fees: (September 01)
Day £5460 – £5970

IBSTOCK PLACE SCHOOL

Clarence Lane, Roehampton,
London SW15 5PY
Tel: (020) 8876 9991
Head: Mrs A Sylvester Johnson
Type: Co-educational Day 3–16
No of pupils: B319 G331
Fees: (September 01)
Day £2610 – £7140

LION HOUSE SCHOOL

The Old Methodist Hall, Gwendolen
Avenue, London SW15 6EH
Tel: (020) 8780 9446
Head: Miss H J Luard
Type: Co-educational Day 3–8
No of pupils: B51 G54
Fees: (September 01)
Day £650 – £1800

THE MERLIN SCHOOL

4 Carlton Drive, Putney Hill,
London SW15 2BZ
Tel: (020) 8788 2769
Head: Mrs J Addis
Type: Co-educational Day 4–8
No of pupils: 170
Fees: (September 01) On application

PROSPECT HOUSE SCHOOL

75 Putney Hill, London SW15 3NT
Tel: (020) 8780 0456
Head: Mr B H Evans and Mrs Gerry
Type: Co-educational Day 3–11
No of pupils: B100 G100
Fees: (September 01)
Day £1035 – £2300

PUTNEY HIGH SCHOOL

35 Putney Hill, London SW15 6BH
Tel: (020) 8788 4886
Head: Mrs E Merchant
Type: Girls Day 4–18
No of pupils: 790
Fees: (September 01)
Day £5145 – £6624

PUTNEY PARK SCHOOL

Woodborough Road, London
SW15 6PY
Tel: (020) 8788 8316
Head: Mrs J Irving
Type: Girls Day 4–16 (Boys 4–11)
No of pupils: B150 G220
Fees: (September 01)
Day £5760 – £6660

SW16

FLAMES ACADEMY

16–16a Wellfield Road, London
SW16 2BP
Tel: (020) 8769 3500
Head: Mr A Andrews
Type: Co-educational Day 7–16
No of pupils: 50
Fees: (September 01)
Day £3885 – £4485

STREATHAM AND CLAPHAM HIGH SCHOOL

42 Abbotswood Road, London
SW16 1AW
Tel: (020) 8677 8400
Head: Miss G M Ellis
Type: Girls Day 3–18 (Boys 3–5)
No of pupils: B5 G802
Fees: (September 01)
Day £5145 – £6624

WALDORF SCHOOL OF SOUTH WEST LONDON

Woodfields, between 16 & 18
Abbottswood Road, London
SW16 1AP
Tel: (020) 8769 6587
Head: Ms U Wooge and Ms J Yulke
Type: Co-educational Day 4–14
No of pupils: B70 G52
Fees: (September 01) On application

SW17

EVELINE DAY SCHOOL
14 Trinity Crescent, Upper Tooting,
London SW17 7AE
Tel: (020) 8672 4673
Head: Ms E Drut
Type: Co-educational Day 3–11
No of pupils: B34 G41
Fees: (September 01)
Day £6761 – £7956

FINTON HOUSE SCHOOL
171 Trinity Road, London SW17 7HL
Tel: (020) 8682 0921
Head: Miss E Thornton
Type: Co-educational Day 4–11
No of pupils: B119 G187
Fees: (September 01)
Day £6450 – £7290

RED BALLOON NURSERY
St Mary Magdalene Church Hall,
Trinity Road, London SW17 7SD
Tel: (020) 8672 4711
Head: Miss C Larkin
Type: Co-educational Day 2–5
No of pupils: 96
Fees: (September 01)
Day £2490 – £2550

THE HEADSTART MONTESSORI NURSERY SCHOOL
St Mary's Church Road, 46
Wimbledon Road, London
SW17 0UQ
Tel: (020) 8947 7359
Head: Ms B Maryth
Type: Co-educational Day 2–5
No of pupils: 24
Fees: (September 01)
Day £1800 – £3960

SW18

HIGHFIELD SCHOOL
256 Trinity Road, Wandsworth
Common, London SW18 3RQ
Tel: (020) 8874 2778
Head: Mrs V J Lowe
Type: Co-educational Day 2–11
No of pupils: B41 G33
Fees: (September 01)
Day £2595 – £5535

THE ROCHE SCHOOL
11 Frogmore, Wandsworth, London
SW18 1HW
Tel: (020) 8877 0823
Head: Dr J Roche
Type: Co-educational Day 3–11
No of pupils: B111 G115
Fees: (September 01)
Day £5430 – £6015

SW19

KING'S COLLEGE JUNIOR SCHOOL
Southside, Wimbledon Common,
London SW19 4TT
Tel: (020) 8255 5335
Head: Mr J A Evans
Type: Boys Day 7–13
No of pupils: 465
Fees: (September 01)
Day £7950 – £9930

KING'S COLLEGE SCHOOL
Wimbledon Common, London
SW19 4TT
Tel: (020) 8255 5300
Head: Mr A C V Evans
Type: Boys Day 13–18
No of pupils: 720
Fees: (September 01) Day £9930

PLAYDAYS NURSERY/ SCHOOL AND MONTESSORI COLLEGE
58 Queens Road, Wimbledon,
London SW19 8LR
Tel: (020) 8946 8139
Head: Ms C Zampalo
Type: Co-educational Day 0–5
No of pupils: B22 G22
Fees: (September 01)
Day £8839 – £10087

THE STUDY PREPARATORY SCHOOL
Camp Road, Wimbledon Common,
London SW19 4UN
Tel: (020) 8947 6969
Head: Mrs L Bond
Type: Girls Day 4–11
No of pupils: 335
Fees: (September 01)
Day £5505 – £6255

WILLINGTON SCHOOL
Worcester Road, Wimbledon,
London SW19 7QQ
Tel: (020) 8944 7020
Head: Mrs R Bowman
Type: Boys Day 4–13
No of pupils: 210
Fees: (September 01)
Day £4740 – £5370

WIMBLEDON COLLEGE PREP SCHOOL
Donhead Lodge, 33 Edge Hill,
Wimbledon, London SW19 4NP
Tel: (020) 8946 7000
Head: Mr G C McGrath
Type: Boys Day 7–13
No of pupils: 295
Fees: (September 01) Day £4188

WIMBLEDON HIGH SCHOOL
Mansel Road, London SW19 4AB
Tel: (020) 8971 0900
Head: Mrs P H Wilkes
Type: Girls Day 4–18
No of pupils: 900
Fees: (September 01)
Day £5145 – £6624

SW20

THE HALL SCHOOL WIMBLEDON
17 The Downs, Wimbledon, London
SW20 8HF
Tel: (020) 8879 9200
Head: Mr T Hobbs and Mr J Hobbs
Type: Co-educational Day 3–16
No of pupils: B350 G300
Fees: (September 01) On application

THE NORWEGIAN SCHOOL
28 Arterberry Road, Wimbledon,
London SW20 8AH
Tel: (020) 8947 6617/6627
Head: Mrs S Hopland
Type: Co-educational Day 3–16
No of pupils: 101
Fees: (September 01)
Day £4900 – £7000

THE ROWANS SCHOOL
19 Drax Avenue, Wimbledon,
London SW20 0EG
Tel: (020) 8946 8220
Head: Mrs J Anderson
Type: Co-educational Day 3–8
No of pupils: B75 G50
Fees: (September 01)
Day £2220 – £4290

URSULINE CONVENT PREPARATORY SCHOOL
18 The Downs, London SW20 8HR
Tel: (020) 8947 0859
Head: Mrs C Grogan
Type: Girls Day 3–11 (Boys 3–7)
No of pupils: B76 G172
Fees: (September 01)
Day £2280 – £3855

W1

GREAT BEGINNINGS MONTESSORI SCHOOL
82a Chiltern Street, Marylebone, London W1U 5AQ
Tel: (020) 7486 2276
Head: Mrs W Innes
Type: Co-educational Day 2–6
No of pupils: B25 G25
Fees: (September 01) On application

LONDON MONTESSORI CENTRE LTD
18 Balderton Street, London W1Y 1TG
Tel: (020) 7493 0165
Head: Mrs S Adams
Type: Co-educational Day 2–5
No of pupils: 30
Fees: (September 01) On application

PORTLAND PLACE SCHOOL
56–58 Portland Place, London W1B 1NJ
Tel: (020) 7307 8700
Head: Mr R Walker
Type: Co-educational Day 11–18
No of pupils: B130 G90
Fees: (September 01)
Day £7920 – £8700

QUEEN'S COLLEGE*
43–49 Harley Street, London W1N 2BT
Tel: (020) 7291 7000
Head: Miss M M Connell
Type: Girls Day 11–18
No of pupils: 380
Fees: (September 01) Day £8445

W2

ALBEMARLE INDEPENDENT COLLEGE*
6–7 Inverness Mews, Bayswater, London W2 3JQ
Tel: (020) 7221 7271
Head: Ms B Mellon and Mr J Eytle
Type: Co-educational Day 16–19
No of pupils: B63 G57
Fees: (September 01)
Day £8250 – £10500

CONNAUGHT HOUSE
47 Connaught Square, London W2 2HL
Tel: (020) 7262 8830
Head: Mr F Hampton and Mrs J A Hampton
Type: Co-educational Day 4–11
No of pupils: B35 G35
Fees: (September 01)
Day £5175 – £7950

DAVIES LAING AND DICK INDEPENDENT VI FORM COLLEGE*
10 Pembridge Square, London W2 4ED
Tel: (020) 7727 2797
Head: Ms E Rickards
Type: Co-educational Day 14–21
No of pupils: B192 G193
Fees: (September 01)
Day £4500 – £12249

DR ROLFE'S MONTESSORI SCHOOL
10 Pembridge Square, London W2 4ED
Tel: (020) 7727 8300
Head: Miss A Arnold
Type: Co-educational Day 2–5
No of pupils: 65
Fees: (September 01)
Day £2850 – £5100

THE HAMPSHIRE SCHOOLS (KENSINGTON GARDENS)
9 Queensborough Terrace, London W2 3TB
Tel: (020) 7229 7065
Head: Mr A G Bray
Type: Co-educational Day 4–13
No of pupils: B80 G80
Fees: (September 01)
Day £5640 – £8055

LANSDOWNE SIXTH FORM COLLEGE
40–44 Bark Place, London W2 4AT
Tel: (020) 7616 4400
Head: Mr H Templeton
Type: Co-educational Day 15–19
No of pupils: B110 G95
Fees: (September 01)
Day £1950 – £10500

PAINT POTS MONTESSORI SCHOOL
Bayswater United Reformed Church, Newton Road, London W2 5LS
Tel: (020) 7376 4571
Head: Miss G Hood
Type: Co-educational Day 2–5
No of pupils: 40
Fees: (September 01) On application

PEMBRIDGE HALL
18 Pembridge Square, London W2 4EH
Tel: (020) 7229 0121
Head: Mrs E Marsden
Type: Girls Day 4–11
No of pupils: 250
Fees: (September 01) Day £7605

RAVENSTONE HOUSE PRE-PREPARATORY AND NURSERY
The Long Garden, Albion Street, Marble Arch, London W2 2AX
Tel: (020) 7262 1190
Head: Mrs A Saunders
Type: Co-educational Day 0–7
No of pupils: B50 G50
Fees: (September 01) On application

TODDLERS AND MUMS MONTESSORI
St Stephens Church, Westbourne Park Road, London W2 5QT
Tel: 020 7402 1084
Head: Mrs M Molavi
Type: Co-educational Day 2–5
No of pupils: B11 G11
Fees: (September 01)
Day £2160 – £2985

WETHERBY SCHOOL
11 Pembridge Square, London W2 4ED
Tel: (020) 7727 9581
Head: Mrs J Aviss
Type: Boys Day 4–8
No of pupils: 172
Fees: (September 01) Day £7530

W3

BARBARA SPEAKE STAGE SCHOOL
East Acton Lane, London W3 7EG
Tel: (020) 8743 1306
Head: Mr D R Speake
Type: Co-educational Day 4–16
No of pupils: B60 G95
Fees: (September 01)
Day £2700 – £3000

EALING MONTESSORI SCHOOL
St Martins Church Hall, Hale Gardens, London W3 9SQ
Tel: (020) 8992 4513
Head: Mrs P Jaffer
Type: Co-educational Day 2–6
No of pupils: B12 G24
Fees: (September 01)
Day £2280 – £3480

INTERNATIONAL SCHOOL OF LONDON*
139 Gunnersbury Avenue, London W3 8LG
Tel: (020) 8992 5823
Head: Mrs E Whelen
Type: Co-educational Day 4–18
No of pupils: B165 G123
Fees: (September 01)
Day £8450 – £12450

THE JAPANESE SCHOOL
87 Creffield Road, Acton, London
W3 9PU
Tel: (020) 8993 7145
Head: Mr K Yamada
Type: Co-educational Day 6–15
No of pupils: B320 G260
Fees: (September 01) Day £1560

KING FAHAD ACADEMY
Bromyard Avenue, East Acton,
London W3 7HD
Tel: (020) 8743 0131
Head: Dr A Al-Ghamdi
Type: Co-educational Day 5–18
No of pupils: B510 G490
Fees: (September 01) On application

W4

THE ARTS EDUCATIONAL SCHOOL*
Cone Ripman House, 14 Bath Road,
Chiswick, London W4 1LY
Tel: (020) 8987 6600
Head: Mr T Sampson
Type: Co-educational Day 8–18
No of pupils: B23 G92
Fees: (September 01)
Day £4836 – £7245

CATERPILLAR MONTESSORI NURSERY SCHOOL
The Green Hall, St Albans Church,
South Parade, Chiswick, London W4
Tel: (020) 8747 8531
Head: Ms A Scott
Type: Co-educational Day 2–5
No of pupils: 70
Fees: (September 01) On application

CHISWICK AND BEDFORD PARK PREPARATORY SCHOOL
Priory House, Priory Avenue,
Bedford Park, London W4 1TX
Tel: (020) 8994 1804
Head: Mrs M B Morrow
Type: Co-educational Day Boys 4–8
Girls 4–11
No of pupils: B70 G115
Fees: (September 01)
Day £4620 – £5550

ELMWOOD MONTESSORI SCHOOL
St Michaels Centre, Elmwood Road,
London W4 3DY
Tel: (020) 8994 8177
Head: Mrs S Herbert
Type: Co-educational Day 2–5
No of pupils: B20 G20
Fees: (September 01) On application

THE FALCONS PRE-PREPARATORY SCHOOL
2 Burnaby Gardens, Chiswick,
London W4 3DT
Tel: (020) 8747 8393
Head: Miss L Wall
Type: Boys Day 3–8
No of pupils: 202
Fees: (September 01)
Day £3000 – £6900

MEADOWS MONTESSORI SCHOOL
Dukes Meadows Community Centre,
Alexandra Gardens, London W4 2TD
Tel: (020) 8742 1327 & (020)
8995 2621
Head: Mrs S Herbert
Type: Co-educational Day 2–5
No of pupils: B20 G20
Fees: (September 01) On application

ORCHARD HOUSE SCHOOL
16 Newton Grove, Bedford Park,
London W4 1LB
Tel: (020) 8742 8544
Head: Mrs S A B Hobbs
Type: Co-educational Day Boys 3–8
Girls 3–11
No of pupils: B80 G140
Fees: (September 01)
Day £3450 – £7350

W5

ASTON HOUSE SCHOOL
1 Aston Road, Ealing, London
W5 2RL
Tel: (020) 8566 7300
Head: Mrs J Lawson
Type: Co-educational Day 2–11
No of pupils: B65 G65
Fees: (September 01)
Day £4260 – £5430

CLIFTON LODGE PREPARATORY SCHOOL*
8 Mattock Lane, Ealing, London
W5 5BG
Tel: (020) 8579 3662
Head: Mr D A P Blumlein
Type: Boys Day 4–13
No of pupils: 180
Fees: (September 01)
Day £4900 – £5350

DURSTON HOUSE
12–14–26 Castlebar Road, Ealing,
London W5 2DR
Tel: (020) 8991 6532
Head: Mr P D Craze
Type: Boys Day 4–13
No of pupils: 430
Fees: (September 01)
Day £6300 – £8100

EALING TUTORIAL COLLEGE
83 New Broadway, Ealing, London
W5 5AL
Tel: (020) 8579 6668
Head: Dr A Clamp
Type: Co-educational Day 16–25
No of pupils: B55 G55
No of boarders: F15
Fees: (September 01) Day £6450

THE FALCONS SCHOOL FOR GIRLS
15 Gunnersbury Avenue, Ealing,
London W5 3XD
Tel: (020) 8992 5189
Head: Miss L Wall
Type: Girls Day 4–11
No of pupils: 107
Fees: (September 01)
Day £2250 – £5550

HARVINGTON SCHOOL
20 Castlebar Road, Ealing, London
W5 2DS
Tel: (020) 8997 1583
Head: Dr F Meek
Type: Girls Day 3–16 (Boys 3–5)
No of pupils: B14 G204
Fees: (September 01)
Day £4170 – £5415

ST AUGUSTINE'S PRIORY
Hillcrest Road, Ealing, London
W5 2JL
Tel: (020) 8997 2022
Head: Mrs F Gumley-Mason
Type: Girls Day 4–18
No of pupils: 480
Fees: (September 01)
Day £4065 – £5925

ST BENEDICT'S JUNIOR SCHOOL
5 Montpelier Avenue, Ealing,
London W5 2XP
Tel: (020) 8862 2050
Head: Mr D A McSweeney
Type: Boys Day 4–11
No of pupils: 240
Fees: (September 01)
Day £6210 – £6800

ST BENEDICT'S SCHOOL
54 Eaton Rise, Ealing, London
W5 2ES
Tel: (020) 8862 2000
Head: Mr C Cleugh
Type: Boys Day 11–18 (Co-ed VIth
Form)
No of pupils: B526 G28
Fees: (September 01) Day £7200

W6

BUTE HOUSE PREPARATORY
SCHOOL FOR GIRLS
Luxemburg Gardens, London
W6 7EA
Tel: (020) 7603 7381
Head: Mrs S Salvidant
Type: Girls Day 4–11
No of pupils: 310
Fees: (September 01) Day £6870

ECOLE FRANCAISE JACQUES
PREVERT
59 Brook Green, London W6 7BE
Tel: (020) 7602 6871
Head: Mr P Trividic
Type: Co-educational Day 4–11
No of pupils: B136 G128
Fees: (September 01)
Day £2971 – £2981

THE GODOLPHIN AND
LATYMER SCHOOL
Iffley Road, Hammersmith, London
W6 0PG
Tel: (020) 8741 1936
Head: Miss M Rudland
Type: Girls Day 11–18
No of pupils: 707
Fees: (September 01) Day £7380

THE JORDANS NURSERY
SCHOOL
Lower Hall, Holy Innocents Church,
Paddenswick Road, London W6 0UB
Tel: (020) 8741 3230
Head: Mrs S Jordan
Type: Co-educational Day 2–5
No of pupils: 50
Fees: (September 01)
Day £2250 – £2715

LATYMER PREPARATORY
SCHOOL*
36 Upper Mall, Hammersmith,
London W6 9TA
Tel: (020) 8748 0303
Head: Mr S P Dorrian
Type: Boys Day 7–11
No of pupils: 144
Fees: (September 01) Day £8100

LATYMER UPPER SCHOOL*
King Street, Hammersmith, London
W6 9LR
Tel: (020) 8741 1851
Head: Mr C Diggory
Type: Boys Day 7–18 (Co-ed VIth
Form)
No of pupils: 1120
Fees: (September 01) Day £8850

LE HERISSON
c/o The Methodist Church,
Rivercourt Road, Hammersmith,
London W6 9JT
Tel: (020) 8563 7664
Head: Ms B Rios
Type: Co-educational Day 2–6
No of pupils: 64
Fees: (September 01)
Day £3000 – £4440

RAVENSCOURT PARK
PREPARATORY SCHOOL
16 Ravenscourt Avenue, London
W6 0SL
Tel: (020) 8846 9153
Head: Mrs M Gardener
Type: Co-educational Day 4–11
No of pupils: B128 G134
Fees: (September 01) Day £6825

RAVENSCOURT THEATRE
SCHOOL
Tandy House, 30–40 Dalling Road,
London W6 0JB
Tel: (020) 8741 0707
Head: Rev R D Blakeley
Type: Co-educational Day 7–16
No of pupils: B43 G41
Fees: (September 01) Day £1500

THE ROSE MONTESSORI
NURSERY SCHOOL
St Alban's Church Hall, Margravine
Road, London W6
Tel: (020) 7381 6002
Head: Ms M Deniya
Type: Co-educational Day 2–5
No of pupils: B12 G12
Fees: (September 01) On application

ST PAUL'S GIRLS' SCHOOL
Brook Green, London W6 7BS
Tel: (020) 7603 2288
Head: Miss E Diggory
Type: Girls Day 11–18
No of pupils: 670
Fees: (September 01) Day £8823

W7

MANOR HOUSE SCHOOL
16 Golden Manor, Hanwell, London
W7 3EG
Tel: (020) 8567 4101
Head: Mr J Carpenter
Type: Co-educational Day 2–11
No of pupils: B100 G70
Fees: (September 01) On application

W8

ASHBOURNE INDEPENDENT
SIXTH FORM COLLEGE*
17 Old Court Place, London W8 4PL
Tel: (020) 7937 3858
Head: Mr M J Hatchard-Kirby and
S J Cook
Type: Co-educational Day 16–19
No of pupils: B90 G60
Fees: (September 01)
Day £10800 – £12000

ASHBOURNE MIDDLE
SCHOOL*
17 Old Court Place, London W8 4PL
Tel: (020) 7937 3858
Head: Mr M J Hatchard-Kirby and
S J Cook
Type: Co-educational Day 14–16
No of pupils: B25 G25
Fees: (September 01)
Day £10600 – £12750

HAWKESDOWN HOUSE
SCHOOL*
27 Edge Street, Kensington, London
W8 7PN
Tel: (020) 7727 9090
Head: Mrs C J Leslie
Type: Boys Day 3–8
No of pupils: 150
Fees: (September 01)
Day £6375 – £7185

THOMAS'S PREPARATORY
SCHOOL
17–19 Cottesmore Gardens, London
W8 5PR
Tel: (020) 7361 6500
Head: Mrs D Maine
Type: Co-educational Day 4–11
No of pupils: B98 G104
Fees: (September 01)
Day £6030 – £8310

W10

BALES COLLEGE
2(J) Kilburn Lane, London W10 4AA
Tel: (020) 8960 5899
Head: Mr W B Moore
Type: Co-educational Day and
Boarding 14+
No of pupils: B50 G50
No of boarders: F18
Fees: (September 01)
FB £10800 – £12300 Day £5250

BASSETT HOUSE SCHOOL
60 Bassett Road, London W10 6JP
Tel: (020) 8969 0313
Head: Mrs A Landen
Type: Co-educational Day 3–8
No of pupils: B72 G58
Fees: (September 01)
Day £3150 – £7200

PETITE ECOLE FRANCAISE
90 Oxford Gardens, London
W10 5UW
Tel: (020) 8960 1278
Head: Ms A Stones
Type: Co-educational Day 2–5
No of pupils: B35 G30
Fees: (September 01) Day £4050

W11

DAVID GAME COLLEGE*
69 Notting Hill Gate, London
W11 3JS
Tel: (020) 7221 6665
Head: Mr D T Game
Type: Co-educational Day and
Boarding 16–24
No of pupils: B190 G150
No of boarders: F150
Fees: (September 01)
FB £10000 – £13620
Day £7000 – £8420

NORLAND PLACE SCHOOL
162–166 Holland Park Avenue,
London W11 4UH
Tel: (020) 7603 9103
Head: Mr D A Alexander
Type: Co-educational Day Boys 4–8
Girls 4–11
No of pupils: B96 G150
Fees: (September 01)
Day £6054 – £7637

SOUTHBANK INTERNATIONAL SCHOOL, KENSINGTON*
36–38 Kensington Park Road,
London W11 3BU
Tel: (020) 7229 8230
Head: Mr N Hughes
Type: Co-educational Day 4–18
No of pupils: B125 G141
Fees: (September 01)
Day £9600 – £14400

W13

AVENUE HOUSE SCHOOL*
70 The Avenue, Ealing, London
W13 8LS
Tel: (020) 8998 9981
Head: Miss C M Barber
Type: Co-educational Day 2–11
No of pupils: B65 G75
Fees: (September 01)
Day £2685 – £5070

EALING COLLEGE UPPER SCHOOL
83 The Avenue, Ealing, London
W13 8JS
Tel: (020) 8248 2312
Head: Mr B Webb
Type: Boys Day 11–18 (Co-ed VIth
Form)
No of pupils: B136 G2
Fees: (September 01) Day £4990

NOTTING HILL AND EALING HIGH SCHOOL GDST
2 Cleveland Road, Ealing, London
W13 8AX
Tel: (020) 8799 8400
Head: Mrs S Whitfield
Type: Girls Day 5–18
No of pupils: 830
Fees: (September 01)
Day £5145 – £6624

W14

ROYAL BALLET SCHOOL
155 Talgarth Road, Barons Court,
London W14 9DE
Tel: (020) 8748 6335
Head: Mr J G Mitchell
Type: Co-educational Boarding and
Day 11–18
No of pupils: B94 G111
No of boarders: F124
Fees: (September 01) FB £19005
Day £14073

ST JAMES INDEPENDENT SCHOOL FOR BOYS (JUNIORS)
29 Earsby Street, London W14 8SH
Tel: (020) 7373 5638
Head: Mr P Moss
Type: Boys Day 4–10
No of pupils: 126
Fees: (September 01)
Day £4950 – £5610

ST JAMES INDEPENDENT SCHOOL FOR GIRLS (JUNIORS)
29 Earsby Street, London W14 8SH
Tel: (020) 7348 1777
Head: Mr P Moss
Type: Girls Day 4–10
No of pupils: 133
Fees: (September 01)
Day £4950 – £5610

ST JAMES INDEPENDENT SCHOOL FOR SENIOR GIRLS
Earsby Street, London W14 8SH
Tel: (020) 7348 1777
Head: Mrs L A Hyde
Type: Girls Day 10–18
No of pupils: 195
Fees: (September 01)
Day £6675 – £6885

THE URDANG ACADEMY OF BALLET
20–22 Shelton Street, London
WC2H 9JJ
Tel: (020) 7836 5709
Head: Miss S Goumain
Type: Co-educational Day 16–23
No of pupils: B28 G104
Fees: (September 01) Day £9480

GREATER MANCHESTER

AUDENSHAW

JOSEPH RAYNER INDEPENDENT SCHOOL
Red Hall, Audenshaw Road,
Audenshaw, Greater Manchester
M34 5HT
Tel: (0161) 355 1434
Head: Mr G Hopkinson
Type: Co-educational Day 4–11
No of pupils: B2 G12
Fees: (September 01) On application

ECCLES

BRANWOOD PREPARATORY SCHOOL
Stafford Road, Monton, Eccles,
Greater Manchester M30 9HN
Tel: (0161) 789 1054
Head: Mr W M Howard
Type: Co-educational Day 4–11
No of pupils: B95 G95
Fees: (September 01)
Day £2055 – £3120

CLARENDON COTTAGE SCHOOL
Ivy Bank House, Half Edge Lane,
Eccles, Greater Manchester M30 9BJ
Tel: (0161) 950 7868
Head: Mrs E Bagnall
Type: Co-educational Day 1–11
No of pupils: B120 G100
Fees: (September 01)
Day £1000 – £4150

MONTON PREP SCHOOL WITH MONTESSORI NURSERIES
The School House, Francis Street,
Monton, Eccles, Greater Manchester
M30 9PR
Tel: (0161) 789 0472
Head: Miss D S Bradburn
Type: Co-educational Day 2–13
No of pupils: B74 G80
Fees: (September 01) On application

MANCHESTER

ABBEY INDEPENDENT COLLEGE
20 Kennedy Street, Manchester
M2 4BY
Tel: (0161) 236 6836
Head: Mr K Byrne
Type: Co-educational Day and
Boarding 15–21
No of pupils: B90 G90
Fees: (September 01)
Day £5700 – £10500

ABBOTSFORD PREPARATORY SCHOOL
211 Flixton Road, Urmston,
Manchester M41 5PR
Tel: (0161) 748 3261
Head: Mr C J Davies
Type: Co-educational Day 3–11
No of pupils: B77 G59
Fees: (September 01)
Day £3060 – £3885

BRIDGEWATER SCHOOL
Drywood Hall, Worsley Road,
Worsley, Manchester M28 2WQ
Tel: (0161) 794 1463
Head: Ms G A Shannon-Little
Type: Co-educational Day 3–18
No of pupils: B287 G225
Fees: (September 01)
Day £2700 – £5220

CHETHAM'S SCHOOL OF MUSIC
Long Millgate, Manchester M3 1SB
Tel: (0161) 834 9644
Head: Mrs C J Moreland
Type: Co-educational Boarding 8–18
No of pupils: B120 G160
No of boarders: F229
Fees: (September 01) FB £19641
Day £15204

KING OF KINGS SCHOOL
142 Dantzic Street, Manchester
M4 4DN
Tel: (0161) 834 4214
Head: Mrs B Lewis
Type: Co-educational Day 2–18
No of pupils: B14 G10
Fees: (September 01)
Day £1530 – £1680

THE MANCHESTER GRAMMAR SCHOOL
Old Hall Lane, Manchester M13 0XT
Tel: (0161) 224 7201
Head: Dr G M Stephen
Type: Boys Day 11–18
No of pupils: 1420
Fees: (September 01) Day £5670

MANCHESTER HIGH SCHOOL FOR GIRLS
Grangethorpe Road, Manchester
M14 6HS
Tel: (0161) 224 0447
Head: Mrs C Lee-Jones
Type: Girls Day 4–18
No of pupils: 927
Fees: (September 01)
Day £3900 – £5520

MANCHESTER ISLAMIC HIGH SCHOOL
55 High Lane, Manchester M21 9FA
Tel: (0161) 881 2127
Head: Mrs M Mohamed
Type: Girls Day 11–16
No of pupils: 216
Fees: (September 01) Day £2350

MANCHESTER MUSLIM PREPARATORY SCHOOL
551 Wilmslow Road, Withington,
Manchester M20 4BA
Tel: (0161) 445 5452
Head: Mrs T Amin
Type: Co-educational Day 3–11
No of pupils: B78 G99
Fees: (September 01)
Day £1620 – £2440

MOOR ALLERTON SCHOOL
131 Barlow Moor Road, Manchester
M20 2PW
Tel: (0161) 445 4521
Head: Mr P S Millard
Type: Co-educational Day 3–11
No of pupils: B100 G40
Fees: (September 01)
Day £3441 – £4626

NORMAN HOUSE SCHOOL
349 Hollinwood Avenue, New
Moston, Manchester M40 0JX
Tel: (0161) 681 3097
Head: Mrs E Mann
Type: Co-educational Day 2–11
No of pupils: B62 G43
Fees: (September 01)
Day £3075 – £3165

ST BEDE'S COLLEGE
Alexandra Park, Manchester
M16 8HX
Tel: (0161) 226 3323
Head: Mr J Byrne
Type: Co-educational Day 4–18
No of pupils: 1000
Fees: (September 01)
Day £3450 – £5232

WILLIAM HULME'S GRAMMAR SCHOOL
Spring Bridge Road, Manchester
M16 8PR
Tel: (0161) 226 2054
Head: Mr S R Patriarca
Type: Co-educational Day 3–18
No of pupils: B534 G219
Fees: (September 01)
Day £3573 – £5475

WITHINGTON GIRLS' SCHOOL
Wellington Road, Fallowfield,
Manchester M14 6BL
Tel: (0161) 224 1077
Head: Mrs J D Pickering
Type: Girls Day 7–18
No of pupils: 650
Fees: (September 01)
Day £3789 – £5418

PRESTWICH

PRESTWICH PREPARATORY SCHOOL
400 Bury Old Road, Prestwich,
Greater Manchester M25 1PZ
Tel: (0161) 773 1223
Head: Mr D R Sheldon
Type: Co-educational Day 2–11
No of pupils: B60 G60
Fees: (September 01) Day £2700

SALFORD

JEWISH HIGH SCHOOL FOR GIRLS
10 Radford Street, Salford, Greater
Manchester M7 4NT
Tel: (0161) 792 2118
Head: Rabbi Y Goldblatt
Type: Girls Day 11–18
No of pupils: 165
Fees: (September 01) On application

TASHBAR PRIMARY SCHOOL
20 Upper Park Rd, Salford, Greater
Manchester M7 4HL
Tel: (0161) 720 8254
Head: Rabbi C S Roberts
Type: Boys Day 3–11
No of pupils: 270
Fees: (September 01)
Day £1020 – £1620

MERSEYSIDE

BIRKENHEAD

BIRKENHEAD SCHOOL
58 Beresford Road, Oxton,
Birkenhead, Merseyside CH43 2JD
Tel: (0151) 652 4014
Head: Mr S J Haggett
Type: Boys Day 3–18
No of pupils: B877 G5
Fees: (September 01)
Day £4311 – £5526

HIGHFIELD SCHOOL
96 Bidston Road, Oxton,
Birkenhead, Merseyside CH43 6TW
Tel: (0151) 652 3708
Head: Mrs S Morris
Type: Co-educational Day Boys 2–11
Girls 2–16
No of pupils: B20 G100
Fees: (September 01)
Day £3000 – £3720

LIVERPOOL

ATHERTON HOUSE SCHOOL
Alexandra Road, Crosby, Liverpool,
Merseyside L23 7TF
Tel: (0151) 924 5578
Head: Mrs A Apel
Type: Co-educational Day 2–11
No of pupils: B45 G48
Fees: (September 01)
Day £2010 – £2655

BEECHENHURST PREPARATORY SCHOOL
145 Menlove Avenue, Liverpool,
Merseyside L18 3EE
Tel: (0151) 722 3279
Head: Mrs C Wright
Type: Co-educational Day 3–11
No of pupils: B50 G50
Fees: (September 01) Day £2790

THE BELVEDERE SCHOOL GDST
17 Belvidere Road, Princes Park,
Liverpool, Merseyside L8 3TF
Tel: (0151) 727 1284
Head: Mrs G Richards
Type: Girls Day 3–18
No of pupils: 600
Fees: (September 01)
Day £3174 – £5442

CARLETON HOUSE PREPARATORY SCHOOL
Lyndhurst Road, Mossley Hill,
Liverpool, Merseyside L18 8AQ
Tel: (0151) 724 4880
Head: Mrs C Line
Type: Co-educational Day 4–11
No of pupils: B88 G62
Fees: (September 01) Day £3510

LIVERPOOL COLLEGE
Liverpool, Merseyside L18 8BG
Tel: (0151) 724 4000
Head: Mrs C Bradley
Type: Co-educational Day 3–18
No of pupils: B600 G400
Fees: (September 01)
Day £3990 – £6255

MCKEE SCHOOL OF EDUCATION, DANCE & DRAMA
2 Carnforth Road, Liverpool,
Merseyside L18 6JS
Tel: (0151) 724 1316
Head: Miss P M McKee
Type: Co-educational Day 3–7
No of pupils: B15 G15
Fees: (September 01)
Day £1695 – £1950

MERCHANT TAYLORS' SCHOOL
Crosby, Liverpool, Merseyside
L23 0QP
Tel: (0151) 928 3308
Head: Mr S J R Dawkins
Type: Boys Day 7–18
No of pupils: 890
Fees: (September 01)
Day £3798 – £5292

MERCHANT TAYLORS' SCHOOL FOR GIRLS
Crosby, Liverpool, Merseyside
L23 5SP
Tel: (0151) 924 3140
Head: Mrs J I Mills
Type: Girls Day 4–18 (Boys 4–7)
No of pupils: B70 G850
Fees: (September 01)
Day £3717 – £5292

NEWBOROUGH SCHOOL
Quarry Street, Woolton, Liverpool,
Merseyside L25 6HD
Tel: (0151) 428 1838
Head: Miss D Prior
Type: Co-educational Day Boys 3–11
Girls 3–16
No of pupils: B50 G80
Fees: (September 01)
Day £1650 – £2175

ST EDWARD'S JUNIOR SCHOOL RUNNYMEDE
North Drive, Sandfield Park,
Liverpool, Merseyside L12 1LF
Tel: (0151) 281 2300
Head: Mr P Sweeney
Type: Co-educational Day 3–11
No of pupils: B190 G140
Fees: (September 01)
Day £3948 – £4162

ST MARY'S COLLEGE
Crosby, Liverpool, Merseyside
L23 3AB
Tel: (0151) 924 3926
Head: Mr W Hammond
Type: Co-educational Day 0–18
No of pupils: B548 G443
Fees: (September 01)
Day £3051 – £5152

STREATHAM HOUSE SCHOOL
Victoria Road West, Blundellsands,
Liverpool, Merseyside L23 8UQ
Tel: (0151) 924 1514
Head: Mrs C Baxter
Type: Girls Day 2–16 (Boys 2–11)
No of pupils: B28 G165
Fees: (September 01)
Day £2355 – £3990

NEWTON-LE-WILLOWS

NEWTON BANK SCHOOL
34 High Street, Newton-Le-Willows,
Merseyside WA12 9SN
Tel: (01925) 225979
Head: Mrs J Butler
Type: Co-educational Day 3–11
No of pupils: B25 G35
Fees: (September 01) Day £2400

PRESCOT

TOWER COLLEGE
Mill Lane, Rainhill, Prescot,
Merseyside L35 6NE
Tel: (0151) 426 4333
Head: Miss R J Oxley
Type: Co-educational Day 3–16
No of pupils: B276 G275
Fees: (September 01)
Day £2928 – £3606

SOUTH WIRRAL

BENTY HEATH SCHOOL AND KINDERGARTEN
Benty Heath Lane, South Wirral,
Merseyside CH64 1SB
Tel: (0151) 327 4594
Head: Mrs J E Tedstone
Type: Co-educational Day 3–7
No of pupils: B25 G22
Fees: (September 01)
Day £375 – £950

SOUTHPORT

SUNNYMEDE SCHOOL
4 Westcliffe Road, Birkdale,
Southport, Merseyside PR8 2BN
Tel: (01704) 568593
Head: Mr S J Pattinson
Type: Co-educational Day 3–11
No of pupils: B63 G61
Fees: (September 01)
Day £2940 – £4485

TOWER DENE PREPARATORY SCHOOL
59–76 Cambridge Road, Southport,
Merseyside PR9 9RH
Tel: (01704) 228556
Head: Mrs A Lewin
Type: Co-educational Day 0–11
No of pupils: B70 G60
Fees: (September 01)
Day £1950 – £2750

WALLASEY

MARYMOUNT CONVENT SCHOOL
Love Lane, Wallasey, Merseyside
CH44 5SB
Tel: (0151) 638 8467
Head: Sister C O'Reilly
Type: Co-educational Day 3–11
No of pupils: B41 G120
Fees: (September 01) Day £2100

WESTBOURNE PREPARATORY SCHOOL
45 Penkett Road, Wallasey,
Merseyside CH45 7QG
Tel: (0151) 639 2722
Head: Mrs H S Hamilton
Type: Co-educational Day 4–11
No of pupils: B30 G30
Fees: (September 01)
Day £1470 – £1545

WIRRAL

AVALON PREPARATORY SCHOOL
Caldy Road, West Kirby, Wirral,
Merseyside CH48 2HE
Tel: (0151) 625 6993
Head: Dr B Scott
Type: Co-educational Day 2–11
No of pupils: B92 G98
Fees: (September 01)
Day £2987 – £3655

BIRKENHEAD HIGH SCHOOL GDST
86 Devonshire Place, Prenton,
Wirral, Merseyside CH43 1TY
Tel: (0151) 652 5777
Head: Mrs C H Evans
Type: Girls Day 3–18
No of pupils: 900
Fees: (September 01)
Day £3174 – £5442

HESWALL PREPARATORY SCHOOL
Carberry, Quarry Road East,
Heswall, Wirral, Merseyside
CH60 6RB
Tel: (0151) 342 7851
Head: Mrs M Hannaford
Type: Co-educational Day 2–11
No of pupils: B25 G25
Fees: (September 01)
Day £1575 – £3000

KINGSMEAD SCHOOL
Bertram Drive, Hoylake, Wirral,
Merseyside CH47 0LL
Tel: (0151) 632 3156
Head: Mr E H Bradby
Type: Co-educational Boarding and
Day 2–16
No of pupils: B147 G87
No of boarders: F24 W4
Fees: (September 01) FB £8085 –
£8790 WB £7785 – £8490
Day £3675 – £5490

MIDDLESEX

ASHFORD

ST DAVID'S SCHOOL
Church Road, Ashford, Middlesex
TW15 3DZ
Tel: (01784) 252494
Head: Ms P Bristow
Type: Girls Day and Boarding 3–18
No of pupils: 400
No of boarders: F25 W6
Fees: (September 01) FB £12570
WB £11790 Day £5370 – £7170

EDGWARE

HOLLAND HOUSE
1 Broadhurst Avenue, Edgware,
Middlesex HA8 8TP
Tel: (020) 8958 6979
Head: Mrs I Tyk
Type: Co-educational Day 4–11
No of pupils: B70 G70
Fees: (September 01) Day £3420

MENORAH GRAMMAR
SCHOOL
Abbots Road, Edgware, Middlesex
HA8 0QS
Tel: (020) 8906 9756
Head: Rabbi A M Goldblatt
Type: Boys Day 11–18
No of pupils: 225
Fees: (September 01) On application

NORTH LONDON
COLLEGIATE SCHOOL
Canons Drive, Edgware, Middlesex
HA8 7RJ
Tel: (020) 8952 0912
Head: Mrs B McCabe
Type: Girls Day 4–18
No of pupils: 1015
Fees: (September 01)
Day £6453 – £7608

ENFIELD

ST JOHN'S SENIOR SCHOOL
North Lodge, The Ridgeway, Enfield,
Middlesex EN2 8BE
Tel: (020) 8366 0035
Head: Mr A Tardios
Type: Co-educational Day 10–18
No of pupils: B98 G77
Fees: (September 01)
Day £4800 – £5700

HAMPTON

ATHELSTAN HOUSE SCHOOL
36 Percy Road, Hampton, Middlesex
TW12 2LA
Tel: (020) 8979 1045
Head: Mrs E M Woolf
Type: Co-educational Day 3–7
No of pupils: 70
Fees: (September 01) On application

DENMEAD SCHOOL
41–43 Wensleydale Road, Hampton,
Middlesex TW12 2LP
Tel: (020) 8979 1844
Head: Mr M T McKaughan
Type: Boys Day 2–13 (Girls 2–7)
No of pupils: B189 G12
Fees: (September 01)
Day £2565 – £5985

GRASSROOTS NURSERY
SCHOOL
The Studio, 24 Ashley Road,
Hampton, Middlesex TW12 2JA
Tel: (020) 8783 1190
Head: Mrs S Mortimer
Type: Co-educational Day 0–5
No of pupils: 35
Fees: (September 01) On application

HAMPTON SCHOOL
Hanworth Road, Hampton,
Middlesex TW12 3HD
Tel: (020) 8979 5526
Head: Mr B R Martin
Type: Boys Day 11–18
No of pupils: 1050
Fees: (September 01) Day £7555

JACK AND JILL SCHOOL
30 Nightingale Road, Hampton,
Middlesex TW12 3HX
Tel: (020) 8979 3195
Head: Miss K S Papirnik
Type: Girls Day 3–7 (Boys 3–5)
No of pupils: B26 G124
Fees: (September 01)
Day £2580 – £4995

THE LADY ELEANOR HOLLES
SCHOOL
102 Hanworth Road, Hampton,
Middlesex TW12 3HF
Tel: (020) 8979 1601
Head: Miss E M Candy
Type: Girls Day 7–18
No of pupils: 885
Fees: (September 01)
Day £5890 – £7824

TWICKENHAM
PREPARATORY SCHOOL
Beveree, 43 High Street, Hampton,
Middlesex TW12 2SA
Tel: (020) 8979 6216
Head: Mr N D Flynn
Type: Co-educational Day Boys 4–13
Girls 4–11
No of pupils: B105 G111
Fees: (September 01)
Day £5175 – £5535

HANWORTH

LITTLE EDEN SDA SCHOOL
& EDEN HIGH SDA SCHOOL
Fortescue House, Park Road,
Hanworth, Middlesex TW13 6PN
Tel: (020) 8751 1844
Head: Mrs L A Osei
Type: Co-educational Day 3–16
No of pupils: B18 G25
Fees: (September 01)
Day £2250 – £2775

HARROW

ALPHA PREPARATORY
SCHOOL
Hindes Road, Harrow, Middlesex
HA1 1SH
Tel: (020) 8427 1471
Head: Mr P J Wylie
Type: Co-educational Day 4–13
No of pupils: B110 G60
Fees: (September 01)
Day £4875 – £5475

BUCKINGHAM COLLEGE
SCHOOL
15 Hindes Road, Harrow, Middlesex
HA1 1SH
Tel: (020) 8427 1220
Head: Mr D F Bell
Type: Boys Day 11–18 (Co-ed VIth
Form)
No of pupils: B164 G1
Fees: (September 01)
Day £5415 – £6375

THE JOHN LYON SCHOOL
Middle Road, Harrow, Middlesex
HA2 0HN
Tel: (020) 8872 8400
Head: Dr C Ray
Type: Boys Day 11–18
No of pupils: 525
Fees: (September 01) Day £7848

ORLEY FARM SCHOOL
South Hill Avenue, Harrow,
Middlesex HA1 3NU
Tel: (020) 8422 1525
Head: Mr I S Elliott
Type: Co-educational Day 4–13
No of pupils: B380 G90
Fees: (September 01)
Day £6105 – £7050

QUAINTON HALL SCHOOL
91 Hindes Road, Harrow, Middlesex
HA1 1RX
Tel: (020) 8427 1304
Head: Mr D P Banister
Type: Boys Day 4–13
No of pupils: 235
Fees: (September 01)
Day £4623 – £5955

ROXETH MEAD SCHOOL
25 Middle Road, Harrow, Middlesex
HA2 0HW
Tel: (020) 8422 2092
Head: Mrs A Collins
Type: Co-educational Day 3–7
No of pupils: B28 G37
Fees: (September 01) Day £4365

HARROW ON THE HILL

HARROW SCHOOL
Harrow on the Hill, Middlesex
HA1 3HW
Tel: (020) 8872 8000
Head: Mr B J Lenon
Type: Boys Boarding 13–18
No of pupils: 790
No of boarders: F790
Fees: (September 01) FB £17955

ISLEWORTH

ASHTON HOUSE SCHOOL
50/52 Eversley Crescent, Isleworth,
Middlesex TW7 4LW
Tel: (020) 8560 3902
Head: Miss M Regan
Type: Co-educational Day 3–11
No of pupils: B70 G80
Fees: (September 01)
Day £3956 – £5367

NORTHWOOD

MERCHANT TAYLORS' SCHOOL
Sandy Lodge, Northwood, Middlesex
HA6 2HT
Tel: (01923) 820644
Head: Mr J R Gabitass
Type: Boys Day 11–18
No of pupils: 780
No of boarders: F5
Fees: (September 01) Day £9120

NORTHWOOD COLLEGE
Maxwell Road, Northwood,
Middlesex HA6 2YE
Tel: (01923) 825446
Head: Mrs A Mayou
Type: Girls Day 3–18
No of pupils: 782
Fees: (September 01)
Day £3897 – £6996

ST HELEN'S SCHOOL FOR GIRLS*
Northwood, Middlesex HA6 3AS
Tel: (01923) 843210
Head: Mrs M Morris
Type: Girls Day and Boarding 4–18
No of pupils: 980
No of boarders: F23 W5
Fees: (September 01) FB £13500
WB £12996 Day £5238 – £7200

ST JOHN'S NORTHWOOD
Potter Street Hill, Northwood,
Middlesex HA6 3QY
Tel: (020) 8866 0067
Head: Mr C R Kelly
Type: Boys Day 4–13
No of pupils: 350
Fees: (September 01)
Day £6000 – £6750

ST MARTIN'S SCHOOL*
40 Moor Park Road, Northwood,
Middlesex HA6 2DJ
Tel: (01923) 825740
Head: Mr M J Hodgson
Type: Boys Day 3–13
No of pupils: 400
Fees: (September 01)
Day £2175 – £6900

PINNER

BUCKINGHAM COLLEGE PREPARATORY SCHOOL
458 Rayners Lane, Pinner, Middlesex
HA5 5DT
Tel: (020) 8866 2737
Head: Mr L Smith
Type: Boys Day 4–11
No of pupils: 126
Fees: (September 01)
Day £4080 – £5415

HEATHFIELD SCHOOL
Beaulieu Drive, Pinner, Middlesex
HA5 1NB
Tel: (020) 8868 2346
Head: Miss C Juett
Type: Girls Day 3–18
No of pupils: 575
Fees: (September 01)
Day £3888 – £6624

INNELLAN HOUSE SCHOOL
44 Love Lane, Pinner, Middlesex
HA5 3EX
Tel: (020) 8866 1855
Head: Mrs R Edwards
Type: Co-educational Day 3–8
No of pupils: B32 G51
Fees: (September 01)
Day £3286 – £3506

REDDIFORD
36–38 Cecil Park, Pinner, Middlesex
HA5 5HH
Tel: (020) 8866 0660
Head: Mr B Hembry
Type: Co-educational Day 3–11
No of pupils: B188 G126
Fees: (September 01)
Day £2100 – £5205

RUISLIP

EILMAR MONTESSORI SCHOOL & NURSERY
Sidmouth Drive, Ruislip Gardens,
Ruislip, Middlesex HA4 0BY
Tel: (01895) 635796
Head: Ms M A Portland
Type: Co-educational Day 2–5
No of pupils: B34 G34
Fees: (September 01)
Day £2791 – £5016

SHEPPERTON

HALLIFORD SCHOOL
Russell Road, Shepperton, Middlesex
TW17 9HX
Tel: (01932) 223593
Head: Mr J R Crook
Type: Boys Day 11–19 (Co-ed VIth
Form)
No of pupils: B312 G8
Fees: (September 01) Day £6450

STAINES

STAINES PREPARATORY
SCHOOL TRUST
3 Gresham Road, Staines, Middlesex
TW18 2BT
Tel: (01784) 452916/450909
Head: Mr P Roberts
Type: Co-educational Day 3–11
No of pupils: B250 G150
Fees: (September 01)
Day £3990 – £4605

STANMORE

PETERBOROUGH & ST
MARGARET'S SCHOOL
Common Road, Stanmore,
Middlesex HA7 3JB
Tel: (020) 8950 3600
Head: Mrs D M Tomlinson
Type: Girls Day 4–16
No of pupils: 235
Fees: (September 01)
Day £4095 – £6060

TWICKENHAM

THE MALL SCHOOL
185 Hampton Road, Twickenham,
Middlesex TW2 5NQ
Tel: (020) 8977 2523
Head: Mr T P MacDonogh
Type: Boys Day 4–13
No of pupils: 290
Fees: (September 01)
Day £5130 – £5940

NEWLAND HOUSE SCHOOL
Waldegrave Park, Twickenham,
Middlesex TW1 4TQ
Tel: (020) 8892 7479
Head: Mr D J Ott
Type: Co-educational Day Boys 4–13
Girls 4–11
No of pupils: B293 G145
Fees: (September 01)
Day £4170 – £6210

ST CATHERINE'S SCHOOL
Cross Deep, Twickenham, Middlesex
TW1 4QJ
Tel: (020) 8891 2898
Head: Miss D Wynter
Type: Girls Day 3–16
No of pupils: 348
Fees: (September 01)
Day £4710 – £6165

ST JAMES INDEPENDENT
SCHOOL FOR BOYS (SENIOR)
Pope's Villa, 19 Cross Deep,
Twickenham, Middlesex TW1 4QG
Tel: (020) 8892 2002
Head: Mr N Debenham
Type: Boys Day 10–18
No of pupils: 265
No of boarders: W32
Fees: (September 01)
WB £7435 – £7645
Day £6675 – £6885

SUNFLOWER MONTESSORI
SCHOOL
8 Victoria Road, Twickenham,
Middlesex TW1 3HW
Tel: (020) 8891 2675
Head: Mrs J Yandell
Type: Co-educational Day 2–7
No of pupils: 79
Fees: (September 01)
Day £1905 – £3900

UXBRIDGE

THE AMERICAN
COMMUNITY SCHOOLS
Hillingdon Court, 108 Vine Lane,
Hillingdon, Uxbridge, Middlesex
UB10 0BE
Tel: (01895) 813734
Head: Mr C Taylor
Type: Co-educational Day 4–19
No of pupils: B340 G302
Fees: (September 01)
Day £4400 – £12700

ST HELEN'S COLLEGE
Parkway, Hillingdon, Uxbridge,
Middlesex UB10 9JX
Tel: (01895) 234371
Head: Mr D A Crehan
Type: Co-educational Day 3–11
No of pupils: B126 G142
Fees: (September 01)
Day £2580 – £4392

WEMBLEY

BUXLOW PREPARATORY
SCHOOL
5/6 Castleton Gardens, Wembley,
Middlesex HA9 7QJ
Tel: (020) 8904 3615
Head: Mrs B L Lancaster
Type: Co-educational Day 4–11
No of pupils: B64 G61
Fees: (September 01) Day £3930

ST CHRISTOPHER'S SCHOOL
71 Wembley Park Drive, Wembley,
Middlesex HA9 8HE
Tel: (020) 8902 5069
Head: Mrs S M Morley
Type: Co-educational Day 4–11
No of pupils: 121
Fees: (September 01) On application

NORFOLK

CROMER

BEESTON HALL SCHOOL
West Runton, Cromer, Norfolk
NR27 9NQ
Tel: (01263) 837324
Head: Mr I K MacAskill
Type: Co-educational Boarding and
Day 7–13
No of pupils: B103 G72
No of boarders: F110
Fees: (September 01)
FB £10920 – £11670
Day £8160 – £8730

DISS

RIDDLESWORTH HALL
Diss, Norfolk IP22 2TA
Tel: (01953) 681246
Head: Mr C Campbell
Type: Co-educational Boarding and
Day Boys 2–11 Girls 2–13
No of pupils: B13 G104
No of boarders: F14 W13
Fees: (September 01) FB £11400
WB £10650 Day £4650 – £6825

HOLT

GRESHAM'S PREPARATORY SCHOOL
Cromer Road, Holt, Norfolk
NR25 6EY
Tel: (01263) 712227
Head: Mr A H Cuff
Type: Co-educational Day and
Boarding 3–13
No of pupils: B184 G151
No of boarders: F17 W36
Fees: (September 01)
FB £11340 – £11910
WB £10500 – £11130
Day £4115 – £9045

GRESHAM'S SCHOOL
Holt, Norfolk NR25 6EA
Tel: (01263) 713271
Head: Mr J H Arkell
Type: Co-educational Boarding and
Day 13–18
No of pupils: B217 G303
No of boarders: F139 W191
Fees: (September 01) FB £16335
WB £15270 Day £12540

HUNSTANTON

GLEBE HOUSE SCHOOL
2 Cromer Road, Hunstanton,
Norfolk PE36 6HW
Tel: (01485) 532809
Head: Mr R E Crosley
Type: Co-educational Boarding and
Day 0–13
No of pupils: B81 G48
No of boarders: W40
Fees: (September 01)
WB £7770 – £8430
Day £3960 – £7080

KINGS LYNN

DOWNHAM MONTESSORI SCHOOL
The Old Rectory, Stow Bardolph,
Kings Lynn, Norfolk PE34 3HT
Tel: (01366) 388066
Head: Mrs E J Laffeaty-Sharpe
Type: Co-educational Day 2–11
No of pupils: B72 G68
Fees: (September 01)
Day £3150 – £4350

SILFIELD SCHOOL
85 Gayton Road, Gaywood, Kings
Lynn, Norfolk PE30 4EH
Tel: (01553) 774642
Head: Mr C E K Phillips and
Mrs E M Phillips
Type: Co-educational Day 3–11
No of pupils: B17 G30
Fees: (September 01)
Day £1320 – £2460

NORTH WALSHAM

ST NICHOLAS KINDERGARTEN & PREPARATORY SCHOOL
Yarmouth Road, North Walsham,
Norfolk NR28 9AT
Tel: (01692) 403143
Head: Mrs M Webster
Type: Co-educational Day 3–11
No of pupils: B72 G70
Fees: (September 01)

NORWICH

ALL SAINTS SCHOOL
School Road, Lessingham, Norwich,
Norfolk NR12 0DJ
Tel: (01692) 582083
Head: Mrs J Gardiner
Type: Co-educational Day 2–16
No of pupils: B35 G35
Fees: (September 01)
Day £1680 – £2760

HETHERSETT OLD HALL SCHOOL
Hethersett, Norwich, Norfolk
NR9 3DW
Tel: (01603) 810390
Head: Mrs J M Mark
Type: Girls Boarding and Day 4–18
(Boys 4–7 years)
No of pupils: B4 G271
No of boarders: F47
Fees: (September 01)
FB £10590 – £13140
Day £4185 – £6600

LANGLEY PREPARATORY SCHOOL & NURSERY
Beech Hill, 11 Yarmouth Road,
Thorpe St Andrew, Norwich, Norfolk
NR7 0EA
Tel: (01603) 433861
Head: Mr P J Weeks
Type: Co-educational Day 2–11
No of pupils: B95 G55
Fees: (September 01)
Day £3450 – £5070

LANGLEY SCHOOL*
Langley Park, Loddon, Norwich,
Norfolk NR14 6BJ
Tel: (01508) 520210
Head: Mr J G Malcolm
Type: Co-educational Boarding and
Day 10–18
No of pupils: B240 G85
No of boarders: F72 W11
Fees: (September 01)
FB £11400 – £13800
WB £10500 – £12600
Day £5580 – £7200

THE NEW ECCLES HALL SCHOOL

Quidenham, Norwich, Norfolk
NR16 2NZ
Tel: (01953) 887217
Head: Mr R W Allard
Type: Co-educational Day and
Boarding 3–16
No of pupils: 170
No of boarders: F72
Fees: (September 01)
FB £9855 – £11685
Day £3720 – £6195

THE NORWICH HIGH SCHOOL FOR GIRLS GDST

95 Newmarket Road, Norwich,
Norfolk NR2 2HU
Tel: (01603) 453265
Head: Mrs V C Bidwell
Type: Girls Day 4–18
No of pupils: 900
Fees: (September 01)
Day £3951 – £5442

NORWICH SCHOOL

School House, 70 The Close,
Norwich, Norfolk NR1 4DQ
Tel: (01603) 623194
Head: Mr C D Brown
Type: Boys Day 8–18 (Co-ed VIth
Form)
No of pupils: B780 G64
Fees: (September 01)
Day £6033 – £6273

NOTRE DAME PREPARATORY SCHOOL

147 Dereham Road, Norwich,
Norfolk NR2 3TA
Tel: (01603) 625593
Head: Mrs V Short
Type: Co-educational Day 3–11
No of pupils: B67 G100
Fees: (September 01)
Day £2280 – £2760

ST CHRISTOPHER'S SCHOOL

George Hill, Old Catton, Norwich,
Norfolk NR7 6DE
Tel: (01603) 425179
Head: Mrs C Cunningham
Type: Co-educational Day 2–9
No of pupils: B80 G60
Fees: (September 01)
Day £522 – £3180

STRETTON SCHOOL

1 Albermarle Road, Norwich,
Norfolk NR2 2DF
Tel: (01603) 451285
Head: Mrs Y D Barnett
Type: Co-educational Day 2–9
No of pupils: 110
Fees: (September 01) On application

TAVERHAM HALL

Taverham, Norwich, Norfolk
NR8 6HU
Tel: (01603) 868206
Head: Mr W D Lawton
Type: Co-educational Boarding and
Day 3–13
No of pupils: B121 G88
No of boarders: W25
Fees: (September 01) WB £9405
Day £1575 – £8175

THORPE HOUSE SCHOOL

7 Yarmouth Road, Norwich, Norfolk
NR7 0EA
Tel: (01603) 433055
Head: Mrs R McFarlane
Type: Girls Day 3–16
No of pupils: 280
Fees: (September 01)
Day £2790 – £4185

TOWN CLOSE HOUSE PREPARATORY SCHOOL

14 Ipswich Road, Norwich, Norfolk
NR2 2LR
Tel: (01603) 620180
Head: Mr R Gordon
Type: Co-educational Day and
Boarding 3–13
No of pupils: B297 G103
No of boarders: W10
Fees: (September 01) WB £8790
Day £3915 – £6240

WOOD DENE SCHOOL

Aylmerton Hall, Aylmerton,
Norwich, Norfolk NR11 8QA
Tel: (01263) 837224
Head: Mrs D M Taylor
Type: Co-educational Day 2–17
No of pupils: B80 G120
Fees: (September 01)
Day £2150 – £3900

SWAFFHAM

SACRED HEART CONVENT SCHOOL

17 Mangate Street, Swaffham,
Norfolk PE37 7QW
Tel: (01760) 721330
Head: Sister Francis Ridler
Type: Co-educational Day and
Boarding Boys 3–11 Girls 3–16
No of pupils: B31 G198
No of boarders: W30
Fees: (September 01) FB £10200
WB £7425 Day £3525 – £4845

THETFORD

THETFORD GRAMMAR SCHOOL

Bridge Street, Thetford, Norfolk
IP24 3AF
Tel: (01842) 752840
Head: Mr J R Weeks
Type: Co-educational Day 5–18
No of pupils: B163 G134
Fees: (September 01)
Day £4890 – £5910

NORTHAMPTONSHIRE

BLACKTHORN

ST PETER'S INDEPENDENT SCHOOL
Lingswood Park, Blackthorn,
Northamptonshire NN3 8TA
Tel: (01604) 411745
Head: Mr G J Smith
Type: Co-educational Day 4–18
No of pupils: 170
Fees: (September 01) On application

BRACKLEY

BEACHBOROUGH SCHOOL
Westbury, Brackley,
Northamptonshire NN13 5LB
Tel: (01280) 700071
Head: Mr A J Boardman
Type: Co-educational Day and Boarding 2–13
No of pupils: B146 G93
No of boarders: W41
Fees: (September 01) WB £10500
Day £5430 – £8550

WINCHESTER HOUSE SCHOOL
Brackley, Northamptonshire
NN13 7AZ
Tel: (01280) 702483
Head: Mr J R G Griffith
Type: Co-educational Boarding and Day 7–13
No of pupils: B139 G72
No of boarders: F30 W49
Fees: (September 01) F/WB £12180
Day £7380 – £9240

WINCHESTER HOUSE SCHOOL PRE-PREP
70 Manor Road, Brackley,
Northamptonshire NN13 6EE
Tel: (01280) 703070
Head: Mrs E J Hamilton
Type: Co-educational Day 3–7
No of pupils: B59 G24
Fees: (September 01)
Day £840 – £5280

KETTERING

OUR LADY'S CONVENT PREPARATORY SCHOOL
Hall Lane, Kettering,
Northamptonshire NN15 7LJ
Tel: (01536) 513882
Head: Mrs L Burgess
Type: Co-educational Day 2–11
No of pupils: B83 G66
Fees: (September 01) Day £3540

ST PETER'S SCHOOL
52 Headlands, Kettering,
Northamptonshire NN15 6DJ
Tel: (01536) 512066
Head: Mr P Jordan
Type: Co-educational Day 2–11
No of pupils: B54 G83
Fees: (September 01)
Day £3636 – £4485

NORTHAMPTON

BOSWORTH INDEPENDENT COLLEGE*
Nazareth House, Barrack Road,
Northampton, Northamptonshire
NN2 6AF
Tel: (01604) 239995
Head: Mr M McQuin
Type: Co-educational Boarding and Day 14–19
No of pupils: B132 G98
No of boarders: F166 W1
Fees: (September 01) FB £13350
Day £6990

MAIDWELL HALL
Maidwell, Northampton,
Northamptonshire NN6 9JG
Tel: (01604) 686234
Head: Mr R A Lankester
Type: Co-educational Boarding and Day 3–13 (Girls day only)
No of pupils: B123 G15
No of boarders: F80
Fees: (September 01) FB £12870
Day £4200 – £9300

NORTHAMPTON CHRISTIAN SCHOOL
The Parish Rooms, Park Avenue
North, Northampton,
Northamptonshire NN3 2HT
Tel: (01604) 715900
Head: Mrs Z Blakeman
Type: Co-educational Day 4–16
No of pupils: B7 G11
Fees: (September 01)
Day £1986 – £2216

NORTHAMPTON HIGH SCHOOL
Newport Pagnell Road,
Hardingstone, Northampton,
Northamptonshire NN4 0UU
Tel: (01604) 765765
Head: Mrs L A Mayne
Type: Girls Day 3–18
No of pupils: 830
Fees: (September 01)
Day £3900 – £5850

NORTHAMPTON PREPARATORY SCHOOL
Great Houghton Hall, Northampton,
Northamptonshire NN4 7AG
Tel: (01604) 761907
Head: Mr M T E Street
Type: Co-educational Day 4–13
No of pupils: B178 G85
Fees: (September 01)
Day £3435 – £6600

OVERSTONE PARK SCHOOL
Overstone Park, Overstone,
Northampton, Northamptonshire
NN6 0DT
Tel: (01604) 643787
Head: Mrs M F Brown
Type: Co-educational Day 0–16
No of pupils: 160
Fees: (September 01)
Day £4410 – £5250

PARKSIDE SCHOOL
1–5 Vigo Crescent, Browns Way,
Bedford Road, Northampton,
Northamptonshire NN1 5NL
Tel: (01604) 637124
Head: Miss K M Madden
Type: Co-educational Day 2–16
No of pupils: B115 G135
Fees: (September 01)
Day £2940 – £4048

QUINTON HOUSE
The Hall, Upton, Northampton,
Northamptonshire NN5 4UX
Tel: (01604) 752050
Head: Mr C H Oliver
Type: Co-educational Day 3–18
No of pupils: B166 G166
Fees: (September 01)
Day £3174 – £5181

ST MATTHEWS SCHOOL
100 Park Avenue North,
Northampton, Northamptonshire
NN3 2JB
Tel: (01604) 712647
Head: Mrs S M Knight
Type: Co-educational Day 2–8
No of pupils: B30 G30
Fees: (September 01)
Day £3800 – £4500

SPRATTON HALL
Spratton, Northampton,
Northamptonshire NN6 8HP
Tel: (01604) 847292
Head: Dr R A Barlow
Type: Co-educational Day 4–13
No of pupils: B216 G176
Fees: (September 01)
Day £3900 – £6195

WESTON FAVELL MONTESSORI NURSERY SCHOOL
473 Wellingborough Road,
Northampton, Northamptonshire
NN3 3HN
Tel: (01604) 712098
Type: Co-educational Day 2–5
No of pupils: 45
Fees: (September 01) On application

PITSFORD

NORTHAMPTONSHIRE GRAMMAR SCHOOL
Pitsford Hall, Pitsford,
Northamptonshire NN6 9AX
Tel: (01604) 880306
Head: Mr S H Larter
Type: Co-educational Day 3–18
No of pupils: B252 G108
Fees: (September 01)
Day £3924 – £6918

WELLINGBOROUGH

WELLINGBOROUGH SCHOOL
Wellingborough, Northamptonshire
NN8 2BX
Tel: (01933) 222427
Head: Mr F R Ullmann
Type: Co-educational Day 3–18
No of pupils: B470 G280
Fees: (September 01)
Day £4095 – £7386

NORTHUMBERLAND

ALNWICK

ROCK HALL SCHOOL
Rock Hall, Alnwick,
Northumberland NE66 3SE
Tel: (01665) 579224
Head: Ms L A Bosanquet
Type: Co-educational Day 2–13
No of pupils: B14 G26
Fees: (September 01)
Day £3870 – £4620

ST OSWALD'S SCHOOL
Spring Gardens, South Road,
Alnwick, Northumberland
NE66 2NU
Tel: (01665) 602739
Head: Mr R Croft
Type: Co-educational Day 3–16
No of pupils: B55 G53
Fees: (September 01)
Day £3100 – £4650

BERWICK-UPON-TWEED

LONGRIDGE TOWERS SCHOOL
Berwick-upon-Tweed,
Northumberland TD15 2XQ
Tel: (01289) 307584
Head: Dr M J Barron
Type: Co-educational Day and
Boarding 4–18
No of pupils: B149 G141
No of boarders: F26 W9
Fees: (September 01) FB £10560 –
£11400 WB £9795 – £10635
Day £3360 – £5625

STOCKSFIELD

MOWDEN HALL SCHOOL
Newton, Stocksfield,
Northumberland NE43 7TP
Tel: (01661) 842147
Head: Mr A Lewis
Type: Co-educational Boarding and
Day 3–13
No of pupils: 233
No of boarders: F130 W10
Fees: (September 01) F/WB £11370
Day £2430 – £8190

NOTTINGHAMSHIRE

MANSFIELD

MANSFIELD PREPARATORY SCHOOL
Welbeck Road, Mansfield,
Nottinghamshire NG19 9LA
Tel: (01623) 420940
Head: Mrs S Mills
Type: Co-educational Day 3–11
No of pupils: B31 G23
Fees: (September 01) Day £1695

SAVILLE HOUSE SCHOOL
11 Church Street, Mansfield
Woodhouse, Mansfield,
Nottinghamshire NG19 8AH
Tel: (01623) 625068
Head: Mrs P Dunn
Type: Co-educational Day 3–11
No of pupils: B70 G70
Fees: (September 01)
Day £1675 – £1880

NEWARK

EDGEHILL SCHOOL
Main Street, Edingley, Newark,
Nottinghamshire NG22 8BE
Tel: (01623) 882868
Head: Mrs A Burton
Type: Co-educational Day 2–11
No of pupils: B27 G26
Fees: (September 01)
Day £585 – £3165

HIGHFIELDS SCHOOL
London Road, Newark,
Nottinghamshire NG24 3AL
Tel: (01636) 704103
Head: Mr P F Smith
Type: Co-educational Day 2–11
No of pupils: B95 G89
Fees: (September 01)
Day £3525 – £3585

RODNEY SCHOOL
Kirklington, Newark,
Nottinghamshire NG22 8NB
Tel: (01636) 813281
Head: Miss G R T Howe
Type: Co-educational Boarding and
Day 7–18
No of pupils: B32 G39
No of boarders: F29 W4
Fees: (September 01)
F/WB £9501 – £9951
Day £4734 – £6066

WELLOW HOUSE SCHOOL
Wellow, Newark, Nottinghamshire
NG22 0EA
Tel: (01623) 861054
Head: Dr M D W Tozer
Type: Co-educational Day and
Boarding 2–13
No of pupils: B86 G68
No of boarders: W13
Fees: (September 01) WB £8100
Day £3450 – £6390

NOTTINGHAM

ATTENBOROUGH PREPARATORY SCHOOL
The Strand, Attenborough, Beeston,
Nottingham NG9 6AU
Tel: (0115) 943 6725
Head: Mrs M Cahill
Type: Co-educational Day 4–11
No of pupils: B59 G28
Fees: (September 01)
Day £1815 – £2400

CAREY DAYS AT THE MOUNT
Conway Close, Off Woodborough
Road, Nottingham NG3 4FS
Tel: (0115) 985 9333
Head: Miss S Thomas
Type: Co-educational Day 0–5
No of pupils: 100
Fees: (September 01) Day £5100

COTESWOOD HOUSE SCHOOL
19 Thackeray's Lane, Woodthorpe,
Nottingham NG5 4HT
Tel: (0115) 967 6551
Head: Miss E Gamble
Type: Co-educational Day 3–11
No of pupils: B20 G20
Fees: (September 01) On application

DAGFA HOUSE SCHOOL
Broadgate, Beeston, Nottingham
NG9 2FU
Tel: (0115) 913 8330
Head: Mr A Oatway
Type: Co-educational Day 3–16
No of pupils: B165 G115
Fees: (September 01)
Day £2640 – £4640

GREENHOLME SCHOOL
392 Derby Road, Nottingham
NG7 2DX
Tel: (0115) 978 7329
Head: Mrs M J Nicholson and
Miss P M Breen
Type: Co-educational Day 3–11
No of pupils: B141 G68
Fees: (September 01)
Day £4350 – £4620

GROSVENOR SCHOOL
Edwalton, Nottingham NG12 4BS
Tel: (0115) 923 1184
Head: Mr C G J Oldershaw
Type: Co-educational Day 4–13
No of pupils: B107 G64
Fees: (September 01)
Day £3855 – £4260

HAZEL HURST SCHOOL
400 Westdale Lane, Mapperley,
Nottingham NG3 6DG
Tel: (0115) 960 6759
Head: Mrs P A Murray
Type: Co-educational Day 2–8
No of pupils: B25 G31
Fees: (September 01)
Day £2691 – £2961

HOLLYGIRT SCHOOL
Elm Avenue, Nottingham NG3 4GF
Tel: (0115) 958 0596
Head: Mrs M Connolly
Type: Girls Day 4–16
No of pupils: 340
Fees: (September 01)
Day £3831 – £5067

THE KING'S SCHOOL
Collygate Road, The Meadows,
Nottingham NG2 2EJ
Tel: (0115) 953 9194
Head: Mr R Southey
Type: Co-educational Day 4–16
No of pupils: B90 G68
Fees: (September 01) Day £2484

MOUNTFORD HOUSE SCHOOL
373 Mansfield Road, Nottingham
NG5 2DA
Tel: (0115) 960 5676
Head: Mrs D Williams
Type: Co-educational Day 3–11
No of pupils: B70 G29
Fees: (September 01)
Day £1119 – £3900

NOTTINGHAM HIGH SCHOOL
Waverley Mount, Nottingham
NG7 4ED
Tel: (0115) 978 6056
Head: Mr C S Parker
Type: Boys Day 11–18
No of pupils: 806
Fees: (September 01) Day £6474

NOTTINGHAM HIGH SCHOOL FOR GIRLS GDST
9 Arboretum Street, Nottingham
NG1 4JB
Tel: (0115) 941 7663
Head: Mrs A C Rees
Type: Girls Day 4–18
No of pupils: 1102
Fees: (September 01)
Day £3951 – £5442

NOTTINGHAM HIGH SCHOOL PREPARATORY SCHOOL
Waverley Mount, Nottingham
NG7 4ED
Tel: (0115) 845 2214
Head: Mr P M Pallant
Type: Boys Day 7–11
No of pupils: 165
Fees: (September 01) Day £5409

PLUMTREE SCHOOL
Church Hill, Plumtree, Nottingham
NG12 5ND
Tel: (0115) 937 5859
Head: Mr N White
Type: Co-educational Day 3–11
No of pupils: B76 G51
Fees: (September 01) Day £3075

ST JOSEPH'S SCHOOL
33 Derby Road, Nottingham
NG1 5AW
Tel: (0115) 941 8356
Head: Mr J Crawley
Type: Co-educational Day 1–11
No of pupils: B115 G72
Fees: (September 01) Day £3900

SALTERFORD HOUSE SCHOOL
Salterford Lane, Calverton,
Nottingham NG14 6NZ
Tel: (0115) 965 2127
Head: Mrs M Venables
Type: Co-educational Day 2–11
No of pupils: B110 G104
Fees: (September 01)
Day £3015 – £3075

TRENT COLLEGE
Long Eaton, Nottingham NG10 4AD
Tel: (0115) 849 4949
Head: Mr J S Lee
Type: Co-educational Boarding and
Day 3–18
No of pupils: B490 G300
No of boarders: F60 W105
Fees: (September 01)
FB £13384 – £14241
WB £9510 – £13160
Day £3940 – £8773

TRENT FIELDS KINDERGARTEN
19/21 Trent Boulevard, West
Bridgford, Nottingham NG2 5BB
Tel: (0115) 982 1685
Head: Mrs G A Robinson
Type: Co-educational Day 2–5
No of pupils: 70
Fees: (September 01) Day £6000

WAVERLEY HOUSE PNEU SCHOOL
13 Waverley Street, Nottingham
NG7 4DX
Tel: (0115) 978 3230
Head: Mr T J Collins
Type: Co-educational Day 3–11
No of pupils: B65 G63
Fees: (September 01)
Day £500 – £1443

RETFORD

AL KARAM SECONDARY SCHOOL
Eaton Hall, Retford,
Nottinghamshire DN22 0PR
Tel: (01777) 706441
Head: Mr M I H Pirzada
Type: Boys Boarding 11–16
No of pupils: 115
No of boarders: F115
Fees: (September 01)
FB £3300 – £6000

BRAMCOTE LORNE SCHOOL
Gamston, Retford, Nottinghamshire
DN22 0QQ
Tel: (01777) 838636
Head: Mr J H Gibson
Type: Co-educational Boarding and
Day 3–13
No of pupils: B117 G98
No of boarders: F20 W20
Fees: (September 01)
FB £7350 – £8400 WB £6750 – £7800
Day £3000 – £6150

ORCHARD SCHOOL
South Leverton, Retford,
Nottinghamshire DN22 0DJ
Tel: (01427) 880395
Head: Mrs S Fox
Type: Co-educational Day 2–16
No of pupils: B85 G70
Fees: (September 01)
Day £2490 – £3975

RANBY HOUSE
Retford, Nottinghamshire DN22 8HX
Tel: (01777) 703138
Head: Mr A C Morris
Type: Co-educational Day and
Boarding 3–13
No of pupils: B201 G134
No of boarders: F75
Fees: (September 01) FB £9375
Day £4050 – £7200

SUTTON IN ASHFIELD

LAMMAS SCHOOL
Lammas Road, Sutton in Ashfield,
Nottinghamshire NG17 2AD
Tel: (01623) 516879
Head: Mr C M Peck
Type: Co-educational Day 4–16
No of pupils: B80 G70
Fees: (September 01)
Day £2775 – £3075

WORKSOP

WORKSOP COLLEGE
Worksop, Nottinghamshire S80 3AP
Tel: (01909) 537127
Head: Mr R A Collard
Type: Co-educational Boarding and
Day 13–18
No of pupils: B255 G125
No of boarders: F120 W95
Fees: (September 01) F/WB £14460
Day £9900

OXFORDSHIRE

ABINGDON

ABINGDON SCHOOL*
Park Road, Abingdon, Oxfordshire
OX14 1DE
Tel: (01235) 521563
Head: Mr M Turner
Type: Boys Boarding and Day 11–18
No of pupils: 800
No of boarders: F65 W70
Fees: (September 01) F/WB £2294
Day £6669

COTHILL HOUSE
PREPARATORY SCHOOL
Frilford Heath, Abingdon,
Oxfordshire OX13 6JL
Tel: (01865) 390800
Head: Mr A D Richardson
Type: Boys Boarding 8–13
No of pupils: 250
No of boarders: F250
Fees: (September 01) FB £13500

JOSCA'S PREPARATORY
SCHOOL
Frilford, Abingdon, Oxfordshire
OX13 5NX
Tel: (01865) 391570
Head: Mr C J Davies
Type: Boys Day 4–13 (Girls 4–7)
No of pupils: B179 G1
No of boarders: W1
Fees: (September 01) Day £6157

MANOR PREPARATORY
SCHOOL
Faringdon Road, Abingdon,
Oxfordshire OX13 6LN
Tel: (01235) 523789
Head: Mrs D A Robinson
Type: Co-educational Day Boys 3–7
Girls 3–11
No of pupils: B38 G322
Fees: (September 01)
Day £3000 – £6000

MILLBROOK HOUSE*
Milton, Abingdon, Oxfordshire
OX14 4EL
Tel: (01235) 831237
Head: Mr S R M Glazebrook
Type: Boys Day and Boarding 7–14
No of pupils: 45
No of boarders: F25
Fees: (September 01)
FB £12750 Day £7000

OUR LADY'S CONVENT
JUNIOR SCHOOL
St John's Road, Abingdon,
Oxfordshire OX14 2HB
Tel: (01235) 523147
Head: Sister J Frances
Type: Co-educational Day 4–11
No of pupils: B55 G75
Fees: (September 01)
Day £3525 – £3615

OUR LADY'S CONVENT
SENIOR SCHOOL
Radley Road, Abingdon, Oxfordshire
OX14 3PS
Tel: (01235) 524658
Head: Mrs G Butt
Type: Girls Day 11–18
No of pupils: 360
Fees: (September 01) Day £5985

RADLEY COLLEGE
Abingdon, Oxfordshire OX14 2HR
Tel: (01235) 543000
Head: Mr A W McPhail
Type: Boys Boarding 13–18
No of pupils: 620
No of boarders: F620
Fees: (September 01)
FB £16410 – £17550

SCHOOL OF ST HELEN &
ST KATHARINE
Faringdon Road, Abingdon,
Oxfordshire OX14 1BE
Tel: (01235) 520173
Head: Mrs C Hall
Type: Girls Day 9–18
No of pupils: 595
Fees: (September 01) Day £6381

BANBURY

BLOXHAM SCHOOL*
Bloxham, Banbury, Oxfordshire
OX15 4PE
Tel: (01295) 720206
Head: Mr D K Exham
Type: Co-educational Boarding and
Day 11–18 (Day only 11–13)
No of pupils: B250 G115
No of boarders: F190 W11
Fees: (September 01) FB £17175
WB £11120 Day £8855 – £13290

THE CARRDUS SCHOOL
Overthorpe Hall, Banbury,
Oxfordshire OX17 2BS
Tel: (01295) 263733
Head: Miss S Carrdus
Type: Girls Day 3–11 (Boys 3–8)
No of pupils: B25 G120
Fees: (September 01)
Day £1845 – £5730

ST JOHN'S PRIORY SCHOOL
St John's Road, Banbury, Oxfordshire
OX16 5HX
Tel: (01295) 259607
Head: Mrs J M Walker
Type: Co-educational Day 2–11
No of pupils: B75 G85
Fees: (September 01)
Day £1200 – £4050

SIBFORD SCHOOL
Sibford Ferris, Banbury, Oxfordshire
OX15 5QL
Tel: (01295) 781200
Head: Ms S Freestone
Type: Co-educational Boarding and
Day 5–18
No of pupils: B220 G154
No of boarders: F57 W67
Fees: (September 01) FB £13524 WB
£9591 – £12597
Day £4205 – £6705

TUDOR HALL SCHOOL
Banbury, Oxfordshire OX16 9UR
Tel: (01295) 263434
Head: Miss N Godfrey
Type: Girls Boarding 11–18
No of pupils: 262
No of boarders: F233
Fees: (September 01) FB £14700
Day £9180

CHIPPING NORTON

KINGHAM HILL SCHOOL*
Kingham, Chipping Norton,
Oxfordshire OX7 6TH
Tel: (01608) 658999
Head: Mr M J Morris
Type: Co-educational Boarding and
Day 11–18
No of pupils: B182 G70
No of boarders: F213
Fees: (September 01)
F/WB £12711 – £13740
Day £7905 – £8568

WINDRUSH VALLEY SCHOOL
The Green, London Lane, Ascott-U-Wychwood, Chipping Norton, Oxfordshire OX7 6AN
Tel: (01993) 831 793
Head: Mr G A Wood
Type: Co-educational Day 3–11
No of pupils: B60 G60
Fees: (September 01)
Day £3168 – £3447

FARINGDON

FERNDALE SCHOOL
5–7 Bromsgrove, Faringdon, Oxfordshire SN7 7JF
Tel: (01367) 240618
Head: Mr C Curl
Type: Co-educational Day 3–11
No of pupils: B88 G90
Fees: (September 01)
Day £4005 – £4695

ST HUGH'S SCHOOL
Carswell Manor, Faringdon, Oxfordshire SN7 8PT
Tel: (01367) 870223
Head: Mr D Cannon
Type: Co-educational Boarding and Day 4–13
No of pupils: B168 G110
No of boarders: W40
Fees: (September 01)
F/WB £9990 – £10650
Day £4980 – £8760

ST MARY'S PRIORY NURSERY SCHOOL
St Mary's Priory, Fernham, Faringdon, Oxfordshire SN7 7PP
Tel: (01367) 242602
Head: Mrs W L Thompson
Type: Co-educational Day 3–5
No of pupils: 24
Fees: (September 01) On application

HENLEY-ON-THAMES

RUPERT HOUSE
90 Bell Street, Henley-on-Thames, Oxfordshire RG9 2BN
Tel: (01491) 574263
Head: Mrs G M Crane
Type: Co-educational Day Boys 4–7 Girls 4–11
No of pupils: B54 G173
Fees: (September 01)
Day £2415 – £5850

ST MARY'S SCHOOL
13 St Andrew's Road, Henley-on-Thames, Oxfordshire RG9 1HS
Tel: (01491) 573118
Head: Mrs S Bradley
Type: Co-educational Day 2–11
No of pupils: B75 G75
Fees: (September 01)
Day £858 – £6040

SHIPLAKE COLLEGE
Henley-on-Thames, Oxfordshire RG9 4BW
Tel: (0118) 940 2455
Head: Mr N V Bevan
Type: Boys Day and Boarding 13–18 (Day Girls 16–18)
No of pupils: B270 G9
No of boarders: F120 W100
Fees: (September 01) FB £15405
Day £10392

OXFORD

ABACUS COLLEGE*
Threeways House, George Street, Oxford OX1 2BJ
Tel: (01865) 240111
Head: Dr R Carrington and Mrs J Wasilewski
Type: Co-educational Day and Boarding 15–19
No of pupils: B100 G50
No of boarders: F70
Fees: (September 01)
FB £8950 – £11200
Day £5250 – £7500

CHERWELL COLLEGE*
Greyfriars, Paradise Street, Oxford OX1 1LD
Tel: (01865) 242670
Head: Mr A Thompson
Type: Co-educational Day and Boarding 16+
No of pupils: B85 G65
No of boarders: F90 W10
Fees: (September 01) F/WB £15750
Day £10500

CHRIST CHURCH CATHEDRAL SCHOOL
3 Brewer Street, Oxford OX1 1QW
Tel: (01865) 242561
Head: Mr J R Smith
Type: Boys Day and Boarding 2–13
No of pupils: B149 G3
No of boarders: F21
Fees: (September 01)
FB £4437 – £11040
Day £2004 – £7116

D'OVERBROECK'S COLLEGE*
1 Park Town, Oxford OX2 6SN
Tel: (01865) 310000
Head: Mr S Cohen and Dr R K Knowles
Type: Co-educational Day and Boarding 13–19 (Day only 13–16)
No of pupils: 280
No of boarders: F100
Fees: (September 01) FB £15615
Day £6210 – £9660

DRAGON SCHOOL
Bardwell Road, Oxford OX2 6SS
Tel: (01865) 315400
Head: Mr R S Trafford
Type: Co-educational Boarding and Day 3–13
No of pupils: B568 G268
No of boarders: F280
Fees: (September 01) FB £13830
Day £6210 – £9660

EDWARD GREENE'S TUTORIAL ESTABLISHMENT
45 Pembroke Street, Oxford OX1 1BP
Tel: (01865) 248308
Head: Mr E P C Greene
Type: Co-educational Day 12–20
No of pupils: B14 G22
No of boarders: F18
Fees: (September 01)
Day £3360 – £16800

EMMANUAL CHRISTIAN SCHOOL
Sandford Road, Littlemore, Oxford OX4 4PU
Tel: (01865) 395236
Head: Mrs R J Stokes
Type: Co-educational Day 4–11
No of pupils: B27 G36
Fees: (September 01) Day £2616

HEADINGTON SCHOOL OXFORD
Oxford, Oxfordshire OX3 7TD
Tel: (01865) 759113
Head: Mrs H A Fender
Type: Girls Day and Boarding 3–18 (Co-ed 3–7)
No of pupils: B16 G825
No of boarders: F112 W62
Fees: (September 01) FB £12075 – £13650 WB £11625 – £13230
Day £3480 – £7485

MAGDALEN COLLEGE SCHOOL
Cowley Place, Oxford OX4 1DZ
Tel: (01865) 242191
Head: Mr A D Halls
Type: Boys Day 7–18
No of pupils: 600
Fees: (September 01)
Day £5445 – £7080

NEW COLLEGE SCHOOL
2 Savile Road, Oxford OX1 3UA
Tel: (01865) 243657
Head: Mrs P Hindle
Type: Boys Day 4–13
No of pupils: 145
Fees: (September 01)
Day £3750 – £5790

OXFORD HIGH SCHOOL GDST
Belbroughton Road, Oxford OX2 6XA
Tel: (01865) 559888
Head: Miss O F S Lusk
Type: Girls Day 3–18 (Boys 3–7)
No of pupils: B45 G860
Fees: (September 01)
Day £1847 – £5442

OXFORD TUTORIAL COLLEGE
12 King Edward Street, Oxford OX1 4HT
Tel: (01865) 793333
Head: Mr B Davey
Type: Co-educational Day 16+
No of pupils: B57 G53
Fees: (September 01)
Day £3990 per subject

RYE ST ANTONY SCHOOL
Pullens Lane, Oxford OX3 0BY
Tel: (01865) 762802
Head: Miss A M Jones
Type: Girls Boarding and Day 3–18 (Boys 3–8)
No of pupils: B20 G380
No of boarders: F90 W20
Fees: (September 01) FB £10350 – £11985 WB £9600 – £11250
Day £4140 – £6900

ST CLARE'S, OXFORD*
139 Banbury Road, Oxford OX2 7AL
Tel: (01865) 552031
Head: Mr B Roberts
Type: Co-educational Boarding and Day 16–20
No of pupils: B143 G220
No of boarders: F348
Fees: (September 01)
FB £18010 – £18300 Day £11260

ST EDWARD'S SCHOOL
Woodstock Road, Oxford OX2 7NN
Tel: (01865) 319200
Head: Mr D Christie
Type: Co-educational Boarding and Day 13–18
No of pupils: B410 G215
No of boarders: F440
Fees: (September 01) FB £17490
Day £13125

SUMMER FIELDS
Oxford, Oxfordshire OX2 7EN
Tel: (01865) 454433
Head: Mr R Badham-Thornhill
Type: Boys Boarding and Day 8–13
No of pupils: 250
No of boarders: F240
Fees: (September 01) FB £13200
Day £9750

WYCHWOOD SCHOOL
74 Banbury Road, Oxford OX2 6JR
Tel: (01865) 557976
Head: Mrs S M P Wingfield Digby
Type: Girls Boarding and Day 11–18
No of pupils: 150
No of boarders: F25 W35
Fees: (September 01) FB £10290
WB £9990 Day £6750

WALLINGFORD

CRANFORD HOUSE SCHOOL
Moulsford, Wallingford, Oxfordshire OX10 9HT
Tel: (01491) 651218
Head: Mrs A B Gray
Type: Girls Day 3–16 (Boys 3–7)
No of pupils: B49 G224
Fees: (September 01)
Day £4485 – £7215

MOULSFORD PREPARATORY SCHOOL
Moulsford, Wallingford, Oxfordshire OX10 9HR
Tel: (01491) 651438
Head: Mr M J Higham
Type: Boys Boarding and Day 5–13
No of pupils: 220
No of boarders: W51
Fees: (September 01)
WB £9435 – £10155
Day £4830 – £8085

WANTAGE

ST ANDREW'S
Wallingford Street, Wantage, Oxfordshire OX12 8AZ
Tel: (01235) 762345
Head: Mrs M Parkes
Type: Co-educational Day and Boarding 3–11
No of pupils: B43 G39
No of boarders: W1
Fees: (September 01)
WB £7191 – £7275
Day £1188 – £4488

ST MARY'S SCHOOL*
Newbury Street, Wantage, Oxfordshire OX12 8BZ
Tel: (01235) 773800
Head: Mrs S Sowden
Type: Girls Boarding and Day 11–18
No of pupils: 189
No of boarders: F173
Fees: (September 01) FB £16425
Day £10950

WITNEY

COKETHORPE SCHOOL*
Witney, Oxfordshire OX29 7PU
Tel: (01993) 703921
Head: Mr P J S Cantwell
Type: Co-educational Boarding and Day 7–18 (Day girls only)
No of pupils: B330 G180
No of boarders: F20 W20
Fees: (September 01)
F/WB £10500 – £15750
Day £5310 – £9480

THE KING'S SCHOOL
12 Wesley Walk, High Street, Witney, Oxfordshire OX8 6ZJ
Tel: (01993) 709985
Head: Mr K Elmitt
Type: Co-educational Day 11–16
No of pupils: B70 G50
Fees: (September 01) On application

THE KING'S SCHOOL, PRIMARY
New Yatt Road, Witney, Oxfordshire OX8 6TA
Tel: (01993) 778463
Head: Miss J Morgan
Type: Co-educational Day 5–11
No of pupils: B63 G56
Fees: (September 01) Day £3500

RUTLAND

OAKHAM

BROOKE PRIORY SCHOOL
Station Approach, Oakham, Rutland
LE15 6QW
Tel: (01572) 724778
Head: Mrs E Bell
Type: Co-educational Day 4–11
No of pupils: B92 G75
Fees: (September 01)
Day £3510 – £4290

OAKHAM SCHOOL*
Chapel Close, Oakham, Rutland
LE15 6DT
Tel: (01572) 758758
Head: Mr A R M Little
Type: Co-educational Boarding and
Day 10–18
No of pupils: B530 G525
No of boarders: F580
Fees: (September 01)
FB £13770 – £16110
Day £8790 – £9630

UPPINGHAM

UPPINGHAM SCHOOL
Uppingham, Rutland LE15 9QE
Tel: (01572) 822216
Head: Dr S C Winkley
Type: Co-educational Boarding and
Day 13–18
No of pupils: B520 G180
No of boarders: F659
Fees: (September 01) FB £16275
Day £11400

SHROPSHIRE

BRIDGNORTH

DOWER HOUSE SCHOOL
The Dower House, Quatt,
Bridgnorth, Shropshire WV15 6QW
Tel: (01746) 780309
Head: Mr J Shaw
Type: Co-educational Day 3–11
No of pupils: B50 G70
Fees: (September 01)
Day £1290 – £3870

BUCKNELL

BEDSTONE COLLEGE
Bedstone, Bucknell, Shropshire
SY7 0BG
Tel: (01547) 530303
Head: Mr M S Symonds
Type: Co-educational Boarding and
Day 3–18
No of pupils: B141 G91
No of boarders: F136
Fees: (September 01)
FB £9327 – £13800
Day £5274 – £7320

ELLESMERE

ELLESMERE COLLEGE
Ellesmere, Shropshire SY12 9AB
Tel: (01691) 622321
Head: Mr B J Wignall
Type: Co-educational Boarding and
Day 9–18
No of pupils: B328 G142
No of boarders: F190 W90
Fees: (September 01)
FB £11460 – £14700 WB £12600
Day £5730 – £9600

LUDLOW

MOOR PARK SCHOOL
Ludlow, Shropshire SY8 4DZ
Tel: (01584) 876061
Head: Mrs J Morris
Type: Co-educational Boarding and
Day 3–13
No of pupils: B115 G115
No of boarders: F18 W55
Fees: (September 01)
F/WB £8850 – £10770
Day £3675 – £7875

NEWPORT

CASTLE HOUSE SCHOOL
Chetwynd End, Newport, Shropshire
TF10 7JE
Tel: (01952) 811035
Head: Mr R M Walden
Type: Co-educational Day 3–11
No of pupils: B60 G55
Fees: (September 01)
Day £1500 – £3960

OSWESTRY

BELLAN HOUSE
PREPARATORY SCHOOL
Bellan House, Church Street,
Oswestry, Shropshire SY11 2ST
Tel: (01691) 653453
Head: Mrs S L Durham
Type: Co-educational Day 2–9
No of pupils: B91 G92
Fees: (September 01) On application

MORETON HALL*
Weston Rhyn, Oswestry, Shropshire
SY11 3EW
Tel: (01691) 776020
Head: Mr J Forster
Type: Girls Boarding and Day 8–18
No of pupils: 265
No of boarders: F219
Fees: (September 01) FB £15960
Day £10965

OSWESTRY SCHOOL
Upper Brook Street, Oswestry,
Shropshire SY11 2TL
Tel: (01691) 655711
Head: Mr P D Stockdale
Type: Co-educational Boarding and
Day 2–18
No of pupils: 426
No of boarders: F101 W30
Fees: (September 01)
FB £12500 – £13362
Day £5472 – £7968

SHREWSBURY

ADCOTE SCHOOL FOR GIRLS
Little Ness, Shrewsbury, Shropshire
SY4 2JY
Tel: (01939) 260202
Head: Mrs A Read
Type: Girls Boarding and Day 4–18
No of pupils: 100
No of boarders: F31 W10
Fees: (September 01)
FB £10830 – £13365
WB £9840 – £12195
Day £4065 – £7530

CONCORD COLLEGE*
Acton Burnell Hall, Shrewsbury,
Shropshire SY5 7PF
Tel: (01694) 731631
Head: Mr A L Morris
Type: Co-educational Boarding and
Day 12–18
No of pupils: B160 G140
No of boarders: F280
Fees: (September 01) FB £16200
Day £5800

KINGSLAND GRANGE
Old Roman Road, Shrewsbury,
Shropshire SY3 9AH
Tel: (01743) 232132
Head: Mr M C James
Type: Boys Day 4–13
No of pupils: 150
Fees: (September 01)
Day £3885 – £6240

PACKWOOD HAUGH
Ruyton XI Towns, Shrewsbury,
Shropshire SY4 1HX
Tel: (01939) 260217
Head: Mr N T Westlake
Type: Co-educational Boarding and
Day 4–13
No of pupils: B163 G78
No of boarders: F141
Fees: (September 01) FB £11274
Day £3750 – £8760

PRESTFELDE PREPARATORY SCHOOL
London Road, Shrewsbury,
Shropshire SY2 6NZ
Tel: (01743) 245400
Head: Mr J R Bridgeland
Type: Co-educational Day and
Boarding 3–13
No of pupils: B241 G69
No of boarders: F25
Fees: (September 01) FB £9150
Day £2310 – £7230

ST WINEFRIDE'S CONVENT SCHOOL
Belmont, Shrewsbury, Shropshire
SY1 1TE
Tel: (01743) 369883
Head: Sister Felicity
Type: Co-educational Day 3–11
No of pupils: B57 G74
Fees: (April 02) Day £1965 – £2010

SHREWSBURY HIGH SCHOOL GDST
32 Town Walls, Shrewsbury,
Shropshire SY1 1TN
Tel: (01743) 362872
Head: Mrs M L R Cass
Type: Girls Day 3–18
No of pupils: 605
Fees: (September 01)
Day £3951 – £5442

SHREWSBURY SCHOOL
The Schools, Shrewsbury, Shropshire
SY3 7BA
Tel: (01743) 280525
Head: Mr J Goulding
Type: Boys Boarding and Day 13–18
No of pupils: 700
No of boarders: F557
Fees: (September 01) FB £17085
Day £11985

TELFORD

THE OLD HALL SCHOOL
Holyhead Road, Wellington, Telford,
Shropshire TF1 2DN
Tel: (01952) 223117
Head: Mr R J Ward
Type: Co-educational Day 3–13
No of pupils: B162 G162
Fees: (September 01)
Day £3975 – £6225

WREKIN COLLEGE
Wellington, Telford, Shropshire
TF1 3BH
Tel: (01952) 240131/242305
Head: Mr S G Drew
Type: Co-educational Boarding and
Day 11–19
No of pupils: B200 G150
No of boarders: F114
Fees: (September 01)
FB £13200 – £15180
Day £7590 – £9180

WHITCHURCH

WHITE HOUSE SCHOOL
Heath Road, Whitchurch, Shropshire
SY13 2AA
Tel: (01948) 662730
Head: Mrs H Clarke
Type: Co-educational Day 4–11
No of pupils: B80 G80
Fees: (September 01) Day £2130

SOMERSET

BRUTON

BRUTON SCHOOL FOR GIRLS
Sunny Hill, Bruton, Somerset
BA10 0NT
Tel: (01749) 812277
Head: Mrs B C Bates
Type: Girls Day and Boarding 3–18
No of pupils: 570
No of boarders: F145
Fees: (September 01)
F/WB £9960 – £11610
Day £5100 – £6750

KING'S SCHOOL
Bruton, Somerset BA10 0ED
Tel: (01749) 814200
Head: Mr R I Smyth
Type: Co-educational Boarding and
Day 13–18
No of pupils: B289 G79
No of boarders: F243
Fees: (September 01)
FB £14970 Day £10965

BURNHAM-ON-SEA

ST CHRISTOPHER'S
St Christophers Way,
Burnham-on-Sea, Somerset TA8 2NY
Tel: (01278) 782234
Head: Mrs D Symes
Type: Co-educational Day 3–11
No of pupils: B40 G45
Fees: (September 01) On application

SOUTHLEIGH KINDERGARTEN

11 Rectory Road, Burnham-on-Sea,
Somerset TA8 2BY
Tel: (01278) 783999
Head: Mrs L Easton
Type: Co-educational Day 2–7
No of pupils: B40 G40
Fees: (September 01)
Day £525 – £3000

CHARD

CHARD SCHOOL

Fore Street, Chard, Somerset
TA20 1QA
Tel: (01460) 63234
Head: Mr J G Stotesbury
Type: Co-educational Day 2–11
No of pupils: B60 G60
Fees: (September 01)
Day £2640 – £2841

CLEVEDON

ST BRANDON'S SCHOOL

Elton Road, Clevedon, Somerset
BS21 7SD
Tel: (01275) 875092
Head: Mrs S Vesey
Type: Co-educational Day 3–11
No of pupils: B70 G70
Fees: (September 01)
Day £750 – £3780

CREWKERNE

PERROTT HILL SCHOOL

North Perrott, Crewkerne, Somerset
TA18 7SL
Tel: (01460) 72051
Head: Mr M J Davies
Type: Co-educational Boarding and
Day 3–13
No of pupils: B94 G65
No of boarders: F10 W16
Fees: (September 01) FB £10170
WB £9270 Day £2199 – £7335

ST MARTIN'S INDEPENDENT SCHOOL

24 Abbey Street, Crewkerne,
Somerset TA18 7HY
Tel: (01460) 73265
Head: Mrs J A Murrell
Type: Co-educational Day 4–13
No of pupils: B50 G50
Fees: (September 01)
Day £1200 – £2850

EAST BRENT

ROSSHOLME SCHOOL

East Brent, Somerset TA9 4JA
Tel: (01278) 760219
Head: Mrs S J Webb
Type: Girls Boarding and Day 3–16
(Co-ed 3–7)
No of pupils: 96
No of boarders: F8 W4
Fees: (September 01)
FB £6960 – £8670 WB £6750 – £8460
Day £2520 – £5940

GLASTONBURY

MILLFIELD PRE-PREPARATORY SCHOOL

Magdalene Street, Glastonbury,
Somerset BA6 9EJ
Tel: (01458) 832902
Head: Mrs M J Greenhalgh
Type: Co-educational Day 2–7
No of pupils: B59 G69
Fees: (September 01) On application

MILLFIELD PREPARATORY SCHOOL

Glastonbury, Somerset BA6 8LD
Tel: (01458) 832446
Head: Mr K Cheney
Type: Co-educational Boarding and
Day 7–13
No of pupils: B270 G190
No of boarders: F200
Fees: (September 01) FB £13020
Day £8790

SHEPTON MALLET

ALL HALLOWS

Cranmore Hall, East Cranmore,
Shepton Mallet, Somerset BA4 4SF
Tel: (01749) 880227
Head: Mr C J Bird
Type: Co-educational Boarding and
Day 4–13
No of pupils: B170 G110
No of boarders: F70
Fees: (September 01) F/WB £11130
Day £3720 – £7575

STREET

MILLFIELD SCHOOL*

Street, Somerset BA16 0YD
Tel: (01458) 442291
Head: Mr P M Johnson
Type: Co-educational Boarding and
Day 2–19
No of pupils: 1819
No of boarders: F933
Fees: (September 01) FB £16770
Day £10980

TAUNTON

KING'S COLLEGE

Taunton, Somerset TA1 3DX
Tel: (01823) 328200
Head: Mr R S Funnell
Type: Co-educational Boarding and
Day 13–18
No of pupils: B283 G150
No of boarders: F301
Fees: (September 01) On application

KING'S HALL SCHOOL

Pyrland, Kingston Road, Taunton,
Somerset TA2 8AA
Tel: (01823) 285920
Head: Mr J K Macpherson
Type: Co-educational Boarding and
Day 3–13
No of pupils: B215 G175
No of boarders: F50 W25
Fees: (September 01)
FB £6555 – £11025
WB £6195 – £10635
Day £2595 – £7815

QUEEN'S COLLEGE

Trull Road, Taunton, Somerset
TA1 4QS
Tel: (01823) 272559
Head: Mr C J Alcock
Type: Co-educational Day and
Boarding 2–18
No of pupils: B370 G310
No of boarders: F171
Fees: (September 01)
FB £6345 – £13050
Day £3105 – £8550

QUEEN'S COLLEGE JUNIOR AND PRE-PREPARATORY SCHOOLS

Trull Road, Taunton, Somerset
TA1 4QP
Tel: (01823) 272990
Head: Mr J M Backhouse and
Mrs E Gibbs
Type: Co-educational Day and
Boarding 2–11
No of pupils: B104 G105
No of boarders: F33
Fees: (September 01)
FB £6345 – £9171
Day £2745 – £5868

TAUNTON INTERNATIONAL STUDY CENTRE (TISC)

Taunton School, Taunton, Somerset
TA2 6AD
Tel: (01823) 348100
Head: Mrs S A Harris
Type: Co-educational Boarding 9–17
No of pupils: B33 G22
No of boarders: F55
Fees: (September 01)
FB £15300 – £17850

TAUNTON PREPARATORY SCHOOL

Staplegrove Road, Taunton,
Somerset TA2 6AE
Tel: (01823) 349250
Head: Mr M Anderson
Type: Co-educational Day and
Boarding 3–13
No of pupils: B259 G212
No of boarders: F38
Fees: (September 01)
FB £7875 – £11910
Day £2865 – £6555

TAUNTON SCHOOL

Taunton, Somerset TA2 6AD
Tel: (01823) 349200/349223
Head: Mr J P Whiteley
Type: Co-educational Boarding and
Day 13–18
No of pupils: B260 G185
No of boarders: F177
Fees: (September 01) FB £15195
Day £9765

WATCHET

BUCKLAND SCHOOL

7 St Decumans Road, Watchet,
Somerset TA23 0HR
Tel: (01984) 631314
Head: Mrs Pirt
Type: Co-educational Day 3–10
No of pupils: 40
Fees: (September 01) Day £1800

WELLINGTON

WELLINGTON SCHOOL

South Street, Wellington, Somerset
TA21 8NT
Tel: (01823) 668800
Head: Mr A J Rogers
Type: Co-educational Boarding and
Day 10–18
No of pupils: B435 G408
No of boarders: F145
Fees: (September 01)
FB £10017 – £11250
Day £4980 – £6165

WELLS

WELLS CATHEDRAL JUNIOR SCHOOL

8 New Street, Wells, Somerset
BA5 2LQ
Tel: (01749) 672291
Head: Mr N M Wilson
Type: Co-educational Boarding and
Day 3–11
No of pupils: B86 G108
No of boarders: F9 W1
Fees: (September 01) FB £10434
Day £3612 – £7365

WELLS CATHEDRAL SCHOOL

Wells, Somerset BA5 2ST
Tel: (01749) 672117
Head: Mrs E C Cairncross
Type: Co-educational Boarding and
Day 3–18
No of pupils: B396 G368
No of boarders: F246 W2
Fees: (September 01)
FB £12285 – £14550
Day £3900 – £8640

YEOVIL

CHILTON CANTELO SCHOOL

Chilton Cantelo, Yeovil, Somerset
BA22 8BG
Tel: (01935) 850555
Head: Mr D S von Zeffman
Type: Co-educational Boarding and
Day 7–18
No of pupils: B135 G85
No of boarders: F120
Fees: (September 01)
FB £8910 – £10800
Day £4500 – £5760

HAZLEGROVE (KING'S BRUTON PREPARATORY SCHOOL)

Hazlegrove House, Sparkford, Yeovil,
Somerset BA22 7JA
Tel: (01963) 440314
Head: Rev B Bearcroft
Type: Co-educational Day and
Boarding 3–13
No of pupils: B300 G120
No of boarders: F85
Fees: (September 01)
FB £10290 – £11670
Day £4110 – £8370

THE PARK SCHOOL

Yeovil, Somerset BA20 1DH
Tel: (01935) 423514
Head: Mr P W Bate
Type: Co-educational Day and
Boarding 3–18
No of pupils: B108 G135
No of boarders: F23 W8
Fees: (September 01)
FB £9255 – £10320
WB £8625 – £9690
Day £2850 – £5640

BATH

BATH ACADEMY
27 Queen Square, Bath, North East
Somerset BA1 2HX
Tel: (01225) 334577
Head: Mrs L H Brown
Type: Co-educational Boarding 14–20
No of pupils: B50 G70
No of boarders: F80
Fees: (September 01)
FB £10950 – £13950
Day £6450 – £7950

DOWNSIDE SCHOOL*
Stratton-on-the-Fosse, Radstock,
Bath, North East Somerset BA3 4RJ
Tel: (01761) 235100
Head: Dom A Sutch
Type: Boys Boarding and Day 8–18
No of pupils: 340
No of boarders: F295
Fees: (September 01)
FB £11988 – £15093
Day £6984 – £7767

KING EDWARD'S JUNIOR SCHOOL
North Road, Bath, North East
Somerset BA2 6JA
Tel: (01225) 463218
Head: Mr J Croker
Type: Co-educational Day 7–11
No of pupils: 192
Fees: (September 01) Day £5052

KING EDWARD'S PRE-PREP SCHOOL
Weston Lane, Bath, North East
Somerset BA1 4AQ
Tel: (01225) 421681
Head: Mrs J A Siderfin
Type: Co-educational Day 3–7
No of pupils: B78 G30
Fees: (September 01) On application

KING EDWARD'S SCHOOL, BATH
North Road, Bath, North East
Somerset BA2 6HU
Tel: (01225) 464313
Head: Mr P J Winter
Type: Co-educational Day 3–18
No of pupils: B800 G214
Fees: (September 01)
Day £4230 – £6477

KINGSWOOD PREPARATORY SCHOOL
College Road, Lansdown, Bath,
North East Somerset BA1 5SD
Tel: (01225) 310468
Head: Mrs M H Newbery
Type: Co-educational Day and
Boarding 3–11
No of pupils: B172 G127
No of boarders: F7 W1
Fees: (September 01) FB £10998
Day £4029 – £4791

KINGSWOOD SCHOOL*
Lansdown, Bath, North East
Somerset BA1 5RG
Tel: (01225) 734200
Head: Mr G M Best
Type: Co-educational Boarding and
Day 3–18
No of pupils: B336 G236
No of boarders: F152 W31
Fees: (September 01)
FB £10998 – £15498
WB £10899 – £13698
Day £4029 – £8499

MONKTON COMBE JUNIOR SCHOOL
Combe Down, Bath, North East
Somerset BA2 7ET
Tel: (01225) 837912
Head: Mr C J Stafford
Type: Co-educational Day and
Boarding 2–13
No of pupils: B215 G116
No of boarders: F15 W20
Fees: (September 01)
FB £11430 – £11970
WB £9910 – £10950
Day £4590 – £8340

MONKTON COMBE SCHOOL
Bath, North East Somerset BA2 7HG
Tel: (01225) 721102
Head: Mr M J Cuthbertson
Type: Co-educational Boarding and
Day 2–19
No of pupils: B404 G227
No of boarders: F254
Fees: (September 01)
FB £11430 – £16320
Day £7050 – £11130

PARAGON SCHOOL
Lyncombe House, Lyncombe Vale,
Bath, North East Somerset BA2 4LT
Tel: (01225) 310837
Head: Mr D J Martin
Type: Co-educational Day 3–11
No of pupils: B142 G115
Fees: (September 01)
Day £3735 – £4149

PRIOR PARK COLLEGE
Ralph Allen Drive, Bath,
North East Somerset BA2 5AH
Tel: (01225) 831000
Head: Dr G Mercer
Type: Co-educational Boarding and
Day 11–18
No of pupils: B275 G225
No of boarders: F87 W28
Fees: (September 01) F/WB £14685
Day £7485 – £8145

THE ROYAL HIGH SCHOOL*
Lansdown, Bath, North East
Somerset BA1 5SZ
Tel: (01225) 313877
Head: Mr J Graham-Brown
Type: Girls Boarding and Day 3–18
No of pupils: 925
No of boarders: F100
Fees: (September 01) FB £10692
Day £3906 – £5010

NORTH SOMERSET

WESTON-SUPER-MARE

ASHBROOKE HOUSE
9 Ellenborough Park North, Weston-Super-Mare, North Somerset
BS23 1XH
Tel: (01934) 629515
Head: Mr J C Teasdale
Type: Co-educational Day 3–11
No of pupils: B60 G50
Fees: (September 01)
Day £1071 – £2472

LANCASTER HOUSE SCHOOL
38 Hill Road, Weston-Super-Mare, North Somerset BS23 2RY
Tel: (01934) 624116
Head: Mrs S Lewis
Type: Co-educational Day 4–11
No of pupils: B21 G35
Fees: (September 01)
Day £1540 – £1700

WYNCROFT
5 Charlton Road, Weston-Super-Mare, North Somerset DS23 4HP
Tel: (01934) 626556
Head: Mrs E M D Thorn
Type: Co-educational Day 4–11
No of pupils: 100
Fees: (September 01) On application

WINSCOMBE

THE HALL PRE-PREPARATORY SCHOOL SIDCOT
Sidcot, Winscombe, North Somerset
BS25 1PD
Tel: (01934) 844118
Head: Ms W Wardman
Type: Co-educational Day 3–9
No of pupils: B55 G43
Fees: (September 01) On application

SIDCOT SCHOOL
Winscombe, North Somerset
BS25 1PD
Tel: (01934) 843102
Head: Mr J Walmsley
Type: Co-educational Boarding and Day 3–18
No of pupils: B256 G162
No of boarders: F122 W12
Fees: (September 01)
FB £11505 – £14685
Day £3820 – £7710

STAFFORDSHIRE

ABBOTS BROMLEY

SCHOOL OF ST MARY AND ST ANNE
Abbots Bromley, Staffordshire
WS15 3BW
Tel: (01283) 840232
Head: Mrs M Steel
Type: Girls Boarding and Day 5–18
No of pupils: 242
No of boarders: F46 W22
Fees: (September 01)
FB £9765 – £13746
Day £3510 – £8715

CANNOCK

CHASE ACADEMY
St John's Road, Cannock, Staffordshire WS11 3UR
Tel: (01543) 501800
Head: Mr M D Ellse
Type: Co-educational Day and Boarding 3–18
No of pupils: B74 G49
No of boarders: F1
Fees: (September 01) FB £11100
Day £1668 – £5652

HANBURY

HOWITT HOUSE SCHOOL
New Lodge, Hanbury, Staffordshire
DE13 8TG
Tel: (01283) 820236
Head: Mr M H Davis
Type: Co-educational Day 3–12
No of pupils: B36 G30
Fees: (September 01) Day £3054

LICHFIELD

LICHFIELD CATHEDRAL SCHOOL
The Palace, Lichfield, Staffordshire
WS13 7LH
Tel: (01543) 306170
Head: Mr Allwood
Type: Co-educational Day and Boarding 4–13
No of pupils: B128 G102
No of boarders: F15 W2
Fees: (September 01) FB £8994 – £9315 WB £8178 – £8502
Day £6060 – £6384

MAPLE HAYES HALL DYSLEXIA SCHOOL*
Abnalls Lane, Lichfield, Staffordshire
WS13 8BL
Tel: (01543) 264387
Head: Dr E Neville Brown
Type: Co-educational Boarding and Day 7–17 (Girls day only)
No of pupils: 110
No of boarders: F22 W29
Fees: (September 01)
F/WB £11475 – £14685
Day £9045 – £12255

ST JOHN'S PREPARATORY SCHOOL
28 St John Street, Lichfield, Staffordshire WS13 6BB
Tel: (01543) 263345
Head: Mrs A Watson
Type: Co-educational Day 2–11
No of pupils: B30 G34
Fees: (September 01)
Day £2190 – £4050

NEWCASTLE-UNDER-LYME

EDENHURST SCHOOL
Westlands Avenue, Newcastle-under-Lyme, Staffordshire ST5 2PU
Tel: (01782) 619348
Head: Mr N H F Copestick
Type: Co-educational Day 3–14
No of pupils: B118 G122
Fees: (September 01)
Day £2994 – £5055

NEWCASTLE-UNDER-LYME SCHOOL
Mount Pleasant, Newcastle-under-Lyme, Staffordshire ST5 1DB
Tel: (01782) 631197
Head: Dr R M Reynolds
Type: Co-educational Day 7–18
No of pupils: B500 G561
Fees: (September 01)
Day £4524 – £5115

STAFFORD

BROOKLANDS SCHOOL
167 Eccleshall Road, Stafford, Staffordshire ST16 1PD
Tel: (01785) 251399
Head: Mr C T O'Donnell
Type: Co-educational Day 3–11
No of pupils: B85 G85
Fees: (September 01)
Day £2724 – £4959

ST BEDE'S SCHOOL
Bishton Hall, Wolseley Bridge, Stafford, Staffordshire ST17 0XN
Tel: (01889) 881277
Head: Mr H C Stafford Northcote and A H Stafford Northcote
Type: Co-educational Boarding and Day 2–13
No of pupils: B68 G50
No of boarders: F10 W15
Fees: (September 01) FB £8316
Day £3738 – £6342

ST DOMINIC'S SCHOOL
32 Bargate Street, Brewood, Stafford, Staffordshire ST19 9BA
Tel: (01902) 850248
Head: Mrs M E K Peakman
Type: Girls Day 2–16 (Co-ed 2–7)
No of pupils: B15 G240
Fees: (September 01)
Day £1740 – £7185

STAFFORD GRAMMAR SCHOOL
Burton Manor, Stafford, Staffordshire ST18 9AT
Tel: (01785) 249752
Head: Mr M R Darley
Type: Co-educational Day 11–18
No of pupils: B197 G157
Fees: (September 01) Day £5364

VERNON LODGE PREPARATORY SCHOOL
School Lane, Stretton, Stafford, Staffordshire ST19 9LJ
Tel: (01902) 850568
Head: Mrs P Sills
Type: Co-educational Day 2–11
No of pupils: B67 G38
Fees: (September 01)
Day £3690 – £4440

YARLET SCHOOL
Yarlet, Stafford, Staffordshire ST18 9SU
Tel: (01785) 286568
Head: Mr R S Plant
Type: Co-educational Boarding and Day 2–13
No of pupils: B93 G62
No of boarders: W19
Fees: (September 01) FB £9600
Day £3810 – £8145

STOKE-ON-TRENT

ST DOMINIC'S INDEPENDENT JUNIOR SCHOOL
Hartshill Road, Stoke-on-Trent, Staffordshire ST4 7LY
Tel: (01782) 848588
Head: Mrs J A Oliver
Type: Co-educational Day 3–12
No of pupils: B83 G82
Fees: (September 01)
Day £2228 – £2928

ST JOSEPH'S PREPARATORY SCHOOL
London Road, Trent Vale, Stoke-on-Trent, Staffordshire ST4 5RF
Tel: (01782) 417533
Head: Mrs M B Hughes
Type: Co-educational Day 3–11
No of pupils: B93 G72
Fees: (September 01)
Day £2955 – £3795

STONE

ST DOMINIC'S PRIORY SCHOOL
21 Station Road, Stone, Staffordshire ST15 8EN
Tel: (01785) 814181
Head: Mrs J Hildreth
Type: Girls Day 3–18 (Boys 3–11)
No of pupils: B22 G338
Fees: (September 01)
Day £3294 – £5055

UTTOXETER

ABBOTSHOLME SCHOOL
Rocester, Uttoxeter, Staffordshire ST14 5BS
Tel: (01889) 590217
Head: Dr S D Tommis
Type: Co-educational Boarding and Day 7–18 (Boarders from 11)
No of pupils: B163 G88
No of boarders: F65 W24
Fees: (September 01)
F/WB £13125 – £15318
Day £6000 – £10242

DENSTONE COLLEGE
Uttoxeter, Staffordshire ST14 5HN
Tel: (01889) 590484
Head: Mr D M Derbyshire
Type: Co-educational Boarding and Day 11–18
No of pupils: B278 G119
No of boarders: F131 W29
Fees: (September 01)
F/WB £10800 – £12000
Day £5400 – £7800

SMALLWOOD MANOR PREPARATORY SCHOOL
Uttoxeter, Staffordshire ST14 8NS
Tel: (01889) 562083
Head: Revd C J Cann
Type: Co-educational Day 2–11
No of pupils: B90 G73
Fees: (September 01)
Day £3975 – £5025

STOCKTON-ON-TEES

EAGLESCLIFFE

TEESSIDE HIGH SCHOOL
The Avenue, Eaglescliffe,
Stockton-on-Tees TS16 9AT
Tel: (01642) 782095
Head: Mrs H J French
Type: Girls Day 3–18
No of pupils: 470
Fees: (September 01)
Day £3510 – £5592

NORTON

RED HOUSE SCHOOL
36 The Green, Norton,
Stockton-on-Tees TS20 1DX
Tel: (01642) 553370
Head: Mr C M J Allen
Type: Co-educational Day 3–16
No of pupils: B236 G196
Fees: (September 01)
Day £3516 – £4479

YARM

YARM SCHOOL
The Friarage, Yarm,
Stockton-on-Tees TS15 9EJ
Tel: (01642) 786023/781447
Head: Mr D M Dunn and
Mr D G Woodward
Type: Co-educational Day 4–18
No of pupils: B735 G126
Fees: (September 01)
Day £4140 – £6795

SUFFOLK

BECCLES

THE OLD SCHOOL
Henstead, Beccles, Suffolk NR34 7LG
Tel: (01502) 741150
Head: Mr M J Hewett
Type: Co-educational Day 4–13
No of pupils: B71 G40
Fees: (September 01)
Day £3207 – £4374

BRANDESTON

FRAMLINGHAM COLLEGE JUNIOR SCHOOL
Brandeston Hall, Brandeston, Suffolk
IP13 7AH
Tel: (01728) 685331
Head: Mr S Player
Type: Co-educational Boarding and
Day 4–13
No of pupils: B153 G105
No of boarders: F50 W10
Fees: (September 01) FB £11025
Day £3942 – £6858

BURY ST EDMUNDS

CHERRY TREES SCHOOL
Flempton Road, Risby, Bury
St Edmunds, Suffolk IP28 6QJ
Tel: (01284) 760531
Head: Ms W Compson
Type: Co-educational Day 0–13
No of pupils: B120 G117
Fees: (September 01)
Day £4560 – £5610

CULFORD SCHOOL
Bury St Edmunds, Suffolk IP28 6TX
Tel: (01284) 728615
Head: Mr J Richardson
Type: Co-educational Boarding and
Day 2–18
No of pupils: B380 G270
No of boarders: F175 W25
Fees: (September 01) FB £11778 –
£15276 WB £10482 – £15276
Day £7566 – £9942

MORETON HALL PREPARATORY SCHOOL
Mount Road, Bury St Edmunds,
Suffolk IP32 7BJ
Tel: (01284) 753532
Head: Mr N Higham
Type: Co-educational Boarding and
Day 3–13
No of pupils: B73 G48
No of boarders: F12 W13
Fees: (September 01) FB £10620
WB £9453 Day £4080 – £7704

SOUTH LEE PREPARATORY SCHOOL
Nowton Road, Bury St Edmunds,
Suffolk IP33 2BT
Tel: (01284) 754654
Head: Mr D Whipp
Type: Co-educational Day 2–13
No of pupils: B125 G166
Fees: (September 01)
Day £4725 – £5895

FELIXSTOWE

FELIXSTOWE INTERNATIONAL COLLEGE
Felixstowe, Suffolk IP11 7NA
Tel: (01394) 282388
Head: Mrs J S Lee
Type: Co-educational Boarding 11–17
No of pupils: B10 G8
No of boarders: F18
Fees: (September 01) FB £16500

HALESWORTH

STARTING POINTS PRE-SCHOOL
School Lane, Halesworth, Suffolk
IP19 8BW
Tel: (01986) 874569
Head: Mrs J J Douglass
Type: Co-educational Day 2–5
No of pupils: 45
Fees: (September 01) On application

HAVERHILL

BARNARDISTON HALL PREPARATORY SCHOOL
Barnardiston, Haverhill, Suffolk
CB9 7TG
Tel: (01440) 786316
Head: Lt Col K A Boulter
Type: Co-educational Day and
Boarding 2–13
No of pupils: B148 G119
No of boarders: F58 W5
Fees: (September 01) FB £10425
WB £9450 Day £5070 – £6375

IPSWICH

AMBERFIELD SCHOOL
Nacton, Ipswich, Suffolk IP10 0HL
Tel: (01473) 659265
Head: Mrs L Amphlett Lewis
Type: Girls Day 3–16 (Boys 3–7)
No of pupils: B19 G267
Fees: (September 01)
Day £3690 – £5520

IPSWICH HIGH SCHOOL GDST
Woolverstone, Ipswich, Suffolk
IP9 1AZ
Tel: (01473) 780201
Head: Miss V C MacCuish
Type: Girls Day 3–18
No of pupils: 700
Fees: (September 01)
Day £3174 – £5442

IPSWICH PREPARATORY SCHOOL
Henley Road, Ipswich, Suffolk
IP1 3SQ
Tel: (01473) 408301
Head: Mrs J M Jones
Type: Co-educational Day 3–11
No of pupils: B211 G82
Fees: (September 01)
Day £4251 – £4908

IPSWICH SCHOOL
Henley Road, Ipswich, Suffolk
IP1 3SG
Tel: (01473) 408300
Head: Mr I G Galbraith
Type: Co-educational Day and
Boarding 11–18
No of pupils: B481 G179
No of boarders: F25 W22
Fees: (September 01)
FB £10341 – £12030
WB £9867 – £11334
Day £6231 – £6930

OLD BUCKENHAM HALL SCHOOL
Brettenham Park, Ipswich, Suffolk
IP7 7PH
Tel: (01449) 740252
Head: Mr M A Ives
Type: Co-educational Day and
Boarding 3–13
No of pupils: 205
No of boarders: F62 W20
Fees: (September 01) FB £12375
WB £12225 Day £4770 – £9825

ORWELL PARK
Nacton, Ipswich, Suffolk IP10 0ER
Tel: (01473) 659225
Head: Mr A H Auster
Type: Co-educational Boarding and
Day 3–13
No of pupils: B177 G83
No of boarders: F135
Fees: (September 01)
FB £11325 – £12570
Day £3360 – £9450

ROYAL HOSPITAL SCHOOL
Holbrook, Ipswich, Suffolk IP9 2RX
Tel: (01473) 326200
Head: Mr N K D Ward
Type: Co-educational Boarding 11–18
(VIth Form day pupils)
No of pupils: B420 G260
No of boarders: F680
Fees: (September 01)
FB £150 – £13119 Day £7758

ST JOSEPH'S COLLEGE
Belstead Road, Birkfield, Ipswich,
Suffolk IP2 9DR
Tel: (01473) 690281
Head: Mrs S Grant
Type: Co-educational Day and
Boarding 3–18
No of pupils: B436 G171
No of boarders: F58 W12
Fees: (September 01)
FB £10815 – £11790
WB £10320 – £11295
Day £4185 – £6780

LEISTON

SUMMERHILL SCHOOL
Leiston, Suffolk IP16 4HY
Tel: (01728) 830540
Head: Mrs Z S Readhead
Type: Co-educational Boarding and
Day 6–16
No of pupils: B41 G22
No of boarders: F51
Fees: (September 01) On application

NEWMARKET

FAIRSTEAD HOUSE SCHOOL
Fordham Road, Newmarket, Suffolk
CB8 7AA
Tel: (01638) 662318
Head: Mrs D J Buckenham
Type: Co-educational Day 3–11
No of pupils: B78 G65
Fees: (September 01)
Day £3975 – £4335

SOUTHWOLD

ST FELIX SCHOOL
Southwold, Suffolk IP18 6SD
Tel: (01502) 722175
Head: Mr R Williams
Type: Girls Boarding and Day 11–18
No of pupils: 150
No of boarders: F76 W12
Fees: (September 01)
F/WB £11805 – £13905
Day £7290 – £9180

ST GEORGE'S SCHOOL
Southwold, Suffolk IP18 6SD
Tel: (01502) 723314
Head: Mrs W H Holland
Type: Co-educational Day 2–11
No of pupils: B102 G104
Fees: (September 01)
Day £3240 – £5700

STOWMARKET

FINBOROUGH SCHOOL
The Hall, Great Finborough,
Stowmarket, Suffolk IP14 3EF
Tel: (01449) 773600
Head: Mrs G Caddock
Type: Co-educational Boarding and
Day 2–18
No of pupils: B93 G92
No of boarders: F109 W9
Fees: (September 01)
FB £9900 – £11475
WB £7530 – £9075
Day £3450 – £5850

HILLCROFT PREPARATORY SCHOOL
Walnutree Manor, Haughley Green,
Stowmarket, Suffolk IP14 3RQ
Tel: (01449) 673003
Head: Mr F Rapsey and Mrs G Rapsey
Type: Co-educational Day 2–13
No of pupils: B47 G42
Fees: (September 01)
Day £1260 – £6240

SUDBURY

STOKE COLLEGE
Stoke by Clare, Sudbury, Suffolk
CO10 8JE
Tel: (01787) 278141
Head: Mr J Gibson
Type: Co-educational Day and
Boarding 3–16
No of pupils: B155 G90
No of boarders: W25
Fees: (September 01)
WB £10575 – £11775
Day £4785 – £6675

WOODBRIDGE

THE ABBEY
The Prep School of Woodbridge
School, Woodbridge, Suffolk
IP12 1DS
Tel: (01394) 382673
Head: Mr N J Garrett
Type: Co-educational Day 4–11
No of pupils: B157 G129
Fees: (September 01)
Day £4326 – £6546

ALEXANDERS
INTERNATIONAL SCHOOL
Bawdsey Manor, Bawdsey,
Woodbridge, Suffolk IP12 3AZ
Tel: (01394) 411633
Head: Ms A Alexander
Type: Co-educational Boarding 11–18
No of pupils: B70 G50
No of boarders: F120
Fees: (September 01)
FB £12500 – £13200

FRAMLINGHAM COLLEGE
Framlingham, Woodbridge, Suffolk
IP13 9EY
Tel: (01728) 723789
Head: Mrs G M Randall
Type: Co-educational Boarding and
Day 4–18
No of pupils: B419 G254
No of boarders: F383 W10
Fees: (September 01)
FB £11025 – £13986
Day £6858 – £8991

MOAT BARN NURSERY
Hasketon, Woodbridge, Suffolk
IP13 6JW
Tel: (01473) 738282
Head: Mrs D K McKenzie and
Ms L Spence
Type: Co-educational Day 3–5
No of pupils: 87
Fees: (September 01) On application

WOODBRIDGE SCHOOL
Woodbridge, Suffolk IP12 4JH
Tel: (01394) 385547
Head: Mr S H Cole
Type: Co-educational Day and
Boarding 11–18
No of pupils: B298 G292
No of boarders: F35 W3
Fees: (September 01) F/WB £13752
Day £7728 – £7932

SURREY

ASHTEAD

CITY OF LONDON
FREEMEN'S SCHOOL ✔
Ashtead, Surrey KT21 1ET
Tel: (01372) 277933
Head: Mr D C Haywood
Type: Co-educational Day and
Boarding 7–18
No of pupils: B407 G408
No of boarders: F36
Fees: (September 01)
FB £11493 – £13698
Day £6462 – £8667

DOWNSEND SCHOOL,
ASHTEAD LODGE
22 Oakfield Road, Ashtead, Surrey
KT21 2RE
Tel: (01372) 273778
Head: Mrs L Packman
Type: Co-educational Day 2–6
No of pupils: B38 G28
Fees: (September 01)
Day £1350 – £5055

PARSONS MEAD*
Ottways Lane, Ashtead, Surrey
KT21 2PE ✔
Tel: (01372) 276401
Head: Mrs P M Taylor
Type: Girls Day 3–18
No of pupils: 300
Fees: (September 01)
Day £4485 – £7521

BAGSHOT

HALL GROVE SCHOOL
Bagshot, Surrey GU19 5HZ
Tel: (01276) 473059
Head: Mr A R Graham
Type: Boys Day and Boarding 4–13
No of pupils: 252
No of boarders: W28
Fees: (September 01)
WB £9000 – £9420
Day £5400 – £7170

BANSTEAD

GREENACRE SCHOOL FOR
GIRLS*
Sutton Lane, Banstead, Surrey
SM7 3RA
Tel: (01737) 352114 ✔
Head: Mrs P M Wood
Type: Girls Day 3–18
No of pupils: 410
Fees: (September 01)
Day £4050 – £6900

PRIORY SCHOOL
Bolters Lane, Banstead, Surrey
SM7 2AJ
Tel: (01737) 354479
Head: Mr G D Malcolm
Type: Boys Day 2–13
No of pupils: 198
Fees: (September 01)
Day £2565 – £6435

CAMBERLEY

CLEWBOROUGH HOUSE SCHOOL AT CHESWYCKS
Guildford Road, Frimley Green, Camberley, Surrey GU16 6PB
Tel: (01252) 835669
Head: Miss S L Streete
Type: Co-educational Day 2–11
No of pupils: B190 G122
Fees: (September 01)
Day £890 – £2095

ELMHURST, THE SCHOOL FOR DANCE & PERFORMING ARTS
Heathcote Road, Camberley, Surrey GU15 2EU
Tel: (01276) 65301
Head: Mr J McNamara
Type: Co-educational Boarding and Day 11–19
No of pupils: B23 G150
No of boarders: F152
Fees: (September 01)
FB £12387 – £12849
Day £9660 – £10020

HAWLEY PLACE SCHOOL
Fernhill Road, Blackwater, Camberley, Surrey GU17 9HU
Tel: (01276) 32028
Head: Mr and Mrs T G Pipe
Type: Girls Day 2–16 (Boys 2–11)
No of pupils: B86 G224
Fees: (September 01)
Day £4455 – £5580

LYNDHURST SCHOOL
36 The Avenue, Camberley, Surrey GU15 3NE
Tel: (01276) 22895
Head: Mr R L Cunliffe
Type: Co-educational Day 2–12
No of pupils: B132 G72
Fees: (September 01)
Day £2040 – £4890

ST CATHERINE'S SCHOOL
Park Road, Camberley, Surrey GU15 2LL
Tel: (01276) 23511
Head: Mr R W Burt and Mrs H M Burt
Type: Girls Day 2–11 (Boys 2–5)
No of pupils: B7 G101
Fees: (September 01)
Day £2062 – £5385

CATERHAM

CATERHAM PREPARATORY SCHOOL*
Harestone Valley Road, Caterham, Surrey CR3 6YB
Tel: (01883) 342097
Head: Mrs S Owen-Hughes
Type: Co-educational Day 3–11
No of pupils: B149 G113
Fees: (September 01)
Day £2673 – £6885

CATERHAM SCHOOL*
Harestone Valley Road, Caterham, Surrey CR3 6YA
Tel: (01883) 343028   ✔
Head: Mr R A E Davey
Type: Co-educational Day and Boarding 11–18
No of pupils: B474 G254
No of boarders: F134 W2
Fees: (September 01)
FB £15183 – £16002
Day £8190 – £8580

ESSENDENE LODGE SCHOOL
Essendene Road, Caterham, Surrey CR3 5PB
Tel: (01883) 348349
Head: Mrs S A Haydock
Type: Co-educational Day 2–11
No of pupils: B89 G110
Fees: (September 01)
Day £1020 – £3105

OAKHYRST GRANGE SCHOOL
160 Stanstead Road, Caterham, Surrey CR3 6AF
Tel: (01883) 343344
Head: Mr N J E Jones
Type: Co-educational Day 2–11
No of pupils: B117 G35
Fees: (September 01)
Day £750 – £4080

CHEAM

GLAISDALE SCHOOL
14 Arundel Road, Cheam, Surrey SM2 7AD
Tel: (020) 8288 1488
Head: Mrs H M Potter
Type: Co-educational Day 3–11
No of pupils: 152
Fees: (September 01)
Day £1200 – £3810

CHERTSEY

SIR WILLIAM PERKINS'S SCHOOL
Guildford Road, Chertsey, Surrey KT16 9BN
Tel: (01932) 562161   ✔
Head: Miss S Ross
Type: Girls Day 11–18
No of pupils: 580
Fees: (September 01) Day £6645

COBHAM

THE AMERICAN COMMUNITY SCHOOLS
'Heywood', Portsmouth Road, Cobham, Surrey KT11 1BL
Tel: (01932) 869744   ✔
Head: Mr T J Lehman
Type: Co-educational Boarding and Day 3–19
No of pupils: B670 G608
No of boarders: F99 W15
Fees: (September 01)
FB £19980 – £20760
WB £17820 – £18600
Day £6540 – £12700

THE COBHAM MONTESSORI SCHOOL
23 Spencer Road, Cobham, Surrey KT11 2AF
Tel: (01372) 373744
Head: Mrs B Preiss
Type: Co-educational Day 2–5
No of pupils: 40
Fees: (September 01) On application

FELTONFLEET SCHOOL
Cobham, Surrey KT11 1DR
Tel: (01932) 862264
Head: Mr P Ward
Type: Co-educational Boarding and Day 3–13
No of pupils: B220 G92
No of boarders: F7 W38
Fees: (September 01) WB £10680
Day £7995

NOTRE DAME PREPARATORY SCHOOL
Burwood House, Cobham, Surrey KT11 1HA
Tel: (01932) 869991
Head: Mr D Plummer
Type: Girls Day 2–11 (Boys 2–5)
No of pupils: B20 G350
Fees: (September 01)
Day £795 – £1950

NOTRE DAME SENIOR SCHOOL
Burwood House, Cobham, Surrey
KT11 1HA
Tel: (01932) 869990 ✓
Head: Mrs M McSwiggan
Type: Girls Day 11–18
No of pupils: 340
Fees: (September 01) Day £7125

PARKSIDE SCHOOL
The Manor, Stoke D'Abernon,
Cobham, Surrey KT11 3PX
Tel: (01932) 862749
Head: Mr D Aylward
Type: Boys Day and Boarding 2–14
(Co-ed 2–5)
No of pupils: B390 G30
No of boarders: W10
Fees: (September 01) WB £9810
Day £4710 – £7080

REED'S SCHOOL*
Sandy Lane, Cobham, Surrey
KT11 2ES ✓
Tel: (01932) 863076
Head: Mr D W Jarrett
Type: Boys Boarding and Day 11–18
(Co-ed VIth Form)
No of pupils: B424 G30
No of boarders: F120
Fees: (September 01)
FB £12153 – £14799
Day £9114 – £11187

YEHUDI MENUHIN SCHOOL
Stoke D'Abernon, Cobham, Surrey
KT11 3QQ ✓
Tel: (01932) 864739
Head: Mr N Chisholm
Type: Co-educational Boarding 8–18
No of pupils: B24 G34
No of boarders: F58
Fees: (September 01) On application

CRANLEIGH

CRANLEIGH PREPARATORY SCHOOL*
Horseshoe Lane, Cranleigh, Surrey
GU6 8QH
Tel: (01483) 274199
Head: Mr M W Roulston
Type: Co-educational Boarding and
Day 7–13
No of pupils: 231
No of boarders: F40
Fees: (September 00) FB £11260
Day £8400

CRANLEIGH SCHOOL
Horseshoe Lane, Cranleigh, Surrey
GU6 8QQ
Tel: (01483) 273666 ✓
Head: Mr G Waller
Type: Co-educational Boarding and
Day 13–18
No of pupils: B383 G165
No of boarders: F377
Fees: (September 01) FB £17790
Day £13485

CROYDON

CAMBRIDGE TUTORS COLLEGE*
Water Tower Hill, Croydon, Surrey
CR0 5SX
Tel: (020) 8688 5284 ✓
Head: Mr D A Lowe
Type: Co-educational Boarding and
Day 16–21
No of pupils: B140 G130
Fees: (September 01) FB £14000
Day £9750

NEW LIFE CHRISTIAN SCHOOL
Cairo New Road, Croydon, Surrey
CR0 1XP
Tel: (020) 8680 7671
Head: Mrs E Parker and
Mrs W Emond
Type: Co-educational Day 4–11
No of pupils: 135
Fees: (September 01) Day £2880

OLD PALACE SCHOOL OF JOHN WHITGIFT
Old Palace Road, Croydon, Surrey
CR0 1AX
Tel: (020) 8688 2027 ✓
Head: Mrs J Hancock
Type: Girls Day 4–18
No of pupils: 850
Fees: (September 01)
Day £4719 – £6348

ROYAL RUSSELL SCHOOL
Coombe Lane, Croydon, Surrey
CR9 5BX
Tel: (020) 8657 4433 ✓
Head: Dr J R Jennings
Type: Co-educational Boarding and
Day 3–18
No of pupils: B497 G274
No of boarders: F95 W35
Fees: (September 01) F/WB £13444
Day £4170 – £7050

TRINITY SCHOOL
Shirley Park, Croydon, Surrey
CR9 7AT
Tel: (020) 8656 9541 ✓
Head: Mr C J Tarrant
Type: Boys Day 10–18
No of pupils: 880
Fees: (September 01) Day £7851

WARLINGHAM PARK SCHOOL
Chelsham Common, Warlingham,
Croydon, Surrey CR6 9PB
Tel: (01883) 626844
Head: Mr M R Donald
Type: Co-educational Day 2–11
No of pupils: B72 G69
Fees: (September 01)
Day £2250 – £4200

DORKING

ABINGER HAMMER VILLAGE SCHOOL
Hackhurst Lane, Abinger Hammer,
Dorking, Surrey RH5 6SE
Tel: (01306) 730343
Head: Mrs P A Hammond
Type: Co-educational Day 3–12
No of pupils: B3 G7
Fees: (September 01) On application

BELMONT SCHOOL*
Feldemore, Holmbury St Mary,
Dorking, Surrey RH5 6LQ
Tel: (01306) 730852/730829
Head: Mr D Gainer
Type: Co-educational Boarding and
Day 4–13
No of pupils: B194 G80
No of boarders: W40
Fees: (September 01) WB £10179
Day £3625 – £6996

BOX HILL SCHOOL*
Mickleham, Dorking, Surrey
RH5 6EA ✓
Tel: (01372) 373382
Head: Dr R A S Atwood
Type: Co-educational Boarding and
Day 11–18
No of pupils: B208 G115
No of boarders: F104 W55
Fees: (September 00) FB £12894
WB £11115 Day £5685 – £7527

HURTWOOD HOUSE*
Holmbury St Mary, Dorking, Surrey
RH5 6NU
Tel: (01483) 277416 ✓
Head: Mr K R B Jackson
Type: Co-educational Boarding and
Day 16–18
No of pupils: B140 G150
No of boarders: F140 W140
Fees: (September 01)
FB £18000 – £20000
Day £12000 – £13000

NOWER LODGE SCHOOL
Coldharbour Lane, Dorking, Surrey
RH4 3BT
Tel: (01306) 882448
Head: Mrs S Watt
Type: Co-educational Day 3–11
No of pupils: B104 G60
Fees: (September 01)
Day £4125 – £5475

ST TERESA'S SCHOOL*
Effingham Hill, Dorking, Surrey
RH5 6ST
Tel: (01372) 452037 ✔
Head: Mrs M Prescott
Type: Girls Boarding and Day 11–18
No of pupils: 475
No of boarders: F55 W20
Fees: (September 01) FB £13950
WB £13050 Day £7950

STANWAY SCHOOL
Chichester Road, Dorking, Surrey
RH4 1LR
Tel: (01306) 882151
Head: Mr P H Rushforth
Type: Girls Day 3–11 (Boys 3–8)
No of pupils: B32 G118
Fees: (September 01)
Day £900 – £5655

EFFINGHAM

ST TERESA'S PREPARATORY SCHOOL
Grove House, Guildford Road,
Effingham, Surrey KT24 5QA
Tel: (01372) 453456
Head: Mrs A Stewart
Type: Girls Day and Boarding 2–11
No of pupils: 160
No of boarders: F6 W2
Fees: (September 01) FB £12150
WB £11250 Day £1680 – £2050

EGHAM

THE AMERICAN COMMUNITY SCHOOLS
Woodlee, London Road (A30),
Egham, Surrey TW20 0HS
Tel: (01784) 430611 ✓
Head: Ms M Hadley
Type: Co-educational Day 3–18
No of pupils: B295 G230
Fees: (September 01)
Day £4400 – £12700

BISHOPSGATE SCHOOL
Englefield Green, Egham, Surrey
TW20 0YJ
Tel: (01784) 432109
Head: Mr M Dunning
Type: Co-educational Day and
Boarding 2–13
No of pupils: B180 G100
No of boarders: W14
Fees: (September 01)
WB £9900 – £10500
Day £2250 – £7830

EPSOM

DOWNSEND SCHOOL, EPSOM LODGE
6 Norman Avenue, Epsom, Surrey
KT17 3AB
Tel: (01372) 721824
Head: Mrs J Macbeth
Type: Co-educational Day 2–6
No of pupils: B74 G70
Fees: (September 01)
Day £1350 – £5055

EPSOM COLLEGE ✓
Epsom, Surrey KT17 4JQ
Tel: (01372) 821004
Head: Mr S R Borthwick
Type: Co-educational Boarding and
Day 13–18
No of pupils: B513 G162
No of boarders: F156 W164
Fees: (September 01) FB £16611 WB
£15216 – £16389
Day £11362 – £12168

EWELL CASTLE SCHOOL
Church Street, Ewell, Epsom, Surrey
KT17 2AW ✓
Tel: (020) 8393 1413
Head: Mr R A Fewtrell
Type: Boys Day 3–18 (Girls 3–11
and 16–18)
No of pupils: B410 G40
Fees: (September 01)
Day £1725 – £6495

KINGSWOOD HOUSE SCHOOL
56 West Hill, Epsom, Surrey
KT19 8LG
Tel: (01372) 723590
Head: Mr P Brooks
Type: Boys Day 3–13
No of pupils: 210
Fees: (September 01)
Day £4710 – £6360

ST CHRISTOPHER'S SCHOOL
6 Downs Road, Epsom, Surrey
KT18 5HE
Tel: (01372) 721807
Head: Mrs M V Evans
Type: Co-educational Day 3–7
No of pupils: B81 G76
Fees: (September 01)
Day £2250 – £4290

ESHER

CLAREMONT FAN COURT SCHOOL*
Claremont Drive, Esher, Surrey
KT10 9LY
Tel: (01372) 467841 ✓
Head: Mrs P B Farrar
Type: Co-educational Boarding and
Day 3–18
No of pupils: B302 G277
No of boarders: F22
Fees: (September 01)
FB £12825 – £13245
Day £2445 – £8220

EMBERHURST
94 Ember Lane, Esher, Surrey
KT10 8EN
Tel: (020) 8398 2933
Head: Mrs P Chadwick
Type: Co-educational Day 3–8
No of pupils: B40 G35
Fees: (September 01) On application

GRANTCHESTER HOUSE
5 Hinchley Way, Hinchley Wood,
Esher, Surrey KT10 0BD
Tel: (020) 8398 1157
Head: Mrs A E Fry
Type: Co-educational Day 3–7
No of pupils: B49 G37
Fees: (September 01)
Day £2415 – £4200

MILBOURNE LODGE SCHOOL
43 Arbrook Lane, Esher, Surrey
KT10 9EG ✔
Tel: (01372) 462737
Head: Mr G Hill
Type: Co-educational Day 8–13
No of pupils: B165 G35
Fees: (September 01)
Day £6270 – £6420

ROWAN PREPARATORY SCHOOL
6 Fitzalan Road, Claygate, Esher,
Surrey KT10 0LX
Tel: (01372) 462627
Head: Mrs E Brown
Type: Girls Day 3–11
No of pupils: 310
Fees: (September 01)
Day £2475 – £6660

EWHURST

DUKE OF KENT SCHOOL*
Peaslake Road, Ewhurst, Surrey
GU6 7NS
Tel: (01483) 277313
Head: Dr A Cameron
Type: Co-educational Boarding and
Day 4–13
No of pupils: B117 G88
No of boarders: F35 W20
Fees: (September 01)
FB £9360 – £11220
Day £4405 – £8150

FARNHAM

BARFIELD SCHOOL
Runfold, Farnham, Surrey GU10 1PB
Tel: (01252) 782271
Head: Mr B Hoar
Type: Co-educational Day 3–13
No of pupils: B185 G125
Fees: (September 01)
Day £5010 – £7416

EDGEBOROUGH
Frensham, Farnham, Surrey
GU10 3AH
Tel: (01252) 792495
Head: Mrs M A Jackson and
Mr R A Jackson
Type: Co-educational Boarding and
Day 3–13
No of pupils: B210 G93
No of boarders: W50
Fees: (September 01) WB £10980
Day £5205 – £8550

FRENSHAM HEIGHTS*
Rowledge, Farnham, Surrey
GU10 4EA ✔
Tel: (01252) 792134
Head: Mr P M de Voil
Type: Co-educational Boarding and
Day 3–18
No of pupils: B240 G220
No of boarders: F116
Fees: (September 01)
FB £14700 – £15900
WB £13950 – £15360
Day £9600 – £10650

GODALMING

ALDRO SCHOOL
Lombard Street, Shackleford,
Godalming, Surrey GU8 6AS
Tel: (01483) 810266
Head: Mr D W N Aston
Type: Boys Boarding and Day 7–13
No of pupils: 220
No of boarders: F92
Fees: (September 01) FB £12150
Day £9405

BARROW HILLS SCHOOL
Roke Lane, Witley, Godalming,
Surrey GU8 5NY
Tel: (01428) 683639
Head: Mr M Connolly
Type: Co-educational Day 3–13
No of pupils: B184 G78
Fees: (September 01)
Day £5235 – £7350

CHARTERHOUSE
Godalming, Surrey GU7 2DJ ✔
Tel: (01483) 291501
Head: Rev J S Witheridge
Type: Boys Boarding and Day 13–18
(Co-ed VIth Form)
No of pupils: B614 G97
No of boarders: F670
Fees: (September 01) FB £17598
Day £14541

KING EDWARD'S SCHOOL WITLEY ✔
Petworth Road, Wormley,
Godalming, Surrey GU8 5SG
Tel: (01428) 682572
Head: Mr P Kerr Fulton-Peebles
Type: Co-educational Boarding and
Day 11–18
No of pupils: B283 G195
No of boarders: F330
Fees: (September 01) FB £13185
Day £9030

PRIOR'S FIELD SCHOOL*
Priorsfield Road, Godalming, Surrey
GU7 2RH ✔
Tel: (01483) 810551
Head: Mrs J Dwyer
Type: Girls Boarding and Day 11–18
No of pupils: 288
No of boarders: F45 W50
Fees: (September 01) F/WB £13980
Day £9348

ST HILARY'S SCHOOL
Holloway Hill, Godalming, Surrey
GU7 1RZ
Tel: (01483) 416551
Head: Mrs S Bailes
Type: Co-educational Day Boys 2–8
Girls 2–11
No of pupils: B110 G298
Fees: (September 01)
Day £4290 – £6600

GUILDFORD

DRAYTON HOUSE SCHOOL
35 Austen Road, Guildford, Surrey
GU1 3NP
Tel: (01483) 504707
Head: Mrs J Tyson-Jones
Type: Co-educational Day 3–8
(Nursery 1–3)
No of pupils: B51 G43
Fees: (September 01) On application

GUILDFORD HIGH SCHOOL (CHURCH SCHOOLS CO) ✔
London Road, Guildford, Surrey
GU1 1SJ
Tel: (01483) 561440
Head: Mrs S H Singer
Type: Girls Day 4–18
No of pupils: 900
Fees: (September 01)
Day £4074 – £6933

LANESBOROUGH
Maori Road, Guildford, Surrey
GU1 2EL
Tel: (01483) 880650
Head: Mr K S Crombie
Type: Boys Day 3–13
No of pupils: 350
Fees: (September 01)
Day £1860 – £6393

LONGACRE PREPARATORY SCHOOL

Shamley Green, Guildford, Surrey
GU5 0NQ
Tel: (01483) 893225
Head: Mrs J Nicol
Type: Co-educational Day 2–11
No of pupils: B100 G100
Fees: (September 01)
Day £1935 – £6060

PEASLAKE SCHOOL

Colmans Hill, Peaslake, Guildford,
Surrey GU5 9ST
Tel: (01306) 730411
Head: Mrs J George
Type: Co-educational Day
No of pupils: B21 G25
Fees: (September 01)
Day £208 – £1040

ROYAL GRAMMAR SCHOOL

High Street, Guildford, Surrey
GU1 3BB
Tel: (01483) 880600 ✓
Head: Mr T M Young
Type: Boys Day 11–18
No of pupils: 860
Fees: (September 01) Day £7865

RYDES HILL PREPARATORY SCHOOL

Aldershot Road, Guildford, Surrey
GU2 8BP
Tel: (01483) 563160
Head: Mrs J Lenahan
Type: Girls Day 3–11 (Boys 3–7)
No of pupils: B10 G150
Fees: (September 01)
Day £2175 – £5160

ST CATHERINE'S SCHOOL*

Station Road, Bramley, Guildford,
Surrey GU5 0DF
Tel: (01483) 893363 ✓
Head: Mrs A M Phillips
Type: Girls Day and Boarding 4–18
No of pupils: 710
No of boarders: F30 W100
Fees: (September 01)
F/WB £13875 Day £4230 – £8445

SURREY COLLEGE

Administration Centre, Abbot
House, Sydenham Road, Guildford,
Surrey GU1 3RL
Tel: (01483) 565887
Head: Ms L Cody
Type: Co-educational Day 14+
No of pupils: B60 G50
Fees: (September 01)
Day £4500 – £10200

TORMEAD SCHOOL

27 Cranley Road, Guildford, Surrey
GU1 2JD
Tel: (01483) 575101
Head: Mrs S Marks
Type: Girls Day 4–18 ✓
No of pupils: 684
Fees: (September 01)
Day £3360 – £7170

HASLEMERE

HASLEMERE PREPARATORY SCHOOL

The Heights, Hill Road, Haslemere,
Surrey GU27 2JP
Tel: (01428) 642350
Head: Mr K J Merrick
Type: Boys Day 2–14
No of pupils: B150 G2
Fees: (September 01)
Day £5775 – £7200

ROYAL SCHOOL HASLEMERE*

Farnham Lane, Haslemere, Surrey
GU27 1HQ
Tel: (01428) 605805 ✓
Head: Mrs L Taylor-Gooby
Type: Girls Day and Boarding 3–18
(Boys 3–4)
No of pupils: B4 G327
No of boarders: F47 W13
Fees: (September 01)
FB £11304 – £13626
Day £5094 – £8685

ST IVES SCHOOL

Three Gates Lane, Haslemere, Surrey
GU27 2ES
Tel: (01428) 643734
Head: Mrs S E Cattaneo
Type: Girls Day 3–11 (Boys 3–5)
No of pupils: B8 G137
Fees: (September 01)
Day £4890 – £6825

WISPERS SCHOOL FOR GIRLS*

High Lane, Haslemere, Surrey
GU27 1AD ✓
Tel: (01428) 643646
Head: Mr L H Beltran
Type: Girls Boarding and Day 11–18
No of pupils: 80
No of boarders: F15 W25
Fees: (September 01) F/WB £13425
Day £8655

HINDHEAD

AMESBURY

Hazel Grove, Hindhead, Surrey
GU26 6BL
Tel: (01428) 604322
Head: Mr N Taylor
Type: Co-educational Day and
Boarding 3–13
No of pupils: B210 G115
No of boarders: W10
Fees: (September 01) WB £10320
Day £5235 – £8340

ST EDMUND'S SCHOOL

Portsmouth Road, Hindhead, Surrey
GU26 6BH
Tel: (01428) 604808
Head: Mr A J Walliker
Type: Boys Boarding and Day 2–13
(Co-ed day 2–7)
No of pupils: B211 G5
No of boarders: F20 W5
Fees: (September 01)
FB £9810 – £12150
Day £5190 – £8970

HORLEY

REDEHALL PREPARATORY SCHOOL

Redehall Road, Smallfield, Horley,
Surrey RH6 9QA
Tel: (01342) 842987
Head: Mrs E Boak
Type: Co-educational Day 4–11
No of pupils: B48 G61
Fees: (September 01)
Day £1738 – £1830

KINGSTON-UPON-THAMES

CANBURY SCHOOL*

Kingston Hill, Kingston-upon-
Thames, Surrey KT2 7LN
Tel: (020) 8549 8622
Head: Mr R Metters
Type: Co-educational Day 10–16
No of pupils: B45 G25
Fees: (September 01) Day £6600

HOLY CROSS PREPARATORY SCHOOL

Coombe Ridge House, George Road,
Kingston Hill, Kingston-upon-
Thames, Surrey KT2 7NU
Tel: (020) 8942 0729
Head: Mrs K Hayes
Type: Girls Day 4–11
No of pupils: 250
Fees: (September 01) Day £6300

KINGSTON GRAMMAR SCHOOL*

70–72 London Road, Kingston-upon-Thames, Surrey KT2 6PY ✓
Tel: (020) 8546 5875
Head: Mr C D Baxter
Type: Co-educational Day 10–18
No of pupils: B360 G240
Fees: (September 01)
Day £7803 – £8043

MARYMOUNT INTERNATIONAL SCHOOL*

George Road, Kingston-upon-Thames, Surrey KT2 7PE ✓
Tel: (020) 8949 0571
Head: Sister R Sheridan
Type: Girls Day and Boarding 11–18
No of pupils: 207
No of boarders: F73 W13
Fees: (September 01)
FB £17300 – £18370
WB £17060 – £18130
Day £9630 – £10700

PARK HILL SCHOOL

8 Queens Road, Kingston-upon-Thames, Surrey KT2 7SH
Tel: (020) 8546 5496
Head: Mrs M D Christie
Type: Co-educational Day Boys 3–8
Girls 3–11
No of pupils: B45 G75
Fees: (September 01)
Day £2490 – £4605

ROKEBY SCHOOL

George Road, Kingston-upon-Thames, Surrey KT2 7PB
Tel: (020) 8942 2247
Head: Mr M K Seigel
Type: Boys Day 4–13
No of pupils: 370
Fees: (September 01)
Day £4698 – £6753

SURBITON HIGH SCHOOL

Surbiton Crescent, Kingston-upon-Thames, Surrey KT1 2JT ✓
Tel: (020) 8546 5245
Head: Dr D J Longhurst
Type: Girls Day 4–18 (Boys 4–11)
No of pupils: B140 G965
Fees: (September 01)
Day £4275 – £7239

LEATHERHEAD

CRANMORE SCHOOL

West Horsley, Leatherhead, Surrey KT24 6AT
Tel: (01483) 284137
Head: Mr A J Martin
Type: Boys Day 3–13
No of pupils: 520
Fees: (September 01)
Day £2460 – £6450

DANES HILL PREPARATORY SCHOOL

Leatherhead Road, Oxshott, Leatherhead, Surrey KT22 0JG
Tel: (01372) 842509
Head: Mr R Parfitt
Type: Co-educational Day 2–13
No of pupils: B477 G374
Fees: (September 01)
Day £1104 – £7473

DOWNSEND SCHOOL

1 Leatherhead Road, Leatherhead, Surrey KT22 8TJ
Tel: (01372) 372197
Head: Mr A D White
Type: Co-educational Day 6–13
No of pupils: B249 G249
Fees: (September 01)
Day £5055 – £6525

DOWNSEND SCHOOL, LEATHERHEAD LODGE

13 Epsom Road, Leatherhead, Surrey KT22 8ST
Tel: (01372) 372123
Head: Mrs G Brooks
Type: Co-educational Day 2–6
No of pupils: B77 G63
Fees: (September 01) On application

GLENESK SCHOOL

Ockham Road North, East Horsley, Leatherhead, Surrey KT24 6NS
Tel: (01483) 282329
Head: Mrs S P Johnson
Type: Co-educational Day 2–7
No of pupils: B107 G113
Fees: (September 01)
Day £2325 – £6450

MANOR HOUSE SCHOOL

Manor House Lane, Little Bookham, Leatherhead, Surrey KT23 4EN
Tel: (01372) 458538
Head: Mrs A Morris
Type: Girls Day 2–16
No of pupils: 360
Fees: (September 01)
Day £1725 – £7590

ST JOHN'S SCHOOL

Epsom Road, Leatherhead, Surrey KT22 8SP
Tel: (01372) 373000 ✓
Head: Mr C H Tongue
Type: Boys Boarding and Day 13–18 (Co-ed VIth Form)
No of pupils: B385 G55
No of boarders: F15 W115
Fees: (September 01)
F/WB £15390
Day £10845

LINGFIELD

NOTRE DAME SCHOOL

Lingfield, Surrey RH7 6PH ✓
Tel: (01342) 833176
Head: Mrs N E Shepley
Type: Co-educational Day 2–18
No of pupils: B312 G374
Fees: (September 01)
Day £3540 – £6015

NEW MALDEN

THE STUDY SCHOOL

57 Thetford Road, New Malden, Surrey KT3 5DP
Tel: (020) 8942 0754
Head: Mrs S Mallin
Type: Co-educational Day 3–11
No of pupils: B73 G67
Fees: (September 01)
Day £2400 – £5217

WESTBURY HOUSE

80 Westbury Road, New Malden, Surrey KT3 5AS
Tel: (020) 8942 5885
Head: Mrs M T Morton
Type: Co-educational Day 3–12
No of pupils: B78 G78
Fees: (September 01)
Day £740 – £1655

OXTED

HAZELWOOD SCHOOL

Wolf's Hill, Limpsfield, Oxted, Surrey RH8 0QU
Tel: (01883) 712194
Head: Mr A M Synge
Type: Co-educational Day 3–13
No of pupils: B248 G134
Fees: (September 01)
Day £2550 – £7350

LAVEROCK SCHOOL
19 Bluehouse Lane, Oxted, Surrey
RH8 0AA
Tel: (01883) 714171
Head: Mrs A C Paterson
Type: Girls Day 3–11
No of pupils: 150
Fees: (September 01)
Day £2250 – £5850

PURLEY

LALEHAM LEA
PREPARATORY SCHOOL
29 Peaks Hill, Purley, Surrey CR8 3JJ
Tel: (020) 8660 3351
Head: Mr A C Baseley
Type: Co-educational Day 3–11
No of pupils: B100 G50
Fees: (September 01) Day £3210

LODGE SCHOOL
11 Woodcote Lane, Purley, Surrey
CR8 3HB ✓
Tel: (020) 8660 3179
Head: Miss P Maynard
Type: Girls Day 3–18 (Boys 3–11)
No of pupils: 250
Fees: (September 01)
Day £3630 – £6525

OAKWOOD
Godstone Road, Purley, Surrey
CR8 2AN
Tel: (020) 8668 8080
Head: Mr C Candia
Type: Co-educational Day 2–11
No of pupils: B44 G36
Fees: (September 01)
Day £4200 – £4575

ST DAVID'S SCHOOL
23 Woodcote Valley Road, Purley,
Surrey CR8 3AL
Tel: (020) 8660 0723
Head: Mrs L Nash
Type: Co-educational Day 3–11
No of pupils: B83 G84
Fees: (September 01)
Day £1875 – £3510

WEST DENE SCHOOL
167 Brighton Road, Purley, Surrey
CR8 4HE
Tel: (020) 8660 2404
Head: Mrs S Topp
Type: Co-educational Day 2–11
No of pupils: B52 G50
Fees: (September 01)
Day £3450 – £3540

REDHILL

THE HAWTHORNS SCHOOL
Pendell Court, Bletchingley, Redhill,
Surrey RH1 4QJ
Tel: (01883) 743048
Head: Mr T R Johns
Type: Co-educational Day 2–13
No of pupils: B280 G130
Fees: (September 01)
Day £775 – £2082

REIGATE

BURYS COURT SCHOOL
Leigh, Reigate, Surrey RH2 8RE
Tel: (01306) 611372
Head: Mr D V White
Type: Co-educational Day 3–12
No of pupils: B70 G50
Fees: (September 01) On application

DUNOTTAR SCHOOL
High Trees Road, Reigate, Surrey
RH2 7EL
Tel: (01737) 761945 ✓
Head: Mrs J Hobson
Type: Girls Day 3–18
No of pupils: 400
Fees: (September 01)
Day £2100 – £7125

MICKLEFIELD SCHOOL
10/12 Somers Road, Reigate, Surrey
RH2 9DU
Tel: (01737) 242615
Head: Mrs C Belton
Type: Co-educational Day 2–11
No of pupils: B98 G198
Fees: (September 01)
Day £1065 – £5220

REIGATE GRAMMAR
SCHOOL
Reigate Road, Reigate, Surrey ✓
RH2 0QS
Tel: (01737) 222231
Head: Mr D S Thomas
Type: Co-educational Day 10–18
No of pupils: B513 G277
Fees: (September 01)
Day £7308

REIGATE ST MARY'S
PREPARATORY AND CHOIR
SCHOOL
Chart Lane, Reigate, Surrey RH2 7RN
Tel: (01737) 244880
Head: Mr D T Tidmarsh
Type: Co-educational Day 3–13
No of pupils: B155 G28
Fees: (September 01)
Day £1155 – £5823

ROYAL ALEXANDRA AND
ALBERT SCHOOL*
Gatton Park, Reigate, Surrey
RH2 0TD
Tel: (01737) 642565
Head: Mr P Spencer Ellis
Type: Co-educational Boarding and
Day 7–18
No of pupils: B295 G255
No of boarders: F359 W33
Fees: (September 01)
FB £6900 – £7800
WB £6750 Day £855 – £2340

RICHMOND

BROOMFIELD HOUSE
10 Broomfield Road, Kew Gardens,
Richmond, Surrey TW9 3HS
Tel: (020) 8940 3884
Head: Mrs I O Harrow
Type: Co-educational Day 3–11
No of pupils: B73 G87
Fees: (September 01)
Day £2505 – £5980

THE GERMAN SCHOOL
Douglas House, Petersham Road,
Richmond, Surrey TW10 7AH
Tel: (020) 8940 2510 ✓
Head: Mr G Koehncke
Type: Co-educational Day 5–19
No of pupils: B339 G326
Fees: (September 01)
Day £2370 – £3450

KEW COLLEGE
24/26 Cumberland Road, Kew,
Richmond, Surrey TW9 3HQ
Tel: (020) 8940 2039
Head: Mrs D E Lyness
Type: Co-educational Day 3–11
No of pupils: B115 G128
Fees: (September 01)
Day £2446 – £4545

KING'S HOUSE SCHOOL
68 King's Road, Richmond, Surrey
TW10 6ES
Tel: (020) 8940 1878
Head: Mr N Chaplin
Type: Boys Day 4–13
No of pupils: 370
Fees: (September 01)
Day £4410 – £5955

OLD VICARAGE SCHOOL
48 Richmond Hill, Richmond,
Surrey TW10 6QX
Tel: (020) 8940 0922
Head: Mrs J Harrison
Type: Girls Day 4–11
No of pupils: 168
Fees: (September 01)
Day £4794 – £5328

UNICORN SCHOOL
238 Kew Road, Richmond, Surrey
TW9 3JX
Tel: (020) 8948 3926
Head: Mrs F Timmis
Type: Co-educational Day 3–11
No of pupils: B84 G84
Fees: (September 01)
Day £3150 – £5790

SOUTH CROYDON

CROHAM HURST SCHOOL*
79 Croham Road, South Croydon,
Surrey CR2 7YN
Tel: (020) 8686 7347   ✓
Head: Miss S C Budgen
Type: Girls Day 3–18
No of pupils: 544
Fees: (September 01)
Day £3735 – £6735

CROYDON HIGH SCHOOL GDST
Old Farleigh Road, Selsdon, South
Croydon, Surrey CR2 8YB
Tel: (020) 8651 5020   ✓
Head: Miss L M Ogilvie
Type: Girls Day 3–18
No of pupils: 934
Fees: (September 01)
Day £5145 – £6624

CUMNOR HOUSE SCHOOL
168 Pampisford Road, South
Croydon, Surrey CR2 6DA
Tel: (020) 8660 3445
Head: Mr P Clare-Hunt
Type: Boys Day 4–13
No of pupils: 350
Fees: (September 01)
Day £5025 – £5955

ELMHURST SCHOOL
44–48 South Park Hill Road, South
Croydon, Surrey CR2 7DW
Tel: (020) 8688 0661
Head: Mr B K Dighton
Type: Boys Day 4–11
No of pupils: 250
Fees: (September 01)
Day £4425 – £5235

FENNIES UNDER 5'S AT BEECH HOUSE
15 Church Way, Sanderstead, South
Croydon, Surrey CR2 0JT
Tel: (020) 8651 0446
Head: Mrs S Fenn
Type: Co-educational Day 0–4
No of pupils: 32
Fees: (September 01) On application

SANDERSTEAD JUNIOR SCHOOL
29 Purley Oaks Road, Sanderstead,
South Croydon, Surrey CR2 0NW
Tel: (020) 8660 0801
Head: Mrs A Barns
Type: Co-educational Day 3–12
No of pupils: B50 G50
Fees: (September 01)
Day £2925 – £4365

WHITGIFT SCHOOL
Haling Park, South Croydon, Surrey
CR2 6YT   ✓
Tel: (020) 8688 9222
Head: Dr C A Barnett
Type: Boys Day 10–18
No of pupils: 1100
No of boarders: F6
Fees: (September 01) Day £8514

SURBITON

LINLEY HOUSE
6 Berrylands Road, Surbiton, Surrey
KT5 8RA
Tel: (020) 8399 4979
Head: Mrs S Mallin
Type: Co-educational Day 3–7
No of pupils: B19 G23
Fees: (September 01)
Day £2508 – £4440

SHREWSBURY HOUSE SCHOOL
107 Ditton Road, Surbiton, Surrey
KT6 6RL
Tel: (020) 8399 3066
Head: Mr C M Ross
Type: Boys Day 7–13
No of pupils: 280
Fees: (September 01) Day £7050

SURBITON PREPARATORY SCHOOL
3 Avenue Elmers, Surbiton, Surrey
KT6 4SP
Tel: (020) 8546 5245
Head: Mr S J Pryce
Type: Boys Day 4–11
No of pupils: 140
Fees: (September 01)
Day £4275 – £5940

SUTTON

HOMEFIELD PREPARATORY SCHOOL
Western Road, Sutton, Surrey
SM1 2TE
Tel: (020) 8642 0965
Head: Mr P R Mowbray
Type: Boys Day 3–13
No of pupils: 360
Fees: (September 01)
Day £2685 – £5970

SEATON HOUSE
67 Banstead Road South, Sutton,
Surrey SM2 5LH
Tel: (020) 8642 2332
Head: Mrs V A Richards
Type: Girls Day 3–11 (Boys 3–5)
No of pupils: B20 G180
Fees: (September 01)
Day £1365 – £4050

STOWFORD
95 Brighton Road, Sutton, Surrey
SM2 5SJ
Tel: (020) 8661 9444   ✓
Head: Mr R J Shakespeare
Type: Co-educational Day 7–17
No of pupils: B55 G28
Fees: (September 01)
Day £4400 – £6200

SUTTON HIGH SCHOOL GDST
55 Cheam Road, Sutton, Surrey
SM1 2AX   ✓
Tel: (020) 8642 0594
Head: Mrs A J Coutts
Type: Girls Day 4–18
No of pupils: 742
Fees: (September 01)
Day £5145 – £6624

TADWORTH

ABERDOUR SCHOOL
Brighton Road, Burgh Heath,
Tadworth, Surrey KT20 6AJ
Tel: (01737) 354119
Head: Mr A Barraclough
Type: Co-educational Day 3–13
No of pupils: B241 G120
Fees: (September 01)
Day £2400 – £6450

BRAMLEY SCHOOL
Chequers Lane, Walton-on-the-Hill,
Tadworth, Surrey KT20 7ST
Tel: (01737) 812004
Head: Mrs B Johns
Type: Girls Day 3–11
No of pupils: 130
Fees: (September 01)
Day £2250 – £5550

CHINTHURST SCHOOL
Tadworth Street, Tadworth, Surrey
KT20 5QZ
Tel: (01737) 812011
Head: Mr T J Egan
Type: Boys Day 3–13
No of pupils: 390
Fees: (September 01)
Day £1950 – £5580

THAMES DITTON

WESTON GREEN SCHOOL
Weston Green Road, Thames Ditton,
Surrey KT7 0JN
Tel: (020) 8398 2778
Head: Mrs J Winser
Type: Co-educational Day 2–8
No of pupils: 180
Fees: (September 01)
Day £2550 – £4500

THORPE

TASIS THE AMERICAN SCHOOL IN ENGLAND*
Coldharbour Lane, Thorpe, Surrey
TW20 8TE
Tel: (01932) 565252 ✓
Head: Mr B E Breen
Type: Co-educational Boarding and
Day 4–18
No of pupils: B385 G365
No of boarders: F147 W3
Fees: (September 01) FB £19080
Day £4950 – £11300

WALLINGTON

COLLINGWOOD SCHOOL
3 Springfield Road, Wallington,
Surrey SM6 0BD
Tel: (020) 8647 4607
Head: Mr G M Barham
Type: Co-educational Day 2–11
No of pupils: B112 G64
Fees: (September 01)
Day £1770 – £3675

WALTON-ON-THAMES

DANESFIELD MANOR SCHOOL
Rydens Avenue, Walton-on-Thames,
Surrey KT12 3JB
Tel: (01932) 220930
Head: Mrs L A Muggleton
Type: Co-educational Day 1–11
No of pupils: 169
Fees: (September 01)
Day £3585 – £3921

WESTWARD PREPARATORY SCHOOL
47 Hersham Road, Walton-on-
Thames, Surrey KT12 1LE
Tel: (01932) 220911
Head: Mrs P Robertson
Type: Co-educational Day 3–11
No of pupils: B70 G70
Fees: (September 01)
Day £2925 – £3600

WEYBRIDGE

ST GEORGE'S COLLEGE
Weybridge Road, Addlestone,
Weybridge, Surrey KT15 2QS
Tel: (01932) 839300
Head: Mr J A Peake ✓
Type: Co-educational Day 11–18
No of pupils: B550 G350
Fees: (September 01) On application

ST GEORGE'S COLLEGE JUNIOR SCHOOL
Thames Street, Weybridge, Surrey
KT13 8NL
Tel: (01932) 839400
Head: Fr. M D Ashcroft
Type: Co-educational Day 2–11
No of pupils: 600
Fees: (September 01)
Day £4230 – £5985

WINDLESHAM

WOODCOTE HOUSE SCHOOL
Snows Ride, Windlesham, Surrey
GU20 6PF
Tel: (01276) 472115
Head: Mr N H K Paterson
Type: Boys Boarding and Day 7–14
No of pupils: 100
No of boarders: F75
Fees: (September 01) FB £10425
Day £7350

WOKING

CABLE HOUSE SCHOOL
Horsell Rise, Woking, Surrey
GU21 4AY
Tel: (01483) 760759
Head: Mr R Elvidge
Type: Co-educational Day 3–11
No of pupils: B60 G60
Fees: (September 01)
Day £2200 – £4530

COWORTH PARK SCHOOL
Valley End, Chobham, Woking,
Surrey GU24 8TE
Tel: (01276) 855707
Head: Mrs C A Fairbairn
Type: Co-educational Day Boys 3–7
Girls 3–11
No of pupils: B26 G136
Fees: (September 01)
Day £2415 – £5775

FLEXLANDS SCHOOL
Station Road, Chobham, Woking,
Surrey GU24 8AG
Tel: (01276) 858841
Head: Mrs A Green
Type: Girls Day 3–11
No of pupils: 160
Fees: (September 01)
Day £2460 – £6000

GREENFIELD SCHOOL
Brooklyn Road, Woking, Surrey
GU22 7TP
Tel: (01483) 772525
Head: Mrs J S Becker
Type: Co-educational Day 3–11
No of pupils: B98 G102
Fees: (September 01)
Day £2640 – £4650

HALSTEAD PREPARATORY SCHOOL
Woodham Rise, Woking, Surrey
GU21 4EE
Tel: (01483) 772682
Head: Mrs S Fellows
Type: Girls Day 3–11
No of pupils: 209
Fees: (September 01)
Day £2400 – £6540

HOE BRIDGE SCHOOL*
Hoe Place, Old Woking Road,
Woking, Surrey GU22 8JE
Tel: (01483) 760018
Head: Mr R W K Barr
Type: Co-educational Day 2–14
No of pupils: B330 G100
Fees: (September 01)
Day £975 – £7575

OAKFIELD SCHOOL
Coldharbour Road, Pyrford,
Woking, Surrey GU22 8SJ
Tel: (01932) 342465
Head: Mrs S H Goddard
Type: Co-educational Day Boys 3–7
Girls 3–16
No of pupils: B30 G150
Fees: (September 01)
Day £3735 – £6330

**PRINS WILLEM-ALEXANDER
SCHOOL**
Old Woking Road, Woking, Surrey
GU22 8HY
Tel: (01483) 750409
Head: Mr P Wassink
Type: Co-educational Day 4–12
No of pupils: B96 G83
Fees: (September 01)
Day £5505 – £8640

RIPLEY COURT SCHOOL
Rose Lane, Ripley, Woking, Surrey
GU23 6NE
Tel: (01483) 225217
Head: Mr A J Gough
Type: Co-educational Day 2–13
No of pupils: B174 G53
Fees: (September 01)
Day £3960 – £6435

ST ANDREW'S SCHOOL*
Church Hill House, Wilson Way,
Horsell, Woking, Surrey GU21 4QW
Tel: (01483) 760943
Head: Mr B Pretorius
Type: Co-educational Day 3–13
No of pupils: 267
Fees: (September 01)
Day £4065 – £7905

WOLDINGHAM

WOLDINGHAM SCHOOL*
Marden Park, Woldingham, Surrey
CR3 7YA
Tel: (01883) 349431   ✓
Head: Miss D Vernon
Type: Girls Boarding and Day 11–18
No of pupils: 560
No of boarders: F440
Fees: (September 01) FB £16320
Day £9735

EAST SUSSEX

BATTLE

BATTLE ABBEY SCHOOL*
High Street, Battle, East Sussex
TN33 0AD
Tel: (01424) 772385
Head: Mr R Clark
Type: Co-educational Boarding and
Day 2–18
No of pupils: B117 G153
No of boarders: F54
Fees: (September 01) F/WB £10401 –
£12864
Day £4374 – £7971

BEXHILL-ON-SEA

AMBERLEY SCHOOL
9 Buckhurst Road, Bexhill-on-Sea,
East Sussex TN40 1QF
Tel: (01424) 212472
Head: Ms C Gardner
Type: Co-educational Day 2–5
No of pupils: 45
Fees: (September 01) On application

BRIGHTON

**BRIGHTON AND HOVE HIGH
SCHOOL GDST**
Montpelier Road, Brighton,
East Sussex BN1 3AT
Tel: (01273) 734112
Head: Miss R A Woodbridge
Type: Girls Day 3–18
No of pupils: 804
Fees: (September 01)
Day £3951 – £5442

BRIGHTON COLLEGE
Eastern Road, Brighton, East Sussex
BN2 2AL
Tel: (01273) 704200
Head: Dr A Seldon
Type: Co-educational Day and
Boarding 13–18
No of pupils: B424 G216
No of boarders: F56 W56
Fees: (September 01) FB £16311
WB £14328 Day £10521

**BRIGHTON COLLEGE PRE-
PREPARATORY SCHOOL**
Sutherland Road, Brighton,
East Sussex BN2 0EQ
Tel: (01273) 704259
Head: Mrs S P Wicks
Type: Co-educational Day 3–8
No of pupils: B120 G86
Fees: (September 01)
Day £2019 – £5565

**BRIGHTON COLLEGE PREP
SCHOOL**
Walpole Lodge, Walpole Road,
Brighton, East Sussex BN2 2EU
Tel: (01273) 704210
Head: Mr B Melia and Mrs H Beeby
Type: Co-educational Boarding and
Day 3–13
No of pupils: B311 G199
No of boarders: W2
Fees: (September 01)
WB £8388 – £10299
Day £1311 – £8685

**BRIGHTON STEINER
SCHOOL LIMITED**
John Howard House, Roedean Road,
Brighton, East Sussex BN2 5RA
Tel: (01273) 386300
Head: Mrs T Bishop
Type: Co-educational Day 2–16
No of pupils: 200
Fees: (September 01)
Day £2142 – £5355

DHARMA SCHOOL
White House, Ladies Mile Road,
Patcham, Brighton, East Sussex
BN1 8TB
Tel: (01273) 502055
Head: Mr K Fossey
Type: Co-educational Day 4–11
No of pupils: B30 G35
Fees: (September 01) Day £3000

ROEDEAN SCHOOL
Brighton, East Sussex BN2 5RQ
Tel: (01273) 603181
Head: Mrs P Metham
Type: Girls Boarding and Day 11–18
No of pupils: 436
No of boarders: F398
Fees: (September 01) FB £17925
Day £10800

ST AUBYN'S
High Street, Rottingdean, Brighton,
East Sussex BNZ 7JN
Tel: (01273) 302170
Head: Mr A G Gobat
Type: Co-educational Boarding and
Day 4–13
No of pupils: B135 G45
No of boarders: F16 W18
Fees: (September 01) FB £11985
Day £3750 – £9135

ST MARY'S HALL*
Eastern Road, Brighton, East Sussex
BN2 5JF
Tel: (01273) 606061
Head: Mrs S M Meek
Type: Girls Day and Boarding 3–18
(Boys 3–8)
No of pupils: G273
No of boarders: F62 W21
Fees: (September 01) FB £9198 –
£12762 WB £9198 – £12234
Day £1620 – £7947

EASTBOURNE

EASTBOURNE COLLEGE*
Old Wish Road, Eastbourne,
East Sussex BN21 4JX
Tel: (01323) 452323
Head: Mr C M P Bush
Type: Co-educational Boarding and
Day 13–18
No of pupils: B348 G179
No of boarders: F57
Fees: (September 01) FB £16545
Day £10695

MOIRA HOUSE JUNIOR
SCHOOL*
Upper Carlisle Road, Eastbourne,
East Sussex BN20 7TE
Tel: (01323) 644144
Head: Mrs J Booth-Clibborn
Type: Girls Day and Boarding 2–11
No of pupils: 110
No of boarders: F4
Fees: (September 01) FB £11850
WB £10800 Day £3855 – £7140

MOIRA HOUSE GIRLS'
SCHOOL*
Upper Carlisle Road, Eastbourne,
East Sussex BN20 7TE
Tel: (01323) 644144
Head: Mrs A Harris
Type: Girls Boarding and Day 11–18
No of pupils: 225
No of boarders: F100 W6
Fees: (September 01) FB £13050 –
£15300 WB £11400 – £13650
Day £7710 – £9090

ST ANDREW'S SCHOOL
Meads, Eastbourne, East Sussex
BN20 7RP
Tel: (01323) 733203
Head: Mr F Roche
Type: Co-educational Boarding and
Day 3–13
No of pupils: B278 G178
No of boarders: F28 W16
Fees: (September 01) FB £11910
WB £10890 Day £3390 – £8370

ST BEDE'S
Duke's Drive, Eastbourne,
East Sussex BN20 7XL
Tel: (01323) 734222
Head: Mr C P Pyemont
Type: Co-educational Boarding and
Day 2–13
No of pupils: B280 G150
No of boarders: F60
Fees: (September 01) F/WB £11520
Day £4905 – £8040

FOREST ROW

ASHDOWN HOUSE SCHOOL
Forest Row, East Sussex RH18 5JY
Tel: (01342) 822574
Head: Mr A J Fowler-Watt
Type: Co-educational Boarding 8–13
No of pupils: B154 G72
No of boarders: F219
Fees: (September 01) FB £11985

GREENFIELDS SCHOOL
Priory Road, Forest Row, East Sussex
RH18 5JD
Tel: (01342) 828262
Head: Mr A M McQuade
Type: Co-educational Day and
Boarding 3–18
No of pupils: B96 G79
No of boarders: F25 W3
Fees: (September 01) F/WB £11586
Day £2580 – £7086

MICHAEL HALL*
Kidbrooke Park, Forest Row,
East Sussex RH18 5JA
Tel: (01342) 822275
Head: Mr E Van Manen
Type: Co-educational Day and
Boarding 0–19
No of pupils: B344 G328
No of boarders: F25
Fees: (September 01) FB £11195
WB £10435 Day £2985 – £6435

HAILSHAM

ST BEDE'S SCHOOL*
The Dicker, Hailsham, East Sussex
BN27 3QH
Tel: (01323) 843252
Heads: Mr S Cole and Mr C Pyemont
Type: Co-educational Boarding and
Day 2½–19
No of pupils: B528 G352
No of boarders: F370 W20
Fees: (September 01)
F/WB £11520 – £15360
Day £4905 – £9420

HASTINGS

BUCKSWOOD SCHOOL*
Broomham Hall, Rye Road,
Guestling, Hastings, East Sussex
TN35 4LT
Tel: (01424) 813813
Head: Mr G Sutton
Type: Co-educational Day and
Boarding 11–19
No of pupils: B50 G30
No of boarders: F67
Fees: (September 01)
FB £11440 – £14250 WB £10500
Day £6750

HOVE

BELLERBYS COLLEGE
44 Cromwell Road, Hove,
East Sussex BN3 3ER
Tel: (01273) 323374
Head: Mr N Addison
Type: Co-educational Boarding and
Day 14+
No of pupils: B270 G210
No of boarders: F390
Fees: (September 01)
FB £14325 – £16900
Day £11700 – £13650

DEEPDENE SCHOOL

Hove, East Sussex BN3 4ED
Tel: (01273) 418984
Head: Mrs L V Clark-Darby and
Mrs N Gane
Type: Co-educational Day 1–8
No of pupils: B108 G122
Fees: (September 01)
Day £2760 – £4025

THE FOLD SCHOOL

201 New Church Road, Hove,
East Sussex BN3 4ED
Tel: (01273) 410901
Head: Mrs B Drake
Type: Co-educational Day 3–9
No of pupils: B37 G38
Fees: (September 01)
Day £3060 – £3510

MOWDEN SCHOOL

The Droveway, Hove, East Sussex
BN3 6LU
Tel: (01273) 503452
Head: Mr C E M Snell
Type: Boys Day 4–13
No of pupils: 130
Fees: (September 01)
Day £4500 – £7950

ST CHRISTOPHER'S SCHOOL

33 New Church Road, Hove,
East Sussex BN3 4AD
Tel: (01273) 735404
Head: Mr R J Saunders
Type: Co-educational Day 4–14
No of pupils: B200 G20
Fees: (September 01) Day £4125

STONELANDS SCHOOL OF BALLET & THEATRE ARTS

170A Church Road, Hove,
East Sussex BN3 2DJ
Tel: (01273) 770445
Head: Mrs D Carteur
Type: Co-educational Boarding and
Day 6–16
No of pupils: B6 G36
No of boarders: F10 W10
Fees: (September 01) FB £9825
Day £5520

LEWES

THE OLD GRAMMAR SCHOOL

140 High Street, Lewes, East Sussex
BN7 1XS
Tel: (01273) 472634
Head: Mr D Cook
Type: Co-educational Day 4–18
No of pupils: B223 G127
Fees: (September 01)
Day £3168 – £6219

MAYFIELD

ST LEONARDS-MAYFIELD SCHOOL*

The Old Palace, Mayfield,
East Sussex TN20 6PH
Tel: (01435) 874614
Head: Mrs Julia Dalton
Type: Girls Boarding and Day 11–18
No of pupils: 378
No of boarders: F135 W53
Fees: (September 01) F/WB £15120
Day £9840

SKIPPERS HILL MANOR PREPARATORY SCHOOL

Five Ashes, Mayfield, East Sussex
TN20 6HR
Tel: (01825) 830234
Head: Mr T W Lewis
Type: Co-educational Day 2–13
No of pupils: B98 G60
Fees: (September 01)
Day £2256 – £7755

ROBERTSBRIDGE

BODIAM MANOR SCHOOL

Bodiam, Robertsbridge, East Sussex
TN32 5UJ
Tel: (01580) 830225
Head: Mr C Moore
Type: Co-educational Day 2–13
No of pupils: B95 G96
Fees: (September 01)
Day £3063 – £6324

DARVELL SCHOOL

Darvell Bruderhof, Robertsbridge,
East Sussex TN32 5DR
Tel: (01580) 883300
Head: Mr Arnold Meier
Type: Co-educational Day 2–14
No of pupils: B55 G55
Fees: (September 01) On application

VINEHALL SCHOOL

Robertsbridge, East Sussex TN32 5JL
Tel: (01580) 880413
Head: Mr D C Chaplin
Type: Co-educational Boarding and
Day 2–13
No of pupils: B248 G150
No of boarders: F75
Fees: (September 01) FB £11007
Day £4791 – £8463

SEAFORD

HOPSCOTCH

The Old School, Church Street,
Seaford, East Sussex BN7 3NF
Tel: (01323) 492123
Head: Ms J Cotton
Type: Co-educational Day 0–5
No of pupils: 92
Fees: (September 01) On application

NEWLANDS MANOR SCHOOL*

Sutton Place, Seaford, East Sussex
BN25 3PL
Tel: (01323) 892334 / 490000
Head: Mr O T Price
Type: Co-educational Boarding and
Day 13–18
No of pupils: B125 G66
No of boarders: F95
Fees: (September 01)
FB £12630 – £14100 WB £12465
Day £7815 – £8145

NEWLANDS PREPARATORY SCHOOL*

Eastbourne Road, Seaford,
East Sussex BN25 4NP
Tel: (01323) 892334 / 490000
Head: Mr O T Price
Type: Co-educational Boarding and
Day 2–13
No of pupils: B157 G122
No of boarders: F58 W2
Fees: (September 01)
FB £10800 – £11550 WB £1140
Day £5745 – £7185

ST LEONARDS-ON-SEA

CLAREMONT SCHOOL

Baldslow, St Leonards-on-Sea,
East Sussex TN37 7PW
Tel: (01424) 751555
Head: Mr I Culley
Type: Co-educational Day 2–14
No of pupils: B200 G200
Fees: (September 01)
Day £3300 – £5550

WESTERLEIGH & ST LEONARDS COLLEGE
Hollington Park, St Leonards-on-Sea, East Sussex TN38 0SE
Tel: (01424) 440760
Head: Mrs P Wheeler
Type: Co-educational Day 2–16
No of pupils: B160 G160
Fees: (September 01)
Day £4245 – £5820

UCKFIELD

TEMPLE GROVE
Heron's Ghyll, Uckfield, East Sussex TN22 4DA
Tel: (01825) 712112
Head: Mr M H Kneath
Type: Co-educational Boarding and Day 3–13
No of pupils: B75 G75
No of boarders: F10
Fees: (September 01)
FB £8820 – £10050
Day £5475 – £7680

WADHURST

BRICKLEHURST MANOR PREPARATORY
Stonegate, Wadhurst, East Sussex TN5 7EL
Tel: (01580) 200448
Head: Mrs C Flowers
Type: Co-educational Day Boys 3–8 Girls 3–11
No of pupils: B28 G98
Fees: (September 01)
Day £4995 – £5250

SACRED HEART R.C. PRIMARY SCHOOL
Mayfield Lane, Durgates, Wadhurst, East Sussex TN5 6DQ
Tel: (01892) 783414
Head: Mrs H Castle
Type: Co-educational Day 3–11
No of pupils: B50 G60
Fees: (September 01)
Day £1080 – £3060

WEST SUSSEX

ARUNDEL

SLINDON COLLEGE
Slindon House, Slindon, Arundel, West Sussex BN18 0RH
Tel: (01243) 814320
Head: Mr I P Graham
Type: Boys Boarding and Day 9–16
No of pupils: 100
No of boarders: F20 W30
Fees: (September 01) F/WB £12840
Day £7935

BURGESS HILL

BURGESS HILL SCHOOL FOR GIRLS*
Keymer Road, Burgess Hill, West Sussex RH15 0EG
Tel: (01444) 241050
Head: Mrs S Gorham
Type: Girls Day and Boarding 3–18 (Co-ed nursery)
No of pupils: B65 G700
No of boarders: F44 W6
Fees: (September 01) FB £12720
WB £11235 Day £3600 – £7530

ST PETER'S SCHOOL
Upper St John's Road, Burgess Hill, West Sussex RH15 8HB
Tel: (01444) 235880
Head: Mr H G Stevens
Type: Co-educational Day 2–8
No of pupils: B98 G84
Fees: (September 01) On application

CHICHESTER

GREAT BALLARD SCHOOL
Eartham, Chichester, West Sussex PO18 0LR
Tel: (01243) 814236
Head: Mr R E Jennings
Type: Co-educational Boarding and Day 2–13
No of pupils: B103 G97
No of boarders: F5 W29
Fees: (September 01) F/WB £9789
Day £1623 – £7314

LAVANT HOUSE ROSEMEAD
Chichester, West Sussex PO18 9AB
Tel: (01243) 527211
Head: Mrs M Scott
Type: Girls Day and Boarding 5–18
No of pupils: 150
No of boarders: F25 W25
Fees: (September 01)
F/WB £9425 – £13295
Day £3825 – £7695

THE LITTLEMEAD SCHOOL
Woodfield House, Tangmere Road, Tangmere, Chichester, West Sussex PO20 6EU
Tel: (01243) 787551
Head: Miss J Mills
Type: Co-educational Day and Boarding 5–16
No of pupils: B27 G16
No of boarders: F4 W2
Fees: (September 01) On application

OAKWOOD SCHOOL
Oakwood, Chichester, West Sussex PO18 9AN
Tel: (01243) 575209
Head: Mr A H Cowell
Type: Co-educational Boarding and Day 2–11
No of pupils: B112 G96
No of boarders: W15
Fees: (September 01) WB £8580
Day £2100 – £6426

THE PREBENDAL SCHOOL
53 West Street, Chichester,
West Sussex PO19 1RT
Tel: (01243) 782026/784828
Head: Rev Canon G C Hall
Type: Co-educational Day and
Boarding 3–14
No of pupils: B138 G119
No of boarders: F18 W12
Fees: (September 01) FB £9216
WB £8820 Day £6804

PREBENDAL SCHOOL (NORTHGATE HOUSE)
38 North Street, Chichester,
West Sussex PO19 1LX
Tel: (01243) 784828
Head: Mrs L M Greenall
Type: Co-educational Day 3–7
No of pupils: B53 G42
Fees: (September 01)
Day £1680 – £3030

WESTBOURNE HOUSE SCHOOL
Shopwyke, Chichester, West Sussex
PO20 6BH
Tel: (01243) 782739
Head: Mr S L Rigby
Type: Co-educational Boarding and
Day 3–13
No of pupils: B205 G133
No of boarders: F100
Fees: (September 01) FB £10650
Day £4425 – £8550

COPTHORNE

COPTHORNE SCHOOL
Effingham Lane, Copthorne,
West Sussex RH10 3HR
Tel: (01342) 712311
Head: Mr G C Allen
Type: Co-educational Day and
Boarding 2–13
No of pupils: B160 G104
No of boarders: W10
Fees: (September 01) WB £9285
Day £4425 – £8025

CRAWLEY

WILLOW TREE MONTESSORI SCHOOL
Charlwood House, Charlwood Road,
Lowfield Heath, Crawley,
West Sussex RH11 0QA
Tel: (01293) 565544
Head: Mrs G Kerfante
Type: Co-educational Day 1–11
No of pupils: B80 G80
Fees: (September 01)
Day £2310 – £3600

EAST GRINSTEAD

BRAMBLETYE SCHOOL*
Brambletye, East Grinstead,
West Sussex RH19 3PD
Tel: (01342) 321004
Head: Mr H D Cocke
Type: Co-educational Boarding and
Day 3–13
No of pupils: B171 G44
No of boarders: F86
Fees: (September 01) FB £12300
Day £2760 – £10200

FONTHILL LODGE
Coombe Hill Road, East Grinstead,
West Sussex RH9 4LY
Tel: (01342) 321635
Head: Mrs J Griffiths
Type: Co-educational Day 2–11
(Single-sex education)
No of pupils: B127 G115
Fees: (September 01)
Day £775 – £2230

STOKE BRUNSWICK
Ashurstwood, East Grinstead,
West Sussex RH19 3PF
Tel: (01342) 828200
Head: Mr W M Ellerton
Type: Co-educational Boarding and
Day 3–13
No of pupils: B100 G55
No of boarders: W10
Fees: (September 01) WB £10215
Day £2235 – £8430

HASSOCKS

HURSTPIERPOINT COLLEGE
Hassocks, West Sussex BN6 9JS
Tel: (01273) 833636
Head: Mr S D A Meek
Type: Co-educational Boarding and
Day 7–18
No of pupils: B356 G172
No of boarders: F109 W81
Fees: (September 01)
FB £10500 – £15540
WB £9990 – £14820
Day £7800 – £12030

HAYWARDS HEATH

ARDINGLY COLLEGE*
Haywards Heath, West Sussex
RH17 6SQ
Tel: (01444) 892577
Head: Mr J R Franklin
Type: Co-educational Boarding and
Day 13–18
No of pupils: 391
No of boarders: F253
Fees: (September 01)
FB £11145 – £16125
Day £6000 – £12075

ARDINGLY COLLEGE JUNIOR SCHOOL*
Haywards Heath, West Sussex
RH17 6SQ
Tel: (01444) 892279
Head: Mrs J L Robinson
Type: Co-educational Boarding and
Day 2–13
No of pupils: B111 G93
No of boarders: F36
Fees: (September 01) FB £11145
Day £6000 – £7530

CUMNOR HOUSE SCHOOL
Danehill, Haywards Heath,
West Sussex RH17 7HT
Tel: (01825) 790347
Head: Mr C S Heinrich
Type: Co-educational Boarding and
Day 4–13
No of pupils: B152 G122
No of boarders: F28
Fees: (September 01) FB £11856
Day £4950 – £9420

GREAT WALSTEAD
Lindfield, Haywards Heath,
West Sussex RH16 2QL
Tel: (01444) 483528
Head: Mr H J Lowries
Type: Co-educational Boarding and
Day 2–13
No of pupils: B314 G157
No of boarders: W30
Fees: (September 01)
WB £8490 – £9195
Day £630 – £7620

HANDCROSS PARK SCHOOL
Handcross, Haywards Heath,
West Sussex RH17 6HF
Tel: (01444) 400526
Head: Mr W J Hilton
Type: Co-educational Day and
Boarding 2–13
No of pupils: B174 G112
No of boarders: W7
Fees: (September 01) WB £9819
Day £1917 – £8376

TAVISTOCK & SUMMERHILL SCHOOL

Summerhill Lane, Haywards Heath, West Sussex RH16 1RP
Tel: (01444) 450256
Head: Mr M Barber
Type: Co-educational Day 3–13
No of pupils: B120 G90
Fees: (September 01)
Day £3270 – £5985

HORSHAM

CHRISTS HOSPITAL

Horsham, West Sussex RH13 7LS
Tel: (01403) 211293
Head: Dr P C D Southern
Type: Co-educational Boarding 11–18
No of pupils: B475 G351
No of boarders: F826
Fees: (September 01) FB £13856

FARLINGTON SCHOOL*

Strood Park, Horsham, West Sussex RH12 3PN
Tel: (01403) 254967
Head: Mrs P M Mawer
Type: Girls Day and Boarding 4–18
No of pupils: 415
No of boarders: F25 W15
Fees: (September 01)
FB £10830 – £13230
WB £10560 – £12960
Day £4005 – £8250

PENNTHORPE SCHOOL

Rudgwick, Horsham, West Sussex RH12 3HJ
Tel: (01403) 822391
Head: Mr S Moll
Type: Co-educational Day 2–14
No of pupils: B187 G95
Fees: (September 01)
Day £780 – £7680

LANCING

ARDMORE SCHOOL AND LANCING MONTESSORI CENTRE

Wembley Gardens, Lancing, West Sussex BN15 9LA
Tel: (01903) 755583
Head: Mrs J Cragg and Mrs A Williams
Type: Co-educational Day 2–8
No of pupils: 60
Fees: (September 01) On application

LANCING COLLEGE

Lancing, West Sussex BN15 0RW
Tel: (01273) 452213
Head: Mr P M Tinniswood
Type: Co-educational Boarding and Day 13–18
No of pupils: B339 G71
No of boarders: F301
Fees: (September 01) FB £16680
Day £12180

LITTLEHAMPTON

NEW WEST PRESTON MANOR NURSERY SCHOOL

39 Park Drive, Rustington, Littlehampton, West Sussex BN16 3DY
Tel: (01903) 784282
Head: Mrs J M Drury
Type: Co-educational Day 2–5
No of pupils: 38
Fees: (September 01) On application

MIDHURST

CONIFERS SCHOOL

Egmont Road, Midhurst, West Sussex GU29 9BG
Tel: (01730) 813243
Head: Mrs J Peel
Type: Co-educational Day Boys 3–8 Girls 3–11
No of pupils: B30 G80
Fees: (September 01)
Day £2100 – £4356

ST MARGARET'S SCHOOL CONVENT OF MERCY

Petersfield Road, Midhurst, West Sussex GU29 9JN
Tel: (01730) 813956
Head: Sister M Martina
Type: Co-educational Day 2–11
No of pupils: 380
Fees: (September 01)
Day £1815 – £3531

PEASE POTTAGE

COTTESMORE SCHOOL*

Buchan Hill, Pease Pottage, West Sussex RH11 9AU
Tel: (01293) 520648
Head: Mr M A Rogerson
Type: Co-educational Boarding 7–13
No of pupils: B100 G50
No of boarders: F150
Fees: (September 01) FB £12090

PETWORTH

SEAFORD COLLEGE*

Lavington Park, Petworth, West Sussex GU28 0NB
Tel: (01798) 867392
Head: Mr T J Mullins
Type: Co-educational Boarding and Day 10–18
No of pupils: B268 G96
No of boarders: F61 W90
Fees: (September 01)
F/WB £11550 – £14970
Day £7950 – £9960

PULBOROUGH

ARUNDALE PREPARATORY SCHOOL

Lower Street, Pulborough, West Sussex RH20 2BX
Tel: (01798) 872520
Head: Miss K Lovejoy
Type: Co-educational Day Boys 2–8 Girls 2–11
No of pupils: B24 G84
Fees: (September 01)
Day £1794 – £5610

DORSET HOUSE SCHOOL

The Manor, Church Lane, Bury, Pulborough, West Sussex RH20 1PB
Tel: (01798) 831456
Head: Mr A L James
Type: Boys Boarding and Day 4–13
No of pupils: 150
No of boarders: W46
Fees: (September 01)
F/WB £9780 – £11025
Day £4575 – £9210

WINDLESHAM HOUSE*

Washington, Pulborough, West Sussex RH20 4AY
Tel: (01903) 874700
Head: Mr P Lough
Type: Co-educational Boarding 8–13 (Day pre-prep 4–7)
No of pupils: B160 G110
No of boarders: F270
Fees: (September 01) FB £12255

SELSEY

ACORNS SCHOOL

33 James Street, Selsey, West Sussex PO20 0JG
Tel: (01243) 603545
Head: Mrs E Hobson
Type: Co-educational Day 3–7
No of pupils: 32
Fees: (September 01) Day £1320

SHOREHAM-BY-SEA

SHOREHAM COLLEGE
St Julian's Lane, Shoreham-by-Sea,
West Sussex BN43 6YW
Tel: (01273) 592681
Head: Mr R K Iremonger
Type: Co-educational Day 3–16
No of pupils: B211 G98
Fees: (September 01) On application

SOMPTING

SOMPTING ABBOTTS*
Sompting, West Sussex BN15 0AZ
Tel: (01903) 235960
Head: Mrs P M Sinclair and
Mr R M Johnson
Type: Co-educational Day and
Boarding 3–13
No of pupils: B135 G30
No of boarders: W12
Fees: (September 01) WB £7650
Day £3750 – £5460

STEYNING

SOUTHDOWN NURSERY
Gervays Hall, Jarvis Lane, Steyning,
West Sussex BN44 3GL
Tel: (01903) 814581
Head: Mrs K Richardson
Type: Co-educational Day 3–5
No of pupils: 20
Fees: (September 01)
Day £735 – £1200

THE TOWERS CONVENT SCHOOL
Upper Beeding, Steyning,
West Sussex BN44 3TF
Tel: (01903) 812185
Head: Sister M Andrew
Type: Girls Day and Boarding 3–16
(Boys 3–11)
No of pupils: B12 G216
No of boarders: F40 W12
Fees: (September 01)
FB £7080 – £7446 WB £6696 – £7044
Day £3855 – £4254

TURNERS HILL

WORTH SCHOOL
Turners Hill, West Sussex RH10 4SD
Tel: (01342) 710200
Head: Fr C Jamison
Type: Boys Boarding and Day 11–18
No of pupils: 428
No of boarders: F301
Fees: (September 01)
FB £14394 – £15993
Day £10602 – £11778

WORTHING

BROADWATER MANOR SCHOOL
Broadwater Road, Worthing,
West Sussex BN14 8HU
Tel: (01903) 201123
Head: Mrs E K Woodley
Type: Co-educational Day 2–13
No of pupils: B203 G154
Fees: (September 01)
Day £399 – £4770

OUR LADY OF SION SCHOOL
Gatwicke Road, Worthing,
West Sussex BN11 4BL
Tel: (01903) 204063
Head: Mr M Scullion
Type: Co-educational Day 2–18
No of pupils: B282 G257
Fees: (September 01)
Day £3582 – £5556

SANDHURST SCHOOL
101 Brighton Road, Worthing,
West Sussex BN11 2EL
Tel: (01903) 201933
Head: Mrs A B Glover
Type: Co-educational Day 2–13
No of pupils: B85 G94
Fees: (September 01)
Day £2118 – £2472

TYNE AND WEAR

NEWCASTLE UPON TYNE

AKHURST PREPARATORY SCHOOL
The Grove, Jesmond, Newcastle
upon Tyne, Tyne and Wear NE2 2PN
Tel: (0191) 281 2116
Head: Mr & Mrs R J Derham
Type: Co-educational Day 1–12
No of pupils: B130 G70
Fees: (September 01)
Day £4155 – £4515

ASCHAM HOUSE SCHOOL
30 West Avenue, Gosforth,
Newcastle upon Tyne, Tyne and
Wear NE3 4ES
Tel: (0191) 285 1619
Head: Mr S H Reid
Type: Boys Day 3–13
No of pupils: 270
Fees: (September 01)
Day £4800

CENTRAL NEWCASTLE HIGH SCHOOL GDST
Eskdale Terrace, Newcastle upon
Tyne, Tyne and Wear NE2 4DS
Tel: (0191) 281 1768
Head: Mrs L J Griffin
Type: Girls Day 3–18
No of pupils: 985
Fees: (September 01)
Day £3174 – £5442

DAME ALLAN'S BOYS SCHOOL
Fowberry Crescent, Fenham, Newcastle upon Tyne, Tyne and Wear NE4 9YJ
Tel: (0191) 275 0608
Head: Mr D W Welsh
Type: Boys Day 8–18 (Co-ed VIth Form)
No of pupils: 500
Fees: (September 01)
Day £4251 – £5400

DAME ALLAN'S GIRLS SCHOOL
Fowberry Crescent, Fenham, Newcastle upon Tyne, Tyne and Wear NE4 9YJ
Tel: (0191) 275 0708
Head: Mr D W Welsh
Type: Girls Day 8–18 (Co-ed VIth Form)
No of pupils: 450
Fees: (September 01)
Day £4251 – £5400

EASTCLIFFE GRAMMAR SCHOOL
The Grove, Gosforth, Newcastle upon Tyne, Tyne and Wear NE3 1NE
Tel: (0191) 285 4873
Head: Mr G D Pearson
Type: Co-educational Day 3–18
No of pupils: B170 G60
Fees: (September 01)
Day £3390 – £5280

LA SAGESSE HIGH SCHOOL
North Jesmond, Newcastle upon Tyne, Tyne and Wear NE2 3RJ
Tel: (0191) 281 3474
Head: Miss L Clark
Type: Girls Day 3–18
No of pupils: 350
Fees: (September 01)
Day £3444 – £5952

LINDEN SCHOOL
72 Station Road, Forest Hall, Newcastle upon Tyne, Tyne and Wear NE12 9BQ
Tel: (0191) 266 2943
Head: Mrs S Inness
Type: Co-educational Day 3–11
No of pupils: B72 G73
Fees: (September 01) Day £3450

NEWCASTLE PREPARATORY SCHOOL
6 Eslington Road, Jesmond, Newcastle upon Tyne, Tyne and Wear NE2 4RH
Tel: (0191) 281 1769
Head: Mr G Clayton
Type: Co-educational Day 2–13
No of pupils: B215 G125
Fees: (September 01)
Day £4410 – £5040

NEWCASTLE UPON TYNE CHURCH HIGH SCHOOL
Tankerville Terrace, Jesmond, Newcastle upon Tyne, Tyne and Wear NE2 3BA
Tel: (0191) 281 4306
Head: Mrs L G Smith
Type: Girls Day 2–18
No of pupils: 624
Fees: (September 01)
Day £3990 – £5670

NEWLANDS SCHOOL
34 The Grove, Gosforth, Newcastle upon Tyne, Tyne and Wear NE3 1NH
Tel: (0191) 285 2208
Head: Mr R McDuff
Type: Boys Day 3–13
No of pupils: 183
Fees: (September 01)
Day £4200 – £5675

ROYAL GRAMMAR SCHOOL
Eskdale Terrace, Newcastle upon Tyne, Tyne and Wear NE2 4DX
Tel: (0191) 281 5711
Head: Mr J F X Miller
Type: Boys Day 8–18 (Co-ed VIth form)
No of pupils: 1060
Fees: (September 01)
Day £4581 – £5499

WESTFIELD SCHOOL
Oakfield Road, Gosforth, Newcastle upon Tyne, Tyne and Wear NE3 4HS
Tel: (0191) 285 1948
Head: Mrs M Farndale
Type: Girls Day 3–18
No of pupils: 372
Fees: (September 01)
Day £4737 – £5811

NORTH SHIELDS

THE KING'S SCHOOL
Huntington Place, Tynemouth, North Shields, Tyne and Wear NE30 4RF
Tel: (0191) 258 5995
Head: Dr D Younger
Type: Co-educational Day 4–18
No of pupils: B550 G278
Fees: (September 01)
Day £4320 – £5685

SUNDERLAND

ARGYLE HOUSE SCHOOL
19/20 Thornhill Park, Sunderland, Tyne and Wear SR2 7LA
Tel: (0191) 510 0726
Head: Mr J N Johnson
Type: Co-educational Day 3–16
No of pupils: B156 G81
Fees: (September 01)
Day £3150 – £4320

GRINDON HALL CHRISTIAN SCHOOL
Nookside, Sunderland, Tyne and Wear SR4 8PG
Tel: (0191) 534 4444
Head: Mrs E Gray
Type: Co-educational Day 3–16
No of pupils: B55 G80
Fees: (September 01)
Day £1650 – £3090

SUNDERLAND HIGH SCHOOL
Mowbray Road, Sunderland, Tyne and Wear SR2 8HY
Tel: (0191) 567 4984
Head: Dr A Slater
Type: Co-educational Day 2–18
No of pupils: B315 G258
Fees: (September 01)
Day £3825 – £5490

WHICKHAM

CHASE SCHOOL
Rectory Lane, Whickham, Tyne and Wear NE16 4PD
Tel: (0191) 488 9432
Head: Mrs A Nelson
Type: Co-educational Day 4–11
No of pupils: B22 G19
Fees: (September 01) On application

WARWICKSHIRE

ATHERSTONE

TWYCROSS HOUSE SCHOOL
Twycross, Atherstone, Warwickshire
CV9 3PL
Tel: (01827) 880651
Head: Mr R V Kirkpatrick
Type: Co-educational Day 8–19
No of pupils: B143 G169
Fees: (September 01)
Day £4500 – £4890

KENILWORTH

ABBOTSFORD SCHOOL
Bridge Street, Kenilworth,
Warwickshire CV8 1BP
Tel: (01926) 852826
Head: Mrs J Adams
Type: Co-educational Day 3–11
No of pupils: B93 G64
Fees: (September 01) On application

LEAMINGTON SPA

ARNOLD LODGE SCHOOL
Kenilworth Road, Leamington Spa,
Warwickshire CV32 5TW
Tel: (01926) 778050
Head: Mr A G Jones
Type: Co-educational Day 3–13
No of pupils: B207 G194
Fees: (September 01)
Day £1574 – £1957

EMSCOTE HOUSE SCHOOL AND NURSERY
46 Warwick Place, Leamington Spa,
Warwickshire CV32 5DE
Tel: (01926) 425067
Head: Mrs G J Andrews
Type: Co-educational Day 2–7
No of pupils: B53 G42
Fees: (September 01)
Day £700 – £3900

THE KINGSLEY SCHOOL
Beauchamp Avenue, Leamington
Spa, Warwickshire CV32 5RD
Tel: (01926) 425127
Head: Mrs C Mannion Watson
Type: Girls Day 2–18 (Boys 2–7)
No of pupils: B12 G582
Fees: (September 01)
Day £3825 – £6570

NUNEATON

MILVERTON HOUSE SCHOOL
Holman Way, Park Street,
Attleborough, Nuneaton,
Warwickshire CV11 4EL
Tel: (024) 7664 1722
Head: Mr C D Badham
Type: Co-educational Day 0–11
No of pupils: B150 G150
Fees: (September 01)
Day £2760 – £2880

THE WOLSTAN PREPARATORY SCHOOL
Temple Hall, Wellsborough,
Nuneaton, Warwickshire CV13 6PA
Tel: (01455) 293024
Head: Mr W N Oakley
Type: Co-educational Day 3–10
No of pupils: B80 G77
Fees: (September 01)
Day £3555 – £4260

RUGBY

BILTON GRANGE
Dunchurch, Rugby, Warwickshire
CV22 6QU
Tel: (01788) 810217
Head: Mr Q G Edwards
Type: Co-educational Boarding and
Day 4–13
No of pupils: B234 G148
No of boarders: F48 W24
Fees: (September 01) F/WB £11397
Day £7959 – £9096

THE CRESCENT SCHOOL
Bawnmore Road, Bilton, Rugby,
Warwickshire CV22 7QH
Tel: (01788) 521595
Head: Mrs C Vickers
Type: Co-educational Day 2–11
No of pupils: B89 G95
Fees: (September 01)
Day £4035 – £4320

PRINCETHORPE COLLEGE
Leamington Road, Princethorpe,
Rugby, Warwickshire CV23 9PX
Tel: (01926) 634200
Head: Mr J M Shinkwin
Type: Co-educational Day and
Boarding 11–18 (Girls day
only 11–16)
No of pupils: B430 G220
No of boarders: F25 W19
Fees: (September 01) FB £12330
WB £11364 Day £5535

RUGBY SCHOOL
Rugby, Warwickshire CV22 5EH
Tel: (01788) 556274
Head: Mr P S J Derham
Type: Co-educational Boarding and
Day 11–18
No of pupils: B487 G302
No of boarders: F615
Fees: (September 01) FB £17550
Day £6300 – £14040

STRATFORD-UPON-AVON

THE CROFT SCHOOL
Alveston Hill, Loxley Road,
Stratford-upon-Avon, Warwickshire
CV37 7RL
Tel: (01789) 293795
Head: Mrs P Thompson
Type: Co-educational Day 2–11
No of pupils: B230 G175
Fees: (September 01)
Day £300 – £5500

ELFIN PRE-PREP & NURSEY SCHOOL
26 Evesham Place, Stratford-upon-
Avon, Warwickshire CV37 6HT
Tel: (01789) 292571
Head: Mrs Buczacki
Type: Co-educational Day 2–8
No of pupils: B18 G18
Fees: (September 01)
Day £2049 – £2652

STRATFORD PREPARATORY SCHOOL
Church House, Old Town, Stratford-
upon-Avon, Warwickshire CV37 6BG
Tel: (01789) 297993
Head: Mrs C Quinn
Type: Co-educational Day 2–11
No of pupils: B70 G81
Fees: (September 01)
Day £1320 – £4350

WARWICK

THE KING'S HIGH SCHOOL FOR GIRLS
Smith Street, Warwick CV34 4HJ
Tel: (01926) 494485
Head: Mrs E Surber
Type: Girls Day 10–18
No of pupils: 550
Fees: (September 01) Day £6126

WARWICK PREPARATORY SCHOOL

Bridge Field, Banbury Road,
Warwick CV34 6PL
Tel: (01926) 491545
Head: Mrs D M Robinson
Type: Co-educational Day Boys 3–7
Girls 3–11
No of pupils: B117 G356
Fees: (September 01)
Day £1965 – £5946

WARWICK SCHOOL

Myton Road, Warwick CV34 6PP
Tel: (01926) 776400
Head: Dr P J Cheshire
Type: Boys Day and Boarding 7–18
No of pupils: 1030
No of boarders: F35 W11
Fees: (September 01)
FB £12003 – £13307
WB £11076 – £12480
Day £4911 – £6315

WEST MIDLANDS

BIRMINGHAM

ABBEY COLLEGE

10 St Pauls Square, Birmingham,
West Midlands B3 1QU
Tel: (0121) 236 7474
Head: Dr C Devine and Ms Z Keeling
Type: Co-educational Day 13+
No of pupils: B105 G82
No of boarders: F7 W10
Fees: (September 01)
Day £6000 – £8400

AL HIJRAH SCHOOL

Cherrywood Centre, Burbidge Road,
Bordesley Green, Birmingham, West
Midlands B9 4US
Tel: (0121) 773 7979
Head: Mr M A K Saqib
Type: Co-educational Day 4–18
(Single-sex education)
No of pupils: B128 G128
Fees: (September 01)
Day £1500 – £2100

BIRCHFIELD INDEPENDENT GIRLS SCHOOL

30 Beacon Hill, Aston, Birmingham,
West Midlands B6 6JU
Tel: (0121) 327 7707
Head: Mrs K Chawdhry
Type: Girls Day 11–16
No of pupils: 142
Fees: (September 01) Day £840

THE BLUE COAT SCHOOL*

Somerset Road, Edgbaston,
Birmingham, West Midlands
B17 0HR
Tel: (0121) 454 1425
Head: Mr A D J Browning
Type: Co-educational Boarding and
Day 2–13
No of pupils: B269 G202
No of boarders: F22 W20
Fees: (September 01) FB £10590
WB £9525 Day £4080 – £6165

DARUL ULOOM ISLAMIC HIGH SCHOOL & COLLEGE

521–527 Coventry Road,
Smallheath, Birmingham, West
Midlands B10 0LL
Tel: (0121) 772 6408
Head: Dr A A Rahim
Type: Co-educational Day and
Boarding (Single-sex education)
No of pupils: B101 G17
No of boarders: F14
Fees: (September 01) On application

EASTBOURNE HOUSE SCHOOL

111 Yardley Road, Acocks Green,
Birmingham, West Midlands B27 6LL
Tel: (0121) 706 2013
Head: Mr P J Moynihan
Type: Co-educational Day 3–11
No of pupils: B66 G58
Fees: (September 01)
Day £1722 – £3180

EDGBASTON COLLEGE

249 Bristol Road, Birmingham, West
Midlands B5 7UH
Tel: (0121) 472 1034
Head: Mr R Bruce
Type: Co-educational Day 2–16
No of pupils: 115
Fees: (September 01) On application

EDGBASTON HIGH SCHOOL FOR GIRLS

Westbourne Road, Edgbaston,
Birmingham, West Midlands B15 3TS
Tel: (0121) 454 5831
Head: Miss E Mullenger
Type: Girls Day 2–18
No of pupils: 970
Fees: (September 01)
Day £3615 – £5730

HALLFIELD SCHOOL

48 Church Road, Edgbaston,
Birmingham, West Midlands B15 3SJ
Tel: (0121) 454 1496
Head: Mr J G Cringle
Type: Co-educational Day 2–11
No of pupils: B327 G130
Fees: (September 01)
Day £3825 – £5730

HIGHCLARE SCHOOL

10 Sutton Road, Erdington,
Birmingham, West Midlands
B23 6QL
Tel: (0121) 373 7400
Head: Mrs C A Hanson
Type: Girls Day 1–18
(Boys 1–11 & 16–18)
No of pupils: B180 G533
Fees: (September 01)
Day £3300 – £5880

HONEYBOURNE SCHOOL

621 Fox Hollies Road, Hall Green,
Birmingham, West Midlands
B28 9DW
Tel: (0121) 777 3778
Head: Mrs J A Hillstead
Type: Co-educational Day 2–7
No of pupils: 65
Fees: (September 01) On application

KING EDWARD VI HIGH SCHOOL FOR GIRLS

Edgbaston Park Road, Birmingham,
West Midlands B15 2UB
Tel: (0121) 472 1834
Head: Miss S H Evans
Type: Girls Day 11–18
No of pupils: 540
Fees: (September 01) Day £6060

KING EDWARD'S SCHOOL
Edgbaston Park Road, Birmingham,
West Midlands B15 2UA
Tel: (0121) 472 1672
Head: Mr R M Dancey
Type: Boys Day 11–18
No of pupils: 889
Fees: (September 01)
Day £6216

MANDER PORTMAN WOODWARD
38 Highfield Road, Edgbaston,
Birmingham, West Midlands
B15 3ED
Tel: (0121) 454 9637
Head: Mr M Lloyd
Type: Co-educational Day 14+
No of pupils: B60 G60
Fees: (September 01)
Day £1827 – £10023

NORFOLK HOUSE SCHOOL
4 Norfolk Road, Edgbaston,
Birmingham, West Midlands B15 3PS
Tel: (0121) 454 7021
Head: Mrs H Maresca
Type: Co-educational Day 3–11
No of pupils: B80 G78
Fees: (September 01)
Day £1968 – £3417

PRIORY SCHOOL
39 Sir Harry's Road, Edgbaston,
Birmingham, West Midlands
B15 2UR
Tel: (0121) 440 4103
Head: Mrs E C Brook
Type: Girls Day 2–18 (Boys 2–11)
No of pupils: B61 G250
Fees: (September 01)
Day £3630 – £5985

RATHVILLY SCHOOL
119 Bunbury Road, Birmingham,
West Midlands B31 2NB
Tel: (0121) 475 1509
Head: Ms M Willetts
Type: Co-educational Day 2–11
No of pupils: B50 G50
Fees: (September 01) On application

ROSSLYN SCHOOL
1597 Stratford Road, Hall Green,
Birmingham, West Midlands B28 9JB
Tel: (0121) 744 2743
Head: Mrs J Taylor
Type: Co-educational Day 2–11
No of pupils: 104
Fees: (September 01) On application

ST GEORGE'S SCHOOL, EDGBASTON
31 Calthorpe Road, Birmingham,
West Midlands B15 1RX
Tel: (0121) 625 0398
Head: Miss H J Phillips
Type: Co-educational Day 3–18
No of pupils: B203 G158
Fees: (September 01)
Day £3000 – £5985

WEST HOUSE SCHOOL
24 St James's Road, Edgbaston,
Birmingham, West Midlands
B15 2NX
Tel: (0121) 440 4097
Head: Mr G K Duce
Type: Boys Day 1–11 (Girls 1–4)
No of pupils: B220 G20
Fees: (September 01)
Day £1089 – £6396

COVENTRY

BABLAKE SCHOOL
Coundon Road, Coventry, West
Midlands CV1 4AU
Tel: (024) 7622 8388
Head: Dr S Nuttall
Type: Co-educational Day 7–19
No of pupils: B475 G450
Fees: (September 01)
Day £3985 – £5496

CHESHUNT PRE-PREPARATORY SCHOOL
8 Park Road, Coventry, West
Midlands CV1 2LH
Tel: (024) 7622 1677
Head: Mrs F Ward
Type: Co-educational Day 3–8
No of pupils: 85
Fees: (September 01) On application

COVENTRY MUSLIM SCHOOL
643 Foleshill Road, Coventry, West
Midlands CV6 5JQ
Tel: (024) 7626 1803
Head: Mr M Ashique
Type: Girls Day 4–16
No of pupils: 40
Fees: (September 01) On application

COVENTRY PREPARATORY SCHOOL
Kenilworth Road, Coventry, West
Midlands CV3 6PT
Tel: (024) 7667 5289
Head: Mr M Abraham
Type: Co-educational Day 3–13
No of pupils: B127 G76
Fees: (September 01)
Day £4602 – £6228

DAVENPORT LODGE SCHOOL
21 Davenport Road, Earlsdon,
Coventry, West Midlands CV5 6QA
Tel: (024) 7667 5051
Head: Mrs M D Martin
Type: Co-educational Day 2–8
No of pupils: B88 G67
Fees: (September 01) On application

KING HENRY VIII SCHOOL
Warwick Road, Coventry, West
Midlands CV3 6AQ
Tel: (024) 7667 3442
Head: Mr G D Fisher
Type: Co-educational Day 7–18
No of pupils: B512 G522
Fees: (September 01)
Day £3885 – £5184

PATTISON COLLEGE
90 Binley Road, Coventry, West
Midlands CV3 1FQ
Tel: (024) 7645 5031
Head: Miss B Pattison and
Mrs J A Satchell
Type: Co-educational Day 3–16
No of pupils: B38 G108
Fees: (September 01)
Day £3000 – £3945

SOLIHULL

ARDEN LAWN
Henley-in-Arden, Solihull, West
Midlands B95 6AB
Tel: (01564) 796800
Head: Mrs J Thomas
Type: Co-educational Day 3–18
No of pupils: B270 G200
Fees: (January 02)
Day £4245 – £6150

EVERSFIELD PREPARATORY SCHOOL
Warwick Road, Solihull, West
Midlands B91 1AT
Tel: (0121) 705 0354
Head: Mr K U Madden
Type: Co-educational Day 2–11
No of pupils: B161 G15
Fees: (September 01)
Day £4500 – £5100

KINGSLEY PREPARATORY SCHOOL
53 Hanbury Road, Dorridge,
Solihull, West Midlands B93 8DW
Tel: (01564) 774144
Head: Mrs J A Scott
Type: Co-educational Day 3–11
No of pupils: B20 G20
Fees: (September 01) On application

KINGSWOOD SCHOOL
St James Place, Shirley, Solihull,
West Midlands B90 2BA
Tel: (0121) 744 7883
Head: Mr P Callaghan
Type: Co-educational Day 2–11
No of pupils: B40 G35
Fees: (September 01)
Day £3150 – £4575

RUCKLEIGH SCHOOL
17 Lode Lane, Solihull, West
Midlands B91 2AB
Tel: (0121) 705 2773
Head: Mrs B M Forster
Type: Co-educational Day 2–11
No of pupils: B119 G101
Fees: (September 01)
Day £2430 – £4761

ST MARTIN'S SCHOOL
Malvern Hall, Brueton Avenue,
Solihull, West Midlands B91 3EN
Tel: (0121) 705 1265
Head: Mrs J R Taylor
Type: Girls Day 3–18
No of pupils: 570
Fees: (September 01)
Day £2085 – £5790

SOLIHULL SCHOOL
Warwick Road, Solihull, West
Midlands B91 3DJ
Tel: (0121) 705 4273
Head: Mr J A Claughton
Type: Boys Day 7–18 (Co-ed VIth
Form)
No of pupils: B912 G85
Fees: (September 01)
Day £4605 – £5940

SUTTON COLDFIELD

CHETWYND HOUSE SCHOOL
6 Streetly Lane, Sutton Coldfield,
West Midlands B74 4TT
Tel: (0121) 308 0332
Head: Mr D Ablett
Type: Co-educational Day 3–11
No of pupils: B55 G2
Fees: (September 01) On application

THE SHRUBBERY SCHOOL
Walmley Ash Road, Walmley, Sutton
Coldfield, West Midlands B76 1HY
Tel: (0121) 351 1582
Head: Mrs H Cook
Type: Co-educational Day 3–11
No of pupils: B152 G118
Fees: (September 01)
Day £1854 – £3795

WYLDE GREEN COLLEGE
245 Birmingham Road, Sutton
Coldfield, West Midlands B72 1EA
Tel: (0121) 354 1505
Head: Mr P J Burd
Type: Co-educational Day 1–11
No of pupils: B120 G40
Fees: (September 01)
Day £3138 – £4230

WALSALL

HYDESVILLE TOWER SCHOOL
25 Broadway North, Walsall, West
Midlands WS1 2QG
Tel: (01922) 624374
Head: Mr T D Farrell
Type: Co-educational Day 3–16
No of pupils: B196 G164
Fees: (September 01)
Day £2325 – £5925

MAYFIELD PREPARATORY SCHOOL
Sutton Road, Walsall, West Midlands
WS1 2PD
Tel: (01922) 624104
Head: Mrs C M Jones
Type: Co-educational Day 3–11
No of pupils: B108 G84
Fees: (September 01) Day £4185

WOLVERHAMPTON

BIRCHFIELD SCHOOL
Albrighton, Wolverhampton, West
Midlands WV7 3AF
Tel: (01902) 372534
Head: Mr R P Merriman
Type: Boys Boarding and Day 3–13
No of pupils: 243
No of boarders: W20
Fees: (September 01) WB £8850
Day £4200 – £6600

THE DRIVE PREPARATORY SCHOOL AT TETTENHALL
Wood Road, Tettenhall,
Wolverhampton, West Midlands
WV6 8RX
Tel: (01902) 751125
Head: Mrs N M Parsons
Type: Co-educational Day 2–7
No of pupils: 131
Fees: (September 01) On application

THE DRIVE SCHOOL
Wrottesley Road, Tettenhall,
Wolverhampton, West Midlands
WV6 8RX
Tel: (01902) 751125
Head: Mrs N M Parsons
Type: Co-educational Day 2–7
No of pupils: B60 G40
Fees: (September 01) On application

NEWBRIDGE PREPARATORY SCHOOL
51 Newbridge Crescent, Tettenhall,
Wolverhampton, West Midlands
WV6 0LH
Tel: (01902) 751088
Head: Miss M J Coulter
Type: Girls Day 3–11 (Boys 3–4)
No of pupils: 150
Fees: (September 01)
Day £2976 – £4533

THE ROYAL WOLVERHAMPTON JUNIOR SCHOOL
Penn Road, Wolverhampton, West
Midlands WV3 0EF
Tel: (01902) 349100
Head: Mrs M Saunders
Type: Co-educational Day and
Boarding 2–11
No of pupils: B122 G85
No of boarders: F3
Fees: (September 01) F/WB £12285
Day £3345 – £5160

THE ROYAL WOLVERHAMPTON SCHOOL
Penn Road, Wolverhampton, West
Midlands WV3 0EG
Tel: (01902) 341230
Head: Mr T J Brooker
Type: Co-educational Boarding and
Day 11–18
No of pupils: B193 G108
No of boarders: F160 W20
Fees: (September 01) FB £13560
WB £12300 – £12660
Day £6210 – £6615

TETTENHALL COLLEGE
Wood Road, Wolverhampton, West
Midlands WV6 8QX
Tel: (01902) 751119
Head: Dr P C Bodkin
Type: Co-educational Boarding and
Day 7–18
No of pupils: B225 G124
No of boarders: F73 W12
Fees: (September 01)
FB £10104 – £12306
WB £8199 – £10239
Day £5901 – £7374

WOLVERHAMPTON GRAMMAR SCHOOL
Compton Road, Wolverhampton,
West Midlands WV3 9RB
Tel: (01902) 421326
Head: Dr B Trafford
Type: Co-educational Day 11–18
No of pupils: B481 G275
Fees: (September 01)
Day £6795

WILTSHIRE

CALNE

ST MARY'S SCHOOL*
Calne, Wiltshire SN11 0DF
Tel: (01249) 857200
Head: Mrs C Shaw
Type: Girls Boarding and Day 11–18
No of pupils: 300
No of boarders: F250
Fees: (September 01) FB £17100
Day £11250

CHIPPENHAM

GRITTLETON HOUSE SCHOOL
Grittleton, Chippenham, Wiltshire
SN14 6AP
Tel: (01249) 782434
Head: Mrs C Whitney
Type: Co-educational Day 3–16
No of pupils: B125 G116
Fees: (September 01)
Day £2895 – £5625

CORSHAM

HEYWOOD PREPARATORY SCHOOL
The Priory, Priory Street, Corsham,
Wiltshire SN13 0AP
Tel: (01249) 713379
Head: Mrs P Hall and Mr M Hall
Type: Co-educational Day 3–11
No of pupils: B126 G90
Fees: (September 01)
Day £3285 – £3840

CRICKLADE

MEADOWPARK NURSERY & PRE-PREP
Calcutt Street, Cricklade, Wiltshire
SN6 6BB
Tel: (01793) 752600
Head: Mrs R Kular and
Mrs S Hanbury
Type: Co-educational Day 1–7
No of pupils: B51 G39
Fees: (September 01) Day £4170

PRIOR PARK PREPARATORY SCHOOL
Calcutt Street, Cricklade, Wiltshire
SN6 6BB
Tel: (01793) 750275
Head: Mr G B Hobern
Type: Co-educational Boarding and
Day 7–13
No of pupils: B125 G75
No of boarders: F23 W24
Fees: (September 01)
F/WB £9807 – £9891
Day £6750 – £7119

DEVIZES

DAUNTSEY'S SCHOOL*
High Street, West Lavington,
Devizes, Wiltshire SN10 4HE
Tel: (01380) 814500
Head: Mr S B Roberts
Type: Co-educational Boarding and
Day 11–18
No of pupils: B364 G316
No of boarders: F264
Fees: (September 01) FB £15435
Day £9225

THE MILL SCHOOL
Potterne, Devizes, Wiltshire
SN10 5TE
Tel: (01380) 723011
Head: Mrs L Gill
Type: Co-educational Day 4–11
No of pupils: B54 G43
Fees: (September 01)
Day £2835 – £4425

MARLBOROUGH

KINGSBURY HILL HOUSE*
34 Kingsbury Street, Marlborough,
Wiltshire SN8 1JA
Tel: (01672) 512680
Head: Mr M Innes-Williams
Type: Co-educational Day 3–13
No of pupils: B90 G90
Fees: (September 00)
Day £3000 – £5725

MARLBOROUGH COLLEGE
Marlborough, Wiltshire SN8 1PA
Tel: (01672) 892300
Head: Mr E J H Gould
Type: Co-educational Boarding 13–18
No of pupils: B525 G311
No of boarders: F807
Fees: (September 01) FB £17550
Day £13170

ST ANDREW SCHOOL
Ogbourne St Andrew, Marlborough,
Wiltshire SN8 1SB
Tel: (01672) 841291
Head: Miss S Platt
Type: Co-educational Day 3–11
No of pupils: B18 G23
Fees: (September 01)
Day £1920 – £3600

STEPPING STONES NURSERY AND PRE-PREPARATORY SCHOOL
Oakhill Farm, Froxfield,
Marlborough, Wiltshire SN8 3JT
Tel: (01488) 681067
Head: Miss S Corfield and
Miss A Harron
Type: Co-educational Day 2–7
No of pupils: B82 G75
Fees: (September 01)
Day £735 – £4149

MELKSHAM

STONAR SCHOOL*
Melksham, Wiltshire SN12 8NT
Tel: (01225) 702795/702309
Head: Mrs S Hopkinson
Type: Girls Boarding and Day 4–18
No of pupils: 400
No of boarders: F140 W60
Fees: (September 01)
F/WB £10881 – £12594
Day £3102 – £6996

PEWSEY

ST FRANCIS SCHOOL
Marlborough Road, Pewsey,
Wiltshire SN9 5NT
Tel: (01672) 563228
Head: Mr P W Blundell
Type: Co-educational Day 2–13
No of pupils: B115 G116
Fees: (September 01)
Day £435 – £6225

SALISBURY

AVONDALE SCHOOL
High Street, Bulford, Salisbury,
Wiltshire SP4 9DR
Tel: (01980) 632387
Head: Mr R McNeall and
Mrs S McNeall
Type: Co-educational Day 3–11
No of pupils: B50 G50
Fees: (September 01)
Day £1926 – £3270

CARING DAY CARE
18 Burford Road, Salisbury, Wiltshire
SP2 8AN
Tel: (01722) 322179
Head: Ms N Letley
Type: Co-educational Day 0–5
No of pupils: 35
Fees: (September 01)
Day £544 – £3395

CHAFYN GROVE SCHOOL*
Bourne Avenue, Salisbury, Wiltshire
SP1 1LR
Tel: (01722) 333423
Head: Mr J E A Barnes
Type: Co-educational Boarding and
Day 3–13
No of pupils: B227 G75
No of boarders: F62
Fees: (September 01)
F/WB £9150 – £11280
Day £3960 – £8430

THE GODOLPHIN PREPARATORY SCHOOL
Laverstock Road, Salisbury, Wiltshire
SP1 2RB
Tel: (01722) 430652
Head: Miss C J Collins
Type: Girls Day 3–11
No of pupils: 110
Fees: (September 01)
Day £3765 – £7374

THE GODOLPHIN SCHOOL
Milford Hill, Salisbury, Wiltshire
SP1 2RA
Tel: (01722) 430500
Head: Miss M J Horsburgh
Type: Girls Boarding and Day 11–18
No of pupils: 412
No of boarders: F196
Fees: (September 01) FB £15240
Day £9210

LA RETRAITE SWAN
Campbell Road, Salisbury, Wiltshire
SP1 3BQ
Tel: (01722) 333094
Head: Mrs R A Simmons
Type: Co-educational Day 2–16
No of pupils: B130 G130
Fees: (September 01)
Day £3435 – £6150

LEADEN HALL
70 The Close, Salisbury, Wiltshire
SP1 2EP
Tel: (01722) 334700
Head: Mrs D Watkins
Type: Girls Day and Boarding 3–13
(Boys 3–4)
No of pupils: B4 G248
No of boarders: F40
Fees: (September 01) FB £9300
Day £4245 – £5985

NORMAN COURT PREPARATORY SCHOOL
West Tytherley, Salisbury, Wiltshire
SP5 1NH
Tel: (01980) 862345
Head: Mr K N Foyle
Type: Co-educational Boarding and
Day 3–13
No of pupils: B118 G172
No of boarders: F22 W42
Fees: (September 01)
F/WB £10563 – £11409
Day £4290 – £8529

SALISBURY CATHEDRAL SCHOOL
1 The Close, Salisbury, Wiltshire
SP1 2EQ
Tel: (01722) 555300
Head: Mr R M Thackray
Type: Co-educational Day and
Boarding 3–13
No of pupils: B129 G113
No of boarders: F50
Fees: (September 01) FB £11775
Day £2775 – £8025

SANDROYD
Tollard Royal, Salisbury, Wiltshire
SP5 5QD
Tel: (01725) 516264
Head: Mr M J Hatch
Type: Boys Boarding 7–13 (A few
day places)
No of pupils: 150
No of boarders: F110
Fees: (September 01)
FB £9975 – £12300
Day £7200 – £10200

SOUTH HILLS SCHOOL
Home Farm Road, Salisbury,
Wiltshire SP2 8PJ
Tel: (01722) 744971
Head: Mrs A Proctor
Type: Co-educational Day 0–8
No of pupils: B30 G30
Fees: (September 01)
Day £778 – £3402

SWINDON

MARANATHA CHRISTIAN SCHOOL
Queenlaines Farm, Sevenhampton,
Swindon, Wiltshire SN6 7SQ
Tel: (01793) 762075
Head: Mr P Medlock
Type: Co-educational Day 3–18
No of pupils: B20 G20
Fees: (September 01) On application

PINEWOOD SCHOOL*
Bourton, Swindon, Wiltshire
SN6 8HZ
Tel: (01793) 782205
Head: Mr C A Stuart-Clark
Type: Co-educational Boarding and
Day 3–13
No of pupils: B143 G107
No of boarders: W26
Fees: (September 01) FB £10185
Day £3975 – £6768

TROWBRIDGE

ROUNDSTONE PREPARATORY SCHOOL
Courtfield House, Polebarn Road,
Trowbridge, Wiltshire BA14 7EG
Tel: (01225) 752847
Head: Mrs M E Pearce
Type: Co-educational Day 4–11
No of pupils: B60 G55
Fees: (September 01) On application

WARMINSTER

STOURBRIDGE HOUSE SCHOOL
Castle Street, Mere, Warminster,
Wiltshire BA12 6JQ
Tel: (01747) 860165
Head: Mrs E Coward
Type: Co-educational Day 2–9
No of pupils: B25 G25
Fees: (September 01)
Day £3075 – £3228

WARMINSTER INTERNATIONAL STUDY CENTRE
Church Street, Warminster,
Wiltshire BA12 8PJ
Tel: (01985) 210170
Head: Mr J McKeown
Type: Co-educational Boarding 9–17
No of pupils: 30
No of boarders: F30
Fees: (September 01) FB £17145

WARMINSTER SCHOOL
Church Street, Warminster,
Wiltshire BA12 8PJ
Tel: (01985) 210100
Head: Mr D Dowdles
Type: Co-educational Boarding and
Day 3–18
No of pupils: B250 G250
No of boarders: F220 W11
Fees: (September 01)
FB £10365 – £12600
Day £3000 – £6705

WORCESTERSHIRE

BEWDLEY

MOFFATS SCHOOL
Kinlet Hall, Bewdley, Worcestershire
DY12 3AY
Tel: (01299) 841230
Head: Mr M Daborn
Type: Co-educational Boarding and
Day 4–13
No of pupils: B51 G38
No of boarders: F45
Fees: (September 01) FB £8385
Day £3460 – £5550

BROMSGROVE

BROMSGROVE LOWER SCHOOL
Cobham House, Conway Road,
Bromsgrove, Worcestershire B60 2AD
Tel: (01527) 579600
Head: Mr P Lee-Smith
Type: Co-educational Boarding and
Day 7–13
No of pupils: B244 G172
No of boarders: F80
Fees: (September 01)
FB £10470 – £12090
Day £5865 – £7680

BROMSGROVE PRE-PREPARATORY AND NURSERY SCHOOL
Ottilie Hild School, Avoncroft
House, Hanbury Road, Bromsgrove,
Worcestershire B60 4JS
Tel: (01527) 873007
Head: Mrs S Pickering
Type: Co-educational Day 3–7
No of pupils: B87 G77
Fees: (September 01)
Day £2325 – £4485

BROMSGROVE SCHOOL*
Worcester Road, Bromsgrove,
Worcestershire B61 7DU
Tel: (01527) 579679
Head: Mr T M Taylor
Type: Co-educational Boarding and
Day 7–18
No of pupils: B685 G465
No of boarders: F398
Fees: (September 01)
FB £10470 – £14010
Day £5865 – £8430

MOUNT SCHOOL
Birmingham Road, Bromsgrove,
Worcestershire B61 0EP
Tel: (01527) 877772
Head: Mr S A Robinson
Type: Co-educational Day 3–11
No of pupils: B82 G68
Fees: (September 01)
Day £3285 – £4485

DROITWICH

WHITFORD HALL & DODDERHILL SCHOOL
Crutch Lane, Droitwich,
Worcestershire WR9 0BE
Tel: (01905) 778290
Head: Mrs J Mumby
Type: Girls Day 3–16 (Boys 3–9)
No of pupils: B20 G190
Fees: (September 01)
Day £1965 – £6150

EVESHAM

GREEN HILL SCHOOL
Evesham, Worcestershire WR11 4NG
Tel: (01386) 442364
Head: Mr O Lister
Type: Co-educational Day 3–13
No of pupils: B55 G50
Fees: (September 01)
Day £3195 – £4350

KIDDERMINSTER

HARTLEBURY SCHOOL
Hartlebury, Kidderminster,
Worcestershire DY11 7TE
Tel: (01299) 250258
Head: Mr D R Bolam
Type: Co-educational Day 4–16
No of pupils: B65 G34
Fees: (September 01)
Day £2175 – £6900

HEATHFIELD SCHOOL
Wolverley, Kidderminster,
Worcestershire DY10 3QE
Tel: (01562) 850204
Head: Mr G L Sinton
Type: Co-educational Day 3–16
No of pupils: B156 G106
Fees: (September 01)
Day £1485 – £5850

HOLY TRINITY SCHOOL
Birmingham Road, Kidderminster,
Worcestershire DY10 2BY
Tel: (01562) 822929
Head: Mrs E L Thomas
Type: Co-educational Day Boys 1–11
Girls 1–18
No of pupils: B34 G338
Fees: (September 01)
Day £2775 – £5445

THE KNOLL SCHOOL
33 Manor Avenue, Kidderminster,
Worcestershire DY11 6EA
Tel: (01562) 822622
Head: Mr N J Humphreys
Type: Co-educational Day 2–11
No of pupils: B79 G38
Fees: (September 01)
Day £2658 – £3567

WINTERFOLD HOUSE
Chaddesley Corbett, Kidderminster,
Worcestershire DY10 4PL
Tel: (01562) 777234
Head: Mr W C R Ibbetson-Price
Type: Co-educational Day 3–13
No of pupils: B220 G90
Fees: (September 01)
Day £3675 – £6750

MALVERN

THE DOWNS SCHOOL
Colwall, Malvern, Worcestershire
WR13 6EY
Tel: (01684) 540277
Head: Mr A Ramsay
Type: Co-educational Boarding and
Day 3–13
No of pupils: B70 G70
No of boarders: F5 W10
Fees: (September 01) FB £10560
WB £10320 Day £2460 – £7620

THE ELMS
Colwall, Malvern, Worcestershire
WR13 6EF
Tel: (01684) 540344
Head: Mr L A C Ashby
Type: Co-educational Boarding and
Day 3–13
No of pupils: B96 G74
No of boarders: F83
Fees: (September 01) FB £10560
Day £3900 – £9240

HILLSTONE SCHOOL
(MALVERN COLLEGE)
Abbey Road, Malvern,
Worcestershire WR14 3HF
Tel: (01684) 581600
Head: Mr P H Moody
Type: Co-educational Boarding and
Day 3–13
No of pupils: B110 G100
No of boarders: F53
Fees: (September 01)
FB £6960 – £11115
Day £3210 – £8385

MALVERN COLLEGE*
College Road, Malvern,
Worcestershire WR14 3DF
Tel: (01684) 581500
Head: Mr H C K Carson
Type: Co-educational Boarding and
Day 13–18
No of pupils: B473 G284
No of boarders: F453
Fees: (September 01)
FB £11115 – £17250
Day £6855 – £11085

MALVERN GIRLS' COLLEGE*
Avenue Road, Malvern,
Worcestershire WR14 3BA
Tel: (01684) 892288
Head: Mrs P M C Leggate
Type: Girls Boarding and Day 11–18
No of pupils: 410
No of boarders: F330
Fees: (September 01) FB £17175
Day £11400

ST JAMES'S SCHOOL*
West Malvern, Malvern,
Worcestershire WR14 4DF
Tel: (01684) 560851
Head: Mrs S Kershaw
Type: Girls Boarding and Day 10–18
No of pupils: 125
No of boarders: F43 W40
Fees: (September 01)
F/WB £14985 – £16050
Day £7425 – £9855

MALVERN WELLS

THE ABBEY COLLEGE*
253 Wells Road, Malvern Wells,
Worcestershire WR14 4JF
Tel: (01684) 892300
Head: Mr L Denholme
Type: Co-educational Boarding and
Day 13+
No of pupils: B60 G50
No of boarders: F109 W1
Fees: (September 01) FB £12950
WB £10475 Day £6475

PERSHORE

BOWBROOK HOUSE SCHOOL
Peopleton, Pershore, Worcestershire
WR10 2EE
Tel: (01905) 841242
Head: Mr S W Jackson
Type: Co-educational Day 3–16
No of pupils: B85 G54
Fees: (September 01)
Day £2763 – £4875

TENBURY WELLS

ST MICHAEL'S COLLEGE
Oldwood Road, St Michaels, Tenbury
Wells, Worcestershire WR15 8PH
Tel: (01584) 811300
Head: Mr S Higgins
Type: Co-educational Day and
Boarding 14–19
No of pupils: B60 G60
No of boarders: F45
Fees: (September 01)
FB £12000 – £12600

WORCESTER

ABBERLEY HALL
Worcester, Worcestershire WR6 6DD
Tel: (01299) 896275
Head: Mr J G W Walker
Type: Co-educational Boarding and
Day 2–13
No of pupils: B185 G98
No of boarders: F119
Fees: (September 01) FB £11910
Day £2205 – £9510

THE ALICE OTTLEY SCHOOL
Upper Tything, Worcester,
Worcestershire WR1 1HW
Tel: (01905) 27061
Head: Mrs M Chapman
Type: Girls Day 3–19
No of pupils: 640
Fees: (September 01)
Day £3177 – £6828

BARBOURNE PREPARATORY
SCHOOL
Cypress House, 47 Waterworks
Road, Worcester, Worcestershire
WR1 3EY
Tel: (01905) 24785
Head: Mr N S Ridley
Type: Co-educational Day 0–11
No of pupils: 55
Fees: (September 01) On application

THE GRANGE
Royal Grammar School Worcester
Pre-Prep, Grange Lane, Claines,
Worcester, Worcestershire WR3 7RR
Tel: (01905) 451205
Head: Mrs M Windsor
Type: Co-educational Day 3–8
No of pupils: B130 G70
Fees: (September 01)
Day £3276 – £4152

KING'S HAWFORD
Worcester, Worcestershire WR3 7SE
Tel: (01905) 451292
Head: Mr R Middleton
Type: Co-educational Day 3–11
No of pupils: B130 G98
Fees: (September 01)
Day £3801 – £6798

THE KING'S SCHOOL
Worcester, Worcestershire WR1 2LH
Tel: (01905) 721700
Head: Mr T H Keyes
Type: Co-educational Day 7–18
No of pupils: B581 G376
Fees: (September 01)
Day £4305 – £6681

RIVER SCHOOL
Oakfield House, Droitwich Road,
Worcester, Worcestershire WR3 7ST
Tel: (01905) 457047
Head: Mr G Coyle
Type: Co-educational Day 5–16
No of pupils: B89 G90
Fees: (September 01) Day £2364

ROYAL GRAMMAR SCHOOL
WORCESTER
Upper Tything, Worcester,
Worcestershire WR1 1HP
Tel: (01905) 613391
Head: Mr W A Jones
Type: Boys Day 3–18
No of pupils: B963 G57
Fees: (September 01)
Day £3276 – £6210

ST MARY'S CONVENT
SCHOOL
Mount Battenhall, Worcester,
Worcestershire WR5 2HP
Tel: (01905) 357786
Head: Mrs B Williams
Type: Girls Day 2–18 (Boys 2–8)
No of pupils: 317
Fees: (September 01)
Day £3195 – £5430

SUNNYSIDE SCHOOL
Barbourne Terrace, Worcester,
Worcestershire WR1 3JR
Tel: (01905) 23973
Head: Mrs M Edwards
Type: Co-educational Day 2–9
No of pupils: B70 G70
Fees: (September 01)
Day £1290 – £3150

EAST RIDING OF YORKSHIRE

DRIFIELD

ST FRANCIS PREPARATORY
SCHOOL
25 High Street, Nafferton, Drifield,
East Riding of Yorkshire YO25 0HR
Tel: (01377) 254628
Head: Mr A J Phillips
Type: Co-educational Day 3–16
No of pupils: B50 G40
Fees: (September 01)
Day £415 – £1300

HESSLE

HESSLE MOUNT SCHOOL
Jenny Brough Lane, Hessle, East
Riding of Yorkshire HU13 0JX
Tel: (01482) 643371/641948
Head: Mrs Cutting
Type: Co-educational Day 3–8
No of pupils: 160
Fees: (September 01)
Day £2640 – £2880

HULL

FROEBEL HOUSE SCHOOL
5 Marlborough Avenue, Princes
Avenue, Hull, East Riding of
Yorkshire HU5 3JP
Tel: (01482) 342272
Head: Mrs L A Roberts
Type: Co-educational Day 4–11
No of pupils: B49 G61
Fees: (September 01)
Day £2520 – £2608

HULL HIGH SCHOOL
Tranby Croft, Anlaby, Hull, East Riding of Yorkshire HU10 7EH
Tel: (01482) 657016
Head: Mrs M A Benson
Type: Girls Day 3–18 (Boys 3–11)
No of pupils: B86 G362
Fees: (September 01)
Day £3536 – £5520

HYMERS COLLEGE
Hymers Avenue, Hull, East Riding of Yorkshire HU3 1LW
Tel: (01482) 343555
Head: Mr J C Morris
Type: Co-educational Day 8–18
No of pupils: B569 G399
Fees: (September 01)
Day £4581 – £5232

KINGSTON-UPON-HULL

HULL GRAMMAR SCHOOL
Cottingham Road, Kingston-Upon-Hull, East Riding of Yorkshire HU5 2DL
Tel: (01482) 440144
Head: Mr R Haworth
Type: Co-educational Boarding and Day 2–18
No of pupils: B278 G170
No of boarders: F7
Fees: (September 01)
FB £11805 – £15075
WB £10500 – £11190
Day £2748 – £5304

POCKLINGTON

POCKLINGTON MONTESSORI SCHOOL
Bielby Lane, Pocklington, East Riding of Yorkshire YO42 1NT
Tel: (01759) 305436
Head: Ms R Pressland
Type: Co-educational Day 0–7
No of pupils: B131 G121
Fees: (September 01)
Day £1372 – £1445

POCKLINGTON SCHOOL*
West Green, Pocklington, East Riding of Yorkshire YO42 2NJ
Tel: (01759) 303125
Head: Mr N Clements
Type: Co-educational Boarding and Day 7–18
No of pupils: B418 G310
No of boarders: F127
Fees: (September 01)
FB £10305 – £11970
Day £6090 – £7155

NORTH YORKSHIRE

BEDALE

AYSGARTH PREPARATORY SCHOOL
Bedale, North Yorkshire DL8 1TF
Tel: (01677) 450240
Head: Mr P J Southall
Type: Boys Boarding 3–13 (Co-ed Day 3–8)
No of pupils: B170 G8
No of boarders: F61 W17
Fees: (September 01) F/WB £11985
Day £3825 – £8985

HARROGATE

ASHVILLE COLLEGE
Harrogate, North Yorkshire HG2 9JP
Tel: (01423) 566358
Head: Mr M H Crosby
Type: Co-educational Day and Boarding 4–18
No of pupils: B507 G339
No of boarders: F110 W30
Fees: (September 01)
F/WB £9837 – £11781
Day £3513 – £6330

BELMONT GROSVENOR SCHOOL
Swarcliffe Hall, Birstwith, Harrogate, North Yorkshire HG3 2JG
Tel: (01423) 771029
Head: Mrs R H Innocent
Type: Co-educational Day 2–13
No of pupils: 345
Fees: (September 01)
Day £633 – £5250

BRACKENFIELD SCHOOL
128 Duchy Road, Harrogate, North Yorkshire HG1 2HE
Tel: (01423) 508558
Head: Mrs P Redding
Type: Co-educational Day 2–11
No of pupils: B90 G92
Fees: (September 01)
Day £1500 – £4500

HARROGATE LADIES' COLLEGE
Clarence Drive, Harrogate, North Yorkshire HG1 2QG
Tel: (01423) 504543
Head: Dr M J Hustler
Type: Girls Boarding and Day 10–18
No of pupils: 378
No of boarders: F200 W24
Fees: (September 01) F/WB £13365
Day £8190

HARROGATE TUTORIAL COLLEGE
2 The Oval, Harrogate, North Yorkshire HG2 9BA
Tel: (01423) 501041
Head: Mr K W Pollard
Type: Co-educational Day and Boarding 15–20
No of pupils: B46 G44
No of boarders: F20 W40
Fees: (September 01)
FB £9400 – £11750
WB £8400 – £9900
Day £7000 – £8500

HIGHFIELD PREPARATORY SCHOOL
Clarence Drive, Harrogate, North Yorkshire HG1 2QG
Tel: (01423) 504543
Head: Mrs P Fenwick and Dr M J Hustler
Type: Co-educational Day 5–11
No of pupils: B33 G47
Fees: (September 01)
Day £4170 – £4485

MALTON

WOODLEIGH SCHOOL
Langton, Malton, North Yorkshire
YO17 9QN
Tel: (01653) 658215
Head: Mr D M England
Type: Co-educational Boarding and
Day 3–13
No of pupils: B69 G49
No of boarders: F10 W25
Fees: (September 01)
F/WB £6330 – £7650
Day £2490 – £5850

RIPON

RIPON CATHEDRAL CHOIR SCHOOL
Whitcliffe Lane, Ripon,
North Yorkshire HG4 2LA
Tel: (01765) 602134
Head: Mr C R E Pepys
Type: Co-educational Boarding and
Day 4–13
No of pupils: B71 G49
No of boarders: F18 W5
Fees: (September 01) FB £8910
WB £8235 Day £4350 – £6540

SCARBOROUGH

BAIRNSWOOD NURSERY SCHOOL
Lady Edith's Park, Scarborough,
North Yorkshire YO12 5PB
Tel: (01723) 363100
Head: Mrs A Johnstone
Type: Co-educational Day 3–5
No of pupils: B25 G25
Fees: (September 01) On application

BRAMCOTE SCHOOL
Filey Road, Scarborough,
North Yorkshire YO11 2TT
Tel: (01723) 373086
Head: Mr J P Kirk
Type: Co-educational Boarding and
Day 7–13
No of pupils: B60 G26
No of boarders: F70
Fees: (September 01) FB £11340
Day £8130

SCARBOROUGH COLLEGE*
Filey Road, Scarborough,
North Yorkshire YO11 3BA
Tel: (01723) 360620
Head: Mr T L Kirkup
Type: Co-educational Boarding and
Day 3–18
No of pupils: B268 G241
No of boarders: F28 W8
Fees: (September 01) F/WB £9150
Day £6495

SCARBOROUGH COLLEGE JUNIOR SCHOOL*
Filey Road, Scarborough,
North Yorkshire YO11 3BA
Tel: (01723) 380606
Head: Mr G S Twist
Type: Co-educational Day 3–11
No of pupils: 165
No of boarders: W2
Fees: (September 01)
Day £3624 – £4935

SELBY

READ SCHOOL
Drax, Selby, North Yorkshire
YO8 8NL
Tel: (01757) 618248
Head: Mr R Hadfield
Type: Co-educational Boarding and
Day 3–18
No of pupils: B146 G94
No of boarders: F57 W4
Fees: (September 01)
FB £9795 – £11265
WB £9180 – £10560
Day £4680 – £5205

SETTLE

CATTERAL HALL
Giggleswick, Settle, North Yorkshire
BD24 0DG
Tel: (01729) 893100
Head: Mr R Hunter
Type: Co-educational Boarding and
Day 3–13
No of pupils: B100 G70
No of boarders: F50
Fees: (September 01)
FB £12490 – £13422
Day £4113 – £8973

GIGGLESWICK SCHOOL*
Giggleswick, Settle, North Yorkshire
BD24 0DE
Tel: (01729) 893000
Head: Mr G P Boult
Type: Co-educational Boarding and
Day 11–18
No of pupils: B214 G103
No of boarders: F255
Fees: (September 01) FB £16443
Day £10911

SKIPTON

MALSIS SCHOOL
Cross Hills, Skipton, North Yorkshire
BD20 8DT
Tel: (01535) 633027
Head: Mr J Elder
Type: Co-educational Boarding and
Day 3–13
No of pupils: B130 G45
No of boarders: F60
Fees: (September 01) FB £10500
Day £4200 – £7800

THIRSK

QUEEN MARY'S SCHOOL
Baldersby Park, Topcliffe, Thirsk,
North Yorkshire YO7 3BZ
Tel: (01845) 575000
Head: Mr I H Angus and
Mrs M A Angus
Type: Girls Boarding and Day 3–16
(Boys 3–7)
No of pupils: B15 G250
No of boarders: F10 W55
Fees: (September 01)
F/WB £10650 – £12240
Day £2780 – £8340

WHITBY

BOTTON VILLAGE SCHOOL
Danby, Whitby, North Yorkshire
YO21 2NJ
Tel: (01287) 661206
Type: Co-educational Day 4–14
No of pupils: B53 G41
Fees: (September 01) On application

FYLING HALL SCHOOL

Robin Hood's Bay, Whitby,
North Yorkshire YO22 4QD
Tel: (01947) 880353
Head: Mr M D Bayes
Type: Co-educational Boarding and
Day 5–19
No of pupils: B120 G110
No of boarders: F146 W11
Fees: (September 01)
FB £7800 – £9500 WB £7800
Day £3800 – £4600

YORK

AMPLEFORTH COLLEGE

York, North Yorkshire YO62 4ER
Tel: (01439) 766000
Head: Rev G F L Chamberlain
Type: Boys Boarding and Day 13–18
(Girls 16–18)
No of pupils: B476 G19
No of boarders: F467
Fees: (September 01) FB £16908
Day £8859

BOOTHAM SCHOOL

Bootham, York, North Yorkshire
YO30 7BU
Tel: (01904) 623636
Head: Mr I M Small
Type: Co-educational Boarding and
Day 11–18
No of pupils: B245 G175
No of boarders: F80 W40
Fees: (September 01)
F/WB £9780 – £13596 Day £8889

CLIFTON PREPARATORY
SCHOOL

York, North Yorkshire YO30 6AB
Tel: (01904) 623716
Head: Mrs P Arkley
Type: Co-educational Day 3–8
No of pupils: B84 G68
Fees: (September 01)
Day £3642 – £4209

CUNDALL MANOR SCHOOL

Helperby, York, North Yorkshire
YO6 2RW
Tel: (01423) 360200
Head: Mr P Phillips
Type: Co-educational Boarding and
Day 2–13
No of pupils: 110
No of boarders: F20
Fees: (September 01) FB £10317
Day £4299 – £7134

EBOR PREPARATORY
SCHOOL

116 Clifton, York, North Yorkshire
YO3 6BA
Tel: (01904) 655021
Head: Ms V Tildesley
Type: Co-educational Day 3–11
No of pupils: B70 G50
Fees: (September 01)

HOWSHAM HALL

York, North Yorkshire YO60 7PJ
Tel: (01653) 618374
Head: Mr S J Knock
Type: Co-educational Boarding 5–14
No of pupils: B60 G15
No of boarders: F40
Fees: (September 01) FB £7200
Day £3240 – £4800

THE MINSTER SCHOOL

Deangate, York, North Yorkshire
YO1 7JA
Tel: (01904) 557230
Head: Mr R J Shephard
Type: Co-educational Day 3–13
No of pupils: B100 G80
Fees: (September 01)
Day £3270 – £5040

THE MOUNT JUNIOR
SCHOOL*

Dalton Terrace, York,
North Yorkshire YO24 4DD
Tel: (01904) 667513
Head: Miss J Wilson
Type: Co-educational Day 3–11
No of pupils: B52 G116
Fees: (September 01)
Day £3390 – £5220

THE MOUNT SENIOR
SCHOOL*

Dalton Terrace, York,
North Yorkshire YO24 4DD
Tel: (01904) 667500
Head: Mrs D J Gant
Type: Girls Boarding and Day 11–18
No of pupils: 327
No of boarders: F68 W22
Fees: (September 01)
F/WB £9948 – £13680 Day £8580

QUEEN ETHELBURGA'S
COLLEGE*

Thorpe Underwood Hall, Ouseburn,
York, North Yorkshire YO26 9SS
Tel: (0870) 742 3300
Head: Mr P Dass
Type: Co-educational Boarding and
Day 2–18
No of pupils: B91 G289
No of boarders: F190 W10
Fees: (September 01)
FB £11085 – £16275
WB £10137 – £15087
Day £2925 – £9975

QUEEN MARGARET'S
SCHOOL

Escrick Park, York, North Yorkshire
YO19 6EU
Tel: (01904) 728261
Head: Dr G A H Chapman
Type: Girls Boarding and Day 11–18
No of pupils: 363
No of boarders: F266 W60
Fees: (September 01) F/WB £14148
Day £8964

RED HOUSE SCHOOL

Moor Monkton, York,
North Yorkshire YO26 8JQ
Tel: (01904) 738256
Head: Major A V Gordon
Type: Co-educational Day 3–13
No of pupils: B30 G20
Fees: (September 01) On application

SAINT MARTIN'S
AMPLEFORTH

Gilling Castle, Gilling East, York,
North Yorkshire YO62 4HP
Tel: (01439) 766600
Head: Mr S Mullen
Type: Co-educational Boarding and
Day 3–13
No of pupils: 180
No of boarders: F100
Fees: (September 01) FB £11895
Day £6120

ST OLAVE'S SCHOOL
(JUNIOR OF ST PETER'S)

York, North Yorkshire YO30 6AB
Tel: (01904) 623269
Head: Mr T Mulryne
Type: Co-educational Day and
Boarding 8–13
No of pupils: B200 G127
No of boarders: F55
Fees: (September 01) On application

ST PETER'S SCHOOL
York, North Yorkshire YO30 6AB
Tel: (01904) 623213
Head: Mr A F Trotman
Type: Co-educational Boarding and
Day 13–18
No of pupils: B314 G180
No of boarders: F149
Fees: (September 01) FB £13899 –
£14271
Day £8094 – £8499

TERRINGTON HALL
Terrington, York, North Yorkshire
YO60 6PR
Tel: (01653) 648227
Head: Mr J Glen
Type: Co-educational Boarding and
Day 3–13
No of pupils: B110 G70
No of boarders: F32 W10
Fees: (September 01) F/WB £9750
Day £2985 – £7350

SOUTH YORKSHIRE

BARNSLEY

**BARNSLEY CHRISTIAN
SCHOOL**
Fellowship House, Blucher Street,
Barnsley, South Yorkshire S70 1AP
Tel: (01226) 211011
Head: Mr G J Barnes
Type: Co-educational Day 5–16
No of pupils: B49 G45
Fees: (September 01)
Day £2100 – £2700

DONCASTER

**HILL HOUSE PREPARATORY
SCHOOL**
Rutland Street, Doncaster,
South Yorkshire DN1 2JD
Tel: (01302) 323563
Head: Mr J Cusworth
Type: Co-educational Day 3–13
No of pupils: B154 G110
Fees: (September 01)
Day £4056 – £5613

ST MARY'S SCHOOL
65 Bawtry Road, Doncaster,
South Yorkshire DN4 7AD
Tel: (01302) 535926
Head: Mrs B J Spencer
Type: Co-educational Day 3–16
No of pupils: B74 G106
Fees: (September 01)
Day £3897 – £5967

**SYCAMORE HALL
PREPARATORY SCHOOL**
1 Hall Flat Lane, Balby, Doncaster,
South Yorkshire DN4 8PT
Tel: (01302) 856800
Head: Miss J Spencer
Type: Co-educational Day 3–11
No of pupils: B41 G43
Fees: (September 01) On application

ROTHERHAM

**RUDSTON PREPARATORY
SCHOOL**
59–63 Broom Road, Rotherham,
South Yorkshire S60 2SW
Tel: (01709) 837774
Head: Mrs S Atack
Type: Co-educational Day 2–11
No of pupils: B135 G94
Fees: (September 01)
Day £3228 – £3456

SHEFFIELD

**ASHDELL PREPARATORY
SCHOOL**
266 Fulwood Road, Sheffield,
South Yorkshire S10 3BL
Tel: (0114) 266 3835
Head: Mrs J Upton
Type: Girls Day 4–11
No of pupils: 115
Fees: (September 01)
Day £4650 – £5250

BIRKDALE SCHOOL
Oakholme Road, Sheffield,
South Yorkshire S10 3DH
Tel: (0114) 266 8409
Head: Mr R J Court
Type: Boys Day 4–18 (Co-ed VIth
Form)
No of pupils: B763 G32
Fees: (September 01)
Day £4380 – £6225

**BRANTWOOD INDEPENDENT
SCHOOL FOR GIRLS***
1 Kenwood Bank, Sheffield,
South Yorkshire S7 1NU
Tel: (0114) 258 1747
Head: Mrs E M Swynnerton
Type: Girls Day 4–16
No of pupils: 223
Fees: (September 01)
Day £4050 – £5250

**HANDSWORTH CHRISTIAN
SCHOOL**
231 Handsworth Road, Handsworth,
Sheffield, South Yorkshire S13 9BJ
Tel: (0114) 243 0276
Head: Mrs P Arnott
Type: Co-educational Day 4–16
No of pupils: B55 G63
Fees: (September 01)
Day £1860

**MYLNHURST RC SCHOOL &
NURSERY**
Button Hill, Sheffield,
South Yorkshire S11 9HJ
Tel: (0114) 236 1411
Head: Mr C Emmott
Type: Co-educational Day 3–11
No of pupils: B95 G89
Fees: (September 01)
Day £3450 – £3807

**SHEFFIELD HIGH SCHOOL
GDST**
10 Rutland Park, Sheffield,
South Yorkshire S10 2PE
Tel: (0114) 266 0324
Head: Mrs M A Houston
Type: Girls Day 4–18
No of pupils: 970
Fees: (September 01)
Day £3951 – £5442

WESTBOURNE SCHOOL
50–54 Westbourne Road, Sheffield,
South Yorkshire S10 2QQ
Tel: (0114) 266 0374
Head: Mr C R Wilmshurst
Type: Co-educational Day 4–16
No of pupils: B195 G55
Fees: (September 01)
Day £3900 – £5800

WEST YORKSHIRE

APPERLEY BRIDGE

**WOODHOUSE GROVE
SCHOOL**
Apperley Bridge, West Yorkshire
BD10 0NR
Tel: (0113) 250 2477
Head: Mr D C Humphreys
Type: Co-educational Boarding and
Day 11–18
No of pupils: B385 G229
No of boarders: F80 W15
Fees: (September 01) FB £12405
Day £7050 – £7200

BATLEY

BATLEY GRAMMAR SCHOOL
Carlinghow Hill, Batley, West
Yorkshire WF17 0AD
Tel: (01924) 474980
Head: Mr B Battye
Type: Co-educational Day 4–18
No of pupils: B312 G150
Fees: (September 01)
Day £3498 – £5517

BINGLEY

LADY LANE PARK SCHOOL
Lady Lane, Bingley, West Yorkshire
BD16 4AP
Tel: (01274) 551168
Head: Mrs G Wilson
Type: Co-educational Day 2–11
No of pupils: B89 G81
Fees: (September 01)
Day £3465 – £3690

BRADFORD

**BRADFORD CHRISTIAN
SCHOOL**
Bradford Road, Idle, Bradford, West
Yorkshire BD10 8SA
Tel: (01274) 620738
Head: Mr P J Moon
Type: Co-educational Day 4–16
No of pupils: B73 G74
Fees: (September 01)
Day £1297 – £2658

**BRADFORD GIRLS'
GRAMMAR SCHOOL**
Squire Lane, Bradford, West
Yorkshire BD9 6RB
Tel: (01274) 545395
Head: Mrs L J Warrington
Type: Girls Day 3–18
No of pupils: 843
Fees: (September 01) Day £5985

**BRADFORD GRAMMAR
SCHOOL**
Keighley Road, Bradford, West
Yorkshire BD9 4JP
Tel: (01274) 542492
Head: Mr S R Davidson
Type: Co-educational Day 7–18
No of pupils: B903 G154
Fees: (September 01)
Day £5130 – £6435

BRONTE HOUSE SCHOOL
Apperley Bridge, Bradford, West
Yorkshire BD10 0PQ
Tel: (0113) 250 2811
Head: Mr C B F Hall
Type: Co-educational Boarding and
Day 3–11
No of pupils: B181 G118
No of boarders: F6
Fees: (September 01)
FB £10800 – £11010
WB £8550 – £8610
Day £4230 – £6180

ROSSEFIELD SCHOOL
Parsons Road, Heaton, Bradford,
West Yorkshire BD9 4AY
Tel: (01274) 543549
Head: Mrs A M Ball
Type: Co-educational Day 3–11
No of pupils: B90 G45
Fees: (September 01)
Day £1680 – £2925

SHAW HOUSE SCHOOL
150–152 Wilmer Road, Heaton,
Bradford, West Yorkshire BD9 4AH
Tel: (01274) 496299
Head: Mr R C Williams
Type: Co-educational Day 9–18
No of pupils: B57 G55
Fees: (September 01)
Day £3450 – £4800

BRIGHOUSE

**RASTRICK PREP AND
NURSERY SCHOOL**
Ogden Lane, Rastrick, Brighouse,
West Yorkshire HD6 3HF
Tel: (01484) 400344
Head: Mrs S A Vaughey
Type: Co-educational Day and
Boarding 0–13
No of pupils: B93 G99
Fees: (September 01)
Day £3585 – £5250

HALIFAX

THE GLEDDINGS SCHOOL
Birdcage Lane, Halifax, West
Yorkshire HX3 0JB
Tel: (01422) 354605
Head: Mrs Wilson
Type: Co-educational Day 3–11
No of pupils: B80 G80
Fees: (September 01) On application

HIPPERHOLME GRAMMAR SCHOOL
Bramley Lane, Hipperholme, Halifax, West Yorkshire HX3 8JE
Tel: (01422) 202256
Head: Mr C C Robinson
Type: Co-educational Day 11–18
No of pupils: B160 G125
Fees: (September 01) Day £5370

LIGHTCLIFFE PREPARATORY
Wakefield Road, Wakefield, Halifax, West Yorkshire HX3 8AQ
Tel: (01422) 201330
Head: Mrs J A Pickersgill
Type: Co-educational Day 2–11
No of pupils: B85 G85
Fees: (September 01)
Day £2145 – £3495

HEBDEN BRIDGE

GLEN HOUSE MONTESSORI SCHOOL
Cragg Vale, Hebden Bridge, West Yorkshire HX7 5SQ
Tel: (01422) 884682
Head: Ms M Scaife
Type: Co-educational Day 2–15
No of pupils: B11 G21
Fees: (September 01)
Day £591 – £2775

HUDDERSFIELD

HUDDERSFIELD GRAMMAR SCHOOL
Royds Mount, Luck Lane, Marsh, Huddersfield, West Yorkshire HD1 4QX
Tel: (01484) 424549
Head: Mrs E J Jackson and Mrs J L Straughan
Type: Co-educational Day 3–16
No of pupils: B190 G150
Fees: (September 01)
Day £2190 – £4530

ISLAMIA GIRLS HIGH SCHOOL
Thornton Lodge Road, Thornton Lodge, Huddersfield, West Yorkshire HD1 3JQ
Tel: (01484) 432928
Head: Mr I Meer
Type: Girls Day 11–16
No of pupils: 77
Fees: (September 01) On application

MOUNT SCHOOL
3 Binham Road, Edgerton, Huddersfield, West Yorkshire HD2 2AP
Tel: (01484) 426432
Head: Mr N M Smith
Type: Co-educational Day 3–11
No of pupils: B75 G77
Fees: (September 01) On application

MOUNTJOY HOUSE SCHOOL
63 New North Road, Huddersfield, West Yorkshire HD1 5ND
Tel: (01484) 429967
Head: Mrs C Rogers
Type: Co-educational Day 3–11
No of pupils: 110
Fees: (September 01)
Day £1800 – £2850

ROSEMEADE SCHOOL
12 Bank End Lane, Almondbury, Huddersfield, West Yorkshire HD5 8ES
Tel: (01484) 421076
Head: Mrs H M Hebblethwaite and Mrs C M Howson
Type: Co-educational Day 3–11
No of pupils: B50 G53
Fees: (September 01)
Day £2850 – £3025

ILKLEY

CLEVEDON PREPARATORY HOUSE SCHOOL
Ben Rhydding Drive, Ilkley, West Yorkshire LS29 8BJ
Tel: (01943) 600575
Head: Rev A W Munro
Type: Co-educational Day 0–11
No of pupils: B105 G85
Fees: (September 01)
Day £3420 – £4386

GHYLL ROYD SCHOOL
Greystone Manor, Ilkley Road, Burley in Wharfedale, Ilkley, West Yorkshire LS29 7HW
Tel: (01943) 865575
Head: Mrs J Bonner
Type: Boys Day 2–11
No of pupils: 72
No of boarders: W60
Fees: (September 01)
Day £2910 – £4485

MOORFIELD SCHOOL
Wharfedale Lodge, Ben Rhydding Road, Ilkley, West Yorkshire LS29 8RL
Tel: (01943) 607285
Head: Mrs P Burton
Type: Girls Day 2–11
No of pupils: 160
Fees: (September 01)
Day £720 – £4200

WESTVILLE HOUSE PREPARATORY SCHOOL
Carters Lane, Middleton, Ilkley, West Yorkshire LS29 0DQ
Tel: (01943) 608053
Head: Mr C A Holloway
Type: Co-educational Day 3–11
No of pupils: B93 G52
Fees: (September 01)
Day £2610 – £4860

LEEDS

ALCUIN SCHOOL
64 Woodland Lane, Leeds, West Yorkshire LS7 4PD
Tel: (0113) 269 1173
Head: Mr J Hipshon
Type: Co-educational Day 4–11
No of pupils: B25 G38
Fees: (September 01) Day £1500

THE FROEBELIAN SCHOOL
Clarence Road, Horsforth, Leeds, West Yorkshire LS18 4LB
Tel: (0113) 258 3047
Head: Mr J Tranmer
Type: Co-educational Day 3–11
No of pupils: B93 G97
Fees: (September 01)
Day £2490 – £3780

GATEWAYS SCHOOL
Harewood, Leeds, West Yorkshire LS17 9LE
Tel: (0113) 288 6345
Head: Mrs D Davidson
Type: Girls Day 3–18 (Boys 3–7)
No of pupils: B10 G442
Fees: (September 01)
Day £3267 – £5886

LEEDS GIRLS' HIGH SCHOOL
Headingley Lane, Leeds, West Yorkshire LS6 1BN
Tel: (0113) 274 4000
Head: Ms S Fishburn
Type: Girls Day 3–19
No of pupils: 959
Fees: (September 01)
Day £4221 – £6312

LEEDS GRAMMAR SCHOOL

Alwoodley Gates, Harrogate Road,
Leeds, West Yorkshire LS17 8GS
Tel: (0113) 229 1552
Head: Dr M Bailey
Type: Boys Day 4–18
No of pupils: 1360
Fees: (September 01)
Day £3873 – £6873

LEEDS ISLAMIA GIRLS' SCHOOL

Newton Hill House, Newton Hill
Road, Leeds, West Yorkshire LS7 4JE
Tel: (0113) 262 4001
Head: Mrs Z Arshad
Type: Girls Day 11–16
No of pupils: 100
Fees: (September 01)
Day £500 – £700

MOORLANDS SCHOOL

Foxhill, Weetwood Lane, Leeds,
West Yorkshire LS16 5PF
Tel: (0113) 278 5286
Head: Mr A Jones
Type: Co-educational Day 3–13
No of pupils: B178 G117
Fees: (September 01)
Day £2169 – £4860

RICHMOND HOUSE SCHOOL

170 Otley Road, Leeds, West
Yorkshire LS16 5LG
Tel: (0113) 275 2670
Head: Mr G Milne
Type: Co-educational Day 3–11
No of pupils: B165 G119
Fees: (September 01)
Day £2832 – £4440

ST AGNES PNEU SCHOOL

25 Burton Crescent, Leeds, West
Yorkshire LS6 4DN
Tel: (0113) 278 6722
Head: Mrs S McMeeking
Type: Co-educational Day 2–7
No of pupils: B35 G19
Fees: (September 01)
Day £2235 – £4095

WAKEFIELD TUTORIAL PREPARATORY SCHOOL

Commercial Street, Morley, Leeds,
West Yorkshire LS27 8HY
Tel: (0113) 253 4033
Head: Mrs J A Tanner
Type: Co-educational Day 4–11
No of pupils: B40 G40
Fees: (September 01)
Day £2235 – £2400

PONTEFRACT

ACKWORTH SCHOOL*

Ackworth, Pontefract, West
Yorkshire WF7 7LT
Tel: (01977) 611401
Head: Mr M J Dickinson
Type: Co-educational Boarding and
Day 4–18
No of pupils: 480
No of boarders: F100 W10
Fees: (September 01) F/WB £13116
Day £4053 – £7389

INGLEBROOK SCHOOL

Northgate Close, Pontefract, West
Yorkshire WF8 1HJ
Tel: (01977) 700120
Head: Mrs J Bellamy
Type: Co-educational Day 2–11
No of pupils: B104 G106
Fees: (September 01)
Day £534 – £2184

PUDSEY

FULNECK SCHOOL

Fulneck, Pudsey, West Yorkshire
LS28 8DS
Tel: (0113) 257 0235
Head: Mrs H S Gordon
Type: Co-educational Day and
Boarding 3–18
No of pupils: B214 G196
No of boarders: F28 W5
Fees: (September 01)
FB £9690 – £11760
WB £8985 – £10680
Day £2190 – £6390

RISHWORTH

RISHWORTH SCHOOL

Rishworth, West Yorkshire HX6 4QA
Tel: (01422) 822217
Head: Mr R A Baker
Type: Co-educational Day and
Boarding 3–18
No of pupils: B309 G231
No of boarders: F67 W10
Fees: (September 01)
FB £11670 – £12705
WB £10605 – £11610
Day £3360 – £6570

SHIPLEY

VICTORIA PARK PREPARATORY SCHOOL

7 Victoria Park, Shipley, West
Yorkshire BD18 4RL
Tel: (01274) 581680
Head: Ms P Sanderson
Type: Co-educational Day 3–9
No of pupils: B30 G20
Fees: (September 01)
Day £3120 – £3135

WAKEFIELD

CLIFF SCHOOL

St John's Lodge, 2 Leeds Road,
Wakefield, West Yorkshire WF1 3JT
Tel: (01924) 373597
Head: Mrs K M Wallace
Type: Co-educational Day Boys 2–9
Girls 2–11
No of pupils: B64 G111
Fees: (September 01)
Day £3810

QUEEN ELIZABETH GRAMMAR SCHOOL

154 Northgate, Wakefield, West
Yorkshire WF1 3QX
Tel: (01924) 373943
Head: Mr M R Gibbons
Type: Boys Day 7–18
No of pupils: 658
Fees: (September 01) Day £6075

ST HILDA'S SCHOOL

Dovecote Lane, Horbury, Wakefield,
West Yorkshire WF4 6BB
Tel: (01924) 260706
Head: Mrs A R Mackenzie
Type: Co-educational Day Boys 3–7
Girls 3–11
No of pupils: B48 G90
Fees: (September 01)
Day £3600 – £3780

SILCOATES SCHOOL

Wrenthorpe, Wakefield, West
Yorkshire WF2 0PD
Tel: (01924) 291614
Head: Mr A P Spillane
Type: Co-educational Day 7–18
No of pupils: B430 G249
Fees: (September 01)
Day £4302 – £7272

SUNNY HILL HOUSE SCHOOL
Wrenthorpe Lane, Wrenthorpe,
Wakefield, West Yorkshire WF2 0QB
Tel: (01924) 291717
Head: Mrs H K Cushing
Type: Co-educational Day 2–7
No of pupils: B65 G42
Fees: (September 01) Day £3600

WAKEFIELD GIRLS' HIGH SCHOOL
Wentworth Street, Wakefield, West
Yorkshire WF1 2QS
Tel: (01924) 372490
Head: Mrs P A Langham
Type: Girls Day 3–18 (Boys 3–7)
No of pupils: B60 G1035
Fees: (September 01)
Day £4086 – £6075

WAKEFIELD INDEPENDENT SCHOOL
The Nostell Centre, Doncaster Road,
Nostell, Wakefield, West Yorkshire
WF4 1QG
Tel: (01924) 865757
Head: Mrs K E Caryl
Type: Co-educational Day 3–16
No of pupils: B95 G81
Fees: (September 01)
Day £2865 – £4350

WETHERBY

HIGH TREES SCHOOL
Cinder Lane, Clifford, Wetherby,
West Yorkshire LS23 6HH
Tel: (01937) 541020
Head: Mrs J L Ratcliff
Type: Co-educational Day 2–8
No of pupils: 50
Fees: (September 01) On application

2.2
NORTHERN IRELAND

COUNTY ANTRIM

BELFAST

BELFAST ROYAL ACADEMY
7 Cliftonville Road, Belfast,
County Antrim BT14 6JL
Tel: (028) 9074 0423
Head: Mr W S F Young
Type: Co-educational Day 4–19
No of pupils: B781 G813
Fees: (September 01) On application

CABIN HILL SCHOOL
562–594 Upper Newtownards Road,
Knock, Belfast, County Antrim
BT4 3HJ
Tel: (028) 9065 3368
Head: Mr N I Kendrick
Type: Boys Day and Boarding 3–13
(Co-ed kindergarten)
No of pupils: 375
No of boarders: F11 W24
Fees: (September 01) On application

CAMPBELL COLLEGE
Belfast, County Antrim BT4 2ND
Tel: (028) 9076 3076
Head: Dr R J I Pollock
Type: Boys Boarding and Day 11–18
No of pupils: 680
No of boarders: F18 W24
Fees: (September 01) FB £6510 –
£7440 WB £6410 – £7340
Day £1311 – £1521

HUNTERHOUSE COLLEGE
Finaghy, Belfast, County Antrim
BT10 0LE
Tel: (028) 9061 2293
Head: Mrs M Clark
Type: Girls Day 5–19
No of pupils: 800
Fees: (September 01) Day £80

METHODIST COLLEGE
1 Malone Road, Belfast,
County Antrim BT9 6BY
Tel: (028) 9020 5205
Head: Dr T W Mulryne
Type: Co-educational Day and
Boarding 4–19
No of pupils: B1300 G1100
No of boarders: F170
Fees: (September 01)
FB £4627 – £7930 Day £255 – £325

**ROYAL BELFAST
ACADEMICAL INSTITUTION**
College Square East, Belfast,
County Antrim BT1 6DL
Tel: (028) 9024 0461
Head: Mr R M Ridley
Type: Boys Day 4–18
No of pupils: 1050
Fees: (September 01)
Day £590 – £2300

**VICTORIA COLLEGE
BELFAST**
Cranmore Park, Belfast,
County Antrim BT9 6JA
Tel: (028) 9066 1506
Head: Mrs M Andrews
Type: Girls Day and Boarding 4–18
No of pupils: 1020
No of boarders: F47
Fees: (September 01) FB £4995
Day £280

COUNTY ARMAGH

ARMAGH

THE ROYAL SCHOOL
College Hill, Armagh, County
Armagh BT61 9DH
Tel: (028) 3752 2807
Head: Mr T Duncan
Type: Co-educational Boarding and
Day 4–19
No of pupils: B340 G350
No of boarders: F25 W76
Fees: (September 01) FB £4620
WB £2835 Day £180 – £190

COUNTY DOWN

BANGOR

BANGOR GRAMMAR SCHOOL
13 College Avenue, Bangor, County
Down BT20 5HJ
Tel: (028) 9147 3734
Head: Mr S D Connolly
Type: Boys Day 11–18
No of pupils: 913
Fees: (September 01)
Day £80 – £264

HOLYWOOD

THE HOLYWOOD RUDOLF STEINER SCHOOL
The Highlands, 34 Croft Road,
Holywood, County Down BT18 0PR
Tel: (028) 9042 8029
Type: Co-educational Day 4–17
No of pupils: 210
Fees: (September 01) On application

ROCKPORT SCHOOL
Craigavad, Holywood, County Down
BT18 0DD
Tel: (02890) 428372
Head: Mrs H G Pentland
Type: Co-educational Boarding and
Day 3–16
No of pupils: B108 G112
No of boarders: W21
Fees: (September 01)
WB £5850 – £8100
Day £1950 – £6900

COUNTY LONDONDERRY

COLERAINE

COLERAINE ACADEMICAL INSTITUTION
Castlerock Road, Coleraine, County
Londonderry BT51 3LA
Tel: (028) 7034 4331
Head: Mr R S Forsythe
Type: Boys Day 11–19
No of pupils: 800
Fees: (September 01) Day £100

COUNTY TYRONE

DUNGANNON

ROYAL SCHOOL DUNGANNON
Northland Row, Dungannon, County
Tyrone BT71 6AP
Tel: (028) 8772 2710
Head: Mr P D Hewitt
Type: Co-educational Day and
Boarding 11–19
No of pupils: B320 G337
No of boarders: F30 W15
Fees: (September 01) F/WB £8036
Day £375

2.3
SCOTLAND

ABERDEENSHIRE

ABERDEEN

ABERDEEN WALDORF SCHOOL
Craigton Road, Cults, Aberdeen AB15 9QD
Tel: (01224) 869932
Head: Mrs V Easton
Type: Co-educational Day 3–16
No of pupils: B79 G58
Fees: (September 01)
Day £1000 – £5265

ALBYN SCHOOL FOR GIRLS*
17–23 Queen's Road, Aberdeen AB15 4PB
Tel: (01224) 322408
Head: Miss J Leslie
Type: Girls Day 2½–18 (Boys 2½–5)
No of pupils: B20 G361
Fees: (September 01)
Day £3660 – £6200

INTERNATIONAL SCHOOL OF ABERDEEN
'Fairgirth', 296 North Deeside Road, Milltimber, Aberdeen AB13 9QD
Tel: (01224) 732267
Head: Mr J D Osbo
Type: Co-educational Day 3–18
No of pupils: B191 G169
Fees: (September 01) On application

ROBERT GORDONS COLLEGE
Schoolhill, Aberdeen AB10 1FE
Tel: (01224) 646346
Head: Mr B R W Lockhart
Type: Co-educational Day 4–18
No of pupils: B893 G532
Fees: (September 01)
Day £3750 – £5900

ST MARGARET'S SCHOOL FOR GIRLS
17 Albyn Place, Aberdeen AB10 1RU
Tel: (01224) 584466
Head: Mrs L Mckay
Type: Girls Day 3–18 (Boys 3–5)
No of pupils: B2 G388
Fees: (September 01)
Day £1692 – £5898

TOTAL FINA ELF FRENCH SCHOOL
1–5 Whitehall Place, Aberdeen AB25 4RH
Tel: (01224) 645545
Head: Mr J Albert
Type: Co-educational Day 4–18
No of pupils: 97
Fees: (September 01) On application

ANGUS

DUNDEE

THE HIGH SCHOOL OF DUNDEE
Euclid Crescent, Dundee, Angus DD1 1HU
Tel: (01382) 202921
Head: Mr A M Duncan
Type: Co-educational Day 5–18
No of pupils: B539 G530
Fees: (September 01)
Day £4155 – £5910

MONTROSE

LATHALLAN SCHOOL
Brotherton Castle, Johnshaven, Montrose, Angus DD10 0HN
Tel: (01561) 362220
Head: Mr P Platts-Martin
Type: Co-educational Boarding and Day 3–13
No of pupils: B80 G50
No of boarders: F6 W38
Fees: (September 01)
FB £10869 – £11945
WB £10626 – £11688
Day £4794 – £1757

ARGYLL AND BUTE

HELENSBURGH

LOMOND SCHOOL
10 Stafford Street, Helensburgh,
Argyll and Bute G84 9JX
Tel: (01436) 672476
Head: Mr A D Macdonald
Type: Co-educational Day and
Boarding 3–19
No of pupils: B268 G234
No of boarders: F60 W10
Fees: (September 01)
FB £12930 – £13455
WB £12570 – £13095
Day £1980 – £6285

SOUTH AYRSHIRE

AYR

WELLINGTON SCHOOL
Carleton Turrets, Ayr, South Ayrshire
KA7 2XH
Tel: (01292) 269321
Head: Mrs D A Gardner
Type: Co-educational Day 3–18
No of pupils: B250 G270
Fees: (September 01)
Day £1950 – £6555

BANFFSHIRE

ABERLOUR

ABERLOUR HOUSE
Aberlour, Banffshire AB38 9LJ
Tel: (01340) 871267
Head: Mr N W Gardner and
Mrs C E Gardner
Type: Co-educational Boarding and
Day 7–13
No of pupils: B43 G43
No of boarders: F67
Fees: (September 01) FB £12192
Day £8505

CLACKMANNANSHIRE

DOLLAR

DOLLAR ACADEMY
Dollar, Clackmannanshire FK14 7DU
Tel: (01259) 742511
Head: Mr J S Robertson
Type: Co-educational Day and
Boarding 5–18
No of pupils: B603 G560
No of boarders: F76 W14
Fees: (September 01) FB £11673 –
£13131 WB £10980 – £12438
Day £4428 – £5886

FIFE

DUNFERMLINE

INCHKEITH SCHOOL AND NURSERY
Balgownie House, Culross,
Dunfermline, Fife KY12 8JJ
Tel: (01383) 880330
Head: Mrs P Matthewson Brown
Type: Co-educational Day 2–11
No of pupils: B25 G25
Fees: (September 01)
Day £2985 – £3255

KIRKCALDY

SEA VIEW PRIVATE SCHOOL
102 Loughborough Road, Kirkcaldy,
Fife KY1 3DD
Tel: (01592) 652244
Head: Mrs E A Mason
Type: Co-educational Day 3–12
No of pupils: B25 G26
Fees: (September 01)
Day £1632 – £3510

ST ANDREWS

NEW PARK SCHOOL
98 Hepburn Gardens, St Andrews,
Fife KY16 9LN
Tel: (01334) 472017
Head: Mr A Donald
Type: Co-educational Day 3–13
No of pupils: B73 G37
Fees: (September 01)
Day £1545 – £7110

ST KATHARINES PREPARATORY SCHOOL
The Pends, St Andrews, Fife
KY16 9RB
Tel: (01334) 460470
Head: Mrs J Gibson
Type: Co-educational Boarding and
Day 3–12
No of pupils: B24 G49
No of boarders: F8
Fees: (September 01) FB £12294
Day £5055 – £6981

ST LEONARDS SCHOOL & ST LEONARDS VITH FORM COLLEGE
St Andrews, Fife KY16 9QJ
Tel: (01334) 472126
Head: Mrs W A Bellars
Type: Co-educational Boarding and
Day 12–19
No of pupils: B18 G213
No of boarders: F153
Fees: (September 01) FB £16209
Day £9084

GLASGOW

GLASGOW

CRAIGHOLME SCHOOL
72 St Andrews Drive, Glasgow
G41 4HS
Tel: (0141) 427 0375
Head: Mrs G Burt
Type: Girls Day 3–18 (Boys 3–5)
No of pupils: B13 G537
Fees: (September 01)
Day £2370 – £5745

DAIRSIE HOUSE SCHOOL
54 Newlands Road, Glasgow G43 2JG
Tel: (0141) 632 0736
Head: Mrs S S McKnight
Type: Co-educational Day 3–9
No of pupils: B68 G38
Fees: (September 01)
Day £2004 – £3420

THE GLASGOW ACADEMY
Colebrooke Street, Glasgow G12 8HE
Tel: (0141) 334 8558
Head: Mr D Comins
Type: Co-educational Day 2–18
No of pupils: B616 G510
Fees: (September 01)
Day £4155 – £5985

GLASGOW STEINER SCHOOL
52 Lumsden Street, Glasgow G3 8RH
Tel: (0141) 334 8855
Type: Co-educational Day 3–14
No of pupils: B51 G23
Fees: (September 01)
Day £960 – £4200

THE HIGH SCHOOL OF GLASGOW
637 Crow Road, Glasgow G13 1PL
Tel: (0141) 954 9628
Head: Mr R G Easton
Type: Co-educational Day 3–18
No of pupils: B520 G534
Fees: (September 01)
Day £1980 – £6093

HUTCHESONS' GRAMMAR SCHOOL
21 Beaton Road, Glasgow G41 4NW
Tel: (0141) 423 2933
Head: Mr J G Knowles
Type: Co-educational Day 5–18
No of pupils: B1022 G1029
Fees: (September 01)
Day £4612 – £5562

HUTCHESONS' LILYBANK JUNIOR SCHOOL
4 Lilybank Terrace, Glasgow
G12 8RX
Tel: (0141) 339 9127
Head: Mrs L Mcintosh
Type: Girls Day 3–11 (Boys 3–5)
No of pupils: 130
Fees: (September 01)
Day £4612 – £5418

KELVINSIDE ACADEMY
33 Kirklee Road, Glasgow G12 0SW
Tel: (0141) 357 3376
Head: Mr J L Broadfoot
Type: Co-educational Day 3–18
No of pupils: B435 G213
Fees: (September 01)
Day £3675 – £6360

ST ALOYSIUS' COLLEGE
45 Hill Street, Glasgow G3 6RJ
Tel: (0141) 332 3190
Head: Rev A Porter
Type: Co-educational Day 3–18
No of pupils: B712 G519
Fees: (September 01)
Day £4100 – £4800

ST ALOYSIUS JUNIOR SCHOOL
56–58 Hill Street, Glasgow G3 6RH
Tel: (0141) 572 1859
Head: Ms F McLoone and
Mr T Mooney
Type: Co-educational Day 5–12
No of pupils: 431
Fees: (September 01) On application

LANARKSHIRE

HAMILTON

HAMILTON COLLEGE
Bothwell Road, Hamilton,
Lanarkshire ML3 0AY
Tel: (01698) 282700
Head: Mr A J Leach
Type: Co-educational Day 3–18
No of pupils: B400 G400
Fees: (September 01)
Day £2994 – £3972

SOUTH LANARKSHIRE

RUTHERGLEN

FERNHILL SCHOOL
Fernbrae Avenue, Rutherglen, South
Lanarkshire G73 4SG
Tel: (0141) 634 2674
Head: Mrs L M McLay
Type: Girls Day 4–18 (Boys 4–11)
No of pupils: B50 G260
Fees: (September 01)
Day £3900 – £4650

LOTHIAN

DUNBAR

BELHAVEN HILL
Dunbar, Lothian EH42 1NN
Tel: (01368) 862785
Head: Mr I M Osborne
Type: Co-educational Boarding and
Day 7–13
No of pupils: B60 G40
No of boarders: F85
Fees: (September 01) FB £11685
Day £8520

EDINBURGH

BASIL PATERSON TUTORIAL
COLLEGE*
Dugdale-McAdam House, 23
Abercromby Place, Edinburgh,
Lothian EH3 6QE
Tel: (0131) 556 7698
Head: Mrs I P Shewan
Type: Co-educational Day and
Boarding 14+
No of pupils: B24 G16
No of boarders: F2 W2
Fees: (September 01)
FB £8200 – £13700
WB £7200 – £12700
Day £5000 – £10500

CARGILFIELD
Barnton Avenue West, Edinburgh,
Lothian EH4 6HU
Tel: (0131) 336 2207
Head: Mr M Seymour
Type: Co-educational Boarding and
Day 3–13
No of pupils: B140 G70
No of boarders: F35
Fees: (September 01) F/WB £12300
Day £2400 – £8700

DUNEDIN SCHOOL
5 Gilmerton Road, Edinburgh,
Lothian EH16 5TY
Tel: (0131) 664 1328
Head: Mrs J Foulner
Type: Co-educational Day 7–17
No of pupils: B14 G6
Fees: (September 01) On Application

THE EDINBURGH ACADEMY
42 Henderson Row, Edinburgh,
Lothian EH3 5BL
Tel: (0131) 556 4603
Head: Mr J V Light
Type: Boys Day and Boarding 5–18
(Co-ed VIth Form)
No of pupils: B421 G28
No of boarders: F17 W2
Fees: (September 01)
FB £12153 – £14475
Day £5367 – £6789

EDINBURGH ACADEMY
JUNIOR SCHOOL
10 Arboretum Road, Edinburgh,
Lothian EH3 5PL
Tel: (0131) 552 3690
Head: Mr C R F Paterson
Type: Boys Day 3–11 (Girls 3–5)
No of pupils: B389 G10
Fees: (September 01)
Day £1911 – £4764

THE EDINBURGH RUDOLF
STEINER SCHOOL
60 Spylaw Road, Edinburgh, Lothian
EH10 5BR
Tel: (0131) 337 3410
Head: Mr Farquh
Type: Co-educational Day 3–18
No of pupils: B150 G150
No of boarders: F15 W1
Fees: (September 01) On application

EDINBURGH TUTORIAL
COLLEGE
29 Chester Street, Edinburgh,
Lothian EH3 7EN
Tel: (0131) 225 9888
Head: Mrs J Blackmore and
Ms J Simpson
Type: Co-educational Day 15–18
No of pupils: B20 G20
Fees: (September 01) On application

FETTES COLLEGE*
Carrington Road, Edinburgh,
Lothian EH4 1QX
Tel: (0131) 311 6701
Head: Mr M C B Spens
Type: Co-educational Boarding and
Day 8–18
No of pupils: B351 G241
No of boarders: F387
Fees: (September 01)
FB £12228 – £16884
Day £7668 – £11391

GEORGE HERIOT'S SCHOOL
Lauriston Place, Edinburgh, Lothian
EH3 9EQ
Tel: (0131) 229 7263
Head: Mr A G Hector
Type: Co-educational Day 4–18
No of pupils: B904 G652
Fees: (September 01)
Day £3741 – £5650

GEORGE WATSON'S COLLEGE

Colinton Road, Edinburgh, Lothian
EH10 5EG
Tel: (0131) 447 7931
Head: Mr G H Edwards
Type: Co-educational Day and
Boarding 3–18
No of pupils: B1223 G1034
No of boarders: F16
Fees: (September 01) FB £12250
Day £3870 – £6000

THE MARY ERSKINE SCHOOL

Ravelston, Edinburgh, Lothian
EH4 3NT
Tel: (0131) 337 2391
Head: Mr J N D Gray
Type: Girls Day and Boarding 11–18
No of pupils: 672
No of boarders: F26
Fees: (September 01) FB £12795
Day £6108

MERCHISTON CASTLE SCHOOL*

Colinton, Edinburgh, Lothian
EH13 0PU
Tel: (0131) 312 2200
Head: Mr A R Hunter
Type: Boys Boarding and Day 8–18
No of pupils: 400
No of boarders: F270
Fees: (September 01)
FB £11100 – £16500
Day £6900 – £11385

ST GEORGE'S SCHOOL FOR GIRLS

Garscube Terrace, Edinburgh,
Lothian EH12 6BG
Tel: (0131) 332 4575
Head: Dr J McClure
Type: Girls Day and Boarding 2–18
(Boys 2–5)
No of pupils: B6 G964
No of boarders: F55
Fees: (September 01)
FB £11040 – £12825
Day £3510 – £6525

ST MARGARET'S SCHOOL

East Suffolk Road, Edinburgh,
Lothian EH16 5PJ
Tel: (0131) 668 1986
Head: Mrs E Davis
Type: Girls Day and Boarding 3–18
(Boys 3–8)
No of pupils: B21 G600
No of boarders: F15 W10
Fees: (September 01)
FB £10150 – £12195
WB £9085 – £12195
Day £2270 – £5840

ST MARY'S MUSIC SCHOOL

Coates Hall, 25 Grosvenor Crescent,
Edinburgh, Lothian EH12 5EL
Tel: (0131) 538 7766
Head: Mrs J J Rimer
Type: Co-educational Boarding and
Day 8–18
No of pupils: B30 G35
No of boarders: F24
Fees: (September 01) On application

ST SERF'S SCHOOL

5 Wester Coates Gardens,
Edinburgh, Lothian EH12 5LT
Tel: (0131) 337 1015
Head: Mrs K D Hume
Type: Co-educational Day 5–18
No of pupils: B77 G70
Fees: (September 01)
Day £3220 – £4488

STEWART'S MELVILLE COLLEGE

Queensferry Road, Edinburgh,
Lothian EH4 3EZ
Tel: (0131) 332 7925
Head: Mr J N D Gray
Type: Boys Day and Boarding 12–18
(Co-ed VIth Form)
No of pupils: B748 G110
No of boarders: F13
Fees: (September 01) FB £12879
Day £6108 – £6444

HADDINGTON

THE COMPASS SCHOOL

West Road, Haddington, Lothian
EH41 3RD
Tel: (01620) 822642
Head: Mr M Becher
Type: Co-educational Day 4–11
No of pupils: B54 G57
Fees: (September 01)
Day £2844 – £4626

NEWBRIDGE

CLIFTON HALL

Newbridge, Lothian EH28 8LQ
Tel: (0131) 333 1359
Head: Mr M Adams
Type: Co-educational Day 3–11
No of pupils: B74 G70
Fees: (September 01)
Day £1900 – £6345

MIDLOTHIAN

MUSSELBURGH

LORETTO
Musselburgh, Midlothian EH21 7RE
Tel: (0131) 653 4455
Head: Mr M B Mavor
Type: Co-educational Boarding and
Day 13–18
No of pupils: B174 G97
No of boarders: F218
Fees: (September 01) FB £16548
Day £11043

LORETTO JUNIOR SCHOOL
North Esk Lodge, Musselburgh,
Midlothian EH21 6JA
Tel: (0131) 653 4570
Head: Mr R G Selley
Type: Co-educational Boarding and
Day 5–13
No of pupils: B63 G56
No of boarders: F32 W5
Fees: (September 01)
FB £11694 – £12474
Day £4164 – £8355

MORAYSHIRE

ELGIN

GORDONSTOUN SCHOOL*
Elgin, Morayshire IV30 5RF
Tel: (01343) 837829
Head: Mr M C Pyper
Type: Co-educational Boarding and
Day 13–18
No of pupils: B235 G175
No of boarders: F385
Fees: (September 01)
FB £17625 – £18755
Day £11895 – £13020

ROSEBRAE SCHOOL
Spynie, Elgin, Morayshire IV30 8XT
Tel: (01343) 544841
Head: Mrs B MacPherson
Type: Co-educational Day 2–8
No of pupils: B35 G35
Fees: (September 01)
Day £294 – £2880

PERTHSHIRE

BLAIRGOWRIE

BUTTERSTONE SCHOOL
Meigle, Blairgowrie, Perthshire
PH12 8QY
Tel: (01828) 640528
Head: Mr & Mrs B Whitten
Type: Girls Boarding and Day 2–13
(Co-ed 3–7)
No of pupils: B20 G88
No of boarders: F43
Fees: (September 01) FB £12144
Day £4245 – £8130

CRIEFF

ARDVRECK SCHOOL
Gwydyr Road, Crieff, Perthshire
PH7 4EX
Tel: (01764) 653112
Head: Mr P Watson
Type: Co-educational Boarding and
Day 3–13
No of pupils: B80 G70
No of boarders: F110
Fees: (September 01) FB £11610
Day £7420

MORRISON'S ACADEMY
Crieff, Perthshire PH7 3AN
Tel: (01764) 653885
Head: Mr I Bendall
Type: Co-educational Day and
Boarding 3–18
No of pupils: B259 G232
No of boarders: F62 W5
Fees: (September 01)
FB £13035 – £14520
WB £9735 – £11220
Day £1950 – £5880

DUNBLANE

QUEEN VICTORIA SCHOOL
Dunblane, Perthshire FK15 0JY
Tel: (01786) 822288
Head: Mr B Raine
Type: Co-educational Boarding 11–18
No of pupils: B167 G109
No of boarders: F276
Fees: (September 01)
FB £2133 – £2214

PERTH

**CRAIGCLOWAN
PREPARATORY SCHOOL**
Edinburgh Road, Perth, Perthshire
PH2 8PS
Tel: (01738) 626310
Head: Mr M E Beale
Type: Co-educational Day 4–13
No of pupils: B130 G130
Fees: (September 01) Day £5775

GLENALMOND COLLEGE*
Perth, Perthshire PH1 3RY
Tel: (01738) 842056
Head: Mr I G Templeton
Type: Co-educational Boarding and
Day 12–18
No of pupils: B258 G143
No of boarders: F349
Fees: (September 01)
FB £12375 – £16485
Day £8250 – £10995

**KILGRASTON (A SACRED
HEART SCHOOL)**
Bridge of Earn, Perth, Perthshire
PH2 9BQ
Tel: (01738) 812257
Head: Mrs J L Austin
Type: Girls Boarding and Day 5–18
(Boys day 2–9)
No of pupils: B15 G219
No of boarders: F109
Fees: (September 01)
F/WB £12441 – £14916
Day £5065 – £8794

STRATHALLAN SCHOOL
Forgandenny, Perth, Perthshire
PH2 9EG
Tel: (01738) 812546
Head: Mr B K Thompson
Type: Co-educational Boarding 10–18
No of pupils: B271 G173
No of boarders: F353
Fees: (September 01)
FB £12000 – £16380
Day £7470 – £11280

PITLOCHRY

RANNOCH SCHOOL*
Rannoch, Pitlochry, Perthshire
PH17 2QQ
Tel: (01882) 632332
Head: Mr A Andrews
Type: Co-educational Boarding and
Day 10–18
No of pupils: B76 G37
No of boarders: F106 W3
Fees: (September 01)
FB £12489 – £14775
WB £10113 – £12294 Day £7704

RENFREWSHIRE

KILMACOLM

ST COLUMBA'S SCHOOL
Duchal Road, Kilmacolm,
Renfrewshire PA13 4AU
Tel: (01505) 872238
Head: Mr A Livingstone
Type: Co-educational Day 3–18
No of pupils: B328 G354
Fees: (September 01)
Day £1905 – £5505

NEWTON MEARNS

BELMONT HOUSE
Sandringham Avenue, Newton
Mearns, Renfrewshire G77 5DU
Tel: (0141) 639 2922
Head: Mr S J McCulloch
Type: Co-educational Day 3–18
No of pupils: 330
Fees: (September 01)
Day £3030 – £5685

ROXBURGHSHIRE

MELROSE

**ST MARY'S PREPARATORY
SCHOOL**
Abbey Park, Melrose, Roxburghshire
TD6 9LN
Tel: (01896) 822517
Head: Mr J Brett
Type: Co-educational Day 2–13
No of pupils: B62 G62
Fees: (September 01) WB £10050
Day £5250 – £7890

STIRLING

STIRLING

BEACONHURST GRANGE
52 Kenilworth Road, Bridge of Allan,
Stirling FK9 4RR
Tel: (01786) 832146
Head: Mr D R Clegg
Type: Co-educational Day 3–18
No of pupils: B132 G150
Fees: (September 01)
Day £4350 – £5880

2.4
WALES

BRIDGEND

PORTHCAWL

ST CLARE'S CONVENT SCHOOL
Newton, Porthcawl, Bridgend
CF36 5NR
Tel: (01656) 782509
Head: Mrs C Barnard
Type: Co-educational Day 3–18
No of pupils: B147 G222
Fees: (September 01)
Day £2460 – £5010

ST JOHN'S SCHOOL
Newton, Porthcawl, Bridgend
CF36 5NP
Tel: (01656) 783404
Head: Mrs E D Smith and
Ms D Spearey
Type: Co-educational Day 3–16
No of pupils: B130 G70
Fees: (September 01)
Day £3000 – £6330

CARDIFF

CARDIFF

THE CATHEDRAL SCHOOL
Llandaff, Cardiff CF5 2YH
Tel: (029) 2056 3179
Head: Mr P L Gray
Type: Co-educational Day 3–16
No of pupils: B301 G99
Fees: (September 01)
Day £4140 – £6240

ELM TREE HOUSE SCHOOL
Clive Road, Llandaff, Cardiff
CF5 1GN
Tel: (029) 2022 3388
Head: Mrs C M Thomas
Type: Co-educational Day 2–11
No of pupils: B24 G136
Fees: (September 01)
Day £3135 – £3915

HOWELL'S SCHOOL, LLANDAFF GDST
Cardiff Road, Llandaff, Cardiff
CF5 2YD
Tel: (029) 2056 2019
Head: Mrs J Fitz
Type: Girls Day 3–18
No of pupils: 729
Fees: (September 01)
Day £3174 – £5442

KINGS MONKTON SCHOOL
6 West Grove, Cardiff CF24 3XL
Tel: (029) 2048 2854
Head: Mr R N Griffin
Type: Co-educational Day 3–18
No of pupils: B220 G180
Fees: (September 01)
Day £3516 – £4758

NEW COLLEGE AND SCHOOL
Bute Terrace, Cardiff CF10 2TE
Tel: (029) 2046 3355
Head: Mr W Hoole
Type: Co-educational Boarding and
Day 4–18
No of pupils: B136 G61
No of boarders: F12
Fees: (September 01)
FB £9150 – £14010
Day £3405 – £8850

ST JOHN'S COLLEGE
College Green, Old St. Mellons,
Cardiff CF3 5YX
Tel: (029) 2077 8936
Head: Dr D Neville
Type: Co-educational Day 3–18
No of pupils: B240 G200
Fees: (September 01) On application

WESTBOURNE SCHOOL
4 Hickman Road, Penarth, Cardiff
CF64 2AJ
Tel: (029) 2070 5705
Head: Dr B V Young
Type: Co-educational Day 3–16
No of pupils: B115 G84
Fees: (September 01)
Day £2745 – £5490

CARMARTHENSHIRE

LLANDOVERY

LLANDOVERY COLLEGE
Llandovery, Carmarthenshire
SA20 0EE
Tel: (01550) 723000
Head: Mr P A Hogan
Type: Co-educational Boarding and
Day 7–18
No of pupils: B136 G69
No of boarders: F117 W31
Fees: (September 01) F/WB £12995
Day £8694

LLANELLI

ST MICHAEL'S SCHOOL
Bryn, Llanelli, Carmarthenshire
SA14 9TU
Tel: (01554) 820325
Head: Mr D T Sheehan
Type: Co-educational Day 3–18
No of pupils: B194 G149
Fees: (September 01)
Day £3075 – £5094

CONWY

COLWYN BAY

LYNDON SCHOOL
Grosvenor Road, Colwyn Bay,
Conwy LL29 7YF
Tel: (01492) 532347
Head: Mr M B Collins
Type: Co-educational Day 2–11
No of pupils: B41 G50
Fees: (September 01)
Day £1830 – £3810

RYDAL PENRHOS
PREPARATORY SCHOOL
Pwllycrochan Avenue, Colwyn Bay,
Conwy LL29 7BP
Tel: (01492) 530381
Head: Mr P J Bendall
Type: Co-educational Boarding and
Day 2–11
No of pupils: B88 G67
No of boarders: F18
Fees: (September 01)
F/WB £6387 – £11175
Day £2457 – £6915

RYDAL PENRHOS SENIOR
SCHOOL
Pwllycrochan Avenue, Colwyn Bay,
Conwy LL29 7BT
Tel: (01492) 530155
Head: Mr M S James
Type: Co-educational Boarding and
Day 11–18 (Single-sex education)
No of pupils: B219 G217
No of boarders: F141
Fees: (September 01) On application

LLANDUDNO

ST DAVID'S COLLEGE
Llandudno, Conwy LL30 1RD
Tel: (01492) 875974
Head: Mr W Seymour
Type: Co-educational Boarding and
Day 11–18
No of pupils: B200 G50
No of boarders: F160 W5
Fees: (September 01)
FB £12309 – £14592
Day £8004 – £9921

DENBIGHSHIRE

DENBIGH

HOWELL'S SCHOOL
Denbigh, Denbighshire LL16 3EN
Tel: (01745) 813631
Head: Mrs L Robinson
Type: Girls Boarding and Day 3–18
No of pupils: 386
No of boarders: F80
Fees: (September 01)
FB £6885 – £11835
Day £3285 – £7935

RHYL

NORTHGATE PREPARATORY
57 Russell Road, Rhyl, Denbighshire
LL18 3DD
Tel: (01745) 342510
Head: Mr P G Orton
Type: Co-educational Day 4–11
No of pupils: B23 G23
Fees: (September 01) On application

RUTHIN

RUTHIN SCHOOL
Ruthin, Denbighshire LL15 1EE
Tel: (01824) 702543
Head: Mr J S Rowlands
Type: Co-educational Boarding and
Day 3–18
No of pupils: B167 G73
No of boarders: F78 W17
Fees: (September 01)
FB £9285 – £13240
WB £9285 – £11130
Day £3330 – £8505

GWYNEDD

BANGOR

HILLGROVE SCHOOL
Ffriddoedd Road, Bangor, Gwynedd
LL57 2TW
Tel: (01248) 353568
Head: Mr J G Porter
Type: Co-educational Day 3–16
No of pupils: B80 G30
Fees: (September 01)
Day £1800 – £3000

ST GERARD'S SCHOOL
Ffriddoedd Road, Bangor, Gwynedd
LL57 2EL
Tel: (01248) 351656
Head: Miss A Parkinson
Type: Co-educational Day 3–18
No of pupils: B149 G174
Fees: (September 01)
Day £2715 – £4110

MONMOUTHSHIRE

CHEPSTOW

ST JOHN'S-ON-THE-HILL
Tutshill, Chepstow, Monmouthshire
NP16 7LE
Tel: (01291) 622045
Head: Mr I K Etchells
Type: Co-educational Boarding and
Day 2–13
No of pupils: B177 G125
No of boarders: F27 W2
Fees: (September 01) F/WB £9540
Day £4218 – £7050

MONMOUTH

**HABERDASHERS'
MONMOUTH SCHOOL FOR
GIRLS**
Hereford Road, Monmouth,
Monmouthshire NP25 5XT
Tel: (01600) 711100
Head: Dr B Despontin
Type: Girls Day and Boarding 7–18
No of pupils: 691
No of boarders: F117
Fees: (September 01)
F/WB £12277 – £12751
Day £5607 – £6624

MONMOUTH SCHOOL
Almshouse Street, Monmouth,
Monmouthshire NP25 3XP
Tel: (01600) 713143
Head: Mr T H P Haynes
Type: Boys Day and Boarding 7–18
No of pupils: 660
No of boarders: F150
Fees: (September 01) F/WB £12096
Day £4977 – £7257

NEWPORT

NEWPORT

ROUGEMONT SCHOOL
Llantarnam Hall, Malpas Road,
Newport NP20 6QB
Tel: (01633) 820800
Head: Mr I Brown
Type: Co-educational Day 3–18
No of pupils: B374 G325
Fees: (September 01)
Day £3390 – £5790

PEMBROKESHIRE

SAUNDERSFOOT

NETHERWOOD SCHOOL*
Saundersfoot, Pembrokeshire
SA69 9BE
Tel: (01834) 811057
Head: Mr D H Morris
Type: Co-educational Day and
Boarding 3–18
No of pupils: B87 G82
No of boarders: F21 W15
Fees: (September 01)
FB £8475 – £11985
WB £7275 – £8175
Day £2850 – £5985

POWYS

BRECON

CHRIST COLLEGE
Brecon, Powys LD3 8AG
Tel: (01874) 623359
Head: Mr D P Jones
Type: Co-educational Boarding and
Day 11–18
No of pupils: B205 G100
No of boarders: F184 W45
Fees: (September 01)
F/WB £10710 – £13695
Day £8025 – £10620

WELSHPOOL

**BROOKLAND HALL SCHOOL
& GOLF ACADEMY**
Welshpool, Powys SY21 9BU
Tel: (01938) 552326
Head: Mr M J Hutchinson
Type: Boys Boarding and Day 16–18
Fees: (September 01) On application

SWANSEA

CRAIG-Y-NOS SCHOOL

Clyne Common, Bishopston,
Swansea SA3 3JB
Tel: (01792) 234288
Head: Mr G W Fursland
Type: Co-educational Day 2–11
No of pupils: B85 G62
Fees: (September 01)
Day £2580 – £3390

FFYNONE HOUSE SCHOOL

36 St James' Crescent, Swansea
SA1 6DR
Tel: (01792) 464967
Head: Mr J R Thomas
Type: Co-educational Day Boys 7–18
Girls 11–18
No of pupils: B148 G89
Fees: (September 01) On application

OAKLEIGH HOUSE

38 Penlan Crescent, Uplands
Swansea SA2 0RL
Tel: (01792) 298537
Head: Mrs R Ferriman
Type: Co-educational Day Boys 3–7
Girls 3–11
No of pupils: B46 G116
Fees: (September 01)
Day £2709 – £3045

2.5
OVERSEAS SCHOOLS

EGYPT

CAIRO

**THE BRITISH
INTERNATIONAL SCHOOL***
PO Box 137, Gezira, Cairo, Egypt
Tel: (00) 202 736 5959
Head: Dr P McLaughlin
Type: Co-educational Day 3–18
No of pupils: B302 G307
Fees: (September 01)
Day £2724 – £6294

FRANCE

MOUGINS

MOUGINS SCHOOL*
615 Avenue Dr Maurice Donat, Font
de l'Orme, BP 401,
Mougins 06251 Cedex
Tel: (+33) 4 93 90 15 47
Head: Mr B Hickmore
Type: Co-educational Day 3–18
No of pupils: B203 G170
Fees: (September 01)
Day FF24900 – FF69000

THE NETHERLANDS

THE HAGUE

THE BRITISH SCHOOL IN THE NETHERLANDS*
Foundation School: Tarwekamp 3,
2592 XG The Hague
Junior School: Vlaskamp 19, 2592
AA The Hague
Senior School: Jan Van Hooflaan 3,
2252 BG Voorschoten
Tel: (+31) 70 333 8111
Head: Mr R T Rowell
Type: Co-educational Day 3–18
No of pupils: B924 G880
Fees: (September 01)
Day Euros 8040 – 10920

PHILIPPINES

MANILA

THE BRITISH SCHOOL MANILA*
36th Street University Park,
Fort Bonifacio, Global City, Taguig,
Metro Manila
Tel: (+632) 840 15 70
Head: H Kinsey-Wightman
Type: Co-educational day 4–16
No of pupils: B196 G206
Fees: (September 01) £5700

SPAIN

MADRID

KING'S COLLEGE*
Paseo de los Andes, 35,
28761 Soto de Vinuelas, Madrid
Tel: (+34) 918 034 800
Head: Mr C T Gill Leech
Type: Co-educational Boarding and
Day 1½–18
No of pupils: B660 G640
No of boarders: F20
Fees: (September 01)
FB Ptas.330000 Euros 1983.34
Day Ptas.200500 – 412000
Euros 1205.03 – 2476.17

SWITZERLAND

LAUSANNE

BRILLANTMONT INTERNATIONAL COLLEGE*
Avenue Secretan 16, 1005 Lausanne
Tel: (+41) 21 310 04 00
Director: Mr P Pasche
Type: Co-educational boarding and day 13–19
No of pupils: 140
No of boarders: F90
Fees: (September 01) FB SFr48,000; WB SFr42,700; Day SFr18,500

CHESIÈRES

AIGLON COLLEGE*
Rue Centrale Chesières 1885
Tel: (+41) 24 496 61 61
Head: Dr Rev J Long
Type: Co-educational boarding and day 9–18
No of pupils: B183 G142
No of boarders: F280
Fees: (September 01) FB SFR40,170–SFR60,160 depending on age; Day SFR12,500–SFR39,560 depending on age

SAANEN

JOHN F KENNEDY INTERNATIONAL SCHOOL*
3792 Saanen, Saanen
Tel: (+41) 33 7441373
Head: Mr W M Lovell
Type: Co-educational Boarding and Day 5–14
No of pupils: B30 G30
No of boarders: F30
Fees: (September 01) FB Chf40000 Day Chf22000

PART THREE: SCHOOL PROFILES

COUNTIES OF ENGLAND, SCOTLAND AND WALES

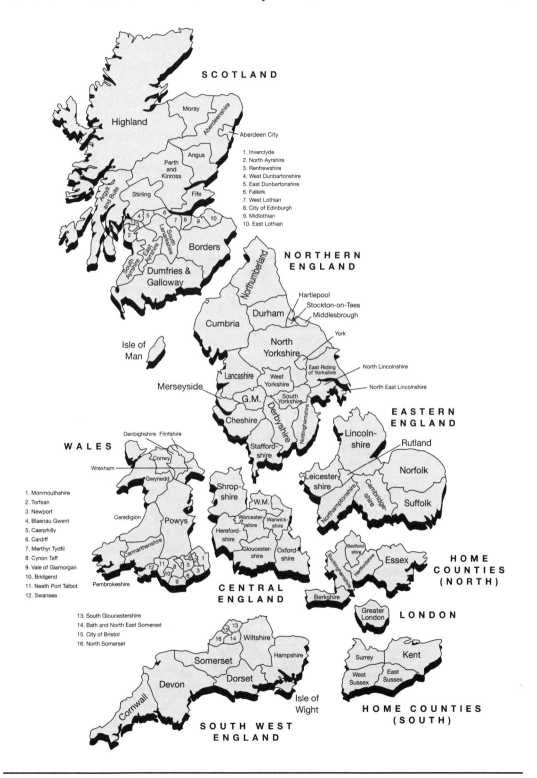

SCOTLAND

Highland

Moray

Aberdeenshire

Aberdeen City

Angus

Perth and Kinross

Argyll and Bute

Stirling

Fife

1. Inverclyde
2. North Ayrshire
3. Renfrewshire
4. West Dunbartonshire
5. East Dunbartonshire
6. Falkirk
7. West Lothian
8. City of Edinburgh
9. Midlothian
10. East Lothian

South Lanarkshire

North Ayrshire

East Ayrshire

Borders

Dumfries & Galloway

NORTHERN ENGLAND

Northumberland

Hartlepool
Stockton-on-Tees
Middlesbrough

Durham

Cumbria

Isle of Man

North Yorkshire

York

Lancashire

West Yorkshire

East Riding of Yorkshire

North Lincolnshire

North East Lincolnshire

Merseyside

G.M.

Derbyshire

South Yorkshire

Nottinghamshire

EASTERN ENGLAND

Cheshire

Lincolnshire

Rutland

Denbighshire   Flintshire

WALES

Conwy

Wrexham

Stafford-shire

Leicester-shire

Norfolk

Northamptonshire

Cambridge-shire

Gwynedd

Shrop-shire

W.M.

Suffolk

1. Monmouthshire
2. Torfean
3. Newport
4. Blaenau Gwent
5. Caerphilly
6. Cardiff
7. Merthyr Tydfil
8. Cynon Taff
9. Vale of Glamorgan
10. Bridgend
11. Neath Port Talbot
12. Swansea

Ceredigion

Powys

Worcester-shire

Warwick-shire

Hereford-shire

Bedford-shire

HOME COUNTIES (NORTH)

Carmarthenshire

Gloucester-shire

Oxford-shire

Buckinghamshire

Hertfordshire

Essex

Pembrokeshire

13. South Gloucestershire
14. Bath and North East Somerset
15. City of Bristol
16. North Somerset

CENTRAL ENGLAND

Berkshire

Greater London

LONDON

Wiltshire

Hampshire

Surrey

Kent

Somerset

West Sussex

East Sussex

Devon

Dorset

Isle of Wight

HOME COUNTIES (SOUTH)

Cornwall

SOUTH WEST ENGLAND

PROFILED SCHOOLS IN NORTHERN ENGLAND

NORTHERN ENGLAND

(Incorporating the counties of Cheshire, Cumbria, Derbyshire, Durham, Hartlepool, Lancashire, North East Lincolnshire, North Lincolnshire, Greater Manchester, Merseyside, Middlesbrough, Northumberland, Nottinghamshire, Staffordshire, Stockton-on-Tees York, East Riding of Yorkshire, North Yorkshire, South Yorkshire, West Yorkshire)

PROFILED SCHOOLS IN SOUTH WEST ENGLAND

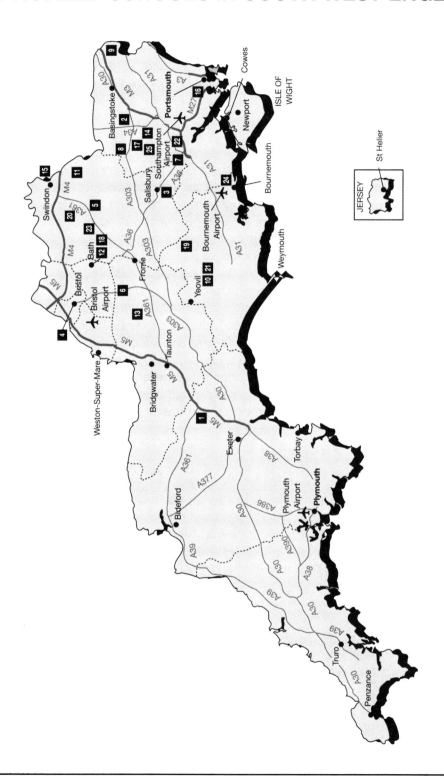

SOUTH WEST ENGLAND

(Incorporating the counties of Bath and North East Somerset, City of Bristol, Cornwall, Devon, Dorset, South Gloucestershire, Hampshire, Isle of Wight, Somerset, North Somerset, Wiltshire)

PROFILED SCHOOLS OF EASTERN ENGLAND

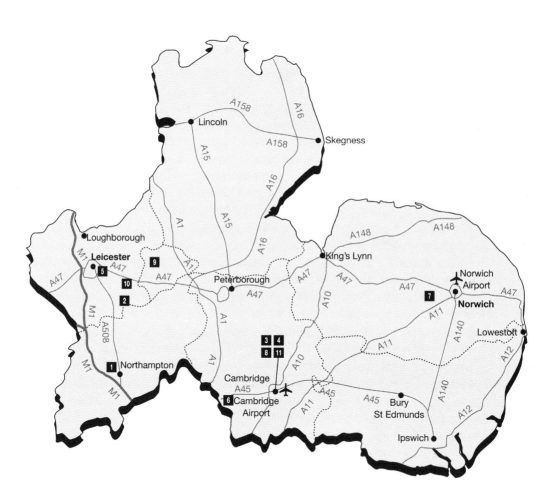

EASTERN ENGLAND

(Incorporating the counties of Cambridgeshire, Leicestershire, Lincolnshire, Norfolk, Northamptonshire, Rutland,Suffolk)

PROFILED SCHOOLS IN THE HOME COUNTIES (NORTH)

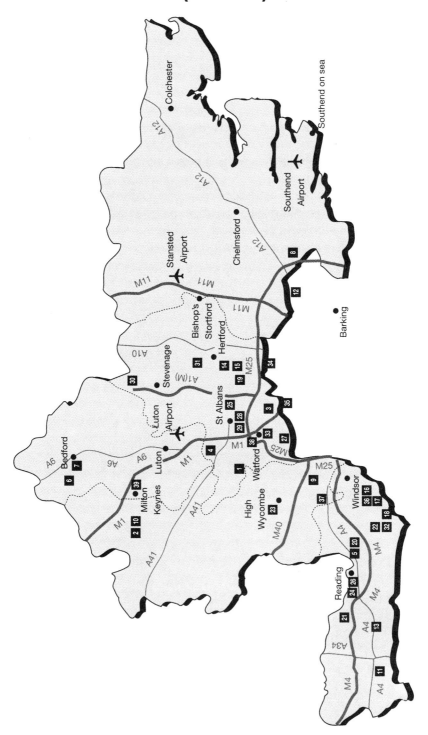

HOME COUNTIES (NORTH)

(Incorporating the counties of Bedfordshire, Berkshire, Buckinghamshire, Essex, Hertfordshire, Middlesex)

PROFILED SCHOOLS IN INNER LONDON

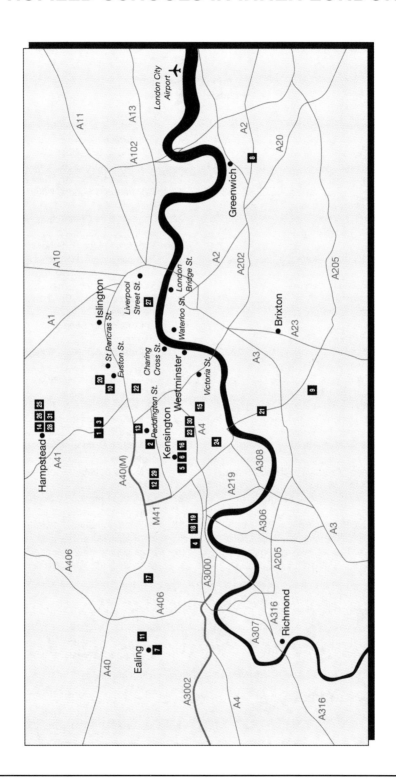

INNER LONDON

PROFILED SCHOOLS IN OUTER LONDON

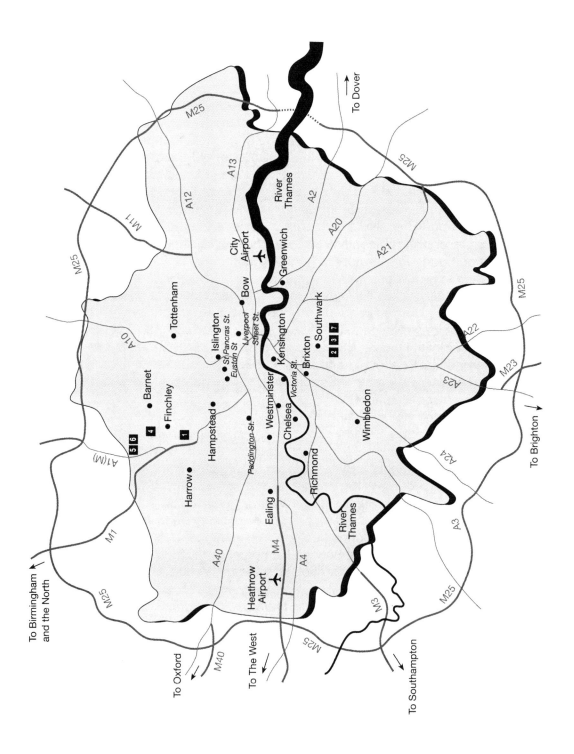

OUTER LONDON

PROFILED SCHOOLS IN SCOTLAND

SCOTLAND

(Incorporating the counties of Aberdeen City, Aberdeenshire, Angus, Argyll and Bute, East Ayrshire, North Ayrshire, South Ayrshire, Borders, City of Edinburgh, Dumfries and Galloway, East Dunbartonshire, West Dunbartonshire, Falkirk, Fife, Highland, Inverclyde, East Lothian, Midlothian, Moray, Perthshire, Renfrewshire, Stirling, South Lanarkshire, West Lothian)

PROFILED SCHOOLS IN WALES

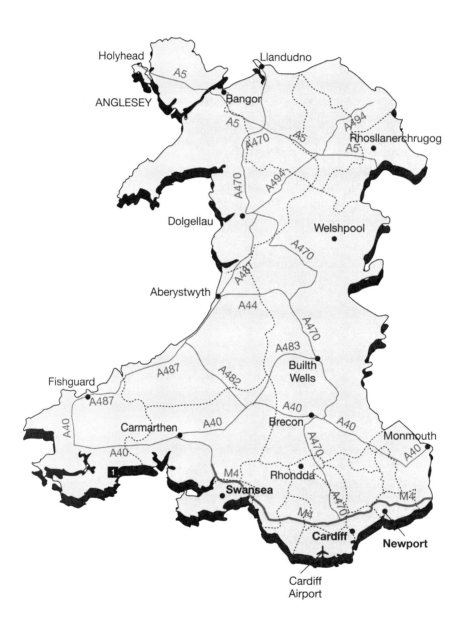

WALES

(Incorporating the counties of Blaenau Gwent, Bridgend, Caerphilly, Cardiff, Carmarthenshire, Ceridigion, Conwy, Cynon Taff, Denbighshire, Flintshire, Gwynedd, Merthyr Tydfil, Monmouthshire, Neath Port Talbort, Newport, Pembrokeshire, Powys, Swansea, Torfean, Vale of Glamorgan, Wrexham)

Map   **Page**
Number   **Number**

PROFILED SCHOOLS IN CENTRAL ENGLAND

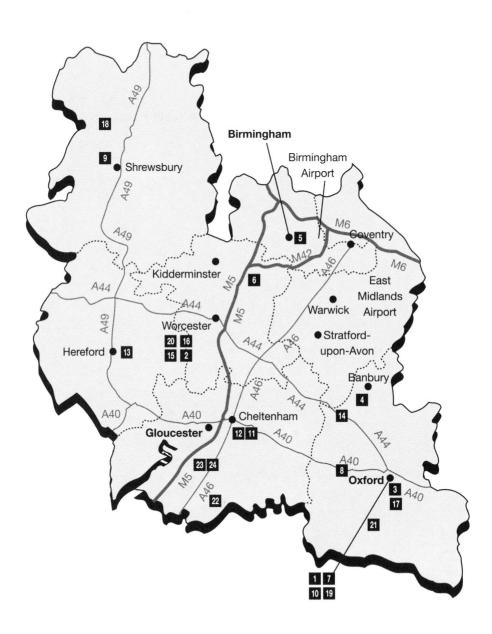

CENTRAL ENGLAND

(Incorporating the counties of Gloucestershire, Herefordshire, Oxfordshire, West Midlands, Shropshire, Warwickshire, Worcestershire)

PROFILED SCHOOLS IN THE HOME COUNTIES (SOUTH)

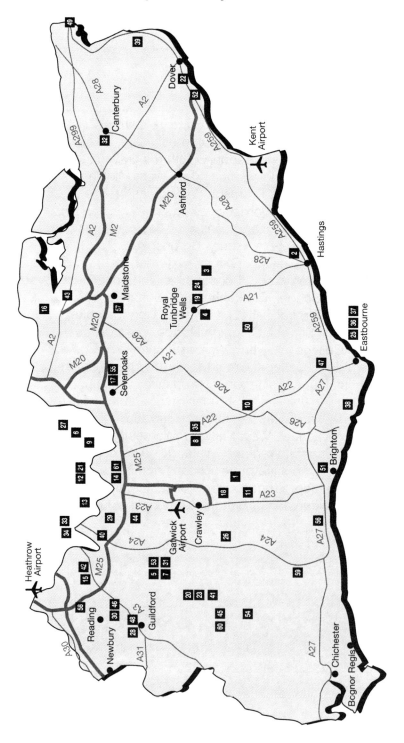

THE HOME COUNTIES (SOUTH)

(Incorporating the counties of Kent, Surrey, East Sussex, West Sussex)

PROFILED SCHOOLS IN EUROPE AND OUTSIDE EUROPE

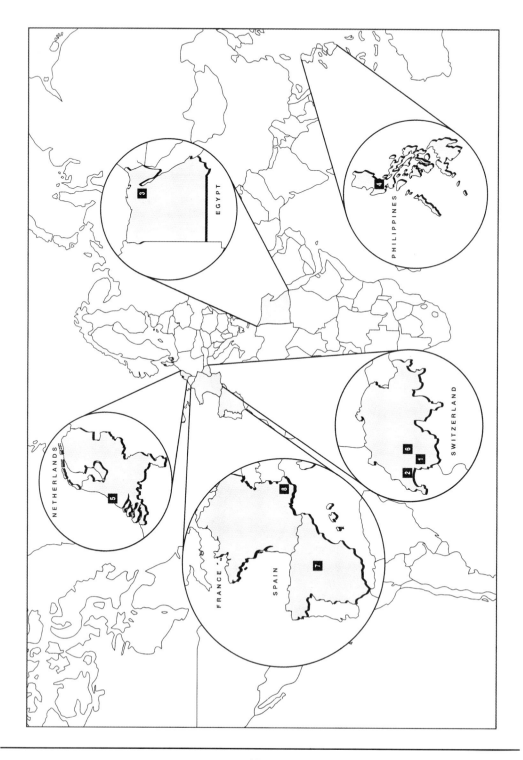

EUROPE AND OUTSIDE EUROPE

Bedford High School

Yes ✓Prelim 20.09.05 no match
Yes. Jenny Morris

Bromham Road, Bedford, Bedfordshire MK40 2BS
Tel: (01234) 360221   Fax: (01234) 353552
E-mail: head@bedfordhigh.co.uk   Web site: www.bedfordhigh.co.uk   www.gabbitas.net

Head Mrs G Piotrowska MA
Founded 1882
Type Girls' independent prep and senior boarding and day
Religious denomination Non-denominational
Member of GSA, GBGSA, BSA
Special needs provision ESOL, DYS
Age range 7–18
No of pupils (day) 755; *(boarding)* 128
Junior 198; *Senior* 477; *Sixth Form* 198
Fees per annum (boarding)(full) £13,269; *(weekly)* £5,970; *(day)* £7,299

Bedford High School has a long tradition of academic excellence, diversity of opportunity and the highest standards in pastoral care.

The Junior School provides an ideal foundation, fostering an enquiring mind and establishing good study skills. In the Senior School a choice may be made from a wide spectrum of GCSE subjects (23) and A Levels (30). Sport, the Creative Arts and ICT are particular strengths and there is a real emphasis on the importance of realising the potential of each individual. Careers guidance begins at 13 years and includes a programme for personal development and health awareness. Almost all Sixth Formers continue their education at university with a number of Oxbridge entrants each year. *Extra-curricular activities (over 40):* debating, dance, harp, lacrosse, the rock band and rowing are a few examples.

Flexi-boarding is offered and the four houses have been recently refurbished and extended to the highest standards.

Centrally sited in Bedford, the School is convenient for all London airports.

Entry is by examination/GCSE results, report and interview. Bursaries and scholarships are available.

Bedford School Study Centre

✓Prelim 20.09.05 no match
she Kenneally reply. NO

67 De Parys Avenue, Bedford, Bedfordshire MK40 2TR
Tel: +44 (0)1234 362300   Fax: +44 (0)1234 362305
E-mail: bssc@bedfordschool.org.uk Web site: www.bedfordschool.org.uk/bssc www.gabbitas.net

Head Mrs O Heffill
Founded 1996
Type Independent co-educational boarding only
Religious denomination Non-denominational
Special needs provision EFL
Age range 11–17
No of pupils (boarding) 30
Girls 10; *boys* 20
Fees per annum (boarding) (full) £20,100

Bedford School Study Centre is a special part of Bedford School. Boys and girls from overseas spend one, two or three terms here before they enter a mainstream school. Our students study English as a Foreign Language, mathematics, science, ICT and sport. Our classes have a maximum of six students, who live and study in one comfortable, friendly building, with the extensive facilities of Bedford School just a few minutes' walk away from the campus, and 24-hour care from the resident house staff. Our students have the best possible start to their UK education, wherever they go next.

Bearwood College

v prelim 20.09.0-

Wokingham, Berkshire RG41 5BG
Tel: (0118) 978 6915   Fax: (0118) 977 3186
E-mail: headmaster@bearwoodcollege.berks.sch.uk
Web site: www.bearwoodcollege.berks.sch.uk   www.gabbitas.net

Head SGG Aiano MA (Cantab)
Founded 1827
Type Co-educational independent senior boarding and day
Religious denomination Church of England (All denominations welcome)
Member of GBA, SHMIS, ISIS, BSA
Special needs provision DYS
Age range 11–18; *boarders from* 11
No of pupils (day) 201; *(boarding)* 130
Girls 68; *boys* 263
Senior 256; *Sixth Form* 75
Fees per annum (boarding) (full) £12,450–£13,875; *(weekly)* £12,450–£13,875; *(day)* £7,650–£8,250

All pupils are positively encouraged to perform to their best, both academically and outside the classroom. The academic programme culminates in a full range of GCSEs and a choice of over 20 A Level subject choices. A generous staff/pupil ratio ensures small classes allowing real focus on each pupil.

Pupils are all engaged in a wide selection of games, both team and individual sports, and other extra-curricular activities. Drama and Music are important features of College life, based in the renowned Bearwood College Theatre and Music School.

Pastoral care is given a high priority. Every pupil is a member of one of the six Houses, under the Housemaster or Housemistress, an assistant and a body of pastoral turors.

Access to Bearwood College is easy. We are close to the motorway network, and within easy reach of Heathrow and Gatwick Airports, and 35 minutes from London by train.

Cheam School

Headley, Newbury, Berkshire RG19 8LD
Tel: (01635) 268381   Fax: (01635) 269345
E-mail: office@cheamschool.co.uk   Web site: www.cheamschool.co.uk

Head Mr MR Johnson
Founded 1645
Type Co-educational independent pre-prep and prep boarding and day
Religious denomination Church of England
Member of BSA, IAPS, ISBA; *accredited by* ISC
Special needs provision 4 qualified teachers; ADD, ADHD, DYS, DYP, HI
Age range 3–13; *boarders from* 8
No of pupils (day) 260; *(boarding)* 93
Girls 143; *boys* 210
Fees per annum (boarding) £13,050; *(day)* £5,520–£9,660

Curriculum: for the 21st century your child needs the best possible preparation: communication, adaptability and confidence will be vitally important. Children are prepared in small classes (maximum 16) for Common Entrance and scholarships to all major public schools. The syllabus covers and exceeds National Curriculum requirements. Those with special needs are well catered for.

Entry requirements: by interview. Two scholarships are offered annually.

Academic and leisure facilities: excellent facilities set in a stimulating yet secure 80 acre estate. New classroom block and Music School including refurbished Chapel, completed September 2001. Modern science block (1996); dedicated IT, Art and Design departments; superb sporting facilities include squash court and 9-hole golf course.

Pastoral care and boarding facilities: each child is under the watchful eye of two house tutors and a form teacher; resident staff and matrons supervise boarders in comfortable dormitories Separate girls' boarding accommodation. Nursery and pre-prep on site.

Downe House

√prod̃in 20·09·05

Cold Ash, Thatcham, Berkshire RG18 9JJ
Tel: (01635) 200286   Fax: (01635) 202026
E-mail: correspondence@downehouse.berks.sch.uk   Web site: www.downehouse.net

Head Mrs E McKendrick BA
Founded 1907
Type Girls' independent senior boarding and day
Religious denomination Church of England
Member of GSA, BSA, ISIS, ISC, ISBA
Age range 11–18; *boarders from* 11
No of pupils (day) 21; *(boarding)* 515
Senior 365; *Sixth Form* 171
Fees per annum (boarding) £17,490; *(day)* £12,678

Curriculum: a wide selection of subjects is available at both GCSE and A Level. Girls are also prepared for university entrance.

Entry requirements and procedures: by Common Entrance and assessment. Five passes at grade C or above for an A Level course. Scholarships at 11+, 12+, 13+ and Sixth Form.

The School is situated only five miles from Newbury with easy access to the motorway network, London and Heathrow Airport. The School has an excellent academic record with nearly all pupils going on to university.

Academic and leisure facilities: Sixth Form complex with study bedrooms. Extensive refurbishment of all boarding. Significant expenditure on ICT with voicemail and e-mail for every girl. New Sports Hall and Indoor swimming pool. One term spent in France in 12+ Year. Leith's Food and Wine certificate is offered in the Sixth Form.

Heathfield School

Prelim. 20.09.05   X Failed

London Road, Ascot, Berkshire SL5 8BQ
Tel: (01344) 898343   Fax: (01344) 890689
E-mail: info@heathfield.ascot.sch.uk   Web site: www.heathfield.ascot.sch.uk   www.gabbitas.net

Head Mrs HM Wright MA (Oxon) MA (Leics)
Founded 1899
Type Girls' independent senior boarding
Religious denomination Church of England
Member of GSA, BSA, ISIS, SHA
Accredited by ISC
Special needs provision DYS (mild)
Age range 11–18; *boarders from* 11
No of pupils 221
Junior 101; *Senior* 67; *Sixth Form* 53
Fees per annum £17,325

Heathfield School, founded in 1899, is one of the few remaining girls' schools where every pupil is a full boarder. Set in 35 acres, the school is 40 minutes from London and 25 minutes from Heathrow. The original Georgian house has been extended over the years and facilities now include a new science block, a computer lab with internet access for all girls, art studios, a superb sports hall, indoor swimming pool and an upper-sixth complex. The School has a beautiful late Victorian chapel.

Heathfield is unashamedly comfortable but competitive and academically rigorous too. Emphasis is always on individual achievement and depth, an ethos underlined by excellent, highly-qualified teachers. The staff:pupil ratio is 1:7. While the more traditional subject combinations remain most popular, there is also excellence in art, drama, music and sport. Twenty-seven subjects are offered up to AS and A Level including Law, Economics, Business Studies and Media Studies. Academic results are consistently impressive and all girls go on to higher education.

Boarding accommodation is excellent, two thirds of the pupils having single bedrooms. All rooms are light, airy and appropriately personalised by the girls. The Upper Sixth live in a separate, self-contained complex which encourages them to prepare for the relative independence of university. Pastoral care throughout the School is recognised as outstanding, with year heads, form staff, tutors, two resident SRNs and ten resident house-mothers all playing their part.

Computers are used in a wide variety of academic areas as well as outside lessons. The Sports Hall is always a hive of activity. There are nineteen clubs, also frequent museum and theatre trips to London and elsewhere, work-shops, field trips and work experience abroad for linguists. At Heathfield the day does not finish at 4pm, nor the week on Friday.

Entry for the majority of pupils is at 11, a few girls join at 12 or 13 or come into the Lower Sixth for AS and A Level studies. Junior entrants take our entrance papers and also the appropriate Common Entrance examination. Entry into the Lower Sixth is via predicted GCSE grades, tests in intended AS and A Level subjects and interview. A number of academic, music and art scholarships for entry to Junior School and Sixth Form are awarded each year.

Hurst Lodge School

√ prelim 20·09·05

Bagshot Road, Ascot, Berkshire SL5 9JU
Tel: (01344) 622154   Fax: (01344) 627049
Email: admissions@hurstlodgesch.co.uk

Principals Mrs A Smit and Miss V Smit
Founded 1941
Type Independent pre-prep, prep and senior
day and boarding
Religious denomination Non-denominational
Member of BSA, ISA, CReSTeD
Special needs provision DYC, DYS
Age range Girls 2½–18; *Boys* 2½–7
Boarders from 9
No of pupils (day) 225; *(boarding)* 25
Girls 230; *boys* 20
Junior 90; *Senior* 146; *Sixth Form* 14
Fees per annum (boarding) £13,545; *(day)*
(junior) £2,535–£6,555; *(senior)* £7,950

Hurst Lodge is a small friendly school, set in grounds of over 20 acres. Girls are accepted from the age of 2½ to 18, while boys leave at 7. Girls may board from 9. The school is 50 minutes from central London and half an hour from Heathrow.

We offer a modern curriculum and traditional values in a caring environment. Through small class sizes and dedicated professional teaching, we encourage each individual to maximize their potential. The infant and junior departments prepare pupils for academic success by focusing on the development of sound numeracy and language skills in all the key subject areas, including English, maths, science, computing, geography, history, drama, religious knowledge, design technology, art, music, ballet and modern dance. Pupils also begin French in the junior school. GCSE and A Level classes are taught on a tutorial basis by enthusiastic subject specialists.

Extra classes are also offered in a wide variety of subjects, including, amongst others, tap and jazz dancing, horse riding and French.

All students are encouraged to develop the qualities necessary for meeting future challenges and attaining a fulfilling adult life. Confidence, respect for others, team-working skills and individuality are especially encouraged. These goals are fostered by offering a curriculum that combines an academic education with creative and performing arts. Success in local and national competitions gives pupils additional self-confidence.

As a CReSTeD school, specialist teaching is available for children who have specific learning difficulties, especially dyslexia.

The school's entrance examination to the senior school is held yearly. However, in some cases pupils may be accepted on the strength of their last school report and a letter of recommendation from their present head teacher.

A wide variety of scholarships and bursaries are available.

Licensed Victuallers' School

✓prelim 20.09.05   ✗failed

London Road, Ascot, Berkshire SL5 8DR
Tel: (01344) 882770   Fax: (01344) 890648
E-mail: Catrin.Milner-Smith@lvsascot.org.uk   Web site: www.lvsascot.windsor.sch.uk

Head Mr IA Mullins BEd (Hons), MSc, MBIM
Founded 1803
Patron Her Majesty The Queen
Type Co-educational independent prep and senior boarding and day
Religious denomination Non-denominational
Member of BSA, ISA, ISIS, GBA, SHMIS
Accredited by ISC
Special needs provision DYS
Age range 4+–18; *boarders from* 7
No of pupils (day) 540; *(boarding)* 180
Junior 200; *Senior* 390; *Sixth Form* 130
Fees per annum (boarding) £11,805–£13,065; *(day)* £4,480–£7,410

Location and Facilities The Licensed Victuallers' School is a fully co-educational day and boarding School of 720 pupils aged 4½–18. The School is set in extensive grounds, just a short distance away from Royal Ascot and ideally situated within easy reach of London and the main international airports.

The striking modern architectural design of the School ensures that the needs of the pupils and staff are fully accommodated. This includes eight specialist laboratories, a magnificent theatre with its state-of-the-art sound and light systems, indoor swimming pool, Sports Hall and movement/dance studio, medical centre and four boarding houses.

Curriculum Both Junior and Senior School follow the 'National Curriculum-plus', with the added feature of a wide range of GCSE, AS Level, A Level and GNVQ options, catering for each individual pupil's strengths. We encourage students to give of their best with a philosophy of 'whole person' education. There is a pupil:teacher ratio of 9.5:1. International students account for approximately 7 per cent of all pupils.

Academic scholarships are available – please request further details.

Luckley-Oakfield School

✓prelim 20.09.05
Yes. MRS. D. Gummery

Luckley Road, Wokingham, Berkshire RG40 3EU
Tel (0118) 978 4175   Fax: (0118) 977 0305   E-mail: registrar@luckley.wokingham.sch.uk
Web site: www.luckley.wokingham.sch.uk   www.gabbitas.net

Head Richard C Blake (Oxon), MPhil (Soton)
Founded 1918
Type Girls' independent senior boarding and day
Religious denomination Church of England
Member of GSA, GBGSA, BSA
Special needs provision ADD, DYS, DYP, HI
Age range 11–18; *boarders from* 11
No of pupils (day) 252; *(boarding)* 72
Senior 265; *Sixth Form* 57
Fees per annum (boarding) (full) £13,131; *(weekly)* £12,117; *(day)* £7,695

Curriculum and examinations: National Curriculum is followed to GCSE including Double award Modular Science, French, German and Spanish. 20 A Levels with AS courses for Year 12 with Key Skills and EAL.

Entry: School's own examination and interview mainly at age 11, 12 or 13.

Academic and leisure facilities: separate Sixth Form residential block, modern science labs, studio, modern ICT resources, and a music centre. Covered swimming pool, Sports Hall, tennis courts and games field.

Extended day option to 5.30pm.

Scholarships: academic awards offered at 11 and 16. Music scholarships offered.

Boarding facilities: Junior and Senior boarding houses in main building, separate Sixth Form accommodation. High standard of pastoral care. Pleasant setting on edge of town. Easy links to M3, M4 and Heathrow.

Pangbourne College

Pangbourne, Reading, Berkshire RG8 8LA
Tel: (0118) 984 2101   Fax: (0118) 984 1239
E-mail: registrar@pangcoll.co.uk   Web site: www.pangbournecollege.com   www.gabbitas.net

Head Dr Kenneth Greig MA(Oxon) PhD(Edin)
Founded 1917
Type Co-educational independent boarding
and day
Religious denomination Church of England
Special needs provision DYS
Member of HMC, SHMIS
Age range 11–18; *boarders from* 11
No of pupils (day) 167; *(boarding)* 221
Girls 87; *boys* 301; *Sixth Form* 116
Fees per annum (boarding) £11,595–£15,960;
(day) £8,130–£11,190

Entry at 11, 13, and 6th form. Generous scholarship provision with Academic, Sport, Music, Art, Technology and All-Rounder Awards available.

Emphasis remains on qualities of leadership, teamwork, self-discipline and service to others. Academically, Pangbourne believes its task is to enable each individual to make the very best of their potential no matter where strengths lie. Excellent Music, Drama, and sport contribute to a vibrant and exciting atmosphere. Specialist coaches have led to success at county, national and international level in a number of sports. Set in fine grounds of 240 acres, including a beautiful stretch of the Thames.

Papplewick

Windsor Road, Ascot, Berkshire SL5 7LH
Tel: (01344) 621488   Fax: (01344) 874639
Web site: www.papplewick.org.uk   www.gabbitas.net

Head Mr DR Llewellyn
Founded 1947
Type Boys' independent prep boarding and day
Religious denomination Church of England
Member of HMC, GBA, BSA
Special needs provision DYS, DYP, MLD, PH, SPLD
Age range 7–13; *boarders from* 7
No of pupils (day) 75; *(boarding)* 134
Fees per annum (boarding) £13,200;
(day) £10,140

Entry requirements: parental choice and interview followed by placing test. It is essential to register boys well in advance of their sixth birthday.

Papplewick enjoys a spacious rural location on the edge of Windsor Great Park. Convenient links with M4, M3, M25, Heathrow and Gatwick. The quality of care and the dedication of staff are outstanding and remain Papplewick's special hallmark.

Average size of class: 12. *Teacher:pupil ratio:* 1:8
Curriculum: all main subjects are studied. Computing is taught throughout the School as are Art, Design and Technology. Steady work towards scholarships and Common Entrance passes is balanced with music, PE and a wide range of competitive sports and games. Magnificent new Sports Hall and Music School.

Queen Anne's School

✓ prelim 20·09·05

6 Henley Road, Caversham, Reading, Berkshire RG4 6DX
Tel: (0118) 918 7300   Fax: (0118) 918 7310
E-mail: admis@queenannes.reading.sch.uk   Web site: www.qas.org.uk   www.gabbitas.net

Head Mrs Deborah Forbes
Founded 1894
Type Girls' independent senior boarding and day
Religious denomination Church of England
Member of GSA, GBGSA
Age range 11–18; *boarders from* 11
No of pupils (day) 159; *(boarding)* 165
Senior 239; *Sixth Form* 85
Fees per annum (full boarding) £16,026; *(day)* £10,836

Located on an attractive campus near Reading, the School is readily accessible from London and Heathrow with excellent road and rail links. Entry by Common Entrance or Queen Anne's own exam. A range of scholarships is available. Facilities include performing arts centre for drama and music, well equipped IT Department, heated indoor swimming pool and new Sports Centre. Recently refurbished boarding accommodation. Separate Sixth Form Houses ease the transition from school to University life. Excellent academic record with all girls going on to higher education with a number each year going to Oxford and Cambridge. A wide range of extra-curricular activities and a varied programme all contribute to a busy but happy life at Queen Anne's.

Reading Blue Coat School

✓ prelim 20·09·05

Holme Park, Sonning-on-Thames, Reading, Berkshire RG4 6SU
Tel: (0118) 944 1005   Fax: (0118) 944 2690
E-mail: vmf@blue-coat.reading.uk   Web site: www.blue-coat.reading.sch.uk   www.gabbitas.net

Head Mr SJW McArthur BSc, MA, CertEd, FCollP
Founded 1646
Type Co-educational independent senior day
Religious denomination Church of England
Member of HMC, SHMIS, GBA
Age range 11–18; girls 16–18
No of pupils 600
Senior 400; *Sixth Form* 200
Fees per annum £7,530

Richard Aldworth founded the School in 1646 for 'Scholars in Blue Coates'. Today the magnificent riverside setting at Sonning-on-Thames provides an excellent campus. The new Science laboratories and the current imaginative development programme enhance the fine facilities at this progressive school, whilst still retaining traditional values. Day places are available to boys from 11 to 18 with girls joining our co-educational Sixth Form.

The School is well known for its academic standards, for Science, the Humanities, Arts, Technology and ICT and the fostering of sporting and artistic development in its pupils. We have a superb tradition of art, drama and music with regular performances and exhibitions. The school has an international reputation for public speaking. Our activities progamme offers a wide range from adventure training and the Duke of Edinburgh's Award to sailing, archery and community service.

The extensive grounds and sports fields provide superb facilities for a wide range of sports including rugby, tennis and rowing.

The school believes in each individual's contribution and in enabling pupils to reach their potential. Whilst examination success is our goal, we also recognise the other facets to education and encourage sports and creativity.

St George's School, Ascot

✓ prelim 20.09.05

Ascot, Berkshire SL5 7DZ
Tel: (01344) 629900   Fax: (01344) 629901
E-mail: office@stgeorges-ascot.org.uk   Web site: www.gabbitas.net

Head Mrs J Grant Peterkin
Founded 1877
Type Girls' independent boarding and day
Religious denomination Church of England
Age range 11–18; *boarders from* 11
No of pupils 300; *(boarding)* 140
Fees per annum (boarding) £16,050;
(day) £10,275

St George's School, Ascot, is an independent school for girls located in the Berkshire countryside. It is situated between the M3, M4 and M25 motorways, allowing for easy access to London, Heathrow and Gatwick.

Entry is by examination at 11, 12 or 13 and, while broadstream, the academic results are outstanding. There are limited places at 16+.

Boarders and day girls benefit from the caring and personal attention of a dedicated teaching and pastoral staff. The main faith is Church of England, but girls from any denomination are welcome. Extra-curricular activities are many and include music, drama, debating, voluntary service, Duke of Edinburgh Award and photography. Sport is excellent and includes lacrosse, tennis, swimming, gymnastics, squash and fitness exercising.

St George's, Ascot is committed to the development of the individual and her talents, to the best of her ability.

St Mary's School, Ascot

✓ prelim 20.09.05
25.09.05   YES. MRS. Lynne Povey.

St Mary's Road, Ascot, Berkshire SL5 9JF
Tel: (01344) 293614   Fax: (01344) 297491
E-mail: admissions@st-marys-ascot.co.uk Web site: www.st-marys-ascot.co.uk www.gabbitas.net

Head Mrs Mary Breen
Founded 1885
Type Girls' independent senior boarding
Religious denomination Roman Catholic
Member of GSA, GBSA; *accredited by* DfEE
Age range 11–18; *boarders from* 11
No of pupils (day) 27; *(boarding)* 324
Senior 247; *Sixth Form* 104
Fees per annum (full boarding) £16,440;
(day) £11,040

St Mary's is a selective independent Roman Catholic boarding school for girls aged 11–18. The School is situated in 44 acres close to the M3, M4 and M25 motorways and within easy access of London and the airports. Entry at 11+, 13+ and 16+ is subject to the School's own entry procedure. Facilities are excellent as are examination results, with 82 per cent AB grades at A Level and 100 per cent ABC grades GCSE (2000). The majority of pupils stay on for the Sixth Form and 99 per cent go on to university. Facilities include a state-of-the-art library with intergrated ICT, a language faculty, a purpose built Upper Sixth House of single study bedrooms, an indoor heated swimming pool, and a newly opened all weather sports surface.

St Piran's Preparatory School

Gringer Hill, Maidenhead, Berkshire SL6 7LZ
Tel: (01628) 627316   Fax: (01628) 632010
E-mail: office@stpirans.co.uk   Web site: www.stpirans.co.uk

Head Mr JA Carroll
Founded 1820
Type Independent co-educational pre-prep and prep day only
Religious denomination Church of England
Member of IAPS; *accredited by* ISI
Age range 3–13;
No of pupils 363
Girls 105; *boys* 258
Fees per annum £3,780–£6,870

Curriculum: National Curriculum subjects up to Year 8. French is offered from Reception to Year 8. German and Spanish are options in the senior years.
Sport: A comprehensive range for all pupils. Facilities include a new sports hall, indoor swimming pool, all weather pitch and Dance Studio.
Facilities: Excellent facilities. Fully networked ICT department and PCs in classrooms. We have two specialist teachers for those who need additional support. Trampolining, drama, games and crafts, amongst others, are activities for Year 5 to Year 8 at the end of the day.
Entry requirements: Entry is by interview, school report and where necessary, a short assessment if entry is higher up in the school.

Clifton College

No email address.

32 College Road, Clifton, Bristol BS8 3JH
Tel: (0117) 3157 000   Fax: (0117) 3157 101
Website: www.cliftoncollegeuk.com   www.gabbitas.net

Head Dr MS Spurr
Founded 1862
Type Co-educational independent senior
boarding and day
Religious denomination Church of England and
Jewish House
Member of HMC
Special needs provision DYS, MLD
Age range 13–18; *boarders from* 13 (8 in prep
school)
No of pupils (day) 240; *(boarding)* 430
Girls 240; *boys* 430
Senior 400; *Sixth Form* 270
Fees per annum (boarding) £16,770;
(day) £11,170

Clifton offers a broad and flexible curriculum
with an unusually large number of subjects on
offer. Entry at 13+ is by Common Entrance or
ability tests. Scholarships are available at 11
(for prep school), 13 and 16 for academic, art,
music and all-round abilities. The School, and
the adjoining Preparatory School (3–13),
occupy a superb site in what has been described
as 'the handsomest suburb in Europe'. Academic excellence, magnificent buildings and
cultural facilities, a pioneering spirit and a high
level of pastoral care in a caring and friendly
atmosphere characterise the Clifton of today.

Akeley Wood School

No email

Buckinghamshire MK18 5AE
Tel: (01280) 814100   Fax: (01280) 822945
Web site: www.gabbitas.net

Principal Mr WH Wilcox
Type Co-educational independent pre-prep,
prep and senior day
Religious denomination Non-denominational
Special needs provision DYS, DYP at the
Charmandean Dyslexia Centre
Age range 2¾–18
No of pupils 829
Girls 334; *boys* 485
Fees per annum £4,398–£6,450

Akeley Wood is an independent co-educational
day school for some 700 pupils between the
ages of 2¾ years and 18.
The Junior School occupies an attractive Georgian house and estate between Buckingham and
Milton Keynes. There is an emphasis on sound
teaching of basic skills, though there is a broad
curriculum and plenty of opportunity for creative activities, physical education and play.
The Lower School is situated at Lillingstone
Dayrell where children reinforce all the skills
they have learned at the Junior School as well as
embarking on an extended curriculum in
readiness for secondary education.
The Senior School, for 11 to 18 year olds,
stands in beautiful countryside between the
villages of Lillingstone Dayrell, Akeley and
Maids Moreton. Pupils are prepared for GCSE
and A Level examinations, with an outstanding
record of success.
The School offers a friendly and purposeful
environment, with small classes and enthusiastic teaching, where good habits of work and
independence of mind can flourish in a happy
and civilised atmosphere.

Caldicott

Crown Lane, Farnham Royal, Buckinghamshire SL2 3SL
Tel: (01753) 649300   Fax: (01753) 649325
E-mail: office@caldicott.com   Web site: www.caldicott.com   www.gabbitas.net

Head Mr SJG Doggart
Founded 1904
Type Boys independent prep boarding and day
Religious denomination Church of England
Member of ISIS, SATIPS, SFIA, IAPS, BSA
Special needs provision DYS
Age range 7–13; *boarders from* 7
No of pupils (day) 110; *(full boarding)* 140
Fees per annum (full boarding) £12,081;
(day) £9,063

Caldicott – a leading IAPS preparatory school
for boys with 250 pupils, situated in 40 acres,
adjacent to Burnham Beeches, yet only 20 minutes from Heathrow. All boys board during
their last two years. Boarding facilities are comfortable and homely. Boys, who are prepared for
Common Entrance/scholarship examinations
to public schools, achieve a high rate of success.
Caldicott has well-equipped academic facilities,
extensive sports facilities, excellent design
workshops, Computer Department, and a purpose built Music School. There are facilities for
most games as well as music, art and drama.
Entry via interview and assessment. Prospectus
available from Headmaster, Caldicott, Farnham
Royal, Bucks SL2 3SL.

The Charmandean Dyslexia Centre   *No email*

Lillingstone Dayrell, Buckingham MK18 5AN
Tel: 01280 860182   Fax: 01280 860194
Web site: www.gabbitas.net

Principal WH Wilcox
Founded 1998
School status Co-educational independent day
Religious denomination Non-denominational
Age range 7–16
Girls 28 *Boys* 71
Fees per annum (day) Tuition fees £8,268

The Charmandean Dyslexia Centre, which opened in September 1998, offers a comprehensive education for pupils aged from 7 to 16 who are held back by Dyslexia and certain other learning difficulties.

Curriculum: All pupils have an Individual Education Plan outlining their needs and targets for each term. Teaching is in small classes with additional periods of intensive specialised tuition directed at overcoming specific difficulties. The main emphasis for the younger children is on English and Mathematics, using a multi-sensory approach. Science, French (mainly oral), History, Geography, Scripture, Art, Design, Music, Drama, Computing (including keyboard skills) and Study Skills all feature in the curriculum.

The mainstream curriculum is followed wherever possible, but it is presented in ways best suited to individual learning patterns.

Physical education: Pupils are able to take part in a varied programme of Physical Education and Games. In the winter terms the main sports for boys are rugby and football; in the summer term the main sports are cricket and athletics. For girls the winter sports are netball and hockey, with rounders, athletics and tennis in the summer. Charmandean has its own covered and heated swimming pool for use throughout the year. There is a full programme of competitive fixtures with other schools.

Drama and Music: Both Drama and Music are an integral part of the Dyslexia Centre curriculum. In addition, individual tuition can be arranged with our peripatetic teachers on a wide variety of musical instruments.

Computing: Benefiting from an up-to-date facility, the pupils are taught keyboard skills and basic computing. Those pupils for whom a laptop computer is an essential classroom aid are thus able to use it to best advantage.

Mrs Hawkins is the Head Teacher and in charge of organising and supervising the work. Every term there is a more formal parents' evening to review pupils' achievements and a detailed written report is sent home.

Entry is by interview, test and a psychological assessment arranged by the school.

(14)

Pipers Corner School

✓ prelim. 20.09.05   ✗ Not delivered

Pipers Lane, Great Kingshill, High Wycombe, Buckinghamshire HP15 6LP
Tel: (01494) 718255   Fax: (01494) 719806
E-mail: pipers@enterprise.net   Web site: www.piperscorner.co.uk   www.gabbitas.net

Head Mrs VM Statterfield MA (Oxon) PGCE
Founded 1930
Type Girls' independent pre-prep, prep and senior boarding and day
Religious denomination Church of England
Member of GSA, GBGSA, BSA
Accredited by ISI
Age range 4–18; *boarders from* 8
No of pupils 450
Pre-prep 35; *Prep* 75; *Senior* 280; *Sixth Form* 60
Fees per annum (boarding) (full) £10,785–£12,960; *(weekly)* £10,650–£12,795; *(day)* £3,390–£7,770

Set in 36 acres of the beautiful Chilterns our spacious campus, with its outstanding facilities, is only half an hour from Heathrow and less than an hour from London.
Pipers is not only for girls with academic, artistic or sporting talent who hit the headlines or gain Oxbridge places, (although ours do!). It is just as proud of students with average abilities who strive to do their best and achieve more than they ever thought they would. Every success is valued. We provide a challenging and well balanced curriculum. Girls achieve high standards and are well prepared for higher education.
In boarding, the atmosphere is calm and relaxed, with the emphasis on family values and with friendly, well-ordered supervision. An exciting variety of weekend activities is organised for the girls.
Entry requirements: Preparatory Department by interview and report; Senior School by entrance examination, interview and report.
Scholarships: academic and service bursaries and Sixth-Form scholarships are available.

Swanbourne House School

Swanbourne, Milton Keynes, Buckinghamshire MK17 0HZ
Tel: (01296) 720264   Fax: (01296) 728188
E-mail: office@swanbourne.org   Web site www.swanbourne.org

Head Mr and Mrs S Goodhart
Founded 1920
Type Co-educational independent pre-pre and prep day and boarding
Member of IAPS, BSA, ISIS, SATIPS
Age range 2¾–13
No of pupils in pre-prep 160
No of pupils in prep 242
Girls 166; *boys* 236
Fees per term (full boarding) £3,750; *(day)* £2,950

Swanbourne House is a successful IAPS preparatory school from which academic scholarships and awards in Arts/Sport and Music are won each year. There are many opportunities for personal development through activities, sport, the Arts, holiday clubs and trips abroad.
Pupils have a form tutor in addition to a Housemaster and are prepared for Public School through Leadership Training, Public School Induction, socials, First Aid, Personal Advice, taking responsibility and Study Skills. Pupils also take part in a French immersion programme for one week and they also attend an outdoor pursuits course.
Facilities: laboratory, computer rooms, astroturf, engineering workshop, comfortable boarding house, Design and Art Centre, language lab, library, amphitheatre, sports hall and a year round swimming pool.

Cambridge Centre for Sixth-form Studies

1 Salisbury Villas, Station Road, Cambridge, Cambridgeshire CB1 2JF *✓ prelim 20·09·05*
Tel: (01223) 716890   Fax: (01223) 517530 *Yes, Itol basis. Head of Modern Language*
E-mail: office@ccss.co.uk   Web site: www.ccss.co.uk   www.gabbitas.net *Mr Adrian Wainwright*

Head Mr PC Redhead
Founded 1981
Type Co-educational independent sixth-form college, boarding and day
Religious denomination Non-denominational
Member of CIFE, ISA, ISIS; *accredited by* ISC
Special needs provision DYS
Age range 15–19; *boarders from* 15
No of pupils (day) 40; *(boarding)* 130
Girls 75; *boys* 95
Senior (GCSE year) 20; *Sixth Form* 150
Fees per annum (boarding) from £12,015; *(day)* from £7,230

A sixth-form college in the fullest sense, CCSS takes students both for two-year A Level and GCSE courses, and for intensive one-year and short-term retake programmes. An extensive range of subjects is offered and subject combination is unrestricted.

The key to the College's academic strength is the teaching structure: students are taught in small classes (maximum eight) and have, in addition, weekly individual tutorials with their subject teachers which prove invaluable in developing skills and confidence and in ironing out difficulties.

All students, whatever the length of their stay, benefit from the College's strong tradition of pastoral care, and are able to participate in a comprehensive range of sporting and extra curricular activities, enthusiastically supported by CCSS staff.

Approximately one–third of students are local and the College provides fully supervised accommodation in its own houses for the students needing to board.

Kimbolton School

✓ prelim 20.09 05
Replied NO

Kimbolton, Huntingdon, Cambridgeshire PE28 OEA
Tel: (01480) 860505   Fax: (01480) 860386
E-mail: headmaster@kimboltonschool.demon.co.uk   Web site: www.kimbolton.cambs.sch.uk

Head Mr RV Peel BSc, FRSA
Founded 1600
Type Co-educational independent pre-prep, prep and senior boarding and day
Religious denomination Christian Ethos
Member of HMC, GBA
Special needs provision DYS, DYC, DYP, HI
Age range 4–18; *boarders from* 11
No of pupils (day) 786; *(boarding)* 53
Girls 368; *boys* 418
Junior 264; *Senior* 395; *Sixth Form* 127
Fees per annum (full boarding) £12,810; *(day)* £3,990–£7,710

Curriculum: a full and wide range of subjects taught to GCSE and A Level including Art, Design Technology, Economics and Business, Food Technology, Politics, Spanish and Social Biology. Computer Studies throughout the School. Full PE programme. Games include

soccer, hockey, cricket, netball and tennis. There is a full programme of indoor activities, including squash, in the new sports complex. New Concert Hall and theatre facilities have recently been provided, along with an Art Centre and Sixth Form Centre. A new indoor swimming pool was opened in June 2000. Pre-preparatory Department from 4–6 years, opened in 1996.

Entry requirements: interview and test 7 to 11; tests in English, Maths and Verbal Reasoning at 11+. Common Entrance at 13+ (internal examinations where appropriate). Sixth Form entry by GCSE results. Scholarships and bursaries available at 11, 13 and Sixth Form.

Kimbolton School Charitable Trust exists to provide high-quality education for local boys and girls from the parish of Kimbolton and also for the education of children from other areas.

The Leys School

prelim 20·09·03
25.09.05 Yes MRS Wiedermann

Trumpington Road, Cambridge, Cambridgeshire CB2 2AD
Tel: (01223) 508900   Fax: (01223) 505303
E-mail: office@theleys.cambs.sch.uk   Web site: www.theleys.cambs.sch.uk   www.gabbitas.net

Head Dr JCA Barrett
Founded 1875
Type Co-educational independent senior
boarding and day
Religious denomination Methodist
Member of HMC
Special needs provision DYS, DYP
Age range 11–18; *boarders from* 11
No of pupils 526; *No of boarders* 273
Senior 326; *Sixth Form* 200
Girls 198; *boys* 328
Fees per annum (boarding) (full) £11,400–
£15,900; *(day)* £7,200–£11,850

The Leys is an Independent boarding and day school situated in the the world famous university City of Cambridge. There is an academic, but caring atmosphere. Pupils are encouraged to achieve their potential. There are strong Science, Language and Mathematics departments. Technology subjects are well-resourced. Arts subjects including Drama are popular choices up to A level. New subjects in Sixth Form include PE and Psychology. Links with the University and local industry. Modern sports complex including astro with over 20 sports offered including rugby, cricket, rowing and water polo. Scholarships available in Art, Music, Drama, Technology, Sport and special awards for some in Tennis nominated by the Lawn Tennis Association.

Sancton Wood School

prelim 20.09.05
Ref 50 Yes, MR Russell Lord

2 St Paul's Road, Cambridge, Cambridgeshire CB1 2BZ
Tel: (01223) 359488   Fax: (01223) 471703
E-mail: sturdy@sturdy.demon.co.uk   Web site: www.sanctonwood.org.uk   www.gabbitas.net

Head Julia Avis BA
Founded 1976
Type Co-educational independent pre-prep
prep and senior day only
Religious denomination Church of England
Special needs provision DEL, DYS, DYP, SP&LD
Age range 1–16
No of pupils 174
Junior 50; *Senior* 71
Girls 69; *boys* 105
Fees per annum (day) £4,350–£5,355

Sancton Wood is a unique, small, family-orientated school in the centre of Cambridge, founded on the principle of small class sizes. The school makes an outstanding contribution to the development of each individual and has a reputation for instilling good manners and self-discipline. Class sizes do not exceed 16 pupils. The staff are highly qualified and committed teachers, who endeavour to develop each pupils' academic and social skills to full capacity. Pupils consistently achieve 100 per cent A–C grades at GCSE. Families choosing Sancton Wood School feel they are an active part of the pursuit of excellence within the ideal educational environment.

Casterton School

✓ *prelim* 20.09.05

Kirkby Lonsdale, Carnforth, Cumbria LA6 2SG
Tel: (015242) 79200   Fax: (015242) 79208
E-mail: admissions@castertonschool.co.uk
Web site: www.castertonschool.co.uk   www.gabbitas.net

Head AF Thomas MA
Founded 1823
Type Independent pre-prep, prep and Girls' senior boarding and day
Religious denomination Church of England
Member of GSA, GBGSA
Special needs provision DYS, HI
Age range 4–18; *boarders from* 8;
(boys 4–11 day only)
No of pupils (day) 136; *(boarding)* 226
Girls 344; *boys* 18
Fees per annum (boarding) (full) £12,870;
(weekly) £10,746; *(day)* £6,876–£7,920

Beautifully situated between the Lake District and the Yorkshire Dales, Casterton School is the most successful girls' boarding and day school in the North West of England. Examination results are consistently outstanding – in 1999, Casterton was one of only ten schools to achieve a 100 per cent pass rate (A–C) at GCSE. Pass rate in excess of 98 per cent are regularly achieved at both GCSE and A-Level. Almost all girls remain at Casterton for their A-Levels and most go on to university.

Casterton offers a wide choice of sports and activities. Full use is made of the school's unique environment and great emphasis is placed upon extra-curricular activities; hockey, netball, lacrosse, athletics, tennis and rounders are played, there is an indoor swimming pool, riding stables and most girls take part in the Duke of Edinburgh Award Scheme. There are very strong traditions in the arts, music and drama with many opportunities for performance. In addition to a continuous programme of improvements, new buildings in the 1990s have included an Arts Centre, a Science/Maths block Preparatory Department, Sports pavilion and the latest project – an all-weather pitch.

The younger girls live in Bronte House; they have access to all of the Senior School facilities and an exciting programme of activities operates every weekend. Between the ages of 12–16, girls live in one of five small and friendly senior boarding houses. There are three separate highly individual Sixth Form Houses with study-bedroom accommodation. These, together with a Social Centre in one of the traditional cottages on campus, provide greater freedom and an excellent preparation for university. Sixth formers play an important part in the care of the younger girls and visitors comment upon the happy and positive atmosphere in the School.

Casterton has close links with a number of neighbouring boys' schools and regular cultural, sporting and social meetings are arranged. Casterton is 95 minutes from Manchester Airport to which a comprehensive escort system is provided.

St Bees School

St Bees, Cumbria CA27 0DS
Tel: (01946) 822263   Fax: (01946) 823657
E-mail: mailbox@st-bees-school.co.uk   Web site: www.st-bees-school.co.uk

prelim - 20·09·05
25·09·05 YES DR. A.J.H. Reeve

Head Mr PJ Capes
Founded 1583
Type Co-educational independent prep and
senior boarding and day
Religious Denomination Church of England
Member of HMC, GBA, BSA
Special needs DYC, DYS, HI, MLD, SPLD, VIS
Age range 11–18
No of pupils (day) 170; *(boarding)* 126
Girls 112; *boys* 184
Junior 96; *Senior* 200; *Sixth Form* 102
Fees per annum (boarding) (full) £11,355–
£15,513; *(weekly)* £9,840–£13,974;
(day) £7,800–£9,909

Curriculum: very broad during the first three
years; Drama, Music, Information Technology
and outdoor pursuits. Sixteen GCSE and 17
A Level courses; over 95 per cent of leavers go
on to higher education.

Entrance: own examinations; Common
Entrance; Sixth Form entrance requires mini-
mum of five GCSEs at grade C or higher.
Scholarships: academic and music at 11+ and
13+ and at 16+. Art, Music and sports into Sixth
Form.
Sport and extra-curricular: outstanding sporting
record and facilities. Lake District nearby used
for outdoor pursuits.
Boarding: weekly, full and flexi.

Windermere St Anne's

prelim 20.09.05 x Failed

Windermere, Cumbria LA23 1NW
Tel: (015394) 46164   Fax: (015394) 88414
E-mail: win@windermerest-annes.cumbria.sch.uk
Web site: www.windermerest-annes.cumbria.sch.uk   www.gabbitas.net

Head Wendy Ellis BA Hons, PGCE
Founded 1863
Type Co-educational independent pre-prep,
prep and senior boarding and day
Religious denomination Non denominational
Special needs provision DYS
Member of SHMIS, Round Square
Age range 2–18; *boarders from* 8
No of pupils (day) 245; *(boarding)* 94
Girls 222; *boys* 117
Junior 134; *Senior* 145; *Sixth Form* 60
Fees per annum (boarding) £11,616–£12,312;
(day) £3,402–£6,804

Windermere St Anne's is an independent boarding and day school with facilities for over 300
senior school pupils. For over 130 years, the
School has created a strong reputation for the
individual development of pupils, from the UK
and overseas, based on academic, cultural and
sporting achievement, supported by close
pastoral care and an international perspective.
The philosophy of the School centres around
development of the individual through a
balanced, full rounded approach to education.
The aim is to ensure that all pupils are able to
fulfil their potential. Targets are set not for the
School but for each pupil and success is judged
by personal achievement. This allows pupils to
progress academically and develop their self-
confidence and self-awareness at the same time.
A nurturing environment exists, with extremely supportive staff. This helps create a
lively, caring, family atmosphere and mutual
trust and respect within the School. Amongst
the pupils, the ethos produces independence,
individual responsibility, and a sense of adventure towards discovery and learning.
Windermere St Anne's has probably one of the
most enviable locations for a school. In the
heart of the Lake District, with views over

Windermere to the fells beyond, the School is
set in 80 acres of wooded parkland, with landscaped gardens and has a private lakeshore
watersports centre.
The School policy is to provide equal opportunities for all pupils and each Year is divided
into Forms with sets in the main subjects. Class
sizes are currently around 15 pupils. The curriculum comprises English, Business Studies,
History, Geography, French, Mathematics,
Physics, Chemistry, Biology, Music, Art, Drama,
Dance, Home Economics, Information
Technology, Design and Technology, Religious
Studies and Physical Education and Games.
Spanish and German are taken in Year 8. A
number of scholarships are available to boys
and girls for entry into all years for academic
and creative disciplines.
The co-educational Junior Department, Elleray,
has close links with the senior school. The
children study a full range of subjects and enjoy
a full activity programme after school.

Mount St Mary's College

Pielin 20.09.05

Spinkhill, Derbyshire S21 3YL
Tel: (01246) 433388   Fax: (01246) 435511
E-mail: headmaster@msmcollege.com   Web site: www.msmcollege.com   www.gabbitas.net

Head Mr PG MacDonald MA (Oxon)
Founded 1842
Type Co-educational independent senior boarding and day
Religious denomination Roman Catholic
Member of HMC
Special needs provision ADD, ADHD, ASP, DYC, DYS, DYP, EPI, HI, MLD
Age range 11–18; *boarders from* 11
No of pupils (day) 174; *(boarding)(full)* 116; *(weekly)* 36
Girls 100; *boys* 190; *Sixth Form* 85
Fees per annum (boarding) (full) £9,195–£12,510; *(weekly)* £8,130–£11,085; *(day)* £6,045–£6,990

Mount St Mary's College, established in 1842, is a co-educational Catholic school welcoming children of all denominations. The school is situated in beautiful surroundings close to the M1 junction 30, with minibus service to local areas. The school offers:

- Excellent teacher pupil ratio
- Specialist Science block, new ICT centre, new music school, and excellent sports facilities
- Scholarships, bursaries and Mount assisted places scheme available

Entry: 11+ via entrance exaimination (Feb). 13+ via common entrance or interview. 16+ by interview and GCSE results.

Barlborough Hall School

Barlborough, Chesterfield, Derbyshire S43 4TJ
Tel: (01246) 810511   Fax: (01246) 570605
E-mail: barlborough.hall@virginnet.co.uk

Head Mrs W Parkinson
Founded 1938
Type Co-educational independent pre-prep and prep boarding and day
Religious denomination Roman Catholic
Member of HMC
Special needs provision DYS, MLD
Age range 3–11; *boarders from* 7
Girls 86; *boys* 118
Fees per annum (day pre-prep) £3,585; *(prep)* £5,310

Barlborough Hall School is an independent Catholic co-educational day and boarding school situated in extensive grounds close to junction 30 of the M1.

The School offers a stimulating education of high quality for children in the 3–11 age range with an emphasis on academic, cultural and social development.

The school provides:

- Academic excellence
- Attractive environment and excellent sporting facilities
- Extensive minibus service
- Strong traditions of music and drama
- Out-of-school care
- A Christian community with happy, confident children aware of the needs of others
- New ICT suite

Blundell's School

Tiverton, Devon EX16 4DN
Tel: (01884) 252543   Fax: (01884) 243232
E-mail: registrars@blundells.org   Web site: www.blundells.org

Head Mr J Leigh MA, FRSA
Founded 1604
Type Co-educational independent prep and
senior boarding and day
Religious denomination Church of England
Member of HMC
Special needs provision DYS
Age range 11–18; *boarders from* 11
No of pupils (day) 150; *(flexi-boarding)* 250;
(boarding) 110
Girls 190; *boys* 320
Junior 120; *Senior* 230; *Sixth Form* 160
Fees per annum (boarding) £10,515–£15,810;
(flexi-boarding) £6,645–£14,290; *(day)* £5,685–
£9,825

Blundell's, a key West Country school, combines balance, excellence, space and tradition
to provide a unique package for 11–18-year-old
day and boarding pupils.
Curriculum: Blundell's offers all traditional subjects at A Level plus Theatre Studies, Music,
Art, History of Art, Photography and Sports
Science. The main curriculum is underpinned
by a full programme of supplementary courses
and lectures at all levels.
Entry requirements: A-Level entry: minimum of
5 GCSEs plus interview and report from present school; 11+ and 13+: Blundell's Entrance
Test or Common Entrance.

Examinations offered: GCSE, A Level, Music.
Academic and Leisure Facilities: Blundell's
impressive sporting reputation is widely known
and its superb facilities, including a new all-
weather pitch, are complemented by an unusually wide range of sporting and extramural
activities to suit all interests, particulary music
and drama. New 40-computer resources centre.
Scholarships: 11+, 13+ and Sixth Form:
academic, music, art and all rounder.
Boarding facilities: life at Blundell's is supported
by a very strong house structure where pupils
live in a family environment, guided by their
houseparents and tutors.

International College, Sherborne School

Newell Grange, Sherborne, Dorset DT9 4EZ   *✓ Prelim 20.09.05*
Tel: (01935) 814743   Fax: (01935) 816863
E-mail: reception@sherborne-ic.net   Web site: www.sherborne-ic.net

Principal Dr CJ Greenfield
Founded 1977
Type Co-educational independent prep and senior boarding
Religious denomination Non-denominational
Member of ISA, GBA, BSA, ECIS
Accredited by ISA
Age range 11–17; *boarders from* 11
No of pupils 120
Girls 38; *Boys* 82
Junior 20; *Senior* 100
Fees per annum £19,500

The International College is unique. It was established in 1977 (as the International Study Centre) to prepare boys – and later girls – from non-British educational backgrounds so that they could function successfully in traditional British boarding schools. Typically these boys and girls spend one year at the International College before moving on to a traditional British boarding school where the majority of students are British. Those students who join in year 10 (usually around 14 or 15 years old) and start a two-year course leading towards GCSE Examinations must stay at the school for the duration of the course.

The college has three major tasks:

- Concentrated improvement in spoken and written English;
- Academic preparation in English in the full range of curriculum subjects;
- A good introduction to British educational procedures and the British way of life.

The arrangements of the College are designed to achieve these tasks. Classes are small, usually between six and eight students to each teacher. All teachers are not only experienced specialists in their own subject, but also have additional training in teaching the English language.

Characteristics: The teaching facilities at the International College include modern classrooms, seven science laboratories, a computer centre and a library with internet access. The College uses the extensive sporting, musical and theatre facilities at Sherborne School including a 25 metre indoor swimming pool.

The International College has gained an unrivalled reputation for providing the very best start to British independent education for children from overseas. Through a carefully supervised programme of study, students gain a sound working knowledge of the main British Curriculum subjects such as Mathematics, the Sciences and Humanities. The College has high standards of discipline and pastoral care. Most weekends there is a busy programme that ensures students are fully occupied on Saturday and Sunday.

St Mary's School

Shaftesbury, Dorset SP7 9LP
Tel: (01747) 854005   Fax: (01747) 851557
E-mail: admin@st-marys-shaftesbury.co.uk
Web site: www.st-marys-shaftesbury.co.uk   www.gabbitas.net

prelim 20·09·05
Yes. Head of Classics - Mr Patrick Dooley

Head Mrs Sue Pennington BA Hons
Founded 1945
Type Girls' independent prep and senior boarding and day
Religious denomination Roman Catholic
Member of BSA, GSA, ISIS
Special needs provision DYC, DYS, DYP, EBD, EPI, PH, W
Age range 9–18; *boarders from* 9
No of pupils (day) 112; *(boarding)* 228
Junior 67; *Senior* 196; *Sixth Form* 77
Fees per annum (boarding) £13,695–£14,430; *(day)* £8,910–£9,375;

Curriculum: a broad and balanced curriculum with all girls learning Latin, Science, Technology and IT from 11. The average number of GCSEs is nine with all girls studying RE, English Language and Literature, French, Mathematics and Balanced Science plus three options.

Entry requirements: own entrance exam and testimonial at 9+, 10+, 11+ and 14+. Common Entrance and testimonial at 12+ and 13+. Five grade C GCSEs and testimonial at 16+. Two Sixth-Form scholarships, music scholarships from 11+, art scholarships from 13+, and all-round awards at 11+, 12+ and 13+.
Subject specialities: very good science facilities and very strong Art and Music Department. Pass rate at GCSE is 99 per cent and A Level 97 per cent.
Facilities: in boarding houses, all with common rooms, quiet rooms and kitchens. Purpose-built Sixth-Form house and Modern Languages Centre, Library, Infirmary and astroturf. Music School, IT Room, Sports Hall, Drama Studio, brand new Junior School, new kitchens and refectory, swimming pool, 55 acres. County champions in netball, athletics and hockey.

 # Sherborne School for Girls

Bradford Road, Sherborne, Dorset DT9 3QN
Tel: (01935) 818287   Fax: (01935) 389444/389445
E-mail: enquiry@sherborne.com   Web site: www.sherborne.com

prelim 20·09·05
Yes   Siobhan Jones

Head Mrs G Kerton-Johnson, BSc UED
Founded 1899
Type Girls' independent senior boarding and day
Religious denomination Church of England
Member of GSA, BSA, SHA
Age range 11–18; *boarders from* 11
No of pupils (day) 28; *(boarding)* 320
Senior 200; *Sixth Form* 150
Fees per annum (boarding) £17,430; *(day)* £12,900
Average size of class: 18
Teacher:pupil ratio: 1:7.2

Curriculum: all the usual subjects up to GCSE; over 30 subjects offered at AS/A Level including the following, Business Studies, Drama and Theatre Studies, Economics, History of Art, Further Mathematics, Music Technology, Russian, Electronics (AS), Law (AS) and Philosophy (AS). Some A/AS Levels are studied jointly with Sherborne School.

Entry requirements and procedures: girls must pass 11+, or 13+ Common Entrance. Entrance into Sixth Form is competitive.
The School stands in its own grounds of 40 acres. Train service between Sherborne and Waterloo. School coach to Heathrow.
Scholarships, exhibitions and bursaries: six academic scholarships and two exhibitions are offered annually as a result of examination and interview; in addition there is an art scholarship plus two scholarships offered for outstanding promise in music. Sixth-Form scholarship held in November. Closing date for 11+, 13+ and music scholarships is 1 December for examinations and auditions in late January or February. Winners of academic or other awards are offered emoluments related to the current fees. Details from the Registrar.
Sherborne School for Girls is a charitable trust (No. 3074527) for the purpose of educating girls in a boarding environment.

Wentworth College +e?

College Road, Southbourne, Bournemouth BH5 2DY
Tel: (01202) 423266   Fax: (01202) 418030
E-mail: wentcolleg@aol.com   Web site: www.wentworthcollege.org.uk

prelim 20.09.03
email failed

Head Miss SD Coe
Founded 1871
Type Girls' independent boarding and day
Religious denomination Inter-denominational
Member of GSA, GBGSA, BSA; *Accredited by* ISC
Special needs provision DYS, DYP, SPLD
Age range 11–18; *boarders from* 11
No of pupils 225; *(full boarding)* 40; *(weekly)* 20
Senior 181; *Sixth Form* 44
Fees per annum (full boarding) £11,550;
(weekly) £11,550; *(day)* £7,275

Wentworth College provides a stimulating and caring environment with committed teachers who respond to the needs of every girl, helping her to reach her full potential. We aim to develop happy, confident young women who are proud of their academic success and personal achievement, and who leave equipped for adult life.

Situated in beautiful grounds on a cliff top just 200 meteres from Bournemouth's award winning beaches and close to the New Forest, the school offers well-equipped teaching and excellent sports facilities. We have a dedicated sixth form study centre and offer numerous extra-curricular activities.

Brentwood School

Ingrave Road, Brentwood, Essex CM15 8AS
Tel: (01277) 243243   Fax: (01277) 243299
E-mail: headmaster@brentwood.essex.sch.uk   Web site: www.brentwoodschool.co.uk

Head John AB Kelsall
Founded 1557
Type Co-educational independent pre-prep,
prep and senior boarding and day
Religious denomination Church of England
Special needs provision ADD, DYP, DYS
Member of HMC, *Accredited by* GBA, IAPS
Age range 3–18; *boarders from* 11
No of pupils (day) 1,025; *(boarding)* 75
Pre-Prep and Prep 371; *Senior* 791;
Sixth Form 309
Fees per annum (full boarding) £14,622;
(day) £8,433

Brentwood School offers a first-class academic education for boys and girls aged 3 to 18 in a complex of modern and refurbished buildings on a 70-acre leafy site at the heart of Brentwood in Essex. Two boarding houses accommodate some 48 boys and 27 girls, aged 11 to 18. The Senior School has approximately 1,100 pupils, the Preparatory School 232 boys and girls aged 7 to 11 and the Pre-preparatory School 139 pupils, aged 3 to 7. Brentwood enables all its pupils to realise fully their individual potential within a happy and friendly environment.

Cranbrook College

Mansfield Road, Ilford, Essex IG1 3BD
Tel: (020) 8554 1757   Fax: (020) 8518 0317
E-mail: cranbrookcollege@aol.com

Head Mr CP Lacey
Founded 1896
Type Boys independent prep and senior day
Religious denomination Non-denominational
Member of ISA
Accredited by ISC
Age range 4–16
No of pupils 210
Senior 120; *Junior* 90
Fees per term (day) £3,840–£5,019

Cranbrook College, founded in 1869, is situated in a residential area close to the centre of Ilford. In the Lower School, boys follow a general primary school course, and in the Upper School they prepare for GCSEs.

The main entry is at age 4 but older boys are admitted when vacancies exist. Admission at 8 and above is subject to a test and boys under 8 are interviewed before admission is confirmed. The School caters for pupils of a wide range of ability and aims to provide a happy, ordered and secure environment in which, through academic work and a wide variety of sports and other activities, each boy has an opportunity to reach the highest standards that are within his capabilty.

Cranbrook College Educational Trust Limited is a Registered Charity, number 312662. It exists to provide 'general instruction of the highest class' for pupils from Ilford and the surrounding area.

Dean Close Preparatory School

Lansdown Road, Cheltenham, Gloucestershire GL51 6QS
Tel: (01242) 512217   Fax: (01242) 258005
E-mail: office@deancloseprep.gloucs.uk
Web site: deancloseprep.gloucs.sch.uk   www.gabbitas.net

Head Mr Stephen Baird BA
Founded 1886
Type Co-educational independent pre-prep and prep boarding and day
Religious denomination Church of England
Member of IAPS, ISIS
Accredited by ISC
Age range 2+–13+; *boarders from* 7
No of pupils (day) 299; *(boarding)* 61
Girls 170; *boys* 190; *Pre-Prep* 111; *Prep* 249
Fees per annum (boarding) £12,300;
(day) £3,960–£8,415

Dean Close Preparatory School is a Christian family school with outstanding facilities and caring staff committed to the development of the individual child in all aspects of education. The School follows the Common Entrance base but firmly embraces the National Curriculum.

An entry test in English and Mathematics appropriate for the age is set but most children come and spend a day in the School.

Academic and music scholarships and exhibitions, and sports awards are offered at 11+.

There are two boarding houses run by house parents and three day houses all offering pastoral care of the highest order. The classrooms are modern and purpose-built and include two science laboratories, a Computer Centre and an Art and Technology Department. The School Hall, Dining Hall and playing fields all enable the children to enjoy first-class facilities, together with the swimming pool, gymnasium, artificial pitches and theatre in the Senior School.

The vast majority of boys and girls move on to Dean Close School at 13+, so ensuring continuity and stability.

30 Dean Close School

Shelburne Road, Cheltenham, Gloucestershire GL51 6HE
Tel: (01242) 522640   Fax: (01242) 258003
E-mail: dcsregistrar@dean-close.demon.co.uk   Web site: www.deanclose.org.uk   www.gabbitas.net

Head Timothy M Hastie-Smith
Founded 1886
Type Co-educational independent senior boarding and day
Religious denomination Church of England
Member of HMC
Special needs provision DYS, SPLD, Learning support unit
Age range 13–18; *boarders from* 13
No of pupils (day) 193; *(boarding)* 267
Girls 207; *boys* 253; *Senior* 260; *Sixth Form* 190
Fees per annum (full boarding) £16,800;
(day) £11,790

Dean Close is truly co-educational, where the number of girls and boys are almost equal. The School aims to broaden the opportunities of each and every pupil through an exceptional array of facilities in sport, music, theatre and art as well as over 100 clubs and societies. Facilities include a heated 25m indoor swimming pool, two astro-turf pitches, an impressive 550-seat theatre/concert hall, a purpose built art centre and a newly built music school.

An underlying Christian ethos generates genuine warmth and mutual respect at all levels within the School.

Westonbirt School

prelim 20.09.05
Yes: MRS. J. Watson.

Tetbury, Gloucestershire, GL8 8QG
Tel: (01666) 880333   Fax: (01666) 880364   E-mail: office@westonbirt.gloucs.sch.uk
Web site: www.westonbirt.gloucs.sch.uk   www.gabbitas.net

Head Mrs Mary Henderson MA
Founded 1928
Type Girls' independent senior boarding and day
Religious denomination Church of England
Special needs provision DYS
Member of Allied Schools, BSA, GSA, ISIS;
Accredited by BSA, GSA, ISIS
Age range 11–18; *boarders from* 11
Senior 140; *Sixth Form* 60
Fees per annum (boarding) £15,720;
(day) £10,956

Providing all the advantages of a small rural girls' school, Westonbirt offers academic excellence for all abilities in a happy community within a beautiful Cotswold setting.

Academic work may come naturally to your daughter, or she may need more encouragement and coaching. In either case Westonbirt's caring, personal approach will ensure that she fulfils her potential.

Pupils typically pass at least nine GCSEs and three full A Levels before going on to study for a degree. Students benefit from extensive careers advice (Westonbirt is an accredited Investor in Careers), and take part in valuable Key Skills programmes to prepare them for the world of work. Non-academic qualifications such as the Duke of Edinburgh Awards and the Leith's Certificate in Food and Wine are also available.

The school's Orangery Theatre, in which frequent drama productions are held, enables the girls to take part both on stage and behind the scenes. This involvement often inspires pupils to take additional qualifications in Speech and Drama.

In the school's 250 acre grounds, your daughter will enjoy extensive sporting facilities including a nine-hole golf-course, grass and hard tennis courts, and an indoor heated swimming pool. She may join the lacrosse team, which frequently qualifies as one of the top ten schools' teams in the UK and makes regular match tours of the USA, or be one of many girls who are asked each year to represent their county, region or country in various sports. Even if your daughter is not particularly fond of sport, she will be encouraged to develop a regular fitness programme for a long-term healthy lifestyle.

Westonbirt is renowned for its enthusiasm and excellent reputation in music. Its accomplished choirs, soloists and ensembles are always in demand to perform at sacred and secular venues throughout the region.

From Years 7 to 11, your daughter will live in a small dormitory in the beautiful Grade I Listed Westonbirt House. In the Sixth Form, she will have her own study bedroom and will be encouraged to develop independence and self-reliance to prepare her for university life.

Wycliffe College

Stonehouse, Gloucestershire GL10 2JQ
Tel: (01453) 822432   Fax: (01453) 827634
E-mail: senior@wycliffe.co.uk   www.wycliffe.co.uk   www.gabbitas.net

prelim 20.09.05
Slynn Corrine replied, YES MRS. Watson.

Head Dr RA Collins MA, DPhil
Founded 1882
Type Co-educational independent senior boarding and day
Religious denomination Inter-denominational
Member of HMC, ISIS, GBA
Special needs provision DYS, EFL, DYP, SPLD
Age range 13–18; *boarders from* 13
No of pupils (day) 143; *(boarding)* 262
Girls 152; *boys* 271
Sixth Form 226
Fees per annum (boarding) £16,515–£18,600; *(day)* £10,755–£11,166

Situated in sixty acres of parkland on the edge of the Cotswolds, Wycliffe creates a strikingly warm and friendly environment in which to learn.

Great pride is taken in Wycliffe's academic reputation. With a focus on individual learning, the superb facilities and lively enthusiasm of the teachers help to inspire a commitment to lifelong learning.

The extensive range of A Level courses includes Theatre, Sport, Business Studies, Media Studies and Computing as well as the more traditional subjects.

A spectrum of sports and activities provide something for everyone.

Wycliffe College Junior School

Ryeford Hall, Stonehouse, Gloucestershire GL10 2LD
Tel: (01453) 820470   Fax: (01453) 825604
E-mail: junior@wycliffe.co.uk   Web site: www.gabbitas.net

Head Mr K Melber BA
Founded 1927
Type Co-educational pre-prep and prep boarding and day
Religious denomination Inter-denominational
Special needs provision DYS, DYP, EFL, SPLD
Age range 7–13; *boarders from* 7
No of pupils (day) 222; *(boarding)* 34
Girls 95; *boys* 161
Fees per annum (boarding) £8,460–£10,635; *(day)* £4,740–£7,515

At Wycliffe Junior School our aim is to educate pupils to become confident and capable of dealing with the challenges that lie ahead of them: to achieve academically in a happy and caring environment, but also to contribute to sport, music, art and drama, as well as other activities which make the School such a special place.

Academic achievements at Wycliffe Junior School are also high and the Key Stage 1 and 2 test results are well above the national average. Scholarships, both academic and non-academic, are available for entry at 10+ and 11+. Forces bursaries are offered.

Morning and afternoon creches in the Pre-Prep and an extended day with supervised preps and evening activities in the Junior School enable the necessary flexibility for working parents. Flexi–boarding is a popular service enjoyed by the children.

An excellent pastoral care system ensures that the academic progress and welfare of the children are monitored very carefully.

Brockwood Park School

✓ prelim 20·09·05

Bramdean, Near Alresford, Hampshire SO24 0LQ
Tel: (01962) 771744   Fax: (01962) 771875
E-mail: admin@brockwood.org.uk   Web site: www.brockwood.org.uk

Heads Bill Taylor and Colin Foster
Founded 1969 by J Krishnamurti
Type Co-educational independent senior
boarding
Religious denomination Non-denominational
Special needs provision MLD
Age range 15–19
No of pupils 60; *Girls* 32; *boys* 28
Fees per annum £10,800

Curriculum: small class size, individualised programmes and a unique atmosphere provide an educational approach to meet the extraordinary demands of our society. Whilst seeking to support academic excellence, the main focus is on holistic learning. The communal nature of the School is an integral part of the educational programme with staff and students living together, sharing responsibility for all aspects of their daily life.

Entry requirements: participation in a prospective student week.
Examinations offered: Cambridge International AS and A Level Examinations.
Academic and leisure activities: the 35-acre estate, including the organic vegetable garden, is used extensively as an educational resource. Classrooms are intimate and fully equipped. Art, music, dance and theatre facilities are extensive. Computer facilities include multimedia, Internet and film-making suite.

Embley Park

✓ prelim 20·09·05

Romsey, Hampshire SO51 6ZE
Tel: (01794) 512206   Fax: (01794) 518737   Junior School (01794) 515737
E-mail: embley.park.school@virgin.net
Web site: www.gabbitas.net

Head David Chapman BA (Dunelm)
Founded 1947
Type Co-educational independent pre-prep, prep and senior boarding and day
Religious denomination Ecumenical/Church of England
Member of GBA, SHMIS, SHA, BSA
Special needs provision DYS, DYP, EPI, MLD, SPLD, VIS
Age range 3–18; *boarders from* 9
No of pupils (day) 337; *(boarding)* 86
Girls 140; *boys* 290
Junior 145; *Senior* 229; *Sixth Form* 49
Fees per annum (senior boarding) £13,905; *(senior day)* £8,505; *(junior day)* £5,070; *(nursery)* £2,385

Embley is a broad-ability school with an IQ threshold of 100, but still achieves, by small classes and setting in key subjects, approx-

imately 85 per cent entry to higher education (Oxbridge 7 per cent). The School sets its own entry test, but Common Entrance is used at 13+. At GCSE a core curriculum is offered but separate subject sciences and two languages can still be attempted. Business Studies with IT, PE and Drama are alternative humanity options. At A Level, 22 subjects are offered with 25 per cent of the Senior School aged 16–18. New facilities include a new junior school, purpose-built science laboratories and a 7,000 square-foot sports hall. Scholarships available; also bursaries (HM Forces, clergy, teachers, single parents, and hardship). Lively family atmosphere.

A main feature of provision is co-education 3–18 years, with boarding available from 9 years. Included in *The Times* 'Top 700 Schools' (state and independent) 2000.

Farleigh School

Red Rice, Andover, Hampshire SP11 7PW
Tel: (01264) 710766   Fax: (01264) 710070
E-mail: office@farleighschool.co.uk   Web site: www.farleighschool.com   www.gabbitas.net

Head Mr JA Allcott
Founded 1953
Type Co-educational independent prep boarding and day
Religious denomination Roman Catholic
Member of IAPS
Special needs provision DYS
Age range 3–13; *boarders from* 7
No of pupils (day) 308; *(boarding)* 107
Girls 162; *boys* 253
Fees per annum (boarding) £12,210; *(day)* £2,331–£9,150

Farleigh School is set in a 25 hectare rural estate close to the A303 (M3), within one and a half hours drive from Heathrow airport. The majority of boarders, both full and weekly, are Roman Catholic, but the School welcomes children of all Christian denominations.

Boarders are accommodated from age 7 to 13. Day children from age 3. The building of a new kindergarten and pre-prep department has now been completed.

The curriculum leads to the Common Entrance and scholarship examinations for senior schools and most subjects are taught in four ability sets. Up-to-date facilities include three science laboratories, a large purpose built Sports Hall and two state-of-the-art IT Suites. The Music Department and the enlarged library have all been refurbished.

A wide range of clubs and activities are arranged after school and at weekends, giving boarders and day children a full and varied life. Many of the staff live in and the pastoral team has been strengthened by the introduction of a House system. There are also two medically qualified matrons and assistants.

Farnborough Hill

Farnborough, Hampshire GU14 8AT
Tel: (01252) 545197 (school);   529811 (enquiries);   Fax: (01252) 513037
E-mail: devdir@farnborough-hill.org.uk   Web site: www.farnborough-hill.org.uk

Head Miss Jacqueline Thomas MA, PGCE
Founded 1889
Type Girls independent senior day
Religious denomination Roman Catholic
Member of GSA
Accredited by ISC
Special needs provision Extra lessons for dyslexics and dyspraxics
Age range 11–18
No of pupils 500
Senior 400; *Sixth Form* 100
Fees per annum £6,525

Farnborough Hill is housed in the historic home of the Empress Eugenie. Facilities include a chapel, gymnasium, indoor swimming pool, laboratories, technology workshops, and extensive playing fields. The School is committed to the education of the whole person in a caring, Christian environment. Academic standards are high; GCSE and A Level pass rates are always close to 100 per cent. Among the many extra-curricular activities there is particular emphasis on sport and the creative arts. Entry is by examination taken in January for the following September. The School offers bursaries and academic, sporting and musical scholarships. Excellent transport links and school coaches bring pupils from Hampshire, Berkshire and Surrey.

The Pilgrims' School

3 The Close, Winchester, Hampshire SO23 9LT
Tel: (01962) 854189   Fax: (01962) 843610
E-mail: pilgrimshead@btinternet.com   Web site: www.gabbitas.net

Head The Rev Dr BA Rees
Re-founded 1931 (From ancient Chantry Roots)
Type Boys' independent prep boarding and day
Religious denomination Church of England
Member of IAPS, CSA, BSA
Age range 7–13; *boarders from* 8
No of pupils (day) 123; *(boarding)* 79
Fees per annum (boarding; full and weekly)
£11,730; *(day)* £9,030

Boys' selective preparatory school (IAPS) for weekly/full boarders and day boys, incorporating the Choristers of Winchester Cathedral and the Quiristers of Winchester College who attend the School with choral scholarships to the value of half the boarding fee. High academic standards and an enviable Scholarship record are hallmarks of the School. There are excellent facilities for music, sport and academic study, with exceptional staff/pupil ratio and pastoral structure. The School is situated in beautiful buildings in the Cathedral Close with adjacent playing fields, and benefits additionally from the sporting and recreational facilities of Winchester College. For futher information, please apply to the Headmaster.

Rookesbury Park School

Wickham, Fareham, Portsmouth, Hampshire PO17 6HT
Tel: (01329) 833108   Fax: (01329) 835090
E-mail: rookesbury.park@ukonline.co.uk   Web site: www.rookesburypark.co.uk

Head Mrs SM Cook BA (Hons), PGCE
Founded 1929
Type Co-educational independent pre-prep and prep boarding and day
Member of IAPS, BSA; *accredited by* ISJC
Special needs provision DYS, EPI, MLD
Age range 3–13; *girls boarding from* 7
No of pupils (day) 90; *(boarding)* 30
Girls 100; *boys* 20
Fees per annum (boarding; full and weekly)
£9,075–£10,500; *(day)* £2,100–£7,050

The School is situated in a beautiful manor house in a parkland setting. Rookesbury has a happy and caring family atmosphere where each child is special. It has a flourishing Pre-Prep Department for boys and girls 3–8 and excellent facilities for science, technology, music and sport. The class sizes are small with an excellent broad based curriculum. A recent OFSTED report found that 'the School is a successful one with many good features where pupils are confident, relaxed and motivated learners who are well behaved and polite'. Excellent results at Common Entrance.

Rookwood School

✓ prelim 20.09.05 (handwritten)

Weyhill Road, Andover, Hampshire SP10 3AL
Tel: (01264) 325900   Fax: (01264) 325909   E-mail: office@rookwood.hants.sch.uk
Web site: www.rookwood.hants.sch.uk   www.gabbitas.net

Head Mrs MP Langley BSc (Hons)
Founded 1934
Type Co-educational independent pre-prep, prep and senior boarding and day
Religious denomination Non-denominational
Member of ISA, ISIS
Special needs provision DEL, DYP, DYS, HI, VIS
Age range 3–16; boarders (girls only) from 7
No of pupils (day) 309; *(boarding)* 11
Girls 213; *boys* 102; *Junior* 249; *Senior* 66
Fees per annum (boarding) £10,200–£12,000; *(day)* £870–£6,750

Rookwood School offers an excellent education throughout the school.

The co-educational Pre-preparatory and Pre-paratory School are each housed in purpose-built quarters, which enhance the teaching facilities and the disciplined and happy environment encourages all the children to give of their personal best.

The Senior School girls' excellent GCSE results are testimony to the high acdemic standards achieved in small classes taught by experienced subject specialists.

A wide range of sports and athletics cater for all abilities and interests, as do extra-curricular activities including choirs, the Duke of Edinburgh Award, Science and Engineering, Enterprise and speech and drama.

Pupils working hard and playing hard are evident everywhere, including the small boarding house with its unique family atmosphere.

Stanbridge Earls

✓ prelim 20.09.05 (handwritten)
email failed (handwritten)

Romsey, Hampshire SO51 0ZS
Tel: (01794) 516777   Fax: (01794) 511201
E-mail: stanbridgeesec@aol.com   Web site: www.gabbitas.net

Head Mr NR Hall BSc (London)
Founded 1952
Type Co-educational senior boarding and day
Religious denomination Inter-denominational
Special needs provision DYS, DYC, DYP, SP&LD, ASP, DEL, ADD, ADHD
Member of GBA, SHMIS, BSA; *corporate member* British Dyslexia Association, CReSTeD
Age range 11–18; boarders from 11
No of pupils (day) 21; *(boarding)* 175
Girls 41; *boys* 155
Junior 40; *Senior* 120; *Sixth Form* 36
Fees per annum (boarding) £14,700–£16,170; *(day)* £10,980–£12,000
Average size of class: 10
Teacher:pupil ratio: 1:6

Curriculum: all the traditional subjects are offered up to GCSE level but there is a great variety of alternatives designed to develop the strengths and interest of every pupil, such as

Drama, Craft, Design and Technology, Motor Vehicle Studies, Photography. Thirteen subjects are available at A Level. Many pupils are dyslexic but everyone takes GCSE.

Entry requirements and procedures: by interview, school report and where appropriate educational psychologists' report.

Academic and leisure facilities available: the School has excellent facilities for all academic subjects. Accelerated learning centre, with 16 experienced specialist teachers, for those with dyslexia. Maths skills centre, with 5 specialist staff, for those with dyscalculia. There is a wide choice of games and the School has a large sports hall, indoor swimming pool, squash courts, floodlit tennis courts, vehicle engineering workshops and playing fields. Sailing is done from Lymington.

The School is registered charity number 307342.

Hereford Cathedral School

✓ prelim 20.09.05
25.09.05 YES MRS SFN De.Souza

Old Deanery, Cathedral Close, Herefordshire HR1 2NG
Tel: (01432) 363522   Fax: (01432) 363525
E-mail: enquiry@cathedralschool.hereford.sch.uk
Web site: www.catherdralschool.hereford.sch.uk   www.gabbitas.net

Head HC Tomlinson BA, FRHistS
Re-founded 1384
Type Co-educational independent senior day
Religious denomination Church of England
Member of HMC, CSA
Age range 11–18
Girls 272; *boys* 322
Senior 440; *Sixth Form* 164
Fees per annum £6,390

History: Hereford Cathedral School, as other secular foundations, developed from the Song School and Library associated with the original Cathedral Church of the eighth century. The earliest extant record, however – the appointment of the first lay headmaster – is 1384. Cathedral and School remain in close harmony; morning assembly is held in the Cathedral, as are all major services and gatherings, and the choristers – who attend the Junior School – are part of the Choral Foundation that maintains the reputation for musical excellence at Hereford.

Composition/numbers: HCS is a Christian foundation in the Anglican tradition; each boy and girl is encouraged to explore Christian beliefs, although children of other faiths and different denominations are welcome. Around six hundred pupils attend the School (164 in the Sixth Form), with a further 330 (aged 3 to 11) in the Junior School, Pre-Preparatory and Nursery Class. There is boarding provision for the choristers.

Entry requirements and scholarships: admission is normally by entrance examination at 11+ or 13+, although tests can be arranged for transfer from other Schools at 12+ and 14+. Students may be admitted to the Sixth Form to take A Level courses provided they have appropriate GCSE qualifications. A substantial number of scholarships (including art and music) and fee-assisted places are awarded each year.

Pastoral care: each pupil is assigned to a personal tutor in one of the day or boarding houses. The housemaster/mistress, assisted by tutors, ensures continuity of advice and care throughout the pupil's career.

Curriculum: the School provides a broad academic base. In the first two years all pupils take English, Religious Studies, Mathematics, Latin, French, Geography, History, Information Technology, Chemistry, Physics, Biology, Technology, Music, Drama, Art, Physical Education and Games. By delaying choices for as long as possible, the aim is to enable pupils to experience subjects in depth before making their course commitments.

Sixth-Form students usually take three A Levels, most also sitting a General Studies paper. All undertake a non-specialist programme; with options including Geology, Information Technology, Current Affairs, Political Theory, Contemporary Issues in Science, German for Business, Magazine Production, Current Affairs, Linguistics, Ecology, Ethics, and Public Speaking. A strong careers team of senior staff includes 8 professional careers officers. Their advice is available throughout the School.

Music and drama: by participation in festivals and local orchestras, and the development of the Music School as focus of music-making in the community, HCS enhances the strong musical tradition of the city. Dramatic performances play an important part in School life, pupils of all ages participating in many and varied productions, including large-scale musicals.

Sport: extensive playing fields, by the River Wye, accommodate cricket, rugby and hockey pitches. The School has tennis, squash and netball courts, and a gymnasium, and the use of the city's leisure centre, all-weather athletics track and hockey pitches, swimming baths and rowing club.

Outdoor pursuits: the School has its own Scout and Venture Scout Groups, Combined Cadet Force (all three services), and is an operating authority for Duke of Edinburgh Award Scheme.

Abbot's Hill

✓ prelim 20·09·05

No

Bunkers Lane, Hemel Hempstead, Hertfordshire HP3 8RP
Tel: (01442) 839107   Fax: (01442) 269981
E-mail: cking@abbotshill.herts.sch.uk   Web site: www.abbotshill.co.uk.net   www.gabbitas.net

Head Mrs K Lewis MA
Founded 1912
Type Co educational independent pre-prep,
prep and senior boarding and day
Religious denomination Church of England
Member of GSA, GBGSA, BSA, AHIS, IAPS
Special needs provision ASP, CP, DYC, DYS, DYP,
EPI
Age range 3–16; *boarders from* 10
Girls 370; *boys* 30
Junior 210; *Senior* 190
Fees per term (boarding) (weekly) £4,500;
(day) £2,720

Abbot's Hill and its Junior School, St Nicholas
House (boys 3–7), are set in 70 acres of parklands close to London and all major motorway
networks.
The School aims to 'educate the whole
person' treating each pupil as an individual by
providing an excellent academic education,
wide ranging extracurricular activities, sport,
and pastoral care.
Weekly and flexible boarding plus day pupils
have a very full and varied school day.
We offer excellent facilities, a wide range of
subjects and dedicated teaching staff.
Abbot's Hill is a charitable trust dedicated to
educating children. Charitable trust Number
311053.

(40) Aldenham School

✓ prelim 20·09·05

Elstree, Hertfordshire WD6 3AJ   Tel: (01923) 858122   Fax: (01923) 854410
E-mail: enquiries@aldenham.com   Web site: www.aldenham.com

Head Mr RS Harman MA
Founded 1597
Type Boys' independent senior boarding and
day (co-educational in Sixth Form and pre-
prep to 7)
Religious denomination Church of England (but
all denominations accepted)
Member of HMC, SHA, GBA, ISIS
Special needs provision DYC, DYS, DYP
Age range 5–7, 11–18; *boarders from* 11
No of pupils *(day)* 305; *(boarding)* 140
Girls 20; *boys* 421; *Senior* 299; *Sixth Form* 123
Fees per annum (boarding) (full) £11,100–
£15,600; *(weekly)* £9,300–£12,900;
(day) £7,350–£10,950

Founded in 1597 Aldenham School stands in
its own 100+ acre site with modern facilities
including a new design technology and computing centre, large sports hall, refurbished
science block and newly opened floodlit artifi-
cal turf pitch and music centre. As a small
school the close knit family units in the boarding houses enable dedicated staff to be available
at all hours to help. Both flexible and weekly
boarding are available to those who live within
easy reach of Aldenham.
A wide curriculum embraces the traditional
arts, sciences and humanities, alongside the
modern subjects such as Technology, Business
Studies, Theatre Studies and Sports Science. A
personal tutor is provided for every pupil.
An extensive games and activities programme
enables every pupil to have the chance to pursue
almost any existing interest or discover something new and challenging. Football, hockey,
sailing and cricket teams are highly successful.
Strong Music and Drama Departments stage
regular productions. A Special Educational
Needs Department supports able pupils with
dyslexia and dyscalculia and provides specialist
English lessons for overseas students (ESL).
Awards for academic potential, sport, music,
art, technology are available.

The Arts Educational School, Tring Park

Tring, Hertfordshire HP23 5LX
Tel: (01442) 824255   Fax: (01442) 891069
E-mail: info@aes-tring.com   Website: www.aes.tring.com   www.gabbitas.net

Head Mrs JD Billing GGSM, CertEd, FRSA
Founded 1919
Type Co-educational independent prep and
senior boarding and day
Religious denomination Inter-denominational
Member of ISA, SHA, BSA, SHMIS
Special needs provision DYS
Age range 8–18
No of pupils (day) 84; *(boarding)* 188
Girls 233; *boys* 39
Junior 113; *Senior* 85; *Sixth Form* 74
Fees per annum (boarding) £11,772–£16,545;
(day) £6,798–£10,290

Tring Park offers exciting educational opportunities for pupils who show talent in one or more of the Performing Arts and we are committed to ensuring that all pupils fulful their potential.

The School is set in 17 acres of attractive and secluded parkland and the main house was formerly a Rothschild Mansion.

Today, the School accommodates up to 200 boarders and 90 day pupils and aims to provide an environment ideally suited to the teaching of the Performing Arts, combined with academic study to the highest level.

Tring Park is part of the Music and Dance Scheme, funded and administered by the DfES, and places are awarded annually under this scheme for talented classical dancers.

Up to the age of 14 all pupils study Dance, Music and Drama combined with a full and virgorous academic curriculum. The pupils all study eight or nine GCSE subjects combined with the Dance, Musical and Theatre or Drama course. Academic study receives equal emphasis and the department provides a broad and balanced curriculum for all pupils. Following success in the A Level examinations, many of our Sixth Form students proceed to higher vocational or academic studies at universities

and colleges. For others, the opportunity to perform becomes a reality immediately.

For those entering the Dance Course, we believe in training the whole dancer in body, mind and in artistic understanding. Dancers are encouraged to fulful their own individual potential and each pupil's progress is monitored carefully.

Those senior pupils joining the Drama Foundation Couse will undertake an intensive and wide-ranging preparation for either direct entry into the theatre, further training at drama school or, with appropriate A Levels, higher education on a relevant degree course.

The Musical Theatre Course is designed to extend the skills of the all-round performer and to focus them in this popular entertainment area.

Throughout the School, pupils have frequent opportunities to present work in Markova Theatre and there are regular public shows given by senior pupils. The range of work undertaken provides pupils with the opportunity to become versatile and able to communicate skilfully, whatever the chosen field.

Haileybury

✓ prelim 20.09.05 ✗ failed

Hertford, Hertfordshire SG13 7NU
Tel: (01992) 463353   Fax: (01992) 470663   E-mail: nickjg@haileybury.herts.sch.uk
Web site: www.haileybury.herts.sch.uk   www.gabbitas.net

Head Mr SA Westley MA
Founded 1862
Type Co-educational independent senior
boarding and day
Religious denomination Church of England
Member of HMC
Accredited by HMC
Special needs provision ADD, DYS, DYP, MLD
Age range 11–13; 13–18
No of pupils (day) 280; *(boarding)* 400
Girls 280; *boys* 400
Lower 100; *Senior* 330 *Sixth Form* 250
Fees per annum (full boarding) £17,505;
(Lower School) £11,160; *(day)* £12,750

Boys and girls, boarding and day, admitted at 11 into the Lower School; at 13 into the Main School and at 16 into the Sixth Form. Magnificent classical buildings set in a 500-acre campus of playing fields, woods and farmland. Yet only 20 miles north of central London and one hour by road from Heathrow. Combines high academic standards with a wide range of activities: especially art, music, drama and sport. Please contact the Registrar for a prospectus.

(42) Heath Mount School

✓ prelim 20.09.05
25.09.03   YES   MRS Williams

Woodhall Park, Watton-at-Stone, Hertford, Hertfordshire SG14 3NG
Tel: (01920) 830230   Fax: (01920) 830357
E-mail: office@heathmount.org   Web site: www.gabbitas.net

Head Rev HJ Matthews BSc, MA, PGCE
Founded 1817
Type Co-educational pre-prep and prep
boarding and day
Religious denomination Church of England
Member of IAPS
Special needs provision ADD (mild), DYS, DYP
Age range 3–13; *boarders from* 8–13
No of pupils (day) 289; *(boarding)* 72
Girls 143; *boys* 218
Fees per annum (boarding) £9,762–£11,325;
(day) £2,385–£8,180

Heath Mount Preparatory School, established over 175 years ago, is located at Woodhall Park, a beautiful Georgian mansion in 40 acres of private parkland. The mansion's vast cellar areas have been imaginatively converted to house up-to-date technology, art and science and computer laboratories and a flourishing Year 8 centre. The School also has its own purpose-built Pre-Prep, Sports and Dance Hall and heated swimming pool. Weekly and half-weekly boarding places are available as well as day places. Children may choose to board for 1–4 nights weekly, signing up for activity evenings run by specialists. The ethos of the school is to offer children a challenge in a happy, stress free environment

Lochinver House School

Heath Road, Potters Bar, Hertfordshire EN6 1LW
Tel: (01707) 653064   Fax: (01707) 653064   E-mail: registrar@lochinverhouse.herts.sch.uk
Web site: www.lochinverhouse.herts.sch.uk   www.gabbitas.net

Head Mr Patrick Atkinson
Founded 1947
Type Boys' independent pre-prep and prep day
Religious denomination Non-denominational
Member of IAPS; *Accredited by* ISJC
Special needs provision DEL, DYS, DYP, HI, SP&LD
Age range 4–13
No of pupils 349
Fees per annum £6,330–£7,062

A major redevelopment programme completed in 1998 has made Lochinver a school which combines modern facilities with the discipline of a traditional prep school education. Boys take Common Entrance and Scholarship exams to major public schools.

Lochinver boasts on-site playing fields and has a flourishing Music School. During his school career a boy will spend time in France and take part in outdoor pursuits courses. The cost of all curriculum related trips is covered by the fees. Lochinver has a fully integrated pastoral care system and offers a wide range of after school activities and a late-stay group for younger boys.

Queenswood

Shepherds Way, Brookmans Park, Hatfield, Hertfordshire AL9 6NS
Tel: (01707) 602500   Fax: (01707) 602597
E-mail: registry@queenswood.herts.sch.uk
Web site: www.queenswood.herts.sch.uk   www.gabbitas.net

Principal Ms Clarissa Farr, Chairman of BSA, 2001/2002
Founded 1894
Type Girls' independent senior boarding and day
Religious denomination Inter-denominational
Member of GSA, BSA
Special needs provision EFL, DYS
Age range 11–18; *boarders from* 11
No of pupils (day) 162; *(boarding)* 228
Girls 390
Senior 202; *Sixth Form* 93
Fees per annum (boarding) £15,330–£16,680; *(day)* £10,350–£11,295

Curriculum: National Curriculum adapted and enriched where educationally beneficial.
Entrance Procedures: at 11+, 13+, Common Entrance or Queenswood papers, interview and report from current Head. Into Sixth Form – examination, interview and report from current Head. A Queenswood Sixth Former will normally have achieved at least 6 B grades at GCSE, with A* or A grades in the subjects to be studied at A, A/S Level.
Academic and Leisure Facilities: purpose built teaching block with departmental suites. Individual study carrels. Campus-wide IT network. Clay court tennis centre. Gymnasium, weights and fitness studios, indoor swimming pool, athletics field. 120 acres of woodlands.
Scholarships: academic, music, creative arts, tennis, hockey, PE, Sixth Form and all rounder scholarships, bursaries.
Boarding facilities: Junior House for all Year 7. Sixth Form Houses. Newly refurbished mixed age houses for Years 8 to 11.

The Royal Masonic School for Girls
prelim 20.09.05

Rickmansworth Park, Rickmansworth, Hertfordshire WD3 4HF
Tel: (01923) 773168　Fax: (01923) 896729　E-mail: enquiries@royalmasonic.herts.sch.uk
Web site: www.royalmasonic.herts.sch.uk　www.gabbitas.net

Head Mrs D Rose MA(Cantab)
Founded 1788
Type Girls' independent pre prep, prep and senior boarding and day
Religious denomination Church of England
Member of GSA, GBSA
Special needs provision mild DYS
Age range 4–18; *boarders from* 7
No of pupils (day) 575; *(boarding)* 250
Junior 200; *Senior* 410; *Sixth Form* 155
Fees per annum (boarding) (full) £11,982
(senior) £7,374 *(junior) (day)* £3,753–£7,290

The School has exceptional facilities including good laboratories, an attractive, circular library and separate areas for ICT, music, drama, craft, art and design. Sporting facilities include a sports hall, indoor swimming pool, tennis courts and superb playing fields.

A wide-ranging curriculum is supported by a fully qualified staff. A favourable staff:pupil ratio ensures that pupils get much individual attention.

Rickmansworth is close to the M25 and London is easily accessible.

Boarding pupils are cared for in well-appointed and spacious Houses. In each House there is a balanced number of boarders and day pupils.

Admission is by the School's own entrance examination and interview. A number of generous scholarships are available.

(45) St Albans High School for Girls
prelim 20-09-05
Yes MRS. Alison Chapman

Townsend Avenue, St Albans, Hertfordshire AL1 3SJ
Tel: (01727) 853800　Fax: (01727) 792516　E-mail: Admissions@stalbans-high.herts.sch.uk
Web site: www.sahs.org.uk　www.gabbitas.net

Head Mrs CY Daly BSc, FRSA
Founded 1889
Type Girls' independent pre-prep, prep and senior day
Religious denomination Church of England
Member of GSA, GBGSA, ISIS
Special needs provision DYS (mild); other special needs may be accommodated but it depends on the individual case
Age range 4–18; *No of pupils* 857
Junior 252; *Senior* 432; *Sixth Form* 173
Fees per annum (senior school) £6,810;
(junior house) £5,655;
(reception class) £5,355 (inc. lunch)

Curriculum: a broad and balanced academic education is provided to include National Curriculum subjects and others. Teaching methods are modern and extensive use is made of resources such as computers and audio-video equipment. Public examination results at GCSE and A Level are of a consistently high standard and for the vast majority, degree courses follow.

Entry requirements and examinations: entry is by examination at 4, 7, 11 and 16 with intermediate ages, subject to vacancies.

Academic and leisure facilities: a wide range of extra-curricular activities are offered with sport, music and drama featuring strongly. Facilities for physical education include a sports hall and playing fields.

Scholarships/bursaries: academic and music scholarships are available on entry at 11, 13 and further academic scholarships at 16.

St Christopher School

(46)

✓ prelim 20.09.03

Barrington Road, Letchworth, Hertfordshire SG4 9AQ
Tel: (01462) 679301   Fax: (01462) 481578
E-mail: Stchris.admin@rmplc.co.uk   Web site: www.stchris.co.uk   www.gabbitas.net

Head Colin Reid MA
Founded 1915
Type Co-educational independent pre-prep, prep and senior boarding and day
Religious denomination Non-denominational
Member of GBA, SHMIS; *accredited by* ISC
Special needs provision DYS, DYP
Age range 3–18; *boarders from* 8–18
No of pupils 592; *(day)* 480; *(boarding)* 112
Girls 249; *boys* 343
Junior 178; *Senior* 301; *Sixth Form* 88
Fees per annum (full boarding) £15,300; *(day)* £2,040–£8,700 *(senior)*

St Christopher School is situated in Letchworth, 35 miles north of London on the A1(M) with easy access to the M25 and all major airports. The fast trains from Kings Cross take 30 minutes. There is a domestic village atmosphere with most of the buildings in the 'Garden City' idiom and surrounded by attractive grounds.

The School provides a complete education from infancy to adulthood. Children of one family, whatever their ages, can attend the same school. The School provides day as well as boarding pupils with a wide range of opportunity throughout every day of the week.

Boarders live in family-style houses having breakfast, evening meal and supper with their houseparents. The diet is vegetarian. There is a strong community feel and many staff live in or adjacent to the School with their own children attending.

The School has long been noted for the value it places on the individual and for the encouragement of self-confidence. It attracts children (and parents) with strong independent attitudes and many children who need to be valued for themselves flourish at St Christopher. There is no school uniform worn apart from in games and all are referred to by first names.

The teaching is of a high standard and academic results are creditable. Most sixth formers proceed to a degree course and the School gives careful advice on future plans. St Christopher does not believe in artificial competition in academic work; thus there are no subject or form orders and no prizes.

The School is strong in the creative and performing arts as well as the core academic subjects such as Science. There are excellent, purpose-built music and technology facilities, a superb theatre and a new 25m indoor swimming pool.

There is a very wide range of sports, games and extra-curricular courses with a special emphasis on outdoor pursuits such as climbing, walking, camping and orienteering. There are major expeditions for all in each year group and regular weekend trips.

The School has strong local support and pupils are involved in a range of ventures among the local community. There are strong international links and regular exchanges with schools in France, Germany and Spain and visits by Sixth Formers to development projects in India.

St Edmund's College

prelim 20·09·05

Old Hall Green, Ware, Hertfordshire SG11 1DS
Tel: (01920) 824247   Fax: (01920) 823011   E-mail: admissions@stedmundscollege.org
Web site: www.stedmundscollege.org   www.gabbitas.net

Head DJJ McEwen
Founded 1568
Type Co-educational independent prep and senior boarding and day
Religious denomination Roman Catholic
Member of HMC, GBA; *accredited by* DfEE, British Council
Special needs provision DYS
Age range 3–18; *boarders from* 11
No of pupils (day) 440; *(boarding)* 160
Girls 260; *boys* 340
Junior 180; *Senior* 370; *Sixth Form* 130
Fees per annum (boarding) (full) £12,030–£13,605; *(weekly)* £11,160–£12,675; *(day)* £4,755–£8,520

England's oldest Catholic school, the College is in 400 acres of private parkland, halfway between central London and Cambridge, with London Stanstead airport only 15 minutes away.

Computers and science laboratories, art/technology workshops, indoor heated pool and multi-sports hall. AVCE courses in Business and Art/Design alongside traditional range of AS and A2 Levels. In 2001 96 per cent of graduates took up university places. Day pupils and boarders accepted. High level of pastoral care. Twin or single bedrooms. Wide range of extra-curricular sports and activities. Full English language support across the curriculum for overseas students and international; summer school in July/August.

St Martha's Senior School

no email

Camlet Way, Hadley, Barnet, Hertfordshire EN5 5PX
Tel: (020) 8449 6889   Fax: (020) 8441 5632
Web site: www.gabbitas.net

Head Miss C Burke MA
Founded 1947
Type Girls' independent senior day
Religious denomination Roman Catholic
Special needs provision DEL, DYS, EPI
Age range 11–18
No of pupils 320
Senior 280; *Sixth Form* 40
Fees per annum £5,100

St Martha's Senior School is a Catholic foundation under the direction of the Sisters of St Martha, which exists in order to promote the spiritual, aesthetic, intellectual and physical well-being of every girl put into its care, in the spirit of the Gospel. Girls are selected through an entrance examination and are placed in one of two parallel forms in which they will remain for the first five years. At the end of Year 7 (first year) girls are placed in different groups, based on ability for French, Mathematics and Science.

During the first three years pupils follow a common academic and creative course which includes all the requirements of the National Curriculum, with additions. At the end of Year 11 GCSE is taken, normally in at least eight subjects. Girls who wish to stay on then enter the Sixth Form, and can follow a wide variety of courses leading to A Levels.

Stanborough School

prelim. 20.09.05
email add ?

Stanborough Park, Garston, Watford, Hertfordshire WD25 9JT
Tel: (01923) 673268   Fax: (01923) 893943
Email: stanboroughpark.herts.sch.uk   Web site: www.gabbitas.net

Head Mr S Rivers
Founded 1902
Type Co-educational independent
Religious denomination Seventh Day Adventist
Member of ISA; *accredited by* ISC
Special needs provision EFL
Age range 3–18; *boarders from* 11
No of pupils (day) 230; *(boarding)* 70
Girls 130; *boys* 170
Junior 150; *Senior* 150; *Sixth Form* 20
Fees per annum (full boarding) £11,000–£13,000, *(weekly)* £9,000–£10,500; *(day)* £3,000–£6,000

History: Stanborough began as a co-educational school for the children of Missionaries. Its well-disciplined, caring environment provides the opportunity for each pupil to achieve excellence. Today, the school is home to pupils from over 40 nationalities.

Location: Stanborough is set in over 40 acres of parkland, located just 20 minutes from London.
Facilities: There are separate buildings for pre-prep, prep and the senior school. The school facilities are classically modern, with the boarding house exclusively offering twin en-suite rooms. Extensive playing fields accommodate cricket, hockey, football, tennis and volleyball. There is a purpose built gymnasium, Information Technology and Design suites, Languages Laboratories, Science and Music suites.
Entry Requirements: Admission by informal interview for pre-prep, formal interview and examination at 8+, 11+ or 13+. Advanced level admission is by 6 GCSE grades A to C.

Bedgebury School

Goudhurst, Kent TN17 2SH
Tel: (01580) 211221   Fax: (01580) 212252
E-mail: info@bedgeburyschool.co.uk   Web site: www.bedgeburyschool.co.uk

✓ prelim 20-09-05
Yes MRs Tina Budd

Head Mrs Hilary Moriarty MA
Founded 1920
Type Girls' independent pre-prep, prep and senior boarding and day
Religious denomination Church of England
Member of GSA, GBSA, ISIS
Special needs provision DYS, DYP
Age range 2½–18; boarders from 8
No of pupils (day) 228; *(boarding) (full)* 57; *(weekly)* 74
Fees per annum (boarding) £9,960–£15,120; *(day)* £2,280–£9,390

The broad education Bedgebury offers builds confidence, inspires enthusiasm and delivers achievement. The Senior School, accommodated in and around a 17th century mansion, is for girls aged from 11 upwards; the Junior School, built in 1998, is for children aged from 2½–11. Outstanding facilities include a 22 acre lake for watersports, an assault course, climbing wall and abseil tower. The art centre has studios for art, ceramics, jewellery and design technology. There is a dedicated information and communication technology centre. The riding centre, with stabling for 60 horses, has two indoor and one outdoor school and a full cross country course in the 206 acres of parkland surrounding the School.

Beechwood Sacred Heart

v. prelim 23.09.05
email failed X

12 Pembury Road, Tunbridge Wells, Kent TN2 3QD
Tel: (01892) 532747   Fax: (01892) 536164
E-mail: bsh@beechwood.org.uk   Web site: www.beechwood.org.uk   www.gabbitas.net

Head Mr NR Beesley
Founded 1915
Type Girls' independent prep and senior boarding and day (co-educational prep)
Religious denomination Catholic
Member of GSA, BSA, CISC, ISIS
Special needs provision ADD, DYC, DYS, DYP, SPLD
Age range 3–18 (boys 3–11); *boarders from* 9
No of pupils (day) 267; *(boarding)* 68
Junior 190; *Senior* 145; *Sixth Form* 40
Fees per annum (boarding) £13,950; *(weekly)* £12,405; *(day)* £8,550

General: Founded in 1915 by the Society of the Sacred Heart, Beechwood is now an independent GSA day and boarding school for girls aged 11–18, with its own integral Preparatory School for boys and girls aged 3–11. The school is set in the extensive and beautiful grounds of an elegant Victorian mansion, yet within walking distance of the railway station and centre of Royal Tunbridge Wells, ideally situated near London, main airports and channel ports.

Beechwood is a happy, friendly school in which every pupil is known and valued. We believe in maintaining traditional values whilst always looking to keep up with modern innovations and developments. We are firmly committed to the single-sex education of girls at secondary level, as we believe that this provides for them a secure environment in which their educational and pastoral needs can be met most effectively. The school is non-selective academically, selection for entry being based on interview and previous school report.

Our own integrated Learning Support Unit provides qualified assessment and support for pupils with specific learning difficulties.

Examination results: A broad curriculum is followed throughout the School. Small classes and committed, professional staff produce excellent results at all levels.

Most recent results: 100 per cent grade A–C pass-rate at GCSE; 90 per cent pass rate, 21.2 points per candidate at A Level, five year A Level average 21.4 points per candidate.

Nearly all Sixth Form leavers proceed to higher education at art college or university.

School facilities: Academic facilities include library, up-to-date computer room, modern well-equipped science building, language and business centre.

Sports facilities include hockey and football pitches, netball and tennis courts, heated outdoor swimming pool, gymnasium.

Sports and activities: We encourage our pupils to participate in a wide variety of sporting experiences. The emphasis is always on fun and participation, although we also achieve considerable competitive success, being the current Kent County basketball champions.

There is also an extensive programme of extra-curricular activities after school and at weekends. The extended day (activities until 6pm) and flexi-boarding provide valuable support for working parents.

Bickley Park School

24 Page Heath Lane, Bickley, Bromley, Kent BR1 2DS
Tel: (020) 8467 2195   Fax: (020) 8325 5511
E-mail: info@bickleyparkschool.co.uk   Web site: bickleyparkschool.co.uk   www.gabbitas.net

Head Mr M Bruce
Founded 1918
Type Boys' (girls 2–5) independent pre prep and prep day
Religious denomination Non-denominational
Member of IAPS, NAHT, SATIPS
Accredited by ISC
Special needs provision DYS, DYP, MLD
Age range 2½–13+
No of pupils 440; *Girls* 30; *boys* 420
Fees per annum (pre-prep) from £2,415;
(prep) from £5,700

Our Nursery, warm and stimulating, guides children through early stages of learning towards a firm foundation in basic literacy and numeracy whilst encouraging social development. In Pre-Prep a class-teacher approach is blended with the start of additional specialist taught subjects.

In the Prep School, reached at age 7 onwards, academic abilities and talents are further nurtured by the deployment of specialists across the curriculum. Drama, music and sport are energetically encouraged.

The curriculum prepares pupils for scholarship/Common Entrance exams to senior schools at 13+, although some boys leave for appropriate schools at 11.

Breaside Preparatory School

41 Orchard Road, Bromley, Kent BR1 2PR
Tel: (020) 8460 0916   Fax: (020) 8466 5664

Head R O'Doherty BA(Hons), MA, CertEd
Founded 1950
Type Co-educational independent pre-prep and prep day
Religious denomination Inter-denominational
Head is a member of NAHT, SATIPS
Special needs provision DYS
Age range 3–11+
No of pupils 300
Girls 98; *boys* 202
Fees per annum £2,730–£5,010

Breaside is a co-educational school with a well-established reputation for friendliness and high achievement. On the Chislehurst side of Bromley it is easily reached from many parts of south-east London.

Curriculum: a strong emphasis is placed on individual attention in small classes. Children are prepared for all senior schools and those with additional promise sit scholarships. The broadly based curriculum aims to help children fulfil their potential. French is taught from Reception and pupils are able to participate in the many games, clubs and activities. The School is well resourced and enjoys the support of belonging to Asquith Court Schools Ltd.

Entry requirements: interview and test after 5 years of age. The School is well worth a visit to experience the busy, caring environment which its dedicated staff create.

51

Cobham Hall

Cobham, Gravesend, Kent DA12 3BL
Tel: (01474) 823371   Fax: (01474) 825906
E-mail: cobhamhall@aol.com   Web site: www.cobhamhall.com

melin 23.09.05
email failed

Head Mrs Rosalind McCarthy BA
Founded 1962
Type Girls' independent boarding and day
Religious denomination Inter-denominational
Member of GSA, BSA, Round Square
Special needs provision ADD, DYC, DYS, DYP
Age range 11–18; *boarders from* 11
No of pupils (day) 70; *(boarding)* 130
Sixth Form 60
Fees per annum (boarding) £14,100–£16,200;
(day) £8,850–£10,950

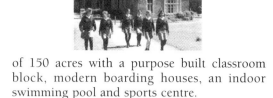

One of Britain's leading girls' schools, Cobham Hall promotes excellence in all subjects and enables the majority of students to proceed to higher education. Specialist help is provided for dyslexic students and our EFL Department offers overseas students intensive language training.

The School is housed in a beautiful 16th century mansion set in landscaped parkland of 150 acres with a purpose built classroom block, modern boarding houses, an indoor swimming pool and sports centre.

Membership of Round Square, an affiliation which unites schools around the world, provides the opportunity for international exchanges.

Cobham Hall is situated 25 miles from central London, with easy access to International airports.

Combe Bank School

Sundridge, Sevenoaks, Kent TN14 6AE
Tel: (01959) 563720   Fax: (01959) 561997
E-mail: enquiries@combebank.kent.sch.uk   Web site: www.combebank.kent.sch.uk

Head Mrs R Martin
Head (preparatory) Mrs R Cranfield
Founded 1972
Type Girls' independent prep and senior day
co-educational Nursery
Religious denomination Ecumenical Catholic
Foundation
Member of GSA, GBGSA, ISIS
Age range 3–18 Boys 3–5 only
Junior 200; *Senior* 230; *Sixth Form* 50
Fees per annum (day) £3,000–£7,845

The decision which faces you is one of the most important in your daughter's life.

Here at Combe Bank we enjoy a tradition of high standards and commitment to care.

Our beautiful surroundings, excellent facilities and dedicated staff, together with the advantages of small class sizes, enable girls of all abilities to become achievers in the academic, sports and creative fields.

The social and moral values, which are taught within our broad and balanced curriculum, help to promote confidence, direction, and lead to a well rounded personality. The important skills and lessons learnt during a girl's education at Combe Bank provide a solid foundation which she carries with her for the rest of her life.

KENT

Cranbrook School

Cranbrook, Kent TN17 3JD
Tel: (01580) 711800   Fax: (01580) 711828
E-mail: registrar@cranbrook.kent.sch.uk
Web site: www.cranbrook.kent.sch.uk   www.gabbitas.net

Handwritten notes: ✓ Prelim 23.09.05
25.09.05 Yes Danielle Parker
Mactachini@cranbrook.kent.sch.uk

Head Mrs A Daly
Founded 1518
Type Co-educational voluntary-aided senior boarding and day
Religious denomination Non-denominational
Special needs provision DYS
Age range 13–18; *boarders from* 13
No of pupils (day) 470; *(boarding)* 245
Girls 312; *boys* 403
Senior 413; *Sixth Form* 290+
Fees per annum (boarding) £6,450

Cranbrook is a co-educational boarding and day school offering a superb all-round education at a very reasonable cost with a wide range of extra-curricular activities in a small country town setting in the beautiful Kentish Weald.

High academic standards of 99 per cent A–C grades at GCSE and 99 per cent pass rate (59 per cent A/B grades) at A Level. 95 per cent of students go on to university/polytechnic.

Music, art and drama thrive and teams compete at the highest levels in all major sports. Musical activities include an orchestra and choral society; many productions for music and drama are held in our superb theatre. Cranbrook has fine facilities for the creative arts including the new design/technology centre. Cranbrook has plentiful playing fields, a swimming pool, sports hall and astro-turf pitches.

Entry at 13+ and 16+ by interview and examination. Details from the Registrar, Cranbrook School. Cranbrook School (VA) exists to promote education in Cranbrook.

Dover College

Effingham Crescent, Dover, Kent CT17 9RH
Tel: (01304) 205969   Fax: (01304) 242208
E-mail: registrar@dovercollege.demon.co.uk
Web site: www.dover-college.kent.sch.uk   www.gabbitas.net

prelim 23.09.05.
e-mail failed ??

Head HW Blackett MA
Founded 1871
Type Co-educational independent prep and senior boarding and day
Religious denomination Church of England
Member of SHMIS
Special needs provision ADD, DYS, DYP, EFL
Age range 7–18; *boarders from* 11
No of pupils (day) 182; *(boarding)* 100
Girls 116; *boys* 166
Senior 170; *Sixth Form* 80
Fees per annum (boarding) £11,178–£14,250;
(weekly) £10,440–£11,220;
(day) £4,050–£8,328

Founded in 1871, Dover College occupies a beautiful 12th century Priory site. The College Close with its medieval and modern buildings creates an attractive enclosed haven of tranquility and learning. Pupils still use the original 12th Century Refectory and Chapel.

Academic Life: Great importance is placed upon literacy, numeracy, information technology and key skills in all years. 4th and 5th form pupils study between six and ten GCSE subjects. Emphasis is placed upon the breadth of education offered: music, art and drama are an integral part of the curriculum and all pupils participate in a variety of sports. Class sizes are small.

Sixth Form: Pupils are able to choose AS/A Levels from a list of 20 subjects. AVCE Business Studies is also on offer and from September 2002 AVCE Leisure and Tourism will be available. The School works in close liaison with Kent Careers Services, to deliver careers education and guidance, enabling pupils to make informed career plans before attending university.

Sport: The School's playing fields are a short distance away. On-site are tennis courts, a modern sports hall and a new astro-turf facility. Swimming takes place at the local indoor swimming pool. Golf and riding are offered locally.

Pastoral Care: Each pupil belongs to a House and boarders reside in one of three boarding houses. A Housemaster/mistress, supported by a team of tutors, runs each House. It is their role to give pastoral support as well as supervising their academic progress.

The International Study Centre: This new centre provides intensive English courses for pupils whose first language is not English. These courses enable pupils to integrate fully into the life of Dover College quickly after their arrival.

Recent Developments: A new computer centre giving pupils regular access to the Internet and e-mail, Junior Department, introduction of football as the major sport during the Michaelmas term, an eleven day timetable, with every other weekend as an activities weekend, and a fully equipped dance studio.

Location: Dover College is the closest school to continental Europe, with easy access via the Eurotunnel. Good rail and road links are within easy reach of the school, making London and the major airports very accessible.

Dulwich Preparatory School, Cranbrook

Coursehorn, Cranbrook, Kent TN17 3NP
Tel: (01580) 712179   Fax: (01580) 715322
E-mail: registrar@dcpskent.org   Web site: www.dcpskent.org

Head MC Wagstaffe
Founded 1939
Type Co-educational independent pre-prep,
prep and boarding and day
Religious denomination Church of England
Member of IAPS
Special needs provision Gifted children catered
for, remedial and dyslexia help given. Several
staff specifically trained.
Age range 3–13; *boarders from* 8
No of pupils (day) 499; *(boarding)* 44
Girls 237; *boys* 306
Fees per annum (boarding) £11,985–£12,300;
(day) £2,805–£8,160

The School is fully co-educational, taking
pupils on a first come, first served basis. There
is a strong academic tradition enabling children
to achieve scholarships to top senior schools,
with special needs help offered to those with
learning difficulties. There is an emphasis on
up-to-date teaching and the School has
achieved notable successes in music and art.
Entry: at 3+ and 4; by testing from 7+ onwards.
Curriculum: National Curriculum followed.
Usual subjects taught, plus French, Art, DT,
Drama, IT, Music and Physical Education.
Examinations offered: pupils prepare for 11+,
Common Entrance and scholarships.
Academic and leisure facilities: Music School, IT
& CDT centre. Theatre/Art Room block under
construction. All-weather pitches, athletics
track, playing fields, tennis courts, sports hall
complex, two swimming pools.
Boarding facilities: from age 8, in two houses.
Six to eight pupils in each dormitory. Travel to/
from airports arranged, plus train travel to/from
London escorted by staff.
Special needs: gifted children catered for. Reme-
dial and dyslexia help given. Several staff
specially trained.

(54) Farringtons and Stratford House

prelim 23.09.05
Replied - No

Perry Street, Chislehurst, Kent BR7 6LR
Tel: (020) 8467 0256   Fax: (020) 8467 5442   E-mail: admissions@farringtons.kent.sch.uk
Website: www.farringtons.org.uk   www.gabbitas.net

Head Mrs CE James MA
Founded 1911
Type Girls' independent pre-prep, prep and
senior boarding and day
Religious denomination Methodist but all
denominations welcome
Member of GSA, GBGSA, ISIS
Special needs provision DYS (mild); ESOL
Age range 2½–18; *boarders from* 7
No of pupils (day) 425; *(boarding)* 66
Junior 240; *Senior* 228; *Sixth Form* 40
Fees per annum (boarding) (full) £12,990–
£14,340; *(weekly)* £12,450–£13,860;
(day) £5,100–£7,290

Farringtons & Stratford House is a warm and
friendly school with a Christian perspective
situated within a beautiful location in Kent.
We have a wide ability intake and a commitment to stretch every girl to the very best of her
ability. We are proud of the way we educate our
girls, combining traditional values with the
skills required for the 21st century.
We are able to boast a range of facilities including: a new computer suite, impressive sports
hall with dance studio and weights room, a
technology centre and a swimming pool.
Our boarding Facilities have just been
refurbished giving girls comfortable study-
bedrooms all freshly decorated with new
carpets, curtains and modern furniture.
Farringtons & Stratford House is situated on a
beautiful 25 acre site in a peaceful Kent village:
yet it is a mere 12 miles from central London. It
is also ideally located close to airports and
the M25.

Kent College

Whitstable Road, Canterbury, Kent, CT2 9DT
Tel: (01227) 763231   Fax: (01227) 787450
E-mail: name@kc-canterbury.kent.sch.uk   Web site: www.kentcollege.co.uk   www.gabbitas.net

Prelim 23.09.05
email failed. X

Head Mr EB Halse
Founded 1885
Type Co-educational independent pre-prep, prep and senior boarding and day
Religious denomination Methodist
Member of HMC, IAPS
Special needs provision DYS
Age range 3–18; *boarders from* 7
No of pupils (day) 557; *(boarding)* 139
Juniors 236; *Senior* 320; *Sixth Form* 140
Fees per annum (full boarding) £15,780; *(day)* £8,790

Kent College is a vibrant coeducational boarding and day school taking children from age 3–18 years. Based in rural surroundings, yet only minutes walk from the historic city centre of Canterbury, you can be assured your child will be able to fulfil their potential, whether it be in the classroom, on the playing fields or in an orchestra or on the stage. Together with the multitude of extra curricular activities life at Kent College is the ideal preparation for university and beyond.

Our International Study Centre provides an environment in which language skills can be developed. We ensure each student is totally involved/engaged socially and educationally.

With extensive facilities including a school farm, we feel well placed to offer a complete service to pupils and parents alike.

Visit us and you'll be convinced!

Northbourne Park School

Betteshanger, Deal, Kent CT14 0NW
Tel: (01304) 611215/611218   Fax: (01304) 619020
E-mail: office@northbourne.kent.sch.uk   Web site: www.northbourne.kent.sch.uk

Head Stephen Sides
Founded 1936
Type Co-educational independent pre-prep and prep boarding and day
Religious denomination Church of England
Member of IAPS, ISIS, BSA
Provision offered for special needs ADD, ADHD, ASP, DYS, DYP, SP&LD, SPLD
Age range 3–13; *boarders from* 7
No of pupils (day) 162; *(boarding)* 49
Junior 51; *Senior* 160
Fees per annum (boarding) (full) £10,260–£12,555; *(weekly)* pro rata; *(day)* £4,740–£8,040

Set in beautiful parklands in the Kentish countryside, there is easy access to Dover and the continent, and Gatwick and London are within an 80-minute drive. An eleven day teaching cycle has enabled pupils to spend a long weekend at home once a fortnight. Many English and French pupils commute from Brussels and Paris on this basis. There are 25 French children and several bilingual families within the school community.

Curriculum/Academic: we prepare children for Common Entrance and individual scholarship examinations. French is taught from age 3. A unique Anglo-French programme is producing bilingual pupils. Spanish is taught from age 9 and German is offered as a club. Information technology is used in most subjects. Academic, choral, music, art and sports scholarships awarded.

Rochester Independent College ✓ Prelim 23·09·05

Star Hill, Rochester, Kent ME1 1XF
Tel: (01634) 828115   Fax: (01634) 405667
E-mail: rochester@mcmail.com   Web site: www.rochester-college.org   www.gabbitas.net

Head Mr B Pain   Mr S de Belder
Founded 1985
Type Independent co-educational senior
boarding and day
Religious denomination Non-denominational
Accredited by BAC
Special needs DYS
Age range 14–20; *boarders from* 16
No of pupils 220
Girls 110; *boys* 100; *No of boarders (full)* 55
Fees per annum (day) £9,300;
(full) £14,340–£15,270

Very small classes together with the enthusiasm of the well-qualified and experienced teachers create a stimulating and enjoyable learning environment. Students who have fun learning, usually achieve excellent results, and in the process gain the confidence to apply for excellent degree courses leading to interesting and exciting careers.

The well-equipped and specially converted listed buildings in the heart of Rochester contain all the facilities required for the wide range of subjects offered at both GCSE and A level for day students and those accommodated in the excellent Halls of Residence. There is also an on-site School of English.

St Lawrence College

Ramsgate, Kent CT11 7AE
Tel: (01843) 592680   Fax: (01843) 851123
E-mail: Headmaster.SLC@dial.pipex.com
Web site: www.st-lawrence-college.com   www.gabbitas.net

Headmaster Mark Slater MA
Founded 1879
Type Co-educational independent junior,
middle and senior boarding and day
Religious denomination Church of England
Member of HMC, IAPS, ISIS
Special needs provision ADD, DYC, DYS, DYP,
EPI, HI, EFL
Age range 3–18; *boarders from* 7
No of pupils (day) 240; *(boarding)* 240
Girls 241; *boys* 239
Junior 100; *Senior* 320; *Sixth Form* 60
Fees per annum (boarding) (full/weekly)
£12,480–£16,560; *(day)* £4,494–£10,632

A busy, thriving, family community, the College
provides a highly successful combination of
modern facilities, academic excellence and a
strong Christian ethos.

An approachable friendly school at which we
listen to the voices of parents and children alike
– justifiably proud of its high academic standards, wide range of cultural and sporting
opportunities, its excellent facilities and exceptionally caring pastoral emphasis. Our main
aim is to draw out the talents of each individual, within a Christian framework which will
serve to guide them throughout their lives.

Our academic track record is impressive, with
95 per cent of all Senior School pupils going on
to the university of their first or second choice
and several successful Oxbridge candidates
most years. There is a wide range of subjects
offered at GCSE and A Level. Class sizes are
small, on average 15 pupils at the Junior School
and 15 pupils at the Senior School, which
encourages more efficient learning.

St Mary's Westbrook

Ravenlea Road, Folkestone, Kent CT20 2JU
Tel: (01303) 854006   Fax: (01303) 249901
E-mail: hm@st-marys-westbrook.co.uk
Web site: www.st-marys-westbrook.co.uk   www.gabbitas.net

Head Mrs LA Watson
Type Co-educational independent boarding and day
Religious denomination All denominations
Member of IAPS, ISA, BSA, Cobisec
Special needs provision ADD, ADHD, ASP, AUT, DYS, DYP, MLD, W
Age range 2–16; *boarders from* 7
No of pupils (day) 241; *(boarding)* 43
Girls 119; *boys* 165
Junior 136; *Senior* 87
Fees per annum (boarding) (full) £10,473–£11,544; *(day)* £4,347–£7,686

St Mary's Westbrook is a co-educational boarding and day school for pupils aged 2 to 16. There is a flourishing Montessori Kindergarten for children aged 2 to 4 and a Pre-Prep Department for children aged 4 to 7.

The curriculum is broad and balanced, with excellent support given by the Skills Development Department. The average class size is 15. English as a Foreign Language is offered and the School has a comprehensive extra-curricular programme.

There are strong musical and sporting traditions. The School prepares students for GCSE examinations and accepts pupils of all ages.

(58)

Sevenoaks School

Sevenoaks, Kent TN13 1HU
Tel: 01732 455133   Fax: 01732 456143
E-mail: regist@soaks.org   Web site: www.soaks.org   www.gabbitas.net

√ Prelim 23.09.05
29/09/05 Yes Simon Carr
Head of Classics

Head TR Cookson MA
Founded 1432
Type Co-educational independent senior
boarding and day
Religious denomination Inter-denominational
Member of HMC
Special needs provision DYS, VIS
Age range 11–18; *boarders from* 11
No of pupils (day) 627; *(boarding)* 333
Girls 456; *boys* 504
Junior 119; *Senior* 420; *Sixth Form* 421
Fees per annum (boarding) £16,194;
(day) £9,873

Sevenoaks is a co-educational, independent, day and boarding school, situated next to the 1,000 acres of Knole Park, 30 minutes from central London and Gatwick Airport, and an hour from Heathrow. Approximately one-third of the 960 students are boarders. Pupils worldwide enter at 11, 13 or 16, taking GCSEs and the International Baccalaureate. Sevenoaks aspires to high academic standards–all students proceed to Oxbridge and major universities–while providing excellent facilities for sport and extra-curricular activities. More than 50 scholarships are awarded annually for academic excellence, art, music and all-round ability. Prospectus and further details from the Registrar.

(59)

Sutton Valence School

Sutton Valence, Maidstone, Kent ME17 3HN
Tel: (01622) 842281   Fax: (01622) 844093
E-mail: enquiries@svs.org.uk   Web site: www.svs.org.uk   www.gabbitas.net

√ Prelim 23.09.05
Yes Kevin Jones.

Head Mr JS Davies
Founded 1576
Type Co-educational independent pre-prep,
prep and senior boarding and day
Religious denomination Church of England
Member of HMC
Special needs provision DYS, DYP
Age range 3–18; *boarders from* 9
No of pupils Senior (day) 311; *(boarding)* 129
Girls 146; *boys* 294; *Junior: girls* 147; *boys* 204
Sixth Form 120
Fees per annum (full boarding) £16,260;
(day) £10,260 *(Junior) (prep)* £2,000

Sutton Valence aims to provide the best academic education possible for each of our pupils while giving them a wide range of extra-curricular and sporting activities designed to develop their talents.

The school is located on a 100 acre site in the safe and picturesque village of Sutton Valence with excellent facilities including a new sports hall. We have a junior boarding house for boys and girls aged 9–13.

We are proud of our success and welcome enquires and visits from prospective parents and pupils. Entrance is by our own examination or common entrance at 11+, 13+ and at 16+. Scholarships are awarded for academic performance, music, art, drama, sport and all-rounder.

Brooke House College

✓ Prelim 23·09·05

Leicester Road, Market Harborough, Leicestershire LE16 7AU
Tel: (01858) 462452   Fax: (01858) 462487
E-mail: brookehse@aol.com   Web site: www.brookehouse.com

Head Mr JC Stanford BA PGCE
Founded 1967
Type Independent co-educational boarding and day
Religious denominations Non-denominational
Special needs provision SP&LD English as a foreign language
Member of CIFE
Accredited by BAC
Age range 14–19; *boarders from* 14
No of pupils 150; *(boarding)* 150
Girls 65; *boys* 85
Fees per annum (boarding) £13,860; *(day)* £9,000

Brooke House is a fully-residential, international college. Intensive, small group tuition is provided by GCSE, 'A' Level and pre-University Foundation courses. The college possesses excellent academic facilities including science laboratories, an art and design studio and a recently-developed computer room. A comprehensive programme of extra-curricular activities is organized for students' free-time. Personal tutors cater for every student's pastoral needs. The college's full-time Universities Admissions Adviser gives advice and guidance. Brooke House has an enviable tradition of assisting international and UK students to gain places at the most prestigious of universities in the UK and the USA.

Irwin College

✓ Prelim · 23·09·05 email failed ✗

164 London Road, Leicester, Leicestershire LE2 1ND
Tel: (0116) 255 2648   Fax: (0116) 285 4935
E-mail: irwin_college@lineone.net   Web site: www.cife.org.uk/irwin/index.htm

Head Mr Stephen Wytcherley
Founded 1972
Type Co-educational independent college of further education, senior boarding and day
Religious Denomination Non-denominational
Member of CIFE
Accredited by BACIFHE
Special needs provision MLD
Age range 14–25; *boarders from* 14
No of pupils (day) 10; *(boarding)* 100
Girls 40; *boys* 70
Senior 40; *Sixth Form* 100
Fees per annum (full boarding) £10,950 *(day)* £4,950

Irwin College offers examination courses for UK and overseas students in GCSE, A and AS Levels, accredited University Foundation Study Courses (guaranteed entry to selection of UK universities on successful completion of the course), Foundation Course in Medical Studies guarantees a place in a registered medical school in the Czech Republic on successful completion. Full academic and pastoral supervision, requiring committed and conscientious study in a warm, friendly and supportive environment with due care shown to all cultural requirements. The College is located opposite a large park near the centre of Leicester, with three supervised comfortable residences five minutes away. Each student has a personal tutor available for consultation over university entrance, careers and personal matters. Classes are small. Full social and sporting programmes. Full English Language courses to IELTS examination.

Oakham School

√ Prelim 23-09-05
Yes. Head of Classics
Holly Eckhardt

Chapel Close, Oakham, Rutland LE15 6DT
Tel: (01572) 758758   Fax: (01572) 758595
E-mail: admissions@oakham.rutland.sch.uk   Web site: www.oakham.org.uk   www.gabbitas.net

Head Anthony Little
Founded 1584
Type Co-educational independent senior boarding and day
Religious Denomination Church of England
Member of HMC, BSA
Special needs provision ADD, DYS, DYP, EPI, HI, VIS
Age range 10–18; *boarders from* 10
No of pupils (day) 472; *(boarding)* 580
Girls 525; *boys* 530
Junior 234; *Senior* 468; *Sixth Form* 350
Fees per annum (full boarding) £16,110; *(day)* £9,630

Oakham School was founded in 1584 by Robert Johnson, Archdeacon of Leicester. Oakham is a genuinely co-educational boarding and day school. There are 15 houses and each pupil belongs to a small tutor group so that his or her progress can be carefully monitored, thus ensuring that each child receives expert tuition, care and guidance.

An innovative school, Oakham has been wholly committed to co-education for more than 30 years and there are equal numbers of boys and girls at every level in the School.

High academic standards are achieved. In 2001, our students received record A Level results, gaining 61 per cent at grades A or B. 52 per cent of all GCSEs taken were awarded A or A*.

Oakham has an excellent reputation for the quality of its musical and dramatic activities. The Art, Design & Technology Department includes as part of its staff an 'artist in residence'. Musicians and actors have performed in America and Germany. Social and cultural visits to Russia, Peru, North Africa, New Guinea, Israel and the Arctic Circle have also taken place.

Games teams compete successfully in local and national competitions. The principal games are rugby football, association football, cricket, hockey, tennis, athletics, lacrosse, swimming, shooting, squash and netball and teams have toured Japan, Canada, the USA, Australia, New Zealand and France.

A modern Information and Communication Technology Department is readily available to all and a magnificent library and study centre opened in 1994. Oakham is at the forefront of curriculum development in science.

Normal points of entry to Oakham are at 10, 11, 13 or 16 years. The scholarship and entrance examinations to the Sixth Form are held in November and Junior entry exams and scholarships in January and February. Common Entrance is in June and the Oakham School entry examination for 13-year-olds is held in January. Students entering the Sixth Form are offered a full programme of the International Baccalaureate as an alternative to AS/A2.

Co-education and the School's proximity to both London and Midland airports make Oakham particularly well suited to families living abroad.

Ratcliffe College

Prelim. 23.09.05
N. Carr – Wants to know why.

Fosse Way, Ratcliffe-on-the-Wreake, Leicestershire LE7 4SG
Tel: (01509) 817000   Fax: (01509) 817004
E-mail: registrar@ratcliffe.leics.sch.uk   Web site: www.ratcliffecollege.com

Head Mr P Farrar MA
Type Co-educational Day and Boarding
Special Needs provision DYS
Age range 3–18
No. of pupils (day) 460; *(boarding)* 100
Boys 360; *Girls* 200
Nursery 25; *Junior* 88; *Senior* 338;
Sixth Form 110
Boarders from 10
Fees per term as at 1.9.01 (boarding) £3,237–
£4,069; *(day)* £1,645–£2,702

Ratcliffe College is a fully co-educational day and boarding school, taking pupils from the age of 3 to 18. It is a Catholic school, welcoming children of all denominations.

Students are educated to GCSE and A level, most students taking nine GCSEs, four AS levels in Year 12 and three A2 levels in Year 13. A broad and balanced curriculum is offered, which aims to identify and provide for individual needs, and recognise and encourage individual talents.

The superb sports facilities, including new swimming pool, a fine sports centre and floodlit all-weather hockey pitch, allow a wide range of games to take place. There is an extensive extra-curricular programme.

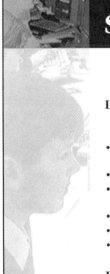

Abercorn School

28 Abercorn Place, London NW8 9XP
Tel: (020) 7286 4785 Fax: (020) 7266 0219
E-mail: a.greystoke@abercornschool.com
Web Site: www.abercornschool.com   www.gabbitas.net

Head Mrs A Greystoke
Founded 1987
Type Co-educational independent pre-prep and prep day
Religious Denomination Non-denominational
Member of ISA
Accredited by ISC
Age range 2½–13½
No of pupils 300; *Girls* 150; *boys* 150
Fees per annum £4,305–£8,010

Abercorn School

The School is situated in leafy St John's Wood. Facilities include a science laboratory, computing room, history/geography resource room and Art and CDT Centre. Abercorn has the enviable reputation for developing young children into individuals with the confidence, self-discipline and talents to achieve across the curriculum. Whilst emphasis is placed upon basic skills in literacy and numeracy, the children are also taught and encouraged to participate in music, sport, computing, art and design technology. French is taught throughout the age groups.

Enthusiastic, qualified staff produce excellent academic results in a happy atmosphere. Communication between the School and parents is encouraged in all aspects of school life.

The American School in London

One Waverley Place, London NW8 0NP
Tel: (020) 7449 1200   Fax: (020) 7449 1350
E-mail: admissions@asl.org   Web Site: www.asl.org

Head Dr William C Mules
Founded 1951
Type Co-educational independent pre-prep, prep and senior day
Accredited by ECIS, MSACS
Age range 4–18
No of pupils 1,270; *Girls* 640; *boys* 630
Fees per annum £12,650–£14,750

The American School in London is a co-educational, non-profit institution which offers an outstanding American education. The curriculum leads to an American high school diploma, and the strong Advanced Placement program enables students to enter the top universities in the US, the UK and other countries.

The core curriculum of English, Maths, Science, and Social Studies is enriched with .courses in Modern Languages, Computer, Fine Arts, and Physical Education. Small classes allow teachers to focus on individuals; students are encouraged to take an active role in learning to develop the skills necessary for independent critical thinking and expression. Many extra-curricular activities including sports, music, drama, and community service are available for students of all ages.

The American School in London welcomes students of all nationalities, including non-English speakers below the age of 11, who meet the scholastic standards. Entry is at any time throughout the year.

The Arts Educational School, London

Cone Ripman House, 14 Bath Road, Bedford Park, London, W4 1LY
Tel: (020) 8987 6600   Fax: (020) 8987 6601
E-mail: head@artsed.co.uk   www.gabbitas.net

Head Mr T Sampson MA, Cert Ed, LRAM, ACSD
Founded 1919
Type Co-educational independent prep and senior day
Religious Denomination Non-denominational
Member of ISA *accredited by* ISC
Special needs DYS
Age range 8–16
No of pupils 115
Girls 92; *boys* 23
Junior 17 (in prep); *Senior* 99
Fees per annum (day) (prep) £4,836; *(lower/upper school)* £7,245

The Arts Educational School was founded in 1919 and now occupies a large site in a pleasant residential area of West London where it is well served by public transport.

The school offers an integrated curriculum of academic study, dance, music and drama. The preparatory department gives boys and girls confidence, self-discipline and the opportunity to develop their talents in the creative and performing arts. Transfer to the lower school is in Year 7 and all pupils follow a course leading to eight or nine GCSEs and a range of music, drama and dance courses. All pupils have access to outstanding performance facilities, rehearsal rooms, proscenium and studio theatres.

Pupils leave the school to continue their education at independent day or boarding schools or at specialised vocational colleges.

Admission is at 8+, 11+ and 13+ by written examinations, interviews and audition.

The Arts Educational School is a Registered Charitable Trust no. 311087 which exists solely for educational puposes.

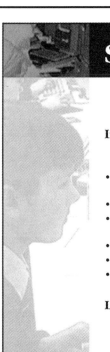

Ashbourne Middle School

17 Old Court Place, London W8 4PL
Tel: (020) 7937 3858   Fax: (020) 7937 2207
E-mail: admin@ashbournecoll.co.uk   Web site: www.ashbournecoll.co.uk   www.gabbitas.net

Head MJ Hatchard-Kirby MSc, BApSc
Founded 1984
Type Co-educational independent prep day
Member of CIFE
Accredited by BAC
Age range 14–16
No of pupils 50
Girls 25; *boys* 25
Fees per annum £10,600

Ashbourne aims to unlock the academic potential through tuition in small groups whose size never exceeds ten.

Wonderfully situated near Kensington Gardens, Ashbourne is a few minutes away from many excellent museums. The curriculum is wide ranging and includes Computing integrated with Art, Photography and Drama. The atmosphere is relaxed and the relation between staff and students informal; nevertheless the College insists on the highest standards of commitment and opens its doors on Saturdays for students who have fallen behind in their work.

Ashbourne suits students who need a closely supervised, structured approach to work in order to achieve examination success. High academic expectations together with individual attention have been the key to Ashbourne's success in revitalising the academic work of many Students.

Ashbourne Independent Sixth Form College

17 Old Court Place, London W8 4PL
Tel: (020) 7937 3858   Fax: (020) 7937 2207
E-mail: admin@ashbournecoll.co.uk   Web site: www.ashbournecoll.co.uk   www.gabbitas.net

Heads Mr MJ Hatchard-Kirby MSc, BApSc;
Mr Jim Sharpe BSC, MSc, PGCE (PCET)
Type Co-educational independent Sixth-Form College day
Member of CIFE
Accredited by BAC
Age range 16–19
No of pupils 150
Fees per annum £12,000

Wonderfully situated near Kensington Gardens Ashbourne is a few minutes away from the Albert Hall, the Imperial College of Science and many excellent museums.

The atmosphere is adult and unencumbered by petty restrictions. Working in small groups which never exceed ten, the College emphasises independence while insisting on strict commitment to work and attendance. A wide ranging curriculum includes the Medical School Programme whose mentor is Professor John Foremen, Dean of Students at University College London, and a Department for Multimedia which integrates Computing with Media, Film Studies, Art, Photography and Drama.

Ashbourne suits students who need a closely supervised, structured approach to work in order to achieve examination success. Through individual attention and the insistence on aiming high the College aims to unlock academic potential.

Avenue House

70 The Avenue, Ealing, London, W13 8LS
Tel: (020) 8998 9981   Fax: (020) 8991 1533

Head Carolyn Barber
Founded 1995
Type Co-educational pre-prep and prep day
Religious Denomination Non-denominational
Age range 2½–11
No of pupils 140
Girls 75; *boys* 65
Fees per annum (day) Half day £2,685; Full day
£5,070

Avenue House is a happy, caring, academic school situated in a quiet leafy area of Ealing. Founded in January 1995, the aim of this co-educational pre-preparatory and preparatory school is to provide an environment where each child can realise his or her educational potential to the full. Pupils are encouraged to develop their own individual talents and personalities, enabling them to become self-confident, enthusiastic and caring children who learn to value the importance of diligent work from an early age.

Pupils are taught in small classes where they can achieve their full potential in academic subjects, music, drama, sport and public examinations. All pupils are monitored individually and frequent meetings with parents and the School are actively encouraged. We believe a positive approach to learning leads to excellence.

Children in the Nursery are taught in a stimulating environment. Apart from being introduced to their numbers and a variety of initial reading schemes, French, Computers, Cooking, Drama, PE, Art, Craft, Music and Movement form a vital part of the nursery sessions. Weekly swimming lessons are given at the Gurnell Swimming Pool by specialist instructors.

The Preparatory School curriculum, whilst adhering closely to the National Curriculum, is based on the need to prepare pupils for the relevant public examination of the parents' choice. In conjunction with the traditional academic subjects Computers, Music, Art, Craft, Drama, swimming, gymnastics and games are taught. Although the emphasis is still on developing all the children's talents, we also believe in the traditional values of courtesy, kindness and consideration for others.

In addition to its own library and purpose-built gymnasium the School has the use of a purpose-built science laboratory. The School also offers a pre- and after-school care service for parental convenience.

Educational visits play an important role in helping children relate their class work to the real world. For this reason the pupils are taken on outings where they can benefit from having first-hand knowledge of London and its surrounding area.

At Avenue House we believe a happy child is most likely to succeed.

Blackheath Nursery and Preparatory School

4 St Germans Place, Blackheath, London SE3 0NJ
Tel: (020) 8858 0692   Fax: (020) 8858 7778

Head Mrs EA Cartwright
Type Independent Co-educational day only
Religious denomination Non-denominational
Special needs provision DYS
Age range 3–11; *No of pupils* 270
Fees per annum (day) £2,340–£5,250

The ethos of the school is to provide a happy, stimulating and thought-provoking environment in which the children can develop and flourish to their full potential. We want our pupils to be confident and to know that they are valued as individuals, each with a very important contribution to make to the life of the school.

'The quality of teaching and assessment is very good, with excellent interaction between teachers and children . . . Children's personal and social development is given a high priority, with emphasis on developing their self-confidence and self-esteem'. Ofsted 1999

Blackheath Nursery and Preparatory School, Charitable Status No 312732, exists to provide high quality education for local boys and girls.

Broomwood Hall

74 Nightingale Lane, London SW12 8NR
Tel: (020) 8673 1616   Fax: (020) 8675 0136
E-mail: broomwood@northwoodschools.com

Headmistress Mrs KAH Colquhoun BEd, DipT
Founded 1984
Type Girls' independent prep day,
co-educational independent pre-prep day
Religious denomination Christian (non-
denominational)
Age range Girls 4–13; boys 4–8
Girls 225; *boys* 165
Fees per annum £6,000–£7,500

We are a pre-preparatory school for boys and girls (4–8) and preparatory school for girls from 8–13, located in the heart of Wandsworth midway between Clapham and Wandsworth Commons and at our new Pre-Preparatory department on Garrads Road, overlooking Tooting Common. Our main emphasis is on preparation for entry to boarding schools at 8 (boys) and 13 (girls) via Common Entrance, and London day schools. Boys have a preferential entry at 8 to Northcote Lodge (qv). We also prepare girls for Common Entrance 11+ or 12+. We cater for children of *all* abilities, setting a high academic standard for able children whilst encouraging the less able without applying undue pressure. The Christian ethos emphasises the development of good manners, responsibility and a sense of duty.

Pre-prep entry is in September following a child's fourth birthday. Admission is by personal interview with both parents and the child at the age of 3. Parents must live locally (Clapham/Battersea/Wandsworth/Tooting). Entry to the girls' Preparatory School is at any time after 8.

Northcote Lodge

26 Bolingbroke Grove, London SW11 6EL
Tel: (020) 7924 7170   Fax: (020) 7801 9027
E-mail: northcote@northwoodschools.com

Headmaster Paul Cheeseman BA
Founded 1993
Type Boys independent prep day
Religious denomination Christian (non-
denominational)
Age range 8–13
No of pupils 150
Fees per annum £7,500–£8,700

Northcote Lodge is the sister school of Broomwood Hall (qv). It is intended specifically for those who seek a traditional prep school education for their sons, yet who would like them to remain at home as part of their families. Ideally located on the edge of Wandsworth Common, it combines the feel of a country prep school with the advantages of a day school in London. The curriculum is geared towards Common Entrance to the major public schools at 13 – it does not cater for those seeking entry to senior schools at 11+. The School caters for boys of all abilities; a scholarship class enables the brightest to be pushed through at a faster rate, whilst careful streaming and setting encourage the less able so they achieve the best possible Common Entrance result.

All homework is done at school. The day is longer than usual to accommodate this, but the boys know that when they get home, work is behind them and there is no further pressure.

The Cavendish School

179 Arlington Road, London NW1 7EY
Tel: (020) 7485 1958   Fax: (020) 7267 0098
E-mail: admissions@cavendish-school.co.uk
Web site: www.cavendish-school.co.uk   www.gabbitas.net

Head Mrs Linda Hayes BA (Hons)
Founded 1875
Type Girls' independent pre-prep and prep day
Religious denomination Roman Catholic
Member of IAPS; *accredited by* ISJC
Age range 3–11
No of pupils 180
Fees per annum £5,424–£5,769

Parents seeking a happy, exceptionally well resourced, academic girls' preparatory school should consider The Cavendish School – a Catholic preparatory school accepting all denominations, housed in spacious Victorian school buildings and a modern block with two secluded playgrounds. Founded in 1875, The Cavendish School specialises in providing a well-balanced curriculum in a caring, family atmosphere. A broad range of subjects and extra-curricular activities, ballet, BAYS, science, gymnastics and games is taught by highly qualified experienced staff. An after school care facility is provided.

The School aims to stimulate the children's attainment of sound academic standards whilst also encouraging the development of their creative skills, confidence and happiness.

Clifton Lodge Preparatory School

8 Mattock Lane, Ealing, London W5 5BG
Tel: (020) 8579 3662   Fax: (020) 8810 1332
E-mail: admin@cliftonlodge.ealing.sch.uk   Web site: www.cliftonlodge.ealing.sch.uk

Head DAP Blumlein
Founded 1979
Type Boys' independent prep day
Religious Denomination Christian
Age range 4–13
Junior 40; *Senior* 140
Fees per annum £4,900–£5,350

Clifton Lodge is a school that stands for standards: standards of proper behaviour, and standards of personal achievement. We believe that boys want to be a success in life and this they can only obtain by hard work, confidence in their own ability and a properly disciplined approach, whatever the activity. Clifton Lodge seeks at all times to impart these values.

The School is geared to give much individual attention, with boys being able to work at their own level, enabling them to realise their own potential.

The curriculum is based on the need to prepare boys for entry to public school at 13+ through the Common Entrance examination, public school scholarships or other equivalent examinations, and Clifton Lodge is justifiably proud of its excellent record of success in these. Whereas this provides the core of the academic programme, nevertheless we consider it essential to educate all pupils as broadly as possible and much time is also given to music (regular choral and instrumental recitals are given), sport (football, rugby, cricket, tennis, athletics, etc) and drama, these avenues providing boys with valuable opportunities to develop further talents and to build up their self-confidence.

The School is of Christian denomination and the daily assembly, attended by the whole community, is based around these ideas.

Choral scholarships: the School has an established choral tradition and choristerships to the value of one third of the basic fees are available to boys who become full choristers.

67. Wellington College, Crowthorne
Head: Mr A.H. Munro
23.09.05 Latin – Yes. Head of classics: Mrs R. Walker

Devonshire House Preparatory School

2 Arkwright Road, Hampstead, London NW3 6AE
Tel: (020) 7435 1916   Fax: (020) 7431 4787
Web site: www.gabbitas.net

Head Mrs SPT Donovan BEd (Hons)
Founded 1989
Type Co-educational independent pre-prep and prep day
Religious Denomination Non-denominational
Member of ISIS; *accredited by* Independent Schools Association
Age range 2–13
No of pupils 430
Girls 190; *boys* 240
Fees per annum £6,600–£7,455;
Nursery £5,625

Curriculum: early literacy and numeracy are very important and the traditional academic subjects form the core curriculum. Specialist teaching and the combined sciences form an increasingly important part of the timetable as the children grow older. Expression in all forms of communication is encouraged with classes also having lessons in Art, Music, Drama, French, and Information and Design Technology. Much encouragement is given to pupils to help to widen their horizons and broaden their interests. The School fosters a sense of responsibility amongst the pupils.

Entry requirements: the offer of places is subject to availability and to an interview. Children wishing to enter the School over the age of 6 will normally be required to take a formal written test.

Academic and leisure facilities: the School is situated in fine premises in the heart of Hampstead with their own walled grounds. The aim is to achieve high academic standards whilst developing enthusiasm and initiative throughout a wide range of interests. It is considered essential to encourage pupils to develop their own individual personalities and a good sense of personal responsibility.

Scholarships: the School offers academic and music scholarships.

DUCKS (Dulwich College Kindergarten & Infants School)

Eller Bank, 87 College Road, London SE21 7HH
Tel: 020 8693 1538   E-mail: ducks@rmplc.co.uk

Head Mrs F Johnstone
Founded 1992
Type Co-educational independent pre-prep day
Age range 3 months–7 years
No of pupils 220
Fees per annum £6,285

DUCKS is situated in beautiful, semi-rural surroundings off the main Dulwich College campus.

The Kindergarten offers a caring and stimulating environment for girls and boys from 3 months to 3 years.

The Infants School has places for 140 girls and boys aged between 3 and 7 years. The children work in new, purpose-built classrooms and have access to extensive playgrounds. DUCKS follows the Early Learning Goals and Key Stage 1 Curriculum but also offers specialist Music, Dance, French, Games, Swimming and PE. Children are prepared for the entrance exams for local schools at 7+.

For further information or to visit DUCKS, please contact Mrs Rosalind Uddin.

68 Dulwich College

Dulwich Common, London SE21 7LD
Tel/Fax: (020) 8299 9263
E-mail: the.registrar@dulwich.org.uk   Web site: www.dulwich.org.uk   www.gabbitas.net

Head GG Able
Founded 1619
Type Boys' independent prep and senior boarding and day
Religious Denomination Church of England
Member of HMC, GBA, BSA, ISIS
Age range 7–18; *boarders from* 11
No of pupils (day) 1,340; (boarding) 110
Junior 476; *Senior* 583; *Sixth Form* 391
Fees per annum (boarding) (full) £17,070;
(weekly) £16,395; *(day)* £8,730

Broad academic curriculum to GCSE and A Level. The great majority of pupils proceed to university. Admission at 7+ on aptitude test, interview and school report, and at 10+, 11+ and 13+ on written examination, interview and school report; at 16+ on interview, school report and six or more passes at GCSE with grade A or B in English Language and the three subjects to be studied at A Level.

Situated in a leafy suburb close to good rail links. Well-equipped libraries, science, language and computing laboratories, workshops, music and art schools, sports hall, swimming pool, theatre and extensive playing fields. Art, Music and Drama flourish. Scholarships for academic ability, Music, Art and Design and Technology. Three well-equipped boarding houses.

Garden House School

Girls' School 49–53 Sloane Gardens, London SW1W 8ED
Boys' School 28 Pont Street, London SW1X 0AB
Girls' School Tel: (020) 7730 1652   Fax: (020) 7730 0470
Boys' School Tel: (020) 7589 7708   Fax: (020) 7589 3773
Kindergarten (boys and girls) 28 Sloane Gardens
Web site: www.gabbitas.net

Head of Girls' Upper School Mrs J Webb
Head of Girls' Lower School Mrs W Challen
Heads of Boys' School Mr S Poland; Mr M Giles
Principal Mrs J Oddy
Founded 1951
Type Boys' and Girls' independent day
Religious denomination Inter-denominational
Age range (co-educational Kindergarten) 3–4;
Girls 4–11; Boys 4–8
Fees per annum Kindergarten: £4,050; £4,050–
£8,850 Fees include ballet/dancing from 3
years and lunch from 5 years. A 10 per cent
reduction is given to siblings.

Curriculum: Garden House follows the National Curriculum whilst preparing girls for Common Entrance to senior schools and boys for entry to Preparatory schools.

As well as the usual academic subjects, which often result in scholarships, we encourage other skills. As a central London school, we use surrounding open spaces, sports halls and swimming pools to achieve high sporting standards. Netball, gym, swimming, tennis, rounders, fencing, football, cricket and athletics are all an integral part of the school week. We enjoy field trips and outward bound courses as well as frequent visits to art galleries, museums and botanical gardens. We encourage visiting specialists in fields as diverse as butterfly farming, juggling and banking to spend time working with the children.

We continually update our media department and employ computer specialists who envisage an ongoing exploration into information technology.

We rejoice in the performing arts. The majority of our pupils learn a musical instrument and we have two choirs, general and chamber, an orchestra and smaller ensembles. The school year ends with a Summer Show and Speech Day. Since its inception, Garden House has excelled in Cechetti Ballet and Scottish Dancing, as well as Art, winning regional and national prizes. Drama and poetry are especially enjoyed as we prepare the children for music and drama certificates. The girls and boys are educated in separate buildings but retain close links with one another.

School Successes: A stimulating learning environment, with an emphasis on good manners and style, gives Garden House children a head start; senior schools are impressed by their enthusiasm and self-confidence. There is a hard working, happy atmosphere in the classrooms and our Children gain entry often with scholarships, to top boarding and day schools.

How to apply: We encourage you to visit the School. An application form can be obtained from the School Office which, once completed, your child's name is placed on our waiting list. Pupils join Garden House at 3 or 4 years of age, after an interview and assessment.

Appointments for visiting can be made by contacting the above numbers. We look forward to welcoming you and your children to Garden House School.

Hawkesdown House School

27 Edge Street, Kensington, London W8 7PN
Tel: (020) 7727 9090   Fax: (020) 7727 9988
E-mail: hawkesdown @hotmail.com   www.gabbitas.net

Head Mrs CJ Leslie BA, Cert. Ed.
Founded 2000
Type Boys independent pre-prep day only
Religious denomination Non-denominational
Age range 3–8
No of pupils approx. 150
Fees per annum £6,375–£7,185

Hawkesdown House is an independent school for boys from the ages of three to eight. Early literacy and numeracy are of prime importance and the traditional academic subjects form the core curriculum. A balanced education helps all aspects of learning and a wide range of interests is encouraged. The School finds and fosters individual talents in each pupil. Boys are prepared for entry at eight to the main London and other preparatory schools.

Sound and thorough early education is important for success, and also for self-confidence.

The thoughtful and thorough teaching and care at Hawkesdown House ensure high academic standards and promote initiative, kindness and courtesy. Hawkesdown House provides an excellent education in a safe, happy and caring atmosphere. Many of the boys coming to the School are from within walking distance and the School is part of the Kensington community. There are clear expectations and the boys are encouraged by positive motivation and by recognition and praise for achievement, progress and effort. Individual attention and pastoral care for each of the boys is of great importance.

Hawkesdown House has a fine building in Edge Street, off Kensington Church Street.

Parents who would like further information or to visit the School and meet the Headmistress, should contact the School Office for a prospectus or an appointment.

International School of London

139 Gunnersbury Avenue, London W3 8LG
Tel: (020) 8992 5823   Fax: (020) 8993 7012
E-mail: islondon@dial.pipex.com   Web site: www.islondon.com

Head Mrs Elaine Whelen
Founded 1972
Type Co-educational independent day
Member of ECIS, LISA
Accredited by ECIS
Age range 4–18
No of pupils 288
Girls 123; *boys* 165
Junior 113; *Senior* 126; *Sixth Form* 49
Fees per annum £8,450–£12,450

The International School of London exists to serve the needs of the international community in London. It aims to maximise the achievement of each of its students across the breadth of the curriculum and in personal and social fields. The School aims to develop in each student a global outlook which seeks to understand and appreciate the attitudes of others. All pupils are valued and treated equally. ISL follows a British curriculum in primary and up to GCSE. Sixth Form students prepare for the International Baccalaureate. Home language is available in French, Arabic, Italian, German, Danish, Polish, Norwegian, Russian, Hindi, Dutch, Turkish, Spanish, Japanese, Korean, Portuguese and any other on demand. A full intensive English (ESL) programme is available for non-English speaking pupils. Door-to-door transport is available. ISL has full IT facilities, Sports Hall, playground and audio visual suite. Admission is based on previous school records and an interview.

The King Alfred School

North End Road, London NW11 7HY
Tel: (020) 8457 5200   Fax: (020) 8457 5264
E-mail: KAS@kingalfred.barnet.sch.uk Web site: www.kingalfred.barnet.sch.uk www.gabbitas.net

Head Ms Lizzie Marsden
Founded 1898
Type Co-educational independent prep and senior day
Religious denomination Non-denominational
Member of GBA; *accredited by* ISA
Special needs provision DYS
Age range 4–18
Girls 251; *boys* 248
Junior 229; *Senior* 223; *Sixth Form* 48
Fees per annum £6,150–£8,790

This well-established North London independent day school is unique and was well ahead of its time at its foundation. It is still co-educational, all age, secular and embraces a wide ability range. KAS provides a rigorous, academic education for all and has very good examination results, despite its non-selective policy. Subjects offered include Music Technology, Spanish, Photography and IT and classes are usually small. The school encourages all aspects of a child's development from the early years in the Lower School to Sixth Formers being offered responsibilities such as a member of the Pupils' Council or even the Governing Body. Particular emphasis is placed on the need to research and to work independently and to play a full part in the life of the school.

The Latymer Preparatory School

36 Upper Mall, Hammersmith, London W6 9TA
Tel: 020 8748 0303   Fax: 020 8741 4916
E-mail: latymer@prepschool.fsnet.co.uk   Web site: www.latymer-upper.org

Head Mr SP Dorrian
Founded 1995
Type Boys independent prep and senior day
Religious denomination All denominations
Member of IAPS, Junior HMC
Accredited by IAPS
Age range 7–11; *No of pupils* 144
Fees per annum £8,100

Curriculum: Boys are taught the full range of subjects following National Curriculum guidelines, but to an advanced standard. Classes are small which allows for close monitoring and evaluation of each pupil's progress and well-being.

Entry requirements and procedures: The school is academically selective and entry to the school is by Assessment in Maths, English and Verbal Reasoning. Visits for prospective parents occur throughout the Autumn term and can be arranged by telephoning for an appointment.

Academic and leisure facilities: Academic achievement is strong, but in addition there is an extensive range of activities featuring Sport, Music, Art and Drama. The school has a large choir and its own orchestra.

The school is well resourced, sharing catering, sport and theatre facilities with the Upper School.

The major sports are soccer, rugby, cricket, tennis and athletics. There is also a thriving swimming club (the school has its own indoor pool). Karate, fencing and a whole range of clubs take place after school.

Latymer Upper School

King Street, Hammersmith, London W6 9LR
Tel: (020) 8741 1851   Fax: (020) 8748 5212
E-mail: registrar@latymer-upper.org   Web site: www.latymer-upper.org   www.gabbitas.net

Head Mr C Diggory BSc, MA, CMath, FIMA, FRSA
Founded 1624
Type Boys' independent prep and senior day Co-educational Sixth Form
Religious Denomination Non-denominational
Special needs provision DYS, DYP
Member of HMC, IPA
Age range Boys 7–18
No of pupils 1,120
Preparatory 140; *Senior* 630; *Sixth Form* 350
Fees per annum £8,850

Entry requirements: registrations by early December. Competitive examinations and interviews are held for entry at 7, 8, 11 and 13, and at 16 for the Sixth Form for boys and for girls. Academic as well as art, drama, sport and music scholarships are offered every year. The syllabus and past papers in Mathematics and English are available from the Registrar, along with further details.

Curriculum: a full range of academic subjects is offered to GCSE and AS/A2 Level. Languages include Latin, Greek, French, German, Italian and Spanish (European work experience and exchanges are run every year). Science is taught as separate subjects by subject specialists. Results are strong, and all pupils go to university. A School-wide computer network is used to assist pupils in many subjects. Form sizes of 22 pupils and teaching group sizes often smaller than that ensure the personal attention of staff.

The Latymer Preparatory School has its own extensive facilities and riverside site for the 7–11 age range.

Pastoral care: the School has a strong tradition of excellent pastoral care. The School has three Divisions (Lower School, Middle School, Sixth Form) and individual Year Groups are led by a Head of Year. Teams of form tutors deliver a coherent programme promoting involvement in the community, charity work, and the personal, social and academic development of their form.

Music and drama: these activities play a large part in the life of the School. There are several orchestras and choirs and concerts each term. There are five major drama productions each year, and opportunities for all to perform in Gild events. Some orchestras and drama productions are run jointly with The Godolphin and Latymer School. The new £4m Latymer Arts Centre (including a 300-seat theatre) opened in January 2000.

Sport: there are fine facilities for sport. The School has a boat house in the grounds with direct river access, a large Sports Hall, a squash court and an indoor swimming pool on site. The playing fields are 2 miles away at Wood Lane. Emphasis is on involvement, participation and choice.

The School does well in the major sports of rugby, soccer, rowing, cricket and athletics and runs more than one team per year group. It also offers other sports such as fencing, swimming and golf to cater for individual interests. The school maintains excellent fixture lists in all major sports.

Outdoor pursuits: every pupil has the opportunity to have a residential experience and take part in outdoor pursuits as part of the annual School activities week. A very active Parents' Gild ensures that no one is excluded from an activity for financial reasons.

The Duke of Edinburgh's Award Scheme flourishes in the School with several boys and girls achieving the Gold Award each year.

Mill Hill School

The Ridgeway, Mill Hill, London NW7 1QS
Tel: (020) 8959 1221   Fax: (020) 8906 2614
Web site: www.gabbitas.net

No email

Head Mr WR Winfield MA
Founded 1807
Type Co-educational independent senior
boarding and day
Religious Denomination Non-denominational
Member of HMC, ISIS, SHA
Age range 13–18
No of pupils (day) 417; *(boarding)* 167
Girls 148; *boys* 462
Fees per annum (boarding) £16,125;
(day) £10,464

Founded in 1807, Mill Hill School offers education to boys and girls aged 13 to 18 years. The Schools occupy a magnificent parkland site of 120 acres, only 10 miles from central London and yet within easy reach of Heathrow Airport and other transport links. The boarders form the heart of a vibrant, open and cosmopolitan community where the contribution of every child is valued.

Curriculum: Mill Hill School offers exciting teaching methods set against a traditional background. At age 13 pupils follow a broad curriculum in which the core subjects are separately streamed by ability. GCSE French may be taken in the second year but all other subjects are taken in the third year.

In the Lower Sixth, pupils take a one-year course to AS Level in four subjects. In the upper sixth they continue with three of these to A Level. Pupils are specially prepared in all subjects for Oxford and Cambridge.

Academic performance: the School has achieved excellent public examination results year on year. Notable strengths are History, Art, Science, Modern Languages and Business Education. In 2001 43 per cent of our GCSE results were A* or A grades, with a 96 per cent pass rate. At AS Level, 51 per cent of pupils gained A

or B grades. Academic and careers guidance is provided throughout a pupil's career at the School, with particular care taken over AS and A Level and university course choices. More than 95 per cent of our leavers go on to university.

Drama, art, multi-media and IT: Mill Hill has an outstanding reputation for music, drama and art. A new drama centre has recently been opened. In 1999 new facilities for Art/Design and Music were opened. In 2000, work on a new £500,000 library was completed. The School has over 200 computers and is a leader in IT and Internet communication.

Sports and other extra-curricular activities: historically great sports achievers, we offer over 26 sporting disciplines, and are frequent participants in national and overseas inter-school contests. Extra-curricular activities include a Community Service group, the Duke of Edinburgh Award Scheme and a Combined Cadet Force, along with a wide range of other clubs and societies.

European Initiative: leaders in developing an integrated European education policy.

Scholarships: the School offers a range of academic and music scholarships and bursary awards.

Entrance examinations: entrance at 13+ and 14+ is by tests and interviews and a head's confidential reference. Entrance at 16+ is by interview and school reference and is normally conditional on GCSE performance. Entrance and scholarship examinations are held in January.

For further information please contact the admissions office.

The Mount

Milespit Hill, Mill Hill, London NW7 2RX
Tel: (020) 8959 3403   Fax: (020) 8959 1503
E-mail: JKirsten.jackson.47@hotmail.com   Web site: www.mountschool.com www.gabbitas.net

Head Mrs J Kirsten Jackson BSc, MA
Founded 1925
Type Girls' independent pre-prep, prep and senior day
Religous denomination Inter-denominational
Member of ISA, ISIS, GBGSA; *accredited by* ISC
Special needs provision DEL, DYC, DYS, DYP
Age range 4–18
No of pupils 370
Junior 90; *Senior* 240; *Sixth Form* 40
Fees per annum £5,010–£5,820

This is a friendly, family school with a caring and supportive atmosphere, set in 5 acres of delightful grounds in a designated green belt area near Mill Hill East station and the 240 and 221 buses. There are good and improving facilities for all subjects. Good use is made of exhibitions and theatres in London.

A wide range of GCSE and A Level subjects are offered and each pupil is encouraged to strive for their personal best. The girls are successful in gaining admission to a wide range of courses at university both in the UK and abroad. The EFL department helps overseas students with their English if necessary.

North Bridge House School

no email

1 Gloucester Avenue, London, NW1 7AB
Tel: Nursery school (020) 7435 9641   Junior school (020) 7435 2884
Lower prep school (020) 7485 0661   Upper prep & senior school (020) 7267 6266
Fax: (020) 7284 2508   Web site: www.gabbitas.net

Principal WH Wilcox
Founded 1939
Type Co-educational independent pre-prep, prep and senior day
Religious denomination Non-denominational
Provision offered for special needs DYS, DYP
Age range 2½–18
No of pupils 881
Girls 389; *boys* 492; *Junior* 634; *Senior* 228
Fees per annum £7,425

North Bridge House provides a complete education from Nursery at 2½ years to 18. The School comprises four buildings, two of them large Victorian houses in Hampstead and two others prominently fronting the approach to Regents Park at Parkway.
North Bridge House offers a busy and happy environment where pupils are encouraged to develop a critical spirit, self-confidence, clarity of expression and social awareness and where good habits of work and independence of mind can flourish and provide the pupils with a sound foundation for their future development. We have an outstanding record of success and send 70 to 80 children annually to the London Public Day Schools. In 1987 a Senior School was established and has long been achieving excellent results at GCSE. Our successful pupils have been welcomed into the Sixth Form at such schools as Westminster, City of London, UCS, Highgate, South Hampstead, Francis Holland and Channing.
The Sixth Form, opened in September 2001, offers a wide range of AS and A Level subjects including: English, Mathematics, French, Science, History, Geography, Art and Photography, IT, CDT, Media Studies, PE and Sport, and Music.

Queen's College

43–49 Harley Street, London W1G 8BT
Tel: (020) 7291 7070   Fax: (020) 7291 7090
E-mail: queens@qcl.org.uk   Web site: www.qcl.org.uk   www.gabbitas.net

Head Miss MM Connell MA (Oxon)
Founded 1848
Type Girls' independent senior day
Religious denomination Anglican
Member of GSA, GBGSA; *accredited by* ISI
Age range 11–18
No of pupils 380
Senior 300; *Sixth Form* 80
Fees per annum £8,445

Queen's College, founded in 1848 by Professor FD Maurice, was the first-ever academic institution to receive a charter for the education of women. Former students include Dorothea Beale, Sophie Jex-Blake, Gertrude Bell and Katherine Mansfield. Housed in beautiful 18th-century buildings in the very heart of London, the College is equipped with bright modern Science and Language laboratories. IT provision is excellent with a large network and state-of-the-art facilities. We pay close attention to academic standards, with all girls going on to university, but we also encourage individuality, self-motivation and independence of mind, welcoming different talents, abilities and interests. We offer a very wide range and combination of subjects and opportunities to enjoy almost everything from art and music to information technology and visits abroad. Our location is one of our greatest assets, and all students benefit from London's galleries, museums, theatres, exhibitions and concerts. Admission is by examination and interview. Scholarships and bursaries available. Contact Admissions Secretary for details.

Queen's Gate School

No email -

133 Queen's Gate, London SW7 5LE
Tel: (020) 7589 3587   Fax: (020) 7584 7691   Web site: www.gabbitas.net

Head Mrs AM Holyoak CertEd
Founded 1891
Type Girls' independent prep and senior day
Religious Denomination Non-denominational
Member of GSA, SHA
Age range 4–18
No of pupils 390
Junior 120; *Senior* 220; *Sixth Form* 50
Fees per annum £6,150–£7,950

Curriculum and academic life: the curriculum is rich, varied, well balanced and as wide as possible during the years leading to the GCSE examinations, and is frequently reviewed to take into account new approaches to teaching and scientific and technological change.

All girls sit GCSE examinations in English Language, English Literature, Mathematics, a Modern Language, and a Science, and have the option of taking courses in additional Science subjects, the Humanities, a range of Modern Languages, Classics, Business Studies, Computer Studies, Art and Design, Graphic Design, Music and Drama. Decisions on options are made after full consultation with parents.

Small classes ensure maximum guidance with course work and much individual attention. Each girl's work is frequently assessed and progress and achievement are carefully monitored. Detailed reports are written for parents.

Entry requirements and procedures: for Junior School: girls enter the preliminary form aged four without formal testing, but visit the School for a morning of assessment in the autumn term prior to the September entry. Girls wishing to enter after this take tests in Maths and English. Girls in Year 6 are required to pass the London Day Schools 11+ entrance examination before moving up into the Senior School.

Senior School: girls sit the London Day School Examination at 11+ and the School's own entrance examinations at 12+, 13+ and 16+. Before acceptance all girls are interviewed.

Sixth Form: girls entering the Sixth Form are required to have at least five GCSE passes, grades A–C with at least an A grade in those subjects they wish to pursue to A2. They are expected to study four or five A/S Levels and to continue three of those subjects to A2.

Examinations offered: Edexcel, OCR, AQA.

Academic and leisure facilities: the School has well-equipped science and computer laboratories and is conveniently placed to take full advantage of the resources offered by central London education. It is within easy walking distance of the Science Museum, Geological and Natural History Museums and the Victoria and Albert Museum, Hyde Park and Kensington Gardens.

The girls play netball, hockey, lacrosse and tennis and, as well as having their own gymnasium, enjoy the facilities of local sports hall, athletics grounds and swimming pools.

Scholarships: one 8+ scholarship (external and internal), two internal Sixth-Form scholarships.

Queen's Gate School Trust is a registered charity which exists to provide high quality education for girls in central London.

Redcliffe School

47 Redcliffe Gardens, London SW10 9JH
Tel: (020) 7352 9247   Fax: (020) 7352 6936   E-mail: admissions@redcliffeschool.com
Web site: www.redcliffeschool.com   www.gabbitas.net

Head Miss RE Cunnah MA
Founded 1948
Type Co-educational independent pre-prep and prep day
Religious Denomination Christian multi-denominational
Member of IAPS
Special needs provision DYS, DYP
Age range Boys 4–8; *girls* 4–11
No of pupils 100
Girls 67; *boys* 33
Fees per annum £6,750

Redcliffe School is a small, friendly school. It caters for a range of abilities and enables children to reach a high academic standard whilst developing the potential of each individual. Basic skills are accentuated within a broad and balanced curriculum incorporating creative and practical activities.

Rosemead Preparatory School

70 Thurlow Park Road, West Dulwich, London SE21 8HZ
Tel: (020) 8670 5865   Fax: (020) 8761 9159
E-mail: rosemead1@aol.com   Web site: www.gabbitas.net

Head Mrs RL Lait BA, MBA (Ed), CertEd
Founded 1942
Type Co-educational independent pre-prep and prep day
Religious denomination Non-denominational
Member of ISA, ISIS; *accredited by* ISA, ISC
Age range 3–11
Girls 135; *boys* 135
Fees per annum £3,930–£4,560

Rosemead is a well-established preparatory school with a fine record of academic achievement. Children are prepared for entrance to independent London day schools at age 11 years, many gaining awards and scholarships. The School has a happy, family atmosphere with boys and girls enjoying a varied, balanced curriculum which includes Maths, English, Science, French, Information and Communication Technology, Arts and Humanities. Music and Drama are strong subjects with tuition available in most orchestral instruments and various music groups meeting frequently. A full programme of Physical Education includes gymnastics, most major games, dance and (from age 6) swimming. Classes make regular visits to places of interest. A residential field studies course is arranged for the junior pupils along with various school holidays. Main entry to the School is at ages 3 and 4 years following informal assessment. The School is administered by a board of governors elected annually by the parents.

The Royal School, Hampstead

65 Rosslyn Hill, Hampstead, London NW3 5UD
Tel: (020) 7794 7708   Fax: (020) 7431 6741
E-mail: royschham@aol.com   Web site: www.royalschoolhampstead.net   www.gabbitas.net

Patron HRH Princess Alexandra, the Hon. Lady Ogilvy, GVCO
Principal Mrs CA Sibson, MA (Oxon)
Founded 1855
Type Girls' independent day and boarding
Religious denomination All religions welcome
Member of ISA, ISIS, BSA
Special needs provision MLD
Age range 4–18; boarders from 11
No of pupils enrolled as at 1.6.01 200
Junior 92; *Senior* 96; *Sixth Form* 12
Fees per annum (boarding) (full) £9,279–£11,529 *(weekly)* £7,659–£9,585; *(day)* £4,926–£5,799

Curriculum: Balanced curriculum, including two modern languages plus Latin, and three sciences leading to GCSE, AS and A2. EFL is offered as required. There is a variety of sports with access to excellent facilities, plus music, drama, ballet, Duke of Edinburgh, Young Enterprise, art and karate. The school has a low pupil to teacher ratio.

Entry requirements: Entry is by interview and previous school reports. An entrance test is taken when applicable. Scholarships and Bursaries are available.

The school is small, homely and happy with a staff dedicated to the academic and personal development of each child as an individual. It offers day, weekly and full boarding options including 'flexi-boarding'.

The school is situated in pleasant surroundings only 250m from Hampstead Tube Station. It has comfortable, spacious and light classrooms, and a separate Sixth Form Study Centre with personal work stations, IT, common room and kitchen facilities. There is a large car park for the arrival and departure of pupils.

St Margaret's

18 Kidderpore Gardens, London, NW3 7SR
Tel: (020) 7435 2439   Fax: (020) 7431 1308
E-mail: staff@st-margarets.co.uk   suzannemeaden@infinnet.co.uk
Web site: www.st-margarets.co.uk   www.gabbitas.net

Head Mrs S Meaden
Founded 1884
Type Girls' independent day prep and senior
Religious denomination Church of England
Member of ISA; *accredited by* ISJC
Special needs provision DYS (moderate), DYP (mild)
Age range 5–16
No of pupils 150
Junior 70; *Senior* 80
Fees per annum £5,850

St Margaret's offers a high standard of teaching in small classes. Pupils follow the National Curriculum. French begins in the infant classes, and in the Senior School Spanish, Russian and Classical Civilisation are offered in addition to the core National Curriculum subjects. All girls go on to full time Sixth-Form education. Recent leavers are now studying at South Hampstead High School, Francis Holland, Channing, Camden School for Girls, Fine Arts College.

The girls frequently visit London theatres, art galleries and concert halls. Extra-curricular activities include gym and drama clubs, self defence, first aid, batik classes and horse riding. Girls may have individual instrumental and speech and drama lessons.

Entrance is by interview at ages 5 and 6 and by interview and written test from the age of 7. A prospectus is available from the School and Suzanne Meaden is happy to see parents at any time.

St Paul's Cathedral School

2 New Change, London EC4M 9AD
Tel: (020) 7248 5156   Fax: (020) 7329 6568
E-mail: admissions@spcs.city-of-london.sch.uk
Web site: www.stpauls.co.uk   www.gabbitas.net

Head AH Dobbin MA (Cantb)
Founded 12th century
Type Co-educational pre-prep and prep;
Boys' boarding
Religious Denomination Church of England
Member of IAPS, CSA
Age range 4–13; *boarders from* 7
No of pupils 153; *(boarding choristers, boys)* 40
Pre-prep 51; *Prep* 102
Girls 29; *boys* 124
Fees per annum (boarding; full and weekly)
£4,314; *(day)* £6,810

Governed by the Dean and Chapter, the original residential choir school expanded in 1989 to include non-chorister day boys. A new co-educational pre-preparatory for 4–7 year olds opened in September 1998. The school will become fully co-educational from September 2002.

Curriculum: a broad curriculum leads to scholarship and Common Entrance examinations at 13 and the School has an excellent record in placing pupils in senior schools of their choice, many with scholarships. A wide variety of sport and musical instrument tuition is offered. Choristers receive an outstanding choral training as members of the renowned St Paul's Cathedral Choir.
Facilities: the refurbishment of the School's facilities has provided a separate Pre-Preparatory Department, improved classrooms and new boarding facilities for the choristers.
Admission: day pupils and pre-preparatory children are interviewed and tested before September entry at 4+ or 7+ years old. Voice trials and tests for choristers are held three times a year for boys of nearly 7 years and upwards.

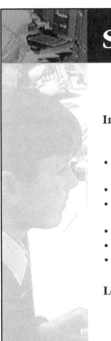

Southbank International School, Kensington

36–38 Kensington Park Road, London W11 3BU
Tel: (020) 7243 3803   Fax: (020) 7727 3290
E-mail: admissions@southbank.org   Web site: www.southbank.org   www.gabbitas.net

Head Mr Nigel Hughes
Founded 1979
Type Co-educational independent pre-prep,
prep and senior day
Member of ISC, ECIS, LISA;
accredited by ISC, IB
Age range 4–18
No of pupils 266
Girls 141; *boys* 125
Junior 100; *Senior* 99; *Sixth Form* 67
Fees per term £3,200–£4,800

Southbank Kensington serves pupils aged 4–18 from over 40 countries, including the UK. Many are children of the expatriate professional and diplomatic community. The International Baccalaureate (IB) curriculum offered at all levels is flexible, challenging and individualised to accommodate pupil diversity, and includes modern languages, mathematics, humanities, experimental science, computing, creative arts and sports. German is offered in the Primary School, French is introduced in the Middle School, and 18 languages are offered in the High School. The High School programme leads to the IB Diploma, a rigorous A Level alternative, which is accepted as a university entrance requirement world-wide, and is recognised by leading institutions in the UK. Pupils may also obtain a US High School Diploma, based on the IB curriculum.

Admissions are based on previous school reports and references and are made year-round, subject to space. A door-to-door bus service serves an extensive area of central and north London.

Southbank International School, Hampstead

16 Netherhall Gardens, London NW3 5TH
Tel: (020) 7243 3803   Fax: (020) 7727 3290
E-mail: admissions@southbank.org   Web site: www.southbank.org   www.gabbitas.net

Head Mrs J Treftz
Founded 1995
Type Co-educational independent pre-prep and
prep day
Member of ISA, LISA, ECIS;
accredited by ISC, IBO
Age range 3–14
No of pupils 176
Girls 86; *boys* 90
Junior 128; *Senior* 48
Fees per term £2,050–£4,300

A branch of the Southbank International School in Kensington, Southbank Hampstead serves pupils aged 3–14 from over 30 countries including the UK. Many are children of the expatriate professional and diplomatic community. The School is in a new, purpose-built property. The integrated curriculum, based on the International Baccalaureate (IB) Primary and Middle Years Programme, is challenging and individualised to accommodate pupil diversity, and places special emphasis on foreign languages (German at Primary Level, French in Middle School), computing and technology skills, creative arts (including a Suzuki music programme in the primary school) and sports. Students completing the Middle School programme are eligible to transfer to the IB Diploma Programme in the High School at the Kensington campus.

Admissions are based on previous academic reports and references, and are made year-round subject to space. Three-year-olds have a half-day option. A door-to-door bus service serves an extensive area of central and north London.

Willoughby Hall Dyslexia Centre

1 Willoughby Road, London NW3 1RP
Tel: 020 7794 3538   Fax: 020 7435 2872
Web site: www.gabbitas.net

Principal WH Wilcox
Founded September 1998
School status Co-educational independent day
Religious denomination Non-denominational
Age range 6–12
Girls 9 *boys* 24
Fees per annum £13,497

Willoughby Hall Dyslexia Centre offers a complete course of education for pupils aged from 6 to 12 years, who are held back by dyslexia and other learning difficulties. The Centre is a development of work done over the last twenty years at North Bridge House School, culminating in the opening of this special facility, itself based on a pilot scheme at our Parkway premises.

The teaching is based on a full-time multi-sensory course which aims to provide the pupils with a thorough knowledge of the skills required in Secondary Education, enabling pupils to return to the mainstream. As dyslexic children can have a very limited span of concentration, the intensive work in therapy can only be maintained for very short periods. This means that other activities such as Art, Music and CDT must be simultaneously available so that they can relax, whenever necessary. The children are taught in a small group from which individuals are drawn out to concentrate on building the skills they have failed to develop earlier and overcoming their specific difficulties.

Each pupil works to an Individual Education Plan. The main emphasis is on English and Mathematics, using a multi-sensory approach. Science, History, Geography, Scripture, Art, Design, Music, Drama, Computing (including keyboarding skills) and Study Skills all feature in the curriculum. We keep as close as possible to the mainstream syllabus.

Pupils are able to take part in a varied programme of Physical education at Willoughby Hall.

Dyslexia Centre pupils are taught keyboard skills and basic computing. Those pupils for whom a laptop computer is an essential classroom aid will thus be able to use it to best advantage.

At the Dyslexia Centre it is understood that parents will want to be very closely involved with their child's education and the Head Teacher and her Deputy will always make time to see parents, even at short notice.

Should you wish to discuss the work of the Willoughby Hall Dyslexia Centre further, please telephone the secretary on 020 7794 3538. Entry to the department is by interview and test. The parent is also required to arrange for an assessment by an Educational Psychologist recommended by the school.

St Helen's School

Eastbury Road, Northwood, Middlesex, HA6 3AS
Tel: (01923) 843210   Fax: (01923) 843211
E-mail: office@sthelensnorthwood.co.uk
Web site: www.sthelensnorthwood.co.uk   www.gabbitas.net

Head Mrs Mary Morris BA (Hons)
Founded 1899
Type Girls' independent, prep and senior
boarding and day
Religious denomination Christian foundation
but accept all faiths
Member of GBGSA, GSA; *accredited by* ISC
Age range 4–18+; *boarders from* 11
No of pupils (day) 980
Junior 358; *Middle and Upper School* 456;
Sixth Form 166
Fees per annum (boarding) £13,500; *(weekly)*
£12,996; *(day)* £5,238–£7,200

St Helen's has a commitment to academic achievement that has given us an enviable reputation for over a hundred years. We provide an excellent academic education for able girls, developing personal integrity alongside intellectual, creative and sporting talents. The staff are highly qualified and enthusiastic, the facilities are excellent, discipline is good and we know and care for every individual pupil.

The curriculum is designed to enable every girl to achieve intellectual and personal fulfilment and to develop her talents to the full. We support the aims of the National Curriculum, but offer a wider range of subjects and teach to greater depth, enabling the girls to explore their interests and talents. The staff are subject specialists who aim to inspire a love of their subjects in their pupils. They help the students learn to study independently and develop good study habits, through stimulating and rigorous teaching.

Music, art, drama and sport are all an integral part of school life and every girl is involved.

The use of Information Communication Technology is a key element in learning and features both within the curriculum and to support the delivery of other subjects.

St Helen's Sixth Form is a flourishing community of approximately 180 girls who take an active role in the life of the school. Each year we welcome new students who join us from other schools. The Sixth Form is in many ways a new beginning, often the most enjoyable and challenging time of school life. Almost all girls go on to Higher Education and significant numbers go to Oxford and Cambridge each year.

A large number of clubs and societies exist which cater for all interests. St Helen's is one of only eight girls' schools to run a Combined Cadet Force, which is done jointly with Merchant Taylors' boys School.

Above all we encourage all girls at St Helen's to chase their dreams and achieve a successful and fulfilling adult life.

St Martin's School

40 Moor Park Road, Northwood, Middlesex HA6 2DJ
Tel: (01923) 825740   Fax: (01923) 835452
E-mail: office@stmartins.org.uk   Web site: www.stmartins.org.uk   www.gabbitas.net

Head Mr MJ Hodgson MA, CertEd
Founded 1922
Type Boys' independent pre-prep and prep day
Religious denomination Church of England
Member of IAPS, ISIS
Age range 3–13
No of pupils 400
Junior 135; *Senior* 265
Fees per annum £2,175–£6,900

Curriculum: boys entering the kindergarten at three, the pre-preparatory at four and the main school at seven are taught by class teachers. Subject specialists take over at nine. We have the benefit of science laboratories, art and design rooms and excellent computer facilities. *Entry requirements:* all candidates take an assessment test.

Examinations offered: children are prepared successfully for Common Entrance or Scholarship Entrance to senior schools.
Academic and sports facilities: St Martin's offers an all-round education. We enjoy an enviable reputation in games and competitive sports. Our choirs, orchestra and stage productions are deservedly renowned, and our activities programme caters for a wide range of hobbies. Our pastoral system encourages children to learn self-reliance and a sense of responsibility in a happy family atmosphere. An extensive development programme is well under way, with a sports complex and a new block of eight classrooms as the latest projects.

Langley School

Langley Park, Loddon, Norwich, Norfolk NR14 6BJ
Tel: (01508) 520210   Fax: (01508) 528058   E-mail: administration@langleyschool.co.uk
Web site: www.langleyschool.co.uk   www.gabbitas.net

Head JG Malcolm BSc, MA, CertEd
Founded 1910
Type Co-educational independent senior boarding and day
Religious denomination Non-denominational
Member of SHMIS, BSA, GBA
Accredited by ISI (inspected Jan 2001)
Special needs provision ADD, ADHD, DYC, DYS, DYP, SP&LD, W
Age range 10–18; *boarders from* 10
No of pupils (day) 242; *(boarding)* 83
Girls 85; *boys* 240
Senior 247; *Sixth Form* 78
Fees per annum (boarding) (full) £11,400–£13,800; *(weekly)* £10,500–£12,600; *(day)* £5,580–£7,200

General: situated in some 50 acres of playing fields and wooded parkland landscaped by Capability Brown, Langley is approximately 100 miles from London and close to Norwich airport for international connections.

A programme of continuous investment has ensured that students benefit from the latest technology and learning opportunities whilst enjoying the heritage and history of a delightful country house. The impressive facilities include a large sports hall, indoor activity centre, lecture/film theatre, performing arts centre, new studios for art, sculpture and ceramics, new 11 laboratory science complex, workshops for technology and electronics and separate computer centres for the teaching of ICT.

Curriculum: an experienced graduate staff employ formal teaching methods with an emphasis on good manners, high standards of academic work and encouraging students to partake in as wide a range of experience as possible. With a staff:student ratio of 1:8 classes are small and there are currently 24 GCSE, A2 and AS Level subjects to choose from including all the Sciences, four Modern Languages, Business Studies, Information Technology, Media Studies, Drama as well as the more traditional subjects. Entry to the Sixth Form is selective and the majority of students take four or five subjects to AS Level in L6 and three to A2 in U6

for entry to University or the professions. Students with specific learning difficulties or whose first language is not English can receive additional help from specialist staff.

Games and Activities: activities cannot be described as extra-curricular as they take place within the normal school day. All students are expected to take part but they can choose from a list of over 70 alternatives each week. The daily programme has options for those interested in Drama, Music, Art, Science, Technology, Academic pursuits, Creative and many more. Within the programme the School also operates an active Combined Cadet Force and D of E Scheme as avenues for adventure training and service.

Sport also plays a major part in the activity programme with opportunities for aerobics, athletics, badminton, basketball, canoeing, climbing, croquet, cross-country, fencing, golf, gymnastics, judo, orienteering, sailing, shooting, squash, swimming, table-tennis, tennis, volleyball and windsurfing as well as the major games of rugby, soccer, hockey, cricket, netball and rounders.

Performing Arts: the Departments of Drama, Music and Art offer a termly programme of studio events featuring workshops, professional artistes, premier events by our resident Community Theatre Company as well as numerous performances by Langley students. In addition, the Arts Umbrella programme offers the opportunity for parents and students to experience the theatrical and musical productions in London and other centres.

Admission and Scholarships: at 10, 11, 12 and 13 it is normal for a student to be offered a place based on interview and satisfactory reports from their previous school or through the Common Entrance Examination. At Sixth Form candidates must have completed a satisfactory GCSE course. Competitive Entrance Scholarships are offered in Music, Drama, Art, Sport, Technology and for academic ability. The auditions, interviews and examination take place in late February and details can be obtained from the School.

Abingdon School

Abingdon, Oxfordshire OX14 1DE
Tel: (01235) 531755   Fax: (01235) 536449
E-mail: registrar@abingdon.com

Head M St John Parker
Founded 1256
Type Boys' independent senior boarding and day
Religious denomination Church of England; others welcome
Member of HMC
Special needs provision DYS, DYP
Age range 11–18; boarders from 11
No of pupils (day) 673; *(boarding)* 124
Junior 130; *Senior* 417; *Sixth form* 250
Fees per annum (boarding) £12,294; *(day)* £6,669

Abingdon is increasingly gaining a national reputation for academic distinction and an adventurous attitude towards extra-curricular and curriculum development. Music and drama flourish, and amongst many other games, rowing is particularly strong. The original buildings have been much extended with further development planned. Pastoral care is of central importance and a friendly and positive attitude makes the School a happy and purposeful place. Boys from primary schools enter at 11, or via two years at Josca's Prep School with which Abingdon merged in 1998. Those from prep schools enter at 13 after Common Entrance, and Sixth Form entry depends on GCSE results.

Bloxham School

Bloxham, Near Banbury, Oxfordshire OX15 4PE
Tel: (01295) 720206   Fax: (01295) 721897   E-mail: registrar@bloxhamschool.co.uk
Web site: www.bloxhamschool.com   www.gabbitas.net

Head Mr David K Exham MA
Founded 1860
Type Independent co-educational senior boarding and day
Religious denomination Church of England
Member of HMC, Woodard Corporation
Accredited by ISI, CReSTeD
Special needs provision DYS
Age range 11–18
No of pupils (day) 167; *(boarding) (full)* 190 *(weekly)* 11
Junior 64; *Senior* 157; *Sixth Form* 147
Girls 115; *boys* 250
Fees per annum (boarding) (full) £17,175; *(weekly)* £11,120; *(day) from* £8,855–£13,290

Bloxham School, which is predominantly boarding, is fully co-educational.
The school offers a supportive, caring and friendly environment that allows those with talent in any area of the school's life to contribute and succeed.
Bloxham attaches great importance to the academic quality of its education. It offers a wide range of GCSE and A/AS Level courses. 98 per cent of pupils go to University, including Oxford and Cambridge.
Bloxham enjoys superb facilities for academic work, sport, technology, the Arts, all found within a campus of great charm. The school offers an impressive array of extra curricular activity across a wide spread of interests and many of the activities are generated by a mix of staff and pupil energy and expertise.
Built around a strong supportive pastoral and tutorial system Bloxham School creates an environment where boys and girls expect to do well – and they usually do!

Cherwell College

Greyfriars, Paradise Street, Oxford, Oxfordshire OX1 1LD
Tel: (01865) 242670   Fax: (01865) 791761
E-mail: chercoll@rmplc.co.uk   Web site: www.cherwell-college.oxon.sch.uk

Head Andy Thompson
Founded 1973
Type Co-educational independent FE boarding and day
Religious denomination Inter-denominational
Member of CIFE
Accredited by BAC
Special needs provision ADD, ADHD, DYS, DYP
Age range 16+; *boarders from* 16+
No of pupils (day) 60; *(boarding)* 90
Girls 65; *boys* 85
Fees per annum (boarding) £15,750; *(day)* £10,500

Cherwell is a well established, fully co-educational day and residental college that prepares students under close personal supervision for their GCSE and A Level examinations.
Cherwell's distinction is that of tuition geared to the needs of the individual, where tutorials are supported by interactive seminars and trials held weekly, lectures, revision classes and practicals for those studying Natural Sciences and Art.
Accommodation arrangements are made. Students may live in a Hall of Residence, with a family or self-cater in a flat or bedsit. Provision is made for all sport at Cherwell.

Cokethorpe

Witney, Oxfordshire OX29 7PU
Tel: (01993) 703921   Fax: (01993) 773499
E-mail: admin@cokethorpe.org   Website: www.cokethorpe.org

Head PJS Cantwell
Founded 1957
Type Co-educational independent prep and senior boarding and day
Religious denomination Inter-denominational
Member of SHMIS; *accredited by* ISC
Special needs provision DEL, DYC, DYS, DYP, MLD, PH, SP&LD, SPLD
Age range 7–18; *boarders from* 10 (boys only)
No of pupils (day) 470; *(boarding)* 40
Girls 180; *boys* 330
Junior 160; *Senior* 350; *Sixth Form* 70
Fees per annum (boarding) £10,500–£15,750; *(day)* £5,310–£9,480

A broad academic and vocational curriculum is followed to GCSE. Traditional A Levels and GNVQs are available to the Sixth Form. Small classes provide everyone with the opportunity of fulfilling their potential. Extra help is available in the learning support department. Entry requirements are interview and headteacher's report at the age of 7 and 9, interview and assessment at 11, 13 and 16 years.
Examinations: GCSE, A and A/S Level, GNVQ levels 2 and 3. New buildings house the library, art and ceramics, information technology and design and technology. There are also modern laboratories, Music School and Sixth Form facilities. The new Sports Hall provides for a wide range of indoor sports. There is a wide range of extra-curricular activities within 50 acres of grounds. In 2001, the Campus was fully networked and a new ICT Resource Centre opened; the network runs ICT including white boards in each classroom and the centre provides 64 open access workstations.
Scholarships are awarded on entrance assessment. Bursaries are available on application for details.

d'Overbroeck's College

1 Park Town, Oxford, Oxfordshire OX2 6SN
Tel: (01865) 310000   Fax: (01865) 552296   E-mail: mail@doverbroecks.com
Web site: www.doverbroecks.com   www.gabbitas.net

Principals Mr S Cohen BSc and Dr RK Knowles
MA, DPhil
Founded 1977
Type Co-educational independent senior
boarding and day
Religious denomination Non-denominational
Member of ISA
Special needs provision DYS, MLD
Age range 13–19; *boarders from* 16
No of pupils 280
Fees per annum (boarding, average) £15,615
(Sixth Form only); (day) £7,995–£11,655

d'Overbroeck's is a co-educational college in
Oxford offering a distinctive and highly successful education for students across the ability
range. It has a friendly and stimulating approach
which provides a strong alternative to a traditional public school whilst placing a great deal
of emphasis on academic achievement. The
College's approach is characterised by small
classes (an average of 5–6 students) a high level
of personal attention and an unusual degree of
flexibility in the range and possible combinations of subjects. The teaching is highly
interactive and seeks to generate enthusiasm
and effective working habits – while at the same
time providing a thorough preparation for public examinations.

All students at the College have their own
Director of Studies who co-ordinates their
academic programme and who is responsible
for their overall welfare. The Directors of
Studies also maintain regular contact with
parents who are kept well informed about their
son and daughter's progress.

There is a full programme of extra curricular
events, sports and clubs. All students are
encouraged to participate in these activities
on a voluntary basis in the Sixth Form.

Kingham Hill School

Kingham, Chipping Norton, Oxfordshire OX7 6TH
Tel: (01608) 658999   Fax: (01608) 658658
E-mail: admissions@kinghamhill.org.uk   Web site: www.kinghamhill.org.uk   www.gabbitas.net

Head Martin Morris BEd, BA (Hons)
Founded 1886
Type Co-educational senior independent
boarding and day
Religious denomination Christian
Member of SHMIS, ISC; *accredited by* CReSTeD
Special needs provision DYC, DYS, DYP
Age range 11–18; *boarders from* 11
No of pupils (day) 39; *(boarding)* 213
Girls 70; *boys* 182
Senior 192; *Sixth Form* 60
Fees per annum (boarding) £12,711–£13,740;
(day) £7,905–£8,568

Kingham Hill is a thriving school for boys and
girls between the ages of 11 and 18.

The school is midway between Oxford, Cheltenham and Stratford-upon-Avon with good
rail links to London (80 minutes). Set in 92
acres, it is a place where pupils have space to
learn and grow.

Curriculum: A wide choice of academic options
is offered to gain the full potential from each
child; a leading vocational Sixth Form.

Boarding: Strong pastoral care through small
boarding houses run by husband and wife
teams.

Development: A £2 million programme during
2000/2001 has provided a floodlit sports pitch
and Sixth Form social centre. A new indoor
swimming pool complex is set for completion
in 2002.

Millbrook House

Milton, Abingdon, Oxfordshire OX14 4EL
Tel: (01235) 831237   Fax: (01235) 821556
E-mail: millbrook@millbrookhouse.org.uk   Web site: www.millbrookhouse.org.uk

Head SRM Glazebrook BSc
Founded 1963
Type Boys' independent prep boarding and day
Religious denomination Church of England
Member of CReSTeD
Special needs provision DYC, DYS, DYP
Age range 7–14; *boarders from* 7
No of pupils 45
Fees per annum (full boarding) from £12,750
(day) from £7,000

Millbrook caters for:

- children who require a first class preparatory school education
- overseas children who require extra English language tuition with specialist TEFL teachers
- children who need extra tuition to help them pass the Common Entrance Examination to Public Schools

The classes are small (under ten) plus one-on-one teaching if necessary. The emphasis is on confidence building and motivation to succeed. We offer intensive tuition, tailored to suit the needs of the individual child. We also go to great lengths to find the right public school. Sport includes cricket, tennis, soccer, hockey, swimming and rugby.

St Mary's School, Wantage

Newbury Street, Wantage, Oxfordshire OX12 8BZ
Tel: (01235) 773800   Fax: (01235) 760467
E-mail: stmarysw@rmplc.co.uk   Web site: www.stmarys.oxon.sch.uk   www.gabbitas.net

Head Mrs S Sowden BSc, AKC
Founded 1873
Type Girls' independent senior boarding and day
Religious denomination Church of England
Member of GSA; *Accredited by* ISI
Special needs provision DYC, DYS, DYP, EPI, MLD, SPLD
Age range 11–18; *boarders from* 11
No of pupils (day) 16; *(boarding)* 173
Senior 138; *Sixth Form* 51
Fees per annum (full boarding) £16,425; *(day)* £10,950

As a Christian foundation, we aim to give each girl a stable set of values, ensuring the best possible preparation for life beyond the School. Strong academic results are achieved without excessive pressure. Particular strengths are in Art, Music and ICT. A new wireless computer system means that the girls use their laptops anywhere on the 13 acre campus to contact their tutors, central printers, or their parents via the internet. A specialist support unit provides for all special needs including the gifted child and those with dyslexia and other specific learning difficulties.

We take weekends seriously. Girls are full-time boarders or local day girls (who may sleep any number of nights on a regular or occasional basis).

Concord College

Acton Burnell Hall, Shrewsbury, Shropshire SY5 7PF
Tel: (01694) 731631   Fax: (01694) 731389
E-mail: theprincipal@concordcollegeuk.com   Web site: www.concordcollegeuk.com

Head AL Morris
Founded 1949
Type Co-educational independent boarding and day
Member of CIFE; *accredited by* BAC
Age range 12–18; *boarders from* 12+
No of pupils (day) 20; (boarding) 280
Girls 140; *boys* 160
Senior 60; *Sixth form* 240
Fees per annum (boarding) £16,200; (day) £5,800

Courses offered: GCSE and A Levels
Nature of tuition: classes small. Average class size: 10. Student:teacher ratio: 8:1.
Concord has a reputation for excellent examination results and was placed at No. 51 for A Level results in the Financial Times list of the UK's Top 1000 Schools (June 2001). Concord has an impressive campus with attractive buildings, playing fields and gardens. It has modern and well-equipped laboratories, library and excellent computer facilities.

Its graduate teachers work hard with the students and provide a sympathetic but disciplined environment. Students also attend supervised private study for two hours each day. Students are carefully prepared for their examinations and are advised and assisted in gaining university places, with particular success for university entrance in Engineering, Accountancy, Law and the Medical Sciences.

Most sports are offered. Facilities include a large sports centre and an indoor swimming pool.

A truly international college, there were students from 44 countries attending the college in 1998–99. The students are ambitious and conscientious and this creates an environment in which our British students greatly benefit from the energetic and purposeful competition.

86

Moreton Hall

Weston Rhyn, Oswestry, Shropshire SY11 3EW
Tel: (01691) 776020   Fax: (01691) 778552
E-mail: jfmhall@aol.com   www.moretonhall.org   www.gabbitas.net

Head Jonathan Forster
Founded 1913
Type Girls' independent prep and senior
boarding and day
Religious denomination Church of England
Member of SHA, GSA, GBGSA, ISCO, ISIS
Age range 8–18; *boarders from* 11
No of pupils (day) 46; *(boarding)* 219
Junior 60; *Senior* 115 *Sixth Form* 90
Fees per annum (boarding) £15,960;
(day) £10,965

Curriculum: going well beyond the National Curriculum, some 20 subjects are available at GCSE, varying from the traditional academic subjects such as Latin and the Sciences, to the practical subjects such as Drama, Dance and Physical Education. Modern languages available include French, German and Spanish. A Levels in History of Art, Human Biology, Business Studies, and Theatre Studies extend the range of the curriculum. Information Technology is a compulsory subject up to Sixth Form, optional thereafter.

Entry requirements: girls are admitted to the School, normally in September, at the age of 11, either by Common Entrance or by the School's entrance examination, which is held at the end of January each year. Sixth Form Entrance is by examination and interview and numbers are limited. Since September 2000 girls from the age of 8 have been admitted to Moreton First.

Academic and leisure facilities: Moreton Hall has recently completed an ambitious building and refurbishment programme. The new laboratories, information technology rooms and Art Design Centre are housed within a short distance of the central classroom, careers and Library complex.

An exceptionally well-equipped Sports Centre comprising a Sports Hall and floodlit tennis courts, along with heated swimming pool, nine-hole golf course and playing fields are set in one hundred acres of beautiful park land at the foot of the Berwyn hills. The School offers a wide range of sporting options, including Lacrosse, Netball, Hockey, Cricket, Tennis and Athletics. Sailing and Riding are also popular. Moreton Enterprises, a Sixth form managed company, offers the girls real business experience. A new radio station and recording studio were opened in 1997.

Scholarships: a number of scholarships and Bursaries are awarded to girls entering Lower VI or to assist a pupil in the School to complete her education. Awards for Music, Drama, Art and for outstanding sporting talent are made at 11+, 12+, 13+ and 16+.

Boarding facilities: younger girls are housed in the Norton-Roberts building under the supervision of resident houseparents. Boarding houses at Moreton Hall are all linked informally with houses at Shrewsbury School, meeting regularly for musical, dramatic and social occasions.

Downside School

Stratton on the Fosse, Radstock, Bath, BA3 4RJ
Tel: (01761) 235100   Fax: (01761) 235105
E-mail: registrar@downside.co.uk   Web site: www.downside.co.uk

Head Dom Antony Sutch MA
Founded 1605
Type Boys' independent prep and senior
boarding and day
Religious denomination Catholic
Member of HMC
Age range 8–18; *boarders from* 8
No of pupils (day) 45; *(boarding)* 295
Junior 60; *Senior* 280; *Sixth Form* 100
Fees per annum (boarding) £11,988–£15,093;
(day) £6,984–£7,767

Downside offers a broad, balanced academic education to GCSE and A Level. Entry at 8/10+, 13+ or 16+ but can be at other stages depending upon assessment, report and interview. Day pupils benefit from the many opportunities available in a caring Benedictine community whilst having the flexibility to return home after classes or after prep. Pupils in the Fifth Form (Year 11) and above have individual study bedrooms.

Downside has a strong sporting and musical tradition. Facilities include a theatre, recently upgraded ICT facilities, design, art and ceramics centres, sports hall and indoor pool.

Details of scholarships and awards from the registrar.

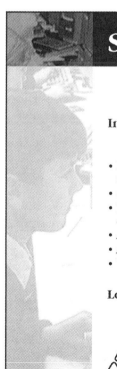

Kingswood School

Lansdown, Bath, BA1 5RG
Senior School: Tel: (01225) 734200   Fax: (01225) 734205
Prep School: Tel: (01225) 310468   Fax: (01225) 247179
E-mail: registrar@kingswood.bath.sch.uk
Web site: www.kingswood.bath.sch.uk   www.gabbitas.net

Principal Gary M Best MA
Prep School Head Miss Anita Gleave
Founded 1748
Type Co-educational independent prep and
senior boarding and day
Religious denomination Methodist foundation
but all denominations welcome
Member of HMC, GBA, ISIS, BSA, IAPS
Age range 3–18; *boarders from* 7
No of pupils Senior School (day) 398; (boarding)
174; *Prep* (day) 290; (boarding) 9
Girls 236; *boys* 336
Prep 299; *Sixth Form* 170
Fees per annum (boarding) £10,998–£15,498;
(weekly) £10,899–£13,698;
(day) £4,029–£8,499

Kingswood School believes that each individual child has a variety of talents and abilities needing development to the full. That is why education at Kingswood goes far beyond the 'classroom' teaching and each pupil is offered a unique educational experience. The school has a dedicated and caring staff committed to encouraging their pupils to reach this goal in every way, in an atmosphere of enthusiasm, enjoyment, security and respect for others. Kingswood is a co-educational school for pupils aged 3–18 and is dedicated to providing continuity of education from nursery through to Sixth Form in a happy, caring and disciplined environment, based on Christian principles. Its strengths include the level of pastoral care provided for both day and boarding pupils and the wide range of extra-curricular activities that go towards the development of a broader outlook for each individual child. It offers excellent facilities for both boarders and day pupils in one of the most beautiful school sites in the south of England – standing in 218 acres of parkland at Lansdown on the northside of the world-heritage city of Bath and is within easy reach of major road, rail and air links.

Drama, Sport and Music are key elements within both the curriculum and in extra-curricular activities with a brand new Music School opened in May 2000, with its own recording studios. There is also a 'state-of-the-art' theatre. Academic Scholarships, Special Talent Awards, HM Forces Remissions and Bursaries are available for entry in September 2002. Please contact the registrar on 01225 734210 for an appointment to visit or see the web site for further information: www.kingswood.bath.sch.uk

A new CD Rom prospectus is now available.

Millfield School

Millfield, Street, Somerset, BA16 0YD
Tel: (01458) 442291   Fax: (01458) 447276   E-mail: admissions@millfield.somerset.sch.uk
Web site: www.millfield.somerset.sch.uk   www.gabbitas.net

Head PM Johnson
Founded 1935
Type Co-educational independent pre-prep
prep and senior boarding and day
Religious denomination Multi-denominational
Member of HMC, IAPS
Special needs provision DYS
Age range 2–19; *boarders from* 7
Pre-prep 129; *Junior* 456; *Senior* 675;
Sixth Form 559
Fees per annum on application

Millfield welcomes students from all social and academic backgrounds, one of the few independent schools that can claim to offer a fully comprehensive intake.

The importance of a balanced education at Millfield is a well tried and tested formula. It has high academic standards, an exceptionally high teacher:pupil ratio, and world-class facilities, which include 23 tennis courts (including an indoor tennis centre), athletics track, fencing salle, equestrian centre with polo pitch and show jumping arena and an Olympic-size swimming pool. Other facilities on campus include a theatre, fine arts gallery, observatory and science laboratories and an award-winning library.

Registered charity no. 310283.

The Royal High School, Bath (GDST)

Lansdown Road, Bath BA1 5SZ
Tel: (01225) 313877/313873   Fax: (01225) 465446
E-mail: royalhigh@bat.gdst.net
Web site: www.gdst.net/royalhighbath   www.gabbitas.net

Headmaster Mr J Graham-Brown BA (Hons)
Type Girls boarding and day (GDST school)
Religious denomination Non-denominational
Member of LCST DipSld(Dyslexia) awarded by
the Dyslexia Association, AMBDA
Special needs provision DEL, DYS, DYP, EBD,
EPI, HI, MLD, VIS
Age range 3–18; *boarders from* 10
No of pupils (day) 800; *(boarding)* 100
Nursery 28; *Junior* 292; *Senior* 597
Fees per term (boarding) £3,564;
(day) £1,058–£1,814 (10 per cent discount for
service children)

With excellent results at both GCSE and Advanced Level and a 12:1 teacher to pupil ratio, the Royal High School aims to foster a dynamic and supportive environment in which girls of academic ability are encouraged to pursue a wide range of intellectual, cultural and recreational interests.

A recent extensive re-development programme has ensured that junior and senior pupils enjoy outstanding facilities including a sports hall and modern science block.

New high quality boarding is complemented by a strong day community where academic excellence is valued, balanced with participation in sport, music, drama, clubs, societies and extra curricular activities.

Maple Hayes Hall Dyslexia School

Abnalls Lane, Lichfield, Staffordshire WS13 8BL
Tel: (01543) 264387   Fax: (01543) 262022
E-mail: brown-dr@dyslexia-maplehayes.staffs.sch.uk
Web site: www.dyslexia.gb.com   www.gabbitas.net

Head Dr E Neville Brown
Founded 1982
Type Co-educational independent boarding and day (girls day only)
Religious denomination Inter-denominational
Member of ISIS, ISA, ISC, ECIS; *accredited by* DfES
Special needs provision DYC, DYS, DYP, SPLD
Age range 7–17; *boarders from* 7
No of pupils (day) 70; *(boarding) (boys only)* 40
Fees per annum (weekly boarding) £11,475–£14,685; *(day)* £9,045–£12,255

Maple Hayes Hall is one of the select few schools for dyslexics and underachievers which is inspected and approved by the Department for Education and Skills. The School is set in extensive grounds near Lichfield and caters for up to 120 children from 7 to 17 years. We have a worldwide reputation for our unique and effective teaching methods and for our examination results. After taking GCSE with us, most students go on to higher education at college or university.

We provide a good all-round education without the stigma of withdrawal to a special unit and our youngsters compete well in the Midland and National Independent School sports championships.

Children's learning is under the supervision of a chartered psychologist and an assessment service is available. Private and LEA placements are welcome. In addition to bursaries for private placements, there is a bursary scheme for children of very high intelligence. Admission is by interview and psychologist's report.

Belmont School

Feldemore, Holmbury St Mary, Dorking, Surrey RH5 6LQ
Tel: (01306) 730829/730852   Fax: (01306) 731220
E-mail: schooloffice@belmontschool.org   Web site: www.belmont-school.org   www.gabbitas.net

Head David Gainer BEd Hons (London)
Founded 1870
Type Independent co-educational pre-prep and prep boarding and day
Religious denomination Church of England
Member of IAPS
Age range 4–13; *boarders from* 7
No of pupils (day) 234; (boarding) 40
Girls 80; *boys* 194
Fees per annum (weekly boarding) £10,179; (day) £3,625–£6,996

A very happy co-educational IAPS school for children aged 4 to 13, with good weekly boarding facilities from 7 upwards. No Saturday school leads to full family weekend.

Excellent academic and sporting traditions in a caring, friendly environment. Beautiful grounds in rural Surrey within easy reach of central London. A magnificent 'home from home'.

A purpose-built Dyslexia Unit (Moon Hall) with highly trained specialist staff. Sixty-acre estate with playing fields, all-weather hockey pitch, gymnasium, sports hall and open air swimming pool.

Completely refurbished main house, with extensive modern facilities. Fully-equipped computer room and new art and CDT area. New dining room building recently completed. Emphasis on broad curriculum and exposure to very wide range of extra-curricular activities. Very good interaction between day and boarding pupils.

A new multipurpose sports hall has just been completed.

Further information and prospectus from the headmaster's secretary.

Box Hill School ✓

Mickleham, Dorking, Surrey RH5 6EA
Tel: (01372) 373382   Fax: (01372) 363942
E-mail: registrar@boxhillschool.org.uk   Web site: www.boxhillschool.org.uk   www.gabbitas.net

Head Dr RAS Atwood BA, PhD
Founded 1959
Type Co-educational independent senior boarding and day
Religious denomination Non-denominational
Member of SHMIS, ISCO, Round Square
Accredited by ISJC
Special needs provision DYS
Age range 11–18; *boarders from* 11
No of pupils (day) 164; *(boarding)* 159
Girls 115; *boys* 208
Senior 223; *Sixth Form* 100
Fees per annum (boarding) (full) £12,894; *(weekly)* £11,115; *(day)* £5,685–£7,527

Average size of class: 15
Teacher:pupil ratio: 1:8.5
Entry requirements and procedures: interview; written tests in Maths and English; confidential report from previous school; Common Entrance where appropriate.
Educational extras: most extras are genuinely personal (ie transport, toiletries, clothes). Some A Level texts must be purchased and all Sixth Form parents are asked to provide £40 to £50 for cultural outings and theatre trips.
Curriculum: wide range of subjects in Years 7 to 9 including Art, Music, Computing, Design. Expeditions to York, Pilgrim's Way, and the Lakes combine academic work with outdoor pursuits. Years 10 and 11: English, English Literature, Mathematics, individual or combined Sciences, choice of 12 other options. Form 6: choice of 20 A Levels.
Subject specialities and academic track record: strong in Maths and English, also Art, Physical Education, Drama, Computing, Design/Technology. In art over past three years two thirds of grades A or A*. Special needs: two full time dyslexia specialists. ESL courses for overseas students.
Examinations offered: wide choice at both GCSE and A Level; no attempt to force pupils into a mould. Small tutor groups. Subjects chosen from nearly all exam groups and boards.

Destination and career prospects of leavers: nearly all A Level leavers go on to university. Some do gap years as junior staff at sister schools abroad.
Academic and leisure facilities include: science and design/technology blocks, classroom block, computing and electronics rooms, recently extended art facility, drama studio, multi-purpose hall/gymnasium, 35 acres of playing fields with outdoor heated swimming pool, plus a fitness room and cyber cafe.
Termly exchanges and visits with sister schools in Germany, Australia, Switzerland, USA and Canada offer unique opportunities, particularly for languages. Project work undertaken in India.
The School is situated in an attractive country village, within easy distance of Gatwick and Heathrow airports and the M25, and 45 minutes from central London by train.
The School is a registered charity providing a broad education for children both boarding and day.
Scholarships, exhibitions and bursaries: there is a sliding scale of day fees in Years 7, 8 and 9. Two half fees scholarships are offered at 11 plus and two at 13 plus. There are bursaries varying from 10 per cent to 20 per cent at the same ages. Ten scholarships are awarded each year for Sixth-Form entry.

Canbury School

Kingston Hill, Kingston upon Thames, Surrey KT2 7LN
Tel: (020) 8549 8622   Fax: (020) 8974 6018

Head Mr R Metters BEd
Founded 1982
Type Co-educational independent senior day
Religious denomination Non-denominational
Member of ISA
Age range 10–16
No of pupils 70
Girls 25; *boys* 45
Fees per annum £6,600

Curriculum: we cover a full range of GCSE subjects, most pupils taking a total of eight or nine.

Entry requirements: there are tests in English and Maths. The headmaster interviews each candidate. A trial day or two at the School can be arranged prior to entry.

Subjects offered: in Years 7, 8 and 9 we emphasise English, Mathematics and Science in line with the requirements of the National Curriculum. Our extended curriculum includes Spanish, French, Geography, History, Information Technology, Art, Drama, Music and Personal and Moral Education. Later, Physics, Chemistry and Biology are taken as doubly-certificated GCSE subjects. Individual arrangements can be made for pupils to prepare for GCSE in German, Chinese and other languages. Business Studies and Spanish are offered in Years 10 and 11 as an option leading to the GCSE.

Facilities: IT computer facilities are accessible to all pupils. There is an excellent art room. Pupils are transported to a wide range of sports facilities within the borough.

Canbury School is different in placing emphasis on small classes. No class has more than 15 pupils. Full concentration is placed on bringing out the talents of each pupil. Pupils participate in the school council which makes decisions in some areas of school life.

Caterham School

Harestone Valley Road, Caterham, Surrey CR3 6YA
Tel: (01883) 343028   Fax: (01883) 347795
E-mail: caterhamschool@caterham.rmplc.co.uk   Web site: www.caterhamschool.surrey.sch.uk

Head Mr R Davey MA
Founded 1811
Type Co-educational independent pre-prep, prep and senior boarding and day
Religious denomination URC
Member of HMC, IAPS, GBA; *accredited by* ISC
Special needs provision ADD, DYC, DYS, DYP, SPLD, TOU
Age range 3–18; *boarders from* 11
No of pupils (day) 860 *(boarders)* 133
Girls 382; *boys* 611
Prep 263; *Senior* 513; *Sixth Form* 217
Fees per annum (full boarding) £15,183–£16,002; *(day)* £2,673–£8,580

Caterham School's commitment to academic excellence combined with its achievements in sport, music and drama, testify to its success in providing an all-round education. This fully co-educational HMC boarding and day school offers boys and girls from 3 to 18 a friendly and stimulating environment designed to educate for life. The School is served by a committed and caring staff.

Individuals are taught respect for others, concern for the community and self discipline. The School is large enough to provide a full range of academic courses and extra-curricular activities but small enough to allow everybody to be known and to make their mark.

The School is located conveniently in a beautiful 80 acre site of wooded valley with easy access from the M25 and with good rail and bus links.

Claremont Fan Court School ✓

Claremont Drive, Esher, Surrey KT10 9LY
Tel: (01372) 467841   Fax: (01372) 471109   E-mail: admissions@claremont.surrey.sch.uk
Web site: www.claremont-school.co.uk   www.gabbitas.net

Principal Patricia B Farrar
Founded 1922
Type Co-educational independent pre-prep,
prep and senior boarding and day
Religious denomination Christian
Member of GBA, ISBA, ISIS, SHA, SHMIS
Special needs provision DYS, DYP
Age range 3–18; *boarders from* 11 (Christian
Scientists only)
No of pupils (day) 579; (boarding) 22
Girls 277; *boys* 302
Junior (Upper and Lower) 274; *Senior* 247;
Sixth Form 58
Fees per term (boarding) £4,275–£4,415;
(weekly) £3,615–£3,755; *(day)* £815–£2,740

The School is situated in the Claremont Estate,
one of the premier historic sites in the country.
The original house and the famous landscape
garden were first laid out by Sir John Vanbrugh
for the Duke of Newcastle early in the 18th
century. Later Capability Brown built the present Palladian mansion for Clive of India and
landscaped the grounds in his typical manner.
For over a century Claremont was a royal
residence and played an important part in
Queen Victoria's early years.

Aims: an excellent academic programme with
small class sizes provides the pupils with a wide
and varied curriculum. Each child receives a
breadth of educational, cultural, social and
sporting opportunities, through which the
potential of each individual can be realised.
High expectations and moral values are established and developed within small classes in a
happy, positive environment, free from the
excessive pressures sometimes placed on young
people today.

Curriculum: The expectation of high academic
achievement and personal growth is established

in the junior years. The syllabus follows
National Curriculum guidelines but our expectations of attainment are well beyond the
national levels. The academic programme in
Senior School ensures that all pupils attain
the highest qualifications of which they are
capable for entry into university or college.

Students from Claremont Fan Court School
also have a strong tradition of excellence in
Technology, Drama, Music, Art and Sport.
Facilities include five ICT suites, a fully
equipped Design Technology studio and workshop, and a specialised Textiles and Food
technology unit. Major drama productions are
performed in the Joyce Grenfell Centre for the
Performing Arts. The Music Department benefits from excellent Music Technology facilities.
A new fully equipped Sports Centre and Gymnasium have recently enhanced sports at
Claremont. Teams compete regularly with
neighbouring schools, with individuals com-
peting at county and national levels.

Entry to the School: Applications for entry into
the School are welcome at all levels. Principal
intakes are at 3+, 4+, 7+, 11+, 13+ and Sixth
Form.

Scholarships: Academic scholarships are available at Years 3, 7, 9 and Sixth Form. Music, Art
and Sport scholarships are also available.

Cranleigh Preparatory School

Horseshoe Lane, Cranleigh, Surrey GU6 8QH
Tel: (01483) 274199   Fax: (01483) 277136
E-mail: enquiries@cranleigh-school.demon.co.uk   Web site: www.gabbitas.net

Head Michael Roulston MBE, n Ed
Founded 1881
Type Boys' independent prep boarding and day
Religious denomination Church of England
Member of IAPS, ISIS
Age range 7–13; *boarders from* 7
No of pupils (day) 130; *(boarding)* 50
Fees per annum (boarding) £11,260; *(day)*
£8,400

Founded in 1881, the School stands in its own beautiful 35 acres. It is essentially a boarding school, the benefits of which are available to day boys. Boarding life is busy and fun, with committed staff, full weekends, and regular exeats. Mr and Mrs Roulston and boarding staff also live in the main building.

Boys enter from age 7, and are prepared for Common Entrance or scholarships. Two-thirds proceed to Cranleigh School, across the road. A broad, balanced but academic curriculum includes computing, Art and design, pottery, woodwork, metalwork, music (including three choirs and an orchestra), and many time-tabled activities.

Sport is strong and varied. Rugby, soccer, hockey, cricket, tennis, swimming and athletics are the main sports, among many others.

Facilities are excellent, the latest development is a building (October 1996) to house a new Computer Department and classrooms.

Croham Hurst School

79 Croham Road, South Croydon, Surrey CR2 7YN
Tel: (020) 8686 7347   Fax: (020) 8688 1142
E-mail: crohamh@aol.com

Head Miss SC Budgen
Founded 1889
Type Girls' independent pre-prep, prep and senior day
Religious denomination Inter-denominational
Member of GSA, ISIS, GBGSA
Special needs provision DYS, EFL
Age range 3–18
Junior 171; *Senior* 305; *Sixth Form* 68
Fees per annum £3,735–£6,735

Croham Hurst occupies an attractive open site and is easily accessible by public transport.

The School maintains a reputation for high academic achievement and is committed to developing the individual potential of each girl. We have a proven record of excellent results at GCSE and A Level and an established tradition of university entrance, including Oxbridge.

Many girls begin their education in the lively, stimulating environment of the on-site Junior School. This is sustained in the Senior School by the broad curriculum in the first three years, where National Curriculum subjects are supplemented by Classical Studies, Latin, German, Spanish and Textiles. We offer an extensive range of option courses, providing a choice from 24 subjects at GCSE and 20 at A Level. Girls are encouraged to achieve high standards and their learning is supported by small teaching groups and the flexibility to provide 'tailor-made' timetables in order to accommodate the needs of the individual pupils' personal talents and interests can be extended through an exciting programme of extra-curricular activities.

Entrance is by interview and test relevant to age. Bursaries and scholarships, including Sixth-Form scholarships, are available.

Duke of Kent School

Ewhurst, Cranleigh, Surrey GU6 7NS
Tel: (01483) 277313   Fax: (01483) 273862
E-mail: dok.school@virgin.net   Web site: dukeofkent.surrey.sch.org.uk   www.gabbitas.net

Head Dr Alan Cameron
Founded 1976
Type Co-educational independent pre-prep and prep boarding and day
Religious denomination Inter-denominational
Member of IAPS; *Accredited by* IAPS
Special needs provision DYS
Age range 4–13; *boarders from* 7
No of pupils (day) 150; *(boarding)* 55
Girls 88; *boys* 117
Fees per annum (day) £4,405–£8,150; *(boarding)* £9,360–£11,220

A happy and caring co-educational day and boarding school situated in a beautiful location in the Surrey hills with easy access to Gatwick, Heathrow and major stations. It has outstanding facilities including science and computer labs, modern classroom block and dormitories, music school, workshops, indoor heated pool, large sports hall, spacious playing fields and grounds. *Curriculum:* all main subjects required for Common Entrance and public school scholarships plus Art, Music, Drama, CDT, Computer Studies, hobbies and a structured games programme.
Entry: placement tests and interviews. Bursaries and scholarships available.

Frensham Heights

Rowledge, Farnham, Surrey GU10 4EA
Tel: (01252) 792134   Fax: (01252) 794335
E-mail: Headmaster@frensham-heights.org.uk   Web site: www/demon.co.uk./frensham-heights

Head Peter M de Voil MA, FRSA
Founded 1925
Type Co-educational independent junior and senior boarding and day
Religious denomination Non-denominational
Member of HMC, BSA
Special needs provision DYS, TESL
Age range 3–18; *boarders from* 11
No of pupils (day) 347; *(boarding)* 113
Girls 220; *boys* 240
Junior 120; *Senior* 250; *Sixth Form* 90
Fees per annum (boarding) (full) £14,700–£15,900; *(weekly)* £13,500–£15,360; *(day) (senior school upwards)* £9,600–£10,656

Frensham Heights is a fully co-educational HMC boarding (full or weekly) and day school of 460 pupils aged between 3 and 18. The School's philosophy endorses liberal values and promotes strong personal relationships and respect for the individual. It achieves distinguished results in the performing and creative arts. Classes are small and academic results are excellent. New facilities include a £2m Performing Arts Centre, an indoor sports Hall, modern science laboratories, a fully equipped ICT Suite and an adventure centre for Outdoor Education. The School is situated in beautiful grounds near Farnham, 45 minutes from Heathrow and Gatwick airports.

Greenacre School for Girls

Sutton Lane, Banstead, Surrey SM7 3RA
Tel: (01737) 352114   Fax: (01737) 373485
E-mail: admin@greenacre.school.com
Web site: www.greenacre.school.com   www.gabbitas.net

Head Mrs PM Wood, BA
Founded 1933
Type Girls' independent nursery through to senior day
Religious denomination Non-denominational
Member of GSA, GBGSA, ISIS, ISBA
Age range 3–18
No of pupils 410
Junior 168; *Senior* 209; *Sixth Form* 33
Fees per annum £4,050–£6,900

Greenacre, founded in 1933, provides a full education to girls from age 3 to 18. High academic achievements are expected and excellent results show the hard work of pupils, as well as the commitment of the staff. The girls are prepared for the ever changing world in which they must live, blending traditional values into the modern world. Staff encourage them to develop their talents which are unique to each of them.

The Sixth Form Centre provides excellent facilities and the long established tutorial system provides support to them throughout their courses, with over 20 subjects to choose from at AS and A Level. Careers advice is always available. The School's facilities offer a swimming pool, Sports Hall and modern Science Building. Extra curricular activities include Duke of Edinburgh Scheme, computer, music and drama clubs. Strong performances are achieved in Drama by productions performed to governors, staff, parents and friends.

Hoe Bridge School

Hoe Place, Old Woking Road, Woking, Surrey GU22 8JE
Tel: (01483) 760018   Fax: (01483) 757560
E-mail: hoebridge@hoebridge.surrey.sch.uk   Web site: www.hoebridge.surrey.sch.uk

Prep School Head RWK Barr;
Pre-Prep Head Mrs LM Renfrew
Type Co-educational independent
Religious denomination Non-denominational
Member of IAPS; *accredited by* ISC
Special needs provision DYS, MLD
Age range 2½–14
No of pupils 430; *girls* 100; *boys* 330
Fees per annum (day) £975–£7,575

The Pre-Preparatory Department is for children aged between 2½ and 7. This is a very attractive purpose-built school with its own play areas in landscaped grounds. There is a specially designed Nursery Unit which forms part of the School.

The Prep School prepares boys and girls between the ages of 7 and 14 for the scholarship and Common Entrance requirements of all senior independent schools. The curriculum includes those subjects, games and activities necessary for a child's development.

The School is situated on the outskirts of Woking and stands in its own grounds of 20 acres. These afford admirable facilities for all games and outdoor pursuits, including rugby, soccer, hockey, netball, basketball, cricket, athletics, tennis and swimming.

A 17th century mansion forms the heart of the school but extensive architect designed buildings have been added over the past ten years. These include laboratories, changing rooms, classrooms and a multi-purpose Sports Hall.

The school has a Design Centre set in a restored 17th century tower and stable block. This provides superb facilities for art, design technology and information technology. ICT is networked throughout the school and there are two computer suites.

A new Music School was opened in September 2001, and plans are underway for a new Arts Centre to be added in 2002.

Hurtwood House ✓

Holmbury St Mary, Dorking, Surrey RH5 6NU
Tel: (01483) 277416   Fax: (01483) 267586
E-mail: hurtwood2@aol.com   Web site: www.hurtwood-house.co.uk   www.gabbitas.net

---

Head KRB Jackson
Founded 1970
Type Co-educational independent senior
boarding and day
Religious denomination Non-denominational
Member of ISA; *accredited by* ISC

Age range 16–18; *boarders from* 16
No of pupils (day) 10; *(boarding)* 280
Girls 150; *boys* 140
Fees per annum (full boarding) £18,000–
£20,000; *(day)* £12,000–£13,000

THE SCHOOL WITH THE BEST PERFORMANCE

HURTWOOD HOUSE

For further details, please contact:
Richard Jackson
Hurtwood House
Holmbury St Mary
Dorking, Surrey, RH5 6NU
T: 01483 277416
F: 01483 267586
E: hurtwood2@aol.com
www.hurtwood-house.co.uk

Not only does Hurtwood House have the biggest and best Drama and Media Departments in England, with superb professional facilities, but it is also hugely successful academically and is one of The Times 'top 10' mixed independent schools this year.

Uniquely, our 300 boarding students join us after GCSE, when they are ready for the fresh challenge of a sixth-form where life is as exciting and stimulating as it is at university. Structured and secure, innovative and dynamic, Hurtwood House is one of England's most successful and exciting schools.

Kingston Grammar School   ✓

70–72 London Road, Kingston on Thames, Surrey KT2 6PY
Tel: (020) 8546 5875   Fax (020) 8547 1499
E-mail: head@Kingston-grammar.surrey.sch.uk   Web site: www.kingston-grammar.surrey.sch.uk

Head Mr CD Baxter
Founded 1561
Type Co-educational independent prep and senior day
Religious denomination Church of England but all faiths welcomed
Member of HMC
Age range 10–18
No of pupils 600
Girls 240; *boys* 360
Junior 25; *Senior* 415; *Sixth Form* 160
Fees per annum £7,803–£8,043

In Years 1 and 2 pupils follow a wide curriculum including Latin, French, German and Technology. In the Third Year an option scheme introduces Spanish. Further options are undertaken in the Fourth Year where the pupils select ten subjects for GCSE. A number take Mathematics in the Fourth Year. In the Sixth Form a comprehensive range of A2 Levels and AS Levels are available. At all levels pupils receive careers advice and have a timetable constructed based on their options.

Entry requirements: entry at 10+ and 11+ is by examination in January, at 13+ by Common Entrance or our own examination. At 16+ entrance is by interview and GCSE results. Academic, art, music and sports awards are available.

Kingston Grammar School Foundation, a registered charity, exists to provide high quality education for girls and boys.

Marymount International School   ✓

George Road, Kingston upon Thames, Surrey KT2 7PE
Tel: (020) 8949 0571   Fax: (020) 8336 2485   E-mail: admissions@marymount.kingston.sch.uk
Web site: www.marymount.kingston.sch.uk   www.gabbitas.net

Head Sister Rosaleen Sheridan RSHM
Founded 1955
Type Girls' independent prep and senior boarding and day
Religious denomination Roman Catholic
Member of Sisters of the Sacred Heart of Mary, GSA, ECIS; *accredited by* ECIS, ISC, MSA (USA)
Special needs provision MLD
Age range 11–18; *boarders from* 11
No of pupils (day) 120; *(boarding)* 87
Grades 6–10 116; *Grades 11–12* 91
Fees per annum (boarding) (full) £17,300–£18,370; *(weekly)* £17,060–£18,130; *(day)* £9,630–£10,700

Curriculum: International Baccalaureate (IB) and American College Preparatory. Marymount was the first school in the UK to be accredited to offer the IB Middle Years Programme – a pre-IB course for Grades 6–10. The IB diploma course follows in Grades 11–12.

Entry requirements: reports for previous three years.

Boarding facilities: a new boarding extension provides modern recreational facilities and additional boarding accommodation, with single rooms for seniors.

Facilities: Computer Centre, Sports Hall, Theatre, Music Centre, modern science block. The 7-acre campus is conveniently situated for London and its airports. Marymount is an independent school with students of over 40 nationalities.

Parsons Mead School

no email

Ottways Lane, Ashtead, Surrey KT21 2PE
Tel: (01372) 276401   Fax: (01372) 278796   Web site: www.gabbitas.net

Head Mrs P Taylor BA(Hons)
Founded 1897
Type Girls' independent nursery, pre-prep, prep and senior day
Religious denomination Church of England
Member of GSA, AHIS, BSA; *accredited by* ISC
Special needs provision DYS, HI
Age range 3–18
No of pupils 300
Junior 135; *Senior* 135; *Sixth Form* 30
Fees per annum £4,485–£7,521

Parsons Mead provides an excellent all-round education in a happy and caring environment. Classes are small averaging 17. Girls gain excellent results at KS1, KS2, GCSE and A Level. Former pupils are studying for degrees at many leading universities including Oxford. Music, Drama and sport flourish. The School has a sports hall, heated outdoor pool and drama studio. Clubs and societies include Brownies, Young Engineers, Young Enterprise and Duke of Edinburgh Award Scheme. Facilities are constantly upgraded. In 1998 a new Junior building and Sixth Form centre were opened. Day boarding is available from 7.30am and until 6.30pm and flexible occasional boarding is popular. Minibuses run from Tadworth, Kingston/Surbiton and from Ashtead Station.

Prior's Field ✓

Godalming, Surrey GU7 2RH
Tel: (01483) 810551   Fax: (01483) 810180   E-mail: admin@priorsfield.surrey.sch.uk
Web site: www.priorsfield.demon.co.uk   www.gabbitas.net

Head Mrs J Dwyer, BEd Hons (Cantab)
Founded 1902
Type Girls' independent boarding and day
Religious denomination Non-denominational
Member of GSA
Special needs provision DYS
Age range 11–18; *boarders from* 11
No of pupils (day) 193; *(boarding)* 95
Senior 236; *Sixth Form* 52
Fees per term (boarding) £4,660; *(day)* £3,116

Prior's Field is set in 25 acres of Surrey countryside outside Guildford and succeeds in securing excellent examination results in a friendly atmosphere where small classes build confidence and encourage motivation. A wide range of AS and A Level subjects are offered and most leavers proceed to university. Reduced fees for service daughters and annual scholarships. Duke of Edinburgh, Young Enterprise and visits abroad breed self reliance. A new Sports Hall has been completed. Sports include netball, hockey, athletics and regional standard tennis. There is a tradition of choral training and drama productions. Individual study bedrooms for Senior girls and Sixth Formers. Entry 11+, 13+ and 6th Form.

Reed's School, Cobham

Sandy Lane, Cobham, Surrey KT11 2ES
Tel: (01932) 869044   Fax: (01932) 869046   Web site: www.gabbitas.net

Head D W Jarrett
Founded 1813
Type Boys' boarding and day; girls' sixth form
Religious denomination Church of England
Member of HMC, SHMIS
Age range 11–18; *boarders from* 11
No of pupils (day) 193; *(boarding)* 95
Girls 30; *boys* 424
Fees per annum (boarding) £12,153–£14,799; *(day)* £9,114–£11,187

The headmaster is assisted by a permanent full-time teaching staff of 42 including a school chaplain and pupils are prepared for GCSE, AS and A level examinations with a variety of boards. Up to the beginning of GCSE courses, the school broadly follows the National Curriculum. At GCSE all boys take English, maths, French and science; most pupils take 9 or 10 subjects. A wide range of A level subjects is available including some courses taught in conjunction with a local girls school.

Registration and Entry: pupils may be registered at any time and entry is at ages 11+, 12+, 13+ and sixth form. Entry at 11+ and 12+ is by special examination, whilst that at 13+ is normally by Common Entrance. Sixth form entry is determined by GCSE results, school report and interview. Foundation bursaries are available to boys who are in need of a boarding education.

Scholarships: academic, music, art, technology, all-round and sports scholarships up to the value of half fees are offered each year for pupils entering at 11+ and 13+ respectively. Sixth-Form scholarships to the value of half fees are offered in November each year.

Facilities: seven science laboratories, specialist classrooms for languages, CDT, art, music, geography, printing and computing. Full facilities for rugby, hockey, cricket, tennis, squash, swimming, including sports hall, swimming pool, two artificial hockey pitches and nine tennis courts. A new library, day-boy centre and Sixth-Form Hall were added in 1966 and new laboratories and classrooms in 1998. A new Music School opened in 2001. There are three separate boarding houses, The Close for 11 and 12+, a middle school house and a sixth-form house.

The ethos of the school is directed towards academic achievement, and it offers a wide range of activities to encourage character development. Pupils participate in the Duke of Edinburgh's Award Scheme, there is a CCF contingent comprising RAF and Army units.

The school is situated just off the A3 in 40 acres of Surrey heathland within easy reach of Heathrow and Gatwick airports.

Application should be made to the Admissions Secretary.

Royal School Haslemere ✓

Farnham Lane, Haslemere, Surrey GU27 1HQ
Tel: (01428) 605805   Fax: (01428) 607451
E-mail: admissions@royal.surrey.sch.uk   Web site: www.royal.surrey.sch.uk   www.gabbitas.net

Head Mrs Lynne Taylor-Gooby BEd, MA
Founded 1840
Type Girls' (co-educational nursery)
independent pre-prep, prep and senior
boarding and day
Religious denomination Church of England
Member of GSA, BSA; *accredited by* GSA
Special needs provision DYS, MLD
Age range 3–18; *boarders from* 5
No of pupils (day) 279; *(boarding)* 63
Junior 153; *Senior* 159; *Sixth Form* 36
Fees per term (boarding) £3,768–£4,542;
(day) £1,698–£2,895

The School is located in an area of outstanding natural beauty. The Senior School is situated on the outskirts of the Surrey town of Haslemere, less than an hour by both road and rail from central London and Gatwick and Heathrow international airports. Set in a 30-acre site, the School is a blend of Edwardian and modern buildings, which provide first-class facilities. Boarding facilities are spacious and comfortable and there is a varied range of activities available out of school hours to both boarders and day girls alike. There is a supportive network of pastoral care with both the boarding and teaching staff as well as the senior girls having a role to play.

The Royal School places great emphasis on encouraging its girls to become outward looking, independent and considerate to others. The intake includes a wide ability range; expert academic teaching and an affirmative environment enables girls to achieve exceptional success in all public examinations and the School is justifiably proud of its alumni who have gone on to make their mark in many different fields.

Class sizes are small, averaging less than 20 girls. Facilities for computer studies, modern languages, performing arts, science and sport are excellent and many after-school activities are offered, including Young Enterprise, all levels of the Duke of Edinburgh's Award scheme, computer studies, Art, music drama and competitive sports. The School provides a full programme of activities for its students in the final weeks of the summer term following public examinations.

Our Junior School is a lively, flourishing establishment on its own 25-acre site, for girls aged 3 to 11 years and boys from 3 years. There is a strong emphasis on traditional teaching in small classes, with sensitive pastoral care. Academic standards are high.

Conscious of the needs of parents, The School offers a range of after-school care for all ages, and flexible boarding from 7 years. Day girls come from an extensive area, many taking advantage of the fleet of modern minibuses, which travel to Farnham and Haslemere stations, as well as the outlying, rural areas.

Scholarships are available at 11+ and 16, (academic, exhibition or in specific areas such as Art, dance, drama, music or physical education). Some bursaries are also available on application.

For further information, please contact Mrs H Davies, Admissions Registrar, Ext 252.

St Andrew's School, Woking

Church Hill House, Wilson Way, Horsell, Woking, Surrey GU21 4QW
Tel: (01483) 760943   Fax: (01483) 740314
E-mail: admin@st.andrews.woking.sch.uk
Web site: www.st-andrews.woking.sch.uk   www.gabbitas.net

Head Mr B Pretorius BEd
Founded 1936
Type Co-educational independent pre-prep and prep day
Religious denomination Church of England
Member of IAPS; *accredited by* ISI
Special needs provision DYS, MLD
Age range 3–13
No of pupils (day) 267
Fees per annum £4,065–£7,905

Curriculum: children are prepared for Common Entrance and scholarships to a wide range of senior schools with top awards won every year. New teaching facilities for all subjects including Science, Computing and Music. Separate rooms for Art, Pottery and Woodwork.

Academic and leisure activities: there is a sports hall, all weather tennis courts, heated pool and ample grounds for games. Major games are soccer, hockey, cricket, swimming, tennis and athletics. Evening activities include badminton, table-tennis, chess, drama and woodwork.
Entry requirements: 7+ scholarship. Entry tests for children over 6.

St Catherine's School   102

Station Road, Bramley, Guildford, Surrey GU5 0DF
Tel: (01483) 893363   Fax: (01483) 899608;   Junior School Tel: (01483) 899665
E-mail: schooloffice@st-catherines.surrey.sch.uk
Web site: www.st-catherines.surrey.sch.uk   www.gabbitas.net

Head Mrs AM Phillips MA Cantab
Founded 1885
Type Girls' independent pre-prep, prep and senior boarding and day
Religious denomination Church of England
Member of GSA, BSA
Special needs provision DYC, DYS, W
Age range 4–18; *boarders from* 11
No of pupils (day) 562; *(boarding) (full)* 30; *(weekly)* 100
Junior 185; *Senior* 392; *Sixth Form* 115
Fees per annum (boarding; full and weekly) £13,875; *(day)* £4,230–£8,445

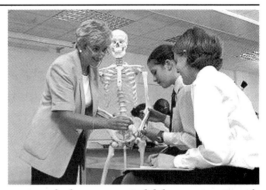

St Catherine's is fortunately situated at the heart of the attractive Surrey village of Bramley, 3 miles south of Guildford with its excellent facilities and main-line station. Access to Heathrow and Gatwick is easy via the A3 and M25. Teaching facilities are first-rate, with well-equipped classrooms and laboratories. Boarding accommodation has recently been refurbished to provide smaller study-bedrooms for 2–4 girls, and comfortable common rooms. Not only are the results at A Level and GCSE outstanding, but sport, drama, art and music flourish, as girls are encouraged to take part in a variety of activities outside the classroom.

St Teresa's School

Beech Avenue, Effingham Hill, Dorking, Surrey RH5 6ST
Tel: (01372) 452037   Fax: (01372) 450311
E-mail: info@stteresas.surrey.sch.uk Web site: www.stteresas.surrey.sch.uk   www.gabbitas.net

Senior Head Mrs ME Prescott BA (Hons), PGCE, FRSA
Preparatory Head Mrs AM Stewart MA (Hons), PGCE
Founded 1928
Type Girls' independent Pre-prep, Prep and senior boarding and day
Religious denomination Roman Catholic
Member of GSA, IAPS, GBGSA, BSA
Age range (preparatory school) 2–11; *(senior school)* 11–18; *boarders from* 7
No of pupils (day) 395; *(boarding)* 75
Preparatory 140; *Senior* 262; *Sixth Form* 68
Fees per annum (full boarding) £13,950; *(weekly boarding)* £13,050; *(day)* £7,950

St Teresa's, situated in beautiful rural surroundings, is only 40 minutes drive from Heathrow and Gatwick Airports and less than one hour's travelling distance from London. Local pupils have the amenity of coach services from a wide area. The early years in the Nursery and Pre-Preparatory departments are critical in terms of successful physical, social and intellectual development. In the Preparatory Department in addition to the main core subjects, music, sport, choir and orchestra play a vital role in the life of the School. There are many extra-curricular activities and the School has an extended day policy.

Entrance to the Senior School is at 11+ but girls who enter at 12+ and 13+ are warmly welcomed. Scholarships are available at all three levels of entry as well as Sixth Form. There are three forms in each year and all girls follow a very wide range of academically challenging subjects. As well as those who come up through the School, St Teresa's Sixth Form welcomes girls from elsewhere. 22 AS and A Level subjects are on offer and virtually all girls proceed to university including Cambridge and Oxford. Art, music, public speaking and sport are an integral part of life at St Teresa's with local and national recognition. There are 60+ extra-curricular activities on offer including Duke of Edinburgh's Award Scheme, Work Experience and the Young Enterprise Scheme.

The Boarding facilities are first class and the dormitories and rooms are organised on a year basis. Interesting activities are planned each weekend, however, built into the system, is the flexibility that girls may leave at any time during the weekend by arrangement.

TASIS The American School in England

Coldharbour Lane, Thorpe, Surrey TW20 8TE ✓
Tel: (01932) 565252   Fax: (01932) 564644
E-mail: ukadmissions@tasis.com   uksummer@tasis.com
Web site: www.tasis.com   www.gabbitas.net

Head Mr Barry Edward Breen
Founded 1976
Type Co-educational independent pre-prep,
prep and senior boarding and day
Religious denomination Non-denominational
Age range 4–18; *boarders from* 14
Member of ECIS, NEASC
No of pupils (day) 600; *(boarding)* 150
Girls 365; *boys* 385
Junior 420; *Senior* 330
Tuition per annum (full boarding) £19,080;
(day) £4,950–£11,300

TASIS England, frequently cited as the premier American school in the United Kingdom, is now into its third decade of offering an American college-preparatory curriculum to day students from grades Pre–K through 12 and to boarding students from Grades 9–12. Mrs M Crist Fleming, who established The American School in Switzerland in 1956, founded TASIS England in 1976. Located on a stunningly beautiful historic estate of Georgian mansions and 17th century cottages some 18 miles southwest of London, TASIS combines an excellent academic program with exceptional facilities for art, drama, music, computers, and sports. Small classes and over 100 dedicated, experienced faculty members provide highly individualised attention and an outstanding environment for learning.

TASIS England embraces four divisions: Early childhood, (Grades PK-2; ages 4–7) Lower (Grades 3–5; ages 8–10), Middle (Grades 6–8; ages 11–13), and Upper (Grades 9–12; ages 14–18). Students in each division regularly benefit from the opportunity to work closely with visiting artists, actors, musicians, and sports professionals. The comprehensive athletics program includes intramurals in the Lower School and interscholastic games for Middle School, JV, and Varsity teams. Throughout the year, students enjoy numerous field trips, weekend activities, and In-Program travel to London, elsewhere within the UK, and abroad. TASIS' ongoing commitment to provide its

students with the very best educational experience was recently underscored with the opening of the expanded Fine Arts Department. Virtually doubling the previous facility, the two storey addition enhances the School's acclaimed programs in drawing, painting, print-making, sculpture, and photography. The addition is the latest stage in the School's development plan, which has included the 400-seat Fleming Theatre, a new college counselling centre, and expanded dining facilities for the Upper and Middle Schools.

But it is only the combination of these facilities with a strong traditional academic program that has given TASIS its valued reputation both here and abroad. Each year TASIS students accept places at some of the finest universities within the UK, US, Canada, and elsewhere.

Admissions decisions for the academic school year are made on a rolling basis upon receipt of a completed application form together with the application fee, three teachers' recommendations, and three years of transcripts. Standardised test scores and a student questionnaire are requested, but are not required. An interview is recommended unless distance is a prohibiting factor. For additional information, please contact Mr Terry Giffen, Director of Admissions.

TASIS England also offers a Summer Program for day and boarding students from ages 12–18. Local and international students participate in: intensive courses offered for high school credit, enrichment programs, theatre workshops, ESL, TOEFL, and SAT Review. Students also enjoy extensive sports activities, and travel, both international and within the UK. For more information please contact Faie Gilbert, Director of Summer Admissions.

Wispers School for Girls, Haslemere ✓

High Lane, Haslemere, Surrey GU27 1AD
Tel: (01428) 643646 Fax: (01428) 641120 E-mail: Head@wispers.prestel.co.uk
Web site: www.wispers.org.uk   www.gabbitas.net
Station: Haslemere (Waterloo–Portsmouth Line)

Head Mr LH Beltran BA Hons (Exeter), PGCE (Leeds)
Founded 1947
Type Girls' independent senior boarding (full and weekly) and day
Age range 11–18   *No of pupils* 120
Fees per annum (boarding) £13,425; *(day)* £8,655

BRAVELY
- A clear vision and purpose for educating girls in the 21st Century

FAITHFULLY
- Outstanding opportunities offered, in excellent facilities, for the study of academic and vocational subjects individually suited to the pupils. Summer 2001 GCSE pass rate (A*–C) 89 per cent; A Level pass rate 100 per cent.

HAPPILY
- A heightened sense of community where governors, staff, parents and girls work together for the success of the school.

A FIRST CLASS SCHOOL SERVING THE LOCAL COMMUNITY

Registered as a Charity Number 307039

In Partnership with Surrey County Council and the University of Surrey
ADULT EDUCATION CENTRE 2001/2002

Woldingham School ✓

Marden Park, Woldingham, Surrey CR3 7YA
Tel: (01883) 349431   Fax: (01883) 348653   E-mail: registrar@woldingham.surrey.sch.uk
Web site: www.woldingham.surrey.sch.uk   www.gabbitas.net

Head Miss Diana Vernon BA
Founded 1842
Type Girls' independent senior boarding and day
Religious denomination Roman Catholic
Age range 11–18; *boarders from* 11
No of pupils (day) 120; *(boarding)* 440
Senior 410; *Sixth Form* 150
Fees per annum (full boarding) £16,320; *(day)* £9,735

Curriculum: most girls take nine to eleven GCSEs. All acquire at least a 'working knowledge' of two European languages and take science to 16+ either on an integrated or separate subject basis. The aim is to provide 'breadth and balance' so that alternative academic pathways are available at 16+. Sixth Formers study four AS Level subjects in the Lower Sixth and continue with three or four to A2 Level in the Upper Sixth. All Sixth Formers follow a General Studies programme.

Entry requirements and procedures: as a Roman Catholic school in the ecumenical tradition, Woldingham welcomes members of other traditions in sympathy with its educational philosophy. Girls normally enter at 11+ having taken the Common Entrance Examination.

This age group also attend the school for a one-day informal assessment during the previous autumn. Entry is also at 13+ and 16+ and some vacancies maybe available in other years. The Registrar will provide details. Sixth Form entrants should be capable of taking at least four AS Levels in Lower Sixth and three A2 Levels in Upper Sixth.

Examinations and Boards offered: GCSE Core Curriculum of 7 or 8 subjects with 3 options chosen from a further 10. Choice of 4 AS subjects from 23 in the Lower Sixth with 3 continued to A2 in the Upper Sixth. Sixth Form students prepared for entry to UK and American Universities including Oxbridge.

Boarding facilities: girls are organised on a year group basis, pastoral supervision and support being provided by senior teachers (Heads of Years) and assistant teachers. At Marden House 110 boarders, aged 11–13, share small dormitories. Senior House accommodates girls aged 13–17, with over half in single study bedrooms. Opened in 1992, Berwick House provides outstanding facilities with single rooms for Upper Sixth girls. A new sports centre opened in 1995, a new Art Centre opened January 1998, and new Drama and Music Centres and 600 seat auditorium opened in February 1999.

Ardingly College

Haywards Heath, West Sussex RH17 6SQ
Tel: (01444) 892577   Fax: (01444) 892266
E-mail: registrar@ardingly.com   Web site: www.ardingly.com   www.gabbitas.net

Head John Franklin
Founded 1858
Type Co-educational independent pre-prep,
prep and senior boarding and day
Religious denomination Church of England
Member of IAPS, HMC, Woodard S
Age range 2½–18; *boarders from* 7+
No of pupils (day) 416; *(boarding)* 279
Girls 279; *boys* 411
Junior & Pre-Prep 294; *Senior* 212;
Sixth Form 179
Fees per annum (boarding) £11,145–£16,125;
(day) (not incl Pre-Prep) £6,000–£12,075

One College: Ardingly College is one of Britain's leading independent co-educational boarding and day schools. There is a single campus which is shared by the Pre-Prep and Junior School of about 110 boys and 90 girls from 2–13, and the Senior School of about 250 boys and 170 girls from 13–18.

Location: the School is set in lovely English countryside, only 35 miles from central London, 18 miles north of Brighton and just nine miles from Gatwick Airport, which makes it particularly attractive to those who live overseas.

Ardingly is an academic school. As a general pattern, pupils will be expected to take nine GCSEs in the Fifth Form and four A/AS Levels in the Sixth Form or the International Baccalaurate. Class sizes throughout the school are small – fewer than 20 pupils for GCSE and about 12 per set for A Levels.

90 per cent of all Ardinians go on to further education. Ten or so candidates apply for Oxford or Cambridge and a good proportion is accepted each year. This sets high standards of expectation throughout the School. Ardinians are taught very much as individuals. There is splendid pastoral care with individual tutors for each pupil and a well-organised house system.

Most subjects studied here are the traditional ones common to many schools, but there are some, particularly in the Sixth Form, which are fairly unusual (English Language, Theatre Studies, Fine Art, Craft Art, Archaeology, Statistics and Physical Education).

Ardingly has an enviable reputation for excellence in sport, music and the creative arts. Outside the classroom there is a tremendous range of activity and pupils are encouraged to sample as much of it as they possibly can.

Scholarships: we offer academic, all-round, art, craft, design and technology, drama, language, music science and sports scholarships, which may be supplemented by a discretionary bursary.

Battle Abbey School

High Street, Battle, East Sussex TN33 0AD
Tel: (01424) 772385   Fax: (01424) 773573   E-mail: office@battleabbeyschool.btinternet.com
Web site: www.battleabbeyschool.com   www.gabbitas.net

Head Mr RC Clark BA, MA(Ed)
Founded 1922
Type Co-educational independent pre-prep,
prep and senior boarding and day
Religious denomination Christian non-
denominational
Member of SHMIS, GBGSA, ISIS
Accredited by ISIS
Special needs provision DYC, DYS (five trained
specialists), DYP, SP&LD
Age range 2½–18, *boarders from* 8
No of pupils (day) 270 *(boarding)* 54
Girls 153; *boys* 117
Junior 101; *Senior* 169; *Sixth Form* 46
Fees per annum (boarding) £10,401–£12,864;
(day) £4,374–£7,971

Battle Abbey School, which occupies one of the most famous historical sites in the world – that of the 1066 Battle of Hastings, is an independent, co-educational school for pupils from 2½ to 18. Boarders are accepted from the age of 8. The School is large enough to encourage healthy competition and to develop the social skills and awareness of others, learnt by being part of a lively community, but it is small enough to have many of the attributes of a large family. Teaching classes are small throughout the school, allowing individual attention and the opportunity for all pupils to achieve their maximum potential.

Brambletye

Lewes Road, East Grinstead, West Sussex RH19 3PD
Tel: (01342) 321004   Fax: (01342) 317562   E-mail: brambletye@brambletye.rmplc.co.uk
Web site: www.brambletye.com   www.gabbitas.net

Head Mr HD Cocke BA, CertEd (Oxon)
Founded 1919
Type Co-educational independent pre-prep and
prep boarding and day
Religious denomination Church of England
Member of IAPS, *Accredited by* ISC
Special needs provision DYS, DYP
Age range 3–13; *boarders from* 7
No of pupils (day) 129; *(boarding)* 86
Girls 44; *boys* 171
Fees per annum (full boarding) £12,300;
(day) £2,760–£10,200

Brambletye is an Educational Trust, which became fully co-educational in September 2000.
Children may start as boarders or day pupils, but there is an expectation that all boys and girls will board in their final three years.
Pupils are prepared for Common Entrance and Scholarships to a wide range of Independent Senior Schools.
Brambletye stands in its own 130 acre estate. It has its own Theatre, Art Department, indoor swimming pool, hard tennis courts, 6-hole golf course, Computer Centre and library. A new Sports Hall was opened in May 2000, and a new Pre-Preparatory building in September 2000.

Buckswood School

Broomham Hall, Rye Road, Guestling Nr Hastings, TN35 4LT
Tel: (01424) 813813   Fax: (01424) 812100
E-mail: achieve@buckswood.co.uk   Web site: www.buckswood.co.uk   www.gabbitas.net

Registrar Mrs Lynda Fletcher
Type Co-educational independent senior
boarding and day
Religious denomination non-denominational
Member of ARELS, ECIS; *accredited by* British
Council
Special needs provision DYS, MLD, SP&LD,
SPLD
Age range 11–19; *boarders from* 11
No of pupils (day) 13; *(boarders)* 67
Girls 30; *boys* 50   *Senior* 50; *Sixth Form* 30
Fees per annum (boarding) (full) £11,400–
£14,250; *(weekly)* £10,500; *(day)* £6,750

A truly international educational environment awaits your child at Buckswood. Parents select Buckswood because they know it is a school that contributes something special to their children's education. Its size allows the School to preserve a more home-like atmosphere, where the care and welfare of students is a priority.

Buckswood follows the British Curriculum and small classes for GCSE and A levels ensure pupils receive more individual attention.
We have a large campus near the seaside town of Hastings with a swimming pool, horse riding, large sports grounds and tennis – sports and activities play an important part of a Buckswood all-round education

Burgess Hill School for Girls

Keymer Road, Burgess Hill, West Sussex RH15 0EG
Tel: (01444) 241050   Fax: (01444) 870314   E-mail: registrar@burgesshill-school.com
Web site: www.burgesshill-school.com   www.gabbitas.net

Head Mrs S Gorham
Founded 1906
Type Girls' independent pre-prep, prep and senior boarding and day
Member of GSA
Religious denomination Inter-denominational
Special needs provision DYS
Age range 3–18; (boys from 3–5); boarders from 13
No of pupils (day) 765 (incl. nursery); *(boarding)* 50
Junior 255; *Senior* 319; *Sixth Form* 81
Fees per annum (boarding) £12,720; *(weekly boarding)* £11,235; *(day)* £3,600–£7,530

Burgess Hill School stands in 14 acres of beautiful grounds close to the centre of the town and is a 20-minute drive from Gatwick.

The excellent facilities include a fully equipped Science block, a new Technology laboratory, a new Learning Resources Centre, an Art & Design Studio, a Textiles centre, a Music centre and Drama Studio. The Sixth Form have their own centre with individual study areas, common rooms and an HE centre holding extensive careers advice.

The main aim of the School is to challenge the students to achieve goals well beyond their own expectations in all the activities they pursue. We educate for life and develop consideration for others, a love of learning, self-esteem and self-discipline. The curriculum is broad and challenging and relevant to the needs of young people. There is a wide choice of subjects both at GCSE and A-Level.

There are well appointed boarding houses adjoining the School grounds. The rooms and common rooms are spacious, light and pleasantly furnished and the atmosphere is informal and friendly.

The School also runs a daily bus service to and from a number of outlying districts including Turners Hill, Henfield, Cowfold, Lewes, Uckfield, Newick, East Grinstead and Worthing.

For further details please contact the Registrar.

Cottesmore School

Buchan Hill, Pease Pottage, West Sussex RH11 9AU
Tel: (01293) 520648   Fax: (01293) 614784
E-mail: schooloffice@cottesmoreschool.com   Web site: www.cottesmoreschool.com

Head MA Rogerson MA (Cantab)
Founded 1894
Type Co-educational independent boarding
Religious denomination Church of England
Special needs provision DYS, DYP, MLD
Age range 7–13; *boarders from* 7
No of pupils 150
Girls 50; *boys* 100
Fees per term £4,030
Fees per annum £12,090

Cottesmore is an all boarding school, situated one mile from Exit 11 of the M23, ten minutes from Gatwick Airport and one hour from central London and Heathrow Airport.

Curriculum: boys and girls are taught together in classes averaging 14 in number. The teacher:pupil ratio is 1:9. Children are fully prepared for Common Entrance and scholarship examinations.

Music: the musical tradition is strong, with more than 80 per cent of children learning a variety of instruments; there is a chapel choir, a school orchestra, and several musical ensembles.

Drama: several plays are produced every year, with major productions open to parents.

Sport: the major games are association and rugby football, cricket, hockey, netball and rounders. Numerous other sports are taught and encouraged. They include tennis, squash, golf, riding, athletics, cross country running, swimming (facilities include a 20 metre indoor pool), windsurfing, fishing, boating, gymnastics, shooting, judo, archery and trampolining. The school competes at a national level in several of these sports.

New development: a technology and computer centre was recently opened, comprising a highly specified IT suite, a junior laboratory, craftroom, art studio, ceramics room and technology workshop.

Hobbies and activities: these include pottery, photography, stamp collecting, chess, bridge, model-making, model railway, tenpin bowling, roller hockey, gardening, ballet, modern dancing, drama, craft, carpentry, printing, cooking and debating.

The boys and girls lead a full and varied life and are encouraged to take part in as wide a variety of activities as possible. With a third of the children having parents living and working abroad, weekends-in are a vital part of school life and are made busy and fun for all.

Entry requirements: entry is by Headmaster's interview and a report from the previous school. For a prospectus and more information, please write to, or telephone, the Headmaster's secretary.

Eastbourne College

Old Wish Road, Eastbourne, East Sussex BN21 4JX
Tel: (01323) 452323   Fax: (01323) 452354
E-mail: registrar@eastbourne-college.co.uk   Web site: www.eastbourne-college.co.uk

Head Mr CMP Bush MA (Oxon)
Founded 1867
Type Co-educational independent senior
boarding and day
Religious denomination Church of England
Member of HMC, BSA
Special needs provision DYS
Age range 13–18; *boarders from* 13
Girls 179; *boys* 348
Senior 300; *Sixth Form* 227
Fees per annum (full boarding) £16,545;
(day) £10,695

Eastbourne College is situated at the heart of a quiet, friendly town, a few minutes' walk from many amenities and adjacent to local theatres, the sea and Sussex Downs. Gatwick and Heathrow are within easy reach.

There are five boarding houses and four day houses at the College. First-class accommoda-tion ensures a reputation for excellent pastoral care.

Almost all pupils study ten subjects to GCSE, and most will study four at AS Level in 2001. Over 90 per cent of pupils go on to university, several annually to Oxford and Cambridge. There is an extensive careers advice programme. The School's size and strong boarding tradition ensure plenty of opportunity for all. Sport and the arts are especially strong. A new Learning Resources Centre opened in October 1998, and a new Science building will be completed in 2002.

Farlington School

Strood Park, Horsham, West Sussex RH12 3PN
Tel: (01403) 254967   Fax: (01403) 272258   E-mail: theoffice@farlington.w-sussex.sch.uk
Web site: www.farlington.w-sussex.sch.uk   www.gabbitas.net

Head Mrs PM Mawer BA
Founded 1896
Type Girls' independent pre-prep, prep and
senior boarding and day
Religious denomination Church of England (but
open to all denominations)
Member of GSA, BSA, IAPS
Accredited by IAPS, GSA, BSA
Special needs provision DYS, DYP
Age range 4–18; *boarders from* 8
No of pupils (day) 375 *(boarding)* 40
Junior 155; *Senior* 205; *Sixth Form* 55
Fees per annum (boarding) (full) £10,830–
£13,230; *(weekly)* £10,560–£12,960;
(day) £4,005–£8,250

Curriculum: broadly-based academic curricu-lum. Wide range of subjects offered at GCSE; 19 subjects at A Level and AS-Level.
Entry requirements and procedures: our own exam and interview.

Examinations offered: GCSE, A Level, AS Level. In 2001 A Level pass rate 100 per cent with 33.3 per cent A grades; GCSE A* to C grades 96.8 per cent; 58.1 per cent at A* and A.
Academic and leisure facilities: new sports hall, new Library, new Sixth Form Centre, new prep building; new computer facilities. Science building with five large laboratories, and inter-active white boards. All-weather pitch, outdoor heated swimming pool, student-run farm; recording studio.
Scholarships: music, art, drama, PE, academic, Sixth Form.
Boarding facilities: weekly or full in small, friendly boarding house.

Michael Hall (Steiner Waldorf School)

Kidbrooke Park, Forest Row, Sussex RH18 5JA
Tel: (01342) 822275   Fax: (01342) 826593
E-mail: info@michaelhall.co.uk   Web site: www.michaelhall.co.uk

Chairman of College Mr Ewout van Manen
Founded 1925
Type Co-educational, boarding and day
Religious denomination Non-denominational
Age range 0–19; *boarders from* 12
No of pupils (day) 647; *(boarding)* 25
Girls 328; *boys* 344
Lower school 491; *Upper School* 137
Fees per annum (full boarding) up to £11,195;
(weekly boarding) up to £10,435; *(day)* up to
£6,435

Protecting the right to childhood
Creating abilities for life
Offering a structured and imaginative approach
and an international curriculum, Michael Hall
has gained wide recognition as a creative and
compassionate alternative to more traditional
avenues of education
* Full age range from pre-school to university
  entrance
* Unique international curriculum based on
  child development
* Languages from age six
* GCSE and A Level
* Arts, crafts, sport, sciences and humanities
* Intensive English courses for foreign stu-
  dents
* Over 620 day and boarding pupils
* Set in rural Sussex, within reach of main
  cultural centres

Moira House Junior School

Upper Carlisle Road, Eastbourne, East Sussex BN20 7TE
Tel: (01323) 644144   Fax: (01323) 649720
E-mail: enquiries@moirahouse.co.uk
Web site: www.moirahouse.co.uk   www.gabbitas.net

Head Mrs Jane Booth-Clibborn
Founded 1875
Type Girls' independent pre-prep and prep day
Religious denomination Christian Inter-
denominational
Members of GSA, BSA, SHMIS
Accredited by ISC, ISI
Special needs provision DYS, DYP, EFL
Age range 2½–11; *boarders from* 9
No of pupils 110
Fees per term (boarding) (full) £3,950;
(weekly) £3,600; *(day)* £1,285–£2,380

The Junior School is very much part of Moira
House, but retains its individual identity.
Whilst sharing the swimming pool, games
fields, Swann Hall and dining room it has its
own library, activities centre and garden.

Entry may be at any stage, but tests in core
subjects are given to girls over 7, preferably
during a day visit to School. Curriculum
includes French, performing arts and
swimming in addition to sound foundations
in English, Mathematics and Science. From 9,
girls receive specialist teaching before moving
into the Senior School. Scholarships are
offered from 7+, Year 3. An extensive activity
programme complements the curriculum, with
particular strengths in Music and Drama. The
growth of self-confidence is encouraged within
a highly stimulating, caring atmosphere.
The day nursery is open 42 weeks a year,
8.00am to 5.30pm Monday to Friday, for girls
between 2½ and 4 years old.

Moira House Girls' School

Upper Carlisle Road, Eastbourne, East Sussex BN20 7TE
Tel: (01323) 644144   Fax: (01323) 649720
E-mail: enquiries@moirahouse.co.uk
Web site: www.moirahouse.co.uk   www.gabbitas.net

Principal Ann Harris BEd (Hons), ARCM
Founded 1875
Type Girls' independent pre-prep, prep and senior
Religious denomination Christian Inter-denominational
Member of GSA, BSA, SHMIS
Provision offered for special needs DYS, DYP, EFL
Age range 2½–18+; boarders from 9
No of pupils (day) 230; *(boarding)* 105
Junior 110; *Senior* 155; *Sixth Form* 70
Fees per term (boarding) £3,950–£5,100; *(weekly)* £3,800–£4,550; *(day)* £2,570–£3,030

Foundation: Moira House was founded in 1875 by Mr and Mrs Charles Ingham, regarded in their time as gifted pioneers in the field of female education.

Situation: we are situated on high ground in Eastbourne, near Beachy Head, with views over the sea. Our grounds open directly on to the Sussex Downs.

Facilities: each subject has its own resource at base and there has been an extensive building programme over the last 20 years. All our sports facilities are on site, including a 25-metre indoor heated pool. We are members of the local David Lloyd Club for racket sports.

Faith: the School is inter-denominational and the majority of the school attends Family Service at the parish church, whose vicar is our chaplain and prepares girls for Confirmation.

Boarding: we have two boarding houses including a separate Sixth Form House. There is a Senior Day Girl House.

Curriculum: in the Junior School we offer a wide curriculum. In the Senior School, we follow formal academic courses in the normal curriculum in arts and sciences. There are 20 GCSE examination subjects, 18 A Level examination subjects, including Business Studies, and Sports Studies.

Special needs: we have a full-time Special Needs teacher and EFL teacher.

Careers counselling: the strong programme of careers counselling has been developed by our careers counsellor, Howard Barlow, well known as author of *How To Pass A Levels* and *University Places*.

Drama, music and sport: these have always been strengths of our School. Plays and concerts are regularly performed, both in School and in the community of Eastbourne. We have a strong programme of inter-school sport, including biennial hockey and netball tours overseas.

Activity: over 30 activities are offered each term in a strong programme which include the Duke of Edinburgh Award, the Young Enterprise Scheme, Shakespeare on the Platform, Youth Parliament and community service.

International links: there are usually three exchanges each year plus skiing and outdoor pursuits in Europe and a sports and music tour of Australia in 2000.

Entry: entry is by examination and interview at any age to the Junior School and the Senior School at 11+, 13+ and 16+. Scholarships and bursaries are available. Please refer to the scholarships section.

Charitable status: Moira House School is a registered charity (no 307072). It exists to provide excellent education for young women.

Newlands School

Eastbourne Road, Seaford, East Sussex BN25 4NP
Tel: (01323) 490000   Fax: (01323) 898420
E-mail: newlands1@msn.com   Web site: www.newlands-school.com   www.gabbitas.net

Headmaster Mr Oliver Price BEd (Hons)
Founded 1854
Type Nursery, Pre-Preparatory, Preparatory and Manor (senior) school
Religious denomination Inter-denominational
Member of IAPS, ISA
Age range 2½–18; boarders from 6
No of pupils (day) 320; *(boarding)* 160
Girls 190; *boys* 290
Pre-prep 100; *Prep* 170; *Manor* 190;
Sixth Form 33
Fees per annum (day) Prep from £5,745,
Manor £7,815 *(boarding)* Prep from £10,800
Manor from £12,630

Our school: Newlands offers an opportunity for educational continuity from nursery to university entrance on one site.

Newlands is a friendly, happy school with a strong academic tradition. At Newlands we place an emphasis on fully developing your child's potential in a happy and caring environment. The wide range of activities available make it possible for every pupil to achieve success and confidence in one field or another. Classes are small and a pupil's progress is monitored carefully.

Location: Newlands is situated on one 21-acre campus in a pleasant coastal town surrounded by an area of outstanding natural beauty. Good communication links exist with Gatwick (37 miles), Heathrow (78 miles) and London (65 miles).

High academic standards: At Newlands, we expect pupils to attain optimum results in external examinations, as is evident by our strong academic record. A Level, and GCSE results show year on year improvement.

The arts flourish with thriving music, drama, dance and art departments. There is a strong choral tradition and annual dramatic productions.

Theatre Arts Course: A Theatre Arts Course is available to students who wish to specialise in dance, drama, music and art within an academic environment.

Entry requirements: Interview and school reports are required for the Preparatory School. Interview and/or school reports are needed for the Manor (senior) part of the school.

Scholarship: Academic, drama, dance, sport, music and theatre arts scholarships are available at the Preparatory and Manor parts of the school. We also prepare Preparatory pupils for scholarships to Newlands Manor at 13 years. There is a generous discount for service families as fees are in line with the BSA.

Academic and sports facilities: Our facilities include five high-tech computer rooms, science

laboratories, a large art studio, a language laboratory, a design technology workshop, an assembly hall/theatre and music room.

There are the equivalent of eight football pitches, a heated indoor swimming pool, a hard playing surface for three tennis/netball courts, a gymnasium, and .22 rifle range. There are many opportunities for sports including soccer, hockey, rugby, netball, cricket, athletics, volleyball, basketball, squash, rounders, badminton, tennis, horse-riding and cross-country running. A new multi-purpose hall is appropriate for most indoor games as well as other activities.

Accelerated Learning Unit: This nationally renowned centre has specialist teachers who provide one-to-one tuition for gifted pupils, dyslexic pupils and those learning English as a foreign language.

The staff provide individual programmes of learning on a one-to-one basis.

All members of staff are fully qualified with diplomas in Special Education Needs or Certificate/Diplomas in Teaching English as a foreign language.

The centre is approved by CReSTeD (Council for the Registration of Schools Teaching Dyslexic Pupils), having a category B listing, supported by the British Dyslexia Association and the Dyslexia Institute.

Gifted pupils receive intensive tuition in their area of giftedness, so that they can achieve success at an earlier age.

Modern technology allows dyslexic pupils to produce work of a high standard.

Study skills and examination techniques are taught in order to prepare pupils for their GCSE and A-Level courses. The centre offers continuity of education support throughout a pupil's time at Newlands.

Transport and pastoral care: When required, pupils are escorted to Gatwick, Stansted and Heathrow airports and met on incoming flights. Newlands' minibuses can provide transport to Victoria Station and as far as Romsey, Aldershot and Maidstone.

Guardians can be arranged for overseas pupils. The well-established pastoral care system at Newlands includes housemasters and housemistresses who provide a caring approach for our pupils.

Newlands School exists to provide quality education for boys and girls.

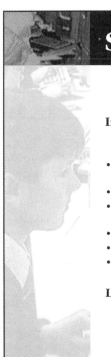

St Bede's School, Hailsham

Senior School: The Dicker, Hailsham, East Sussex BN27 3QH
Tel: (01323) 843252   Fax: (01323) 442628
Preparatory School: Duke's Drive, Eastbourne, East Sussex BN20 7XL
Tel: (01323) 734222   Fax: (01323) 720119
Web site: www.stbedeschool.org   www.gabbitas.net

No email!

Heads Stephen Cole and Christopher Pyemont
Founded 1978 &1895
Type Co-educational independent
Religious denomination Inter-denominational
Members of SHMIS, GBA, IAPS, ISIS
Age range 2½–19 *Boarders from* 7+
No of students aged 8–19 (boarding) 380;
(day) 500
Girls 352 *Boys* 528
Prep & pre-prep 386 *Senior* 350 *Sixth form* 230
Fees per term (not including pre-prep) (boarding)
£3,840–£5,120; *(day)* £2,680–£3,140

St Bede's is one of Britain's leading independent co-educational schools. The School is proudly and purposefully non-selective and the generous staffing ratio of 1:8 enables outstanding results to be achieved. The Senior School is located on a separate campus to the Pre-Prep and Prep Schools which gives students a change of teaching staff and environment as well as the opportunity to mature.

Location: The Senior School is found at the heart of the village of Upper Dicker based on a small country estate set in beautiful countryside. The Prep School is situated nearby on the seafront in Eastbourne. Both schools are easily accessible by road and rail from London's airports and Channel seaports. Transport to and from school can be arranged for boarders and a school bus service is available for day students.

Curriculum: St Bede's provides an extremely wide-ranging and flexible programme. In the early years at the Prep School there is a strong emphasis on literacy and numeracy as well as skills such as languages and computing. Academic standards are high and all students are prepared for Common Entrance and Scholarship exams.

At the Senior School, students spend the first year following a widely-based curriculum prior to making their choice from the 30 GCSE (Key Stage 4) subjects offered. Similarly at AS and A level 30 subjects are offered including media studies, theatre studies and pure and applied mathematics. The school also offers a number of Advanced Vocational Courses (AVCEs), a professional dance course and specialist coaching in tennis and swimming.

Facilities: Both schools have imaginatively converted and added to their original Edwardian buildings to provide excellent teaching and sporting facilities. Each site provides an indoor sports centre, indoor swimming pool, EFL centre, art, design and technology studios and an impressive computer network. In addition the Senior School offers drama studios, riding stables, a practice golf course, ceramics and graphic design studios.

Sporting and Club Activities: Both schools are particularly strong in football, tennis, cricket, squash and swimming. The Prep School has a very strong games playing tradition and encourages students of all abilities to participate in sport. At the Senior School games are organised as part of an extensive club activities programme which takes place every day. In all there are over 140 club activities ranging from all kinds of sport and outdoor pursuits to activities within the fields of art, drama, music, journalism, science, agriculture and technology.

Scholarships and Bursaries: A generous number of academic, art, music, dance, drama, allrounder and sports scholarships are available at both schools and scholarships may be awarded to those entering the Sixth Form.

St Leonards-Mayfield School

The Old Palace, Mayfield, East Sussex TN20 6PH
Tel: (01435) 874600   Fax: (01435) 872627
E-mail: enquiry@stlm.e-sussex.sch.uk   Web site: www.stlm.e-sussex.sch.uk   www.gabbitas.net

Head Mrs Julia Dalton
Founded 1872
Type Girls' independent senior boarding and day
Religious denomination Roman Catholic
Special needs provision DYS, HI, VIS
Member of GSA, SHA, ISIS, ISCO, ISBA
Age range 11–18
No of pupils (day) 189; *(boarding)* 189
Senior 257; *Sixth Form* 120
Fees per annum (boarding) (full and weekly) £15,120; *(day)* £9,840

St Leonards-Mayfield School is a leading Roman Catholic boarding and day school for girls aged 11–18. It is set in an attractive Sussex village, surrounded by an area of outstanding natural beauty. The beautiful school buildings are based on the medieval palace of the Archbishops of Canterbury. There is comfortable boarding accommodation and excellent pastoral care.

St Leonards-Mayfield academic standards are consistently high and the dedicated, professional and caring staff ensures a happy atmosphere. The strong spirit in the school derives from its foundation in early Victorian times and can be summarised as a spirit of trust and respect, which fosters the gifts of each girl, enabling her to grow into an intelligently caring and sensitively confident adult. Girls are encouraged to achieve high standards across a broad curriculum.

Sciences are exceptionally strong at St Leonards-Mayfield, with first class facilities, including a new science block. Creative writing is another strength, with girls writing prize-winning poetry, prose and drama. A wide range of languages, classical and modern, is offered. There is a modern music school, and two orchestras and five choirs give girls the opportunity to sing major choral works alongside professional soloists. Creative arts are well catered for, with teaching by practicing artists. The art and ceramics departments are visionary in their encouragement of imaginative ideas and the use of materials and techniques.

The school provides a lively and wide range of sports, including equestrian. Other sports offered are hockey, netball, swimming, tennis, rounders, athletics, volleyball and gymnastics. The facilities for sport are excellent and for riders there is a sand school and cross country course in the grounds.

Girls also have the chance to take on the challenge of the Duke of Edinburgh Award scheme. Many girls achieve their Gold Awards before finishing their A levels at St Leonards-Mayfield. St Leonards-Mayfield has a reputation for giving girls the intellectual skills and confidence to tackle challenging careers in Science, Technology and Medicine, as well as offering outstanding creative stimulus within the stability of a secure and happy environment.

St Mary's Hall

Eastern Road, Brighton, East Sussex BN2 5JF
Tel: (01273) 606061   Fax: (01273) 620782
E-mail: communicate@stmaryshall.co.uk
Web site: www.stmaryshall.co.uk   www.gabbitas.net

Head Mrs SM Meek MA
Founded 1836
Type Girls' independent pre-prep, prep and senior boarding and day
Religious denomination Church of England
Member of GSA, GBGSA, ISIS, BSA;
Accredited by DFEE
Age range 3–18; *boarders from* 8+
No of pupils (excluding Sixth Form) (day) 273; *(boarding)* 83
Junior 133; *Senior* 192; *Sixth Form* 64
Fees per annum (boarding) £9,198–£12,762; *(day)* £1,620–£7,947

St Mary's Hall was founded in 1836 for the daughters of the Church of England clergy. The School is proud of its traditions of care and respect for the individual and its capacity to provide the best of modern education in a thriving family atmosphere.

St Mary's Hall has the fine chapel of St Mark's and each day begins with an act of Christian worship, although all faiths are treated with respect. All dietary needs are met from our on-site facilities.

With approximately 400 pupils, each girl is seen as an individual. The School is large enough to support good facilities stimulating a lively pursuit of music, drama and the visual arts.

Curriculum and examinations: seventeen subjects are offered at GCSE; pupils normally sitting between eight and ten. A wide variety of subjects are available at A Level including Theatre Studies, History of Art, Law, Economics and Business Studies. Most girls continue to higher education degree courses. The musically gifted are encouraged to sit appropriate specialist examinations.

Academic and leisure facilities: there are two well appointed technology rooms with network CD ROM and Internet facilities. The art block includes two pottery kilns and a dark room. Drama Studies take place in a studio theatre with a computerised stage lighting system. The playing field, all-weather tennis courts and a 25 metre heated indoor swimming pool are all on site.

Boarding facilities: boarding accommodation ranges from the nearby Regency splendour of Sussex Square to a modern purpose-built house in the School grounds which also accommodates younger boarders.

Scholarships: St Mary's Hall is a charity established to promote the education of girls. Entry is by examination and interview. Academic, music and sport scholarships, clergy and Armed Forces bursaries together with St Mary's Hall Assisted Places are available.

Prospective pupils are welcome to spend a day at the School or, if boarding is being considered, to stay overnight. Visits by prospective parents are welcome at all times.

Seaford College, Petworth

Petworth, West Sussex GU28 0NB
Tel: (01798) 867392   Fax: (01798) 867606
E-mail: seaford@freeuk.com   Web site: www.seaford.org.uk   www.gabbitas.net

Head Mr TJ Mullins BA
Founded 1884
Type Co-educational independent boarding and day
Religious denomination Church of England
Member of SHMIS, GBA
accredited by ISI
Special needs provision DYC, DYS, DYP, MLD
Age range 10–18; *boarders from* 10
No of pupils (day) 207; *(boarding)* 157
Girls 96; *boys* 268; *Junior* 86; *Senior* 278
Fees per annum (boarding) (full or weekly)
£11,550–£14,970; *(day)* £7,950–£9,960

Seaford College was founded in 1884 and is a fully co-educational school for boarding and day pupils aged 10–18. Situated within 360 acres at the foot of the South Downs, the College is close to the historic town of Petworth and just seven miles from the closest railway station. Heathrow and Gatwick airports are within an hour's drive. Pupils may board weekly or full-time and a bus service collects day pupils from a wide area.

Curriculum: A wide range of subjects is offered at GCSE and a wide choice of A Level options is available to the large Sixth Form. 96 per cent of leavers go on to university.

Entry requirements and procedures: Entrance to the Junior House at 10+ and 11+ is based on an IQ test and interview with the headmaster. Pupils are admitted at 13+ following Common Entrance examination. Sixth Form entry is dependent on GCSE results and an interview. Overseas pupils must pass an English exam set by the College and past academic achievements will also be taken into account.

Academic and leisure facilities: The College boasts an impressive and successful Art, Design and Technology Centre.

Outstanding sports facilities including 6 rugby pitches and an artificial hockey pitch of international standard along with staff who have coached at international level, have helped the College gain an excellent sporting record.

The hockey and rugby teams have toured South Africa, Australia, Canada and New Zealand and our pupils have played at county and national level.

Music and drama feature strongly in the life of the College. The Chapel Choir enjoys an international reputation and they have sung for Her Majesty Queen Elizabeth, the Queen Mother as well as touring America, Russia, France and South America.

Scholarships: Scholarships are offered for academic, Design and Technology, music (instrumental or choral), sport or art but must be accompanied by a good all-round academic standard.

Bursaries: Bursaries are available to Forces families and siblings.

Boarding facilities: Boys aged 13–17 are divided between three houses, in the care of live-in houseparents. The older boys have individual studies and the younger boys sleep in dormitories. Second year A Level students are accommodated in a separate House, offering more privileges and responsibility and helping with the transition from the protection of school life to the relative freedom of university. The girls' boarding house, comprising dormitories for pre-GCSE girls, and single and twin rooms for lower sixth is located in the Mansion House. Dormitory facilities are provided in the Junior House for girls and boys aged 10–13.

For further information and a prospectus please contact the Headmaster's Secretary.

Sompting Abbotts School

Church Lane, Sompting, West Sussex BN15 0AZ
Tel: (01903) 235960   Fax: (01903) 210045
E-mail: office@somptingabbotts-prep-school.co.uk
Web site: www.somptingabbotts-prep-school.co.uk   www.gabbitas.net

Principal Mrs PM Sinclair
Head Mr RM Johnson Cert Ed
Founded 1921
Type Co-educational independent pre-prep and prep boarding and day
Religious denomination Church of England
Member of IAPS
Age range 3–13; *boarders from* 7
No of pupils (day) 165; *(weekly boarding)* 10
Girls 30; *boys* 135
Fees per annum (weekly boarding) £7,650; *(day)* £3,750–£5,460

Sompting Abbots School is situated on the edge of the South Downs, set in 30 acres, facing the sea with views towards Beachy Head and the Isle of Wight. The aim of the school is to provide a well-balanced education in a caring environment whilst developing the individual needs of each child.

The School has a vibrant Pre-Preparatory Department, which includes lively and stimulating Nursery and Reception classes. In the Preparatory Department, a well-equipped Computer Room and Science Laboratory is enjoyed by all ages, the Art and Drama Departments offer wide scope for creativity, and peripatetic teachers provide tuition for a range of musical instruments.
Weekly boarding is available for the boys from Monday 8.30am–Friday 6.30pm and flexi-boarding is also available.

Windlesham House

Washington, Pulborough, West Sussex RH20 4AY
Tel: (01903) 873207   Fax: (01903) 873017
Web site: www.windlesham.com   www.gabbitas.net

No email

Head Philip Lough MA (Oxon)
Founded 1837
Type Co-educational independent pre-prep day and prep boarding
Religious denomination Church of England
Member of IAPS
Special needs provision ADD, DYS, DYP, MLD
Age range 4–13; *boarders from* 8
No of pupils (day) 60; *(boarding)* 260
Girls 145; *boys* 175
Fees per annum (full boarding) £12,200

Curriculum: very broad curriculum offered to enable all children to discover and develop their personal strengths and talents. Strong academic record and emphasis on creative arts, drama, music and sport. Entrance requirements: no entrance examination. Parents seeking a place for their child at Windlesham should contact the registrar. Flexible entrance policy.

Academic/leisure facilities: recently upgraded science labs, ICT, dorms and classrooms. Theatre/sports hall, swimming pool (indoor), gymnasium, dance/drama studio, tennis and squash courts, small astro-turf pitch, extensive playing fields and grounds (60 acres).
Boarding: this is very much a family school where all children board from 8. Warm, friendly, child-centred atmosphere. Individuality is respected (dress code rather than uniform) and relationships between staff and children are excellent. We produce happy, rounded and confident children. Newly upgraded dormitory areas.
Pre-prep: opened September 1997 in newly created premises offering a wide curriculum and making use of the excellent facilities of the main school.

The Blue Coat School

Somerset Road, Edgbaston, Birmingham, West Midlands B17 OHR
Tel: (0121) 454 1425   Fax: (0121) 454 7757
E-mail: admissions@bluecoat.bham.sch.uk
Web site: www.bluecoat.bham.sch.uk   www.gabbitas.net

Head ADJ Browning
Founded 1722
Type Co-educational independent pre-prep and prep boarding and day
Religious denomination Church of England
Member of BSA, IAPS, ISC, ISIS;
Accredited by ISC
Special needs provision DYP, DYS, MLD
Age range 2–13; *boarders from* 7
No of pupils (day) 429; *(boarding) (full)* 22; *(weekly)* 20
Girls 202; *boys* 269
Fees per annum (boarding) (full) £10,590; *(weekly)* £9,525; *(day)* £6,165

Scholar or scuba diver? Flautist or flexi-boarder? Potter . . . or Harry Potter? Girl or boy? At Blue Coat, tremendous opportunities await all pupils. Set in 15 acres of grounds, two miles from the city centre, the School is easily accessible by rail, motorway and Birmingham International Airport.

Pupils follow a broad programme of study that we call 'National Curriculum Plus'. Specialist teaching and small classes ensure excellent performance at all levels. The music department is especially strong, offering instrumental tuition, ensembles, a robed Chapel Choir, and links with Birmingham Conservatoire.

Blue Coat has something for everyone, with over 40 extra-curricular activities operating each week, including Brownies, Spanish, sign language and woollen crafts.

Chafyn Grove

Bourne Avenue, Salisbury, Wiltshire SP1 1LR
Tel: (01722) 333423   Fax: (01722) 323114
E-mail: officecgs@lineone.net   Web site: www.chafyngrove.co.uk   www.gabbitas.net

Head James Barnes
Founded 1876
Type Co-educational independent pre-prep and prep boarding and day
Religious denomination Non-denominational
Member of ISIS
Accredited by IAPS, BSA
Special needs provision ADD, ADHD, DYC, DYP, DYS, SP&LD.
Age range 3–13; *boarders from* 7+
No of pupils (day) 240; *(boarding)* 62
Girls 75; *boys* 227
Fees per annum (full boarding) £9,150–£11,280; *(day)* £3,960–£8,430

The aim of the school is to prepare its pupils academically, culturally, morally and physically for the next stage of their education. Boarding is an important element at Chafyn Grove and we are proud of our happy family environment. There is a fine academic record to 13+ with many scholarships won to senior public schools. Music, ICT, Design Technology, PE, Art, Pottery, Woodwork and Drama are part of the regular curriculum and there are many optional activities.

Ten acres of playing fields surround the school and the facilites include a swimming pool, mucic school, two libraries, 3 hard tennis courts, 2 glass backed squash courts, a creative arts centre, sport hall, excellent science block and a computer centre. A new Nursery Department opened January 2002 for children aged 3.

Dauntsey's School

High Street, West Lavington, Devizes, Wiltshire SN10 4HE
Tel: (01380) 814500   Fax: (01380) 814501
E-mail: information@dauntseys.wilts.sch.uk
Web site: www.dauntseys.wilts.sch.uk   www.gabbitas.net

Head Mr SB Roberts
Founded 1542
Type Co-educational independent senior boarding and day
Religious denomination Inter-denominational
Member of HMC
Special needs provision DYS (mild only), MLD
Age range 11–18; *boarders from* 11
No of pupils (day) 416 *(boarding)* 264
Girls 316; *boys* 364
Junior 250; *Senior* 220; *Sixth Form* 210
Fees per annum (boarding) £15,435; *(day)* £9,225

Dauntsey's is a very happy and successful co-educational independent school. Excellent facilities are available for academic work, music, drama, art and sport. There are several new buildings: sports hall, swimming pool, CDT and maths centres, science laboratories, humanities area, and an all-weather hockey and tennis surface. A new 5-studio Art School was opened in 1999 and a new library and IT suite in 2000. There have also been major extensions to the boarding houses, music school and dining hall. Outward-bound activities flourish including a very active sailing club which sails the famous *Jolie Brise* (winner of Tall Ships 2000).

There is an emphasis on pastoral care and Christian values although worship is not narrowly denominational. There is a flexible system on exeats for boarders.

Careers advice is thorough and there is a programme of work experience. Most pupils go on to university and each year several go to Oxbridge.

Visitors are always welcome. Please contact the Registrar for a prospectus and details of the entry procedure.

Kingsbury Hill House

34 Kingsbury Street, Marlborough, Wiltshire SN8 1JA
Tel: (01672) 512680   Fax: (01672) 511635   Web site: www.gabbitas.net

Head Mr M Innes-Williams
Founded 1945
Type Co-educational independent pre-prep and prep day
Age range 3–13
Girls 90; *boys* 90
Junior 180
Fees per term £990–£1,880
Fees per annum £3,000–£5,725

Kingsbury Hill House School occupies a fine double fronted Georgian house situated close to the eastern end of Marlborough's historic High Street. Further classrooms, a large gymnasium, science room and art school are located around the enclosed formal gardens, which include a large playground and two tennis/netball courts. Sporting facilities are located on site and in the outstanding settings of Marlborough Common and Savernake Forest nearby.

The School has Nursery, Pre-Preparatory and Preparatory Departments and prepares children for CEE and scholarship at 11+, 12+ and 13+.
The School maintains a fine academic tradition, but also believes that loyalty, a sense of fair play, and good manners are as important for the development of the child.
The staff includes a dyslexia specialist and there are thriving music and drama clubs. The School provides a happy and stimulating start to education so that children may develop within a firm, yet friendly environment and achieve excellence in academic, sporting and creative pursuits, thus developing a spirit of independence.

Pinewood School

Bourton, Swindon, Wiltshire SN6 8HZ
Tel: (01793) 782205   Fax: (01793) 783476
e-mail: janey@pinewood.biblio.net
Website: www.pinewoodschool.oxon.sch.uk   www.gabbitas.net

Head CA Stuart-Clark
Founded 1875
Type Co-educational independent pre-prep and prep boarding and day
Religious denomination Church of England
Member of IAPS, ISIS
Special needs provision DYS, MLD, PH
Age range 3–13; *boarders from* 8
No of pupils (day) 224; *(boarding)* 26
Girls 107; *boys* 143
Fees per annum (boarding) £10,185;
(day) £3,975–£6,768

Pinewood is set in acres of wonderful, rolling countryside, yet close to major routeways and towns. The School offers a quality, family-style, forward-looking education, a vibrant blend of tradition and buzz. Resources include purpose-built Music School and Junior Forms Wing, and conversions of the original buildings to provide a flourishing Pre-Prep, Art & Design Workshops, Research and Reference Library and dedicated ICT Room.

Pinewood achieves excellent academic results for entry to the major public schools through inspirational teaching within a happy, genuinely friendly and stimulating learning environment. Sport is keenly coached and competed in matches and House competitions. There is a wide programme of activities and clubs, visits by speakers and educational trips.

Pinewood is an open school: open to the countryside, open to comment and input and always open for parents to visit and look, meet and discuss.

St Mary's School, Calne

Wiltshire SN11 0DF
Tel: (01249) 857200   Fax: (01249) 857207
E-mail: registrar@stmaryscalne.wilts.sch.uk
Web site: www.stmaryscalne.sch.uk   www.gabbitas.net

Head Mrs Carolyn J Shaw BA (London)
Founded 1873
Type Girls' independent senior boarding and day
Religious denomination Church of England
Member of GSA, IAPS, GBGSA
Special needs provision DYS
Age range 11–18; *boarders from* 11
No of pupils (day) 50; *(boarding)* 250
Fees per annum (full boarding) £17,100; *(day)* £11,250

St Mary's School, Calne offers a stimulating academic education in an attractive, informal and supportive environment, with excellent pastoral care and a successful tutor system. Girls are encouraged to develop independence of judgement and a sense of responsibility.

Entry is via the 11+, 12+ and 13+ Common Entrance examinations or into the Sixth Form; scholarships available at all levels.
Public examination results are consistently impressive. Years 7 to 9 follow a broad curriculum; six core subjects and up to four others are taken at GCSE; normally three subjects are studied at A Level from a large number on offer, to include AS Levels. Well-equipped Careers library and full-time Careers staff.
A wide range of evening and weekend activities is offered: Art, Drama, Music and Sports are all very strong and popular in the girls' spare time, as is the Duke of Edinburgh Award.
St Margaret's Preparatory School is the co-educational day preparatory department and shares the grounds and facilities of St Mary's School, Calne.

Stonar School

Cottles Park, Atworth, Melksham, Wiltshire SN12 8NT
Tel: (01225) 702795/702309   Fax: (01225) 790830
E-mail: office@stonar.wilts.co.uk
Web site: www.stonar.wilts.sch.uk   www.gabbitas.net

Head Mrs Sue Hopkinson BA (Oxon)
Founded 1921
Type Girls' independent pre-prep, prep and senior boarding and day
Religious denomination non-denominational
Member of GSA
Special needs provision DYS, DYP, HI, MLD, VIS
Age range 4–18; *boarders from* 8
No of pupils (day) 200; *(boarding)* 200
Junior 100; *Senior* 190; *Sixth Form* 100
Fees per annum (boarding) £12,594; *(day)* £6,996

Stonar School is a cheerful, purposeful and progressive centre of learning for girls, set in eighty acres of English parkland close to the heritage city of Bath. The school develops the talents and abilities of every individual, providing a breadth of opportunity to achieve their

potential across and beyond the formal curriculum, while offering a positive work ethic and quality pastoral care. Curiosity, creativity, confidence and independence are encouraged so that pupils leave school well equipped for the challenges of adult life and keen to contribute to the wider community.
Well placed in National League tables, Stonar has modern, architect-designed Sixth Form houses and prep school, interspersed with delightful older buildings. Up-to-the-minute IT facilities with personal email are offered, as well as many extra-curricular opportunities using the school's superb on-site Sports Hall, Astroturf, Theatre, Music School, Art Studio and Equestrian Centre.

The Abbey College, Malvern

253 Wells Road, Malvern Wells, Worcestershire WR14 4JF
Tel: (01684) 892300   Fax: (01684) 892757
E-mail: abbey@cix.co.uk   Web site: www.abbey-college.co.uk   www.gabbitas.net

Principal Mr L Denholm
Founded 1874
Type Co-educational independent boarding and day
Religious denomination Non-denominational
Member of BAC, ARELS
Accredited by BAC, ARELS, British Council
Special needs provision
Age range 13+; *boarders from* 13
No of pupils 110
No of pupils (boarding) 109; *(weekly)* 1
Girls 50; *boys* 60
Senior 40; *Sixth Form* 70
Fees per annum (boarding) (full) £12,950; *(weekly)* £10,475; *(day)* £6,475

The Abbey College is located on a beautiful 70 acre campus in Malvern, central England. The College is easily accesible being 2½ hours from London (by car or train), 50 minutes from Birmingham, and within 1¼ hours of Oxford, Stratford, Bristol and Bath.

The Abbey's campus – and the course fees – include everything the student needs. Lessons, accommodation, meals, airport transfer, use of all facilities, welfare, healthcare, sports and social programmes and various outings are all included in the cost. The College provides a private, safe and peaceful environment for study, in a genuinely international residential community of over 30 different nationalities.

The College offers two main types of courses: Academic and English Language. The Academic school (minimum age 13), offers IGCSE, GCSE, AS, A-Level and Foundation/Access courses in a variety of subjects such as Art, Accounting, Biology, Business Studies, Chemistry, Computing, English, Mathematics and Physics. There is also a unique Foundation/Access course for Medicine in conjunction with the renowned Charles University, Prague. All lessons are taught by fully qualified graduate teachers in small classes (average six in one class) and we have an excellent record of sending students to good universities. The College has particular strengths in the science and business-related subjects.

The English Language courses fall in to two main categories – English All Year and Summer/Easter Vacation Courses. The English All Year programmes can be studied in conjunction with an English exam (KET, PET, FCE, CPE, IELTS, TOEFL, IGCSE, AS/A-Level and Trinity). The Vacation courses, run since 1969, offer general English lessons combined with a full programme of excursions, sports and social activities, and are available at all levels for age ranges 8–11, 12–17 and 18+.

Although the school is deliberately small in population, with a maximum of less than 120 students in the academic year, it has continued to send large numbers of students for top-level courses. Entry is by previous school results and reports. Scholarships worth 25 per cent, 50 per cent, 75 per cent and 100 per cent of tuition (which is half of the overall cost) are available to outstanding students. Inspections of the College are regularly carried out by independent bodies and reports are available to parents.

Bromsgrove School

Worcester Road, Bromsgrove, Worcestershire B61 7DU
Tel: (01527) 579679   Fax: (01527) 576177
E-mail: admissions.upper@bromsgrove-school.co.uk
Web site: www.bromsgrove-school.co.uk   www.gabbitas.net

Head TM Taylor MA, DipEd
Founded 1553
Type Co-educational independent prep and senior boarding and day
Religious denomination Church of England
Member of HMC, IAPS
Special needs provision DYS
Age range 7–18; *boarders from* 7
No of pupils (day) 725; *(boarding)* 398
Girls 465; *boys* 658
Junior 393; *Senior* 468; *Sixth Form* 262
Fees per annum (boarding) (full) £10,470–£14,010; *(day)* £5,865–£8,430

Curriculum: the School is at the forefront of curriculum development, whilst maintaining traditional teaching values. It prides itself on achieving high standards from pupils of a wide range of ability. It offers an impressive range of subjects, including Design and Technology, Spanish, Business Studies and the performing arts. With close monitoring of the academic progress of each pupil, the School obtains high academic success with a pass rate of 99 per cent at A Level. The overall pass rate for GCSE (A–C) in 2001 was 91 per cent with 39 per cent at A* and A grades. 95 per cent of pupils continue to University with significant success at Oxbridge.

Entry requirements: entry between ages 7 to 11 is based upon assessment tests and at 13 by interview and tests, or Common Entrance. Pupils' entry into the Sixth Form is determined by their GCSE results.

Examinations offered: the School seeks to offer the most appropriate examination for each subject. A, AS and GCSE subjects are offered through the various examination boards. A number of modular courses have been introduced where appropriate and VCEs in Business, Art and Design, Leisure and Recreation and Science are also available.

Careers: there is an excellent careers department. The School enjoys close links with industry and pupils undertake work experience placements. Pupils undertake self-appraisal and mock interview practice.

Academic and leisure facilities: the School is situated in a leafy, 100 acre, self-contained campus, near the town of Bromsgrove; it is easily accessible, being convenient for the motorway network (via M6/M5 or M40/M42) and Birmingham International Airport. There are excellent facilities for study and recreation. Academic facilities include a design centre, modern laboratories, music school and drama studio. In May 1994, the School opened a £2.5 million library and resources centre including 'state of the art' library, lecture theatre, careers room and information technology facilities. In September 1997, a £600,000 extension was completed to the Mathematics and Modern Languages Department. A new £2.5 million art, design and technology building was opened in November 1999 and in September 2001 a new £1 million Girls' Sixth Form boarding extension opened with 20 single rooms each with ensuite facilities.

The School is opportunity-orientated and provides a very wide range of extra-curricular and sporting activities.

Facilities include a heated indoor swimming pool, sports hall, floodlit 'all-weather' pitch and climbing wall, as well as extensive grass pitches within the campus. Sport, music and drama thrive as extra-curricular activities.

Boarding: while the School offers boarding and day education, the ethos is that of a vibrant boarding community. Every pupil has their own desk in their house, be it modern purpose-built accommodation or an older building which has been carefully modernised. A full programme of activities, cultural trips and expeditions is offered.

Malvern College

College Road, Malvern WR14 3DF
Tel: (01684) 581500   Fax: (01684) 581615
E-mail: registrar@malcol.org   Web site: www.malcol.org   www.gabbitas.net

Head Mr HCK Carson
Founded 1865
Type Independent co-educational pre-prep,
prep and senior boarding and day
Religious denomination Church of England
Member of HMC
Special needs DYS, SPLD
Age range (Pre-prep) 3–7; *(Prep)* 7–13;
(Senior) 13–18 boarders from 7
No of pupils 757
Junior 218; *Senior* 263; *Sixth form* 276
Girls 284; *boys* 473
No of boarders (full) 453
Fees per annum (full boarding) £11,115–
£17,250; *(day)* £6,855–£11,085

Malvern College is a thriving co-educational boarding and day school which the Inspectors' Report describes as 'a fine school and a friendly community in which very good personal relationships prevail'.

The College has an excellent reputation for pastoral care and academic excellence. A wide variety of sports is available, and arts including music and drama are performed to a high standard. The Sixth Form offers both A levels and the International Baccalaureate (in 2001 the IB results corresponded to AAB at A level). Malvern College prides itself on developing in students respect, independence, self-reliance and values which make them creative and responsible members of society.

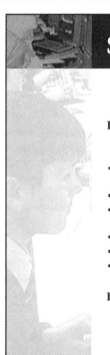

Malvern Girls' College

Avenue Road, Great Malvern, Worcestershire WR14 3BA
Tel (01684) 892288   Fax (01684) 566204
E-mail: registrar@mgc.worcs.sch.uk   Web site: www.mgc.worcs.sch.uk   www.gabbitas.net

Head Mrs Philippa MC Leggate BA, MEd, PGCE
Founded 1893
Type Girls' independent senior boarding and day
Religious denomination Church of England
Member of GSA, BSA, ECIS
Special needs provision DYS
Age range 11–18; *boarders from* 11
No of pupils (day) 80; *(boarding)* 330
Senior 240: *Sixth Form* 170
Fees per annum (full boarding) £17,175; *(day)* £11,400

In a class of its own, Malvern Girls' College offers a high quality academic programme in a friendly boarding environment. With an emphasis on care for the individual, each girl is encouraged actively to develop her own talents and personality. The College offers extensive opportunities for participation in sport and a wide range of extra-curricular activities, which help to develop confident and independent young women. The College is situated in one of the most beautiful areas of Britain, at the foot of the Malvern Hills. Founded in 1893, the College enjoys a deserved reputation for excellent academic results.

The College is committed to providing for the education of the whole person, so when every girl leaves she is well-equipped to fulfil her own individual potential with a sense of social commitment, responsibility and enthusiasm. The Head emphasises that the College caters for a wide range of ability on entry.

Malvern Girls' College provides a broad curriculum with more than 20 subjects offered at GCSE, AS and A^2 Level. Academic staff are well-qualified, lively and enthusiastic. Teaching in small groups encourages quality discussion, analysis and problem solving.

The College's new science centre reinforces a long tradition of excellence in science. There is also considerable investment in Information Technology. There is a strong musical tradition in the College, with more than three quarters of pupils playing at least one instrument.

Boarding life revolves around the six Houses, including a Junior House for 11–12 year olds, and two Sixth Form Houses. Day boarders are regarded as full members of the Houses and take part in all House activities. Pastoral care is excellent, supported by dedicated housestaff.

Girls are encouraged to take part in community service. Every year, members of the Lower Sixth Form undertake a week's community service placement.

The College has been awarded the Sports Council's Sportsmark Gold award for its physical education provision in teaching more than 21 sports. Facilities include an indoor swimming pool, astro-turf games, and squash courts. There is a varied weekend programme of activities for all age groups, including abseiling, canoeing, dry slope skiing, rock climbing, photography, watersports and expeditions leading to the Duke of Edinburgh Award.

Admission is through the College's own examinations, or through Common Entrance examination, together with an interview with the Head. The College offers Academic Entrance Scholarships and Exhibitions, as well as entrance awards for excellence in Art, Music, and Physical Education.

St James's School

West Malvern, Worcestershire WR14 4DF
Tel: (01684) 560851   Fax: (01684) 569252   E-mail: kershawhm@aol.com
Web site: www.st-james-school.co.uk   www.gabbitas.net

Head Mrs S Kershaw BA, PGCE, FRSA
Founded 1896
Type Girls' independent senior boarding and day
Religious denomination Church of England
Member of GSA
Special needs provision DEL, DYC, DYS, DYP, EPI, SPLD
Age range 10–18; *boarders from* 10+
No of pupils (day) 42; *(boarding) (full)* 43; *(weekly)* 40
Senior 85; *Sixth Form* 40
Fees per annum (boarding) (full and weekly) £14,985–£16,050; *(day)* £7,425–£9,855
NB: Fees include lunch and text books.

At St James's School, girls learn in a single-sex environment where they acquire the leadership skills to help them succeed in the wider world. Above all we make learning as enjoyable as possible, supplementing traditional approaches with innovative teaching methods to ensure that they remain interested and focused on each subject.

By offering a wider choice of subjects than demanded by National Curriculum guidelines, we meet the needs of girls with exceptional talents and wide-ranging interests. As a result we lead many girls on to new and unexpected heights.

In all our teaching we believe that the more individual attention we give our girls, the more effective the results, which is why we keep classes small. This personal approach allows us to track each girl's progress and develop

teaching strategies which will motivate, challenge and support her so that she gains the most from her efforts. Skilled help is available through our Learning Enhancement Department for girls with specific learning difficulties (Dyslexia). The Department works in close co-operation with mainstream subject teachers and House staff, suggesting learning techniques and strategies which benefit all our students in their studies.

St James's School is set in an area of outstanding natural beauty on the western slopes of the Malvern Hills in 47 acres of grounds. Its facilities are the envy of many larger schools. There is a 250-seat theatre in a separate Music and Drama block, as well as Art and Pottery studios. The Harvey-Jones School for international business, opened in September 1998, has its own purpose built IT and conference facilities used by all our senior pupils. St James's is the only independent school at present to hold the Herefordshire & Worcestershire Quality Mark for Careers Education Guidance. The School has a separate Sixth Form Centre with individual study bedrooms. Extensive sports facilities include an outdoor heated swimming pool, athletics track and fitness centre.

We place strong emphasis on the quality of our pastoral care so all our girls feel happy and secure.

The School offers academic scholarships as well as exhibitions (worth one sixth of tuition fees) in Music, Drama, Art and Sport.

Ackworth School

Ackworth, Pontefract, West Yorkshire WF7 7LT
Tel: (01977) 611401   Fax: (01977) 616225   E-mail: ackworth@aol.com
Web site: www.ackworth.w-yorks.sch.uk   www.gabbitas.net

Head Martin J Dickinson
Founded 1779
Type Co-educational independent pre-prep, prep and senior boarding and day
Religious denomination Society of Friends (Quakers)
Member of HMC, SHMIS
Special needs provision DYS, EFL
Age range 4–18; *boarders from* 10
No of pupils 480
Junior 130; *Senior* 270; *Sixth Form* 80
Fees (Senior School) per annum (boarding) £13,116; *(day)* £4,053–£7,389

Ackworth is a boarding and day school for boys and girls aged 4 to 18. Boarding starts at 10 and boarders have well presented accommodation in rooms for two or three. Ackworth has superb teaching facilities (the refurbished theatre is the latest addition), and a stable, devoted staff, who have established a tradition of excellence in academic results. Each year 95 per cent of Sixth Form leavers go to university. Music, drama and sporting facilities are outstanding and results show in first rate sporting achievement and a fine musical and theatrical tradition. The School is friendly and welcoming.

Entry is by academic test. Academic, music and art scholarships are available.

Brantwood Independent School for Girls

1 Kenwood Bank, Sheffield, Yorkshire S7 1NU
Tel: (0114) 258 1747   Fax: (0114) 258 1847

no email

Head Mrs EM Swynnerton BA (Hons), DipEd
Founded 1910
Type Girls' independent day
Member of ISIS *accredited by* ISA
Special needs provision DYS
Age range 4–16
No of pupils 223
Junior 104; *Senior* 119
Fees per annum £4,050–£5,250

Brantwood School offers its pupils small class sizes and individual attention.
Senior School curriculum: English Language, English Literature, History, Geography, French, German, Mathematics, IT, Technology, Physics, Chemistry, Biology, RE, Art, Music, Drama, Physical Education, Games.
Junior School curriculum: English, Mathematics, Science, Technology, IT, History, Geography, RE, Art, Speech Training, Drama, Ballet, Music, Physical Education, Games, French.

Examination Boards: AQA, OCR, Edexcel.
Senior School entry: entrance test. *Junior entry*: individual interview.
The School believes in a system which values each child, building on their strengths and supporting weaknesses. We encourage individual development and aim to maximise success in public examinations.

Giggleswick School

Settle, North Yorkshire BD24 0DE
Tel: (01729) 893000   Fax: (01729) 893150
E-mail: registrar@giggleswick.org.uk   Web site: www.giggleswick.org.uk

Head Mr GP Boult
Founded 1512
Type Co-educational independent pre-prep,
prep and senior boarding and day
Religious denomination Church of England
Member of HMC, IAPS, TABS
Special needs provision ADD, DYC, DYS, DYP
Age range 3–18; *boarders from* 7
No of pupils (day) 197; *(boarding)* 287
Girls 191; *boys* 293
Junior 125; *Senior* 315; *Sixth Form* 160
Fees per annum Senior School (boarding)
£16,443; *(day)* £10,911
Junior School (boarding) £12,489–£13,422;
(day) £8,358–£8,973

Gigglewick is one of the leading co-educational boarding schools in the North of England with 80 per cent of pupils in the Senior School boarding. The School is set in magnificent Dales scenery only an hour away from Manchester and Leeds with good access to the motorways and international airports. Small classes and a low staff to pupil ratio lead to excellent academic standards. The academic, leisure and boarding facilities are first class. A recently completed £4.5 million development programme has included an innovative Learning and Information Centre, a floodlit synthetic hockey pitch and a new Languages Facility. Plans for the coming year include a new library and teaching centre for Giggleswick's Junior School, Catteral Hall.

Pocklington School   129

West Green, Pocklington, York, East Yorkshire YO42 2NJ
Tel: (01759) 303125   Fax: (01759) 306366   E-mail: mainoffice@pocklington.e-yorks.sch.uk
Web site: www.pocklington.e-yorks.sch.uk   www.gabbitas.net

Head Mr N Clements MA, BSc
Founded 1514
Type Co-educational independent prep and
senior boarding and day
Religious denomination Church of England
Age range 7–18; *boarders from* 9
No of pupils (day) 601; *(boarding)* 127
Girls 310; *boys* 418
Junior 149; *Senior* 415; *Sixth Form* 164
Fees per annum (full boarding) £10,305–
£11,970; *(day)* £6,090–£7,155

Pocklingtion School is set in extensive grounds on the edge of Pocklington, a market town 12 miles east of York. Communications are good with effective bus service coverage for day pupils and a fast road link to York and the motorway network.

The Curriculum has been designed to stretch and motivate pupils who consistently achieve excellent academic results at both GCSE and A Level. Most go on to Higher Education including Oxbridge and other top institutions.

An impressive range of extra curricular and sporting activities is available to all pupils.

Academic and music scholarships and exhibitions are available at most entry levels including the Sixth Form.

The Mount School York

"Rated the Top Girls' Independent Day and boarding school" in the North of England for 'A' Levels *The Times* 24 August 2001

Dalton Terrace, York, North Yorkshire YO24 4DD
Tel: Registrar (01904) 667507   Fax: (01904) 667524   E-mail: registrar@mount.n-yorks.sch.uk
Web site: www.mount.n-yorks.sch.uk   www.gabbitas.net

Head Mrs Diana Gant
Founded 1785
Type Girls' independent boarding and day senior school, co-educational pre-prep and prep
Religious denomination Quaker
Member of GSA, BSA
Special needs provision DYS
Age range 3–18; *boarders from* 11
No of pupils (day) 423; (boarding) 90
Girls; 371; *boys* 52
Junior 168; *Senior* 255; *Sixth Form* 72
Fees per annum (full and weekly boarding) £9,948–£13,680; (day) £3,390–£8,580

The Mount School York balances academic excellence with outstanding pastoral care. It develops individuals while teaching responsibility to the community and a global outlook. Mount pupils are self-possessed but not arrogant. A broad curriculum at GCSE leads to a wide choice of A and AS Levels, with almost all proceeding to degree courses. The School is strong in all academic departments.

Facilities: redesigned boarding accommodation in the Middle School completed in September 1998: specialist rooms for all subjects; excellent facilities for Music, Science, Maths, Arts and Technology, cross-curricular policy for computers. Several high quality drama productions each year and many concerts and opportunities for musical performance. Good opportunities for sports and outdoor activities, 16 acres of grounds and playing fields, 25 metre indoor pool, new sports hall and fitness suite opened 2000. The school has regional and national representatives in several sports, international orienteers and fencers. 50 extra-curricular subjects offered including 12 musical ensembles. Duke of Edinburgh Scheme very strong. High profile music, drama and visual arts, exciting programme of foreign visits throughout school. Foreign exchanges are frequent.

Ethos: the Quaker ethos means an open minded welcome to the rich diversity of philosophies or religious traditions from which pupils come, encouraging everyone's strengths and promoting high standards and moral values.

Entry is by our own examination and interview. Scholarships and bursaries are available.

TREGELLES: Junior Department opened in 1991. Single age classes in each year group. A stimulating and creative environment promoting excellent work habits and excitement about learning.

Queen Ethelburga's College

Thorpe Underwood Hall, Ouseburn, York YO26 9SS
Tel: (0870) 742 3300   Fax: (0870) 742 3310
E-mail: admin@queenethelburgas.edu   Web site: www.queenethelburgas.edu   www.gabbitas.net

Head Mr Peter Dass
Founded 1912
Type Co-educational independent prep and
senior boarding and day
Religious denomination Church of England
Member of GSA, GBGSA, BHS
Special needs provision ADD, DYC, DYS, HI
Age range 2½–18; *boarders from* 6
No of pupils (day) 180; *(boarding)* 200
Girls 289; *boys* 91
Junior 150; *Senior* 230; *Sixth Form* 85
Fees per annum (full boarding) £11,085–
£16,275; *(day)* £2,925–£9,975

Broad based curriculum following National
Curriculum in key subject areas. Entry to Preparatory School by assessment and interview.
Students move through to Senior School. External entry to Senior School is by test and
interview. Senior Students are prepared for
GCSE, A Levels and advanced vocational courses including Fashion and Design, Photography, Travel and Tourism, Business and
BHSAI for riders. Recent heavy investment has
been made in living accommodation, equestrian
centre, business and computing suite, cookery
area, purpose built laboratories and lecture
theatre. There is a large programme of sport
and extra activities. Scholarships for academic
excellence and riding competence are available.

Scarborough College & Lisvane School

Filey Road, Scarborough, North Yorkshire YO11 3BA
Tel: (01723) 360620   Fax: (01723) 377265   E-mail: admin@scarboroughcollege.co.uk
Web site: www.scarboroughcollege.co.uk   www.gabbitas.net

Head Mr TL Kirkup
Founded 1898
Type Co-educational independent pre-prep,
prep and senior boarding and day
Religious denomination Inter-denominational
Member of SHMIS, IAPS, GBA, BSA
Special needs provision DYS, DYP, SPLD
Age range 3–18; *boarders from* 9
No of pupils (day) 469; *(boarding)* 40
Girls 241; *boys* 268
Junior 163; *Senior* 256; *Sixth Form* 75
Fees per annum (boarding) (full) £9,150;
(weekly) £9,150; *(day)* £6,495

Scarborough College entered the 21st century
as North Yorkshire's top independent school for
boys and girls.
Scarborough College and its Junior School,
Lisvane, are stimulating environments where
girls and boys are taught to live co-operatively together and respect one another. Well-
disciplined classes enable every child to achieve
academic success through hard work. Public
examination results are excellent. The College
has a strong reputation in sport. Music, drama
and public speaking all flourish. There is
English language tuition for overseas students
and a learning support Department. At
Scarborough College, your child will be given
every opportunity to learn and develop as a
confident individual.

(133)

Albyn School for Girls, Aberdeen

17–23 Queen's Road, Aberdeen AB15 4PB
Tel: (01224) 322408   Fax: (01224) 209173
E-mail: information@albynschool.co.uk   Web site: www.albynschool.co.uk   www.gabbitas.net

Head Miss Jennifer Leslie MA (Hons), CertEd
Founded 1867
Type Girls' day only independent pre-prep, prep and senior. Co-educational nurseries for children aged 2½–5 years old
Religious denomination Non-denominational
Member of SCIS, SGS
Special needs provision CP, DEL, DYS, DYP, EPI, HI, PH, SPLD (mild), VIS
Age range 2½–18
No of pupils 381
Girls 361; *boys* 20
Junior 173; *Senior* 146; *Sixth Form* 62
Fees per annum £3,660–£6,200

Albyn School is one of Scotland's most highly regarded independent day schools delivering academic excellence in a caring environment. Set in four attractive granite buildings in the West End of Aberdeen, Albyn is a well-equipped establishment with modern facilities such as science laboratories and computing rooms. Besides a spacious playground on-site, we have an excellent sports facility at Milltimber comprising a pavilion, tennis courts, hockey pitches and a running track. Academic standards are very high. Upper School specialists in Art and Design, Computing, French, PE and Music teach Lower School pupils at various stages. Extra-curricular activities are many and varied.

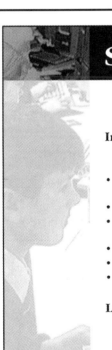

Basil Paterson Tutorial College

23 Abercromby Place, Edinburgh, Lothian EH3 6QE
Tel: (0131) 556 7698   Fax: (0131) 557 8503
E-mail: study@bp-tut.demon.co.uk   Web site: www.basilpaterson.co.uk

Head Mrs Iris Shewan MA
Founded 1929
Type Independent tutorial college
Accredited by BAC
Special needs provision ADD, ADHD, ASP, DEL, DYS, DYP, EPI, HI, VIS
Age range 14+
No of pupils (day) 35
Girls 16; *boys* 24
Fees per annum (boarding with host family accommodation) (full boarding) £8,200–£13,700; *(weekly)* £7,200–£12,700; *(day)* £5,000–£10,500

Basil Paterson College occupies a spacious 19th century building in Edinburgh's famous Georgian New Town, five minutes from the city centre. The college has two schools, combining academic studies with the teaching of English as a foreign language. This combination offers a flexible range of courses for British and overseas students.

The Tutorial College offers a wide range of courses in preparation for A-Levels, AS-Levels, Scottish Highers, GCSE and Standard Grade examinations. The permanent staff consists of mature, qualified and experienced teachers, all of whom are specialists in their fields. Each conducts small classes, thus allowing students individual attention. Student advisers are present to monitor progress, offer advice and assist with academic and personal matters.

The school is accredited by the British Accreditation Council. A full social programme is on offer to students from both schools.

Fettes College

Carrington Road, Edinburgh, Midlothian, EH14 1QX
Tel: (0131) 311 6701   Fax: (0131) 311 6714
E-mail: enquiries@fettes.com   Web site: www.fettes.com

Head Mr MCB Spens MA
Founded 1870
Type Co-educational independent prep and senior boarding and day
Religious denomination Inter-denominational
Member of HMC, GBA, BSA, IAPS
Age range 8–18; *boarders from* 8
No of pupils (day) 205; *(boarding)* 387
Girls 241; *boys* 351
Prep 161; *Senior* 237; *Sixth Form* 190
Fees per annum (boarding) £12,228–£16,884; *(day)* £7,668–£11,391

The curriculum provides GCSE courses in English, Latin, Greek, French, German, Spanish, Religious Studies, Business Studies, History, Geography, Mathematics, Physics, Chemistry, Biology, Technology, Drama, Art, Music and PE. Compulsory courses in Information Technology are also included. The option system permits pupils to select the combination of subjects best suited to their abilities.

In the Sixth Form there is the attractive alternative of the specialisation offered by GCE A Levels, or the wealth of stimulation offered by the Higher grade examinations of the Scottish Certificate of Education. Through these two systems over 95 per cent of pupils gain university entry qualifications and a good number each year secure places at Oxford and Cambridge.

Scholarships and entrance examinations for the Prep School are held in February. Boys and girls from preparatory schools take the scholarship examination in March or the Common Entrance examination. Candidates from maintained schools can take the School's own entrance examination in English and Mathematics.

Candidates for the Sixth Form take the Sixth Form scholarship and entrance examination in November, or can be considered on report and interview only. The Headmaster is prepared to give individual consideration to other candidates.

Scholarships to maximum value of 50 per cent fees are available for candidates aged 11+ or 13+ at entry and also for entry to the Sixth Form: these awards can be supplemented by bursaries in case of financial need.

Foundation awards and bursaries are available to those candidates whose parents cannot meet the full fees. The value of these awards depends on the parents' financial means. These awards are made not only on the basis of academic standards but also on the ability and enthusiasm of the candidate to contribute strongly to the sporting and cultural activities of the School.

Music and Art scholarships and All-rounder Awards of up to the value of 50 per cent are also available. Bursaries provide 12.5 per cent reduction in fees for children of HM forces.

Fettes stands in a magnificent park of 85 acres, a mile and a half from the centre of Edinburgh and within which are situated all School's facilities. Full advantage is taken of the academic and cultural opportunities which Edinburgh affords and at the same time the sea and countryside are close by offering an excellent environment for outdoor pursuits.

The major sports for boys and girls are all offered. The School has its own indoor swimming pool, fives, squash, badminton and basketball courts as well as an all-weather sports surface. A new Sports Centre will be completed in 2002.

Leadership is fostered throughout the School with special courses as well as through the Combined Cadet Force, Outside Service and Duke of Edinburgh's Award Scheme.

Merchiston Castle School

Colinton, Edinburgh, Midlothian EH13 0PU
Tel: (0131) 312 2200   Fax: (0131) 441 6060
Web site: www.merchiston.co.uk   www.gabbitas.net

Head AR Hunter BA
Founded 1833
Type Boys' independent boarding and day
Religious denomination Inter-denominational
Member of HMC, ISBA
Special needs provision DYS
Age range 8–18; *boarders from* 8
No of pupils (day) 137; *(boarding)* 280
Junior 97; *Senior* 175; *Sixth Form* 146
Fees per annum (boarding) £11,100–£16,500;
(day) £6,900–£11,385

Merchiston is one of Scotland's leading independent schools, situated four miles from the town centre of Edinburgh, one of Europe's most historic and thriving cultural cities. It is set in 100 acres of exceptionally beautiful parkland and is a Scottish school not solely by virtue of its location, but in its adherence to Scottish values and traditions. It is renowned for its academic and sporting excellence.

Full range of subjects to GCSE, A Levels or Highers. In 2001, an impressive 68 per cent of A Level candidates gained A and B grades, whilst at GCSE 55 per cent of grades were awarded at A and A*. 98 per cent gained university places with 86 per cent achieving their first choice. Regular winners of national engineering, electronic and mathematics prizes. Outstanding sporting achievements including pupils participating at international level in seven different sports. Strongly featured Music Department with prestigious School choir and pipe band. Friendly integral Junior School – Pringle (8–12 years). Strong links with two girls' schools. As a result of expansion, new Junior School facilities are under construction. Recently opened: new IT suite, Music School and library. Indoor swimming pool, and sports hall. Extensive extra-curricular opportunities. Admission though School's own exam. Scholarships and bursaries available.

Gordonstoun School

Elgin, Moray, IV30 5RF
Tel: (01343) 837829   Fax: (01343) 837808   E-mail: admissions@gordonstoun.org.uk
Web site: www.gordonstoun.org.uk   www.gabbitas.net

Head Mr MC Pyper
Founded 1934
Type Co-educational independent senior boarding and day
Religious denomination Non-denominational
Special needs provision ADD, DEL, DYS, DYP, EPI, SPLD, VIS
Age range 13–18; *boarders from* 13
No of pupils (day) 25; *(boarding)* 385
Girls 175; *boys* 235
Senior 200; *Sixth Form* 210
Fees per annum (full boarding) £17,625–£18,755; *(day)* £11,895–£13,020

Gordonstoun benefits from its setting between the sea and mountains in magnificent Moray countryside. It is also well located for easy access to the international airports at Aberdeen and Inverness.

Founded in 1934 by Dr Kurt Hahn, Gordonstoun is much more than a first class conventional school. An integrated curriculum caters for pupils of a wide ability range and produces excellent results according to their talents. A full personal development programme of sporting and creative activities, outdoor education including a unique sail training programme, is backed by excellent facilities and highly committed staff ensuring pastoral care of the highest quality.

Glenalmond College

Perth, Perthshire PH1 3RY
Tel: (01738) 842056   Fax: (01738) 842063
E-mail: registrar@glenalmondcollege.co.uk   Web site: www.glenalmondcollege.co.uk

Head Mr IG Templeton
Founded 1841
Type Co-educational independent senior boarding and day
Religious denomination Episcopelian/non-denominational
Member of HMC
Special needs provision DYS, ESL
Age range 12–18; *boarders from* 12
No of pupils (day) 52; *(boarding)* 349
Girls 143; *boys* 258
Junior 11; *Senior* 234; *Sixth Form* 156
Fees per annum (boarding) £12,375–£16,485; *(day)* £8,250–£10,995

Full range of subjects to GCSE, choice of A Level or Scottish Highers in Sixth Form. Very strong music, art, theatre.
Splendid facilities for technology and there are excellent computing opportunities, including new internet access throughout the school.

Golf course, salmon river, artificial ski-slope, indoor and outdoor shooting, skiing, water sports enhance a wide range of sports facilities. There is a new second astroturf pitch and a new Science block opened in October 2001. Glenalmond is also strong on public speaking and debating. There are good European links. Easy access to Glasgow and Edinburgh and to airports. Art, Music and academic scholarships and All-rounder awards. Bursaries are available for service children and clergy children.
The College is a registered charity providing quality education for boys and girls.

Rannoch School

Rannoch By Pitlochry, Perthshire PH17 2QQ
Tel: (01882) 632332   Fax: (01882) 632443
E-mail: headmaster@rannoch.co.uk   Web site: www.rannoch.co.uk   www.gabbitas.net

Head Mr Arthur Andrews DipEd
Founded 1959
Type Co-educational independent prep and senior boarding and day
Religious denomination Inter-denominational
Member of SHMIS, GBA, Round Square: Registered with Scottish Education Dept
Special needs provision ADD, ADHD, DYC, DYS, DYP, EPI, MLD, SPLD
Age range 10–18; *boarders from* 10
No of pupils (day) 2; *(boarding)* 110
Girls 36; *boys* 76
Junior 21; *Senior* 35; *Sixth Form* 56
Fees per annum (boarding) (full) £12,489–£14,775; *(weekly)* £10,113–£12,294; *(day)* £7,704 (10% discount for service personnel)
Av. class size: 10; *Teacher:pupil ratio* 1:6

Rannoch, a co-educational 10–18 boarding school, combines personal tuition in small classes with outdoor educational challenges,

inspiring all pupils to discover their real capabilities.
The results are impressive ... from Standard and Higher Grade achievers (including those with learning challenges) to over 600 pupils attaining the Duke of Edinburgh Gold Award. Music, choir and drama are integral aspects of a wide curriculum that encourages personal responsibility, service to the community (locally and internationally) and, ultimately, engenders self-reliance and builds pupils' confidence to rise to the challenge of adulthood.
Companies send senior managers to Rannoch for team training, imagine the head-start for your child after seven years at Rannoch!

Netherwood School

Saundersfoot, Pembrokeshire SA69 9BE
Tel: (01834) 811057   Fax: (01834) 811023
E-mail: netherwood.school@virgin.net   Web site: www.gabbitas.net

Principal Mr DH Morris BA, CertEd, FRGS, FCollP
Founded 1947
Type Co-educational independent pre-prep, prep and senior boarding and day
Religious denomination Church of England
Member of AHIS, NAHT;
Accredited by Welsh Office
Special needs provision DYS, PH, VIS
Age range 3–18; *boarders from* 6
No of pupils (boarding) 37; *(day)* 132
Girls 82; *boys* 87
Junior 68; *Senior* 101
Fees per annum (boarding)(full) £8,475–£9,075; *(weekly)* £7,275–£8,175; *(day)* £2,850–£4,275
Sixth Form (boarding) £11,985; *(day)* £5,985

Safe, enclosed environment based on an elegant listed building, next to the beautiful Pembrokeshire coastline. Day and boarding grown as a large family since 1947. National Curriculum followed closely, SATs are followed at all stages. Very thorough schemes of work followed, reported on via Records of Achievement.

In 1998 100 per cent of all Year 11 pupils gained between 5 and 11 A*–C grades at GCSE, sitting a minimum of 9 subjects each. Currently offering A Levels and AVCEs. Motto – 'Through Friendship and Understanding we Prosper'.

Mougins School

615 Avenue Dr Maurice Donat, Font de l'Orme, BP 401, Mougins 06251 Cedex, France
Tel: +33 4 93 90 15 47   Fax: +33 4 93 75 31 40
E-mail: information@mougins-school.com
Web site: www.mougins-school.com   www.gabbitas.net

Head Brian G Hickmore
Founded 1964
Type Co-educational independent pre-prep, prep and senior day
Religious denomination Non-denominational
Member of COBISEC
Special needs provision ADD, ADHD, DYS, MLD, W
Age range 3–18
No of pupils 373
Girls 170; *boys* 203
Junior 159; *Senior* 131; *Sixth Form* 45
Fees per annum FF24,900–FF69,000

Mougins School is situated 10km north of Cannes on a purpose built campus. Facilities include Library, 2 Science Laboratories, Information Technology Centre, Art Room, Music Room, Dining Room, synthetic Football Pitch.

The School has a one form entry system catering for students aged from 3 to 18 with over thirty nationalities. Studies are based on the UK National Curriculum modified to meet the needs of an international market. Tests are taken at 7, 11, and 14 followed by IGCSE, GCSE, AS and A Level examinations. ESOL is available as well as Special Needs Provision.

The caring family atmosphere complements the high quality of the teaching and helps to enhance the academic, cultural and physical development of our students, producing excellent results, not only academically, but also in the sporting and artistic domains.

A fleet of three School buses allows us to organise field trips, sporting activities and competitions outside the School as well as residential educational visits.

The British School in The Netherlands

Foundation School: Tarwekamp 3, 2592 XG The Hague, The Netherlands
Junior School: Vlaskamp 19, 2592 AA The Hague, The Netherlands
Senior School: Jan Van Hooflaan 3, 2252 BG Voorschoten, The Netherlands
Tel: 31 70 333 8111   Fax: 31 70 333 8100
E-mail: foundation@britishschool.nl   junior@britishschool.nl   senior@britishschool.nl
Web site: www.britishschool.nl

Principal Mr RT Rowell
Founded 1935
Type Co-educational independent pre-prep, prep and senior day
Member of COBISEC, HMC, ECIS, Governing Bodies Association
Special needs provision individually assessed
Age range 3–18
No of pupils 1,804
Girls 880; *boys* 924
Foundation 240; *Junior* 842; *Senior* 565; *Sixth Form* 157
Fees per annum Euros 8,040–10,920

The British School in The Netherlands occupies two extensive green field sites in The Hague and Voorschoten, plus a smaller Foundation School for the youngest children. Each site provides excellent facilities to support the educational, recreational and sporting programmes offered. It is an international, co-educational day school for children aged 3–18 years, following a British curriculum. Pupils follow a broad and challenging programme. The curriculum is enriched by international field trips and participation in European sports fixtures, debating competitions and a host of extra curricular activities. The BSN offers GCSE and the new A Level examinations in a wide range of subjects. The academic success rate is consistently high with most students continuing with further education at universities throughout the world. Admission is granted throughout the year following an interview.

King's College

Paseo de los Andes, 35, 28761 Soto de Viñuelas, Madrid, Spain
Tel: +34 918 034 800   Fax: + 34 918 036 557
E-mail: soto@kingsgroup.com   Web site: www.kingscollege.es

Head Christopher T Gill Leech MA (Cantab)
Founded 1969
Type Co-educational independent pre-prep, prep and senior boarding and day
Religious denomination Non-denominational
Member of HMC, COBISEC, ECIS, NABSS; *accredited by* ISC, Spanish Ministry of Education
Special needs provision W
Age range 1½–18 boarders from 11
No of pupils (day) 1,280; *(boarding)* 20
Girls 640; *boys* 660
Junior 700; *Senior* 530; *Sixth Form* 70
Fees per term (boarding) Ptas. 330,000 additional (Euros 1,983.34 additional); *(day)* Ptas. 200,500 (Euros 1,205.03)–Ptas. 412,000 (Euros 2,476.17)

Founded in 1969, King's College is the largest British school in Spain.

It is a co-educational day and boarding school following the English National Curriculum which prepares pupils for IGCSE and GCE A Levels and offers a wide range of subjects at both levels. There are optional Spanish studies and preparation for Spanish University entrance examinations.

With 1,300 pupils of more than 30 nationalities, the School has a complement of 85 fully qualified teachers. All academic staff have British qualifications, except the Spanish teachers and some who teach modern languages. The average length of stay of the staff is over seven years.

Over the last 30 years, the College has earned a reputation for high academic standards and excellent examination results with students going on to universities in Britain, USA, Spain, amongst others. A very experienced Careers and University Entrance Advisory Department is available to all students.

King's College is a modern purpose-built school set in a 12 acre site, surrounded by countryside but well connected to Madrid.

The School has its own catering service and offers three course midday meals. There is an optional bus service with a modern fleet of 17 vehicles covering Madrid and outlying areas.

Academic facilities: King's College offers excellent academic facilities including seven science laboratories, two multimedia computer centres, two libraries, music rooms, art studio, etc.

Sports facilities: on-site sports facilities include: gymnasium, judo room, fitness centre, 25-metre heated indoor swimming pool, eleven-a-side and five-a-side football pitches, floodlit multisports area, tennis courts, stables and riding school.

Boarding facilities: there are recently refurbished boarding facilities for boys and girls with rooms for one to three pupils over the age of 11. At present the Residence includes pupils from the UK, Russia, Germany, as well as students from expatriate families living in Spain. Resident students enjoy free access to King's Sports Centre for afternoon/evening activities.

Extra-curricular activities: the full range of extra curricular activities offered by the School broadens students general education, helping them to develop worthwhile leisure-time activities. Ballet, handicrafts, piano, judo, violin, riding, swimming and tennis are all offered as optional classes.

Admission: the procedure for admission varies according to the age of the pupil. Importance is given to previous school records and from age 7 to 16 years candidates are required to sit entrance tests in Mathematics and English.

Aiglon College

Rue Centrale Chesières 1885, Switzerland
Tel: 00 41 24 496 61 61   Fax: 00 41 24 496 61 62
E-mail: info@aiglon.ch   Web site: www.aiglon.ch

Head Dr Rvd Jonathan Long
Founded 1949
Type Co-educational independent prep and senior boarding and day
Religious denomination Christian allegiance
Member of HMC, Round Square, ECIS, NEASC
Age range 9–18; boarders from 9
No of pupils (day) 40; *(boarding)* 280
Girls 142; *boys* 183
Junior 84; *Senior* 137; *Sixth Form* 104
Fees per annum (boarding) Sfr40,170–Sfr60,160 depending on age; *(day)* Sfr12,500–Sfr39,560 depending on age

The British International School in Switzerland is situated in the French-Swiss Alps and has 332 students, aged 9 to 18. The headmaster is an overseas member of The Headmaster's Conference and the School is registered as a non-profit making trust in the Netherlands, Switzerland, the UK, USA and Canada.

Founded in 1949, Aiglon aims to provide, within a safe, caring and supportive framework, a rigorous and challenging education in intellectual, physical, moral, emotional and spiritual self-discipline and self-discovery. The academic programme is demanding and prepares students for British GCSE and A Level examinations as well as the American College Board. Aiglon students are currently enrolled in leading universities on both sides of the Atlantic.

Academic study is complemented by a high degree of pastoral care and a challenging programme of sports and outdoor activities including skiing and mountain expeditions. The School has a separate Junior School for boys and girls aged 9 to 13 with bilingual (French/English) primary section, and six Senior boarding houses all situated on a south facing slope at 4,000 ft. Facilities include an outstanding new building housing science laboratories, a Computer Centre, an extensive Music Department and on-campus radio; in addition there are language laboratories, a library, an Art School and several sports surfaces. The School also has access to a swimming pool, an ice skating rink, a Sports Centre with indoor tennis and squash courts, and extensive ski slopes just five minutes walk from the School. Admission is through the School's entrance tests or the Common Entrance Examinations and a number of places are also available in the Lower Sixth for candidates with good GCSE qualifications.

Language summer schools in English and French combined with outdoor activities are offered in July and August.

Further information may be obtained from the head of admissions.

144

Brillantmont International College

Avenue Secretan 16, 1005 Lausanne, Switzerland 1005
Tel: 00 41 21 310 04 00   Fax: 00 41 21 320 84 17
E-mail: info@brillantmont.ch   Web site: www.brillantmont.ch   www.gabbitas.net

Director Philippe Pasche
Founded 1882
Type Co-educational independent prep and
senior boarding and day
Religious denomination Non-denominational
Member of FSEP, AVDEP, SGIS; *accredited by*
ECIS, NEASC
Age range 13–19
No of pupils (day) 50; *boarding* 90
Boarders from age of 13
Fees per annum (boarding) (full) SFr48,000;
(weekly) SFr42,700; *(day)* SFr18,500

Brillantmont prepares students to IGCSE, AS, A Level and AICE (Cambridge International Examinations) in English, French, German, Italian, Spanish, Maths, Biology, Chemistry, Physics, Computer Studies, History, Economics, Art.

Located in the centre of Lausanne, the French speaking area of Switzerland, Brillantmont has a reputation for teaching languages and offers a wide variety of cultural and sporting events.

Our strengths are: to offer an excellent preparation for university; to have an international students' body from 35 nations; to offer tuition in small classes; to have a boarding school where the development of the student's personality and talents is a major concern.

The school is situated seven minutes from the centre of Lausanne. The campus comprises seven buildings adjacent to one another in a park of four acres. School facilities include two science laboratories, one computerised language laboratory, a video room, a computer laboratory, a media centre, and a library.

A wide variety of extra-curricular activities is available: art, music, photography, drama, cinema, yearbook, ballet, Community Service, creative writing and journalism. The sports programme offers: volleyball, basketball, track, athletics, cross-country, swimming, badminton, tennis, bicycling, windsurfing, rowing, skating, skiing, hockey, football, squash and musculation.

The location of the school in Lausanne enables Brillantmont to offer an enriched cultural programme. Our pupils can benefit from a wide range of cultural events, and are encouraged to visit art galleries, museums and multicultural festivals and to attend concerts, plays and dance performances, presented by artists of international reputation.

The student community includes representatives from about 35 countries, offering an exceptional chance to learn about each others' traditions and different ways of life and customs, to organize international evenings, and to practise foreign languages.

The bonds of friendship forged at Brillantmont last a lifetime and can lead to contacts and exchanges which are the key to greater international understanding.

Applicants to British or European universities receive counselling in the choice of a university; these pupils also tour universities in England. Career counselling is available.

Students are admitted on their previous school record accompanied by a recommendation from their former principal.

John F Kennedy International School

3792 Saanen, Saanen, Switzerland   Tel: +41 33 7441373
Fax: +41 33 744 8982   E-mail: lovell@jfk.ch   Web site: www.jfk.ch   www.gabbitas.net

Head William M Lovell, Director
Type Co-educational independent prep and
pre-prep boarding and day
Accredited by Department of Education Cantan
of Bern, Switzerland
Special needs provision MLD
Age range 5–14; *boarders from* 6
No of pupils 60; *(boarding)* 30
Girls 30; *boys* 30
Fees per annum (full boarding) Chf40,000
(day) Chf22,000

Located in the beautiful Gstaad area, JFK is an English language international school for students between the ages of 5 and 14.

Main features include excellent preparation for secondary schools, small classes, EFL programmes, daily French classes, a caring atmosphere and a rich offering of sports and activities including daily skiing in winter.

Our mission is to provide a well-rounded education enhancing academic, social, physical and moral growth. Fundamental to our programme is the strong belief that each child is a unique individual with differing needs and abilities. Curriculum is designed to meet individual differences aiding our students to become continuous learners and confident, productive members of society.

Our summer camp in July and August combines language instruction in English or French with a variety of sports, outdoor activities and camping.

The British International School, Cairo

PO Box 137, Gezira, Cairo, Egypt
Tel: (00) 202 736 5959   Fax: (00) 202 736 4168
E-mail: biscairo@hotmail.com   Web site: www.bisc.edu.eg   www.gabbitas.net

Head Dr P McLaughlin BA (hons), PhD
Founded 1976
Type Co-educational independent pre-prep, prep and senior day
Religious denomination Inter-denominational
Member of COBISEC, ECIS
Age range 3–18
Girls 307; *boys* 302
Primary 361; *Senior* 201; *Sixth Form* 47
Fees per annum £2,724–£6,294

The British International School, Cairo has an uncompromising commitment to excellence and to delivering the highest standards in teaching and learning. Our public examination results in both the Primary and Senior Schools place us amongst the first division of independent and selective schools in the United Kingdom league tables. BISC's development plan is building on its existing reputation for outstanding achievement to make it a world class institution.

The School follows the programmes of study and assessment procedures of the National Curriculum for England and Wales but offers NC Plus, with the full General Certificate of Secondary Education being taken at 16. Pre-university preparation is completed with the highly prestigious, two-year, International Baccalaureate (IB) programme. Recognised both in the United Kingdom and worldwide, the IB has resulted in the School placing students at Oxford and Cambridge, other top UK universities and such major institutions as MIT and Swathmore in the USA.

The Primary School, as it is called, comprises all pupils between the ages of 3 and 11. There is one Nursery class of 32 children with a full time Nursery teacher and three assistants. From Reception up to Year 6 there are two classes per year group of between 20 and 24 children. The early years (Key Stage 1) classes have excellent support, with full-time assistant teachers. Key Stage 2 classes also have a full-time assistant teacher which enables the teaching of small groups in the core subjects of English and

Mathematics. Standards are high, with exemplary SATs results both at KS1 and KS2.

The Senior School has a teacher:pupil ratio of 1:9, a policy of limiting class sizes and an extensive tutor support system with a teaching staff consisting of UK university graduates who have had extensive international experience. The student body has a strong British representation and encompasses a total of 40 nationalities.

BISC is a well-equipped school with 'state of the art' science laboratories, computer centres, libraries, air-conditioned classrooms, and access to an all-weather athletic track, swimming pool and astro-turf areas.

The value of being a relatively small school is that we are able to give the individual attention which the modern student needs, and in so doing to foster such aspects as responsibility, flexibility of mind and an awareness of the needs of others.

Application procedures will be initiated by an interview with the Principal and placement is subject to an assessment of suitability, together with the availability of places.

The British School Manila

36th Street University Park, Fort Bonifacio, Global City, Taguig, Metro Manila, Philippines
Tel: 00 (632) 840 15 70   Fax: 00 (632) 840 15 20
E-mail: admissions@britishschoolmanila.org   Web site: www.britishschoolmanila.org

Head Helen Kinsey-Wightman, BA (Hons),
Cert Ed, MA (EdMan)
Founded 1976
Type Co-educational independent day
Religious denomination Non-denominational
Member of ECIS, FOBISSEA, IAPS
Accredited by ECIS
Age range 4–16
No of pupils 402
Girls 206; *boys* 196
Junior 319; *senior* 83
Fees per annum £5,700

The British School Manila provides a British-style education for children from 4–16 years of age. Places are allocated to children of expatriates residing in the Philippines and British children make up the larger population, although increasingly more children are coming from the host nation. All children take an assessment prior to admission to determine their correct academic placement. We follow the UK National Curriculum, setting the National School Tests at KS1, KS2 and KS3, as well as 11+, 12+ and 13+ if requested. Children sit GCSEs at the end of KS4.

The school moved to a new, ultramodern facility in September 2001.

Cambridge Arts & Sciences (CATS) incorporating Cambridge School of Art & Design (CSAD)

Round Church Street, Cambridge, Cambridgeshire CB5 8AD
Tel: (01223) 314431   Fax: (01223) 467773
E-mail: cats@dial.pipex.com   Web site: www.ceg-uk.com   www.gabbitas.net

Co-Principals Peter Mclaughlin BEd, CertED; Elizabeth Armstrong BA (Hons), DipPsych
Founded 1985
Type Co-educational independent sixth-form college, boarding and day
Religious denomination Non-denominational
Member of ISA, ISIS; *accredited by* BAC, ISC
Special needs provision ADD, ADHD, DYC, DYS, DYP, EBD, EPI, MLD
Age range 15–19+; *boarders from* 15
No of pupils (day) 20; *(boarding)* 180
Girls 99; *boys* 101
GCSE and Foundation 30; *Sixth Form* 160
Fees per annum (boarding) £13,925–£15,650; *(day)* £10,625–£12,150

The College is set in a central campus which surrounds the famous Cambridge Union. Facilities include six art studios, three science laboratories, a photographic studio, dark room, music and music teaching facility, video editing suite and computer laboratory. All students are members of the Cambridge Union and they attend its lectures and debating workshops. There are no restrictions on the combinations of subjects which are studied. Class sizes are limited to seven and the staff:student ratio is 1:3. A premium is placed on individual attention and students have a personal tutor who monitors well-being and progress. Wide range of sports, extra-curricular activities and study trips offered. Entry is by interview and school reference. CATS is a thriving community with a dynamic, family atmosphere. In the last seven years all applicants have secured places in higher education. CSAD offers an Art & Design/Media Foundation course for post A-Level students who wish to go on to Art School.

Albany College

21–24 Queen Road, Hendon, NW4 2TL
Tel: (020) 8202 5965   Fax: (020) 8202 8460
E-mail: info@albany-college.co.uk   Web site: www.albany-college.co.uk   www.gabbitas.net

Head RJ Arthy
Founded 1974
Type College
Religious denomination Inter-denominational
Member of CIFE *accredited by* BAC
Special needs provision DYS, MLD
Age range 14–18
No of pupils 200
Senior 30; *Sixth Form* 170
Girls 90; *boys* 110
Fees per annum (day) £9,600

Albany is a highly successful, well-established caring and cosmopolitan independent 5th and 6th Form College. Our teaching and academic counselling is extremely effective. Albany students have won the Richard Smart Memorial prize for academic excellence for the past four years. In June 2001 27 students gained at least 2 A grade A level passes, and there were 45 perfect module scores, with the majority of students gaining places at traditional established universities. In February 2000, Albany was specially singled out by the Daily Telegraph for our high A level grade improvements for re-sit candidates. Our well-equipped facilities are located on two sites which are a short walking distance from each other and the college also offers thriving extra curricular programme.

Albany has a highly qualified and dedicated professional teaching and administrative team whose enthusiasm and commitment have enabled our students to attain outstanding results. Our aim is that students leave the college with the confidence and skills necessary to be happy and successful throughout life.

Albemarle Independent College

6–7 Inverness Mews, Bayswater, London W2 3JQ
Tel: (020) 7221 7271   Fax: (020) 7792 3910
E-mail: admin@albemarle.org.uk   Web site: www.albemarle.org.uk

Co-Principals Beverley Mellon, James Eytle
Type Co-educational independent sixth form college day
Religious denomination Non-denominational
Special needs provision DYS
Age range 16–19
Girls 57; *boys* 63
Fees per annum £8,250–£10,500

Albemarle is an A-level specialist college, offering full AS and A-level courses and short resit courses in a wide range of subjects. Tuition is in small groups of six to seven, and students benefit considerably from individual help outside of classes.

Abermarle has an excellent record of success at A Level *(100 per cent A, B, C grades–first time students June 2000)* and 92 per cent of students achieve a place at their first choice university. This year eight students gained scholarships to the universities of Warwick, Nottingham, Oxford and LSE. Each student has a personal tutor who monitors progress, and provides advice on study skills and choice of degree course.

Work experience placements, university tours and careers talks by visiting professionals are key elements of the careers programme at Albemarle. Accommodation close to the college can also be arranged.

David Game College

69 Notting Hill Gate, London W11 3JS
Tel: (020) 7221 6665   Fax: (020) 7243 1730
E-mail: david-game@easynet.co.uk   Web site: www.davidgame-group.com   www.gabbitas.net

Head David Game MA (Oxon), MPhil (London)
Founded 1974
Type Co-educational independent sixth-form college boarding and day
Accredited by BACIFHE
Age range 16–24
No of pupils 340; *No of boarders* 150
Girls 150; *boys* 190
Fees per annum (tuition only) £7,000–£8,420; (self-catering residential and host family) £3,000–£5,200

The college is one of London's leading international centres for pre-university education, and offers a transitional environment as an alternative to the traditional school Sixth Form. All major subjects are offered at A, A/S and GCSE levels, and there are one year, 18 months, 2 years and re-take options.

As an alternative, the nine month continuously assessed University Foundation Programme, combines a modular framework, study skills tuition and specialist subject choice, offers guaranteed entry to degree courses at over 60 universities.

This can be followed at the College by the University Diploma Programme, a first year degree equivalent course giving progression to the second year of degree courses in business and IT related subjects.

Both programmes have September and January start dates with University progression the following October.

The college is centrally located in modern purpose designed premises adjacent to Notting Hill Gate underground station.

Student residences are conveniently located nearby.

Davies, Laing & Dick (DLD)

10 Pembridge Square, Notting Hill, London W2 4ED
Tel: (020) 7727 2797   Fax: (020) 7792 0730
E-mail: dld@dld.org   Web site: www.dld.org   www.gabbitas.net

Principal Ms Elizabeth Rickards MA
(St Andrews) PGCE, FRSA
Founded 1931
Type Co-educational independent sixth form
day
Member of CIFE
Accredited by BAC
Special needs provision ADD, DYS, DYP
Age range 14–21
No of pupils 385
Girls 193; *boys* 192
Sixth Form 245; *Re-take* 80
Fees per term (day) from £1,175–£4,083
Fees per annum (day) £4,500 *(one course)*–
£12,249 *(3 A Levels)*

Davies, Laing and Dick is housed in a large Victorian building in Pembridge Square, some five minutes' walk from Kensington Gardens. The student roll is currently 385 students: over half of these students are Sixth Formers spending two years preparing for A Levels; the others are A Level retake students re-sitting to secure university places on over-subscribed degree courses such as Medicine, Law or English at premier league universities. There is also a GCSE department specialising in one year GCSE courses.

Apart from the traditional school subjects, other unusual subjects are offered at A Level including Photography, Psychology, Film and Media studies, Philosophy, Theatre Studies and Music Technology. There is a portfolio art course for students wishing to go on to a Foundation course at Art School.

Students are expected to be strongly committed to their studies. They are supported in this by excellent study facilities: two laboratories, three art studios, a fully staffed library, an additional study area/exams room and a computer room. Support is also extended through a vigilant personal tutor system. Fortnightly reports in all subjects, daily class attendance monitoring, and where necessary, timetabled supervised study ensure that students are able to achieve their potential. Teachers are highly qualified and carefully chosen for their ability to communicate and encourage. The average set size is 6:1.

For relaxation there is a large canteen/common room. There is also a sports and social programme; lectures and extra mural visits are frequently organised. A welfare officer is able to arrange accommodation with host families or in student residences.

High standards of teaching are the norm at DLD; in turn we expect high standards from our students in terms of commitment to study, behaviour and courtesy. Appointments to visit the college can be made both during the academic year as well as in the Easter and Summer holidays.

Westminster Tutors

86, Old Brompton Road, London SW7 3LQ
Tel: 020 7584 1288   Fax: 020 7584 2637
E-mail: info@westminstertutors.co.uk   Web site: www.westminstertutors.co.uk

Principal Mr PC Brooke/Mr JJ Layland
Founded 1934
Type Independent day only senior
co-educational college
Religious denomination Non-denominational
Age range 16–19
No of pupils 120
Girls 60 *boys* 60
Fees per annum From £3,675 for one A Level
subject to £10,650 for 3 A Level subjects

Westminster Tutors has been well known and widely respected for over 65 years. We are a small co-educational college with a friendly, informal atmosphere. With no more than 7 students per class, a great deal of attention can be paid to each student, helping them to achieve their full potential.

We specialise in A-level courses taken over one or two years or, in the case of intensive re-take courses, as little as three months. We also offer GCSE courses as well as Christmas and Easter revision courses. Students do not always require the traditional 5 GCSE passes to be accepted onto our A-Level courses nonetheless, over 80 per cent of the grades achieved by recent A-level students have been A–C. Nearly all of our students go on to Higher Education and we have been preparing students for Oxford and Cambridge Entrance for sixty-five years with outstanding success.

Westminster Tutors is situated in new attractive premises on the Old Brompton Road, close to South Kensington underground and Hyde Park.

Abacus College

Threeways House, George Street, Oxford, Oxfordshire OX1 2BJ
Tel: (01865) 240111   Fax: (01865) 247259
E-mail: principal@abacuscollege.net   Web site: www.abacuscollege.net   www.gabbitas.net

Joint Principal Dr Roy Carrington; Mrs Jenny Wasilewski
Founded 1968
Type Co-educational independent sixth-form college boarding and day
Religious denomination Non-denominational
Accredited by BACIFHE
Special needs provision W
Age range 15–19; *boarders from* 15+
No of pupils (boarding) 110; *(day)* 40
Girls 50; *boys* 100
Senior 20; *Sixth Form* 130
Fees per annum (boarding) £8,950–£11,200; *(day)* £5,250–£7,500

Curriculum and examinations: Abacus College has been preparing students for GCE A Level and GCSE examinations for 30 years and is recognised as efficient by BACIFHE. A broad range of subjects is offered and tuition is in small groups or on a one-to-one basis. The principals and all key tutors are experienced graduates with a minimum of five years with the college.

The Abacus College University Foundation Programme is a 30-week full-time course which offers students an alternative route to British university degree courses and which has been designed by the College in consultation with university admissions tutors. The September and January starts give university entrance in October following.

Students should contact the College with their qualifications and complete an application form.

The College's purpose-built facilitiies include excellent classrooms, laboratory, library and computer room, plus a comfortable students' common room.

Accommodation is available in mini-hostels or with families and is full board or self-catering.

St Clare's, Oxford

139 Banbury Road, Oxford, Oxfordshire OX2 7AL
Tel: (01865) 552031   Fax: (01865) 513359
E-mail: ib.admissions@stclares.ac.uk   Web site: www.stclares.ac.uk   www.gabbitas.net

Head Boyd Roberts MA (Oxon), Cert Ed, CBiol, MIBiol
Founded 1953
Type Co-educational independent sixth-form college, boarding and day
Member of ECIS, NAFSA, CIFE, ARELS; *accredited by* BAC, BC for ELT
Age range 16–20; *boarders from* 16
No of pupils (day) 15; *(boarding)* 348
Girls 220; *Boys* 143
Fees per annum (full boarding) £18,010–£18,300; *(weekly boarding)* £18,010; *(day)* £11,260

St Clare's is a co-educational, day and residential college in Oxford. Founded in 1953, it has grown out of a scheme to establish links between British and European students after the war. The College is a registered charity which aims to promote international understanding and high academic standards in its students.

Around 350 students from over 40 countries study during the academic year; the largest national group being British. The minimum age is 16, and the atmosphere is informal and friendly, encouraging personal responsibility. The College is located in a pleasant residential area about 1½ kms from Oxford city centre, and occupies 19 Victorian houses to which purpose-built facilities have been added. These include an outstanding academic resources centre (35,000 volumes, audio-visual centre, computer suite), and four science laboratories, art studio, hall, music room, dining room and student cáfe. Students live in college houses under the care of a resident warden.

Courses are offered at pre-university and university levels, and in English language. The two year pre-university course leads to the International Baccalaureate diploma, designed to educate the whole person and to qualify for entrance to the world's most demanding universities. Residental students choose six subjects, providing a programme balanced in depth and breadth. They also complete a research project, follow a course in critical thinking and take part in extra-curricular activities.

A one-year university foundation course preparing them for entry to British universities is also offered.

Teaching staff are selected for their strong academic background and teaching skills. Many are involved in IB curriculum development and examining and the College (which has offered the IB since 1977), regularly assists schools introducing the programme. The staff:student ratio is below 1:7.

Students are assigned a Personal Tutor who oversees welfare and progress, meeting students individually weekly.

There is an extensive programme of social, cultural, service and sporting activities, and students are encouraged to take full advantage of all the opportunities which Oxford provides. Entry is on the basis of academic results, interview and confidential school record. Scholarships and bursaries are available.

Almost all IB diploma students proceed to higher education in Britain or elsewhere assisted by two higher education advisers, one employed full-time.

Bosworth Independent College

Nazareth House, Barrack Road, Northampton, NN2 6AF
Tel: (01604) 239995   Fax: (01604) 239996
E-mail: bosworthcollege@hotmail.com   Web site: under construction

Head Mr Michael McQuin MEd
Founded 1977
Type Co-educational independent day and boarding college
Member of CIFE and BAC
Special needs provision DEL, DYS, DYP, EBD, EPI, MLD
Age range 14–19; *boarders from* 14
No of pupils 230
No of pupils (full) 198
Girls 98; *boys* 132
Fees per annum (full) £13,350; *(day)* £6,990

Bosworth is a small and friendly residential and day college for British and Overseas students. Excellent academic success and care for our students have made Bosworth a leading Independent College.

Bosworth offers a wide range of GCSE, A-Level and University Foundation Courses. Courses are usually taken over one year, eighteen months or two years. English as a Foreign Language courses are available and the College runs an Easter Revision School as well as a thriving Summer School for overseas students. Our average class size is 7 and each student is allocated a Personal Tutor to oversee academic progress and welfare.

Students from Bosworth go on to attend top universities, including LSE, Imperial College, Oxford and Cambridge and we have an excellent tradition in placing students for medicine.

Cambridge Tutors College

Water Tower Hill, Croydon, Surrey CR0 5SX
Tel: (020) 8688 5284/7363   Fax: (020) 8686 9220
E-mail: admin@ctc.ac.uk   Web site: www.ctc.ac.uk

Principal Mr DA Lowe MA (Cantab) FRSA
Founded 1958
Type Co-educational independent sixth form/
tutorial boarding and day
Religious denomination Non-denominational
Member of CIFE, ECIS, *Accredited* by BAC
Special needs provision DEL
Age range 16–21, *boarders from* 16
No of pupils (day) 110 *(boarding)* 160
Girls 130; *boys* 140
Senior (GCSE) 20; *Sixth Form* 250
Fees per annum (boarding) £14,000
(day) £9,750

Cambridge Tutors College is an international sixth form college for about 270 young people founded in 1958 by graduates of Cambridge University, offering pre-university level courses. Over the years it has built a solid reputation for excellent A Level teaching and for the high take-up of student places at top universities. Teachers are highly qualified and experienced and the College is situated in an attractive parkside location in south Croydon, 20 minutes from central London. The College's distinguishing features are small group tuition, regular weekly testing under examination conditions, an international dimension and an adult context for study.

One year Foundation courses for Science (Kings, London) and Medicine (St Georges, Grenada) are offered.

Winchester College

College Street, Winchester, Hampshire SO23 9NA
Tel: (01962) 621100   Fax: (01962) 621106
E-mail: information@wincoll.ac.uk   Web site: www.wincoll.ac.uk   www.gabbitas.net

Head Dr EN Tate MA, PhD
Founded 1382
Type Boys' independent boarding and day
Religious denomination Church of England
Member of HMC
Age range 13–18; *boarders from* 13
No of pupils 680
Senior 398; *Sixth Form* 277
Fees per annum (boarding) (full) £18,360;
(day) £17,442

Winchester College is a boarding school for boys aged 13–18. It was founded in 1382 by William of Wykeham, Bishop of Winchester and Chancellor to Richard II, and has the longest unbroken history of any school in the country. Its setting is one of unrivalled beauty and spaciousness.

Winchester enjoys an international reputation for its outstanding academic record. This can be seen not just in its excellent examination results but also in the quality of the intellectual training it provides. Nearly all of it pupils go on to good universities and about 50 each year win places at Oxford or Cambridge.

The high academic standards are matched by similar achievements in Music, Art, Drama and a wide range of sporting activities. The school has extensive playing fields and generous provision for pupils to develop their cultural and athletic interests.

There 680 boys in the school, most of whom are boarders, but day boys are accepted.

Generous Academic and Music Awards are offered annually to boys entering the school at age 13 and 16.

13+ Academic Scholarships and Exhibitions: the examination of candidates for scholarships and exhibitions is held at the College in early May: about 15 scholarships and about 6 exhibitions are offered. Scholarships have a basis value of half of the full fee, with additional means-tested help where necessary. Exhibitions have a maximum value of one-third of the full fee. Candidates must be under 14 and at least 12 on 1 September in the year in which they sit the exam. Entry forms, which must be returned by mid-April, are available from the Master in College, Winchester College, College Street, Winchester SO23 9NA.

Sixth Form Academic Awards: The entrance examination for both awards and places takes place at the College early in the Spring term. Up to four scholarships with a maximum value of half of the full fee are offered. Entry forms, which must be returned by mid-November the previous year, are obtainable from the Headmaster's Secretary (address as above).

Details of Music Awards can also be obtained from the Headmaster's Secretary.

St Albans School

Abbey Gateway, St Albans, Hertfordshire AL3 4HB
Tel: (01727) 855521   Fax: (01727) 843447
E-mail: hm@st-albans-school.org.uk   Web site: www.st-albans.herts.sch.uk   www.gabbitas.net

Head AR Grant MA (Cantab)
Founded 948
Type Boys' independent senior day; co-educational sixth form
Religious denomination Non-denominational
Member of HMC
Age range 11–18
No of pupils 735
Girls 33; *boys* 702
Senior 500; *Sixth Form* 235
Fees per annum £7,878

Following the abolition of the Government's Assisted Places Scheme, the School is able to offer some assistance with fees in certain circumstances of proven need, from its own endowed bursary fund. All bursaries are means-tested. A variable number of academic scholarships worth up to 50 per cent of the annual fees is awarded on academic merit at 11+, 13+ and 16+. Scholarships for music and art are offered at 13+. Bursaries towards music tuition are provided for pupils from each year in the School. Further details of all awards from the Headmaster.

The School is a registered charity and aims to provide an excellent education enabling pupils to achieve the highest standard of academic success according to ability, and to develop their character and personality so as to become caring and self-disciplined adults.

Moira House Girls School

Upper Carlisle Road, Eastbourne, East Sussex BN20 7TE
Tel: (01323) 644144   Fax: (01323) 649720
E-mail: enquiries@moirahouse.co.uk
Web site: www.moirahouse.co.uk   www.gabbitas.net

Principal of Senior School Mrs A Harris BEd
(Hons), ARCM
Head of Junior School Mrs J Booth-Clibborn
Cert.Ed

The Ingham Scholarships: the Senior School
Sixth-Form Scholarships worth up to 75 per
cent of the fees are available each year.
Ingham Academic Scholarships worth up to 50
per cent of the fees for either day girls or
boarders aged 11–13 years are available each
year.

In addition, exhibitions are offered in the
Senior School for sport, music, art, drama.
The Junior School
A number of Ingham Annual Scholarships
worth up to 50 per cent of the fees are available.
Application
Full details for the Ingham Sixth-Form and
Senior School Scholarships are available from
the Principal's secretary.
Full details for the Ingham Junior School
Scholarships are available from the secretary
of the Head of the Junior School.

Royal Alexandra and Albert School

Gatton Park, Reigate, Surrey RH2 0TW
Tel: (01737) 642576   Fax: (01737) 642294
E-mail: headmaster@gatton-park.org.uk   Web site: www.gatton-park.org.uk

Head Mr P Spencer Ellis BA MPhil NPQH
Founded 1758
Type Voluntary aided co-educational junior and senior boarding and day
Religious denomination Protestant (with Chapel and Chaplain)
Member of STABIS, BSA
Age range 7–18; *boarders from* 7
No of pupils 550; *girls* 255; *boys* 295
Junior 110; *Senior* 400; *Sixth Form* 40
Fees per annum (Sixth form) £7,800; *(senior and junior boarding)* £6,900; *(day)* £2,340
Average size of class: Junior 22; Senior 20

Curriculum: Curriculum: The National Curriculum is followed up to Key Stage 3 (Years 7–9). Pupils then take a wide range of GCSE and GNVQ intermediate courses at Key Stage 4.
Sixth Form: our partnership with local colleges enables students to access to a wide range of courses and subjects.

Entry Requirements: school reference and interview. Applicants must be proficient in English. No English as a second language provision is available.
Academic and Leisure Facilities: well-equipped computer suites, science laboratories. Design technology facilities include a new Computer Aided Design – Manufacturing (CAD-CAM) suite. Sports Hall, Gymnasium, Fitness room, indoor swimming pool and Riding School. Extra-curricular activities include D of E awards, Scouts, Army Cadets, dance, choir and band.
Site and location: The School, which is in close proximity to the M25 and Heathrow and Gatwick airports, is set in 260 acres of landscaped Surrey parkland. There are 11 boarding houses including a Palladian Mansion which houses the sixth form boarders.

PART FOUR: REFERENCE SECTION

4.1
SCHOLARSHIPS

The following is based on information provided by schools. Further details of scholarships available at individual schools may be found in Part Three: School Profiles. The abbreviations are as follows:

A	Art	I	Instrumental music
AA	Academic ability	O	All round ability
D	Drama	S	Science
G	Games	6	VIth Form entry

ENGLAND

BEDFORDSHIRE

Bedford High School, Bedford	6 AA I
Bedford Modern School, Bedford	A AA D G I
Bedford Preparatory School, Bedford	AA
Bedford School, Bedford	6 A AA D I O
Moorlands School, Luton	A AA I

BERKSHIRE

The Abbey School, Reading	6 AA I
Bearwood College, Wokingham	A AA D G I O
Bradfield College, Reading	6 A AA I O
The Brigidine School, Windsor	6 D O
Brockhurst School, Newbury	AA
Cheam School, Newbury	AA
Claires Court School, Maidenhead	6 A AA D G I O
Claires Court Schools, The College, Maidenhead	6 A AA D G I O
Dolphin School, Reading	A AA D G I O
Downe House School, Newbury	6 A AA I
Eagle House, Sandhurst	AA I
Eton College, Windsor	6 AA I
Heathfield School, Ascot	6 A AA D G I O S
Hemdean House School, Reading	AA D I O
Highfield School, Maidenhead	AA
Holme Grange School, Wokingham	AA O
Hurst Lodge, Ascot	6 A AA D G I O
Langley Manor School, Slough	AA G I O
Leighton Park School, Reading	A AA I
Licensed Victuallers' School, Ascot	6 AA G I O
Luckley-Oakfield School, Wokingham	6 AA I
Marist Convent Senior School, Ascot	6 AA O

Marlston House School, Newbury	AA
The Oratory Preparatory School, Reading	AA G I
The Oratory School, Reading	6 A AA G I
Padworth College, Reading	6 AA
Papplewick, Ascot	AA I
Queen Anne's School, Reading	6 A AA G I O
Reading Blue Coat School, Reading	6 AA I
Ridgeway School (Claires Court Junior), Maidenhead	A AA D G I O
St Edward's School, Reading	O
St Gabriel's School, Newbury	6 AA I
St George's School, Ascot	AA I
St George's School, Windsor	AA I
St Joseph's Convent School, Reading	6 AA
St Mary's School, Ascot, Ascot	6 A AA I S
St Piran's Preparatory School, Maidenhead	AA
Thorngrove School, Newbury	AA I O
Upton House School, Windsor	AA
Wellington College, Crowthorne	A AA I

BRISTOL

Badminton School, Bristol	6 A AA D G I O S
Bristol Cathedral School, Bristol	6 AA I
Bristol Grammar School, Bristol	6 I O
Clifton College, Bristol	6 A AA I O
Clifton College Preparatory School, Bristol	AA I O
Clifton High School, Bristol	6 AA G I
Colston's Collegiate School, Bristol	6 A AA D G I O
Colston's Girls' School, Bristol	6 A AA I O S
The Downs School, Bristol	AA O
Fairfield PNEU School, Bristol	AA

Queen Elizabeth's Hospital, Bristol	6 AA I
The Red Maids' School, Westbury-on-Trym	6 AA I
Redland High School, Redland	6 A AA G I
St Ursula's High School, Westbury-on-Trym	AA
Tockington Manor School, Tockington	O

BUCKINGHAMSHIRE

Ashfold School, Aylesbury	A AA G I
Bury Lawn School, Milton Keynes	6 AA
Davenies School, Beaconsfield	A AA G I O
Gateway School, Great Missenden	O
Godstowe Preparatory School, High Wycombe	AA
High March School, Beaconsfield	AA
Holy Cross Convent, Gerrards Cross	6 O
Ladymede, Aylesbury	AA O
Milton Keynes Preparatory School, Milton Keynes	A AA I
Pipers Corner School, High Wycombe	6 I
St Mary's School, Gerrards Cross	6 AA I
Stowe School, Buckingham	6 A AA I O
Swanbourne House School, Milton Keynes	A G
Thorpe House School, Gerrards Cross	AA
Wycombe Abbey School, High Wycombe	6 A AA I

CAMBRIDGESHIRE

Bellerbys College, Cambridge	AA O
Cambridge Arts & Sciences (CATS), Cambridge	6 A AA O
Cambridge Centre for VIth Form Studies (CCSS), Cambridge	AA O
Kimbolton School, Huntingdon	6 A AA G I O
The King's School, Ely	6 A AA D G I O
The Leys School, Cambridge	6 A AA D G I O
Madingley Pre-Preparatory School, Cambridge	O
Mander Portman Woodward, Cambridge	6 AA O
Oundle School, Peterborough	6 A AA D I O
The Perse School, Cambridge	6 A AA I
The Perse School for Girls, Cambridge	6
Peterborough High School, Peterborough	AA I O
St Faiths School, Cambridge	A AA D G I O
St John's College School, Cambridge	I
St Mary's School, Cambridge	6
Sancton Wood School, Cambridge	D O
Wisbech Grammar School, Wisbech	I

CHANNEL ISLANDS

Elizabeth College, Guernsey	I O
St George's Preparatory School, Jersey	AA O
St Michael's Preparatory School, Jersey	AA
Victoria College, Jersey	6 AA

CHESHIRE

Abbey Gate College, Chester	6 AA I O
Alderley Edge School for Girls, Alderley Edge	AA I
Cheadle Hulme School, Cheadle	A D I
Cransley School, Northwich	A AA G I O S
Culcheth Hall, Altrincham	AA

The Grange School, Northwich	6 AA D G I
Hammond School, Chester	AA I
Hulme Hall Schools, Cheadle	AA
The King's School, Macclesfield	AA I
Macclesfield Preparatory School, Macclesfield	AA G O
Mostyn House School, South Wirral	AA
North Cestrian Grammar School, Altrincham	AA
Oriel Bank High School, Stockport	I
The Ryleys, Alderley Edge	AA O
Stockport Grammar School, Stockport	I
Terra Nova School, Holmes Chapel	AA

CORNWALL

The Bolitho School, Penzance	6 A AA I
Polwhele House School, Truro	AA I
Roselyon Preparatory School, Par	AA I O
St Joseph's School, Launceston	A AA D G I O
St Petroc's School, Bude	A AA D G I O S
St Piran's School, Truro	AA O
Treliske School, Truro	AA G I O
Truro High School, Truro	6 A AA I
Truro School, Truro	6 A AA I
Wheelgate House School, Newquay	AA I O

CUMBRIA

Austin Friars School, Carlisle	A AA G I
Casterton School, Carnforth	6 A AA D G I O S
Harecroft Hall School, Seascale	AA
Hunter Hall School, Penrith	AA O
Lime House School, Carlisle	6 A AA D G I O S
Our Lady's, Chetwynde, Barrow-in-Furness	6 AA G I O
St Bees School, St Bees	6 A AA G I
Sedbergh School, Sedbergh	6 A AA G I O
Windermere St Anne's School, Windermere	6 A AA D G I

DERBYSHIRE

Derby Grammar School for boys, Derby	6 AA I
Derby High School, Derby	6 AA I O
Foremarke Hall, Derby	AA I
Mount St Mary's College, Spinkhill	6 AA I O
Ockbrook School, Derby	A AA D G I
Repton School, Repton	6 A AA I O
St Anselm's, Bakewell	AA I
St Elphin's School, Matlock	6 AA D I
St Wystan's School, Repton	AA G I O

DEVON

The Abbey School, Torquay	AA O
Blundell's School, Tiverton	6 A AA G I O
Edgehill College, Bideford	6 AA G I O
Exeter Cathedral School, Exeter	AA I
Exeter Junior School, Exeter	AA
Exeter School, Exeter	6 A AA D I
Gramercy Hall School, Torbay	AA G I
Grenville College, Bideford	6 A AA D G I O S
Kelly College, Tavistock	6 A AA G I O

Lanherne Nursery and Junior School, Dawlish	O
The Maynard School, Exeter	6 I
Mount House School, Tavistock	AA
St Aubyn's School, Tiverton	AA O
St Bernard's Preparatory School, Newton Abbot	A AA G I O
St Christophers School, Totnes	O
St Dunstan's Abbey School, Plymouth	A AA D G I
St John's School, Sidmouth	A AA D G I O
St Margaret's School, Exeter	6
St Michael's, Barnstaple	A AA G I O
St Peter's School, Exmouth	A D I O
Shebbear College, Beaworthy	6 A AA D G I O
Stover School, Newton Abbot	6 A AA G I O
Tower House School, Paignton	A AA D G I O
Trinity School, Teignmouth	6 A AA D G I O S
West Buckland Preparatory School, Barnstaple	AA O
West Buckland School, Barnstaple	6 AA G I O
Wolborough Hill School, Newton Abbot	A AA G I O

DORSET

Bryanston School, Blandford Forum	6 A AA G I O
Canford School, Wimborne	6 A AA I O
Castle Court Preparatory School, Wimborne	AA I
Clayesmore Preparatory School, Blandford Forum	A AA G I O
Clayesmore School, Blandford Forum	6 A AA I O
Dorchester Preparatory School, Dorchester	AA
Dumpton School, Wimborne	A AA G I O
Hanford School, Blandford Forum	I
Homefield School Senior & Preparatory, Christchurch	AA G I
Knighton House, Blandford Forum	A AA G O
Milton Abbey School, Blandford Forum	6 A AA D G I
The Old Malthouse, Swanage	A AA G I O
The Park School, Bournemouth	AA I O
Port Regis, Shaftesbury	A AA G I O
St Antony's-Leweston School, Sherborne	6 A AA D G I
St Martin's School, Bournemouth	AA
St Mary's School, Shaftesbury	6 A AA I O S
Sherborne Preparatory School, Sherborne	AA I O
Sherborne School, Sherborne	6 A AA G I O S
Sherborne School for Girls, Sherborne	A AA I
Talbot Heath, Bournemouth	6 AA G O
Thornlow Preparatory School, Weymouth	AA G
Wentworth College, Bournemouth	6 A AA D G I

COUNTY DURHAM

Barnard Castle School, Barnard Castle	6 A AA G I
Bow School, Durham	AA G I O
The Chorister School, Durham	I
Durham High School For Girls, Durham	6 AA G I
Durham School, Durham	6 A AA G I O
Hurworth House School, Darlington	AA G O
Polam Hall, Darlington	6 AA G I

ESSEX

Alleyn Court Preparatory School, Southend-on-Sea	A AA G I
Bancroft's School, Woodford Green	6 AA I

Brentwood School, Brentwood	6 A AA I
Chigwell School, Chigwell	A AA I
Colchester High School, Colchester	AA O
College Saint-Pierre, Leigh-on-Sea	O
Crowstone Preparatory School, Westcliff-on-Sea	O
Felsted Preparatory School, Dunmow	AA I
Felsted School, Dunmow	6 A AA D I O
Friends' School, Saffron Walden	6 A AA G I O
Glenarm College, Ilford	AA
Gosfield School, Halstead	6 AA D G I O
Herington House School, Brentwood	D G I O
Holmwood House, Colchester	AA I O
Loyola Preparatory School, Buckhurst Hill	AA
New Hall School, Chelmsford	6 A AA D I O S
Park School for Girls, Ilford	AA
St Aubyn's School, Woodford Green	AA
St Hilda's School, Westcliff-on-Sea	O
St Mary's School, Colchester	O
St Nicholas School, Harlow	AA
Thorpe Hall School, Southend-on-Sea	AA

GLOUCESTERSHIRE

The Abbey School, Tewkesbury	I
Berkhampstead School, Cheltenham	AA
Bredon School, Tewkesbury	A AA G O
Cheltenham College, Cheltenham	6 A AA G I O S
Cheltenham College Junior School, Cheltenham	A AA D G I O
The Cheltenham Ladies' College, Cheltenham	6 A AA I
Dean Close Preparatory School, Cheltenham	AA G I O
Dean Close School, Cheltenham	6 A AA G I
Hatherop Castle School, Cirencester	AA D G I O
The King's School, Gloucester	6 A AA G I O
Rendcomb College, Cirencester	6 A AA D G I
The Richard Pate School, Cheltenham	AA
Rose Hill School, Wotton-under-Edge	AA I
St Edward's School, Cheltenham	6 AA G I
Westonbirt School, Tetbury	6 A AA D G I O
Wycliffe College, Stonehouse	6 A AA D G I O
Wycliffe Junior School, Stonehouse	A AA D G I O

SOUTH GLOUCESTERSHIRE

Silverhill School, Winterbourne	O

HAMPSHIRE

Alton Convent School, Alton	6
The Atherley School, Southampton	6 A AA D G I
Ballard School, New Milton	A AA G I O
Bedales School, Petersfield	6 A AA D I
Boundary Oak School, Fareham	AA I
Brockwood Park School, Alresford	O
Churchers College, Petersfield	6 AA I
Daneshill House, Basingstoke	AA I
Ditcham Park School, Petersfield	AA I
Dunhurst (Bedales Junior School), Petersfield	I
Durlston Court, New Milton	A AA G I
Embley Park School, Romsey	6 A AA G I O
Farleigh School, Andover	AA O

Farnborough Hill, Farnborough	6 AA G I
Forres Sandle Manor, Fordingbridge	AA I O
The Gregg School, Southampton	AA I
Highfield School, Liphook	AA G
Hordle Walhampton School, Lymington	AA I O
King Edward VI School, Southampton	AA I
Littlefield School, Liphook	A AA D G I
Lord Wandsworth College, Hook	6 A AA D I O
Mayville High School, Southsea	A AA D G I
Meoncross School, Fareham	O
North Foreland Lodge, Basingstoke	6 A AA D I
The Pilgrims' School, Winchester	I
The Portsmouth Grammar School, Portsmouth	6 A AA D G I O
Portsmouth High School GDST, Southsea	AA
Prince's Mead School, Winchester	AA I
Rookesbury Park School, Portsmouth	AA I
Rookwood School, Andover	AA
St Anne's Nursery & Pre-Preparatory School, Lee-on-the-Solent	AA
St Mary's College, Southampton	AA
St Neot's School, Hook	O
St Nicholas School, Fleet	AA
St Swithun's School, Winchester	6 AA I
Sherborne House School, Eastleigh	G O
Stanbridge Earls School, Romsey	A AA
Stockton House School, Aldershot	AA O
The Stroud School, Romsey	A AA G I O
Winchester College, Winchester	6 AA I
Wykeham House School, Fareham	AA
Yateley Manor Preparatory School, Yateley	AA I

HEREFORDSHIRE

The Hereford Cathedral Junior School, Hereford	A AA I
The Hereford Cathedral School, Hereford	6 A AA I
Lucton Pierrepont School, Leominster	AA O
St Richard's, Bromyard	AA

HERTFORDSHIRE

Abbot's Hill, Hemel Hempstead	A AA D G I O
Aldenham School, Elstree	6 A AA G I O
Aldwickbury School, Harpenden	AA
The Arts Educational School, Tring	D I
Berkhamsted Collegiate Preparatory School, Berkhamsted	AA
Berkhamsted Collegiate School, Berkhamsted	6 A AA I
Bishop's Stortford College, Bishop's Stortford	6 A AA I O
Egerton-Rothesay School, Berkhamsted	A AA G I
Haberdashers' Aske's Boys' School, Elstree	AA I
Haberdashers' Aske's School for Girls, Elstree	AA I
Haileybury, Hertford	6 A AA I O
Haresfoot Preparatory School, Berkhamsted	A AA D O
Heath Mount School, Hertford	AA I O
CKHR Immanuel College, Bushey	6 AA
The Junior School, Bishop's Stortford College, Bishop's Stortford	A AA I O

Lockers Park, Hemel Hempstead	A AA G I O
The Princess Helena College, Hitchin	6 A AA I O
The Purcell School, Bushey	I
Queenswood, Hatfield	6 A AA D G I O
The Royal Masonic School for Girls, Rickmansworth	6 A AA G I
St Albans High School for Girls, St Albans	6 AA I O
St Albans School, St Albans	6 A AA I
St Andrew's Montessori School, Watford	AA I
St Columba's College, St Albans	6 AA I
St Edmund's College, Ware	AA I
St Francis' College, Letchworth	AA I
St Margaret's School, Bushey	6 A AA I O S
St Nicholas House, Hemel Hempstead	AA
Sherrardswood School, Welwyn	6 AA O
Stanborough School, Watford	6
Stormont, Potters Bar	AA
Westbrook Hay, Hemel Hempstead	A AA G I O
York House School, Rickmansworth	AA G

ISLE OF MAN

King William's College, Castletown	6 A AA G I O

ISLE OF WIGHT

Ryde School, Ryde	AA
Westmont School, Newport	AA I O

KENT

Ashford School, Ashford	6 AA D G I O
Babington House School, Chislehurst	AA D G I O
Baston School, Bromley	AA O
Bedgebury School, Cranbrook	6 A AA D G I S
Beechwood Sacred Heart, Tunbridge Wells	6 A AA D G I O S
Benenden School, Cranbrook	6 A AA G I
Bethany School, Cranbrook	6 A AA D G I
Bishop Challoner School, Bromley	AA
Breaside Preparatory School, Bromley	AA
Bromley High School GDST, Bromley	6 A AA G I
Cobham Hall, Gravesend	6 A AA D G I O S
Combe Bank School, Sevenoaks	AA O
Cranbrook School, Cranbrook	I
Derwent Lodge School for Girls, Tonbridge	AA
Dover College, Dover	6 A G I
Farringtons & Stratford House, Chislehurst	6 A AA G I
Friars School, Ashford	AA I
Gad's Hill School, Rochester	O
Hilden Grange School, Tonbridge	AA I
Holmewood House, Tunbridge Wells	A AA G I O
Holy Trinity College, Bromley	6 AA I
The Junior School, St Lawrence College, Ramsgate	AA O
Kent College, Canterbury	6 A AA G I
Kent College Pembury, Tunbridge Wells	6 AA D I
King's Preparatory School, Rochester, Rochester	AA I
The King's School, Canterbury	6 A AA I
King's School Rochester, Rochester	6 A AA G I
Marlborough House School, Hawkhurst	A AA G I O

Merton Court Preparatory School, Sidcup	AA D G I
Northbourne Park School, Deal	A AA G I O
Rochester Independent College, Rochester	6 A AA D O S
Rose Hill School, Tunbridge Wells	A AA D G I O
Sackville School, Tonbridge	6 A AA G I
St Christopher's School, Canterbury	O
St Edmund's Junior School, Canterbury	A AA D G I O
St Edmund's School, Canterbury	6 A AA D G I O
St Lawrence College, Ramsgate	6 AA I O
St Mary's Westbrook, Folkestone	A AA G I O
St Michael's School, Sevenoaks	AA D G I O
Sevenoaks School, Sevenoaks	6 A AA I O S
Solefield School, Sevenoaks	I
Sutton Valence School, Maidstone	6 A AA D G I O
Tonbridge School, Tonbridge	A AA I
Walthamstow Hall, Sevenoaks	AA I
Wellesley House School, Broadstairs	AA G I
Yardley Court, Tonbridge	AA O

LANCASHIRE

Arnold School, Blackpool	6 A AA G I
Bentham Grammar School, Lancaster	6 A AA G I O
Bolton School (Girls' Division), Bolton	6 AA
Bury Grammar School, Bury	6 AA
Bury Grammar School (Girls'), Bury	AA
Clevelands Preparatory School, Bolton	AA O
Heathland College, Accrington	AA I
The Hulme Grammar School, Oldham	6 AA
King Edward VII and Queen Mary School, Lytham St Annes	6 A AA D G I O
Kingswood College at Scarisbrick Hall, Ormskirk	6 O
Kirkham Grammar School, Preston	6 AA I
Moorland School, Clitheroe	AA G I O
Oakhill College, Clitheroe	AA O
Queen Elizabeth's Grammar School, Blackburn	6
Rossall Preparatory School, Fleetwood	A AA I O
Rossall School, Fleetwood	6 A AA G I O S
St Anne's College Grammar School, Lytham St Annes	AA
St Joseph's Convent School, Burnley	I
St Mary's Hall, Stonyhurst	A AA I
Stonyhurst College, Clitheroe	6 A AA I O
Westholme School, Blackburn	6 A AA I

LEICESTERSHIRE

Brooke House College, Market Harborough	6 AA O
The Dixie Grammar School, Market Bosworth	6 AA G I
Grace Dieu Manor School, Leicester	G
Irwin College, Leicester	AA
Leicester Grammar School, Leicester	6 A AA G I O
Leicester High School For Girls, Leicester	6 AA I
Loughborough Grammar School, Loughborough	6 AA I
Loughborough High School, Loughborough	AA I
Our Lady's Convent School, Loughborough	O
Ratcliffe College, Leicester	6 AA I
Stoneygate School, Leicester	AA

LINCOLNSHIRE

Copthill School, Stamford	AA
The Fen Preparatory School, Sleaford	AA
Lincoln Minster School, Lincoln	6 AA I
Maypole House School, Alford	AA O
Stamford High School, Stamford	6 A AA I
Stamford School, Stamford	6 A AA I O
Witham Hall, Bourne	AA I O

NORTH EAST LINCOLNSHIRE

St James' School, Grimsby	6 AA G I O

LONDON

Abercorn Place School, NW8	O
Albany College, NW4	6
The Albany College, NW4	6
Alleyn's School, SE22	6 A AA G I
The Arts Educational School, W4	AA D I
Ashbourne Independent Sixth Form College, W8	6 A AA D O S
Ashbourne Middle School, W8	6 A AA D O S
Belmont (Mill Hill Junior School), NW7	AA D I S
Blackheath High School GDST, SE3	6 A AA I S
Blackheath Preparatory School, SE3	AA
Broomwood Hall School, SW12	A AA O
Channing School, N6	6 AA I
City of London School, EC4V	6 AA I
City of London School for Girls, EC2Y	6 A AA I
Clifton Lodge Preparatory School, W5	I
Colfe's School, SE12	6 A AA G I
Collingham, SW5	6
Davies Laing and Dick Independent VI Form College, W2	6 AA O
Devonshire House Preparatory School, NW3	AA I
Dulwich College, SE21	6 A AA I
Durston House, W5	AA
Ealing College Upper School, W13	6 AA
Ealing Tutorial College, W5	AA
Eaton House The Manor, SW4	AA
Eaton Square Schools, SW1V	O
Eltham College, SE9	6 AA G I
Emanuel School, SW11	A AA I O
Falkner House, SW7	I
Forest Girls' School, E17	6 A AA I
Forest School, E17	6 A AA I
Francis Holland School, SW1W	6 AA
Francis Holland School, NW1	6 I
Garden House Boys' School, SW1X	AA I O
Garden House Girls' School, SW1W	AA I O
The Godolphin and Latymer School, W6	I
The Hall School Wimbledon, SW20	A AA D G I O S
The Hampshire Schools (Kensington Gardens), W2	AA G I O
The Hampshire Schools (Knightsbridge Under School), SW7	AA I O
The Hampshire Schools (Knightsbridge Upper School), SW7	AA I O
Hampstead Hill Pre-Preparatory & Nursery School, NW3	O
Harvington School, W5	D I
Heathside Preparatory School, NW3	AA

410

Hendon Preparatory School, NW4	AA G O
Highgate Junior School, N6	AA
Highgate School, N6	AA I
Ibstock Place School, SW15	I
International Community School, NW1	6 AA O
International School of London, W3	6
The Italia Conti Academy of Theatre Arts, EC1M	D
James Allen's Girls' School, SE22	6 A AA I
Keble Preparatory School, N21	AA O
The King Alfred School, NW11	O
King's College Junior School, SW19	AA I
King's College School, SW19	6 A AA I S
Lansdowne Sixth Form College, W2	AA D O
Latymer Upper School, W6	6 A D G I
Lycee Francais Charles de Gaulle, SW7	6
Mander Portman Woodward, SW7	6 AA
Mill Hill School, NW7	A AA G I O
More House, SW1X	6 AA I
The Mount School, NW7	6 AA O
Newton Prep, SW8	AA
Normanhurst School, E4	AA
North Bridge House Lower School, NW1	AA I
North Bridge House Prep & Senior School, NW1	I
Northcote Lodge, SW11	AA
Notting Hill and Ealing High School GDST, W13	6 AA I O
Palmers Green High School, N21	AA I
Parkgate House School, SW4	AA I
The Pointer School, SE3	AA D G O
Portland Place School, W1B	AA
Prospect House School, SW15	O
Putney High School, SW15	6 AA I
Queen's College, W1N	6 A AA I
Queen's Gate School, SW7	6 O
Redcliffe School, SW10	O
Riverston School, SE12	AA G I O
The Roche School, SW18	AA
The Royal School, Hampstead, NW3	6 AA
St Augustine's Priory, W5	6 I O
St Benedict's Junior School, W5	I
St Benedict's School, W5	I
St Dunstan's College, SE6	6 A AA G I
St Margaret's School, NW3	AA
St Mary's School Hampstead, NW3	AA
St Paul's Cathedral School, EC4M	I
St Paul's Girls' School, W6	6 A AA I
St Paul's Preparatory School, SW13	AA I
St Paul's School, SW13	6 AA I
Sinclair House School, SW6	O
South Hampstead High School, NW3	6 AA I
Southbank International School, Kensington, W11	O
Southbank International School, Hampstead, NW3	O
Streatham and Clapham High School, SW16	6 AA I S
Sussex House School, SW1X	I
Sydenham High School GDST, SE26	6 AA I
Sylvia Young Theatre School, NW1	D I
Thomas's Preparatory School, SW11	O
Thomas's Preparatory School, W8	AA
Thomas's Preparatory School Clapham, SW11	AA G I
Trevor Roberts', NW3	I
The Tuition Centre, NW4	AA
University College School, NW3	AA I
The Village School, NW3	AA
Westminster Abbey Choir School, SW1P	I
Westminster Cathedral Choir School, SW1P	I
Westminster School, SW1P	6 AA I
Westminster Under School, SW1P	I
Wimbledon High School, SW19	6 AA I
Woodside Park International School, N11	AA G I O

GREATER MANCHESTER

Abbey Independent College, Manchester	6 AA
Branwood Preparatory School, Eccles	O
Bridgewater School, Manchester	6 O
Chetham's School of Music, Manchester	I
Manchester High School for Girls, Manchester	AA I
Norman House School, Manchester	AA O
William Hulme's Grammar School, Manchester	6 AA I

MERSEYSIDE

Avalon Preparatory School, Wirral	AA
The Belvedere School GDST, Liverpool	6 AA D I
Birkenhead High School GDST, Wirral	AA I
Birkenhead School, Birkenhead	AA I
Heswall Preparatory School, Wirral	AA O
Kingsmead School, Wirral	AA G I
Liverpool College, Liverpool	6 AA I O
Merchant Taylors' School, Liverpool	6 AA
Merchant Taylors' School for Girls, Liverpool	6 O
St Edward's Junior School Runnymede, Liverpool	I
St Mary's College, Liverpool	6 AA
Streatham House School, Liverpool	AA
Tower College, Prescot	AA I
Tower Dene Preparatory School, Southport	6 D

MIDDLESEX

Buckingham College Preparatory School, Pinner	AA
Buckingham College School, Harrow	6 AA
Halliford School, Shepperton	AA
Hampton School, Hampton	A AA G I O
Harrow School, Harrow on the Hill	6 A AA G I O
Heathfield School, Pinner	6 AA I
The John Lyon School, Harrow	AA G I
The Lady Eleanor Holles School, Hampton	6 AA I
Merchant Taylors' School, Northwood	6 AA I
North London Collegiate School, Edgware	AA I
Northwood College, Northwood	6 AA I
St Catherine's School, Twickenham	A AA G I O
St Christopher's School, Wembley	AA
St David's School, Ashford	6 A AA G I O
St Helen's School for Girls, Northwood	6 A AA D G I
St James Independent School for Boys (Senior), Twickenham	O
Sunflower Montessori School, Twickenham	I

NORFOLK

All Saints School, Norwich	AA I
Glebe House School, Hunstanton	A AA G I O
Gresham's Preparatory School, Holt	AA
Gresham's School, Holt	6 A AA D G I S
Hethersett Old Hall School, Norwich	6 AA O
Langley Preparatory School & Nursery, Norwich	AA I
Langley School, Norwich	6 A AA D G I
The New Eccles Hall School, Norwich	I
The Norwich High School for Girls GDST, Norwich	6 AA I
Norwich School, Norwich	6 AA I
Riddlesworth Hall, Diss	A AA I
Sacred Heart Convent School, Swaffham	A AA D G I O
Taverham Hall, Norwich	AA I
Thetford Grammar School, Thetford	6 AA I
Wood Dene School, Norwich	A AA D

NORTHAMPTONSHIRE

Beachborough School, Brackley	AA O
Bosworth Independent College, Northampton	6 AA O S
Northampton High School, Northampton	6 AA
Northampton Preparatory School, Northampton	A AA I
Northamptonshire Grammar School, Pitsford	6 A AA G I
Quinton House, Northampton	6 AA O
St Peter's School, Kettering	AA G I
Wellingborough School, Wellingborough	6 A AA G I
Winchester House School, Brackley	A AA I O

NORTHUMBERLAND

Longridge Towers School, Berwick-upon-Tweed	6 AA G I
St Oswald's School, Alnwick	6 AA O

NOTTINGHAMSHIRE

Coteswood House School, Nottingham	A AA D G I O
Dagfa House School, Nottingham	O
Hollygirt School, Nottingham	AA I
Nottingham High School, Nottingham	AA
Ranby House, Retford	AA
Rodney School, Newark	AA D
Trent College, Nottingham	6 A AA D G I O
Wellow House School, Newark	A AA G I O
Worksop College, Worksop	6 A AA G I O

OXFORDSHIRE

Abacus College, Oxford	O
Abingdon School, Abingdon	6 A AA I
Bloxham School, Banbury	6 A AA G I O S
Cherwell College, Oxford	6 AA
Christ Church Cathedral School, Oxford	I

Cokethorpe School, Witney	6 A AA D G I O
Cranford House School, Wallingford	I O
d'Overbroeck's College, Oxford	6 AA
Ferndale School, Faringdon	AA
Headington School Oxford, Oxford	6 AA I
Josca's Preparatory School, Abingdon	AA
Kingham Hill School, Chipping Norton	6 A AA I
Magdalen College School, Oxford	AA G I
Millbrook House, Abingdon	AA O
New College School, Oxford	I
Our Lady's Convent Senior School, Abingdon	6 AA
Oxford High School GDST, Oxford	6 A AA G I
Oxford Tutorial College, Oxford	AA
Radley College, Abingdon	A AA G I
Rye St Antony School, Oxford	6 AA O
St Clare's, Oxford, Oxford	6
St Edward's School, Oxford	6 A AA I O
St Mary's School, Wantage	6 A AA G I O
School of St Helen & St Katharine, Abingdon	6 AA I
Shiplake College, Henley-on-Thames	6 A G I
Sibford School, Banbury	6 AA I O
Summer Fields, Oxford	AA I
Tudor Hall School, Banbury	A AA I
Wychwood School, Oxford	6 A AA I S

RUTLAND

Oakham School, Oakham	6 A AA D I O
Uppingham School, Uppingham	6 A AA I O

SHROPSHIRE

Adcote School for Girls, Shrewsbury	6 AA
Bedstone College, Bucknell	6 A AA G I O
Bellan House Preparatory School, Oswestry	AA I O
Concord College, Shrewsbury	6 O
Dower House School, Bridgnorth	AA I O
Ellesmere College, Ellesmere	6 A AA I O S
Moor Park School, Ludlow	AA
Moreton Hall, Oswestry	6 A AA D G I O
The Old Hall School, Telford	AA I
Oswestry School, Oswestry	6 A AA G I O
Packwood Haugh, Shrewsbury	A AA G I
Prestfelde Preparatory School, Shrewsbury	AA I O
Shrewsbury High School GDST, Shrewsbury	6 AA
Shrewsbury School, Shrewsbury	6 A AA I
Wrekin College, Telford	6 A AA G I O

SOMERSET

All Hallows, Shepton Mallet	A AA I O
Bruton School for Girls, Bruton	6 AA I O S
Buckland School, Watchet	I
Chilton Cantelo School, Yeovil	O
Hazlegrove (King's Bruton Preparatory School), Yeovil	AA O
King's College, Taunton	6 A AA D G I O S
King's Hall School, Taunton	AA D G I

King's School, Bruton	6 A AA I O
Millfield Preparatory School, Glastonbury	A AA D G I O
Millfield School, Street	6 A AA G I O
The Park School, Yeovil	6 A AA D I
Perrott Hill School, Crewkerne	A AA G I O
Queen's College, Taunton	6 AA G I
Queen's College Junior and Pre-Preparatory Schools, Taunton	AA G I O
Rossholme School, East Brent	AA D G I O
St Brandon's School, Clevedon	O
St Christopher's, Burnham-on-Sea	I O
St Martin's Independent School, Crewkerne	6 A AA G I O
Taunton Preparatory School, Taunton	AA G I
Taunton School, Taunton	6 AA G I O
Wellington School, Wellington	AA
Wells Cathedral Junior School, Wells	AA I
Wells Cathedral School, Wells	6 A AA I S

NORTH EAST SOMERSET

Downside School, Bath	6 A AA G I O
King Edward's School, Bath, Bath	6 AA D G I
Kingswood Preparatory School, Bath	AA I
Kingswood School, Bath	6 A AA D G I O
Monkton Combe Junior School, Bath	AA O
Monkton Combe School, Bath	6 A AA I O
Paragon School, Bath	O
Prior Park College, Bath	6 A AA I O
The Royal High School, Bath	6 AA

NORTH SOMERSET

The Hall Pre-Preparatory School Sidcot, Winscombe	AA
Sidcot School, Winscombe	6 A I O

STAFFORDSHIRE

Abbotsholme School, Uttoxeter	6 A AA G I O
Brooklands School, Stafford	AA
Chase Academy, Cannock	AA G I O
Denstone College, Uttoxeter	6 A AA D G I O
Edenhurst School, Newcastle-under-Lyme	O
Howitt House School, Hanbury	AA
Lichfield Cathedral School, Lichfield	AA I
Newcastle-under-Lyme School, Newcastle-under-Lyme	6 AA
St Dominic's Independent Junior School, Stoke-on-Trent	AA
St Dominic's Priory School, Stone	AA I
St Dominic's School, Stafford	AA D G I
School of St Mary and St Anne, Abbots Bromley	6 A AA D G I
Stafford Grammar School, Stafford	6 A AA D G I O
Vernon Lodge Preparatory School, Stafford	AA O

STOCKTON-ON-TEES

Yarm School, Yarm	AA I

SUFFOLK

Amberfield School, Ipswich	A AA I
Cherry Trees School, Bury St Edmunds	AA
Culford School, Bury St Edmunds	6 A AA G I
Fairstead House School, Newmarket	AA
Felixstowe International College, Felixstowe	AA O
Finborough School, Stowmarket	6 A AA G I O
Framlingham College, Woodbridge	6 A AA D I O S
Framlingham College Junior School, Brandeston	AA I
Hillcroft Preparatory School, Stowmarket	AA G I
Ipswich High School GDST, Ipswich	6 AA I
Ipswich School, Ipswich	6 A AA I
Moreton Hall Preparatory School, Bury St Edmunds	AA I O
Old Buckenham Hall School, Ipswich	I
Orwell Park, Ipswich	A AA I O
Royal Hospital School, Ipswich	6 A AA G I O
St Felix School, Southwold	6 A AA D G I
St George's School, Southwold	AA I O
St Joseph's College, Ipswich	6 AA G I O
South Lee Preparatory School, Bury St Edmunds	AA
Stoke College, Sudbury	AA I
Woodbridge School, Woodbridge	6 A AA I

SURREY

Aberdour School, Tadworth	AA
Amesbury, Hindhead	AA G I
Barfield School, Farnham	AA G I O
Belmont School, Dorking	AA
Box Hill School, Dorking	6 A AA D G I O
Burys Court School, Reigate	I
Cambridge Tutors College, Croydon	6 AA
Canbury School, Kingston-upon-Thames	AA O
Caterham Preparatory School, Caterham	AA
Caterham School, Caterham	A AA I O
Charterhouse, Godalming	6 A AA I O
City of London Freemen's School, Ashtead	6 A AA D G I
Claremont Fan Court School, Esher	6 A AA G I
Clewborough House School at Cheswycks, Camberley	AA
Cranleigh Preparatory School, Cranleigh	AA I
Cranleigh School, Cranleigh	6 A AA D I
Croham Hurst School, South Croydon	6 AA
Croydon High School GDST, South Croydon	6 AA G I
Cumnor House School, South Croydon	AA G I
Danes Hill Preparatory School, Leatherhead	A AA I O
Duke of Kent School, Ewhurst	AA O
Dunottar School, Reigate	6 AA I
Edgeborough, Farnham	O
Elmhurst, The School for Dance & Performing Arts, Camberley	6
Epsom College, Epsom	6 A AA G I O
Essendene Lodge School, Caterham	O
Ewell Castle School, Epsom	6 AA G O
Feltonfleet School, Cobham	A AA I O
Frensham Heights, Farnham	6 A AA D I O S
Greenacre School for Girls, Banstead	6 AA

Guildford High School (Church Schools Co),
   Guildford   6 AA I
Haslemere Preparatory School,
   Haslemere   A AA D G I O
Hawley Place School, Camberley   A AA D G I O
The Hawthorns School, Redhill   AA I O
Hazelwood School, Oxted   AA G I O
Homefield Preparatory School, Sutton   AA
Hurtwood House, Dorking   6 D O S
King Edward's School, Godalming   6 A AA IS
Kingston Grammar School,
   Kingston-upon-Thames   6 A AA G I S
Kingswood House School, Epsom   AA G
Lanesborough, Guildford   I
Lodge School, Purley   AA I
Longacre Preparatory School, Guildford   AA
Lyndhurst School, Camberley   AA
Manor House School, Leatherhead   A AA G I O
Marymount International School,
   Kingston-upon-Thames   AA
Milbourne Lodge School, Esher   AA
Notre Dame Preparatory School, Cobham   O
Notre Dame School, Lingfield   6 AA O
Notre Dame Senior School, Cobham   6 AA
Nower Lodge School, Dorking   AA D
Oakfield School, Woking   AA O
Old Palace School of John Whitgift, Croydon   AA I
Parkside School, Cobham   AA
Parsons Mead, Ashtead   6 A AA I
Prior's Field School, Godalming   6 A AA D I
Reed's School, Cobham   6 A AA G I O
Reigate Grammar School, Reigate   6 AA I
Reigate St Mary's Preparatory and
   Choir School, Reigate   I
Rokeby School, Kingston-upon-Thames   A AA G I
Royal Grammar School, Guildford   6 AA I
Royal Russell School, Croydon   6 AA
Royal School Haslemere, Haslemere   6 A AA D G I O
St Andrew's School, Woking   AA I
St Catherine's School, Camberley   AA
St Catherine's School, Guildford   6 A AA G I
St Edmund's School, Hindhead   AA
St George's College, Weybridge   6 A AA I O
St Hilary's School, Godalming   AA I
St John's School, Leatherhead   6 A AA I O
St Teresa's School, Dorking   6 A AA G I O
Sir William Perkins's School, Chertsey   6 AA I
Surbiton High School,
   Kingston-upon-Thames   6 A AA G I
Surrey College, Guildford   O
Sutton High School GDST, Sutton   6 AA I
Tormead School, Guildford   6 AA
Trinity School, Croydon   6 A AA G I O
West Dene School, Purley   I
Whitgift School, South Croydon   6 A AA D O
Wispers School for Girls, Haslemere   A D I
Woldingham School, Woldingham   AA I
Yehudi Menuhin School, Cobham   I

EAST SUSSEX

Battle Abbey School, Battle   6 A AA G I O
Bellerbys College, Hove   AA
Bodiam Manor School, Robertsbridge   AA G I

Brighton and Hove High School
   GDST, Brighton   6 AA
Brighton College, Brighton   6 A AA D G I O
Brighton College Prep School, Brighton   AA I O
Buckswood School, Hastings   AA I O
Claremont School, St Leonards-on-Sea   A AA D G I O
Eastbourne College, Eastbourne   6 A AA I O S
The Fold School, Hove   AA
Moira House Junior School, Eastbourne   O
Moira House Girls' School, Eastbourne   AA D G I O
Newlands Manor School, Seaford   6 A AA D G I O
Newlands Preparatory School, Seaford   6 A AA D G I O
The Old Grammar School, Lewes   6 AA I O
Roedean School, Brighton   6 A AA D G I O
St Andrew's School, Eastbourne   AA G O
St Aubyn's, Brighton   A AA G I O
St Bede's, Eastbourne   A AA D G I O
St Bede's School, Hailsham   6 A AA D G I O
St Leonards-Mayfield School,
   Mayfield   A AA I
St Mary's Hall, Brighton   6 AA G I
Skippers Hill Manor Preparatory School,
   Mayfield   AA D G O
Stonelands School of Ballet & Theatre Arts,
   Hove   D O
Temple Grove, Uckfield   O
Vinehall School, Robertsbridge   AA I O
Westerleigh & St Leonards College,
   St Leonards-on-Sea   AA I O

WEST SUSSEX

Ardingly College, Haywards Heath   6 A AA D G I O S
Ardingly College Junior School,
   Haywards Heath   A AA G I
Arundale Preparatory School, Pulborough   A AA G I
Burgess Hill School for Girls, Burgess Hill   6 6 AA D G I
Copthorne School, Copthorne   AA G I
Dorset House School, Pulborough   I
Farlington School, Horsham   6 A AA G I O
Great Ballard School, Chichester   A AA D G I O
Great Walstead, Haywards Heath   AA G I
Handcross Park School, Haywards Heath   AA G I
Hurstpierpoint College, Hassocks   6 A AA G I O
Lancing College, Lancing   6 A AA G I O
Lavant House Rosemead, Chichester   6 AA I
Oakwood School, Chichester   AA O
Our Lady of Sion School, Worthing   6 AA
The Prebendal School, Chichester   I
Seaford College, Petworth   6 A AA G I
Shoreham College, Shoreham-by-Sea   AA I O
Slindon College, Arundel   AA O
Stoke Brunswick, East Grinstead   AA I O
The Towers Convent School, Steyning   AA
Westbourne House School, Chichester   I
Windlesham House, Pulborough   AA G I
Worth School, Turners Hill   6 AA I

TYNE AND WEAR

Ascham House School, Newcastle upon Tyne   AA
Central Newcastle High School GDST,
   Newcastle upon Tyne   6 AA
Dame Allan's Boys School, Newcastle upon Tyne   6 AA

Dame Allan's Girls School, Newcastle upon Tyne	6 AA
Eastcliffe Grammar School, Newcastle upon Tyne	6 A AA I O
La Sagesse High School, Newcastle upon Tyne	6 AA O
Newcastle Preparatory School, Newcastle upon Tyne	A AA I O
Newcastle Upon Tyne Church High School, Newcastle upon Tyne	AA I
Sunderland High School, Sunderland	6 AA I
Westfield School, Newcastle upon Tyne	6 A AA D G I

Leaden Hall, Salisbury	AA
Marlborough College, Marlborough	A AA 6 G I O
Norman Court Preparatory School, Salisbury	A AA D G I O
St Francis School, Pewsey	A AA G I O
St Mary's School, Calne	6 A AA I O
Salisbury Cathedral School, Salisbury	AA G I
Sandroyd, Salisbury	AA G I O
Stonar School, Melksham	6 A AA D G I O
Warminster School, Warminster	6 AA O

WARWICKSHIRE

Abbotsford School, Kenilworth	AA
Arnold Lodge School, Leamington Spa	A AA I O
Bilton Grange, Rugby	AA G I O
The Croft School, Stratford-upon-Avon	AA O
The King's High School for Girls, Warwick	6 AA I
The Kingsley School, Leamington Spa	6 A AA D I
Rugby School, Rugby	6 A AA G I
Warwick School, Warwick	6 A AA I

WEST MIDLANDS

Abbey College, Birmingham	6 AA
Al Hijrah School, Birmingham	AA
Arden Lawn, Solihull	6 A AA G I O
Bablake School, Coventry	6 AA I O
Birchfield School, Wolverhampton	A AA G O
The Blue Coat School, Birmingham	AA I O
Edgbaston College, Birmingham	AA I
Edgbaston High School for Girls, Birmingham	6 AA G I
Eversfield Preparatory School, Solihull	AA
Hallfield School, Birmingham	AA
Highclare School, Birmingham	6 AA O
Hydesville Tower School, Walsall	AA G I O
King Edward VI High School for Girls, Birmingham	AA
King Edward's School, Birmingham	6 A AA I
King Henry VIII School, Coventry	AA I
Mander Portman Woodward, Birmingham	AA
Norfolk House School, Birmingham	AA
The Royal Wolverhampton Junior School, Wolverhampton	AA I O
The Royal Wolverhampton School, Wolverhampton	6 AA G G I O
St George's School, Edgbaston, Birmingham	6 AA I
St Martin's School, Solihull	6 AA I
Solihull School, Solihull	6 A AA D I S
Tettenhall College, Wolverhampton	6 A AA G I O
Wolverhampton Grammar School, Wolverhampton	6 AA I

WILTSHIRE

Chafyn Grove School, Salisbury	A AA O
Dauntsey's School, Devizes	6 A AA G I O S
The Godolphin School, Salisbury	6 A AA G I O
Grittleton House School, Chippenham	AA D G I
Kingsbury Hill House, Marlborough	AA O
La Retraite Swan, Salisbury	A AA G I

WORCESTERSHIRE

Abberley Hall, Worcester	A AA I
The Abbey College, Malvern Wells	6 AA O S
The Alice Ottley School, Worcester	6 A AA G I
Bromsgrove Lower School, Bromsgrove	AA I O
Bromsgrove School, Bromsgrove	6 A AA I O
The Downs School, Malvern	A AA G I O
The Elms, Malvern	AA G O
Green Hill School, Evesham	O
Hartlebury School, Kidderminster	A AA D G I S
Heathfield School, Kidderminster	AA
Hillstone School (Malvern College), Malvern	A AA D G I O
Holy Trinity School, Kidderminster	6 AA I O S
King's Hawford, Worcester	AA
The King's School, Worcester	AA I
The Knoll School, Kidderminster	AA
Malvern College, Malvern	6 A AA D G I O
Malvern Girls' College, Malvern	6 A AA G I
Moffats School, Bewdley	AA I O
Royal Grammar School Worcester, Worcester	6 AA I O
St James's School, Malvern	6 A AA D G I O
St Mary's Convent School, Worcester	6 AA I O
Whitford Hall & Dodderhill School, Droitwich	AA I
Winterfold House, Kidderminster	A AA G I O

EAST RIDING OF YORKSHIRE

Hull Grammar School, Kingston-Upon-Hull	6 AA O
Hull High School, Hull	6 AA
Pocklington School, Pocklington	6 A AA G I O

NORTH YORKSHIRE

Ampleforth College, York	6 AA I
Ashville College, Harrogate	6 AA I O
Aysgarth Preparatory School, Bedale	I
Bootham School, York	6 A AA I O S
Bramcote School, Scarborough	AA I
Catteral Hall, Settle	AA I O
Cundall Manor School, York	AA G I
Fyling Hall School, Whitby	6 AA G
Giggleswick School, Settle	6 A AA D G I O
Harrogate Ladies' College, Harrogate	6 AA I O
Harrogate Tutorial College, Harrogate	6 AA O
Howsham Hall, York	AA G O
Malsis School, Skipton	AA I O
The Minster School, York	I

The Mount Senior School, York 6 A AA I
Queen Ethelburga's College, York 6 A AA D G I
Queen Margaret's School, York 6 A AA I
Queen Mary's School, Thirsk A AA I
Read School, Selby 6 AA
Red House School, York AA
Ripon Cathedral Choir School, Ripon AA I
St Martin's, Ampleforth AA
St Olave's School (Junior of St Peter's), York AA
St Peter's School, York 6 AA I
Scarborough College, Scarborough 6 A AA I
Terrington Hall, York A AA D G I O
Woodleigh School, Malton A AA D G I

SOUTH YORKSHIRE

Birkdale School, Sheffield 6 AA I
Sheffield High School GDST, Sheffield 6 AA I
Westbourne School, Sheffield A AA G O

WEST YORKSHIRE

Ackworth School, Pontefract 6 A AA I

Batley Grammar School, Batley 6 AA
Bradford Girls' Grammar School, Bradford I
Bronte House School, Bradford AA
Clevedon Preparatory House School, Ilkley A AA G
Fulneck School, Pudsey 6 AA G I O
Gateways School, Leeds 6 A AA D G I
Hipperholme Grammar School, Halifax 6 AA
Huddersfield Grammar School, Huddersfield AA I
Leeds Girls' High School, Leeds 6 AA I
Leeds Grammar School, Leeds 6 AA I
Moorlands School, Leeds A AA G I
Queen Elizabeth Grammar School, Wakefield 6 AA I
Rastrick Prep and Nursery School, Brighouse O
Rishworth School, Rishworth 6 AA D G I O
Shaw House School, Bradford AA O
Silcoates School, Wakefield 6 AA I O
Wakefield Girls' High School, Wakefield 6 AA
Wakefield Independent School, Wakefield AA
Wakefield Tutorial Preparatory School, Leeds O
Westville House Preparatory School, Ilkley O
Woodhouse Grove School,
    Apperley Bridge 6 A AA G I O

NORTHERN IRELAND

COUNTY ANTRIM

Campbell College, Belfast A AA I
Hunterhouse College, Belfast AA
Methodist College, Belfast 6 I

COUNTY TYRONE

Royal School Dungannon, Dungannon AA I

SCOTLAND

ABERDEENSHIRE

Albyn School for Girls, Aberdeen A AA G I O
Robert Gordons College, Aberdeen 6 AA G I O
St Margaret's School for Girls, Aberdeen AA I

ANGUS

The High School of Dundee, Dundee O
Lathallan School, Montrose A AA D G I O

ARGYLL AND BUTE

Lomond School, Helensburgh 6 AA I

SOUTH AYRSHIRE

Wellington School, Ayr AA

BANFFSHIRE

Aberlour House, Aberlour AA

CLACKMANNANSHIRE

Dollar Academy, Dollar AA

FIFE

New Park School, St Andrews AA
St Katharines Preparatory School, St Andrews AA O
St Leonards School & St Leonards VIth
    Form College, St Andrews 6 A AA D G I

GLASGOW

Craigholme School, Glasgow AA
The Glasgow Academy, Glasgow 6 AA
The High School of Glasgow, Glasgow AA
Hutchesons' Grammar School, Glasgow 6 AA
Kelvinside Academy, Glasgow 6 AA

LANARKSHIRE

Hamilton College, Hamilton AA I

LOTHIAN

Cargilfield, Edinburgh	AA O
The Edinburgh Academy, Edinburgh	6 A AA I
Edinburgh Academy Junior School, Edinburgh	AA
Fettes College, Edinburgh	6 A AA G I O
George Heriot's School, Edinburgh	A AA I
George Watson's College, Edinburgh	6 AA G I
The Mary Erskine School, Edinburgh	AA I
Merchiston Castle School, Edinburgh	6 A AA I O
St George's School for Girls, Edinburgh	6 A AA D G I O S
St Margaret's School, Edinburgh	6 AA D G I
St Mary's Music School, Edinburgh	I
Stewart's Melville College, Edinburgh	AA I

MIDLOTHIAN

Loretto, Musselburgh	A D G S

MORAYSHIRE

Gordonstoun School, Elgin	6 A AA D G I O

PERTHSHIRE

Ardvreck School, Crieff	AA
Butterstone School, Blairgowrie	AA O
Craigclowan Preparatory School, Perth	AA O
Glenalmond College, Perth	6 A AA I O
Morrison's Academy, Crieff	6 AA
Rannoch School, Pitlochry	6 A AA G I O
Strathallan School, Perth	6 A AA I O

ROXBURGHSHIRE

St Mary's Preparatory School, Melrose	A AA I O

STIRLING

Beaconhurst Grange, Stirling	AA O

WALES

BRIDGEND

St Clare's Convent School, Porthcawl	AA
St John's School, Porthcawl	AA O

CARDIFF

The Cathedral School, Cardiff	AA G I O
Howell's School, Llandaff GDST, Cardiff	6 AA I
Kings Monkton School, Cardiff	6 A AA G I
New College and School, Cardiff	A AA G I
Westbourne School, Cardiff	AA

CARMARTHENSHIRE

Llandovery College, Llandovery	6 AA G I O
St Michael's School, Llanelli	AA G I O

CONWY

Rydal Penrhos Preparatory School, Colwyn Bay	O
Rydal Penrhos Senior School, Colwyn Bay	6 AA G I
St David's College, Llandudno	A AA G I

DENBIGHSHIRE

Howell's School, Denbigh	6 A AA D G I
Ruthin School, Ruthin	6 A AA D G I O S

GWYNEDD

Hillgrove School, Bangor	AA

MONMOUTHSHIRE

Haberdashers' Monmouth School For Girls, Monmouth	6 AA I
Monmouth School, Monmouth	6 AA G I O
St John's-on-the-Hill, Chepstow	A AA D G I O

NEWPORT

Rougemont School, Newport	6 AA I O

PEMBROKESHIRE

Netherwood School, Saundersfoot	AA G I

POWYS

Christ College, Brecon	6 A AA I O

SWANSEA

Ffynone House School, Swansea	6 A AA D G I O S

4.2
BURSARIES AND
RESERVED ENTRANCE AWARDS

The following is compiled by information provided by schools. Further information about awards made by individual schools may be found in Part Three: School Profiles. The abbreviations used are as follows:

C	Choral	H	Financial or domestic hardship
E	Christian Missionary or	M	Medical profession
	full-time worker	T	Teaching profession
F	Her Majesty's Forces*	+	The Clergy
FO	Foreign Office		

* F1 – The Royal Navy F2 – The Royal Marines F3 – The Army F4 – The Royal Air Force

ENGLAND

BEDFORDSHIRE

Bedford High School, Bedford	F H
Bedford Modern School, Bedford	H
Bedford Preparatory School, Bedford	F H
Bedford School, Bedford	+ F H T
Dame Alice Harpur School, Bedford	H
Moorlands School, Luton	H T

BERKSHIRE

The Abbey School, Reading	H
Bearwood College, Wokingham	E F
The Brigidine School, Windsor	H
Brockhurst & Marlston House Pre-Preparatory School, Newbury	F H
Brockhurst School, Newbury	F
Dolphin School, Reading	H T
Downe House School, Newbury	H
Elstree School, Reading	+ E T
Eton College, Windsor	H
Heathfield School, Ascot	H
Hemdean House School, Reading	H
Highfield School, Maidenhead	H
Hurst Lodge, Ascot	F FO H
Lambrook Haileybury, Bracknell	T
Leighton Park School, Reading	+ H T
Licensed Victuallers' School, Ascot	H

Luckley-Oakfield School, Wokingham	F
Marist Convent Senior School, Ascot	H
The Oratory Preparatory School, Reading	F H
Our Lady's Preparatory School, Crowthorne	H
Queen Anne's School, Reading	+ T
Reading Blue Coat School, Reading	E H T
St Andrew's School, Reading	+
St Joseph's Convent School, Reading	H
St Michaels School, Newbury	H
St Piran's Preparatory School, Maidenhead	E H T
Silchester House School, Maidenhead	H
Upton House School, Windsor	H
Wellington College, Crowthorne	F3 H
White House Preparatory School, Wokingham	H

BRISTOL

Badminton School, Bristol	H T
Clifton College, Bristol	+ F H T
Clifton College Preparatory School, Bristol	C F T
Clifton High School, Bristol	H
Colston's Collegiate School, Bristol	F1 F2 F3
Colston's Girls' School, Bristol	H
The Downs School, Bristol	+ F
Fairfield PNEU School, Bristol	H
Overndale School, Bristol	H
Queen Elizabeth's Hospital, Bristol	H

The Red Maids' School, Bristol	H
Redland High School, Bristol	H
Tockington Manor School, Bristol	F T

BUCKINGHAMSHIRE

Ashfold School, Aylesbury	E H T
Bury Lawn School, Milton Keynes	H
Caldicott School, Farnham Royal	H T
Davenies School, Beaconsfield	H
Gayhurst School, Gerrards Cross	+ E H
Godstowe Preparatory School, High Wycombe	T
Heatherton House School, Amersham	H T
Holy Cross Convent, Gerrards Cross	+ F3 F4 H
Ladymede, Aylesbury	H
Milton Keynes Preparatory School, Milton Keynes	H
Pipers Corner School, High Wycombe	F
St Mary's School, Gerrards Cross	+
Stowe School, Buckingham	H
Swanbourne House School, Milton Keynes	+ F1 F3
Thornton College Convent of Jesus and Mary, Milton Keynes	F T
Thorpe House School, Gerrards Cross	H T

CAMBRIDGESHIRE

Bellerbys College, Cambridge	H
Cambridge Centre for VIth Form Studies (CCSS), Cambridge	F H
Kimbolton School, Huntingdon	H
The King's School, Ely	+ F H
The Leys School, Cambridge	F H
Mander Portman Woodward, Cambridge	H
Oundle School, Peterborough	H T
The Perse School for Girls, Cambridge	H
Peterborough High School, Peterborough	F1 F2 F3 H
St John's College School, Cambridge	H
Sancton Wood School, Cambridge	H T

CHANNEL ISLANDS

St George's Preparatory School, Jersey	H T
St Michael's Preparatory School, Jersey	+ H
Victoria College, Jersey	H

CHESHIRE

Abbey Gate College, Chester	H
Alderley Edge School for Girls, Alderley Edge	H
Beech Hall School, Macclesfield	+ E H
Culcheth Hall, Altrincham	H
The Grange School, Northwich	H
Hillcrest Grammar School, Stockport	H
Hulme Hall Schools, Cheadle	H T
The King's School, Chester	H
Macclesfield Preparatory School, Macclesfield	E
Mostyn House School, South Wirral	H T
North Cestrian Grammar School, Altrincham	H
Oriel Bank High School, Stockport	H
Pownall Hall School, Wilmslow	+ T
The Queen's School, Chester	H

Ramillies Hall School, Cheadle	F H T
Terra Nova School, Holmes Chapel	H
Yorston Lodge School, Knutsford	+

CORNWALL

The Bolitho School, Penzance	F H
Polwhele House School, Truro	+ H T
Roselyon Preparatory School, Par	F H
St Petroc's School, Bude	H
St Piran's School, Truro	H
Treliske School, Truro	H
Truro High School, Truro	H
Truro School, Truro	H
Wheelgate House School, Newquay	H

CUMBRIA

Austin Friars School, Carlisle	H
Casterton School, Carnforth	E H T
Harecroft Hall School, Seascale	+ F H
Hunter Hall School, Penrith	H
Lime House School, Carlisle	E F FO H M T
Our Lady's, Chetwynde, Barrow-in-Furness	H
St Bees School, St Bees	+ F H
St Ursulas Convent School, Wigton	H
Sedbergh School, Sedbergh	F H
Wellspring Christian School, Carlisle	E H
Windermere St Anne's School, Windermere	F H

DERBYSHIRE

Derby Grammar School for Boys, Derby	H
Derby High School, Derby	E H
Foremarke Hall, Derby	H
Mount St Mary's College, Spinkhill	H
Repton School, Repton	F H
St Anselm's, Bakewell	+ F
St Elphin's School, Matlock	E F H T

DEVON

Blundell's School, Tiverton	F H
Edgehill College, Bideford	+ E F H
Exeter Cathedral School, Exeter	+ H
Exeter Junior School, Exeter	H
Exeter School, Exeter	H
Exeter Tutorial College, Exeter	H
Gramercy Hall School, Torbay	H T
Grenville College, Bideford	+ F H
Kelly College, Tavistock	E F H T
The Maynard School, Exeter	H
Mount House School, Tavistock	T
Park School, Totnes	H
St Aubyn's School, Tiverton	+
St Christophers School, Totnes	H
St John's School, Sidmouth	F H
St Michael's, Barnstaple	+ H T
St Wilfrid's School, Exeter	H
Sands School, Ashburton	H
Shebbear College, Beaworthy	+ E F H T
Stover School, Newton Abbot	F H

Tower House School, Paignton   H
Trinity School, Teignmouth   + E F H M T
West Buckland Preparatory School, Barnstaple   H
West Buckland School, Barnstaple   + F H

DORSET

Canford School, Wimborne   F1
Castle Court Preparatory School, Wimborne   + E H
Clayesmore Preparatory School,
  Blandford Forum   + E F H
Clayesmore School, Blandford Forum   + E F H T
Dumpton School, Wimborne   H T
Homefield School Senior & Preparatory,
  Christchurch   + F H
Knighton House, Blandford Forum   F T
The Park School, Bournemouth   H
Port Regis, Shaftesbury   T
St Antony's-Leweston School, Sherborne   H
Sherborne Preparatory School, Sherborne   F H
Sherborne School, Sherborne   F H T
Sherborne School for Girls, Sherborne   H
Talbot Heath, Bournemouth   H
Wentworth College, Bournemouth   F

COUNTY DURHAM

Barnard Castle School, Barnard Castle   F
The Chorister School, Durham   + H
Durham High School For Girls, Durham   + H
Durham School, Durham   F H
Hurworth House School, Darlington   H
Polam Hall, Darlington   H

ESSEX

Alleyn Court Preparatory School,
  Southend-on-Sea   + H T
Bancroft's School, Woodford Green   H
Brentwood School, Brentwood   H T
Chigwell School, Chigwell   H T
Colchester High School, Colchester   H
Cranbrook College, Ilford   T
Dame Johane Bradbury's School, Saffron Walden   H
Felsted School, Dunmow   F
Friends' School, Saffron Walden   H
Holmwood House, Colchester   H
New Hall School, Chelmsford   F H
St Hilda's School, Westcliff-on-Sea   H
St Michael's School, Leigh-on-Sea   E
St Nicholas School, Harlow   H T

GLOUCESTERSHIRE

Beaudesert Park, Stroud   F
Bredon School, Tewkesbury   F
The Cheltenham Ladies' College, Cheltenham   H
Dean Close Preparatory School,
  Cheltenham   + E F H T
Dean Close School, Cheltenham   + E F H T
Hatherop Castle School, Cirencester   F H
Ingleside PNEU School, Cirencester   H

The King's School, Gloucester   + F H T
Rendcomb College, Cirencester   F H
Rose Hill School, Wotton-under-Edge   F H
St Edward's School, Cheltenham   H
School of the Lion, Gloucester   E H
Westonbirt School, Tetbury   + F1 F2 F3 FO H
Wycliffe College, Stonehouse   H T
Wycliffe Junior School, Stonehouse   F H

HAMPSHIRE

The Atherley School, Southampton   H
Ballard School, New Milton   H T
Bedales School, Petersfield   H
Churchers College, Petersfield   H
Daneshill House, Basingstoke   H T
Ditcham Park School, Petersfield   T
Dunhurst (Bedales Junior School), Petersfield   H
Durlston Court, New Milton   F H T
Embley Park School, Romsey   F FO H T
Farnborough Hill, Farnborough   H
Forres Sandle Manor, Fordingbridge   F
The Gregg School, Southampton   H
Highfield School, Liphook   + E F1 F2 F3
Hordle Walhampton School, Lymington   H
King Edward VI School, Southampton   H
Littlefield School, Liphook   H
Mayville High School, Southsea   H
North Foreland Lodge, Basingstoke   H
The Pilgrims' School, Winchester   H
The Portsmouth Grammar School, Portsmouth   H T
Portsmouth High School GDST, Southsea   H
Rookesbury Park School, Portsmouth   F H
St Nicholas School, Fleet   +
St Swithun's School, Winchester   H
Salesian College, Farnborough   H
Stanbridge Earls School, Romsey   H
Stockton House School, Aldershot   H
The Stroud School, Romsey   +
Wykeham House School, Fareham   H

HEREFORDSHIRE

The Hereford Cathedral School, Hereford   + F H T
St Richard's, Bromyard   F

HERTFORDSHIRE

Abbot's Hill, Hemel Hempstead   H T
Aldenham School, Elstree   H
Berkhamsted Collegiate Preparatory School,
  Berkhamsted   H
Berkhamsted Collegiate School,
  Berkhamsted   F3 H M T
Bishop's Stortford College,
  Bishop's Stortford   H T
Edge Grove, Aldenham   + E F FO H M T
Egerton-Rothesay School, Berkhamsted   H
Haberdashers' Aske's Boys' School, Elstree   H
Haberdashers' Aske's School for Girls, Elstree   + H
Haileybury, Hertford   E H T
Harpenden Preparatory School, Harpenden   H
Heath Mount School, Hertford   F T

The Junior School, Bishop's Stortford College, Bishop's Stortford	H
Lockers Park, Hemel Hempstead	F T
Norfolk Lodge Nursery & Preparatory School, Barnet	H
The Princess Helena College, Hitchin	+ F H
The Purcell School, Bushey	H
St Albans High School for Girls, St Albans	+ E H
St Albans School, St Albans	H
St Columba's College, St Albans	H
St Edmund's College, Ware	+ F H T
St Francis' College, Letchworth	H
St Margaret's School, Bushey	+ F H
Westbrook Hay, Hemel Hempstead	F
York House School, Rickmansworth	H T

ISLE OF MAN

King William's College, Castletown	+ F H T

ISLE OF WIGHT

Ryde School, Ryde	H
Westmont School, Newport	+ H

KENT

Ashford School, Ashford	H
Baston School, Bromley	H
Bedgebury School, Cranbrook	+ F H
Beechwood Sacred Heart, Tunbridge Wells	H
Bethany School, Cranbrook	+ E F H
Bickley Park School, Bromley	H T
Bishop Challoner School, Bromley	H
Bromley High School GDST, Bromley	H
Cobham Hall, Gravesend	H
Dover College, Dover	F
Farringtons & Stratford House, Chislehurst	F
Gad's Hill School, Rochester	T
The Granville School, Sevenoaks	H
Hilden Grange School, Tonbridge	H
Holmewood House, Tunbridge Wells	F
Holy Trinity College, Bromley	H
Junior King's School, Canterbury	+
The Junior School, St Lawrence College, Ramsgate	+ E F
Kent College, Canterbury	+ F H
Kent College Pembury, Tunbridge Wells	E F
King's Preparatory School, Rochester, Rochester	+ E F H
King's School Rochester, Rochester	E F H
Marlborough House School, Hawkhurst	+ F T
Merton Court Preparatory School, Sidcup	H T
Northbourne Park School, Deal	F H
Rochester Independent College, Rochester	H
Sackville School, Tonbridge	H
St Christopher's School, Beckenham	H
St Edmund's Junior School, Canterbury	+ F FO
St Edmund's School, Canterbury	F FO H
St Lawrence College, Ramsgate	E F
St Mary's Westbrook, Folkestone	+ F
St Michael's School, Sevenoaks	H
Sevenoaks School, Sevenoaks	H
Solefield School, Sevenoaks	H T

Sutton Valence School, Maidstone	F H T
Tonbridge School, Tonbridge	H
Vernon Holme (Kent College Infant & Junior School), Canterbury	F
Walthamstow Hall, Sevenoaks	+ E H
Wellesley House School, Broadstairs	+ H T
Yardley Court, Tonbridge	H

LANCASHIRE

Arnold School, Blackpool	H
Beech House School, Rochdale	H
Bentham Grammar School, Lancaster	+ F H T
Bolton School (Boys' Division), Bolton	H
Bolton School (Girls' Division), Bolton	H
Bury Grammar School (Girls'), Bury	H
Heathland College, Accrington	H
The Hulme Grammar School, Oldham	H
The Hulme Grammar School for Girls, Oldham	H T
Kingswood College at Scarisbrick Hall, Ormskirk	H T
Kirkham Grammar School, Preston	F H
Moorland School, Clitheroe	F
Queen Elizabeth's Grammar School, Blackburn	+ H
Rossall Preparatory School, Fleetwood	+ F3
Rossall School, Fleetwood	+ F
Stonyhurst College, Clitheroe	H

LEICESTERSHIRE

Leicester Grammar School, Leicester	H
Leicester High School For Girls, Leicester	H
Loughborough Grammar School, Loughborough	+ E F H
Loughborough High School, Loughborough	H
Manor House School, Ashby-de-la-Zouch	+ H
PNEU School, Loughborough	+
Ratcliffe College, Leicester	F
Stoneygate School, Leicester	+ E H

LINCOLNSHIRE

The Fen Preparatory School, Sleaford	E F T
Maypole House School, Alford	H
St Hugh's School, Woodhall Spa	F1 F2 F3 T
Stamford High School, Stamford	H
Stamford School, Stamford	H T
Witham Hall, Bourne	F H T

NORTH EAST LINCOLNSHIRE

St James' School, Grimsby	+ F FO H T

NORTH LINCOLNSHIRE

Brigg Preparatory School, Brigg	+

LONDON

The Albany College, NW4	H
Albany College, NW4	H
The American School in London, NW8	H

Arnold House School, NW8	H
The Arts Educational School, W4	H
Ashbourne Middle School, W8	H
Bales College, W10	H
Belmont (Mill Hill Junior School), NW7	H
Blackheath High School GDST, SE3	H
Channing School, N6	H
City of London School, EC4V	H T
City of London School for Girls, EC2Y	H
Collingham, SW5	H T
Dallington School, EC1V	H
Davies Laing and Dick Independent VI Form College, W2	H
Dulwich College, SE21	H
Dulwich College Preparatory School, SE21	H
Durston House, W5	H
Ealing College Upper School, W13	H
Eaton House The Manor, SW4	H
Eltham College, SE9	E H
Fine Arts College, NW3	H
Forest Girls' School, E17	+
Forest School, E17	+ F
Francis Holland School, SW1W	+ H
Francis Holland School, NW1	+
Garden House Boys' School, SW1X	H
Garden House Girls' School, SW1W	H
Gatehouse School, E2	H
The Godolphin and Latymer School, W6	H
Hampstead Hill Pre-Preparatory & Nursery School, NW3	H
Hellenic College of London, SW1X	H
Hereward House School, NW3	+
Highgate Junior School, N6	+ H
Highgate School, N6	H
International School of London, W3	H
James Allen's Girls' School, SE22	H
King Fahad Academy, W3	H
King's College School, SW19	H
Lansdowne Sixth Form College, W2	H
Latymer Upper School, W6	H
Lyndhurst House Preparatory School, NW3	H
Mander Portman Woodward, SW7	H T
Mill Hill School, NW7	F1 F2 F3 H
More House, SW1X	H
The Mount School, NW7	H
Naima Jewish Preparatory School, NW6	H
Normanhurst School, E4	E F3
The Norwegian School, SW20	F FO
Notting Hill and Ealing High School GDST, W13	H
Palmers Green High School, N21	H
The Pointer School, SE3	+ E F1 F2 F3 H
Putney High School, SW15	H
Queen's College, W1N	H
Riverston School, SE12	+ H
The Roche School, SW18	H
Royal Ballet School, W14	H
The Royal School, Hampstead, NW3	H
St Benedict's School, W5	H
St James Independent School for Girls (Juniors), W14	H
St James Independent School for Senior Girls, W14	H
St Margaret's School, NW3	H
St Paul's Cathedral School, EC4M	H

St Paul's Girls' School, W6	H
St Paul's Preparatory School, SW13	H
St Paul's School, SW13	H
Sarum Hall, NW3	H
Sinclair House School, SW6	H
South Hampstead High School, NW3	H
Southbank International School, Kensington, W11	H T
Southbank International School, Hampstead, NW3	H
Streatham and Clapham High School, SW16	H
Sydenham High School GDST, SE26	H
Sylvia Young Theatre School, NW1	H
Trevor Roberts', NW3	H
University College School, NW3	H
The Village School, NW3	+ H
Westminster Cathedral Choir School, SW1P	H
Westminster School, SW1P	H T
Westminster Under School, SW1P	H
The White House Prep & Woodentops Kindergarten, SW12	H
Willington School, SW19	H
Woodside Park International School, N11	H

GREATER MANCHESTER

Abbey Independent College, Manchester	M
The Manchester Grammar School, Manchester	H
Manchester High School for Girls, Manchester	H
Monton Prep School with Montessori Nurseries, Eccles	H T
William Hulme's Grammar School, Manchester	H
Withington Girls' School, Manchester	H

MERSEYSIDE

Avalon Preparatory School, Wirral	H
The Belvedere School GDST, Liverpool	H
Birkenhead High School GDST, Wirral	H
Birkenhead School, Birkenhead	H
Highfield School, Birkenhead	H
Kingsmead School, Wirral	+ E F H T
Liverpool College, Liverpool	+ E F H
Merchant Taylors' School, Liverpool	H
Merchant Taylors' School for Girls, Liverpool	H
Streatham House School, Liverpool	H
Sunnymede School, Southport	H T
Tower Dene Preparatory School, Southport	F M T

MIDDLESEX

Alpha Preparatory School, Harrow	T
The American Community Schools, Uxbridge	+ E H
Hampton School, Hampton	H T
Harrow School, Harrow on the Hill	+ H
Heathfield School, Pinner	H
The John Lyon School, Harrow	H
The Lady Eleanor Holles School, Hampton	H
The Mall School, Twickenham	+ H
Merchant Taylors' School, Northwood	H T
Newland House School, Twickenham	H
North London Collegiate School, Edgware	H
Quainton Hall School, Harrow	T

St Christopher's School, Wembley	H
St David's School, Ashford	F1 F2 F3 H
St Helen's School for Girls, Northwood	H
St James Independent School for Boys (Senior), Twickenham	H
Twickenham Preparatory School, Hampton	H

NORFOLK

Glebe House School, Hunstanton	+ T
Gresham's Preparatory School, Holt	H
Gresham's School, Holt	H T
Langley Preparatory School & Nursery, Norwich	F H
Langley School, Norwich	E F H
The New Eccles Hall School, Norwich	F H
The Norwich High School for Girls GDST, Norwich	H
Norwich School, Norwich	H
Sacred Heart Convent School, Swaffham	E H T
Taverham Hall, Norwich	+ F
Thetford Grammar School, Thetford	H
Wood Dene School, Norwich	H

NORTHAMPTONSHIRE

Beachborough School, Brackley	H
Maidwell Hall, Northampton	+ H
Northampton High School, Northampton	H
Northampton Preparatory School, Northampton	+ H T
Northamptonshire Grammar School, Pitsford	H
Quinton House, Northampton	H
St Peter's School, Kettering	H
Wellingborough School, Wellingborough	H

NORTHUMBERLAND

Longridge Towers School, Berwick-upon-Tweed	+ F FO
Mowden Hall School, Stocksfield	F H T
St Oswald's School, Alnwick	E H T

NOTTINGHAMSHIRE

Bramcote Lorne School, Retford	+ F FO T
Greenholme School, Nottingham	E F FO H T
Grosvenor School, Nottingham	+ F
Nottingham High School for Girls GDST, Nottingham	H
Ranby House, Retford	F H
Rodney School, Newark	H
Trent College, Nottingham	+ F H
Wellow House School, Newark	H
Worksop College, Worksop	+ E F1 F2 H

OXFORDSHIRE

Abingdon School, Abingdon	H
Bloxham School, Banbury	+ H T
The Carrdus School, Banbury	H T

Cherwell College, Oxford	F H
Cokethorpe School, Witney	H
Cranford House School, Wallingford	H
Headington School Oxford, Oxford	+
Josca's Preparatory School, Abingdon	H
Kingham Hill School, Chipping Norton	E F H
Magdalen College School, Oxford	H
Millbrook House, Abingdon	F H T
Our Lady's Convent Senior School, Abingdon	H
Oxford High School GDST, Oxford	H
Oxford Tutorial College, Oxford	H
Rye St Antony School, Oxford	F
St Edward's School, Oxford	+ F
School of St Helen & St Katharine, Abingdon	H
Shiplake College, Henley-on-Thames	F
Sibford School, Banbury	+ H
Summer Fields, Oxford	H
Windrush Valley School, Chipping Norton	H
Wychwood School, Oxford	H

RUTLAND

Oakham School, Oakham	H
Uppingham School, Uppingham	+ H

SHROPSHIRE

Adcote School for Girls, Shrewsbury	+ F H
Bedstone College, Bucknell	F H
Bellan House Preparatory School, Oswestry	+ F T
Concord College, Shrewsbury	F
Dower House School, Bridgnorth	H
Ellesmere College, Ellesmere	H T
Kingsland Grange, Shrewsbury	+ H T
Moor Park School, Ludlow	H
Moreton Hall, Oswestry	+ E F FO H T
Oswestry School, Oswestry	F H T
Packwood Haugh, Shrewsbury	+ F H T
Prestfelde Preparatory School, Shrewsbury	F H T
Shrewsbury School, Shrewsbury	H
Wrekin College, Telford	F H T

SOMERSET

Bruton School for Girls, Bruton	F1 F2 F3 H
Buckland School, Watchet	H
Chard School, Chard	H
Chilton Cantelo School, Yeovil	F FO
Hazlegrove (King's Bruton Preparatory School), Yeovil	H
King's College, Taunton	+ E F H
King's Hall School, Taunton	+ F
King's School, Bruton	+ H T
Millfield Preparatory School, Glastonbury	F
Millfield School, Street	F
The Park School, Yeovil	+ E F H
Perrott Hill School, Crewkerne	+ F H T
Queen's College, Taunton	F FO
Queen's College Junior and Pre-Preparatory Schools, Taunton	+ F H
Rossholme School, East Brent	H
St Christopher's, Burnham-on-Sea	F H
St Martin's Independent School, Crewkerne	F H

Taunton Preparatory School, Taunton	+ F H
Taunton School, Taunton	E F
Wellington School, Wellington	F H T
Wells Cathedral Junior School, Wells	+
Wells Cathedral School, Wells	H

NORTH EAST SOMERSET

Downside School, Bath	H
King Edward's School, Bath, Bath	H
Kingswood Preparatory School, Bath	E F1 F3
Kingswood School, Bath	+ E F H
Monkton Combe Junior School, Bath	+ E F H
Monkton Combe School, Bath	+ E F H T
Paragon School, Bath	H
Prior Park College, Bath	H
The Royal High School, Bath	F

NORTH SOMERSET

Sidcot School, Winscombe	H

STAFFORDSHIRE

Abbotsholme School, Uttoxeter	+ E F FO H T
Chase Academy, Cannock	E F H
Denstone College, Uttoxeter	+ F H T
Edenhurst School, Newcastle-under-Lyme	+ T
Howitt House School, Hanbury	+ H T
Lichfield Cathedral School, Lichfield	+ F FO H
Newcastle-under-Lyme School, Newcastle-under-Lyme	H
St Dominic's Priory School, Stone	H
St Dominic's School, Stafford	H
School of St Mary and St Anne, Abbots Bromley	+ F
Stafford Grammar School, Stafford	H

STOCKTON-ON-TEES

Yarm School, Yarm	H

SUFFOLK

Amberfield School, Ipswich	H
Barnardiston Hall Preparatory School, Haverhill	+ F FO H T
Culford School, Bury St Edmunds	F H
Framlingham College, Woodbridge	F H
Framlingham College Junior School, Brandeston	F1 F3 H
Hillcroft Preparatory School, Stowmarket	H
Ipswich High School GDST, Ipswich	H
Ipswich School, Ipswich	F3 H
Moreton Hall Preparatory School, Bury St Edmunds	F H
Old Buckenham Hall School, Ipswich	+ H T
Orwell Park, Ipswich	H T
Royal Hospital School, Ipswich	F1 F2
St Felix School, Southwold	F1 F3 F4
St George's School, Southwold	H T
St Joseph's College, Ipswich	H
Stoke College, Sudbury	H
Woodbridge School, Woodbridge	H

SURREY

Aldro School, Godalming	H
The American Community Schools, Egham	H
The American Community Schools, Cobham	H T
Box Hill School, Dorking	H T
Cambridge Tutors College, Croydon	H
Canbury School, Kingston-upon-Thames	H
Caterham Preparatory School, Caterham	+ E F FO H T
Caterham School, Caterham	E F FO H T
Charterhouse, Godalming	H
Clewborough House School at Cheswycks, Camberley	+ F H T
Coworth Park School, Woking	+
Cranleigh School, Cranleigh	+ F FO
Croydon High School GDST, South Croydon	H
Drayton House School, Guildford	H
Duke of Kent School, Ewhurst	F
Dunottar School, Reigate	H
Edgeborough, Farnham	F H
Elmhurst, The School for Dance & Performing Arts, Camberley	F1 F3 F4 H
Epsom College, Epsom	M
Essendene Lodge School, Caterham	H
Ewell Castle School, Epsom	H
Frensham Heights, Farnham	H
Glenesk School, Leatherhead	H
Greenacre School for Girls, Banstead	H
Guildford High School (Church Schools Co), Guildford	+ H
Halstead Preparatory School, Woking	H
Haslemere Preparatory School, Haslemere	T
Hawley Place School, Camberley	H
The Hawthorns School, Redhill	+ H
Holy Cross Preparatory School, Kingston-upon-Thames	H T
King Edward's School, Witley, Godalming	+ H E
Kingston Grammar School, Kingston-upon-Thames	+ E H
Kingswood House School, Epsom	+ H T
Lyndhurst School, Camberley	H
Marymount International School, Kingston-upon-Thames	H
Notre Dame Preparatory School, Cobham	H
Notre Dame Senior School, Cobham	H
Parkside School, Cobham	F FO H T
Parsons Mead, Ashtead	+ F
Prior's Field School, Godalming	F H
Reed's School, Cobham	H
Reigate Grammar School, Reigate	H
Royal Alexandra and Albert School, Reigate	H
Royal Grammar School, Guildford	H
Royal Russell School, Croydon	F FO
Royal School Haslemere, Haslemere	+ F H T
St Catherine's School, Guildford	H
St Edmund's School, Hindhead	H T
St John's School, Leatherhead	+
St Teresa's School, Dorking	T
Sanderstead Junior School, South Croydon	H
Shrewsbury House School, Surbiton	T
Sir William Perkins's School, Chertsey	H

Stowford, Sutton	E H
Surbiton High School, Kingston-upon-Thames	+ H
Sutton High School GDST, Sutton	H
TASIS The American School in England, Thorpe	H
Tormead School, Guildford	H
Trinity School, Croydon	H
Whitgift School, South Croydon	H
Wispers School for Girls, Haslemere	F H
Yehudi Menuhin School, Cobham	H

EAST SUSSEX

Ashdown House School, Forest Row	+ T
Battle Abbey School, Battle	F H
Bricklehurst Manor Preparatory, Wadhurst	H
Brighton and Hove High School GDST, Brighton	H
Brighton College, Brighton	+ F3 H T
Brighton College Prep School, Brighton	+ F3
Buckswood School, Hastings	F
Eastbourne College, Eastbourne	H
The Fold School, Hove	H
Moira House Junior School, Eastbourne	H T
Moira House Girls' School, Eastbourne	E F H T
Mowden School, Hove	+ H T
Newlands Manor School, Seaford	F FO H T
Newlands Preparatory School, Seaford	F H
St Andrew's School, Eastbourne	F
St Aubyn's, Brighton	H T
St Bede's, Eastbourne	F T
St Bede's School, Hailsham	F H
St Leonards-Mayfield School, Mayfield	H
St Mary's Hall, Brighton	+ F H
Temple Grove, Uckfield	H
Vinehall School, Robertsbridge	+ E F T
Westerleigh & St Leonards College, St Leonards-on-Sea	H T

WEST SUSSEX

Ardingly College, Haywards Heath	+ F
Ardingly College Junior School, Haywards Heath	H T
Christs Hospital, Horsham	F1 F2 F4 H
Copthorne School, Copthorne	H
Cottesmore School, Pease Pottage	H
Dorset House School, Pulborough	F H T
Farlington School, Horsham	+ F1 F2 F3 H
Fonthill Lodge, East Grinstead	H
Great Ballard School, Chichester	F
Great Walstead, Haywards Heath	+ E F H T
Hurstpierpoint College, Hassocks	+ E F H T
Lancing College, Lancing	H T
Oakwood School, Chichester	F1 F3 F4
Our Lady of Sion School, Worthing	H
Pennthorpe School, Horsham	H
St Peter's School, Burgess Hill	H
Seaford College, Petworth	F
Shoreham College, Shoreham-by-Sea	+ H
Slindon College, Arundel	F H
Stoke Brunswick, East Grinstead	F H
Tavistock & Summerhill School, Haywards Heath	H
Windlesham House, Pulborough	F1 F2 F3

TYNE AND WEAR

Central Newcastle High School GDST, Newcastle upon Tyne	H
Eastcliffe Grammar School, Newcastle upon Tyne	H
Grindon Hall Christian School, Sunderland	+ E T
Newcastle Preparatory School, Newcastle upon Tyne	H
Newcastle Upon Tyne Church High School, Newcastle upon Tyne	+
Newlands School, Newcastle upon Tyne	H
Sunderland High School, Sunderland	E H
Westfield School, Newcastle upon Tyne	H

WARWICKSHIRE

Arnold Lodge School, Leamington Spa	H T
Bilton Grange, Rugby	+ F H T
The King's High School for Girls, Warwick	H
The Kingsley School, Leamington Spa	H
Warwick School, Warwick	H

WEST MIDLANDS

Bablake School, Coventry	H
The Blue Coat School, Birmingham	H
Edgbaston High School for Girls, Birmingham	H
Eversfield Preparatory School, Solihull	+
King Edward VI High School for Girls, Birmingham	H
Mander Portman Woodward, Birmingham	H T
Newbridge Preparatory School, Wolverhampton	+
Pattison College, Coventry	H
The Royal Wolverhampton Junior School, Wolverhampton	F1 F3 H
The Royal Wolverhampton School, Wolverhampton	F H
St George's School, Edgbaston, Birmingham	+
Solihull School, Solihull	+
Tettenhall College, Wolverhampton	F H T
West House School, Birmingham	+ T
Wolverhampton Grammar School, Wolverhampton	H

WILTSHIRE

Chafyn Grove School, Salisbury	H
The Godolphin School, Salisbury	H
Grittleton House School, Chippenham	H
Kingsbury Hill House, Marlborough	H T
La Retraite Swan, Salisbury	H
Leaden Hall, Salisbury	+
Marlborough College, Marlborough	+ H
Pinewood School, Swindon	+ T
St Francis School, Pewsey	H
St Mary's School, Calne	+ H
Sandroyd, Salisbury	H T
Warminster School, Warminster	+ F H

WORCESTERSHIRE

Abberley Hall, Worcester	H
The Abbey College, Malvern Wells	H

The Alice Ottley School, Worcester	+
Bromsgrove Lower School, Bromsgrove	F H
Bromsgrove School, Bromsgrove	E F H T
The Downs School, Malvern	E F H T
The Elms, Malvern	+ F
Green Hill School, Evesham	H
Hartlebury School, Kidderminster	H
Hillstone School (Malvern College), Malvern	F1 F2 F3 FO
King's Hawford, Worcester	+
The King's School, Worcester	H
Malvern College, Malvern	F H T
Malvern Girls' College, Malvern	H T
Moffats School, Bewdley	+ F H T
River School, Worcester	H
Royal Grammar School Worcester, Worcester	H
St James's School, Malvern	F H
St Mary's Convent School, Worcester	H
Winterfold House, Kidderminster	H

EAST RIDING OF YORKSHIRE

Hull Grammar School, Kingston-Upon-Hull	H
Pocklington School, Pocklington	F H

NORTH YORKSHIRE

Ampleforth College, York	H
Ashville College, Harrogate	+ E F H T
Aysgarth Preparatory School, Bedale	F H T
Belmont Grosvenor School, Harrogate	+ F T
Bootham School, York	H
Catteral Hall, Settle	F
Cundall Manor School, York	F FO
Fyling Hall School, Whitby	F H
Giggleswick School, Settle	F H T
Harrogate Ladies' College, Harrogate	+ H
Harrogate Tutorial College, Harrogate	H
Howsham Hall, York	+ H T
Malsis School, Skipton	F H T

Queen Ethelburga's College, York	+ F M
Queen Margaret's School, York	+ F
Queen Mary's School, Thirsk	E F H T
Read School, Selby	H
Red House School, York	H
Ripon Cathedral Choir School, Ripon	F
St Martin's, Ampleforth, York	H
St Olave's School (Junior of St Peter's), York	F H T
St Peter's School, York	+ F H
Scarborough College, Scarborough	F2 F3 F4 H
Terrington Hall, York	E F FO T
Woodleigh School, Malton	F1 F2 F3

SOUTH YORKSHIRE

Ashdell Preparatory School, Sheffield	H
Birkdale School, Sheffield	H
Handsworth Christian School, Sheffield	H
Rudston Preparatory School, Rotherham	H T
Sheffield High School GDST, Sheffield	H
Westbourne School, Sheffield	H

WEST YORKSHIRE

Ackworth School, Pontefract	H
Batley Grammar School, Batley	H
Bradford Girls' Grammar School, Bradford	H
Bradford Grammar School, Bradford	+ H
Bronte House School, Bradford	+ F H
Fulneck School, Pudsey	+ E F H
Gateways School, Leeds	H
Hipperholme Grammar School, Halifax	H
Huddersfield Grammar School, Huddersfield	H
Leeds Girls' High School, Leeds	H
Queen Elizabeth Grammar School, Wakefield	H
Rishworth School, Rishworth	F
Shaw House School, Bradford	H T
Silcoates School, Wakefield	+ E
Wakefield Girls' High School, Wakefield	H
Woodhouse Grove School, Apperley Bridge	+ E F FO H

NORTHERN IRELAND

COUNTY ANTRIM

Cabin Hill School, Belfast	+ E F H
Methodist College, Belfast	+
Royal Belfast Academical Institution, Belfast	H

COUNTY ARMAGH

The Royal School, Armagh	+

COUNTY DOWN

The Holywood Rudolf Steiner School, Holywood	H

COUNTY LONDONDERRY

Coleraine Academical Institution, Coleraine	+ E

COUNTY TYRONE

Royal School Dungannon, Dungannon	E F

SCOTLAND

ABERDEENSHIRE

Robert Gordons College, Aberdeen	H
St Margaret's School for Girls, Aberdeen	H

ANGUS

The High School of Dundee, Dundee	+ H
Lathallan School, Montrose	F FO H T

ARGYLL AND BUTE

Lomond School, Helensburgh   F

BANFFSHIRE

Aberlour House, Aberlour   H

FIFE

St Katharines Preparatory School,
    St Andrews   F1 F3 H T
St Leonards School & St Leonards
    VIth Form College, St Andrews   + F H T
Sea View Private School, Kirkcaldy   H

GLASGOW

Craigholme School, Glasgow   H
The Glasgow Academy, Glasgow   H
The High School of Glasgow, Glasgow   H
Hutchesons' Grammar School, Glasgow   H

LOTHIAN

Cargilfield, Edinburgh   F H
Clifton Hall, Newbridge   F H T
The Edinburgh Academy, Edinburgh   H
Fettes College, Edinburgh   H T
George Heriot's School, Edinburgh   H

George Watson's College, Edinburgh   H
The Mary Erskine School, Edinburgh   H
Merchiston Castle School, Edinburgh   F
St George's School for Girls, Edinburgh   H
St Margaret's School, Edinburgh   F H

MIDLOTHIAN

Loretto, Musselburgh   H

MORAYSHIRE

Gordonstoun School, Elgin   F3 F4 H
Rosebrae School, Elgin   H

PERTHSHIRE

Ardvreck School, Crieff   F
Craigclowan Preparatory School, Perth   H T
Glenalmond College, Perth   E F H T
Kilgraston (A Sacred Heart School), Perth   F1 F3 H T
Morrison's Academy, Crieff   H
Queen Victoria School, Dunblane   F
Rannoch School, Pitlochry   + F H T
Strathallan School, Perth   F H T

ROXBURGHSHIRE

St Mary's Preparatory School, Melrose   F H

WALES

BRIDGEND

St John's School, Porthcawl   H

CARDIFF

Elm Tree House School, Cardiff   H
Howell's School, Llandaff GDST, Cardiff   H

CARMARTHENSHIRE

Llandovery College, Llandovery   F3 H T
St Michael's School, Llanelli   H

CONWY

Rydal Penrhos Preparatory School, Colwyn Bay   E H
Rydal Penrhos Senior School, Colwyn Bay   F
St David's College, Llandudno   F H

DENBIGHSHIRE

Howell's School, Denbigh   F FO
Ruthin School, Ruthin   + F H

GWYNEDD

Hillgrove School, Bangor   E

MONMOUTHSHIRE

Haberdashers' Monmouth School For Girls,
    Monmouth   H
Monmouth School, Monmouth   F H T
St John's-on-the-Hill, Chepstow   F H

NEWPORT

Rougemont School, Newport   H

PEMBROKESHIRE

Netherwood School, Saundersfoot   H

POWYS

Christ College, Brecon   F H

SWANSEA

Ffynone House School, Swansea   H
Oakleigh House, Swansea   H

4.3
SPECIALIST SCHOOLS

Schools in the directory which specialise in the theatre, dance or music are listed below. For full details about entrance requirements and the curriculum parents are advised to contact schools direct.

Arts Schools

The Arts Educational Schools, London W4
The Arts Educational School, Tring
Barbara Speake Stage School, London W3
Italia Conti Academy of Theatre Arts, London EC1
McKee School of Education, Dance and Drama, Liverpool
Pattison College, Coventry
Ravenscourt Theatre School, London W6
Sylvia Young Theatre School, London NW1

Dance Schools

Elmhurst, The School for Dance and the Performing Arts, Camberley
Hammond School, Chester
The Royal Ballet School, London W14
Stonelands School of Ballet and Theatre Arts, East Sussex
The Urdang Academy of Ballet, London WC2

Music Schools

Chethams' School of Music, Manchester
The Purcell School, Bushey
St Mary's Music School, Edinburgh
The Yehudi Menuhin School, Cobham

4.4

SINGLE-SEX SCHOOLS

BOYS' SCHOOLS

ENGLAND

BEDFORDSHIRE

Bedford Modern School, Bedford	7–18
Bedford Preparatory School, Bedford	7–13
Bedford School, Bedford	13–18

BERKSHIRE

Bradfield College, Reading	13–18 (Co-ed VIth Form)
Brockhurst School, Newbury	3–13
Claires Court School, Maidenhead	11–18 (Co-ed VIth Form)
Crosfields School, Reading	4–13
Elstree School, Reading	3–13 (Girls 3–7)
Eton College, Windsor	12–18
Horris Hill, Newbury	7–13
Ludgrove, Wokingham	8–13
The Oratory School, Reading	11–18
Papplewick, Ascot	7–13
Presentation College, Reading	4–18 (Co-ed VIth Form)
Reading Blue Coat School, Reading	11–18 (Co-ed VIth Form)
Ridgeway School (Claires Court Junior), Maidenhead	5–11
St Edward's School, Reading	5–13
St John's Beaumont, Windsor	4–13
Sunningdale School, Sunningdale	8–13
Wellington College, Crowthorne	13–18 (Co-ed VIth Form)

BRISTOL

Bristol Cathedral School, Bristol	10–18 (Co-ed VIth Form)
Queen Elizabeth's Hospital, Bristol	11–18

BUCKINGHAMSHIRE

The Beacon School, Amersham	3–13
Caldicott School, Farnham Royal	7–13
Davenies School, Beaconsfield	4–13
Gayhurst School, Gerrards Cross	4–13
Kingscote School, Gerrards Cross	3–7
Stowe School, Buckingham	13–18 (Co-ed VIth Form)
Thorpe House School, Gerrards Cross	3–13

CAMBRIDGESHIRE

The Perse School, Cambridge	11–18 (Co-ed VIth Form)

CHANNEL ISLANDS

Elizabeth College, Guernsey	2–18 (Co-ed VIth Form)
Victoria College, Jersey	11–19 (VIth Form with Jersey Girls College)
Victoria College Preparatory School, Jersey	7–11

CHESHIRE

Altrincham Preparatory School, Altrincham	4–12
The King's School, Chester	7–18 (Girls 16–18)
North Cestrian Grammar School, Altrincham	11–18
The Ryleys, Alderley Edge	3–13
St Ambrose Preparatory School, Altrincham	4–11

DERBYSHIRE

Derby Grammar School for Boys, Derby	7–18

DORSET

Milton Abbey School, Blandford Forum	13–18
The Old Malthouse, Swanage	3–13 (Girls 3–9)
Sherborne School, Sherborne	13–18

COUNTY DURHAM

Bow School, Durham	3–13
Hurworth House School, Darlington	3–18

ESSEX

Colchester High School, Colchester	3–16 (Girls 3–11)
Cranbrook College, Ilford	4–16
Daiglen School, Buckhurst Hill	4–11
Loyola Preparatory School, Buckhurst Hill	3–11

HAMPSHIRE

The Pilgrims' School, Winchester	7–13
Salesian College, Farnborough	11–18
Winchester College, Winchester	13–18

HERTFORDSHIRE

Aldenham School, Elstree	11–18 (Co-ed VIth Form)
Aldwickbury School, Harpenden	4–13 (Girls 4–7)
Haberdashers' Aske's Boys' School, Elstree	7–18
Lochinver House School, Potters Bar	4–13
Lockers Park, Hemel Hempstead	7–13
Northwood Preparatory School, Rickmansworth	4–13 (Girls 3–4)
St Albans School, St Albans	11–18 (Co-ed VIth Form)
St Columba's College, St Albans	4–18
York House School, Rickmansworth	4–13 (Co-ed 2–5)

KENT

Bickley Park School, Bromley	2–13
Darul Uloom London, Chislehurst	11–0
Harenc School Trust, Sidcup	3–11
The New Beacon, Sevenoaks	5–13
Solefield School, Sevenoaks	4–13
Tonbridge School, Tonbridge	13–18
Yardley Court, Tonbridge	7–13

LANCASHIRE

Bolton School (Boys' Division), Bolton	8–18
Bury Grammar School, Bury	7–18
The Hulme Grammar School, Oldham	3–18

LEICESTERSHIRE

Loughborough Grammar School, Loughborough	10–18

LINCOLNSHIRE

Stamford School, Stamford	11–18

LONDON

Arnold House School, NW8	5–13
Brondesbury College For Boys, NW6	11–16
City of London School, EC4V	10–18

Clifton Lodge Preparatory School, W5	4–13
Dulwich College, SE21	7–18
Dulwich College Preparatory School, SE21	3–13 (Girls 3–5)
Durston House, W5	4–13
Ealing College Upper School, W13	11–18 (Co-ed VIth Form)
Eaton House School, SW1W	4–9
Eaton House The Manor, SW4	2–13 (Girls 2–4)
Eltham College, SE9	7–18 (Co-ed VIth Form)
The Falcons Pre-Preparatory School, W4	3–8
Garden House Boys' School, SW1X	3–8
The Hall School, NW3	4–13
Hawkesdown House School, W8	3–8
Hereward House School, NW3	4–13
Highgate Junior School, N6	7–13
Highgate School, N6	13–18
Keble Preparatory School, N21	4–13
King's College Junior School, SW19	7–13
King's College School, SW19	13–18
Latymer Preparatory School, W6	7–11
Latymer Upper School, W6	7–18 (Co-ed VIth Form)
Lyndhurst House Preparatory School, NW3	7–13
Mechinah Liyeshivah Zichron Moshe, N16	11–16
Northcote Lodge, SW11	8–13
Pardes Grammar Boys' School, N3	11–17
St Anthony's Preparatory School, NW3	5–13
St Benedict's Junior School, W5	4–11
St Benedict's School, W5	11–18 (Co-ed VIth Form)
St James Independent School for Boys (Juniors), W14	4–10
St Paul's Preparatory School, SW13	7–13
St Paul's School, SW13	13–18
St Philip's School, SW7	7–13
Sussex House School, SW1X	8–13
Tower House School, SW14	4–13
University College School, NW3	11–18
University College School, Junior Branch, NW3	7–11
Westminster Abbey Choir School, SW1P	8–13
Westminster Cathedral Choir School, SW1P	8–13
Westminster School, SW1P	13–18 (Co-ed VIth Form)
Westminster Under School, SW1P	7–13
Wetherby School, W2	4–8
Willington School, SW19	4–13
Wimbledon College Prep School, SW19	7–13
Yetev Lev Day School for Boys, N16	3–11

GREATER MANCHESTER

The Manchester Grammar School, Manchester	11–18
Tashbar Primary School, Salford	3–11

MERSEYSIDE

Birkenhead School, Birkenhead	3–18
Merchant Taylors' School, Liverpool	7–18

MIDDLESEX

Buckingham College Preparatory School, Pinner	4–11
Buckingham College School, Harrow	11–18 (Co-ed VIth Form)
Denmead School, Hampton	2–13 (Girls 2–7)

Halliford School, Shepperton   11–19 (Co-ed VIth Form)
Hampton School, Hampton   11–18
Harrow School, Harrow on the Hill   13–18
The John Lyon School, Harrow   11–18
The Mall School, Twickenham   4–13
Menorah Grammar School, Edgware   11–18
Merchant Taylors' School, Northwood   11–18
Quainton Hall School, Harrow   4–13
St James Independent School for Boys (Senior),
  Twickenham   10–18
St John's Northwood, Northwood   4–13
St Martin's School, Northwood   3–13

NORFOLK

Norwich School, Norwich   8–18 (Co-ed VIth Form)

NOTTINGHAMSHIRE

Al Karam Secondary School, Retford   11–16
Nottingham High School, Nottingham   11–18
Nottingham High School Preparatory School,
  Nottingham   7–11

OXFORDSHIRE

Abingdon School, Abingdon   11–18
Christ Church Cathedral School, Oxford   2–13
Cothill House Preparatory School, Abingdon   8–13
Josca's Preparatory School, Abingdon   4–13 (Girls 4–7)
Magdalen College School, Oxford   7–18
Millbrook House, Abingdon   7–14
Moulsford Preparatory School, Wallingford   5–13
New College School, Oxford   4–13
Radley College, Abingdon   13–18
Shiplake College,
  Henley-on-Thames   13–18 (Day Girls 16–18)
Summer Fields, Oxford   8–13

SHROPSHIRE

Kingsland Grange, Shrewsbury   4–13
Shrewsbury School, Shrewsbury   13–18

NORTH EAST SOMERSET

Downside School, Bath   9–18

SURREY

Aldro School, Godalming   7–13
Charterhouse, Godalming   13–18 (Co-ed VIth Form)
Chinthurst School, Tadworth   3–13
Cranmore School, Leatherhead   3–13
Cumnor House School, South Croydon   4–13
Elmhurst School, South Croydon   4–11
Ewell Castle School, Epsom   3–18 (Co-ed VIth Form)
Hall Grove School, Bagshot   4–13
Haslemere Preparatory School, Haslemere   2–14
Homefield Preparatory School, Sutton   3–13
King's House School, Richmond   4–13

Kingswood House School, Epsom   3–13
Lanesborough, Guildford   3–13
Parkside School, Cobham   2–14 (Co-ed 2–5)
Priory School, Banstead   2–13
Reed's School, Cobham   11–18 (Co-ed VIth Form)
Rokeby School, Kingston-upon-Thames   4–13
Royal Grammar School, Guildford   11–18
St Edmund's School, Hindhead   2–13 (Co-ed day 2–7)
St John's School,
  Leatherhead   13–18 (Co-ed VIth Form)
Shrewsbury House School, Surbiton   7–13
Surbiton Preparatory School, Surbiton   4–11
Trinity School, Croydon   10–18
Whitgift School, South Croydon   10–18
Woodcote House School, Windlesham   7–14

EAST SUSSEX

Mowden School, Hove   4–13

WEST SUSSEX

Dorset House School, Pulborough   4–13
Slindon College, Arundel   9–16
Worth School, Turners Hill   11–18

TYNE AND WEAR

Ascham House School, Newcastle upon Tyne   3–13
Dame Allan's Boys School,
  Newcastle upon Tyne   8–18 (Co-ed VIth Form)
Newlands School, Newcastle upon Tyne   3–13
Royal Grammar School,
  Newcastle upon Tyne   8–18 (Co-ed VIth form)

WARWICKSHIRE

Warwick School, Warwick   7–18

WEST MIDLANDS

Birchfield School, Wolverhampton   3–13
King Edward's School, Birmingham   11–18
Solihull School, Solihull   7–18 (Co-ed VIth Form)
West House School, Birmingham   1–11 (Girls 1–4)

WILTSHIRE

Sandroyd, Salisbury   7–13

WORCESTERSHIRE

Royal Grammar School Worcester, Worcester   3–18

NORTH YORKSHIRE

Ampleforth College, York   13–18 (Co-ed VIth Form)
Aysgarth Preparatory School,
  Bedale   3–13 (Co-ed Day 3–8)

SOUTH YORKSHIRE

Birkdale School, Sheffield   4–18 (Co-ed VIth Form)

WEST YORKSHIRE

Ghyll Royd School, Ilkley	2–11
Leeds Grammar School, Leeds	4–18
Queen Elizabeth Grammar School, Wakefield	7–18

NORTHERN IRELAND

COUNTY ANTRIM

Cabin Hill School, Belfast	3–13 (Co-ed kindergarten)
Campbell College, Belfast	11–18
Royal Belfast Academical Institution, Belfast	4–18

COUNTY DOWN

Bangor Grammar School, Bangor   11–18

COUNTY LONDONDERRY

Coleraine Academical Institution, Coleraine   11–19

SCOTLAND

LOTHIAN

The Edinburgh Academy, Edinburgh	5–18 (Co-ed VIth Form)
Edinburgh Academy Junior School, Edinburgh	3–11 (Girls 3–5)

Merchiston Castle School, Edinburgh	8–18
Stewart's Melville College, Edinburgh	12–18 (Co-ed VIth Form)

WALES

MONMOUTHSHIRE

Monmouth School, Monmouth   7–18

POWYS

Brookland Hall School & Golf Academy, Welshpool	16–18

GIRLS

ENGLAND

BEDFORDSHIRE

Bedford High School, Bedford	7–18
Dame Alice Harpur School, Bedford	7–18

BERKSHIRE

The Abbey School, Reading	4–18
The Brigidine School, Windsor	3–18 (Boys 3–7)
Claires Court Schools, The College, Maidenhead	3–16 (Boys 3–5)
Downe House School, Newbury	11–18
Eton End PNEU, Slough	3–11 (Boys 3–7)
Heathfield School, Ascot	11–18
Hurst Lodge, Ascot	2–18 (Boys 2–7)
Luckley-Oakfield School, Wokingham	11–18
Marist Convent Senior School, Ascot	11–18
Marlston House School, Newbury	6–13
Padworth College, Reading	14–20
Queen Anne's School, Reading	11–18
St Gabriel's School, Newbury	3–18 (Boys 3–8)
St George's School, Ascot	11–18
St Joseph's Convent School, Reading	3–18
St Mary's School, Ascot, Ascot	11–18
Upton House School, Windsor	3–11 (Boys 3–7)
White House Preparatory School, Wokingham	3–11 (Boys 3–4)

BRISTOL

Badminton School, Bristol	4–18
Clifton High School, Bristol	3–18 (Boys 3–11)
Colston's Girls' School, Bristol	10–18
The Red Maids' School, Bristol	11–18
Redland High School, Bristol	3–18

BUCKINGHAMSHIRE

Godstowe Preparatory School, High Wycombe	3–13 (Boys 3–8)
Heatherton House School, Amersham	2–11 (Boys 2–5)
High March School, Beaconsfield	3–12 (Boys 3–5)
Holy Cross Convent, Gerrards Cross	3–18
Maltman's Green School, Gerrards Cross	3–11
Pipers Corner School, High Wycombe	4–18
St Mary's School, Gerrards Cross	3–18
Thornton College Convent of Jesus and Mary, Milton Keynes	2–16 (Boys 2–7+)
Wycombe Abbey School, High Wycombe	11–18

CAMBRIDGESHIRE

The Perse School for Girls, Cambridge	7–18
Peterborough High School, Peterborough	3–18 (Boys 3–11)
St Catherines Preparatory School, Cambridge	3–11
St Mary's School, Cambridge	11–18

CHANNEL ISLANDS

Beaulieu Convent School, Jersey	4–18
Helvetia House School, Jersey	4–11
The Ladies' College, Guernsey	4–18

CHESHIRE

Alderley Edge School for Girls, Alderley Edge	3–18
Bowdon Preparatory School For Girls, Altrincham	2–11
Cransley School, Northwich	3–16 (Boys 3–11)
Culcheth Hall, Altrincham	2–16
Loreto Preparatory School, Altrincham	4–11 (Boys 4–7)
Oriel Bank High School, Stockport	3–16
The Queen's School, Chester	5–18

CORNWALL

St Joseph's School, Launceston	3–16 (Boys 3–11)
Truro High School, Truro	3–18 (Boys 3–5)

CUMBRIA

Casterton School, Carnforth	4–18 (Day boys 4–11)

DERBYSHIRE

Derby High School, Derby	3–18 (Boys 3–11)
Ockbrook School, Derby	3–18
St Elphin's School, Matlock	2–18 (Boys 2–7)

DEVON

The Maynard School, Exeter	7–18
St Dunstan's Abbey School, Plymouth	2–18
St Margaret's School, Exeter	7–18
Stover School, Newton Abbot	2–18

DORSET

Hanford School, Blandford Forum	7–13
Knighton House, Blandford Forum	3–13 (Day boys 3–7)
St Antony's-Leweston School, Sherborne	11–18
St Mary's School, Shaftesbury	9–18
Sherborne School for Girls, Sherborne	11–18
Talbot Heath, Bournemouth	3–18 (Boys 3–7)
Wentworth College, Bournemouth	11–18

COUNTY DURHAM

Durham High School For Girls, Durham	3–18
Polam Hall, Darlington	4–18

ESSEX

Braeside School for Girls, Buckhurst Hill	3–16
New Hall School, Chelmsford	4–18 (Boys day 4–11)
Park School for Girls, Ilford	7–18
St Hilda's School, Westcliff-on-Sea	2–16 (Boys 2–7)
St Mary's School, Colchester	4–16

GLOUCESTERSHIRE

The Cheltenham Ladies' College, Cheltenham	11–18
Gloucestershire Islamic Secondary School For Girls, Gloucester	11–16
Kitebrook House, Moreton-in-Marsh	4–13 (Boys 4–8)
Westonbirt School, Tetbury	11–18

HAMPSHIRE

Alton Convent School, Alton	2–18 (Co-ed 2–11)
The Atherley School, Southampton	3–18 (Boys 3–11)
Farnborough Hill, Farnborough	11–18
North Foreland Lodge, Basingstoke	11–18
Portsmouth High School GDST, Southsea	4–18
St Nicholas School, Fleet	3–16 (Boys 3–7)
St Swithun's School, Winchester	11–18
Wykeham House School, Fareham	2–16

HEREFORDSHIRE

The Margaret Allen School, Hereford	2–11

HERTFORDSHIRE

Abbot's Hill, Hemel Hempstead	11–16
Haberdashers' Aske's School for Girls, Elstree	4–18
The Princess Helena College, Hitchin	11–18
Queenswood, Hatfield	11–18
Rickmansworth PNEU School, Rickmansworth	3–11
The Royal Masonic School for Girls, Rickmansworth	4–18
St Albans High School for Girls, St Albans	4–18
St Francis' College, Letchworth	3–18
St Hilda's School, Bushey	3–11
St Hilda's School, Harpenden	2–11
St Margaret's School, Bushey	4–18

St Martha's Senior School, Barnet	11–18
St Nicholas House, Hemel Hempstead	3–11 (Boys 3–7)
Stormont, Potters Bar	4–11

KENT

Ashford School, Ashford	3–18
Babington House School, Chislehurst	3–16 (Boys 3–7)
Baston School, Bromley	2–18
Bedgebury School, Cranbrook	2–18 (Boys Day 2–7)
Beechwood Sacred Heart, Tunbridge Wells	3–18 (Boys 3–11)
Benenden School, Cranbrook	11–18
Bromley High School GDST, Bromley	4–18
Cobham Hall, Gravesend	11–18
Combe Bank School, Sevenoaks	3–18 (Boys 3–5)
Derwent Lodge School for Girls, Tonbridge	7–11
Farringtons & Stratford House, Chislehurst	2–18
The Granville School, Sevenoaks	3–11 (Boys 3–5)
Holy Trinity College, Bromley	2–18 (Boys 3–5)
Kent College Pembury, Tunbridge Wells	3–18
Walthamstow Hall, Sevenoaks	3–18

LANCASHIRE

Bolton Muslim Girls School, Bolton	11–16
Bolton School (Girls' Division), Bolton	4–18 (Boys 4–8)
Bury Grammar School (Girls'), Bury	4–18 (Boys 4–7)
The Hulme Grammar School for Girls, Oldham	3–18
Tauheedul Islam Girls High School, Blackburn	11–16
Westholme School, Blackburn	3–18 (Boys 3–7)

LEICESTERSHIRE

Leicester High School For Girls, Leicester	3–18
Loughborough High School, Loughborough	11–18
Our Lady's Convent School, Loughborough	3–18 (Boys 3–5)

LINCOLNSHIRE

Stamford High School, Stamford	11–18

LONDON

Beis Soroh Schneirer, N3	3–9
Blackheath High School GDST, SE3	3–18
Bute House Preparatory School for Girls, W6	4–11
The Cavendish School, NW1	3–11
Channing Junior School, N6	4–11
Channing School, N6	11–18
City of London School for Girls, EC2Y	7–18
Falkner House, SW7	3–11 (Co-ed 3–4)
Forest Girls' School, E17	11–18 (Co-ed VIth Form)
Francis Holland School, SW1W	4–18
Francis Holland School, NW1	11–18
Garden House Girls' School, SW1W	3–11 (Boys 3–8)

Glendower Preparatory School, SW7	4–11
The Godolphin and Latymer School, W6	11–18
Grange Park Preparatory School, N21	4–11
Harvington School, W5	3–16 (Boys 3–5)
Islamia Girls School, NW6	11–16
James Allen's Girls' School, SE22	11–18
Kensington Prep School, SW6	4–11
Lubavitch House Senior School for Girls, N16	11–18
Madni Girls School, E1	12–18
More House, SW1X	11–18
The Mount School, NW7	4–18
Notting Hill and Ealing High School GDST, W13	5–18
Palmers Green High School, N21	3–16
Pembridge Hall, W2	4–11
Putney High School, SW15	4–18
Putney Park School, SW15	4–16 (Boys 4–11)
Queen's College, W1N	11–18
Queen's Gate School, SW7	4–18
The Royal School, Hampstead, NW3	4–18
St Augustine's Priory, W5	4–18
St Christina's RC Preparatory School, NW8	3–11 (Boys 3–7)
St James Independent School for Girls (Juniors), W14	4–10
St James Independent School for Senior Girls, W14	10–18
St Joseph's Convent School, E11	3–11
St Margaret's School, NW3	5–16
St Mary's School Hampstead, NW3	2–11 (Boys 2–7)
St Paul's Girls' School, W6	11–18
Sarum Hall, NW3	3–11
South Hampstead High School, NW3	4–18
Streatham and Clapham High School, SW16	3–18 (Boys 3–5)
The Study Preparatory School, SW19	4–11
Sydenham High School GDST, SE26	4–18
Tayyibah Girls School, N16	5–18
The Falcons School for Girls, W5	4–11
Ursuline Convent Preparatory School, SW20	3–11 (Boys 3–7)
The Village School, NW3	4–11
Wimbledon High School, SW19	4–18

GREATER MANCHESTER

Jewish High School for Girls, Salford	11–18
Manchester High School for Girls, Manchester	4–18
Manchester Islamic High School, Manchester	11–16
Withington Girls' School, Manchester	7–18

MERSEYSIDE

The Belvedere School GDST, Liverpool	3–18
Birkenhead High School GDST, Wirral	3–18
Merchant Taylors' School for Girls, Liverpool	4–18 (Boys 4–7)
Streatham House School, Liverpool	2–16 (Boys 2–11)

MIDDLESEX

Heathfield School, Pinner	3–18
Jack and Jill School, Hampton	3–7 (Boys 3–5)
The Lady Eleanor Holles School, Hampton	7–18

North London Collegiate School, Edgware	4–18
Northwood College, Northwood	3–18
Peterborough & St Margaret's School, Stanmore	4–16
St Catherine's School, Twickenham	3–16
St David's School, Ashford	3–18
St Helen's School for Girls, Northwood	4–18

NORFOLK

Hethersett Old Hall School, Norwich	4–18 (Boys 4–7)
The Norwich High School for Girls GDST, Norwich	4–18
Thorpe House School, Norwich	3–16

NORTHAMPTONSHIRE

Northampton High School, Northampton	3–18

NOTTINGHAMSHIRE

Hollygirt School, Nottingham	4–16
Nottingham High School for Girls GDST, Nottingham	4–18

OXFORDSHIRE

The Carrdus School, Banbury	3–11 (Boys 3–8)
Cranford House School, Wallingford	3–16 (Boys 3–7)
Headington School Oxford, Oxford	3–18 (Co-ed 3–7)
Our Lady's Convent Senior School, Abingdon	11–18
Oxford High School GDST, Oxford	3–18 (Boys 3–7)
Rye St Antony School, Oxford	3–18 (Boys 3–8)
St Mary's School, Wantage	11–18
School of St Helen & St Katharine, Abingdon	9–18
Tudor Hall School, Banbury	11–18
Wychwood School, Oxford	11–18

SHROPSHIRE

Adcote School for Girls, Shrewsbury	4–18
Moreton Hall, Oswestry	9–18
Shrewsbury High School GDST, Shrewsbury	3–18

SOMERSET

Bruton School for Girls, Bruton	3–18
Rossholme School, East Brent	3–16 (Co-ed 3–7)

NORTH EAST SOMERSET

The Royal High School, Bath	3–18

STAFFORDSHIRE

St Dominic's Priory School, Stone	3–18 (Boys 3–11)
St Dominic's School, Stafford	2–16 (Co-ed 2–7)
School of St Mary and St Anne, Abbots Bromley	5–18

STOCKTON-ON-TEES

Teesside High School, Eaglescliffe	3–18

SUFFOLK

Amberfield School, Ipswich	3–16 (Boys 3–7)
Ipswich High School GDST, Ipswich	3–18
St Felix School, Southwold	11–18

SURREY

Bramley School, Tadworth	3–11
Croham Hurst School, South Croydon	3–18
Croydon High School GDST, South Croydon	3–18
Dunottar School, Reigate	3–18
Flexlands School, Woking	3–11
Greenacre School for Girls, Banstead	3–18
Guildford High School (Church Schools Co), Guildford	4–18
Halstead Preparatory School, Woking	3–11
Hawley Place School, Camberley	2–16 (Boys 2–11)
Holy Cross Preparatory School, Kingston-upon-Thames	4–11
Laverock School, Oxted	3–11
Lodge School, Purley	3–18 (Boys 3–11)
Manor House School, Leatherhead	2–16
Marymount International School, Kingston-upon-Thames	11–18
Notre Dame Preparatory School, Cobham	2–11 (Boys 2–5)
Notre Dame Senior School, Cobham	11–18
Old Palace School of John Whitgift, Croydon	4–18
Old Vicarage School, Richmond	4–11
Parsons Mead, Ashtead	3–18
Prior's Field School, Godalming	11–18
Rowan Preparatory School, Esher	3–11
Royal School Haslemere, Haslemere	3–18 (Boys 2–4)
Rydes Hill Preparatory School, Guildford	3–11 (Boys 3–7)
St Catherine's School, Camberley	2–11 (Boys 2–5)
St Catherine's School, Guildford	4–18
St Ives School, Haslemere	3–11 (Boys 3–5)
St Teresa's Preparatory School, Effingham	2–11
St Teresa's School, Dorking	11–18
Seaton House, Sutton	3–11 (Boys 3–5)
Sir William Perkins's School, Chertsey	11–18
Stanway School, Dorking	3–11 (Boys 3–8)
Surbiton High School, Kingston-upon-Thames	4–18 (Boys 4–11)
Sutton High School GDST, Sutton	4–18
Tormead School, Guildford	4–18
Wispers School for Girls, Haslemere	11–18
Woldingham School, Woldingham	11–18

EAST SUSSEX

Brighton and Hove High School GDST, Brighton	3–18
Moira House Junior School, Eastbourne	2–11
Moira House Girls' School, Eastbourne	11–18
Roedean School, Brighton	11–18
St Leonards-Mayfield School, Mayfield	11–18
St Mary's Hall, Brighton	3–18 (Boys 3–8)

WEST SUSSEX

Burgess Hill School for Girls, Burgess Hill	3–18 (Co-ed nursery)
Farlington School, Horsham	4–18
Lavant House Rosemead, Chichester	5–18
The Towers Convent School, Steyning	3–16 (Boys 3–11)

TYNE AND WEAR

Central Newcastle High School GDST, Newcastle upon Tyne	3–18
Dame Allan's Girls School, Newcastle upon Tyne (Co-ed VIth Form)	8–18
La Sagesse High School, Newcastle upon Tyne	3–18
Newcastle Upon Tyne Church High School, Newcastle upon Tyne	2–18
Westfield School, Newcastle upon Tyne	3–18

WARWICKSHIRE

The King's High School for Girls, Warwick	10–18
The Kingsley School, Leamington Spa	2–18 (Boys 2–7)

WEST MIDLANDS

Birchfield Independent Girls School, Birmingham	11–16
Coventry Muslim School, Coventry	4–16
Edgbaston High School for Girls, Birmingham	2–18
Highclare School, Birmingham	1–18 (Boys 1–11 & 16–18)
King Edward VI High School for Girls, Birmingham	11–18
Newbridge Preparatory School, Wolverhampton	3–11 (Boys 3–4)
Priory School, Birmingham	2–18 (Boys 2–11)
St Martin's School, Solihull	3–18

WILTSHIRE

The Godolphin Preparatory School, Salisbury	3–11
The Godolphin School, Salisbury	11–18
Leaden Hall, Salisbury	3–13 (Boys 3–4)
St Mary's School, Calne	11–18
Stonar School, Melksham	4–18

WORCESTERSHIRE

The Alice Ottley School, Worcester	3–19
Malvern Girls' College, Malvern	11–18
St James's School, Malvern	10–18
St Mary's Convent School, Worcester	2–18 (Boys 2–8)
Whitford Hall & Dodderhill School, Droitwich	3–16 (Boys 3–9)

EAST RIDING OF YORKSHIRE

Hull High School, Hull	3–18 (Boys 3–11)

NORTH YORKSHIRE

Harrogate Ladies' College, Harrogate	10–18
The Mount Senior School, York	11–18
Queen Margaret's School, York	11–18
Queen Mary's School, Thirsk	3–16 (Boys 3–7)

SOUTH YORKSHIRE

Ashdell Preparatory School, Sheffield	4–11
Brantwood Independent School for Girls, Sheffield	4–16
Sheffield High School GDST, Sheffield	4–18

WEST YORKSHIRE

Bradford Girls' Grammar School, Bradford	3–18
Gateways School, Leeds	3–18 (Boys 3–7)
Islamia Girls High School, Huddersfield	11–16
Leeds Girls' High School, Leeds	3–19
Leeds Islamia Girls' School, Leeds	11–16
Moorfield School, Ilkley	2–11
Wakefield Girls' High School, Wakefield	3–18 (Boys 3–7)

NORTHERN IRELAND

COUNTY ANTRIM

Hunterhouse College, Belfast	5–19
Victoria College Belfast, Belfast	4–18

SCOTLAND

ABERDEENSHIRE

Albyn School for Girls, Aberdeen	2–18 (Boys 2–5)
St Margaret's School for Girls, Aberdeen	3–18 (Boys 3–5)

GLASGOW

Craigholme School, Glasgow	3–18 (Boys 3–5)
Hutchesons' Lilybank Junior School, Glasgow	3–18 (Boys 3–5)

SOUTH LANARKSHIRE

Fernhill School, Rutherglen	4–18 (Boys 4–11)

LOTHIAN

The Mary Erskine School, Edinburgh	11–18
St George's School for Girls, Edinburgh	2–18 (Boys 2–5)
St Margaret's School, Edinburgh	3–18 (Boys 3–8)

PERTHSHIRE

Butterstone School, Blairgowrie	2–13 (Co-ed 3–7)
Kilgraston (A Sacred Heart School), Perth	5–18 (Boys day 2–9)

WALES

CARDIFF

Howell's School, Llandaff GDST, Cardiff	3–18

DENBIGHSHIRE

Howell's School, Denbigh	3–18

MONMOUTHSHIRE

Haberdashers' Monmouth School For Girls, Monmouth	7–18

4.5
RELIGIOUS AFFILIATION

The following index lists all schools specifying a particular denomination. However, it should be noted that this is intended as a guide only and that many of the schools listed also welcome children of other faiths. Schools which claim to be non- or inter-deonminational are not listed. Parents should check precise details with individual schools. A full list of each school's entries elsewhere in the book is given in the main index at the back.

BUDDHIST

Dharma School, Brighton

CHRISTIAN

Abinger Hammer Village School, Dorking
Alder Bridge School, Reading
Amberfield School, Ipswich
Ardvreck School, Crieff
The Ark School, Reading
Avondale School, Salisbury
Barnsley Christian School, Barnsley
Benedict House Preparatory School, Sidcup
Benty Heath School and Kindergarten, South Wirral
Berkhamsted Collegiate Preparatory School, Berkhamsted
Berkhamsted Collegiate School, Berkhamsted
Bradford Christian School, Bradford
Bromley High School GDST, Bromley
Broomwood Hall School, SW12
Castle Court Preparatory School, Wimborne
Castle House School, Newport
Caterham Preparatory School, Caterham
Caterham School, Caterham
Cedars School, Rochester
Cedars School, Aldermaston
Chase Academy, Cannock
Chorcliffe School, Chorley
Christ the King School, Sale
Claremont Fan Court School, Esher
Clifton Lodge Preparatory School, W5
Daiglen School, Buckhurst Hill
Dame Alice Harpur School, Bedford
Danes Hill Preparatory School, Leatherhead
Darvell School, Robertsbridge
Derby Grammar School for boys, Derby
Derwent Lodge School for Girls, Tonbridge
Ditcham Park School, Petersfield
Dolphin School, SW11
Dower House School, Bridgnorth
Downham Montessori School, Kings Lynn

Edgbaston College, Birmingham
Emmanual Christian School, Oxford
Emmanuel School, Exeter
Emmanuel School, Derby
Eversfield Preparatory School, Solihull
Falkner House, SW7
Filgrave School, Newport Pagnell
The Firs School, Chester
Fosse Bank New School, Tonbridge
The Froebelian School, Leeds
Gatehouse School, E2
Gateway Christian School, Ilkeston
Ghyll Royd School, Ilkley
The Grange, Worcester
Grange Park Preparatory School, N21
Grangewood Independent School, E7
Hamilton College, Hamilton
Handsworth Christian School, Sheffield
Haslemere Preparatory School, Haslemere
Herne Hill School, SE24
Heswall Preparatory School, Wirral
Hillgrove School, Bangor
Hydesville Tower School, Walsall
Joseph Rayner Independent School, Audenshaw
Kent College Pembury, Tunbridge Wells
Kimbolton School, Huntingdon
King of Kings School, Manchester
The King's School, Nottingham
King's School, Plymouth
The King's School Senior, Eastleigh
The King's School, Primary, Witney
Kings Primary School, Southampton
Kings School, Harpenden
Kingham Hill School, Chipping Norton
Kingsfold Christian School, Preston
Kingsmead School, Wirral
Kingsway School, Wigan
La Retraite Swan, Salisbury
Langley Manor School, Slough
Lincoln Minster School, Lincoln
Littlefield School, Liphook
Lorenden Preparatory School, Faversham

The Lyceum, EC2A
Maranatha Christian School, Swindon
Marlin Montessori School, Berkhamsted
Maypole House School, Alford
Meadowpark Nursery & Pre-Prep, Cricklade
Michael Hall, Forest Row
Monton Prep School with Montessori Nurseries, Eccles
Mount Zion (Christian Primary) School, Bristol
Mountjoy House School, Huddersfield
New Life Christian School, Croydon
Norfolk House Preparatory & Kids Corner Nursery, Sandbach
Norfolk House School, Birmingham
Northampton Christian School, Northampton
Notre Dame School, Lingfield
Oakleigh House, Swansea
Paragon Christian Academy, E5
The Park School, Yeovil
Phoenix School, Westoning
The Pointer School, SE3
The Portsmouth Grammar School, Portsmouth
Primrose Montessori School, N5
Priory School, Sandown
Rastrick Prep and Nursery School, Brighouse
Red House School, Norton
Rickmansworth PNEU School, Rickmansworth
River School, Worcester
Sacred Heart Preparatory School, Chew Magna
St Andrew's Montessori School, Watford
St Aubyn's School, Woodford Green
St Aubyn's School, Tiverton
St Christophers School, Totnes
St Crispin's School (Leicester) Ltd., Leicester
St Francis de Sales Prep School, Tring
St Francis' College, Letchworth
St Helen's School for Girls, Northwood
St Hilda's School, Westcliff-on-Sea
St John's Senior School, Enfield
St Joseph's College, Ipswich
St Mary's Preparatory School, Lincoln
St Mary's Westbrook, Folkestone
St Oswald's School, Alnwick
Scarborough College Junior School, Scarborough
School of the Lion, Gloucester
Sherborne House School, Eastleigh
Stanway School, Dorking
Stoneygate College, Leicester
Stowford, Sutton
Sunflower Montessori School, Twickenham
Sunninghill Preparatory School, Dorchester
The Ark School, Reading
Thomas's Kindergarten, SW1W
Torwood House School, Redland
Trinity School, Stalybridge
Twickenham Preparatory School, Hampton
Victoria College, Jersey
Vine School, Southampton
Wakefield Tutorial Preparatory School, Leeds
Warlingham Park School, Croydon
Warwick Preparatory School, Warwick
Wellspring Christian School, Carlisle
Westbury House, New Malden
Westmont School, Newport
Weston Green School, Thames Ditton
Willington School, SW19

Woodford Green Preparatory School, Woodford Green
Yardley Court, Tonbridge
Yarm School, Yarm

CHRISTIAN ROMAN CATHOLIC

La Sagesse High School, Newcastle upon Tyne
St Thomas Garnet's School, Bournemouth

CHURCH IN WALES

The Cathedral School, Cardiff
Christ College, Brecon
Llandovery College, Llandovery
Lyndon School, Colwyn Bay

CHURCH OF ENGLAND

Abberley Hall, Worcester
Abbey Gate College, Chester
Abbey Gate School, Chester
The Abbey School, Tewkesbury
The Abbey School, Reading
The Abbey, Woodbridge
Abbot's Hill, Hemel Hempstead
Abbotsbury School, Newton Abbot
Aberdour School, Tadworth
Abingdon School, Abingdon
Acorn School, Nailsworth
Adcote School for Girls, Shrewsbury
Airthrie School, Cheltenham
Aldenham School, Elstree
Aldro School, Godalming
Aldwickbury School, Harpenden
The Alice Ottley School, Worcester
Alleyn Court Preparatory School, Southend-on-Sea
Alleyn's School, SE22
Amesbury, Hindhead
Arden Lawn, Solihull
Ardingly College, Haywards Heath
Ardingly College Junior School, Haywards Heath
Arnold House School, NW8
Arnold Lodge School, Leamington Spa
Ashbourne PNEU School, Ashbourne
Ashdown House School, Forest Row
The Atherley School, Southampton
Attenborough Preparatory School, Nottingham
Aysgarth Preparatory School, Bedale
Ballard School, New Milton
Bancroft's School, Woodford Green
Barfield School, Farnham
Barnardiston Hall Preparatory School, Haverhill
Baston School, Bromley
Beachborough School, Brackley
The Beacon School, Amersham
Bearwood College, Wokingham
Beaudesert Park, Stroud
Bedford Preparatory School, Bedford
Bedford School, Bedford
Bedgebury School, Cranbrook
Bedstone College, Bucknell
Beech Hall School, Macclesfield
Beechenhurst Preparatory School, Liverpool

Beechwood Park School, St Albans
Beeston Hall School, Cromer
Bellan House Preparatory School, Oswestry
Belmont School, Dorking
Benenden School, Cranbrook
Berkhampstead School, Cheltenham
Bethany School, Cranbrook
Bilton Grange, Rugby
Birchfield School, Wolverhampton
Bloxham School, Banbury
The Blue Coat School, Birmingham
Blundell's School, Tiverton
Bodiam Manor School, Robertsbridge
The Bolitho School, Penzance
Bow School, Durham
Bradfield College, Reading
Bradford Grammar School, Bradford
Brambletye School, East Grinstead
Bramcote Lorne School, Retford
Bramcote School, Scarborough
Bramley School, Tadworth
Bredon School, Tewkesbury
Brentwood School, Brentwood
Brigg Preparatory School, Brigg
Brighton College, Brighton
Brighton College Pre-preparatory School, Brighton
Brighton College Prep School, Brighton
Bristol Cathedral School, Bristol
Broadwater Manor School, Worthing
Brockhurst & Marlston House Pre-Preparatory School,
    Newbury
Brockhurst School, Newbury
Bromsgrove Lower School, Bromsgrove
Bromsgrove Pre-preparatory and Nursery School,
    Bromsgrove
Bromsgrove School, Bromsgrove
Bronte School, Gravesend
Brookland Hall School & Golf Academy, Welshpool
Broomfield House, Richmond
Bryanston School, Blandford Forum
Buckingham College Preparatory School, Pinner
Burys Court School, Reigate
Cable House School, Woking
Caldicott School, Farnham Royal
Cameron House, SW3
Casterton School, Carnforth
Chafyn Grove School, Salisbury
Chard School, Chard
Charterhouse, Godalming
Cheam School, Newbury
Cheltenham College, Cheltenham
Cheltenham College Junior School, Cheltenham
Chigwell School, Chigwell
Chilton Cantelo School, Yeovil
The Chorister School, Durham
Christ Church Cathedral School, Oxford
Christs Hospital, Horsham
Claremont School, St Leonards-on-Sea
Clayesmore Preparatory School, Blandford Forum
Clayesmore School, Blandford Forum
Clifton College, Bristol
Clifton College Preparatory School, Bristol
Colfe's School, SE12
Colston's Collegiate School, Bristol
Conway Preparatory School, Boston

Coopersale Hall School, Epping
Copthorne School, Copthorne
Cothill House Preparatory School, Abingdon
Cottesmore School, Pease Pottage
Coventry Preparatory School, Coventry
Cranford House School, Wallingford
Cranleigh Preparatory School, Cranleigh
Cranleigh School, Cranleigh
The Crescent School, Rugby
The Croft School, Stratford-upon-Avon
Cumnor House School, South Croydon
Cumnor House School, Haywards Heath
Cundall Manor School, York
Dair House School Trust Ltd, Farnham Royal
Daneshill House, Basingstoke
Dean Close Preparatory School, Cheltenham
Dean Close School, Cheltenham
Deepdene School, Hove
Denmead School, Hampton
Denstone College, Uttoxeter
Derby High School, Derby
The Dormer House PNEU School, Moreton-in-Marsh
Dorset House School, Pulborough
Dover College, Dover
Downe House School, Newbury
Dragon School, Oxford
Duke of Kent School, Ewhurst
Duke of York's Royal Military School, Dover
Dulwich College, SE21
Dulwich College Preparatory School, SE21
Dulwich Preparatory School, Cranbrook, Cranbrook
Dumpton School, Wimborne
Duncombe School, Hertford
Durham High School For Girls, Durham
Durham School, Durham
Durlston Court, New Milton
Eagle House, Sandhurst
Eastbourne College, Eastbourne
Edenhurst School, Newcastle-under-Lyme
Edge Grove, Aldenham
Edgeborough, Farnham
Edgehill School, Newark
Elizabeth College, Guernsey
Ellesmere College, Ellesmere
Elmhurst, The School for Dance & Performing Arts,
    Camberley
The Elms, Malvern
Elstree School, Reading
Emanuel School, SW11
Epsom College, Epsom
Eton End PNEU, Slough
Ewell Castle School, Epsom
Exeter Cathedral School, Exeter
Exeter Junior School, Exeter
Exeter School, Exeter
Fairfield PNEU School, Bristol
Farlington School, Horsham
Felsted Preparatory School, Dunmow
Felsted School, Dunmow
Feltonfleet School, Cobham
The Fen Preparatory School, Sleaford
Flexlands School, Woking
Fonthill Lodge, East Grinstead
Foremarke Hall, Derby
Forest Girls' School, E17

Forest Preparatory School, E17
Forest School, E17
Forres Sandle Manor, Fordingbridge
Foxley PNEU School, Reading
Framlingham College, Woodbridge
Framlingham College Junior School, Brandeston
Francis Holland School, SW1W
Francis Holland School, NW1
Friars School, Ashford
Gayhurst School, Gerrards Cross
Giggleswick School, Settle
Glebe House School, Hunstanton
The Godolphin School, Salisbury
Godstowe Preparatory School, High Wycombe
Great Ballard School, Chichester
Grenville College, Bideford
Gresham's Preparatory School, Holt
Gresham's School, Holt
Grey House Preparatory School, Basingstoke
Guildford High School (Church Schools Co), Guildford
Haberdashers' Aske's Boys' School, Elstree
Haberdashers' Aske's School for Girls, Elstree
Haileybury, Hertford
The Hall School, NW3
Halstead Preparatory School, Woking
Hammond School, Chester
Handcross Park School, Haywards Heath
Hanford School, Blandford Forum
Harrogate Ladies' College, Harrogate
Harrow School, Harrow on the Hill
Hatherop Castle School, Cirencester
Hazelwood School, Oxted
Hazlegrove (King's Bruton Preparatory School), Yeovil
Headington School Oxford, Oxford
Heath Mount School, Hertford
Heathfield School, Ascot
Heathland College, Accrington
Helvetia House School, Jersey
Hemdean House School, Reading
The Hereford Cathedral Junior School, Hereford
The Hereford Cathedral School, Hereford
Hethersett Old Hall School, Norwich
Highfield Preparatory School, Harrogate
Highfield School, Liphook
Highgate Junior School, N6
Highgate Pre-Preparatory School, N6
Highgate School, N6
Hilden Grange School, Tonbridge
Hilden Oaks School, Tonbridge
Hillcroft Preparatory School, Stowmarket
Hillstone School (Malvern College), Malvern
Holme Grange School, Wokingham
Holme Park Preparatory School, Kendal
Hordle Walhampton School, Lymington
Hull Grammar School, Kingston-Upon-Hull
Hull High School, Hull
Hurlingham Private School, SW15
Hurstpierpoint College, Hassocks
Innellan House School, Pinner
Ipswich School, Ipswich
James Allen's Girls' School, SE22
James Allen's Preparatory School, SE22
The Jordans Nursery School, W6
Junior King's School, Canterbury
The Junior School, St Lawrence College, Ramsgate

Kelly College, Tavistock
Kelly College Junior School, Tavistock
King Edward's School, Birmingham
King William's College, Castletown
King's College, Taunton
King's College Junior School, SW19
King's College School, SW19
King's Hall School, Taunton
King's Hawford, Worcester
King's Preparatory School, Rochester, Rochester
The King's School, Chester
The King's School, Macclesfield
King's School, Bruton
The King's School, Canterbury
The King's School, Ely
The King's School, Gloucester
King's School Rochester, Rochester
The King's School, Worcester
Kingscote School, Gerrards Cross
Kingshott, Hitchin
Kingsland Grange, Shrewsbury
The Kingsley School, Leamington Spa
Kingston Grammar School, Kingston-upon-Thames
The Knoll School, Kidderminster
The Lady Eleanor Holles School, Hampton
Lambrook Haileybury, Bracknell
Lanesborough, Guildford
Lanherne Nursery and Junior School, Dawlish
Lavant House Rosemead, Chichester
Leicester Grammar Junior School, Leicester
Leicester Grammar School, Leicester
Leicester High School For Girls, Leicester
Lichfield Cathedral School, Lichfield
The Littlemead School, Chichester
Liverpool College, Liverpool
Lockers Park, Hemel Hempstead
Long Close School, Slough
Luckley-Oakfield School, Wokingham
Ludgrove, Wokingham
Magdalen College School, Oxford
Maidwell Hall, Northampton
The Mall School, Twickenham
Malsis School, Skipton
Malvern College, Malvern
Malvern Girls' College, Malvern
Manor Preparatory School, Abingdon
Mansfield Infant College, Ilford
Marlborough House School, Hawkhurst
Marlston House School, Newbury
Meadowbrook Montessori School, Bracknell
Merchant Taylors' School, Northwood
Merton Court Preparatory School, Sidcup
Merton House (Downswood), Chester
Milbourne Lodge School, Esher
Millbrook House, Abingdon
Milton Abbey School, Blandford Forum
The Minster School, York
Monkton Combe Junior School, Bath
Monkton Combe School, Bath
Moorland School, Clitheroe
Moreton Hall, Oswestry
Morley Hall Preparatory School, Derby
Moulsford Preparatory School, Wallingford
Mount House School, Tavistock
Mowden Hall School, Stocksfield

Mowden School, Hove
Netherwood School, Saundersfoot
The New Beacon, Sevenoaks
New College School, Oxford
New School, Exeter
Newcastle Upon Tyne Church High School,
    Newcastle upon Tyne
Norfolk House School, N10
Norman Court Preparatory School, Salisbury
North Foreland Lodge, Basingstoke
Northampton High School, Northampton
Northbourne Park School, Deal
Northcote Lodge, SW11
Northwood Preparatory School, Rickmansworth
Nower Lodge School, Dorking
Oakham School, Oakham
Oaklands School, Loughton
Oakwood School, Chichester
Old Buckenham Hall School, Ipswich
The Old Hall School, Telford
The Old Malthouse, Swanage
Old Palace School of John Whitgift, Croydon
The Old School, Beccles
Old Vicarage School, Richmond
Oriel Bank High School, Stockport
Orley Farm School, Harrow
Oundle School, Peterborough
Oundle School Laxton Junior, Peterborough
Packwood Haugh, Shrewsbury
Pangbourne College, Reading
Papplewick, Ascot
Park Hill School, Kingston-upon-Thames
Parkside School, Northampton
Parsons Mead, Ashtead
Peaslake School, Guildford
Pennthorpe School, Horsham
Perrott Hill School, Crewkerne
The Perse School, Cambridge
Peterborough & St Margaret's School, Stanmore
Peterborough High School, Peterborough
Pilgrims Pre-Preparatory School, Bedford
The Pilgrims' School, Winchester
Pinewood School, Swindon
Pipers Corner School, High Wycombe
Plumtree School, Nottingham
Pocklington School, Pocklington
The Prebendal School, Chichester
Prebendal School (Northgate House), Chichester
Prestfelde Preparatory School, Shrewsbury
Prince's Mead School, Winchester
The Princess Helena College, Hitchin
Putney Park School, SW15
Quainton Hall School, Harrow
Queen Anne's School, Reading
Queen Elizabeth's Grammar School, Blackburn
Queen Ethelburga's College, York
Queen Margaret's School, York
Queen Mary's School, Thirsk
Queen's College, W1N
The Querns School, Cirencester
Radley College, Abingdon
Ranby House, Retford
Rathvilly School, Birmingham
Ravenscourt Theatre School, W6
Read School, Selby

Reading Blue Coat School, Reading
Red House School, York
Reddiford, Pinner
Reed's School, Cobham
Reigate St Mary's Preparatory and Choir School, Reigate
Rendcomb College, Cirencester
Repton School, Repton
Riddlesworth Hall, Diss
Ripon Cathedral Choir School, Ripon
Rishworth School, Rishworth
Robert Gordons College, Aberdeen
Rock Hall School, Alnwick
Rodney School, Newark
Roedean School, Brighton
Rose Hill School, Wotton-under-Edge
Roselyon Preparatory School, Par
Rossall Preparatory School, Fleetwood
Rossall School, Fleetwood
Rosslyn School, Birmingham
Roxeth Mead School, Harrow
The Royal Masonic School for Girls, Rickmansworth
Royal Russell School, Croydon
Royal School Haslemere, Haslemere
The Royal Wolverhampton Junior School,
    Wolverhampton
The Royal Wolverhampton School, Wolverhampton
Rugby School, Rugby
Rushmoor School, Bedford
Russell House School, Sevenoaks
Ruthin School, Ruthin
Ryde School, Ryde
Sackville School, Tonbridge
Saddleworth Preparatory School, Oldham
St Agnes PNEU School, Leeds
St Albans High School for Girls, St Albans
St Andrew's School, Eastbourne
St Andrew's School, Reading
St Andrew's School, Rochester
St Andrew's School, Woking
St Anselm's, Bakewell
St Aubyn's, Brighton
St Bede's, Eastbourne
St Bees School, St Bees
St Catherine's School, Guildford
St Christopher's, Burnham-on-Sea
St Christopher's School, Epsom
St Christopher's School, Hove
St Christopher's School, Wembley
St Colette's School, Cambridge
St David's School, Ashford
St David's School, Purley
St Dunstan's Abbey School, Plymouth
St Dunstan's College, SE6
St Edmund's Junior School, Canterbury
St Edmund's School, Canterbury
St Edmund's School, Hindhead
St Edward's School, Oxford
St Elphin's School, Matlock
St Francis Preparatory School, Drifield
St Francis School, Pewsey
St Gabriel's School, Newbury
St George's School, Ascot
St George's School, Windsor
St George's School, Edgbaston, Birmingham
St Hilda's School, Harpenden

St Hilda's School, Wakefield
St Hugh's School, Faringdon
St Hugh's School, Woodhall Spa
St Ives School, Haslemere
St James' School, Grimsby
St James's School, Malvern
St John's College School, Cambridge
St John's Northwood, Northwood
St John's Preparatory School, Lichfield
St John's School, Leatherhead
St John's School, Sidmouth
St John's-on-the-Hill, Chepstow
St Lawrence College, Ramsgate
St Margaret's School, NW3
St Margaret's School, Bushey
St Martin's Independent School, Crewkerne
St Martin's School, Bournemouth
St Martin's School, Northwood
St Mary's Hall, Brighton
St Mary's School, Gerrards Cross
St Mary's School, Calne
St Mary's School, Colchester
St Mary's School, Wantage
St Michael's, Barnstaple
St Michael's School, Sevenoaks
St Michael's School, Leigh-on-Sea
St Neot's School, Hook
St Nicholas House, Hemel Hempstead
St Nicholas School, Fleet
St Olave's Preparatory School, SE9
St Olave's School (Junior of St Peter's), York
St Paul's Cathedral School, EC4M
St Paul's Preparatory School, SW13
St Paul's School, SW13
St Peter's School, Kettering
St Peter's School, York
St Petroc's School, Bude
St Piran's Preparatory School, Maidenhead
St Ronan's, Hawkhurst
St Swithun's School, Winchester
St Wilfrid's School, Exeter
St Wystan's School, Repton
Salisbury Cathedral School, Salisbury
Sancton Wood School, Cambridge
Sanderstead Junior School, South Croydon
Sandroyd, Salisbury
Sarum Hall, NW3
Saville House School, Mansfield
School of St Helen & St Katharine, Abingdon
School of St Mary and St Anne, Abbots Bromley
Seaford College, Petworth
Sedbergh School, Sedbergh
Shaw House School, Bradford
Sherborne Preparatory School, Sherborne
Sherborne School, Sherborne
Sherborne School for Girls, Sherborne
Sherrardswood School, Welwyn
Shiplake College, Henley-on-Thames
Shoreham College, Shoreham-by-Sea
Shrewsbury House School, Surbiton
Shrewsbury School, Shrewsbury
Silchester House School, Maidenhead
Smallwood Manor Preparatory School, Uttoxeter
Snaresbrook College Preparatory School, E18
Solefield School, Sevenoaks

Solihull School, Solihull
Sompting Abbotts, Sompting
Southdown Nursery, Steyning
Spratton Hall, Northampton
Starting Points Pre-School, Halesworth
Steephill School, Longfield
Stepping Stones Nursery and Pre-Preparatory School, Marlborough
Stoke Brunswick, East Grinstead
Stonelands School of Ballet & Theatre Arts, Hove
Stoneygate School, Leicester
Stourbridge House School, Warminster
Stover School, Newton Abbot
Stowe School, Buckingham
The Stroud School, Romsey
The Study School, New Malden
Summer Fields, Oxford
Sunderland High School, Sunderland
Sunningdale School, Sunningdale
Sunnyside School, Worcester
Surbiton High School, Kingston-upon-Thames
Surbiton Preparatory School, Surbiton
Sussex House School, SW1X
Sutton Valence Preparatory School, Maidstone
Sutton Valence School, Maidstone
Swanbourne House School, Milton Keynes
Talbot Heath, Bournemouth
Taverham Hall, Norwich
Temple Grove, Uckfield
Thomas's Kindergarten, Battersea, SW11
Thomas's Preparatory School, SW11
Thomas's Preparatory School Clapham, SW11
Thorpe Hall School, Southend-on-Sea
Thorpe House School, Gerrards Cross
Tockington Manor School, Bristol
Tonbridge School, Tonbridge
Town Close House Preparatory School, Norwich
Trent College, Nottingham
Trentvale Preparatory School, Keadby
Trevor Roberts', NW3
Truro High School, Truro
Tudor Hall School, Banbury
Twyford School, Winchester
Uplands School, Poole
Uppingham School, Uppingham
Upton House School, Windsor
Victoria Park Preparatory School, Shipley
Wakefield Independent School, Wakefield
Warminster School, Warminster
Warwick School, Warwick
Wellesley House School, Broadstairs
Wellingborough School, Wellingborough
Wellington College, Crowthorne
Wellington School, Wellington
Wells Cathedral Junior School, Wells
Wells Cathedral School, Wells
West Buckland Preparatory School, Barnstaple
West Buckland School, Barnstaple
Westbourne House School, Chichester
Westbrook Hay, Hemel Hempstead
Westminster Abbey Choir School, SW1P
Westminster School, SW1P
Westminster Under School, SW1P
Weston Favell Montessori Nursery School, Northampton
Westonbirt School, Tetbury

Whitford Hall & Dodderhill School, Droitwich
Widford Lodge, Chelmsford
The Willow School, SW8
Winchester College, Winchester
Winchester House School, Brackley
Winchester House School Pre-Prep, Brackley
Windlesham House, Pulborough
Wisbech Grammar School, Wisbech
Witham Hall, Bourne
Wolborough Hill School, Newton Abbot
Wood Dene School, Norwich
Woodbridge School, Woodbridge
Woodleigh School, Malton
Worksop College, Worksop
Wrekin College, Telford
Wycombe Abbey School, High Wycombe
Wykeham House School, Fareham
Yateley Manor Preparatory School, Yateley
York House School, Rickmansworth
Yorston Lodge School, Knutsford

CHURCH OF SCOTLAND

Butterstone School, Blairgowrie
The Glasgow Academy, Glasgow
Queen Victoria School, Dunblane

EPISCOPELIAN

Glenalmond College, Perth

GREEK ORTHODOX

Hellenic College of London, SW1X

HEBREW

The Kerem School, N2

JEWISH

Akiva School, N3
CKHR Immanuel College, Bushey
Clifton College, Clifton (1 Jewish House)
Jewish High School for Girls, Salford
Kerem House, N2
The Kerem School, N2
Lubavitch House Senior School for Girls, N16
Mechinah Liyeshivah Zichron Moshe, N16
Menorah Grammar School, Edgware
Naima Jewish Preparatory School, NW6
Pardes Grammar Boys' School, N3
Tashbar Primary School, Salford
Yesodey Hatorah Jewish School, N16
Yetev Lev Day School for Boys, N16

METHODIST

Ashville College, Harrogate
Bronte House School, Bradford

Culford School, Bury St Edmunds
Edgehill College, Bideford
Farringtons & Stratford House, Chislehurst
Kent College, Canterbury
Kingswood Preparatory School, Bath
Kingswood School, Bath
The Leys School, Cambridge
Queen's College, Taunton
Queen's College Junior and Pre-Preparatory Schools, Taunton
Rydal Penrhos Preparatory School, Colwyn Bay
Rydal Penrhos Senior School, Colwyn Bay
Shebbear College, Beaworthy
Treliske School, Truro
Truro School, Truro
Vernon Holme (Kent College Infant & Junior School), Canterbury
Woodhouse Grove School, Apperley Bridge

MORAVIAN

Fulneck School, Pudsey

MUSLIM

Al Hijrah School, Birmingham
Al Karam Secondary School, Retford
Al-Muntada Islamic School, SW6
Balham Preparatory School, SW12
Birchfield Independent Girls School, Birmingham
Bolton Muslim Girls School, Bolton
Brondesbury College For Boys, NW6
Coventry Muslim School, Coventry
Darul Uloom Islamic High School & College, Birmingham
Gloucestershire Islamic Secondary School For Girls, Gloucester
Islamia Girls High School, Huddersfield
Islamia Girls School, NW6
Jamahiriya School, SW3
Leeds Islamia Girls' School, Leeds
Manchester Islamic High School, Manchester
Tayyibah Girls School, N16

QUAKER

Ackworth School, Pontefract
Bootham School, York
Friends' School, Saffron Walden
The Hall Pre-Preparatory School Sidcot, Winscombe
Leighton Park School, Reading
The Mount Junior School, York
The Mount Senior School, York
Sibford School, Banbury
Sidcot School, Winscombe

ROMAN CATHOLIC

Alderley Edge School for Girls, Alderley Edge
All Hallows, Shepton Mallet
Alton Convent School, Alton

Ampleforth College, York
Austin Friars School, Carlisle
Barlborough Hall School, Chesterfield
Barrow Hills School, Godalming
Beechwood Sacred Heart, Tunbridge Wells
Bishop Challoner School, Bromley
The Brigidine School, Windsor
Bury Catholic Preparatory School, Bury
Carleton House Preparatory School, Liverpool
The Cavendish School, NW1
Claires Court School, Maidenhead
Claires Court Schools, The College, Maidenhead
Combe Bank School, Sevenoaks
Convent of Mercy, Guernsey
Cranmore School, Leatherhead
Downside School, Bath
Farleigh School, Andover
Farnborough Hill, Farnborough
FCJ Primary School, Jersey
Fernhill School, Rutherglen
Grace Dieu Manor School, Leicester
Holy Cross Convent, Gerrards Cross
Holy Cross Preparatory School, Kingston-upon-Thames
Holy Trinity College, Bromley
Holy Trinity School, Kidderminster
Kilgraston (A Sacred Heart School), Perth
Laleham Lea Preparatory School, Purley
Loreto Preparatory School, Altrincham
Loyola Preparatory School, Buckhurst Hill
Marist Convent Senior School, Ascot
Marymount Convent School, Wallasey
Marymount International School,
    Kingston-upon-Thames
Moor Park School, Ludlow
More House, SW1X
Moreton Hall Preparatory School, Bury St Edmunds
Mount St Mary's College, Spinkhill
Mylnhurst RC School & Nursery, Sheffield
New Hall School, Chelmsford
Notre Dame Preparatory School, Norwich
Notre Dame Preparatory School, Cobham
Notre Dame Senior School, Cobham
Oakhill College, Clitheroe
Oakwood, Purley
The Oratory Preparatory School, Reading
The Oratory School, Reading
Our Lady of Sion School, Worthing
Our Lady's Convent Junior School, Abingdon
Our Lady's Convent Preparatory School, Kettering
Our Lady's Convent School, Loughborough
Our Lady's Convent Senior School, Abingdon
Our Lady's Preparatory School, Crowthorne
Presentation College, Reading
Prior Park College, Bath
Prior Park Preparatory School, Cricklade
Ratcliffe College, Leicester
Ridgeway School (Claires Court Junior), Maidenhead
Rydes Hill Preparatory School, Guildford
Sacred Heart Convent School, Swaffham
Sacred Heart R.C. Primary School, Wadhurst
St Ambrose Preparatory School, Altrincham
St Anthony's Preparatory School, NW3
St Anthonys School, Cinderford
St Antony's-Leweston Preparatory School, Sherborne
St Antony's-Leweston School, Sherborne

St Augustine's Priory, W5
St Benedict's Junior School, W5
St Benedict's School, W5
St Bernard's Preparatory School, Slough
St Catherine's Preparatory School, Stockport
St Catherine's School, Twickenham
St Catherines Preparatory School, Cambridge
St Christina's RC Preparatory School, NW8
St Clare's Convent School, Porthcawl
St Columba's College, St Albans
St Dominic's Independent Junior School,
    Stoke-on-Trent
St Dominic's Priory School, Stone
St Dominic's School, Stafford
St Edmund's College, Ware
St Edward's Junior School Runnymede, Liverpool
St Edward's School, Cheltenham
St George's College, Weybridge
St George's College Junior School, Weybridge
St Gerard's School, Bangor
St John's Beaumont, Windsor
St John's College, Southsea
St John's School, Sidmouth
St Joseph's Convent, Chesterfield
St Joseph's Convent School, E11
St Joseph's Convent School, Reading
St Joseph's Convent School, Burnley
St Joseph's Preparatory School, Stoke-on-Trent
St Joseph's School, Nottingham
St Leonards-Mayfield School, Mayfield
St Margaret's School Convent of Mercy, Midhurst
St Martha's Senior School, Barnet
St Mary's College, Southampton
St Mary's College, Liverpool
St Mary's Convent School, Worcester
St Mary's Hall, Stonyhurst
St Mary's School, Shaftesbury
St Mary's School, Cambridge
St Mary's School, Ascot, Ascot
St Mary's School Hampstead, NW3
St Michaels School, Newbury
St Monica's School, Carlisle
St Philip's School, SW7
St Philomena's Preparatory School,
    Frinton-on-Sea
St Pius X Preparatory School, Preston
St Richard's, Bromyard
St Teresa's School, Dorking
St Teresa's Preparatory School, Effingham
St Teresa's School, Princes Risborough
St Ursula's High School, Bristol
St Winefride's Convent School, Shrewsbury
Salesian College, Farnborough
Sinclair House School, SW6
Stella Maris Junior School, Stockport
Stonyhurst College, Clitheroe
Thornton College Convent of Jesus and Mary,
    Milton Keynes
The Towers Convent School, Steyning
Ursuline Convent Preparatory School, SW20
Virgo Fidelis Convent, SE19
Vita Et Pax School, N14
Westminster Cathedral Choir School, SW1P
Wimbledon College Prep School, SW19
Winterfold House, Kidderminster

Woldingham School, Woldingham
Worth School, Turners Hill

Newbold School, Bracknell
Stanborough School, Watford

SEVENTH DAY ADVENTIST

Dudley House School, Grantham
Fletewood School, Plymouth
Hyland House, E17

UNITED REFORMED CHURCH

Silcoates School, Wakefield
Sunny Hill House School, Wakefield

4.6
PROVISION FOR DYSLEXIA

The index is intended as a general guide only and is compiled upon the basis of information given to Gabbitas by schools. Parents should note that there are wide variations in provision. Some schools offer dedicated special needs; others provide more limited help. In some cases, dyslexic pupils, although offered additional help once enrolled, may be expected to meet the school's normal entrance requirements. Parents are therefore advised to contact individual schools to establish the precise nature and extent of provision offered. Help may also be obtained from the Council for Registration of Schools Teaching Dyslexic Pupils (CReSTeD), the British Dyslexia Association and the Dyslexia Institute (see the reference section for details). * denotes a school registered with CReSTeD (Autumn 2001).

ENGLAND

BEDFORDSHIRE

Bedford High School, Bedford
Bedford Modern School, Bedford
Bedford Preparatory School, Bedford
Bedford School, Bedford
Broadmead School, Luton
Moorlands School, Luton
Polam School, Bedford
Rushmoor School, Bedford

BERKSHIRE

The Abbey School, Reading
Alder Bridge School, Reading
Bearwood College, Wokingham
Bradfield College, Reading
The Brigidine School, Windsor
Brockhurst School, Newbury
Cheam School, Newbury
Claires Court School, Maidenhead
Claires Court Schools, The College, Maidenhead
Dolphin School, Reading
Downe House School, Newbury
Eagle House, Sandhurst
Elstree School, Reading
Eton College, Windsor
Eton End PNEU, Slough
Foxley PNEU School, Reading
Greenhill Pre-Prep and Nursery School, Newbury
Hemdean House School, Reading
Herries School, Maidenhead

Highfield School, Maidenhead
The Highlands School, Reading
Holme Grange School, Wokingham
Hurst Lodge, Ascot *
Lambrook Haileybury, Bracknell
Langley Manor School, Slough
Leighton Park School, Reading
Licensed Victuallers' School, Ascot
Long Close School, Slough
Luckley-Oakfield School, Wokingham
Ludgrove, Wokingham
Marist Convent Senior School, Ascot
Marlston House School, Newbury
The Oratory Preparatory School, Reading
The Oratory School, Reading
Our Lady's Preparatory School, Crowthorne
Pangbourne College, Reading
Presentation College, Reading
Queen Anne's School, Reading
Reading Blue Coat School, Reading
Ridgeway School (Claires Court Junior), Maidenhead
St Andrew's School, Reading
St Bernard's Preparatory School, Slough
St Edward's School, Reading
St Gabriel's School, Newbury
St George's School, Ascot
St George's School, Windsor
St John's Beaumont, Windsor
St Joseph's Convent School, Reading
St Mary's School, Ascot, Ascot
St Michaels School, Newbury
St Piran's Preparatory School, Maidenhead

Silchester House School, Maidenhead
Sunningdale School, Sunningdale
Thorngrove School, Newbury
Upton House School, Windsor
Waverley School, Wokingham
Wellington College, Crowthorne
White House Preparatory School, Wokingham

BRISTOL

Badminton School, Bristol
Bristol Cathedral School, Bristol
Bristol Grammar School, Bristol
Cleve House School, Bristol
Clifton College, Bristol
Clifton College Preparatory School, Bristol*
Clifton High School, Bristol
Colston's Collegiate School, Bristol
Colston's Girls' School, Bristol
The Downs School, Bristol
Mount Zion (Christian Primary) School, Bristol
Queen Elizabeth's Hospital, Bristol
Redland High School, Bristol
Sacred Heart Preparatory School, Chew Magna
St Ursula's High School, Bristol
Tockington Manor School, Bristol

BUCKINGHAMSHIRE

Akeley Wood Junior School, Milton Keynes
Akeley Wood School, Buckingham
Ashfold School, Aylesbury
The Beacon School, Amersham
Bury Lawn School, Milton Keynes
Caldicott School, Farnham Royal
The Charmandean Dyslexia Centre, Buckingham
Chesham Preparatory School, Chesham
Crown House School, High Wycombe
Dair House School Trust Ltd, Farnham Royal
Davenies School, Beaconsfield
Filgrave School, Newport Pagnell
Gateway School, Great Missenden
Gayhurst School, Gerrards Cross
Godstowe Preparatory School, High Wycombe
High March School, Beaconsfield
Holy Cross Convent, Gerrards Cross
Kingscote School, Gerrards Cross
Ladymede, Aylesbury
Milton Keynes Preparatory School, Milton Keynes
St Mary's School, Gerrards Cross
St Teresa's School, Princes Risborough
Stowe School, Buckingham
Swanbourne House School, Milton Keynes
Thornton College Convent of Jesus and Mary,
  Milton Keynes
Thorpe House School, Gerrards Cross

CAMBRIDGESHIRE

Cambridge Arts & Sciences (CATS), Cambridge
Cambridge Centre for VIth Form Studies (CCSS),
  Cambridge

Horlers Pre-Preparatory School, Cambridge
Kimbolton School, Huntingdon
The King's School, Ely*
Kirkstone House School, Peterborough
The Leys School, Cambridge
Mander Portman Woodward, Cambridge
Oundle School, Peterborough
Oundle School Laxton Junior, Peterborough
The Perse School for Girls, Cambridge
Peterborough High School, Peterborough
St Andrew's, Cambridge
St Catherines Preparatory School, Cambridge
St Faiths School, Cambridge
St John's College School, Cambridge
St Mary's School, Cambridge
Sancton Wood School, Cambridge
Whitehall School, Huntingdon
Wisbech Grammar School, Wisbech

CHANNEL ISLANDS

St George's Preparatory School, Jersey
St Michael's Preparatory School, Jersey
Victoria College, Jersey

CHESHIRE

Abbey Gate School, Chester
Alderley Edge School for Girls, Alderley Edge
Beech Hall School, Macclesfield
Cransley School, Northwich
Culcheth Hall, Altrincham
The Firs School, Chester
Greenbank, Cheadle
Hammond School, Chester
Hillcrest Grammar School, Stockport
Hulme Hall Schools, Cheadle
Hulme Hall Schools (Junior section), Cheadle
The King's School, Macclesfield
Lady Barn House School, Cheadle
Loreto Preparatory School, Altrincham
Merton House (Downswood), Chester
Mostyn House School, South Wirral
North Cestrian Grammar School, Altrincham
Oriel Bank High School, Stockport
The Queen's School, Chester
Ramillies Hall School, Cheadle*
The Ryleys, Alderley Edge
Terra Nova School, Holmes Chapel
Trinity School, Stalybridge
Woodford Prep & Nursery School, Stockport
Yorston Lodge School, Knutsford

CORNWALL

The Bolitho School, Penzance
Polwhele House School, Truro
Roselyon Preparatory School, Par
St Joseph's School, Launceston
St Petroc's School, Bude
St Piran's School, Truro
Treliske School, Truro

Truro High School, Truro
Truro School, Truro
Wheelgate House School, Newquay

CUMBRIA

Austin Friars School, Carlisle
Casterton School, Carnforth
Harecroft Hall School, Seascale
Holme Park Preparatory School, Kendal
Lime House School, Carlisle
Our Lady's, Chetwynde, Barrow-in-Furness
St Bees School, St Bees*
St Ursulas Convent School, Wigton
Sedbergh School, Sedbergh
Wellspring Christian School, Carlisle
Windermere St Anne's School, Windermere

DERBYSHIRE

Ashbourne PNEU School, Ashbourne
Barlborough Hall School, Chesterfield
Derby Grammar School for Boys, Derby
Derby High School, Derby
Foremarke Hall, Derby
Mount St Mary's College, Spinkhill*
Ockbrook School, Derby
The Old Vicarage School, Derby
Repton School, Repton
St Anselm's, Bakewell
St Elphin's School, Matlock*
St Joseph's Convent, Chesterfield
St Peter & St Paul School, Chesterfield
St Wystan's School, Repton

DEVON

The Abbey School, Torquay
Bendarroch School, Exeter
Blundell's School, Tiverton
Buckeridge International College, Teignmouth
The Dolphin School, Exmouth
Edgehill College, Bideford
Emmanuel School, Exeter
Exeter Cathedral School, Exeter
Exeter Tutorial College, Exeter
Gramercy Hall School, Torbay
Grenville College, Bideford*
Hylton Kindergarten & Pre-preparatory School, Exeter
Kelly College, Tavistock
Kelly College Junior School, Tavistock
King's School, Plymouth
Lanherne Nursery and Junior School, Dawlish
Magdalen Court School, Exeter
Manor House School, Honiton
The Maynard School, Exeter
Mount House School, Tavistock
New School, Exeter
Osho Ko Hsuan School, Chulmleigh
Park School, Totnes
Plymouth College, Plymouth
Plymouth College Preparatory School, Plymouth

St Aubyn's School, Tiverton
St Christophers School, Totnes
St Dunstan's Abbey School, Plymouth
St John's School, Sidmouth
St Margaret's School, Exeter
St Michael's, Barnstaple
St Wilfrid's School, Exeter
Sands School, Ashburton
Shebbear College, Beaworthy
Stover School, Newton Abbot
Trinity School, Teignmouth
West Buckland Preparatory School, Barnstaple
West Buckland School, Barnstaple

DORSET

Bryanston School, Blandford Forum
Canford School, Wimborne
Castle Court Preparatory School, Wimborne
Clayesmore Preparatory School, Blandford Forum*
Clayesmore School, Blandford Forum*
Dorchester Preparatory School, Dorchester
Dumpton School, Wimborne
Hanford School, Blandford Forum
Homefield School Senior & Preparatory, Christchurch
Knighton House, Blandford Forum
Milton Abbey School, Blandford Forum
The Old Malthouse, Swanage
The Park School, Bournemouth
Port Regis, Shaftesbury
St Antony's-Leweston Preparatory School, Sherborne
St Antony's-Leweston School, Sherborne
St Mary's School, Shaftesbury
St Thomas Garnet's School, Bournemouth
Sherborne Preparatory School, Sherborne
Sherborne School, Sherborne
Sherborne School for Girls, Sherborne
Sunninghill Preparatory School, Dorchester
Talbot Heath, Bournemouth
Thornlow Preparatory School, Weymouth*
Uplands School, Poole
Wentworth College, Bournemouth
Yarrells School, Poole

COUNTY DURHAM

Barnard Castle School, Barnard Castle
Bow School, Durham
The Chorister School, Durham
Durham High School For Girls, Durham
Durham School, Durham
Hurworth House School, Darlington
Polam Hall, Darlington
Raventhorpe Preparatory School, Darlington

ESSEX

Alleyn Court Preparatory School, Southend-on-Sea
Avon House, Woodford Green*
Bancroft's School, Woodford Green
Brentwood School, Brentwood
Chigwell School, Chigwell

Colchester High School, Colchester
College Saint-Pierre, Leigh-on-Sea
Crowstone Preparatory School, Westcliff-on-Sea
Dame Johane Bradbury's School, Saffron Walden
Elm Green Preparatory School, Chelmsford
Felsted Preparatory School, Dunmow
Felsted School, Dunmow
Friends' School, Saffron Walden
Gidea Park College, Romford
Glenarm College, Ilford
Heathcote School, Chelmsford
Holmwood House, Colchester*
Littlegarth School, Colchester
Loyola Preparatory School, Buckhurst Hill
Maldon Court Preparatory School, Maldon
New Hall School, Chelmsford*
Oakfields Montessori Schools Ltd, Upminster
Raphael Independent School, Romford
St Aubyn's School, Woodford Green
St Cedd's School, Chelmsford
St Hilda's School, Westcliff-on-Sea
St John's School, Billericay
St Margaret's School, Halstead
St Mary's School, Colchester
St Michael's School, Leigh-on-Sea
St Philomena's Preparatory School, Frinton-on-Sea
Thorpe Hall School, Southend-on-Sea
Widford Lodge, Chelmsford
Woodford Green Preparatory School, Woodford Green

GLOUCESTERSHIRE

The Abbey School, Tewkesbury
Acorn School, Nailsworth
Airthrie School, Cheltenham
Beaudesert Park, Stroud
Bredon School, Tewkesbury*
Cheltenham College, Cheltenham
Cheltenham College Junior School, Cheltenham
The Cheltenham Ladies' College, Cheltenham
Dean Close Preparatory School, Cheltenham
Dean Close School, Cheltenham
The Dormer House PNEU School, Moreton-in-Marsh
Hatherop Castle School, Cirencester
Hopelands School, Stonehouse
Ingleside PNEU School, Cirencester
The King's School, Gloucester
The Querns School, Cirencester
Rendcomb College, Cirencester
The Richard Pate School, Cheltenham
Rose Hill School, Wotton-under-Edge
St Edward's School, Cheltenham
Westonbirt School, Tetbury
Wycliffe College, Stonehouse
Wycliffe Junior School, Stonehouse
Wynstones School, Gloucester

SOUTH GLOUCESTERSHIRE

Silverhill School, Winterbourne

HAMPSHIRE

The Atherley School, Southampton
Avonlea School, Ringwood
Ballard School, New Milton
Bedales School, Petersfield
Boundary Oak School, Fareham
Brockwood Park School, Alresford
Brookham School, Liphook
Cedars School, Aldermaston
Chiltern Tutorial Unit, Winchester
Churchers College, Petersfield
Churchers College Junior School, Petersfield
Ditcham Park School, Petersfield
Dunhurst (Bedales Junior School), Petersfield
Durlston Court, New Milton
Embley Park School, Romsey
Farleigh School, Andover
Farnborough Hill, Farnborough
Forres Sandle Manor, Fordingbridge
Grey House Preparatory School, Basingstoke
Highfield School, Liphook
Hordle Walhampton School, Lymington*
The King's School Senior, Eastleigh
Littlefield School, Liphook
Lord Wandsworth College, Hook
Mayville High School, Southsea*
Meoncross School, Fareham
Nethercliffe School, Winchester
North Foreland Lodge, Basingstoke
The Portsmouth Grammar School, Portsmouth
Rookesbury Park School, Portsmouth
Rookwood School, Andover
St Anne's Nursery & Pre-Preparatory School, Lee-on-the-Solent
St John's College, Southsea
St Neot's School, Hook
St Nicholas School, Fleet
St Swithun's School, Winchester
St Winifred's School, Southampton
Salesian College, Farnborough
Sherborne House School, Eastleigh
Stanbridge Earls School, Romsey*
Stockton House School, Aldershot
The Stroud School, Romsey
Twyford School, Winchester
Winchester College, Winchester
Yateley Manor Preparatory School, Yateley

HEREFORDSHIRE

Lucton Pierrepont School, Leominster
The Margaret Allen School, Hereford
St Richard's, Bromyard

HERTFORDSHIRE

Abbot's Hill, Hemel Hempstead
Aldenham School, Elstree
The Arts Educational School, Tring
Berkhamsted Collegiate Preparatory School, Berkhamsted
Berkhamsted Collegiate School, Berkhamsted

Duncombe School, Hertford
Edge Grove, Aldenham
Egerton-Rothesay School, Berkhamsted
First Impressions Montessori Schools, Barnet
Haberdashers' Aske's Boys' School, Elstree
Haileybury, Hertford
Haresfoot Preparatory School, Berkhamsted
Harpenden Preparatory School, Harpenden
Heath Mount School, Hertford
CKHR Immanuel College, Bushey
Kingshott, Hitchin
Lochinver House School, Potters Bar
Lockers Park, Hemel Hempstead
Longwood School, Bushey
Marlin Montessori School, Berkhamsted
Norfolk Lodge Nursery & Preparatory School, Barnet
Northwood Preparatory School, Rickmansworth
The Princess Helena College, Hitchin
The Purcell School, Bushey
Queenswood, Hatfield
Rickmansworth PNEU School, Rickmansworth
The Royal Masonic School for Girls, Rickmansworth
St Albans High School for Girls, St Albans
St Albans School, St Albans
St Andrew's Montessori School, Watford
St Christopher School, Letchworth
St Columba's College, St Albans
St Francis' College, Letchworth
St Hilda's School, Bushey
St Joseph's in the Park, Hertford
St Martha's Senior School, Barnet
St Nicholas House, Hemel Hempstead
Sherrardswood School, Welwyn
Stanborough School, Watford
Stormont, Potters Bar
Westbrook Hay, Hemel Hempstead
Westwood, Bushey Heath
York House School, Rickmansworth

ISLE OF MAN

King William's College, Castletown

ISLE OF WIGHT

Priory School, Sandown
Ryde School, Ryde
Westmont School, Newport

KENT

Ashford School, Ashford
Ashgrove School, Bromley
Babington House School, Chislehurst
Baston School, Bromley
Bedgebury School, Cranbrook
Beechwood Sacred Heart, Tunbridge Wells
Benedict House Preparatory School, Sidcup
Bethany School, Cranbrook*
Bickley Park School, Bromley
Bishop Challoner School, Bromley
Bryony School, Gillingham

Cobham Hall, Gravesend*
Combe Bank School, Sevenoaks
Cranbrook School, Cranbrook
Derwent Lodge School for Girls, Tonbridge
Dover College, Dover
Duke of York's Royal Military School, Dover
Dulwich Preparatory School, Cranbrook, Cranbrook
Elliott Park School, Sheerness
Farringtons & Stratford House, Chislehurst
Gad's Hill School, Rochester
The Granville School, Sevenoaks
Hilden Grange School, Tonbridge
Hilden Oaks School, Tonbridge
Holmewood House, Tunbridge Wells
Junior King's School, Canterbury
The Junior School, St Lawrence College, Ramsgate
Kent College, Canterbury
Kent College Pembury, Tunbridge Wells
King's Preparatory School, Rochester, Rochester*
The King's School, Canterbury
King's School Rochester, Rochester*
Lorenden Preparatory School, Faversham
Marlborough House School, Hawkhurst
The Mead School, Tunbridge Wells
The New Beacon, Sevenoaks
Northbourne Park School, Deal
The Old Vicarage, Tonbridge
Rochester Independent College, Rochester
Rose Hill School, Tunbridge Wells
Russell House School, Sevenoaks
Sackville School, Tonbridge
St Andrew's School, Rochester
St David's College, West Wickham
St Edmund's Junior School, Canterbury
St Edmund's School, Canterbury
St Faith's at Ash School, Canterbury
St Lawrence College, Ramsgate
St Mary's Westbrook, Folkestone
St Michael's School, Sevenoaks
St Ronan's, Hawkhurst
Sevenoaks Preparatory School, Sevenoaks
Sevenoaks School, Sevenoaks
Solefield School, Sevenoaks
Somerhill Pre-Preparatory, Tonbridge
Steephill School, Longfield
Sutton Valence Preparatory School, Maidstone
Sutton Valence School, Maidstone
Tonbridge School, Tonbridge
Vernon Holme (Kent College Infant & Junior School),
    Canterbury
Walthamstow Hall, Sevenoaks
Wellesley House School, Broadstairs
West Lodge Preparatory School, Sidcup
Yardley Court, Tonbridge

LANCASHIRE

Arnold School, Blackpool
Bentham Grammar School, Lancaster
Bolton School (Girls' Division), Bolton
Bury Grammar School (Girls'), Bury
Emmanuel Christian School, Poulton-Le-Fylde
Heathland College, Accrington
Highfield Priory School, Preston

King Edward VII and Queen Mary School, Lytham
St Annes
Kingsway School, Wigan
Kingswood College at Scarisbrick Hall, Ormskirk*
Lord's College, Bolton
Moorland School, Clitheroe
Oakhill College, Clitheroe
Queen Elizabeth's Grammar School, Blackburn
Rossall Preparatory School, Fleetwood
Rossall School, Fleetwood
St Anne's College Grammar School, Lytham St Annes
St Mary's Hall, Stonyhurst
St Pius X Preparatory School, Preston
Stonyhurst College, Clitheroe
Westholme School, Blackburn

LEICESTERSHIRE

Brooke House College, Market Harborough
Fairfield School, Loughborough
Grace Dieu Manor School, Leicester
Leicester Grammar Junior School, Leicester
Leicester Grammar School, Leicester
Loughborough Grammar School, Loughborough
Manor House School, Ashby-de-la-Zouch
Our Lady's Convent School, Loughborough
PNEU School, Loughborough
Ratcliffe College, Leicester
St Crispin's School (Leicester) Ltd., Leicester

LINCOLNSHIRE

Ayscoughfee Hall School, Spalding
Conway Preparatory School, Boston
Copthill School, Stamford
The Fen Preparatory School, Sleaford
The Grantham Preparatory School, Grantham
Lincoln Minster School, Lincoln
Maypole House School, Alford
St Hugh's School, Woodhall Spa
St Mary's Preparatory School, Lincoln
Stamford School, Stamford
Witham Hall, Bourne

NORTH EAST LINCOLNSHIRE

St James' School, Grimsby
St Martin's Preparatory School, Grimsby

NORTH LINCOLNSHIRE

Brigg Preparatory School, Brigg
Trentvale Preparatory School, Keadby

LONDON

Akiva School, N3
Albany College, NW4
The Albany College, NW4
Albemarle Independent College, W2
Alleyn's School, SE22

Annemount School, N2
Arnold House School, NW8
The Arts Educational School, W4
Aston House School, W5
Barbara Speake Stage School, W3
Beis Soroh Schneirer, N3
Belmont (Mill Hill Junior School), NW7
Blackheath High School GDST, SE3
Blackheath Preparatory School, SE3
Broomwood Hall School, SW12
Bute House Preparatory School for Girls, W6
Cameron House, SW3
Chiswick and Bedford Park Preparatory School, W4
City of London School, EC4V
City of London School for Girls, EC2Y
Colfe's School, SE12
Collingham, SW5
Connaught House, W2
Dallington School, EC1V
Davies Laing and Dick Independent VI Form College, W2
Devonshire House Preparatory School, NW3
Dolphin School, SW11
The Dominie, SW11*
Dr Rolfe's Montessori School, W2
Duff Miller, SW7
Dulwich College, SE21
Dulwich College Preparatory School, SE21
Durston House, W5
Ealing College Upper School, W13
Ealing Montessori School, W3
Ealing Tutorial College, W5
Eaton House The Manor, SW4
Eaton Square Schools, SW1V
Elmwood Montessori School, W4
Eltham College, SE9
Emanuel School, SW11
Eveline Day School, SW17
Fine Arts College, NW3
Finton House School, SW17
Francis Holland School, SW1W
Francis Holland School, NW1
Fulham Prep School, SW6
Garden House Boys' School, SW1X
Garden House Girls' School, SW1W
Gatehouse School, E2
Glendower Preparatory School, SW7
Grange Park Preparatory School, N21
The Hall School, NW3
The Hall School Wimbledon, SW20
The Hampshire Schools (Kensington Gardens), W2
The Hampshire Schools
(Knightsbridge Under School), SW7
The Hampshire Schools
(Knightsbridge Upper School), SW7
Hampstead Hill Pre-Preparatory & Nursery School, NW3
Harvington School, W5
Hawkesdown House School, W8
Heath House Preparatory School, SE3
Heathside Preparatory School, NW3
Hellenic College of London, SW1X
Hendon Preparatory School, NW4
Hereward House School, NW3
Herne Hill School, SE24
Highfield School, SW18
Highgate Junior School, N6

Highgate School, N6
Hornsby House School, SW12
Ibstock Place School, SW15
International School of London, W3
James Allen's Preparatory School, SE22
Keble Preparatory School, N21
Kensington Prep School, SW6
The Kerem School, N2
The King Alfred School, NW11
Lansdowne Sixth Form College, W2
Latymer Upper School, W6
Lion House School, SW15
Lubavitch House Senior School for Girls, N16
Mander Portman Woodward, SW7
The Montessori House, N10
More House, SW1X
The Mount School, NW7
Newton Prep, SW8
Normanhurst School, E4
North Bridge House Lower School, NW1
North Bridge House Prep & Senior School, NW1
Northcote Lodge, SW11
Orchard House School, W4
Parkgate House School, SW4
Parkside Preparatory School, N17
Pembridge Hall, W2
The Phoenix School, NW3
Playdays Nursery/School and Montessori College, SW19
Portland Place School, W1B
Primrose Montessori School, N5
Princes Avenue School, N10
Prospect House School, SW15
Putney High School, SW15
Putney Park School, SW15
Queen's College, W1N
Rainbow Montessori Nursery School, N6
Ravenscourt Park Preparatory School, W6
Redcliffe School, SW10
Riverston School, SE12
The Roche School, SW18
The Rowans School, SW20
St Anthony's Preparatory School, NW3
St Augustine's Priory, W5
St Benedict's Junior School, W5
St Johns Wood Pre-Preparatory School, NW8
St Margaret's School, NW3
St Martin's, NW7
St Olave's Preparatory School, SE9
St Paul's Cathedral School, EC4M
St Paul's Girls' School, W6
St Philip's School, SW7
Salcombe School, N14
The Schiller International School, SE1
Sinclair House School, SW6
Snaresbrook College Preparatory School, E18
Southbank International School, Hampstead, NW3
The Study Preparatory School, SW19
Sydenham High School GDST, SE26
The Headstart Montessori Nursery School, SW17
Thomas's Preparatory School, W8
Thomas's Preparatory School Clapham, SW11
Toddlers and Mums Montessori, W2
Tower House School, SW14
Trevor Roberts', NW3
The Tuition Centre, NW4

The Vale School, SW7
Vita Et Pax School, N14
Westminster Cathedral Choir School, SW1P
Westminster School, SW1P
Westminster Under School, SW1P
The White House Prep & Woodentops Kindergarten, SW12
Willington School, SW19
Willoughby Hall Dyslexia Centre, NW3
Wimbledon College Prep School, SW19
Woodside Park International School, N11*

GREATER MANCHESTER

Abbey Independent College, Manchester
Abbotsford Preparatory School, Manchester
Chetham's School of Music, Manchester
Clarendon Cottage School, Eccles
The Manchester Grammar School, Manchester
William Hulme's Grammar School, Manchester
Withington Girls' School, Manchester

MERSEYSIDE

The Belvedere School GDST, Liverpool
Birkenhead School, Birkenhead
Carleton House Preparatory School, Liverpool
Heswall Preparatory School, Wirral
Kingsmead School, Wirral
Liverpool College, Liverpool
Marymount Convent School, Wallasey
Merchant Taylors' School, Liverpool
Merchant Taylors' School for Girls, Liverpool
St Mary's College, Liverpool
Streatham House School, Liverpool
Tower Dene Preparatory School, Southport

MIDDLESEX

Alpha Preparatory School, Harrow
Buckingham College School, Harrow
Buxlow Preparatory School, Wembley
Denmead School, Hampton
Hampton School, Hampton
Harrow School, Harrow on the Hill
Heathfield School, Pinner
The John Lyon School, Harrow
The Lady Eleanor Holles School, Hampton
Merchant Taylors' School, Northwood
Northwood College, Northwood
Peterborough & St Margaret's School, Stanmore
Quainton Hall School, Harrow
St Catherine's School, Twickenham
St David's School, Ashford
St Helen's College, Uxbridge
St James Independent School for Boys (Senior), Twickenham
Staines Preparatory School Trust, Staines

NORFOLK

All Saints School, Norwich
Beeston Hall School, Cromer

Downham Montessori School, Kings Lynn
Glebe House School, Hunstanton
Gresham's Preparatory School, Holt
Gresham's School, Holt
Hethersett Old Hall School, Norwich
Langley Preparatory School & Nursery, Norwich
Langley School, Norwich
The New Eccles Hall School, Norwich
The Norwich High School for Girls GDST, Norwich
Notre Dame Preparatory School, Norwich
Riddlesworth Hall, Diss
Sacred Heart Convent School, Swaffham
St Christopher's School, Norwich
Silfield School, Kings Lynn
Taverham Hall, Norwich
Thetford Grammar School, Thetford
Thorpe House School, Norwich
Town Close House Preparatory School, Norwich
Wood Dene School, Norwich

NORTHAMPTONSHIRE

Beachborough School, Brackley
Bosworth Independent College, Northampton
Maidwell Hall, Northampton
Northampton Christian School, Northampton
Northampton High School, Northampton
Northampton Preparatory School, Northampton
Northamptonshire Grammar School, Pitsford
Our Lady's Convent Preparatory School, Kettering
Overstone Park School, Northampton
St Peter's School, Kettering
Spratton Hall, Northampton
Wellingborough School, Wellingborough
Winchester House School, Brackley

NORTHUMBERLAND

Longridge Towers School, Berwick-upon-Tweed
Mowden Hall School, Stocksfield*
St Oswald's School, Alnwick

NOTTINGHAMSHIRE

Attenborough Preparatory School, Nottingham
Bramcote Lorne School, Retford
Dagfa House School, Nottingham
Edgehill School, Newark
Greenholme School, Nottingham
Highfields School, Newark
Hollygirt School, Nottingham
The King's School, Nottingham
Lammas School, Sutton in Ashfield
Mansfield Preparatory School, Mansfield
Mountford House School, Nottingham
Nottingham High School, Nottingham
Nottingham High School for Girls GDST, Nottingham
Nottingham High School Preparatory School, Nottingham
Plumtree School, Nottingham
Ranby House, Retford
St Joseph's School, Nottingham
Salterford House School, Nottingham
Saville House School, Mansfield

Trent College, Nottingham
Waverley House PNEU School, Nottingham
Wellow House School, Newark
Worksop College, Worksop

OXFORDSHIRE

Abingdon School, Abingdon
Bloxham School, Banbury*
Cherwell College, Oxford
Christ Church Cathedral School, Oxford
Cokethorpe School, Witney
Cranford House School, Wallingford
d'Overbroeck's College, Oxford
Dragon School, Oxford
Edward Greene's Tutorial Establishment, Oxford
Headington School Oxford, Oxford
Josca's Preparatory School, Abingdon
Kingham Hill School, Chipping Norton*
Magdalen College School, Oxford
Manor Preparatory School, Abingdon
Millbrook House, Abingdon
Moulsford Preparatory School, Wallingford
Our Lady's Convent Junior School, Abingdon
Our Lady's Convent Senior School, Abingdon
Oxford High School GDST, Oxford
Oxford Tutorial College, Oxford
Rupert House, Henley-on-Thames
Rye St Antony School, Oxford
St Clare's, Oxford, Oxford
St Edward's School, Oxford
St Hugh's School, Faringdon
St John's Priory School, Banbury
St Mary's School, Wantage
School of St Helen & St Katharine, Abingdon
Shiplake College, Henley-on-Thames
Sibford School, Banbury*
Summer Fields, Oxford
Tudor Hall School, Banbury
Windrush Valley School, Chipping Norton
Wychwood School, Oxford

RUTLAND

Brooke Priory School, Oakham
Oakham School, Oakham
Uppingham School, Uppingham

SHROPSHIRE

Adcote School for Girls, Shrewsbury
Bedstone College, Bucknell
Bellan House Preparatory School, Oswestry
Castle House School, Newport
Dower House School, Bridgnorth
Ellesmere College, Ellesmere*
Kingsland Grange, Shrewsbury
Moor Park School, Ludlow
Moreton Hall, Oswestry
The Old Hall School, Telford
Oswestry School, Oswestry
Packwood Haugh, Shrewsbury

Prestfelde Preparatory School, Shrewsbury
Shrewsbury School, Shrewsbury
White House School, Whitchurch
Wrekin College, Telford

SOMERSET

All Hallows, Shepton Mallet
Bruton School for Girls, Bruton
Chard School, Chard
Chilton Cantelo School, Yeovil
Hazlegrove (King's Bruton Preparatory School), Yeovil
King's College, Taunton
King's Hall School, Taunton
King's School, Bruton
Millfield Preparatory School, Glastonbury
Millfield School, Street
The Park School, Yeovil
Perrott Hill School, Crewkerne
Queen's College, Taunton
Queen's College Junior and Pre-Preparatory Schools, Taunton
Rossholme School, East Brent
St Brandon's School, Clevedon
St Christopher's, Burnham-on-Sea
St Martin's Independent School, Crewkerne
Sidcot School, Winscombe*
Taunton Preparatory School, Taunton
Taunton School, Taunton
Wellington School, Wellington
Wells Cathedral Junior School, Wells
Wells Cathedral School, Wells

NORTH EAST SOMERSET

Downside School, Bath
Kingswood Preparatory School, Bath
Kingswood School, Bath
Monkton Combe Junior School, Bath
Monkton Combe School, Bath*
Paragon School, Bath
Prior Park College, Bath
The Royal High School, Bath

NORTH SOMERSET

Ashbrooke House, Weston-Super-Mare
The Hall Pre-Preparatory School Sidcot, Winscombe
Sidcot School, Winscombe

STAFFORDSHIRE

Abbotsholme School, Uttoxeter*
Brooklands School, Stafford
Chase Academy, Cannock
Denstone College, Uttoxeter
Edenhurst School, Newcastle-under-Lyme
Lichfield Cathedral School, Lichfield
Maple Hayes Hall Dyslexia School, Lichfield
St Bede's School, Stafford
St Dominic's School, Stafford
St John's Preparatory School, Lichfield
St Joseph's Preparatory School, Stoke-on-Trent

School of St Mary and St Anne, Abbots Bromley
Smallwood Manor Preparatory School, Uttoxeter
Stafford Grammar School, Stafford
Vernon Lodge Preparatory School, Stafford
Yarlet School, Stafford

STOCKTON-ON-TEES

Red House School, Norton
Teesside High School, Eaglescliffe
Yarm School, Yarm

SUFFOLK

The Abbey, Woodbridge
Amberfield School, Ipswich
Barnardiston Hall Preparatory School, Haverhill
Cherry Trees School, Bury St Edmunds
Culford School, Bury St Edmunds
Fairstead House School, Newmarket
Finborough School, Stowmarket
Framlingham College, Woodbridge
Framlingham College Junior School, Brandeston
Hillcroft Preparatory School, Stowmarket*
Ipswich Preparatory School, Ipswich
Ipswich School, Ipswich
Moreton Hall Preparatory School, Bury St Edmunds
Old Buckenham Hall School, Ipswich
The Old School, Beccles
Orwell Park, Ipswich
Royal Hospital School, Ipswich
St Felix School, Southwold
St George's School, Southwold
St Joseph's College, Ipswich
South Lee Preparatory School, Bury St Edmunds
Stoke College, Sudbury
Woodbridge School, Woodbridge

SURREY

Aldro School, Godalming
The American Community Schools, Egham
Amesbury, Hindhead
Barfield School, Farnham
Barrow Hills School, Godalming
Belmont School, Dorking
Bishopsgate School, Egham
Box Hill School, Dorking*
Bramley School, Tadworth
Cable House School, Woking
Cambridge Tutors College, Croydon
Canbury School, Kingston-upon-Thames
Caterham School, Caterham
Charterhouse, Godalming
Chinthurst School, Tadworth
Claremont Fan Court School, Esher
Clewborough House School at Cheswycks, Camberley
Collingwood School, Wallington
Coworth Park School, Woking
Cranleigh School, Cranleigh
Cranmore School, Leatherhead
Croham Hurst School, South Croydon
Croydon High School GDST, South Croydon

Danes Hill Preparatory School, Leatherhead*
Danesfield Manor School, Walton-on-Thames
Drayton House School, Guildford
Duke of Kent School, Ewhurst
Dunottar School, Reigate
Edgeborough, Farnham
Epsom College, Epsom
Essendene Lodge School, Caterham
Ewell Castle School, Epsom
Feltonfleet School, Cobham
Flexlands School, Woking
Frensham Heights, Farnham
Glenesk School, Leatherhead
Grantchester House, Esher
Greenacre School for Girls, Banstead
Greenfield School, Woking
Hall Grove School, Bagshot
Halstead Preparatory School, Woking
Haslemere Preparatory School, Haslemere
Hawley Place School, Camberley
The Hawthorns School, Redhill
Hazelwood School, Oxted
Hoe Bridge School, Woking
King Edward's School Witley, Godalming
Kingswood House School, Epsom*
Lanesborough, Guildford
Laverock School, Oxted
Lodge School, Purley
Longacre Preparatory School, Guildford
Lyndhurst School, Camberley
Manor House School, Leatherhead
Marymount International School, Kingston-upon-Thames
Micklefield School, Reigate
Notre Dame Preparatory School, Cobham
Notre Dame School, Lingfield
Notre Dame Senior School, Cobham
Nower Lodge School, Dorking
Oakfield School, Woking
Oakhyrst Grange School, Caterham
Old Palace School of John Whitgift, Croydon
Old Vicarage School, Richmond
Park Hill School, Kingston-upon-Thames
Parkside School, Cobham
Parsons Mead, Ashtead
Prior's Field School, Godalming
Priory School, Banstead
Reed's School, Cobham
Reigate Grammar School, Reigate
Reigate St Mary's Preparatory and Choir School, Reigate
Ripley Court School, Woking
Rokeby School, Kingston-upon-Thames
Royal Alexandra and Albert School, Reigate
Royal Grammar School, Guildford
Royal Russell School, Croydon
Royal School Haslemere, Haslemere
Rydes Hill Preparatory School, Guildford
St Andrew's School, Woking
St Catherine's School, Guildford
St David's School, Purley
St Edmund's School, Hindhead
St George's College, Weybridge
St Hilary's School, Godalming
St Ives School, Haslemere
St John's School, Leatherhead
St Teresa's Preparatory School, Effingham

Sanderstead Junior School, South Croydon
Seaton House, Sutton
Sir William Perkins's School, Chertsey
Stanway School, Dorking
Stowford, Sutton*
The Study School, New Malden
Surbiton High School, Kingston-upon-Thames
Surbiton Preparatory School, Surbiton
Surrey College, Guildford
Sutton High School GDST, Sutton
Tormead School, Guildford
Trinity School, Croydon
Unicorn School, Richmond
Warlingham Park School, Croydon
Weston Green School, Thames Ditton
Wispers School for Girls, Haslemere
Woldingham School, Woldingham
Woodcote House School, Windlesham

EAST SUSSEX

Ashdown House School, Forest Row
Battle Abbey School, Battle
Bodiam Manor School, Robertsbridge*
Bricklehurst Manor Preparatory, Wadhurst
Brighton and Hove High School GDST, Brighton
Brighton College, Brighton
Brighton College Pre-preparatory School, Brighton
Brighton College Prep School, Brighton
Brighton Steiner School Limited, Brighton
Buckswood School, Hastings
Claremont School, St Leonards-on-Sea
Darvell School, Robertsbridge
Deepdene School, Hove
Dharma School, Brighton
Eastbourne College, Eastbourne
The Fold School, Hove
Moira House Junior School, Eastbourne
Moira House Girls' School, Eastbourne
Mowden School, Hove
Newlands Manor School, Seaford*
Newlands Preparatory School, Seaford*
The Old Grammar School, Lewes
Roedean School, Brighton
St Andrew's School, Eastbourne
St Aubyn's, Brighton
St Bede's, Eastbourne
St Bede's School, Hailsham
St Leonards-Mayfield School, Mayfield
St Mary's Hall, Brighton
Skippers Hill Manor Preparatory School, Mayfield
Stonelands School of Ballet & Theatre Arts, Hove
Temple Grove, Uckfield
Vinehall School, Robertsbridge
Westerleigh & St Leonards College, St Leonards-on-Sea

WEST SUSSEX

Ardingly College, Haywards Heath
Ardingly College Junior School, Haywards Heath
Arundale Preparatory School, Pulborough
Brambletye School, East Grinstead
Broadwater Manor School, Worthing
Burgess Hill School for Girls, Burgess Hill

Conifers School, Midhurst
Copthorne School, Copthorne
Cottesmore School, Pease Pottage
Cumnor House School, Haywards Heath
Dorset House School, Pulborough
Farlington School, Horsham
Fonthill Lodge, East Grinstead
Great Ballard School, Chichester
Great Walstead, Haywards Heath
Handcross Park School, Haywards Heath
Hurstpierpoint College, Hassocks
Lavant House Rosemead, Chichester
The Littlemead School, Chichester
Oakwood School, Chichester
Pennthorpe School, Horsham
St Margaret's School Convent of Mercy, Midhurst
St Peter's School, Burgess Hill
Sandhurst School, Worthing
Seaford College, Petworth
Shoreham College, Shoreham-by-Sea
Slindon College, Arundel*
Sompting Abbotts, Sompting
Stoke Brunswick, East Grinstead
The Towers Convent School, Steyning
Westbourne House School, Chichester
Windlesham House, Pulborough*
Worth School, Turners Hill

TYNE AND WEAR

Akhurst Preparatory School, Newcastle upon Tyne
Argyle House School, Sunderland
Ascham House School, Newcastle upon Tyne
Central Newcastle High School GDST,
    Newcastle upon Tyne
Dame Allan's Boys School, Newcastle upon Tyne
Dame Allan's Girls School, Newcastle upon Tyne
Eastcliffe Grammar School, Newcastle upon Tyne
Grindon Hall Christian School, Sunderland
Newcastle Preparatory School, Newcastle upon Tyne
Newlands School, Newcastle upon Tyne*
Sunderland High School, Sunderland
Westfield School, Newcastle upon Tyne

WARWICKSHIRE

Abbotsford School, Kenilworth
Arnold Lodge School, Leamington Spa
Bilton Grange, Rugby
The Crescent School, Rugby
The Croft School, Stratford-upon-Avon
Emscote House School and Nursery, Leamington Spa
The King's High School for Girls, Warwick
The Kingsley School, Leamington Spa
Princethorpe College, Rugby
Rugby School, Rugby
Stratford Preparatory School, Stratford-upon-Avon

WEST MIDLANDS

Abbey College, Birmingham
Arden Lawn, Solihull
Bablake School, Coventry
Birchfield School, Wolverhampton

The Blue Coat School, Birmingham
Cheshunt Pre-preparatory School, Coventry
Coventry Preparatory School, Coventry
Davenport Lodge School, Coventry
Edgbaston College, Birmingham
Edgbaston High School for Girls, Birmingham
Eversfield Preparatory School, Solihull
Hallfield School, Birmingham
Highclare School, Birmingham
King Henry VIII School, Coventry
Kingsley Preparatory School, Solihull
Kingswood School, Solihull
Mander Portman Woodward, Birmingham
Mayfield Preparatory School, Walsall
Newbridge Preparatory School, Wolverhampton
Pattison College, Coventry
Priory School, Birmingham
Rosslyn School, Birmingham
The Royal Wolverhampton Junior School,
    Wolverhampton
The Royal Wolverhampton School, Wolverhampton
Ruckleigh School, Solihull
St George's School, Edgbaston, Birmingham
St Martin's School, Solihull
The Shrubbery School, Sutton Coldfield
Tettenhall College, Wolverhampton
West House School, Birmingham
Wolverhampton Grammar School, Wolverhampton
Wylde Green College, Sutton Coldfield

WILTSHIRE

Avondale School, Salisbury
Chafyn Grove School, Salisbury
Dauntsey's School, Devizes
The Godolphin School, Salisbury
Grittleton House School, Chippenham
Kingsbury Hill House, Marlborough
La Retraite Swan, Salisbury
Leaden Hall, Salisbury
Marlborough College, Marlborough
Meadowpark Nursery & Pre-Prep, Cricklade
Norman Court Preparatory School, Salisbury
Pinewood School, Swindon
Prior Park Preparatory School, Cricklade*
Roundstone Preparatory School, Trowbridge
St Francis School, Pewsey
St Mary's School, Calne
Salisbury Cathedral School, Salisbury
Sandroyd, Salisbury
South Hills School, Salisbury
Stonar School, Melksham
Stourbridge House School, Warminster
Warminster School, Warminster

WORCESTERSHIRE

Abberley Hall, Worcester
The Alice Ottley School, Worcester
Bowbrook House School, Pershore
Bromsgrove Lower School, Bromsgrove
Bromsgrove Pre-preparatory and Nursery School,
    Bromsgrove
Bromsgrove School, Bromsgrove

The Downs School, Malvern
The Elms, Malvern
The Grange, Worcester
Green Hill School, Evesham
Hartlebury School, Kidderminster
Heathfield School, Kidderminster
Holy Trinity School, Kidderminster
King's Hawford, Worcester
The King's School, Worcester
The Knoll School, Kidderminster
Malvern College, Malvern
Malvern Girls' College, Malvern
Moffats School, Bewdley
Mount School, Bromsgrove
Royal Grammar School Worcester, Worcester
St James's School, Malvern*
St Mary's Convent School, Worcester
Whitford Hall & Dodderhill School, Droitwich
Winterfold House, Kidderminster

EAST RIDING OF YORKSHIRE

Froebel House School, Hull
Hull Grammar School, Kingston-Upon-Hull
Hymers College, Hull
Pocklington Montessori School, Pocklington
Pocklington School, Pocklington

NORTH YORKSHIRE

Ampleforth College, York
Ashville College, Harrogate
Aysgarth Preparatory School, Bedale
Belmont Grosvenor School, Harrogate
Bootham School, York
Brackenfield School, Harrogate
Bramcote School, Scarborough
Catteral Hall, Settle
Clifton Preparatory School, York
Cundall Manor School, York
Fyling Hall School, Whitby
Giggleswick School, Settle
Harrogate Ladies' College, Harrogate
Harrogate Tutorial College, Harrogate
Highfield Preparatory School, Harrogate
Howsham Hall, York
Malsis School, Skipton
The Mount Junior School, York
The Mount Senior School, York
Queen Ethelburga's College, York
Queen Margaret's School, York
Queen Mary's School, Thirsk
Read School, Selby
Ripon Cathedral Choir School, Ripon

St Olave's School (Junior of St Peter's), York
Scarborough College, Scarborough
Scarborough College Junior School, Scarborough
Terrington Hall, York
Woodleigh School, Malton*

SOUTH YORKSHIRE

Ashdell Preparatory School, Sheffield
Birkdale School, Sheffield
Brantwood Independent School for Girls, Sheffield
Hill House Preparatory School, Doncaster
Mylnhurst RC School & Nursery, Sheffield
St Mary's School, Doncaster
Westbourne School, Sheffield

WEST YORKSHIRE

Ackworth School, Pontefract
Alcuin School, Leeds
Batley Grammar School, Batley
Bradford Christian School, Bradford
Bradford Girls' Grammar School, Bradford
Bradford Grammar School, Bradford
Bronte House School, Bradford*
Clevedon Preparatory House School, Ilkley
Cliff School, Wakefield
The Froebelian School, Leeds
Fulneck School, Pudsey*
Gateways School, Leeds
Ghyll Royd School, Ilkley
Glen House Montessori School, Hebden Bridge
Hipperholme Grammar School, Halifax
Huddersfield Grammar School, Huddersfield
Lady Lane Park School, Bingley
Leeds Girls' High School, Leeds
Leeds Grammar School, Leeds
Lightcliffe Preparatory, Halifax
Moorfield School, Ilkley
Moorlands School, Leeds
Mount School, Huddersfield
Queen Elizabeth Grammar School, Wakefield
Richmond House School, Leeds
Rishworth School, Rishworth
Rossefield School, Bradford
St Agnes PNEU School, Leeds
St Hilda's School, Wakefield
Shaw House School, Bradford
Silcoates School, Wakefield
Wakefield Girls' High School, Wakefield
Wakefield Independent School, Wakefield
Wakefield Tutorial Preparatory School, Leeds
Woodhouse Grove School, Apperley Bridge*

NORTHERN IRELAND

COUNTY ANTRIM

Belfast Royal Academy, Belfast
Methodist College, Belfast
Royal Belfast Academical Institution, Belfast

COUNTY DOWN

Bangor Grammar School, Bangor
Rockport School, Holywood

SCOTLAND

ABERDEENSHIRE
Aberdeen Waldorf School, Aberdeen
Albyn School for Girls, Aberdeen
St Margaret's School for Girls, Aberdeen

ANGUS
The High School of Dundee, Dundee
Lathallan School, Montrose

ARGYLL AND BUTE
Lomond School, Helensburgh

SOUTH AYRSHIRE
Wellington School, Ayr

BANFFSHIRE
Aberlour House, Aberlour

CLACKMANNANSHIRE
Dollar Academy, Dollar

FIFE
New Park School, St Andrews
St Katharines Preparatory School, St Andrews
St Leonards School & St Leonards VIth Form College,
   St Andrews
Sea View Private School, Kirkcaldy

GLASGOW
Craigholme School, Glasgow
The Glasgow Academy, Glasgow
The High School of Glasgow, Glasgow
Hutchesons' Grammar School, Glasgow
Hutchesons' Lilybank Junior School, Glasgow
Kelvinside Academy, Glasgow
St Aloysius' College, Glasgow

LANARKSHIRE
Hamilton College, Hamilton

SOUTH LANARKSHIRE
Fernhill School, Rutherglen

LOTHIAN
Basil Paterson Tutorial College, Edinburgh
Belhaven Hill, Dunbar
Cargilfield, Edinburgh
Clifton Hall, Newbridge
The Compass School, Haddington
The Edinburgh Academy, Edinburgh
Edinburgh Academy Junior School, Edinburgh
The Edinburgh Rudolf Steiner School, Edinburgh
Edinburgh Tutorial College, Edinburgh
Fettes College, Edinburgh
George Heriot's School, Edinburgh
George Watson's College, Edinburgh
Loretto Junior School, Musselburgh
The Mary Erskine School, Edinburgh
Merchiston Castle School, Edinburgh*
St George's School for Girls, Edinburgh
St Margaret's School, Edinburgh
St Serf's School, Edinburgh
Stewart's Melville College, Edinburgh

MIDLOTHIAN
Loretto, Musselburgh

MORAYSHIRE
Gordonstoun School, Elgin
Rosebrae School, Elgin

PERTHSHIRE
Ardvreck School, Crieff
Butterstone School, Blairgowrie
Craiglowan Preparatory School, Perth
Glenalmond College, Perth
Kilgraston (A Sacred Heart School), Perth
Morrison's Academy, Crieff
Queen Victoria School, Dunblane
Rannoch School, Pitlochry
Strathallan School, Perth

RENFREWSHIRE
Belmont House, Newton Mearns

ROXBURGHSHIRE
St Mary's Preparatory School, Melrose

STIRLING
Beaconhurst Grange, Stirling

WALES

BRIDGEND

St John's School, Porthcawl

CARDIFF

The Cathedral School, Cardiff
Elm Tree House School, Cardiff
Howell's School, Llandaff GDST, Cardiff
Kings Monkton School, Cardiff
New College and School, Cardiff

CARMARTHENSHIRE

Llandovery College, Llandovery*

CONWY

Lyndon School, Colwyn Bay
Rydal Penrhos Preparatory School, Colwyn Bay
Rydal Penrhos Senior School, Colwyn Bay
St David's College, Llandudno*

DENBIGHSHIRE

Howell's School, Denbigh
Northgate Preparatory, Rhyl
Ruthin School, Ruthin

GWYNEDD

Hillgrove School, Bangor
St Gerard's School, Bangor

MONMOUTHSHIRE

Haberdashers' Monmouth School For Girls, Monmouth
Monmouth School, Monmouth
St John's-on-the-Hill, Chepstow

NEWPORT

Rougemont School, Newport

PEMBROKESHIRE

Netherwood School, Saundersfoot

POWYS

Christ College, Brecon

SWANSEA

Craig-y-Nos School, Swansea
Ffynone House School, Swansea
Oakleigh House, Swansea

4.7
PROVISION FOR ENGLISH AS A FOREIGN LANGUAGE

This index is intended as a general guide only and is compiled upon the basis of information given to Gabbitas by schools. Parents should note that there are wide variations in provision and are advised to contact individual schools for further details.

ENGLAND

BEDFORDSHIRE

Bedford High School, Bedford
Bedford Modern School, Bedford
Bedford Preparatory School, Bedford
Bedford School, Bedford
Bedford School Study Centre, Bedford
Rushmoor School, Bedford

BERKSHIRE

Bearwood College, Wokingham
Bradfield College, Reading
The Brigidine School, Windsor
Cheam School, Newbury
Claires Court School, Maidenhead
Elstree School, Reading
Heathfield School, Ascot
Holme Grange School, Wokingham
Hurst Lodge, Ascot
Lambrook Haileybury, Bracknell
Leighton Park School, Reading
Licensed Victuallers' School, Ascot
Luckley-Oakfield School, Wokingham
The Oratory Preparatory School, Reading
The Oratory School, Reading
Padworth College, Reading
Pangbourne College, Reading
Papplewick, Ascot
Queen Anne's School, Reading
Reading Blue Coat School, Reading
Ridgeway School (Claires Court Junior), Maidenhead
St George's School, Ascot
St John's Beaumont, Windsor
St Michaels School, Newbury
Upton House School, Windsor

BRISTOL

Badminton School, Bristol
Clifton College, Bristol

Clifton College Preparatory School, Bristol
Colston's Collegiate School, Bristol
The Red Maids' School, Bristol
Tockington Manor School, Bristol

BUCKINGHAMSHIRE

Dair House School Trust Ltd, Farnham Royal
Godstowe Preparatory School, High Wycombe
High March School, Beaconsfield
Milton Keynes Preparatory School, Milton Keynes
Pipers Corner School, High Wycombe
Stowe School, Buckingham
Thornton College Convent of Jesus and Mary, Milton Keynes

CAMBRIDGESHIRE

Cambridge Arts & Sciences (CATS), Cambridge
Cambridge Centre for VIth Form Studies (CCSS), Cambridge
Horlers Pre-Preparatory School, Cambridge
Kimbolton School, Huntingdon
The King's School, Ely
Kirkstone House School, Peterborough
The Leys School, Cambridge
Mander Portman Woodward, Cambridge
Oundle School, Peterborough
Peterborough High School, Peterborough
St Andrew's, Cambridge
St Catherines Preparatory School, Cambridge
St Colette's School, Cambridge
St Mary's School, Cambridge

CHANNEL ISLANDS

St George's Preparatory School, Jersey

CHESHIRE

Alderley Edge School for Girls, Alderley Edge
Culcheth Hall, Altrincham
The Firs School, Chester
Hillcrest Grammar School, Stockport
Loreto Preparatory School, Altrincham
Mostyn House School, South Wirral
North Cestrian Grammar School, Altrincham
Oriel Bank High School, Stockport
Ramillies Hall School, Cheadle
Terra Nova School, Holmes Chapel

CORNWALL

The Bolitho School, Penzance
St Petroc's School, Bude
Truro High School, Truro
Wheelgate House School, Newquay

CUMBRIA

Austin Friars School, Carlisle
Casterton School, Carnforth
Harecroft Hall School, Seascale
Lime House School, Carlisle
Our Lady's, Chetwynde, Barrow-in-Furness
St Bees School, St Bees
Sedbergh School, Sedbergh
Windermere St Anne's School, Windermere

DERBYSHIRE

Ashbourne PNEU School, Ashbourne
Derby High School, Derby
Foremarke Hall, Derby
Mount St Mary's College, Spinkhill
Ockbrook School, Derby
St Elphin's School, Matlock

DEVON

Blundell's School, Tiverton
Buckeridge International College, Teignmouth
Edgehill College, Bideford
Exeter Tutorial College, Exeter
Gramercy Hall School, Torbay
Grenville College, Bideford
Hylton Kindergarten & Pre-preparatory School, Exeter
Kelly College, Tavistock
Magdalen Court School, Exeter
Rudolf Steiner School, Totnes
St Dunstan's Abbey School, Plymouth
St John's School, Sidmouth
St Michael's, Barnstaple
Sands School, Ashburton
Shebbear College, Beaworthy
Stover School, Newton Abbot
Trinity School, Teignmouth
West Buckland Preparatory School, Barnstaple
West Buckland School, Barnstaple

DORSET

Clayesmore Preparatory School, Blandford Forum
Clayesmore School, Blandford Forum
Homefield School Senior & Preparatory, Christchurch
International College, Sherborne School, Sherborne
Knighton House, Blandford Forum
Milton Abbey School, Blandford Forum
The Old Malthouse, Swanage
Port Regis, Shaftesbury
St Antony's-Leweston Preparatory School, Sherborne
St Antony's-Leweston School, Sherborne
St Mary's School, Shaftesbury
St Thomas Garnet's School, Bournemouth
Sherborne Preparatory School, Sherborne
Sherborne School, Sherborne
Sherborne School for Girls, Sherborne
Talbot Heath, Bournemouth
Wentworth College, Bournemouth

COUNTY DURHAM

Barnard Castle School, Barnard Castle
Durham High School For Girls, Durham
Durham School, Durham
Polam Hall, Darlington

ESSEX

Brentwood School, Brentwood
Chigwell School, Chigwell
Felsted School, Dunmow
Glenarm College, Ilford
Gosfield School, Halstead
New Hall School, Chelmsford
St John's School, Billericay
St Michael's School, Leigh-on-Sea
Widford Lodge, Chelmsford

GLOUCESTERSHIRE

Beaudesert Park, Stroud
Cheltenham College, Cheltenham
Cheltenham College Junior School, Cheltenham
Dean Close Preparatory School, Cheltenham
Dean Close School, Cheltenham
The King's School, Gloucester
Rendcomb College, Cirencester
Westonbirt School, Tetbury
Wycliffe College, Stonehouse
Wycliffe Junior School, Stonehouse

HAMPSHIRE

Avonlea School, Ringwood
Brockwood Park School, Alresford
Churchers College, Petersfield
Durlston Court, New Milton
Embley Park School, Romsey
Hordle Walhampton School, Lymington
Mayville High School, Southsea
North Foreland Lodge, Basingstoke

Rookesbury Park School, Portsmouth
St Anne's Nursery & Pre-Preparatory School,
   Lee-on-the-Solent
St John's College, Southsea
St Swithun's School, Winchester
Seafield Pre-School, Fareham
Stanbridge Earls School, Romsey
The Stroud School, Romsey
Twyford School, Winchester

HERTFORDSHIRE

Abbot's Hill, Hemel Hempstead
Aldenham School, Elstree
The Arts Educational School, Tring
Berkhamsted Collegiate Preparatory School, Berkhamsted
Berkhamsted Collegiate School, Berkhamsted
Bishop's Stortford College, Bishop's Stortford
Egerton-Rothesay School, Berkhamsted
Haileybury, Hertford
The Junior School, Bishop's Stortford College,
   Bishop's Stortford
Lochinver House School, Potters Bar
Lockers Park, Hemel Hempstead
Longwood School, Bushey
Marlin Montessori School, Berkhamsted
Norfolk Lodge Nursery & Preparatory School, Barnet
The Princess Helena College, Hitchin
The Purcell School, Bushey
Queenswood, Hatfield
The Royal Masonic School for Girls, Rickmansworth
St Andrew's Montessori School, Watford
St Christopher School, Letchworth
St Edmund's College, Ware
St Francis' College, Letchworth
St Margaret's School, Bushey
Sherrardswood School, Welwyn
Stanborough School, Watford

ISLE OF MAN

King William's College, Castletown

ISLE OF WIGHT

Ryde School, Ryde

KENT

Ashford School, Ashford
Baston School, Bromley
Beechwood Sacred Heart, Tunbridge Wells
Benedict House Preparatory School, Sidcup
Bethany School, Cranbrook
Cobham Hall, Gravesend
Combe Bank School, Sevenoaks
Cranbrook School, Cranbrook
Dover College, Dover
Farringtons & Stratford House, Chislehurst
Hilden Oaks School, Tonbridge

Holmewood House, Tunbridge Wells
Junior King's School, Canterbury
The Junior School, St Lawrence College, Ramsgate
Kent College, Canterbury
Kent College Pembury, Tunbridge Wells
King's Preparatory School, Rochester, Rochester
King's School Rochester, Rochester
Marlborough House School, Hawkhurst
Northbourne Park School, Deal
The Old Vicarage, Tonbridge
Rochester Independent College, Rochester
St Edmund's Junior School, Canterbury
St Edmund's School, Canterbury
St Lawrence College, Ramsgate
St Mary's Westbrook, Folkestone
Sevenoaks Preparatory School, Sevenoaks
Sutton Valence School, Maidstone
Tonbridge School, Tonbridge
Vernon Holme (Kent College Infant & Junior School),
   Canterbury
Walthamstow Hall, Sevenoaks

LANCASHIRE

Bentham Grammar School, Lancaster
King Edward VII and Queen Mary School,
   Lytham St Annes
Kingswood College at Scarisbrick Hall, Ormskirk
Kirkham Grammar School, Preston
Moorland School, Clitheroe
Rossall School, Fleetwood
St Mary's Hall, Stonyhurst
St Pius X Preparatory School, Preston
Stonyhurst College, Clitheroe

LEICESTERSHIRE

Brooke House College, Market Harborough
Grace Dieu Manor School, Leicester
Irwin College, Leicester
Loughborough Grammar School, Loughborough
Manor House School, Ashby-de-la-Zouch
Ratcliffe College, Leicester
St Crispin's School (Leicester) Ltd., Leicester

LINCOLNSHIRE

The Fen Preparatory School, Sleaford
Lincoln Minster School, Lincoln
St Hugh's School, Woodhall Spa
Stamford High School, Stamford
Stamford School, Stamford
Witham Hall, Bourne

NORTH EAST LINCOLNSHIRE

St James' School, Grimsby

NORTH LINCOLNSHIRE

Brigg Preparatory School, Brigg
Trentvale Preparatory School, Keadby

LONDON

Albany College, NW4
The Albany College, NW4
Albemarle Independent College, W2
The American School in London, NW8
The Arts Educational School, W4
Ashbourne Independent Sixth Form College, W8
Barbara Speake Stage School, W3
Belmont (Mill Hill Junior School), NW7
Blackheath High School GDST, SE3
David Game College, W11
Davies Laing and Dick Independent VI Form College, W2
Ealing Tutorial College, W5
Eveline Day School, SW17
Fine Arts College, NW3
Gatehouse School, E2
Goodwyn School, NW7
The Hall School Wimbledon, SW20
The Hampshire Schools (Kensington Gardens), W2
The Hampshire Schools
   (Knightsbridge Under School), SW7
The Hampshire Schools
   (Knightsbridge Upper School), SW7
Hellenic College of London, SW1X
Hendon Preparatory School, NW4
Highgate School, N6
Hill House School, SW1X
Holly Park Montessori, N4
Hornsby House School, SW12
Ibstock Place School, SW15
International School of London, W3
Keble Preparatory School, N21
Kensington Prep School, SW6
The King Alfred School, NW11
King Fahad Academy, W3
Lansdowne Sixth Form College, W2
Le Herisson, W6
Lion House School, SW15
Lycee Francais Charles de Gaulle, SW7
Mander Portman Woodward, SW7
Mill Hill School, NW7
More House, SW1X
The Mount School, NW7
North Bridge House Lower School, NW1
North Bridge House Prep & Senior School, NW1
Orchard House School, W4
Parkside Preparatory School, N17
Portland Place School, W1B
Princes Avenue School, N10
Putney Park School, SW15
Queen's College, W1N
Red Balloon Nursery, SW17
Riverston School, SE12
The Roche School, SW18
Royal Ballet School, W14
St Augustine's Priory, W5
St Christina's RC Preparatory School, NW8
St Johns Wood Pre-Preparatory School, NW8

St Margaret's School, NW3
Salcombe School, N14
The Schiller International School, SE1
Sinclair House School, SW6
Southbank International School, Kensington, W11
Southbank International School, Hampstead, NW3
The Study Preparatory School, SW19
Toddlers and Mums Montessori, W2
The Tuition Centre, NW4
Wimbledon College Prep School, SW19

GREATER MANCHESTER

Bridgewater School, Manchester
Chetham's School of Music, Manchester
Clarendon Cottage School, Eccles
Moor Allerton School, Manchester

MERSEYSIDE

Kingsmead School, Wirral
Marymount Convent School, Wallasey
Newborough School, Liverpool

MIDDLESEX

Buckingham College School, Harrow
Harrow School, Harrow on the Hill
Heathfield School, Pinner
Northwood College, Northwood
St David's School, Ashford
St Helen's School for Girls, Northwood

NORFOLK

Gresham's Preparatory School, Holt
Gresham's School, Holt
Hethersett Old Hall School, Norwich
Langley Preparatory School & Nursery, Norwich
Langley School, Norwich
Riddlesworth Hall, Diss
Silfield School, Kings Lynn
Thorpe House School, Norwich

NORTHAMPTONSHIRE

Bosworth Independent College, Northampton
Northamptonshire Grammar School, Pitsford
Our Lady's Convent Preparatory School, Kettering
St Peter's School, Kettering
Wellingborough School, Wellingborough

NORTHUMBERLAND

Longridge Towers School, Berwick-upon-Tweed
St Oswald's School, Alnwick

NOTTINGHAMSHIRE

Dagfa House School, Nottingham
Greenholme School, Nottingham

Nottingham High School for Girls GDST, Nottingham
Rodney School, Newark
Saville House School, Mansfield
Trent College, Nottingham
Wellow House School, Newark
Worksop College, Worksop

OXFORDSHIRE

Abacus College, Oxford
Bloxham School, Banbury
Cokethorpe School, Witney
Cranford House School, Wallingford
d'Overbroeck's College, Oxford
Edward Greene's Tutorial Establishment, Oxford
Headington School Oxford, Oxford
Kingham Hill School, Chipping Norton
Millbrook House, Abingdon
Oxford Tutorial College, Oxford
Rye St Antony School, Oxford
St Clare's, Oxford, Oxford
St Mary's School, Wantage
Sibford School, Banbury
Tudor Hall School, Banbury
Wychwood School, Oxford

RUTLAND

Brooke Priory School, Oakham
Oakham School, Oakham

SHROPSHIRE

Adcote School for Girls, Shrewsbury
Bedstone College, Bucknell
Castle House School, Newport
Concord College, Shrewsbury
Ellesmere College, Ellesmere
Moor Park School, Ludlow
Moreton Hall, Oswestry
The Old Hall School, Telford
Oswestry School, Oswestry
Packwood Haugh, Shrewsbury
Wrekin College, Telford

SOMERSET

All Hallows, Shepton Mallet
Bruton School for Girls, Bruton
Chilton Cantelo School, Yeovil
King's College, Taunton
King's Hall School, Taunton
King's School, Bruton
Millfield Preparatory School, Glastonbury
Millfield School, Street
The Park School, Yeovil
Queen's College, Taunton
Queen's College Junior and Pre-Preparatory Schools, Taunton
Rossholme School, East Brent
Taunton International Study Centre (TISC), Taunton
Taunton Preparatory School, Taunton
Taunton School, Taunton

Wellington School, Wellington
Wells Cathedral School, Wells

NORTH EAST SOMERSET

Bath Academy, Bath
Downside School, Bath
Kingswood Preparatory School, Bath
Kingswood School, Bath
Monkton Combe School, Bath
Prior Park College, Bath

NORTH SOMERSET

Sidcot School, Winscombe

STAFFORDSHIRE

Abbotsholme School, Uttoxeter
Chase Academy, Cannock
Denstone College, Uttoxeter
St Bede's School, Stafford
School of St Mary and St Anne, Abbots Bromley
Yarlet School, Stafford

STOCKTON-ON-TEES

Teesside High School, Eaglescliffe
Yarm School, Yarm

SUFFOLK

Alexanders International School, Woodbridge
Barnardiston Hall Preparatory School, Haverhill
Culford School, Bury St Edmunds
Felixstowe International College, Felixstowe
Finborough School, Stowmarket
Framlingham College, Woodbridge
Framlingham College Junior School, Brandeston
Ipswich School, Ipswich
Moreton Hall Preparatory School, Bury St Edmunds
Old Buckenham Hall School, Ipswich
Orwell Park, Ipswich
Royal Hospital School, Ipswich
St Felix School, Southwold
St Joseph's College, Ipswich
Woodbridge School, Woodbridge

SURREY

Aldro School, Godalming
The American Community Schools, Cobham
Bishopsgate School, Egham
Box Hill School, Dorking
Cable House School, Woking
Cambridge Tutors College, Croydon
Canbury School, Kingston-upon-Thames
Caterham School, Caterham
City of London Freemen's School, Ashtead
Claremont Fan Court School, Esher
The Cobham Montessori School, Cobham

Cranleigh School, Cranleigh
Danes Hill Preparatory School, Leatherhead
Epsom College, Epsom
Ewell Castle School, Epsom
Frensham Heights, Farnham
Greenacre School for Girls, Banstead
Hall Grove School, Bagshot
Hawley Place School, Camberley
Hurtwood House, Dorking
King Edward's School Witley, Godalming
Lodge School, Purley
Marymount International School, Kingston-upon-Thames
Notre Dame Senior School, Cobham
Nower Lodge School, Dorking
Oakfield School, Woking
Oakwood, Purley
Old Palace School of John Whitgift, Croydon
Parkside School, Cobham
Parsons Mead, Ashtead
Prins Willem-Alexander School, Woking
Prior's Field School, Godalming
Royal Alexandra and Albert School, Reigate
Royal Russell School, Croydon
Royal School Haslemere, Haslemere
St Catherine's School, Guildford
St David's School, Purley
St John's School, Leatherhead
St Teresa's Preparatory School, Effingham
St Teresa's School, Dorking
Stowford, Sutton
The Study School, New Malden
Surbiton High School, Kingston-upon-Thames
Surrey College, Guildford
TASIS The American School in England, Thorpe
Weston Green School, Thames Ditton
Wispers School for Girls, Haslemere
Woldingham School, Woldingham
Woodcote House School, Windlesham
Yehudi Menuhin School, Cobham

EAST SUSSEX

Battle Abbey School, Battle
Bellerbys College, Hove
Bricklehurst Manor Preparatory, Wadhurst
Brighton College, Brighton
Buckswood School, Hastings
Deepdene School, Hove
Eastbourne College, Eastbourne
Greenfields School, Forest Row
Michael Hall, Forest Row
Moira House Junior School, Eastbourne
Moira House Girls' School, Eastbourne
Newlands Manor School, Seaford
Newlands Preparatory School, Seaford
Roedean School, Brighton
St Andrew's School, Eastbourne
St Aubyn's, Brighton
St Bede's, Eastbourne
St Bede's School, Hailsham
St Leonards-Mayfield School, Mayfield
St Mary's Hall, Brighton
Temple Grove, Uckfield
Vinehall School, Robertsbridge

WEST SUSSEX

Ardingly College, Haywards Heath
Ardingly College Junior School, Haywards Heath
Burgess Hill School for Girls, Burgess Hill
Christs Hospital, Horsham
Cumnor House School, Haywards Heath
Farlington School, Horsham
Great Ballard School, Chichester
Hurstpierpoint College, Hassocks
Lavant House Rosemead, Chichester
Sandhurst School, Worthing
Seaford College, Petworth
Shoreham College, Shoreham-by-Sea
Slindon College, Arundel
The Towers Convent School, Steyning
Westbourne House School, Chichester
Windlesham House, Pulborough

TYNE AND WEAR

Eastcliffe Grammar School, Newcastle upon Tyne
Newcastle Preparatory School, Newcastle upon Tyne

WARWICKSHIRE

Abbotsford School, Kenilworth
Bilton Grange, Rugby
Rugby School, Rugby
Warwick School, Warwick

WEST MIDLANDS

Abbey College, Birmingham
Arden Lawn, Solihull
The Blue Coat School, Birmingham
Coventry Preparatory School, Coventry
Hallfield School, Birmingham
Highclare School, Birmingham
King Henry VIII School, Coventry
Kingsley Preparatory School, Solihull
Kingswood School, Solihull
Mander Portman Woodward, Birmingham
Pattison College, Coventry
Priory School, Birmingham
The Royal Wolverhampton Junior School,
    Wolverhampton
The Royal Wolverhampton School, Wolverhampton
St Martin's School, Solihull
Tettenhall College, Wolverhampton

WILTSHIRE

Dauntsey's School, Devizes
The Godolphin School, Salisbury
Grittleton House School, Chippenham
La Retraite Swan, Salisbury
Marlborough College, Marlborough
Meadowpark Nursery & Pre-Prep, Cricklade
Norman Court Preparatory School, Salisbury
Pinewood School, Swindon
Prior Park Preparatory School, Cricklade

Sandroyd, Salisbury
Stonar School, Melksham
Warminster School, Warminster

WORCESTERSHIRE

Abberley Hall, Worcester
The Abbey College, Malvern Wells
Bromsgrove Lower School, Bromsgrove
Bromsgrove Pre-preparatory and Nursery School,
    Bromsgrove
Bromsgrove School, Bromsgrove
The Elms, Malvern
Hillstone School (Malvern College), Malvern
Malvern College, Malvern
Malvern Girls' College, Malvern
St James's School, Malvern
St Michael's College, Tenbury Wells
Winterfold House, Kidderminster

EAST RIDING OF YORKSHIRE

Hull Grammar School, Kingston-Upon-Hull
Pocklington Montessori School, Pocklington

NORTH YORKSHIRE

Ampleforth College, York
Ashville College, Harrogate

Bootham School, York
Brackenfield School, Harrogate
Catteral Hall, Settle
Fyling Hall School, Whitby
Giggleswick School, Settle
Harrogate Tutorial College, Harrogate
Howsham Hall, York
Malsis School, Skipton
The Mount Senior School, York
Queen Margaret's School, York
Read School, Selby
Saint Martin's Ampleforth, York
Scarborough College, Scarborough
Terrington Hall, York
Woodleigh School, Malton

WEST YORKSHIRE

Ackworth School, Pontefract
Alcuin School, Leeds
Bradford Grammar School, Bradford
Fulneck School, Pudsey
Islamia Girls High School, Huddersfield
Leeds Grammar School, Leeds
Richmond House School, Leeds
Rishworth School, Rishworth
Shaw House School, Bradford
Wakefield Independent School, Wakefield
Wakefield Tutorial Preparatory School, Leeds
Woodhouse Grove School, Apperley Bridge

NORTHERN IRELAND

COUNTY ANTRIM

Belfast Royal Academy, Belfast
Methodist College, Belfast
Victoria College Belfast, Belfast

COUNTY ARMAGH

The Royal School, Armagh

COUNTY DOWN

Bangor Grammar School, Bangor
Rockport School, Holywood

COUNTY TYRONE

Royal School Dungannon, Dungannon

SCOTLAND

ABERDEENSHIRE

Aberdeen Waldorf School, Aberdeen
Albyn School for Girls, Aberdeen
International School of Aberdeen, Aberdeen

ARGYLL AND BUTE

Lomond School, Helensburgh

BANFFSHIRE

Aberlour House, Aberlour

CLACKMANNANSHIRE

Dollar Academy, Dollar

FIFE

St Leonards School & St Leonards VIth Form College,
    St Andrews
Sea View Private School, Kirkcaldy

GLASGOW

Hutchesons' Grammar School, Glasgow

LANARKSHIRE

Hamilton College, Hamilton

LOTHIAN

Basil Paterson Tutorial College, Edinburgh
Clifton Hall, Newbridge
The Edinburgh Academy, Edinburgh
The Edinburgh Rudolf Steiner School, Edinburgh
Edinburgh Tutorial College, Edinburgh
Fettes College, Edinburgh
George Watson's College, Edinburgh
Loretto Junior School, Musselburgh
The Mary Erskine School, Edinburgh
Merchiston Castle School, Edinburgh
St George's School for Girls, Edinburgh
St Margaret's School, Edinburgh
St Serf's School, Edinburgh

MORAYSHIRE

Gordonstoun School, Elgin

PERTHSHIRE

Butterstone School, Blairgowrie
Glenalmond College, Perth
Kilgraston (A Sacred Heart School), Perth
Morrison's Academy, Crieff
Rannoch School, Pitlochry

ROXBURGHSHIRE

St Mary's Preparatory School, Melrose

STIRLING

Beaconhurst Grange, Stirling

WALES

BRIDGEND

St Clare's Convent School, Porthcawl

CARDIFF

The Cathedral School, Cardiff
Howell's School, Llandaff GDST, Cardiff
Kings Monkton School, Cardiff
New College and School, Cardiff

CARMARTHENSHIRE

Llandovery College, Llandovery

CONWY

Rydal Penrhos Preparatory School, Colwyn Bay
Rydal Penrhos Senior School, Colwyn Bay
St David's College, Llandudno

DENBIGHSHIRE

Howell's School, Denbigh
Ruthin School, Ruthin

MONMOUTHSHIRE

Haberdashers' Monmouth School For Girls, Monmouth
St John's-on-the-Hill, Chepstow

PEMBROKESHIRE

Netherwood School, Saundersfoot

POWYS

Christ College, Brecon

4.8
EDUCATIONAL ASSOCIATIONS
AND USEFUL ADDRESSES

The Allied Schools
42 South Bar Street
Banbury
Oxon OX16 9XL
Tel: (01295) 256441
General Manager: Nevil Coulson MA, MBA

Provision of financial and management services to member schools and of secretarial services to the Governing Bodies of those schools. The Allied Schools include:

Stowe School
Wrekin College
Canford School
Duke of Kent School (associate)

Harrogate Ladies' College
Westonbirt School
Riddlesworth Hall Preparatory School (associate)

The Association of Educational Guardians for International Students (AEGIS)
Tel: (0116) 2109893
Fax: (0116) 2109894
E-mail: mrb@webleicester.co.uk
Development Director: Margaret Banks

The Association promotes best and legal practice in all areas of guardianship and the care of international students, under 18 years of age, at school or college in the United Kingdom. All members, including school members, are required to adhere to the AEGIS Code of Practice and undertake to follow guidelines on caring for international students. Guardianship organisations are admitted to membership after a successful accreditation inspection.

Association of Heads of Independent Schools
Queen's Gate School
133 Queen's Gate
London SW7 5LE
Honorary Secretary: Mrs A Holyoak

Membership of AHIS is open to the Heads of girls' independent secondary schools and girls' co-educational junior independent schools which are accredited by the Independent Schools Council (see below).

Association of Nursery Training Colleges
Chiltern Nursery Training College
16 Peppard Road
Caversham
Reading RG4 8J2
Tel: (0118) 9471847

Provides information on careers in child care, as nannies, as nursery workers and on National Vocational Qualifications (NVQs) in child care and education offered in the three independent nursery training colleges: Norland College, Hungerford, Chiltern Nursery Training College, Reading and Princess Christian College, Manchester.

Association of Tutors
Sunnycroft
63 King Edward Road
Northampton NN1 5LY
Tel: (01604) 624171   Fax: (01604) 624718
Secretary: Dr D J Cornelius

The professional body for independent private tutors. Members provide advice and individual tuition to students at all levels of education. The tutoring may be supplementary to full course provision or may be on a full course basis.

Boarding Schools' Association (BSA)
Grosvenor Gardens House
35–37 Grosvenor Gardens
London SW1W 0BS
Tel: (020) 7798 1580   Fax: (020) 7798 1581
E-mail: bsa@iscis.uk.net   Website: www.boarding.org.uk
National Director: Adrian Underwood BA (Hons), MA, FRSA

The BSA is committed to the view that boarding education, either for the whole or part of a child's school career, is of benefit to many children and essential for some. It has over 500 member schools that are all accredited ISC boarding schools or OFSTED accredited state boarding schools.

The BSA's aims are:
- To promote the qualities of boarding life provided by all types of boarding schools
- To provide information about boarding and boarding schools that are in membership of BSA
- To organise professional development and training programmes for all staff and governors of boarding schools
- To produce a range of publications on boarding issues and good practice
- To conduct and authorise appropriate research
- To work with other bodies concerned with boarding education
- To maintain regular dialogue with appropriate Government Ministers and their departments, Members of Parliament, and Local Government Officials.

For further information about the BSA Professional Development Programme please contact:-

Tim Holgate BSc (Hons), MSc
BSA Director of Training
4, Manor Farm Cottages
Etchilhampton
Devizes
Wilts SN10 3JR
Tel/Fax: (01380) 860953   E-mail: Tim.Holgate@btinternet.com

British Accreditation Council
The Chief Executive
Westminster Central Hall, Storey's Gate
London SW1H 9NH
Tel: (020) 7223 3468   Fax: (020) 7223 3470
E-mail: info@the-bac.org
Website: www.the-bac.org

British Association for Early Childhood Education (Early Education)
111 City View House
463 Bethnal Green Road
London E2 9QY
Tel: (020) 7739 7594   Fax: (020) 7613 5330

A charitable association which advises on the care and education of young children from birth to eight years. The association also publishes booklets and organises conferences for those interested in early childhood education.

British Dyslexia Association
98 London Road
Reading
Berkshire RG1 5AU
Tel: (0118) 966 2871   Fax: (0118) 935 1927
E-mail: info@dyslexiahelp-bda.demon.co.uk
Website: www.bda-dyslexia.org.uk
(Helpline/Information Service 10am–12.45pm and 2pm-4.45pm Monday to Friday)

Choir Schools Association
The Minster School
Deangate
York YO1 7JA
Tel: (01904) 624900   Fax: (01904) 557232
Administrator: Wendy Jackson

An association of schools educating cathedral and collegiate boy and girl choristers. Membership comprises the following schools:

The Abbey School, Tewkesbury
Bristol Cathedral School, Bristol
The Cathedral School, Lincoln
The Cathedral School, Llandaff
Chetham's School of Music, Manchester
The Chorister School, Durham
Christ Church Cathedral School, Oxford
Exeter Cathedral School, Exeter
Hereford Cathedral Junior School, Hereford
The King's School, Gloucester
The King's School, Worcester
King's College School, Cambridge
The King's School, Ely
King's Preparatory School, Rochester
Lanesborough, Guildford
Lichfield Cathedral School, Lichfield
Magdalen College School, Oxford
The Minster School, Southwell
The Minster School, York
New College School, Oxford

Norwich School, Norwich
The Pilgrim's School, Winchester
Polwhele House, Truro
The Prebendal School, Chichester
Queen Elizabeth Grammar School, Wakefield
Ripon Cathedral Choir School, Ripon
St Edmunds Junior School, Canterbury
St George's School, Windsor
St James's School, Grimsby
St John's College, Cardiff
St John's College School, Cambridge
St Mary's Music School, Edinburgh
St Paul's Cathedral Choir School, London EC4
Salisbury Cathedral School, Salisbury
Wells Cathedral School, Wells
Westminster Abbey Choir School, London SW1
Westminster Cathedral Choir School, London SW1

Associate Members
Ampleforth College, Ampleforth, North Yorkshire
Portsmouth Grammar School, Portsmouth
Reigate St Mary's Preparatory and Choir School, Reigate
St Cedd's School, Chelmsford
St Edward's College, Liverpool
The King's School, Peterborough
Warwick School, Warwick

Council for Independent Further Education (CIFE)
Dr Norma R. Ball
Executive Secretary
75 Foxbourne Road
London SW17 8EN
Tel: (020) 8767 8666
Fax: (020) 8767 9444

CIFE, founded in 1973, is a professional association for independent colleges of further education which specialise in preparing students (mainly over statutory school leaving age) for GCSEs, A and AS levels and university entrance. In addition, some colleges offer English language tuition for students from abroad and degree-level tuition. The aim of the association is to promote good practice and safeguard adherence to strict standards of professional conduct and ethical propriety. Full membership is open to colleges which have been accredited either by the British Accreditation Council for Independent Further and Higher Education (BAC) or by the Independent Schools Council. Candidate membership is available to colleges seeking accreditation by either body within three years which otherwise satisfy CIFE's own stringent criteria for membership. All CIFE colleges, of which are there are currently 31 spread throughout England, with concentrations in London, Oxford and Cambridge, have to abide by exacting codes on conduct and practice; and the character and presentation of their published exam results are subject to regulation, the accuracy of the information presented requiring in addition to be validated by BAC as academic auditor to CIFE. Colleges in full membership are subject to re-inspection from time to time by their accrediting bodies. Further information and a list of colleges are available from the Secretary.

CReSTeD (Council for the Registration of Schools Teaching Dyslexic Pupils)
Registered Charity No: 1052103
Greygarth
Littleworth
Winchcombe
Cheltenham GL54 5BT
Tel/Fax: (01242) 604 852
E-mail: admin@crested.org.uk   Website: www.crested.org.uk
Chairman: Dr S J Chinn

The CReSTeD Register is to help parents and those who advise them to choose shools for dyslexic children. Its main supporters are the British Dyslexia Association and the Dyslexia Institute who, with others, established CReSTeD to produce an authoritative list of schools, both maintained and independent, which have been through an established registration procedure, including a visit by the CReSTeD selected consultant.

Department for Education and Skills
Sanctuary Buildings
Great Smith Street
London SW1P 3BT
Tel: (08700) 012345

The Dyslexia Institute
133 Gresham Road
Staines
Middlesex TW18 2AJ
Tel: (01784) 463851   Fax: (01784) 460747
E-mail: info@dyslexia-inst.org.uk   Website: www.dyslexia-inst.org.uk

A registered charity with teaching, assessment and teacher-training centres throughout the UK. In addition the Dyslexia Institute (DI) provides an information and advice service as well as a growing range of teaching resources including CD-ROM. The aim of the DI is to help dyslexic people of all ages overcome their difficulties in learning to read, write and spell and to achieve their potential. Information may be obtained by sending a stamped address envelope to the address above or by referring to the DI website.

Gabbitas Educational Consultants
Carrington House
126–130 Regent Street
London W1B 5EE
Tel: (020) 7734 0161   Fax: (020) 7437 1764
E-mail: market@gabbitas.co.uk   Website: www.gabbitas.co.uk

Gabbitas offers friendly, independent, expert advice on all stages of education and careers:

- choice of independent schools and colleges
- educational assessment services for parents concerned about their child's progress at school
- sixth form options – A and AS level, International Baccalaureate and vocational courses
- university and degree choices and UCAS applications
- careers assessment and guidance
- extensive guidance for overseas students transferring into the British system
- specialist services including guardianship for overseas students attending UK boarding schools and testing services in English, Maths and Science.

Gabbitas also provides a full range of services for schools, including the appointment of Heads and staff as well as consultancy on any aspect of school management and development.

The Girls' Days School Trust (GDST)
100 Rochester Row
London SW1P 1JP
Tel: (020) 7393 6666

The GDST is a Registered Charity (No 1026057). It was founded in 1872 as a pioneer of girls' education. Today the Trust has over 19,500 pupils attending its 25 schools.

Birkenhead High School, Birkenhead
Blackheath High School, London SE3
Brighton and Hove High School, Brighton
Bromley High School, Bromley
The Belvedere School, Liverpool
Central Newcastle High School, Newcastle-upon-Tyne
Croydon High School, Croydon
Healthfield School, Pinner
Howells School, Cardiff
Ipswich High School, Ipswich
Kensington Preparatory School for Girls, London W8
Norwich High School, Norfolk
Nottingham High School for Girls, Nottingham

Notting Hill and Ealing High School, London W13
Oxford High School, Oxford
Portsmouth High School, Portsmouth
Putney High School, London SW15
The Royal High School, Bath
Sheffield High School, Sheffield
Shrewsbury High School, Shrewsbury
South Hampstead High School, London NW3
Streatham Hill and Clapham High School, London SW16
Sutton High School, Sutton
Sydenham High School, Sydenham, London SE26
Wimbledon High School, London SW19

GDST schools are non denominational. Entry is by interview and test appropriate to the pupil's age. All schools have a junior department. Kensington is a preparatory school only. The Royal High School, Bath also takes boarders. For further details contact schools direct or the GDST office for a general prospectus.

The Girls' Schools Association (GSA)
130 Regent Road
Leicester LE1 7PG
Tel: (0116) 254 1619   Fax: (0116) 255 3792
E-mail: office@girls-schools.org.uk
President: Mrs Sue Singer
General Secretary: Ms Sheila Cooper

The GSA exists to represent the 230 schools whose Heads are in membership. Its direct aim is to promote excellence in the education of girls. This is achieved through a clear understanding of the individual potential of girls and young women. Over 110,000 pupils are educated in schools which cover day and boarding, large and small, city and country, academically elite and broad based education. Scholarships and bursaries are available in most schools.

The Governing Bodies Association and the Governing Bodies of Girls' Schools Association (GBA and GBGSA)
The Ancient Foresters
Bush End
Takeley
Bishops Stortford
Herts CM22 6NN
Tel/Fax: (01279) 871865
Secretary: F V Morgan

The aims of the associations are to advance education in independent schools, to promote good governance and administration in independent schools and to encourage co-operation between their governing bodies. For details please contact the Secretary.

The Headmasters' and Headmistresses' Conference (HMC)
130 Regent Road
Leicester LE1 7PG
Tel: (0116) 285 4810
Fax: (0116) 247 1167
Membership Secretary: D E Prince
Secretary: G H Lucas

Membership of the HMC consists of 245 heads of major boys' and co-educational independent schools. The object of the annual meeting is to discuss matters of common interest to members.

The Incorporated Association of Preparatory Schools (IAPS)
11 Waterloo Place
Leamington Spa
Warwickshire CV32 5LA
Tel: (01926) 887833
Fax: (01926) 888014
E-mail: hq@iaps.org.uk
General Secretary: John Morris

IAPS is the main professional association of Heads of independent preparatory and junior Schools in the UK and overseas. There are some 540 schools whose Heads are in membership, accommodating over 13,000 children.

The Independent Schools Association (ISA)
Boys' British School
East Street
Saffron Walden
Essex CB10 1LS
Tel: (01799) 523619
Secretary: Timothy Ham

There are approximately 300 schools in membership of ISA. These are all schools which have been accredited by the Independent Schools Council Inspection Service. This and the requirement that the school should be "good of its kind" are the criteria for membership ISA represents schools with pupils throughout the age range. The majority of schools are day schools, but a significant number also have boarders. Membership of the Association enables Heads to receive support from the Association in a number of ways and enables pupils to take part in many events organised by ISA.

The Independent Schools' Bursars Association (ISBA)
5 Chapel Close
Old Basing
Basingstoke
Hants RG24 7BZ
Tel: (01256) 330369
Fax: (01256) 330376
E-mail: office@isba.uk.com
Website: www.isba.uk.com
General Secretary: M J Sant

Membership of ISBA includes 780 independent schools. Objectives include the promotion of administrative efficiency and exchange of information between schools.

The Independent Schools Careers Organisation (ISCO)
12A Princess Way
Camberley
Surrey GU15 3SP
Tel (01276) 211888   Fax: (01276) 691833
E-mail: admin@isco.org.uk
Website: www.isco.org.uk

ISCO exists to help young people, from age 15 upwards, to make informed choices about further and higher education and start out on the right career path. It has membership schemes for parents and schools and a network of Regional Directors who work to promote and support careers education and guidance of the highest quality. It provides a range of publications and software, as well as training and conferences for teachers, work experience for sixth formers, information for parents and guidance in individual cases. The magazine Careerscope is published three times a year and is available on subscription.

Independent Schools Examinations Board
Jordan House
Christchurch Road
New Milton
Hants BH25 6QJ
Tel: (01425) 621111

Details of the Common Entrance examinations (see the section on "Examinations and Qualifications") and copies of past papers are available from the Administrator at the address above.

The Independent Schools Council Information Service (ISCIS)
Grosvenor Gardens House
35–37 Grosvenor Gardens
London SW1W 0BS
Tel: (020) 7798 1500
Director: D J Woodhead

Established by the associations of independent schools to provide information about schools to parents and the media.

Independent Schools Council (ISC)
Grosvenor Gardens House
35–37 Grosvenor Gardens
London SW1W 0BS
Tel: (020) 7798 1590   Fax: (020) 7798 1591
General Secretary: Dr Alistair B Cooke OBE

ISC is a federation of the following associations:

Girl's Schools Association (GSA)
Governing Bodies Association (GBA)
Governing Bodies of Girls' Schools Association (GBGSA)
Headmasters' and Headmistresses' Conference (HMC)
Incorporated Association of Preparatory Schools (IAPS)
Independent Schools' Association (ISBA)
Independent Schools' Bursars Association (ISBA)
Society of Headmasters and Headmistresses of Independent Schools (SHMIS)

The total membership of ISC comprises about 1300 schools which are accredited by ISC and inspected on a six-year cycle by the Independent Schools Inspectorate (ISI) under arrangements agreed by the DFES and OFSTED. ISC deals with matters of policy and other issues common to its members and when required speaks collectively on their behalf. It represents its members in discussions with the Department for Education and Skills and with other organisations and represents the collective view of members on independent education, often acting through National ISIS, its media and publications arm.

The Round Square Schools
3 Cronks Hill Close
Meadvale
Redhill
Surrey RH1 6LX
Tel: (01737) 217134
Fax: (01737) 217133
E-mail: Hollandkay@msn.com
Secretary: Kay Holland

An international group of schools which follow the principles of Kurt Hahn, founder of the Salem School in Germany and Gordonstoun in Scotland. There are now 50 member schools in eleven countries: Australia, Canada, England, Germany, India, Kenya, Oman, Scotland, South Africa, Switzerland, Thailand and the United States. Member schools arrange regular exchange visits for pupils and undertake aid projects in India, Kenya, Eastern Europe and Thailand. All member schools uphold the five principles of outdoor adventure, community service, education for democracy, international understanding and environmental conservation. UK member schools are as follows:

Abbotsholme, Uttoxeter (Co-ed)
Box Hill, Dorking (Co-ed)
Cobham Hall, Gravesend (Girls')
Gordonstoun, Elgin (Co-ed)
Hellenic College, London
  (Co-ed, Day)
Rannoch, Pitlochry (Co-ed)
Wellington College, Crowthorne
  (Boys', Girls in Sixth Form)
Westfield, Newcastle upon Tyne
  (Girls')
Windermere St Anne's (Co-ed)

SATIPS
Professional Support for Staff in Independent Schools
Cherry Tress
Stebbing
Nr Great Dunmow
Essex CM6 3ST
Tel/Fax: (01371) 856823
E-mail: erad@dial.pipex.com
General Secretary: Andrew Davis

SATIPS – founded in 1952 – is a source of professional support and encouragement for staff in preparatory, and other schools. We are now one of the foremost providers of subject-based and cross-curricular INSET courses for prep school and other staff. SATIPS is a registered charity. In 1993 the Society widened its appeal by changing its emphasis from purely preparatory school teachers to any school staff, especially those in independent schools. In particular, teachers who have pupils in Key Stages 1, 2 and 3 will find the membership of SATIPS useful: we are particularly interested in making contact with colleagues in the maintained sector. The Society publishes nineteen Broadsheets each term in all subject areas and runs various conferences (mostly one-day) at various venues during the year. We offer school and individual membership.

The Secondary Heads Association (SHA)
130 Regent Road
Leicester LEI 7PG
Tel: (0116) 299 1122
Fax: (0116) 299 1123
E-mail: info@sha.org.uk
Website: www.sha.org.uk
General Secretary: J E Dunford

SHA represents Heads, Deputy Heads, Assistant Heads and senior teachers in all types of secondary schools and colleges.

Service Children's Education (UK)
Trenchard Lines
Upavon
Pewsey
Wilts SN9 6BE
Tel (01980) 618244

To support Service families and entitled civilians in obtaining appropriate educational facilities for their children and to provide high quality, impartial advice on all aspects of education world-wide.

The Society of Headmasters and Headmistresses of Independent Schools (SHMIS)
Celedston
Rhosesmor Road
Halkyn
Holywell
CH8 8DL
Tel/Fax: (01352) 781102
E-mail: gensec@shmis.demon.co.uk
Website: www.shmis.demon.co.uk
General Secretary: I D Cleland

A society of some 95 schools, most of which are co-educational, day and boarding, and all of which educate children up to the age of 18.

Steiner Waldorf Schools Fellowship
Kidbrooke Park
Forest Row
East Sussex RH18 5JA
Tel: (01342) 822115   Fax: (01342) 826004
E-mail: swsf@waldorf.compulink.co.uk
Website: www.steinerwaldorf.org.uk
Chairman: Christopher Clouder

The Steiner Waldorf Schools Fellowship represents the 26 autonomous Steiner Waldorf Schools in the UK and Eire. There are now over 807 schools worldwide. Key character-istics of the education include: careful balance in the artistic, practical and intellectual content of the international Steiner Waldorf curriculum; co-educational from 3 to 19 years. Shared Steiner Waldorf curriculum for all pupils. GCSE and A Level examinations. A broad education based on Steiner's approach to the holistic nature of the human being. Co-operative school management – usually a variable parent payment scheme. Steiner Waldorf education is rapidly gaining in popularity all over the world.

The Woodard Schools
1 The Sanctuary
Westminster
London SW1P 3JT
Tel: (020) 7222 5381
Registrar: P F B Beesley

The Woodard Corporation has 38 schools throughout the country, including 17 Affiliated and Associated schools. All have an Anglican foundation and together they form the largest independent group of Church Schools in England and Wales.

Member Schools

Southern Division

Ardingly College, Haywards Heath
Ardingly College Junior School,
   Haywards Heath
Bloxham School, Banbury
Hurstpierpoint College, Hassocks
Hurstpierpoint Junior School, Hassocks
Lancing College, Lancing

Midland Division

Denstone College, Uttoxeter
Ellesmere College, Ellesmere
Prestefelde, Shrewsbury
Ranby House, Retford
School of St Mary and St Anne, Rugeley
Smallwood Manor Preparatory, Uttoxeter
Worksop College, Worksop

Eastern Division

Peterborough High School,
   Peterborough
St James's School, Grimsby

Western Division

The Cathedral School, Llandaff
Grenville College, Bideford
King's College, Taunton
King's Hall School, Taunton
St Margaret's School, Exeter

Northern Division

The King's School, Tynemouth
Queen Mary's School, Thirsk

Associated Schools

Bow School, Durham
Durham School, Durham

Affiliated Schools

Alderley Edge School for Girls, Alderley Edge
Archbishop Michael Ramsey Technology College, London (Voluntary Aided)
Bishop of Hereford's Bluecoat School, Tupsley (Voluntary Aided)
Bishop Stopford School, Kettering
Bolitho School, Penzance
Crompton House Church of England School
Derby High School, Derby
Derby School, Derby
Grammar School for Boys, Derby
St Aidan's Church of England Technology College
St Elphin's School, Matlock
St Peter's Collegiate School, Wolverhampton (Voluntary Aided)
St Wilfred's Church of England High School and Technology College
St Olaves Grammar School, Orpington
St George's Church of England School, Gravesend
St. Peter's Church of England High School, Stoke on Trent
The King's School, Wolverhampton

GLOSSARY OF ABBREVIATIONS APPEARING IN SCHOOL PROFILES

ABRSM	Associated Board of the Royal Schools of Music
ADD	Attention Deficit Disorder
AEB	Associated Examining Board
AHIS	Association of Heads of Independent Schools
AICE	Advanced International Certificate of Education
ANTC	Association of Nursery Training Colleges
ARCS	Accreditation, Review and Consultancy Service
ARELS	Association of Recognised English Language Services
AVDEP	Association Vaudoise des Ecoles Privees
BACIFHE	British Accreditation Council for Independent Further and Higher Education
BAGA	British Amateur Gymnastics Association
BAYS	British Association for the Advancement of Science
BHS	British Horse Society
BSA	Boarding Schools Association
CAE	Cambridge Certificate in Advanced English
CEE	Common Entrance Examination
CIFE	Conference for Independent Further Examination
COBISEC	Council of British International Schools in the European Community
CReSTeD	Council for the Registration of Schools Teaching Dyslexic Pupils
CSA	Choir Schools Association
DfES	Department for Education and Skills
ECIS	European Council for International Schools
EFL	English as a Foreign Language
ESL	English as a Second Language
ESOL	English for Speakers of Other Languages
FCE	Cambridge First Certificate in English
FOBISSEA	Federation of British International Schools in South-East Asia
FSEP	Federation Suisse des Ecoles Privees
GBA	Governing Bodies Association
GBGSA	Governing Bodies of Girls' Schools Association
GDST	Girls' Day School Trust
GSA	Girls' School Association
HAS	Head Teachers' Association of Scotland
HMC	Headmasters' and Headmistresses' Conference
IAPS	Incorporated Association of Preparatory Schools

IB	International Baccalaureate
IBTA	Independent Business Training Organisation
ICG	Independent Colleges Group
IGCSE	International General Certificate of Secondary Education
ISA	Independent Schools Association
ISBA	Independent Schools Bursars' Association
ISC	Independent Schools Council (formerly Independent Schools Joint Council or ISJC)
ISCO	Independent Schools Careers Organisation
ISIS	Independent Schools Information Service
LAMDA	London Academy of Music and Dramatic Art
LISA	London International Schools Association
MSA	Middle States Association of Colleges and Schools (USA)
NABSS	National Association of British Schools in Spain
NAHT	National Association of Head Teachers
NE/SA	Near East/South Asia
NEAB	Northern Examinations and Assessment Board
NEASC	New England Association of Schools and Colleges
OFSTED	Office of Standards in Education
OUDLE	University of Oxford Delegacy of Local Examinations
PET	Cambridge Preliminary English Test
PSE	Personal and Social Education
RSA CLAIT	Computer Literacy and Informations Technology
SCIS	Scottish Council of Independent Schools
SHA	Secondary Heads Association
SHMIS	Society of Headmasters and Headmistresses of Independent Schools
SpLD	Specific Learning Difficulties
STABIS	State Boarding Schools Information Service
WJEC	Welsh Joint Education Committee

Abbreviations used to denote Special Needs provision in the profiles section are as follows:

ADD	Attention Deficit Disorder	HI	Hearing Impairment
ADHD	Attention Deficit/ Hyperactivity Disorder	MLD	Moderate Learning Difficulties
		PH	Physical Impairment
ASP	Asperger's Syndrome	PMLD	Profound & Multiple Learning Difficulties
AUT	Autism		
CP	Cerebral Palsy	SP&LD	Speech & Language Difficulties
DEL	Delicate		
DOW	Down's Syndrome	SLD	Severe Learning Difficulties
DYC	Dyscalculia	SPLD	Specific Learning Difficulties
DYS	Dyslexia		
EBD	Emotional Behavioural Difficulties	TOU	Tourette's Syndrome
		VIS	Visual Impairment
EPI	Epilepsy	W	Wheelchair Access

MAIN INDEX

A

D

E

F

H

I

J

M

O

Q

R

S

T

W

Y

READER ENQUIRY CARD

If you would like further information about our Advisory, Guardianship or other Services, please complete and return this card. No stamp necessary if posted within the UK.

Name: _____

Address: _____

Tel: _____

Please indicate which area of our services might interest you:

Please tell us where you obtained a copy of this Guide:

Bookshop/Library (name and town):

School/advisory service etc. (please give details).

Borrowed from friend/relative:

READER ENQUIRY CARD

If you would like further information about our Advisory, Guardianship or other Services, please complete and return this card. No stamp necessary if posted within the UK.

Name: _____

Address: _____

Tel: _____

Please indicate which area of our services might interest you:

Please tell us where you obtained a copy of this Guide:

Bookshop/Library (name and town):

School/advisory service etc. (please give details).

Borrowed from friend/relative:

READER ENQUIRY CARD

If you would like further information about our Advisory, Guardianship or other Services, please complete and return this card. No stamp necessary if posted within the UK.

Name: _____

Address: _____

Tel: _____

Please indicate which area of our services might interest you:

Please tell us where you obtained a copy of this Guide:

Bookshop/Library (name and town):

School/advisory service etc. (please give details).

Borrowed from friend/relative:

READER ENQUIRY CARD

If you would like further information about our Advisory, Guardianship or other Services, please complete and return this card. No stamp necessary if posted within the UK.

Name: _____

Address: _____

Tel: _____

Please indicate which area of our services might interest you:

Please tell us where you obtained a copy of this Guide:

Bookshop/Library (name and town):

School/advisory service etc. (please give details).

Borrowed from friend/relative: